PARISH AND BE

CH00762348

What role did the parish play in pe
and Wales, between 1700 and the mid-twentieth century?
By comparison with globalisation and its dislocating effects,
this book stresses how important parochial belonging once
was. Professor Snell discusses themes such as subjective
ideas of belonging, cultures of local xenophobia, settlement
law and practice, marriage patterns, the continuance of out-
door relief in people's own parishes under the new poor
law, the many new parishes of the period and their effects
upon people's local attachments. The book highlights the
continuing vitality of the parish as a unit in people's lives,
and the administration associated with it. It employs a
variety of historical methods, and makes important contributions to the history of welfare, community identity and
belonging. It is highly relevant to the modern themes of
globalisation, de-localisation, and the decline of community, helping to set such changes and their consequences
into local historical perspective.

K. D. M. SNELL is Professor of Rural and Cultural History
at the Centre for English Local History, University of
Leicester. His previous publications include *Annals of the
Labouring Poor: Social Change and Agrarian England, 1660–
1900* (1985) and *Rival Jerusalems: The Geography of Victorian
Religion* (2000).

PARISH AND BELONGING

Community, Identity and Welfare in England and Wales, 1700–1950

K. D. M. SNELL

CAMBRIDGE
UNIVERSITY PRESS

CAMBRIDGE UNIVERSITY PRESS
Cambridge, New York, Melbourne, Madrid, Cape Town, Singapore, São Paulo, Delhi

Cambridge University Press
The Edinburgh Building, Cambridge CB2 8RU, UK

Published in the United States of America by Cambridge University Press, New York

www.cambridge.org
Information on this title: www.cambridge.org/9780521110754

First published 2006
This digitally printed version (with corrections) 2009

A catalogue record for this publication is available from the British Library

ISBN 978-0-521-86292-9 hardback
ISBN 978-0-521-11075-4 paperback

This book is dedicated to Charles Phythian-Adams,
Professor of English Local History,
learned colleague and friend

A human life, I think, should be well rooted in some spot of a native land, where it may get the love of tender kinship for the face of earth, for the labours men go forth to, for the sounds and accents that haunt it, for whatever will give that early home a familiar unmistakable difference amidst the future widening of knowledge: a spot where the definiteness of early memories may be inwrought with affection, and kindly acquaintance with all neighbours, even to the dogs and donkeys, may spread not by sentimental effort and reflection, but as a sweet habit of the blood. At five years old, mortals are not prepared to be citizens of the world, to be stimulated by abstract nouns, to soar above preference into impartiality; and that prejudice in favour of milk with which we blindly begin, is a type of the way body and soul must get nourished at least for a time. The best introduction to astronomy is to think of the nightly heavens as a little lot of stars belonging to one's own homestead.

(George Eliot, *Daniel Deronda* (1876, Harmondsworth, 1984), p. 50)

What life have you if you have not life together?
There is no life that is not in community,
And no community not lived in praise of GOD.
Even the anchorite who meditates alone,
For whom the days and nights repeat the praise of GOD,
Prays for the Church, the Body of Christ incarnate,
And now you live dispersed on ribbon roads,
And no man knows or cares who is his neighbour
Unless his neighbour makes too much disturbance,
But all dash to and fro in motor cars,
Familiar with the roads and settled nowhere.
Nor does the family even move about together,
But every son would have his motor cycle,
And daughters ride away on casual pillions.

(T. S. Eliot, 'Choruses from "The Rock"', II (1934), in his *Collected Poems, 1909–1962* (London, 1974), p. 168)

Driving a pony and trap one's eyes are released from the road-hypnotism of motor travel; one gazes upon the fields and up into the trees. Gardens present themselves like Nature's shop-windows, and domestic moments through open cottage doors. The birds are not frightened from the hedges; paddocked horses look over and greet the stranger . . . It is not merely the handling of reins instead of wheel; one slips into another rhythm of life altogether, as different from the mechanical as the regular jog of the trap is from the jumpy repercussions of the car on the roadway. One's radius both contracts and expands. That is to say, while the circumference of miles at one's disposal is halved, their content is more than doubled. For quiet pace is like a magnifying-glass; regions one has before passed over as familiar suddenly enlarge with innumerable new details and become a feast of contemplation . . . We found we had been living in an undiscovered country . . . One can only take one bite of life, whether one nibble at every land or explore thoroughly a single parish.

(Adrian Bell, *The Cherry Tree* (1932, London, 1949), pp. 115–17)

Contents

Figures

Tables

Preface and acknowledgements

For their help or advice with various parts of this book, I am most grateful to Rod Ambler, John Barrell, Mandy de Belin, Liz Bellamy, Bob Bushaway, Alasdair Crockett, Nick Cull, Ros Davies, Ian Dyck, Christopher Dyer, Angie Edmunds, Paul Ell, David Feldman, Harold Fox, Ian Gregory, Harriet Guest, George Harrison, Cyril Hart, David Hey, Derek Hirst, Jane Humphries, Anna Huppert, Joanna Innes, Prashant Kidambi, Robert Lee, Alan Macfarlane, Dennis Mills, John Morrill, Avner Offer, Brian Outhwaite, David Parry, Charles Phythian-Adams, Sylvia Pinches, Sidney Pollard, Dave Postles, Eileen Power, Barry Reay, Ruth Richardson, Richard Rodger, Julie Rugg, Richard Smith, Peter Solar, Julie-Marie Strange, Rosemary Sweet, Simon Szreter, Sarah Tarlow, James Stephen Taylor, Pat Thane, Mike Thompson, Hiroko Tomida, Margery Tranter, Christine Vialls, Tom Williamson, Sir Tony Wrigley, and to many students at the Centre for English Local History, University of Leicester. I am particularly grateful to Steve Hindle and Steve King, in their capacity as outstanding historians of welfare, for the stimulus of their own writing, and for their comments on some of these chapters. Robert Colls has advised me at many points and I am most thankful for his persistently thoughtful and probing comments. I also acknowledge with gratitude a grant from the British Academy, allowing the *Clergy List* for 1896 to be computerised. Earlier versions of chapters 2, 4 and 8 were respectively published in *Social History*, the *Economic History Review*, and *Past and Present*, and I am most grateful to the editors and referees of those journals for their excellent advice.

This book would not have been completed without generous study leave kindly granted to me by the Vice-Chancellor of the University of Leicester, Professor Bob Burgess.

This is my fourth book with Cambridge University Press, and as always I am extremely grateful to my editors there, Michael Watson and Isabelle Dambricourt, to my copy-editor Linda Randall, and to the Press for their assistance, encouragement and high professional skills.

CHAPTER 1

Introduction – belonging and local attachment

I

'Where do you come from?' must be one of the most frequent opening conversational lines in English. It can be interpreted in a number of ways, yet it always produces a reply and reciprocal interest, and its answer often appears to be confirmed by accent, personality, and appearance. It may establish rapport, but occasionally arouses distrust. Each place, and the many ways in which a person may be attached to it, has different cultural and subjective connotations. These indicate the crucial importance of ideas of belonging, or the wish for it, even in the modern world. Similarly, the search for 'roots', for one's genealogy, fills record offices with people, inspires much local historical research, and manifests the same interest.

In many other areas of culture we also witness the desire for belonging and attachment to place. We hear this in popular song, from nostalgic nineteenth-century emigration songs, like 'The leaving of Liverpool', and earlier ballads like 'Loch Lomond', to 'It's a long way to Tipperary', 'Show me the way to go home', 'Maybe it's because I'm a Londoner', through to the more recent lyrics of 'The green, green grass of home', 'I'm going home', 'Going to my home town', 'Clare to here', and so on. Geordie oil workers, returning from the Scottish rigs, roar in deafening crescendo 'I'm coming home Newcastle, wish I'd never been away', as the train approaches their destination. Thousands more, in football stadiums, chant supportively for their home or adoptive town – even if they do not live or belong there, and even if their 'local' team includes not a single local player. These examples indicate a need to belong, to local community and people, and they often betoken local pride. Television adopts this theme, with programmes such as *Where the Heart Is, Born and Bred, Homeground, Last of the Summer Wine, Coronation Street, EastEnders,* and so on. Even the places where these are set attract visitors hoping for a sense of contiguous locality and incorporation. Such cultural and media expressions, only a few of many that could be cited, show the enduring appeal of local belonging, even if much of this is hopeful or forlorn, revealing as much about a sense of displacement as of belonging. After all, most songs celebrating belonging are about distance, dispersion and dispossession.

There seems little doubt that in both advanced and less developed economies many people have experienced a loss of belonging and local attachment. Insecurity has become a widespread experience, and the problem of non-belonging has become more acute. Multiple or ambiguous belonging are now common, and have permeated identities and personalities. The issues of locality and belonging are ones that have growing urgency for us today, given the pace of globalisation, and its many personal, cultural and economic effects. 'Modernism' and 'postmodernism' are said to have a corrosive effect on belonging and on 'traditional communities', with expansive travel, separation of home and workplace, frequent disruption of work patterns, and removal of people from the neighbourhoods where they were raised. Some theorists even argue that capitalism has long been fundamentally inimical to belonging, that the two are essentially incompatible. Such a view seems increasingly applicable to the experiences of recent decades, although this book offers an alternative picture of earlier periods.

Belonging raises many subjective issues. Take my personal case. I was born and then lived in many African countries until my late teens. As a child I spoke three African languages fluently. My father was an English engineer from Lincoln who became a tropical forestry expert, and my mother left Wales to teach in Hong Kong. I was educated partly in England, but often stayed on Welsh relatives' farms. For me, the contrasts have been acute between African societies, divergent Welsh and English cultures, and local senses of place in Britain. My own upbringing and its frequent dislocations, some in response to post-colonial wars, my views of poverty and ways of living in Africa, and of Welsh farming, quietly influence this book, more so than any theory or historiographical concerns. In other words, this is a book by an outsider lacking a strong sense of belonging, who was attracted to British local history as some highly localised people are attracted to internationalism. That background is mentioned because such an upbringing maps on to the various experiences of countless others faced with disruption of locality and community, with extreme travel, globalisation, and the need to adapt daily or periodically to great cultural contrasts. These themes are subjectively experienced, but they have a wider significance as being intrinsic to 'modernisation' and 'globalisation', to the problems, opportunities and types of person that the modern world produces. They dispose to certain kinds of historical agendas: in my case, to a curiosity about locality, belonging and migration in the past, to an assessment of how 'belonging' used to manifest itself, and to the question of what we are now losing.

The historical questions certainly press upon us. This book is prefaced with a quotation from T. S. Eliot, asking what life there can be other than one lived in community, and lamenting community and mutual care now dispersed on ribbon roads – 'familiar with the roads and settled nowhere'. Eliot converted to the Church of England in 1927, and was fascinated by its rituals. He was deeply pessimistic about the prospects of 'attempting to form a civilized but non-Christian mentality'[1] – views that many would not share. Was he right to stress religion in people's senses of belonging? How did people feel a sense of belonging to places in the past? What territorial units did they belong to? Was the parish or northern township the crucial entity here, given its saliency in local administration? How was 'belonging' structured by law, forms of welfare, local economies, topography, social attitudes, and local customs? In what ways were people's attitudes shown? How were insider–outsider differences focused? What were the forms of local prejudice or confined humanitarianism, and how deeply rooted were they? Why did such attitudes change? What regional differences were there? How did urbanisation affect people's senses of belonging, and did towns try to replicate rural community expectations?

---

[1] T. S. Eliot, *Selected Essays* (1932, London, 1951), p. 387.

In modern nations countless people are not enfranchised 'citizens' where they live, and in that sense they do not 'belong' – what were the historical equivalents of this at parish level in the past? What succeeded as ties of belonging, and what failed?

In these questions, can one discover when and how changes occurred, so that they can be interpreted more readily? These were some of the background issues that I set out to clarify, along with questions of multiple belonging, and these chapters are a partial answer to them. Like all useful history, they aim to provide context for us today. They should help fathom some of our own concerns, and I would not pursue them if I thought otherwise. The sensitivity, skill and utility of any historian comes in taking such modern questions, feeling their immediacy and justifying them to readers, and then in finding ways, sources and methods which convincingly answer them from the historical experience, while endeavouring to be true and exact to the history that one uncovers.

Some of this book concerns centralisation, raising issues to do with its extent, timing, its impact upon local communities, and on how people felt that they belonged to their localities. The prolonged importance of the parish, much stressed in this book, was partly due to the ways in which local communities asserted themselves. A strong case can be made for 'invigorated localism' in the mid-nineteenth century, lasting through to the 1870s or beyond, and much of my evidence supports such a view.[2] It is easy now to overlook or forget how vehement and heated the opposition to centralisation was at that time. Central policy was pragmatically adjusted and often downplayed in response to strident local reception, notably on matters like poor law policy, or the civil and ecclesiastical reform of the parish. Some attacks on central administration need to be taken with a pinch of salt, and local administration in some cases meant not local obligation but local neglect. Nevertheless, 'the Pope of Somerset House' was attacked in the name of 'local responsibility', 'the spirit of Local Self-Government', the right of 'any place striking out any path of improvement for itself', and the need for rights,

---

[2] R. Price, *British Society, 1680–1880: Dynamism, Containment and Change* (Cambridge, 1999), pp. 176–86.

liberties, 'local knowledge', and 'free institutions'. There was widespread condemnation of the 'vices of Centralisation', seeing it as 'subservient sycophancy and moral degradation' and 'dictated monotonous and meaningless routine', which would crush 'the sense of local responsibility' and break up 'local knowledge'. These examples are from Joshua Toulmin Smith, a barrister who also condemned the way in which the new poor law 'was devised in order to destroy . . . the sense of local duty and responsibility', and its 'lessening of the knowledge of and taking part by every district in its own affairs', producing apathy and 'indifference to public and local duties and responsibilities'.[3]

Countless examples from other sources could be added to similar effect. Such quotations give a flavour of how resolute opposition to centralisation once was, highlighting the enduring strength of nineteenth-century localism. This resistance led central authorities (like the Poor Law Commission or Board) to claim defensively that they 'abstained carefully from doing anything which might extinguish the spirit of local independence and self-government'.[4] In the face of bitter local counter-attacks, on many different issues, other central authorities had to tread warily too, and they often made little headway. Indeed, centralising moves often prompted renewed local and civic vigour, as local authorities exerted themselves in opposition to central initiatives regarding the poor law, public health, transport, police, and so on. It was arguably much later, from the 1870s, with more substantial grants-in-aid from central government connected with education, roads, and the like, and most notably with the much larger welfare and other payments by the Treasury in the twentieth century, that centralisation and its bureaucracies became more pronounced and dominant. These issues

---

[3] J. Toulmin Smith, *Local Self-Government and Centralization: The Characteristics of Each* (London, 1851), pp. 158, 205, 360–6, 395–400. He wrote much in similar spirit, and see also his *The Parish: Its Powers and Obligations at Law, as Regards the Welfare of Every Neighbourhood, and in Relation to the State: its Officers and Committees: and the Responsibility of Every Parishioner* (1854, London, 1857). Such language pervaded the Anti-Centralization Society, the anti-new poor law and anti-Public Health Act (1848) campaigns, and many other anti-centralisation movements. This thinking had a limited influence upon the Local Government Act of 1894 and its establishment of parish councils.

[4] Sir G. Nicholls, *A History of the English Poor Law, in Connection with the State of the Country and the Condition of the People*, vol. II (1854, New York, 1967), p. 340.

are fascinating, not least in the context of later twentieth-century centralisation and planning, imposed standardisation, and related debates about the dwindling role of local government. The nineteenth-century arguments also presage debates at another level about the European Union. Finance has continued to be a key issue: among European countries today Britain has one of the highest concentrations of taxing power in central government hands.

However, this is not formally intended as another book on central–local relations, on centralisation as a governmental process, on 'revolutions in government' and their top-down effects. It views centralisation differently, being concerned with its effects on belonging and local identity, and with judging the momentum of centralisation by those effects: with parochial survival and the pace of de-localisation, and the sentiments, structures and cultures of local attachment in neighbourhoods and parishes. It discusses matters such as whether people married locally, whether they accepted settlement by outsiders, divisions between insiders and outsiders, poor relief and the parish, local office-holding, 'new parish' formation, and subjective senses of belonging. It is concerned with the repercussions for the parish and its inhabitants of centralising and globalising trends. Those trends are double-sided coins – central:local – global:local – and I am interested in the less considered local and received dimension, the subjective responses to centralisation and globalisation, and those reactions as seen from below. In other words, I am assessing when and to what extent de-localising trends had their main influence at local level, and uncovering at the micro-level people's attachments to place, and their experience and responses to de-localisation.

Globalisation is now often taken as the broader phenomenon affecting local history. Since the eighteenth century there have been major shifts in the world market economy, the expansion of empire, European emigration, advances in the technology of transport and communications, and the spread of international symbols. These processes did not go unchecked: there were economic downturns and cycles, war-time constraints, retreats from empire. However, the changes have accelerated in the late twentieth century, and strikingly so from the 1970s, with advances in communications, a tendency to cultural uniformity, and radical developments in financial markets. While centralisation made localities or regions more similar, and caused local affiliations to be eclipsed by notions of society and nation, globalisation accentuated de-territorialisation and de-localism across nations. Both centralisation and globalisation connect the local with the general: they are different processes, although one seems dependent upon the other, and their local effects on belonging and identities are comparable. The literature on globalisation, and its effects on localities, identities, and local history, is growing apace.[5] I am not studying globalisation directly here, in the conventional, expansionist way. Rather, I am concerned with its 'other side', with the experienced decline of local administration, associated cultures and a sense of belonging to localities and parishes. Globalisation and centralisation in all countries trigger defensive and sometimes violent reactions, among peoples who see their culture and local ways of life threatened or destroyed. These problems, with all their humanitarian, environmental, cultural, economic and political dimensions, are among the most important of our time. Among the issues linked to them, as an English and Welsh historian I think especially of questions concerning the integrity and survival of the parish or other local entities as civil and religious units, of efforts in the nineteenth century to break down popular notions of identity and belonging, of the extent of people's local horizons, of questions that relate belonging and community to the decline of the organic economy and to its gradual supplanting by new economic forms, of the changing scales and credibility of local and community history, and of questions that concern the limits and boundaries that people set in the exercise of their humanity to others.

---

[5] On the processes of globalisation, among a very large literature, see D. Massey and P. Jess (eds.), *A Place in the World? Places, Cultures and Globalization* (Oxford, 1995); M. Augé, *Non-places: Introduction to an Anthropology of Supermodernity* (1995, London, 2000); M. Waters, *Globalization* (1995, London, 2001); J. Clifford, *Routes: Travel and Translation in the Late Twentieth Century* (London, 1997); K. R. Cox (ed.), *Spaces of Globalization: Reasserting the Power of the Local* (New York, 1997); Z. Bauman, *Globalization: The Human Consequences* (Cambridge, 1998); S. Castles and A. Davidson, *Citizenship and Migration: Globalization and the Politics of Belonging* (Basingstoke, 2000); C. Hines, *Localization: A Global Manifesto* (London, 2000); L. Sklair, *Globalization: Capitalism and its Alternatives* (Oxford, 2002); I. Kaul (ed.), *Providing Global Public Goods: Managing Globalization* (Oxford, 2003).

Given centralising and globalising trends, the significance of the larger contexts in which places are situated has become ever more apparent. Local place has become less a source of identity than hitherto, losing much of its social meaning. Modern communications alter or hide personalities, and undercut the viability and intuitive understandings of face-to-face communities. Many sociologists tell us that community and civic engagement are in serious decline. They document huge turnover, a culture of transience, among people who, residing only a few years in a place and often working long and stressful hours elsewhere, see little reason to become involved with a local community that is breaking up like a dissolving aspirin. Local democracy, and the role of traditional local power structures, seem to become increasingly irrelevant. Decision-making occurs elsewhere, by distant planners, unrepresentative unelected quangos, or in board-rooms, with an eye to shareholders who are not locally tied. Power and capital have become increasingly divorced from obligations and responsibilities to local communities. Indeed, 'human corporate owners are being replaced by non-human computer programmes that move investment funds around according to abstruse formulas, enriching the few while destroying lives and communities'.[6] Power has gone into hiding. Multinational companies readily evade the consequences of their actions, moving away from sites of waste and unemployment, even while they pretend otherwise by calling themselves 'multilocal multi-nationals', still trying to incorporate ideas of 'local' into their transnational corporate image.[7] Community and public trust is fading, especially as power becomes more distant. Ancillary to these developments, travel and mobility now transform senses of history, rendering it shallow and of limited meaning, shifting its political purposes, blurring the possibilities and point of 'community' recall and local discernment, thus even justifying professional historians like myself, who sometimes fill in for the lack of community recollection. All these changes in our society call for a re-thinking of our historical purposes, of what we write history for, and indeed why we read it.

---

[6] Sklair, *Globalization*, p. 285.
[7] *Financial Times* (29 April 2004).

The opinions about locality of George Eliot, and about local perception by Adrian Bell – quotations from them preface this book – are increasingly jostled aside through the technology of modern travel and the separations of work, home and leisure. Adrian Bell could once write that 'To swan around the globe means nothing . . . to burrow into one place is what gives it meaning to you, and ultimately you to yourself.'[8] Yet he formed such opinions back in the 1920s, as part of a generation reacting against the First World War, facing the inter-war rural depression in East Anglia. A persistent theme in his farming work and 'land literature' was an effort to link past, present and future in village life, to find 'some basis of unity, the germ of a new coherence'.[9] The colossal and pointless shadow of the First World War lurked just behind him, as he closed in on the texture and grain of rural life. Yet as the lantern gave way to electricity, pantiles to sheet iron, he saw the 'new' farming methods – modern machinery, motorised transport, factory farming, new marketing and business methods, hedge removals, and so on – and believed that he was describing the passing of a whole culture, with its own distinctive senses of place and belonging, of rural artifacts, horse power, hand technologies and people skilled in them. Even so, for him at least, local places were still unique, singular, and lent themselves to distinctive personal identities.

Into the twenty-first century, localities seem less distinct and singular – they are becoming as homogeneous as the McDonalds containers that litter them, as the mass culture that standardises them. So many of our townscapes could be anywhere or nowhere, like a Lee Friedlander photograph depicting American urban space as nondescript, empty and two-dimensional, a mere cross-sectional view of means of transport, lacking a settled focus.[10] Such areas are less a place than a vapid condition – one cannot belong there, and would not wish to do so. The modern developments have often obliterated the humane vicinity that once gave a form to home and life, as so many people find when they revisit the sites of their childhood. The contrasts

[8] 'The two Suffolks', in M. Watkins (ed.), *The East Anglian Book: A Personal Anthology* (Ipswich, 1971), pp. 133 and 135–8, cited in the *Adrian Bell Society Journal*, 7 (March 2001), p. 9.
[9] K. D. M. Snell, 'Bell, Adrian Hanbury (1901–1980)', *Oxford Dictionary of National Biography* (Oxford, 2004).
[10] For example, Lee Friedlander, 'Albuquerque' (1972), viewable at http://artscenecal. com/ArtistsFiles/FriedlanderL/LFriedlander.html (14 September 2005).

between past and present in respect of 'belonging' are so great for many people that it can sometimes feel as though one is looking back through the light and dark shades of the present, to discover their antithesis in the past – piecing together, so to speak, the historic photographic negative that has depicted us, inverted such that the lights of its local neighbourhoods have become dark, and the darks of its distant horizons have become light. For 'organic' communities and forms of local territorial thought and practice now disintegrate worldwide before waves of cultural contact, rapid transport, economic extension and financial speculation. Most historians, including myself, think of community as formed mainly within a bounded area in which virtually everybody knew each other, to which people felt that they belonged, and which commonly had administrative functions. Yet we now have location-free 'imagined', 'communication', 'simulated', or 'virtual' communities – and there are some theorists who believe that these are communitarian improvements on, and better substitutes for, the past. So many people now live outside territory and community as defined by local space, at least for part of their time. Indeed, to be local is thought by many to be a sign of social deficiency and degradation, of marginalisation and constraint. Measures of 'the quality of life' even stigmatise localism and a failure to be mobile as 'deprivation', and seriously formalise that judgement in quantitative indicators. The 'working community' and its reciprocal networks, as historians sense it through the photography of Frank Meadow Sutcliffe in Whitby, P. H. Emerson on the Norfolk Broads, or the writings of William Cobbett, John Clare, Richard Jefferies, George Sturt, Flora Thompson, Daniel Parry-Jones, Leo Walmsley, Lewis Jones, Adrian Bell, A. G. Street, H. J. Massingham, Alwyn Rees, Raymond Williams, and countless other writers, has often ceased to exist. Indeed, most of those authors were themselves documenting its decline. We are faced with the questions of what we should replace localism with, and of how viable for human needs the replacements will be. Questions of liberal toleration of diversity in a world system, of whether small-scale territorialism and cultural variation can co-exist with globalisation, are unresolved as yet, and are among the most interesting uncertainties of the coming decades. Globalisation might still entail 'a rainbow of localisms' –

as Avner Offer has phrased it to me – languages abound, ethnic cuisines are widely available, in the global street people are still diversely rooted in their 'home' cultures. This may not last much longer. Even so, the need to belong certainly persists. Forms of romantic or mythical belonging, types of imagined community, a diversity of societal planning apparently with 'belonging' in mind – frequently oblivious of or fabricating historical precedent – have figured largely in twentieth-century thought, architecture, and politics, sometimes to disastrous effect. 'New localism' and other such agendas, in opposition to centralisation, are now appearing on the political scene, often looking to the past for inspiration.[11]

Richard Burn, the famous historian of the old poor law, exponent of local practice, and vicar of one of the most 'local' of places (Orton in Westmorland), long ago wrote on the poor law that 'There is a time, when old things shall become new.'[12] This clergyman was subtly adapting to his purpose the utopian wording in Revelation, 21: 4–5: 'And God shall wipe away all tears from their eyes; and there shall be no more death, neither sorrow, nor crying, neither shall there be any more pain: for the former things are passed away. And he that sat upon the throne said, Behold, I make all things new.' That is a fine biblical agenda, particularly for a person like him studying parish welfare. However, that passage is also a standard part of the funeral service. Whether the old can become new for localism and belonging, and whether that is desirable, and how it might become true, and what forms of 'belonging' are sought after or needed, all remain unclear. It is one of the historian's jobs to try to clarify that cloudiness: to look into the past, and through that past to make clear and lucid what others feel in the present as a murky problem of muddled needs and nostalgic wishes.

The momentum of postmodernist experience might now seem unstoppable, barring environmental or other catastrophe. Nevertheless, we should not deal with the future, and define future options, without understanding the past accurately, coming to terms with it, and seeing its striking possibilities. There is no reason why one should not belong, yet communicate widely.

---

[11] D. Carswell *et al.*, *Direct Democracy: An Agenda for a New Model Party* (London, 2005).
[12] R. Burn, *The History of the Poor Laws, with Observations* (London, 1764), preface.

In other words, I want these chapters to return us thoughtfully to a period when 'community' was largely organised around the natural capacity of the human body and spirit, when strong senses of 'belonging' were taken for granted, gave people identities, and were routinely spoken of and legally addressed: to a past when face-to-face local communities predominated, with their character-full personalities, close inter-personal knowledge, often related problems, and painstakingly known boundaries. We need to consider questions about how they operated, how long they lasted, and why they declined. Many of the chapters go well into the twentieth century, as I am interested in long-term change. They are intended to outline some of the main forms of 'belonging' in the past and the issues that accompanied them, to show the prime structures and subjectivities of belonging, and to indicate some of their advantages and shortcomings. Through chosen themes, they will track changes in the senses or realities of belonging in the two and a half centuries after about 1700. Above all, this work holds at its centre the fundamental modern issues of local identity so as to frame an historical argument about how these have changed, and to open up historical ways in which these issues may be debated and assessed in a long-term perspective.

II

I use and stress the term '*parish*' in this book, as in its title. Yet as an Anglo-Welsh historian, baptised in a Welsh Presbyterian Methodist chapel in Llanrhidian in Gower, I do so with a slight sense of concern. For the Welsh were familiar historically with a greater degree of scattered settlement and a much stronger Nonconformist religious culture than existed in many regions of southern and midland England, and for them words like *cymuned* (community, a word having its roots in 'communion' in the religious sense) or *cymdogaeth* (neighbourhood) might often be preferred to *plwyf* (parish). Another word commonly used for the neighbourhood or place where one comes from or belongs is *ardal*. I will still use 'parish', and highlight it here, partly because of its undoubted administrative importance in both countries, and partly because Welsh understandings of *cymuned* or *cymdogaeth* or *ardal* can often supplant or stand alongside my usage of 'parish' when I refer to parish in the sense of locality, community or neighbourhood, as I sometimes do. Such understandings of non-parochial locality have many parallels too in northern and other English regions, although I suspect that the English–Welsh cultural differences are the most salient. There are interesting predicaments arising from marrying Welsh and English, as I know well, and I trust that such usage will not be construed as culturally high-handed. From now on, I shall use 'parish' as a convenient shorthand, as being closest to what I mean in a subjective *and* administrative sense across England and Wales, and by and large exactly what I mean. I shall also often be using 'parish' as a substitute or shorthand for 'township', and indeed for a number of other local entities. Again I do so with a plea for forbearance from northerners, and some others, who will be well aware of the considerable importance that townships often had as administrative units within the parish.

That said, I would like to summarise some of my main findings and emphases. The continuance and *vitality* of the parish as a crucial unit throughout the nineteenth century is stressed repeatedly in this book, whether in cultural, religious or welfare terms, which I take as given and accepted for the eighteenth century. W. E. Tate, like Sidney and Beatrice Webb, in effect wrote off the parish after 1834. All three saw the new poor law as 'The Strangulation of the Parish.'[13] These historians deserve the highest respect; indeed, few others did so much for parish history. Yet it seems to me that they severely underestimated its role after 1834. Whatever my topic, the key role of the parish as a unit for administration, community, and belonging emerges strongly throughout the nineteenth century, and particularly up to the 1870s and 1880s. For some purposes its importance even grew during that century. Industrialisation or 'modernisation' did little to dent or destroy its significance, and the waning of this enormously important historical entity has been much more of a twentieth-century phenomenon. What is more, these parish communities were not zephyrs of the imagination, unsteady

---

[13] W. E. Tate, *The Parish Chest: A Study of the Records of Parochial Administration in England* (1946, Cambridge, 1960), p. 22, citing the Webbs.

or precarious. On the contrary, they were concrete and real, deeply embedded in people's social and economic lives, as well as having strong emotional appeal – they had tangible boundaries that were fixed in the mind, of long medieval lineage, and they were strong legal entities of obligation and control. We will see that this has many implications for community and belonging.

Closely related to this theme is my stress upon the continuing hold of local attachment in the nineteenth century. A strong feeling of local and parochial belonging existed over a very long period, and it declined slowly, and late, along with the civil and ecclesiastical parochial organisation that fostered it. These senses of belonging were so palpable because the parish communities they related to were so real. We are not dealing here with misty, wishful notions of 'community', of the kind espoused since the 1970s, nor with the degraded, washed-out usage of the term that one so often hears today. As this would suggest, I am hoping to press the case for local history in a period when the nation state, national identity, and national expansion allegedly swept the boards. I hope to achieve for the social history of the parish in the nineteenth century what some exceptional early modern historians have accomplished for it: to underline its prominence and continued significance for people's lives, and to inspire more historians to study it.

I am also trying to infuse cultural meaning into administrative history, to extend such history to show how it has many cultural and social causes and ramifications, and to demonstrate how those interacted with administrative reforms. So in dealing with topics like the settlement laws, or the new poor law, or the 'new parishes', I have tried to integrate administrative history with broader social and cultural history. Some of my evidence is from official publications and legal manuals, from bodies such as the Poor Law Board or Parliamentary Select Committees. One has to come to terms with that evidence because it is massive, descriptive, influential and was so central to the administration of settlement, belonging and welfare. It can also be exacting to read and taxing on one's legal aptitude, despite its limitless human content and portrayal of suffering and selective advantage. So in spreading out cultural, folkloric, literary, and other such evidence alongside the official publications and legislation I hope to have produced a variegated work, that conveys cultural depth and meaning to some of the administrative subjects.

Religious issues and organisation, and civil-welfare administration, are topics that are usually separated by largely secularised modern historians. However, I have tried to show how they inter-relate, notably in chapter 7 on the 'new parishes', which considers religious organisation in conjunction with analysis of local identity, parochial reform and civil administration. Religion was unquestionably central in many people's lives and world views, and historians who miss that have a worrying occlusion when describing the past. Furthermore, Edwin Chadwick and Bishop Charles Blomfield had much in common, not least the influence of Bentham. There were fundamental similarities between the Poor Law Commission, and the Ecclesiastical Commission (which was central to church extension and new parish creation): the two key bodies that loom large in relation to chapters 5 and 7, and which were so associated with Chadwick and Blomfield respectively. One Commission ostensibly dealt with the relief of poverty and social welfare, the other with morality and spiritual welfare. Yet in many ways their purposes overlapped, in a Church–State duality often kept apart in the historiography. There are good reasons for discussing them together within the same book: there must be more holistic approaches to the parish. There are equally good reasons for highlighting religious administration in this discussion. In dealing with the state of communities, and with ideas of belonging, one certainly need not be as prescriptively religious as T. S. Eliot was – 'There is no life that is not in community, And no community not lived in praise of GOD'.[14] That was an exaggeration for many areas through much of the nineteenth century. Yet the centrality of community and religious feeling for vast numbers of people was inescapable. If we turn Eliot's present tense into the past tense, and apply his thoughts to contemporary administrative presumptions, we will not be far amiss as historians, and we should conduct our analyses accordingly.

What I call the 'culture of local xenophobia' is discussed in chapter 2. It is on attitudes to local outsiders in the past, the

[14] T. S. Eliot, 'Choruses from "The Rock"', II (1934), in his *Collected Poems, 1909–1962* (London, 1974), p. 168 (his capitalisation).

cultural and administrative forms taken by insider–outsider
divisions and resistances, the role of local boundaries, and *inter
alia* the implications which such attitudes had for ideas of
belonging and the emergence of the working class. This book
is no simple commendation of the historical parish, which certainly had its shadowy and callous sides. I am particularly
concerned here with a tendency to limit the exercise of humanity
to parish confines, with why this occurred, and how it changed.
For example, the more positive effects of Methodist organisation
on local horizons and 'closedness' are stressed. Even so, the
argument shows how persistent local cultures of xenophobia
were, and how crucial a prolonged attachment to the parish or
township was, lasting in many regions throughout the nineteenth century, and often lingering well into the twentieth. This
points to the obstacles these exclusive attitudes and local cultures were for the emergence of the working class, which I thus
take to be a much later development than did E. P. Thompson.

The legal structures and shifting categories of 'belonging' and
precedence that existed at parish level are analysed in chapter 3.
The evolution of settlement and irremovability laws between
1662 and 1948 are discussed, alongside the insider–outsider
hurdles which they created. Even within parishes, settlement
status divided people in a variety of ways. Settlement-law administration had many implications for community, belonging,
local consciousness, class allegiances, labour markets, and inter-
parish rivalries. It is not often realised how very long and
enduring these settlement laws were, from before 1662 to 1948,
and many of their repercussions deeply occupied contemporaries. Many parallels exist with larger-scale divisions today.
England and Wales had complex but clear-cut ideas and rights
of legal 'belonging' to distinct parishes or townships, which
structured belonging in many ways. Yet Scotland and Ireland
lacked these. This essential contrast had crucial repercussions –
after all, why were there no major 'clearances' of people from
England and Wales in this period? Could that be because their
senses of belonging were legally enshrined, whereas the Irish
and Scots, despite gripping senses of belonging, had no such
defence, thus bringing about – through evictions and forced
emigration – the forlorn, elegiac senses of nostalgic belonging
that many associate particularly with the cultures of those two

countries? Among other issues raised are important changes in who became settled and thus 'belonged' legally, what those changes meant for those who 'belonged' in a parish (and for the de-localised who did not), and the significance of the move from parish, to union, and then eventually (in 1948) to national 'settlement' and welfare eligibility.

'Of this parish', as a statement of belonging, is frequently found in the recording of marriages in parish registers. This evidence on marriage is analysed in chapter 4. Long-term shifts in parochial endogamy (marriages with both partners being of the parish) and exogamy are shown, with the notable finding that marital endogamy intensified through the eighteenth and early nineteenth centuries. There were also fascinating regional differences, which are discussed, as are the implications of long-term swings or cycles in marital behaviour. A situation of re-markably high parish endogamy, and narrowness of marital horizons, gave way in the later nineteenth century to a long-term decline in such marriage patterns, which occurred around the same time as the rural exodus. That late nineteenth-century decline in endogamy was decisive and dramatic, showing an opening up of local marriage horizons that was of considerable social significance. Furthermore, like many of the changes dis-cussed in this book, that decline in endogamy occurred surpris-ingly late, pointing again to the crucial and long-extended role of the parish, in this case with regard to marriage choices.

Attention shifts to the administration of welfare and poor relief in chapter 5, notably after 1834. This chapter is a reappra-isal of the new poor law. That law (1834–1929) is usually dis-cussed in a way that highlights the workhouse, and the Poor Law Amendment Act of 1834 is sometimes said to have driven the nails into the coffin of the parish. However, contrary to the intentions in 1834, the workhouse did not dominate the system. Normally well over 80 per cent of poor relief under this sys-tem was *out-door relief*, distributed as hitherto in people's own parishes, where they felt that they 'belonged'. In large regions (including most of Wales), over 90 per cent of relief was so delivered. The *threat* of the workhouse loomed large in working-class consciousness, and yet in-door relief was usually a minority experience. The aim in this chapter is once more to stress the key role of the parish, as the venue for out-relief, much as under the old poor law, showing its forms and continuance, and the ways in which such policies fitted with the deterrence of the workhouse. The chapter redefines the experience of this system, looks at regional, rural–urban, and Welsh–English differences, changes over time, the treatment of various 'classifications' of pauper, the reasons for out-relief continuities from the old poor law, and related issues – all of which bring us back to the parish as the locus for welfare.

Chapter 6 follows on logically from the discussion of the new poor law and the parish. It stresses the important role of parish overseers long into the new poor law, indeed until their abolition, which occurred as late as 1927. One could draw attention to the vigour of the parish and of ideas of local responsibility in the nineteenth century by looking at any parish officers, and this is done here for overseers, showing the enormous number of tasks that they continued to discharge. Once more, parish administration in the nineteenth century is underscored, drawing attention to how neglected that administration has been by historians, and discussing the significance for the community of the voluntary, usually unpaid, work that overseers did.

Well over 4,000 new parishes were created in the nineteenth and early twentieth centuries, and many more were altered, contributing to the separation of the civil from the ecclesiastical. By 1911 a majority of parishes in England and Wales were not coterminous for civil and ecclesiastical purposes. There has been very little attention to this 'new parish' phenomenon. Chapter 7 discusses these parishes, their geography, processes of formation, reasons for them, what they tell us about reforming zeal in the Church of England, and the influences that they and *laissez-faire* church building had on local and community life. It shows how these changes often disrupted holistic parish identities, divided the civil from the ecclesiastical, and often turned the parish into something that was harder to identify with. The discussion goes through to the destruction of churches and parish re-formations during and after the Second World War. A case study is also presented in this chapter of the Forest of Dean in Gloucestershire, to emphasise points about the effects of excessive new parish formation and re-creation.

'Belonging' as a theme is highly subjective, even though it was formally structured, and the interplay between the subjectivity and the structures is part of its fascination. Historians need to search for ways that uncover that subjectivity, however difficult for theoretical and evidential reasons that is. Chapter 8, which is on gravestones, belonging and local attachment, undertakes surveys of church and chapel burial grounds to consider how people expressed their senses of local attachment and belonging on their gravestones. It uses churchyard memorials to discuss how memorialisation with reference to place attachment changed, reinforcing chronologies unearthed in different ways earlier in the book. This chapter interprets this form of memorial evidence, and shows what it can tell us about subjective belonging, de-localisation and the decline of parish or local place attachment.

Why were these particular subjects chosen? They relate strongly to issues of parish and belonging, and they link together as such. In terms of an argument about the late chronology of parochial decline, they are mutually supportive. Yet they are also ones that have importance in respect of other historiographical debates: whether in historical demography, or to do with the emergence of class, or in connection with settlement, welfare and poor law history, Anglican organisational reform, churchyard heritage and memorialisation. In other words, even for readers whose main concerns lie outside the central themes of this book, these discussions are designed to have further interest and connectivity. I do hope, however, that the chapters develop some earlier historiographical themes, which may sometimes seem taken for granted or isolated, and refocus them so as to show their relevance for many modern problems of identity, local administration, senses of place and belonging. For example, the book brings together issues of settlement, belonging and multi-layered structures of exclusion and inclusion, and draws together areas of research on the poor law, so that they contribute more in general terms. This involves a fresh look at the historical subjects themselves, and may provide insights into them in their own right. After all, the issues of parish, belonging, local identities and administration are certainly not new, but have preoccupied many others in the past, in different ways. We will certainly deal better with the dilemmas of our own time when we understand more about how they were conceived and handled hitherto.

The chosen themes of this book are not necessarily pre-eminent in any assessment of belonging and local attachment, although some of them – poor law settlement, the provision of welfare, the changing roles of the parish, the culture of insider–outsider divisions, local office-holding, and perhaps marriage patterns – are likely to be important in most historians' judgements, especially when the focus is (as here) mainly on the sub-elite majority of the population. Nor is *the parish* unreservedly central, a unit to be placed and studied on a pedestal – many other local entities and areas were also of considerable significance for people's senses of belonging, in different contexts. I originally considered chapters on a wider range of topics, but put them aside through a desire to deal thoroughly and in fresh research terms with each. Many of the possibilities take one beyond the parish, to other local areas or cultural regions, to which people may also have felt an attachment. For example, there are outstanding questions relating to local self-subsistence, immediate economic networks, enclosure, the scale of regional trade, and the decline of the organic economy. Or there is the question of the impact of the railway on local communities, and connected to that, the rural exodus and its effects on people's senses of place. Proprietorial ideas of belonging, the relationships between estate structures and parish or township boundaries, and the effects of changing property ownership come to mind as important issues. Then there is the revealing subject of local and civic pride in place – one may think of city, town and village halls, chapel building, church restorations and donated artifacts, ceremonials and rituals, almshouses, celebrations of illustrious local persons, village signs, all of which are richly documented by photographic and other evidence. In fact, countless subjects come to mind on local pride in place, at least in the Victorian period. Some would argue that local pride has sadly diminished over the past half century, and planners, architects, and central government coercion are often blamed for that. Another theme of interest to me was the parish, belonging and insider–outsider divisions in Thomas Hardy's writing; and, extending such literary interest, there were the early mid-twentieth-century English rural writers, such as H. J. Massingham, Adrian Bell and A. G. Street, the 'rediscovering the local' back-to-the-land literature and its senses of place. The study of naturalists and their respective localities is a fascinating one, as a topic relating to the growing and uplifting interest in environmental history – which has managed to combine study of global problems while cherishing the fullness of the local. Here one thinks of the attachment to place of Gilbert White, John Clare, Richard Jefferies, Jim Vincent, W. H. Hudson and other such figures. Again going beyond the parish, there is the study of 'core' local families and their persistence or discontinuance over time. Comparative gendered senses of belonging is another important topic, often at micro-level, with many ramifications.[15] At a religious dimension, there are crucial questions that relate to the Anglican *versus* varying Nonconformist senses of place, with the dissenting circuits and organisational forms as alternatives to the parish. There was also the undoubted significance of what were known as 'countries' (in the sense of local districts, topographical, occupational, cultural, or dialectal regions); and then of *county* identities and loyalties, which were of increasing consequence during the Victorian period, partly no doubt related to the growth of inter-county sport, although I think that a sense of belonging to the county was not as important or long-established as to the parish.

Many of these topics cover other local areas than the parish. While the parish is highlighted in the title of this book, because of its administrative, legal and often subjective importance, it is obvious that many people lived close to parish boundaries, that parish entities were sometimes weak for topographical and other reasons, and that many parishioners had loyalties and senses of belonging elsewhere, whether to relatives, birthplaces, parishes of settlement where they did not reside, to localities within Methodist organisational circuits, to dialectal or working occupational districts, and so on. Such wider allegiances often became stronger over the period covered by this book – for example, friendly society or trade union affiliations. Much of my discussion takes account of these changes, and of different, multiple or ambiguous senses of local attachment. I would not

---

[15] Gendered elements of belonging mainly appear in this book in connection with settlement (chapter 3), marriage (chapter 4), and welfare policies (chapter 5), seeming to be less relevant for other chapters. At the level of micro-history, of hearth and home, and of work, gender is of considerable importance for the theme of belonging.

for a moment wish to rule out such wider areas in relation to the theme of belonging, all of which are highly credible, easily documented, and warrant extended discussion.

It is impossible in one book to deal in a full and balanced way with such a potentially wide range of topics and possibilities. I have separately covered the subjects of British regional novels and local identities,[16] regional religious cultures,[17] and church seating, belonging and the local social order.[18] These connect strongly to the themes of this book. The cultural forms of denominational religion and regional fiction usually addressed broader affiliations and cultural regions than those linked to the parish. Like the discussion of the parish here, local denominational cultures and regional religious identities, and the huge growth of British regional fiction, were prominent features of the nineteenth century. As with the vitality of the parish, these forms of local culture were certainly not impeded or undercut by industrialisation, and indeed they flourished during it.[19] 'Parish and belonging' is a broad subject, hugely important to people in the past, not dismissible as parish-pump gossip. This book's chapters selectively choose from many options, and (given constraints of space) omit revealing possibilities. The theme of belonging can be pursued in many ways, as varied responses to the modern world. Other historians, assuming they feel the importance of these issues, can take up such topics. They may tackle alternative foci of belonging and community – guilds, industrial companies and communities, urban streets and districts, religious groupings, wider units, topographical *pays*, and so on – they will probably conceive of many more of personal interest to themselves, they may intervene more theoretically than I have done, and I hope that they will excuse me for not having broached more options myself.

---

[16] K. D. M. Snell (ed.), *The Regional Novel in Britain and Ireland, 1800–1990* (Cambridge, 1998); and my *The Bibliography of Regional Fiction in Britain and Ireland, 1800–2000* (Aldershot, 2002).

[17] K. D. M. Snell and P. S. Ell, *Rival Jerusalems: The Geography of Victorian Religion* (Cambridge, 2000).

[18] *Ibid.*, ch. 10.

[19] This book, like my previous work, therefore supports the arguments of J. Langton, 'The industrial revolution and the regional geography of England', *Transactions of the Institute of British Geographers*, 9 (1984).

III

I have deliberately not engaged very openly with sociological and cultural theory in this book, even though there is some theoretical literature on the theme of belonging, and far more on communities, identities, globalisation, and secularisation, from across the social sciences and humanities. Some of this literature, for example by Anthony Cohen, Marilyn Strathern and others,[20] is referenced where necessary, as is theoretically inclined work relating to class and local or regional history. It would, however, have made a long book even lengthier to have produced a more theoretical work, and the adaptations and generalisations of more theoretical writing might have compromised an exactness of historical delineation, and substituted for evidence and new research. Some of the theoretical literature contains many historical mistakes, and it is probably best to use it as a jumping-off point, inspiring new questions, rather than regard it with too much respect. Experience also teaches us that historians who link their work strongly to certain theoretical positions find that their writing soon becomes redundant as theoretical fashions change or become shown as poor or constraining history. The historiographical 'theory cycle' is surprisingly short. This should not stop historians contributing to the enhancement of theory. Yet my own view is that historians – who are normally quick to respond to developments in the modern world – should gradually and creatively forge their own lineages, narratives and theory, in well-researched service of the large questions, rather than respectfully adopting much that is currently on offer.

The 'postmodern' community is said to consist of temporary groupings, of free-flowing sociable groups, lacking a fixed basis, self-forming, voluntary, reflexive, open, ambivalent, indefinite, reliant upon electronic communications, hard to define, compatible with expansive individualism, opportunist, often destructively indifferent to localities or draining them of

[20] M. Strathern, *Kinship at the Core: An Anthropology of Elmdon, a Village in North-west Essex in the Nineteen-sixties* (Cambridge, 1981); A. P. Cohen (ed.), *Belonging: Identity and Social Organisation in British Rural Cultures* (Manchester, 1982); A. P. Cohen (ed.), *Symbolising Boundaries: Identity and Diversity in British Cultures* (Manchester, 1986).

content. Such features are exaggerated as a description of current life by many theorists, and then contrasted with historical territorial communities that apparently were stable, ordered, small-scale and closed. Yet, as we will see, the nature of belonging and community in the past was rather different to that: it could be voluntary, reflexive, based on choice, opting for a certain parish over others, shifting allegiance between parishes and away from those that one (or one's family) earlier belonged to. Capitalism did not 'undermine' 'traditional' communities and belonging to them, but, on the contrary, it co-existed with and helped to shape them. Most of the ways in which people gained legal settlement – the ticket to belong – were capitalistic. Traditional forms of 'belonging' persisted with a fluid labour market, high levels of waged labour, and with a degree of personal choice as to where one 'belonged'. Many people opted for a certain settlement, thinking it an advantageous one to belong to. They might do that for reasons of welfare generosity, or because of low rates (if they were ratepayers), or because of occupational compatibility, access to resources, or many other reasons. Even the poor – maybe especially the poor – thought like that, and gained, or shifted (or 'forgot'), settlements and their belonging accordingly. Community could be chosen in the past, like today, but people chose a parish or township, not a network or voluntary and changing range of associates who are little tied in local space. The parish or township communities in the past could constantly reformulate themselves, accepting certain newcomers, allowing them settlements, ejecting others, putting barriers up against yet others. People could enter or exit them.

Such behaviour runs counter to much sociological theory about 'traditional' communities. Nor have we 'lost' such communities in the senses sometimes thought – to think like that is to misunderstand the nature of settlement, belonging and community in the past. We have lost much, but earlier communities were not stable, static, clogged, coherently ordered or layered, pitched like heavy railway sleepers, as supports for subsequent rails, rapid movement, new vistas and theoretical contrasts. Rather, those communities were often fluid, with a regular flux of belonging. The parish was also much structured or internally layered in terms of belonging as a status. Belonging could be a sought after yet temporary footing. Resistance to outsiders was still real and took culturally agreed rituals and forms, frequently defining the parish in oppositional terms to other parishes. Parish identity was something that men and women enlisted themselves into, and that was often reinforced (as often as necessary) by disagreement with other parishes, a process in which such people became conscious and manipulative players. Settlement disputes were ostensibly about who belonged to the parish and so were eligible for welfare there – they were also about the parish's identity and individuality, in contradistinction to other parishes, and the right of each parish to define its own constitution. Parishes would incur much legal expense to that end. The insider–outsider divisions here often meant denying the humanity of people from other parishes *until* they had met certain criteria within one's own parish, earning their legal place in it – as many did.

Belonging, like the parish communities that produced it, was socially, culturally and legally constructed. It was also often elective, individualised, a preference in a range of choices – whether poorly or well understood – and something that could be reconceived and changed, within and across the parish system. The options were wider or narrower in different periods and places, and for many poor people those options declined in the nineteenth century, with such people more often taking paternal settlement, as changeable legal settlement became less accessible. Even so, one's identity as linked to parish affiliation was alterable and open to manipulation – it was not rigidly ordained or beyond control. For this was a highly capitalistic society, and the financial and cultural consequences of transplantable belonging meant that it was contested between different parties, sometimes acquiesced in, even eagerly, sometimes bitterly resisted, in many ways. The disputes over belonging were acrimonious and expensive – between individuals, between communities, between lawyers – and we can make sense of this only by appreciating the importance of parish belonging. Running through all this was the desire to belong, and that was eminently attainable, even by default, and provided considerable personal security and satisfaction. Today, by comparison, we have the flux of movement – a picaresque internationalism – we have the insecurity, and the search for belonging; but the significant decline of the parish or township, for civil and religious reasons, means that we now lack the units of belonging which those entities once provided, and the local knowledge, integration and care that they engendered. None of the alternatives, whether 'society', ethnicity, the nation, or the 'postmodern' 'community' options, provide substitutes which are comparably adequate.

These chapters point to many conclusions and implications, which may vary for each reader. It is my task to elucidate the past – readers can reflect on the present, which is just as complicated as the past, and in some ways less familiar. As history, this books tells a story about unique, structured and culturally accepted forms of belonging, pertaining especially to the parish in the modern period, about how they worked, and about their staged decline, notably from late in the nineteenth century. It does this through quite a wide variety of methods and types of evidence, some of which are more approachable than others. This book moves between the folkloric and the quantitative, with many forms of evidence and methods between. I hope that this reinforces its arguments, fits with respective themes, and gives a fuller picture of the legislative, cultural, economic and other means by which parish identity and forms of belonging were created and expressed. The blended topics, approaches and sources were mainly my own effort to answer questions I set out with. I write largely as a social-science historian influenced by social history 'from below', whose main concern is with the quality of life and structures of human welfare. I have no problems in believing that the past was 'real', that much of that reality can be discerned and outlined, and that certain themes, emphases, patterns, experiences and consistent personal accounts emerge repeatedly from the documentary and quantitative evidence. I also believe that the past is hugely instructive, mainly in the sense that it is a repository of so many options, a means of discovering and evaluating other human and social relationships, showing how they worked or failed hitherto, in the hope of re-establishing a balance between the facets of individual existence. It has been said by some that writing history is a matter of argumentative expertise, a defensive outwardly motivated production; by others that it is an imaginative form of pure textuality – but for me it is more a matter of personal curiosity and enquiry, swayed by present concerns; and accentuated levels of reflexivity and scepticism push me into different methods and sources in a search for their mutual confirmation. In short, the discoveries and arguments of these chapters persuade me as a generalised account of past structures, experiences and valuations. Yet what their conclusions and implications may be for future historiography, for studies of belonging and community, for theoretical schemas about community, modernism and its sequels, may vary considerably, and it feels presumptious to attempt to swing such outcomes. We all know that humankind is engaged in an open-ended, forward-looking project riddled with environmental and human damage, that despite its lessons and influences upon us the past is not readily understandable as a chrysalis or augury of what is to come, that the future will hold many mixes of the local and the global, and that many kinds of history will be deployed to predict, explain, service or criticise that future. My own preferences of course are largely for the local, the immediate, the everyday, the face-to-face, the intimately known: for 'belonging' as tied to place in forms that brought some security, fulfilment and pride in the past. For I have yet to believe that 'postmodern' travel, fluidity, 'weak' and 'thin' networks, and electronic communications – the de-territorialised, diluted, global parish, with its colossal gossip networks, and its many dissenters – has much conduced to tolerance of diversity, or extended inclusion and humanitarianism, or can supply anything remotely commensurate in environmental and human terms with what we are losing. But then I am a historian.

CHAPTER 2

The culture of local xenophobia

The social conscience of a rural people is limited by the parish bounds.[1]

Once men begin to feel cramped in their geographical, social and mental habitat, they are in danger of being tempted by the simple solution of denying one section of the species the right to be considered as human.[2]

'Who's 'im, Bill?'
'A stranger!'
'Eave 'arf a brick at 'im.'[3]

This chapter is on the theme of local identity, exclusion and what I am calling 'the culture of local xenophobia'. 'Xenophobia' is an unattractive word, although perhaps that suits its meaning – it is defined as a fear or dislike of things foreign or strange.[4] I shall use it here as prefaced by 'local'. In other words, this chapter is not dealing with anti-foreigner or anti-outsider sentiments in the more modern international, ethnic or religious senses. In fact, the word 'foreigner' was widely used in the past, even as late as the 1940s, to refer to somebody from another parish or locality, and I will normally use it in that local historical way. Such usage connects back to, and further justifies, the term 'local xenophobia'.

---

[1] F. G. Thomas, *The Changing Village: An Essay on Rural Reconstruction* (1939, London, 1945), p. 90.
[2] C. Lévi-Strauss, *Tristes Tropiques* (1955, Harmondsworth, 1984), p. 190.
[3] *Punch*, 25 February 1854.
[4] I am not strictly concerned here with 'local pride' or 'parochial loyalty'. The latter were more benign or positive terms than local xenophobia, which were sometimes (although not necessarily) linked sentiments. They would necessitate a much wider discussion. However, I will give some examples of parochial loyalty here, stressing its importance, for this is clearly related to my main subject. Further, as its definition implies, 'local xenophobia' does not necessarily imply action, although it often did.

Wider national xenophobic attitudes, whether racist, religious or nationalist, have been much analysed by historians and other academics. Given modern problems, it is very important that study of these issues should occur. By comparison, almost nothing has been written by historians about the subject of local xenophobia, even though that subject bears so much on how, and when, humanitarian attitudes broached parochial confines. The reasons for this neglect are interesting, and probably lie in the course taken by modern social and labour history. There has been great emphasis on the collective features of working-class activity in the eighteenth and nineteenth centuries. E. P. Thompson's *The Making of the English Working Class* (1963), inspiring so much further historiography, placed an overwhelming emphasis on the growth of shared consciousness, upon the ways in which the lower orders came to identify together as a class. Most English working people, Thompson wrote, 'came to feel an identity of interests as between themselves, and as against their rulers and employers', and this apparently happened 'in the years between 1780 and 1832'.[5] A very large body of historical writing, usually empathising with the labouring classes, augmented these views, in some cases altering Thompson's chronology (even by a century or more),[6] dealing with a great variety of communities, regions and forms of work, placing alternative stresses on political, social and economic events and responses to them which exacerbated feelings of class interest. Studies of rural and industrial protest, of the development of trade unions, of the progress of radical agendas in the nineteenth century, have returned repeatedly to Thompson's key theme of the formation of the working class.

The enormous value of this thesis as an organising principle for historical study and debate is indisputable. It has been conspicuous in much of the finest historical research, providing a focus and set of issues that many historians have adopted as central to their scholarly purposes. Even when class, or at least working-class consciousness, was judged by some sociologists

---

[5] E. P. Thompson, *The Making of the English Working Class* (1963, Harmondsworth, 1975), p. 12.
[6] See in particular E. J. Hobsbawm, *Worlds of Labour* (London, 1984), ch. 11, arguing for the emergence of 'the working class' in the later nineteenth century, a view that I share.

to be an increasingly questionable social reality in the later twentieth century, the historiographical momentum inspired by E. P. Thompson continued almost unabated. Whatever the priorities of very recent times, with their liability to influence historiography, most English social historians concerned with the urban and rural labouring poor were resolute and faithful to much of the earlier agenda of the 1960s and 70s. This has led to an ever more refined understanding of certain subjects which have been highlighted as especially worthy of study. Some repetition aside, and allowing for some waning of earlier theoretical purposes, it has promoted scholarly value, given rise to fuller and more professional analysis of evidence, or more original, sometimes interdisciplinary, interpretations of the issues at stake.

Where such a weight of consensus can be detrimental, however, is in precluding or over-shadowing areas of historical understanding which lean in other directions: which imply different questions or ideas about historical trajectory, which may invite conclusions that are contrary to received emphases, or which may query the whole agenda of accepted themes for discussion. A stress on class is clearly highly relevant to an understanding of change during the nineteenth century. Yet as Dorothy Thompson said in a subsequent discussion about her late husband: 'we were probably wrong' about class; we failed to see (I paraphrase her now) that what people kill each other for has to do with ethnicity, otherness, kinship, nations and so on. People don't kill each other for reasons of class.[7] One can think of probable exceptions to this; and if one defines these to be cases of class rather than caste they were highly significant. Even so, looking back at the labour history of the past five decades, at the decline of Marxist influence, and at the ethnic and religious conflicts that face us now, as in the past, I think that we would agree that her emphasis is basically correct. Indeed, some of E. P. Thompson's later work on custom, common right and ritual itself raised issues relating to boundaries and 'otherness' in English rural societies, placing a stress on the

---

[7] Dorothy Thompson interviewed in *A Life of Dissent: Remembering E. P. Thompson*, Channel 4, 18 September 1993. One can document killings that were closely related or attributable to class, but her main comparative emphasis seems valid.

consequences for the emerging working class of the loss of resources like commons, which made the poor 'strangers in their own land'. He was surely right to stress that custom pertained, above all, to the parish.

> The communal economy was parochial and exclusive: if Weldon's rights were 'ours', then Brigstock men and women must be kept out . . . for those who 'belonged' to the parish, there remained some sense that they 'owned' it and had a voice in its regulation . . . Common right, which was in lax terms coterminous with settlement, was *local* right, and hence was also a power to exclude strangers.[8]

He alluded also to questions of localism in discussing a transition from locally supplied markets, where all parties knew something of each other, to the more impersonal relations of large urban markets.[9] Such matters are central for analyses of change from credit based upon local personal repute, to impersonalised cash transactions, and to the issues of scale implicit here. Indeed, the question of what is 'local' – of what areas or spatial limits are involved – and of the role of cultural barriers, has preoccupied many historians.

With such hints and thoughts in mind, I would like to pursue the theme of local xenophobia, and draw attention to its historical prominence. Such a discussion may raise problems for the usual chronologies of 'the making of the working class'. It may not float with the historiographical tide, nor show the labouring poor in a very politically correct or progressive light. However, it opens up areas of labouring sensibility and local identity that have usually been missed by modern British historians, who may occasionally have been prone to romanticise the social and cultural values of the working class. We need to consider the forms that this 'culture of local xenophobia' took, and to raise questions about how prevalent such attitudes were, and when they changed. I shall pay particular attention to the eighteenth, nineteenth and early twentieth centuries, and to rural and cottage-industrial areas of England and Wales. After all, in 1801 nearly four-fifths of the population still lived in rural

---

[8] E. P. Thompson, *Customs in Common* (1991, Harmondsworth, 1993), pp. 179, 184 (his italics); B. D. Palmer, *E. P. Thompson: Objections and Oppositions* (London, 1994), p. 147.
[9] Thompson, *Customs in Common*, p. 292.

areas.[10] I intend this not so much as a critique of class-based interpretations, but rather as a way of moderating their appeal, and adding angles of view which deserve far more study in their own right. For local xenophobia was assuredly one of the root features in the attitudes and cultures of labouring people in the past.

Even if one's intentions were closely akin to E. P. Thompson's in 1963, it would probably be agreed that one partial way of considering the growth of class consciousness would be to see it as a result of a breaking down of localism and of different kinds of boundaries among the labouring poor. Such boundaries might take many forms. They could for example be geographical, grounded upon the confines of a territory of civil or ecclesiastical administration, which had come to have particular significance to the labouring classes over centuries of history. One thinks above all of the parish or, in some regions, of the township or hamlet, which could eclipse the parish in subjective senses of belonging. Alternatively, boundaries could be based upon *skill* and working attainment: demarcations between apprenticed and unskilled workers, or those between different skilled occupations, almost all of which aimed to defend their trades or 'mysteries' against dilution by 'foreigners' and interlopers. This division by skill, strongly legitimated by the 1563 Statute of Artificers, by royal charters, and by guild, company, trade society and trade union customs, was an all-pervasive feature of the eighteenth- and nineteenth-century labour market. It has been very extensively discussed by historians, who have seen it and other aspects of sectionalism as fundamental barriers to the emergence of a more unified working-class consciousness.[11] The gradual erosion of such barriers, or weakening of

---

[10] J. L. Gayler, I. Richards and J. A. Morris, *A Sketch-Map Economic History of Britain* (1957, London, 1965), p. 118.

[11] The points of many historians on the disunity and sectionalism of the nineteenth-century working classes, and on their 'particularistic loyalties and preferences', are well summarised in G. Eley, 'Edward Thompson, social history and political culture: the making of a working-class public, 1780–1850', in H. J. Kaye and K. McClelland (eds.), *E. P. Thompson: Critical Perspectives* (Cambridge, 1990), pp. 24–6. G. Stedman Jones commented that 'by and large throughout the nineteenth and twentieth centuries conflicts of demarcation between different groups of workers were of greater moment than battles between workers and employers'. See his 'The determinist fix:

them in many occupations, and the rise of general unionism and related developments, presaged the more cohesive working class of the 1920s.

In some districts, where certain skills were highly developed, forms of exclusion based upon skill and apprenticeship co-alesced with ideas of local attachment. I think for example of framework knitters in some areas of Leicestershire, of ribbon weavers in Coventry, of some of the ship-building communities, of watch-making in parts of London, of cotton spinners in some of the south Lancashire towns. None of these was exclusively located in such areas, but their industries were quite regionally concentrated. One can also find demarcations in the boundaries of marketing or services, as for example affecting brick-making in some regions – brickmasters not being able to sell their bricks beyond a certain district, as was true in parts of Lancashire.[12] Or neighbouring blacksmiths would sometimes agree not to step on to each other's ground as far as the taking of work was concerned.[13] An association of production or even sales with specific areas was clearly not true of many products. It was compromised in part because the tramping artisan fraternised with other members of his trade society scattered around the country at centres of employment. The form of identity here, insofar as it pertained to skill and work, might well transcend locality: the main barriers between workers comprising those of particular and 'legally' obtained skills which normally con-ferred acceptance or rejection within the 'respectable' branch of their trade. Some other occupations, such as colliers, lacking an apprenticeship system, but sometimes tramping between coal-fields, could also have characteristics in common with these skilled workers as far as extra-local allegiances were concerned,

some obstacles to the further development of the linguistic approach to history in the 1990s', *History Workshop Journal*, 42 (1996), p. 20. See also the interesting comments in R. Hutton, *The Stations of the Sun: A History of the Ritual Year in Britain* (1996, Oxford, 1997), pp. 421–2.

[12] R. N. Price, 'The other face of respectability: violence in the Manchester brickmaking trade, 1859–1870', *Past and Present*, 66 (1975), pp. 114–15.

[13] B. Reay, *Microhistories: Demography, Society and Culture in Rural England, 1800–1930* (Cambridge, 1996), 24; J. Ayres (ed.), *Paupers and Pig Killers: The Diary of William Holland, a Somerset Parson, 1799–1818* (Gloucester, 1984), p. 158.

and their rapidly growing communities were often more open than many others.[14]

With most less skilled occupations, however, the barriers and notions of outsiders more commonly involved geographical limits. Many agricultural workers were affiliated to parish, township, hamlet or estate, and such extremely local units of belonging often eclipsed any wider allegiance. This is not to rule out an attachment or sense of community that related to county, to a multi-parochial town or city, to groupings of parishes which shared certain historical concerns, or a shared resource (e.g. coal in the Forest of Dean), or dense kinship networks, dialect, working habits, costume,[15] key employers, estate structures, or other such features. One can document all these in many ways, and historians have often done so. Yet, as so many would-be poor law reformers lamented in the nineteenth century, it was above all the *parish* to which the poorer rural classes felt that they belonged. Incorporated parishes, and later poor law unions, were bitterly attacked because they violated the principle that the poor should be relieved in their *own* parishes.[16] As William Cobbett remarked, 'every man and woman and child old enough to understand any thing, looks upon his parish as being partly his'.[17] Elsewhere, in *Rural Rides*, Cobbett gave striking examples of extremely local horizons, noting for example a woman, 'about thirty years old', for whom 'the

---

[14] These points about coal-mining communities are well made in R. Thompson, 'A breed apart? Class and community in a Somerset coal-mining parish, *c.* 1750–1850', *Rural History*, 16 (2005).

[15] 'Smocks were often of different colours according to the village they were worn in.' G. Eliot, *Silas Marner* (1861, Harmondsworth, 1969), p. 252 n. 5 by Q. D. Leavis (the editor), although she gave no further reference. The indicative variations of smock designs and colours over larger regions are well documented, for example by A. Armes, *English Smocks* (Leicester, 1974); J. Ayres, *British Folk Art* (New York, 1977), pp. 124–5.

[16] A. J. Peacock, *Bread or Blood: A Study of the Agrarian Riots in East Anglia in 1816* (London, 1965), p. 32; E. A. Goodwyn (ed.), *Selections from Norwich Newspapers, 1760–1790* (Ipswich, 1973), pp. 71, 94, 130–8; A. Digby, *Pauper Palaces* (London, 1978), p. 75; P. Muskett, 'A picturesque little rebellion? The Suffolk workhouses in 1765', *Bulletin of the Society for the Study of Labour History*, 41 (1980), pp. 28–31.

[17] *Political Register* (20 February 1834), pp. 241–2, quoted in I. Dyck, *William Cobbett and Rural Popular Culture* (Cambridge, 1992), p. 161. As we will see in chapter 3, this sense of attachment to one's 'home' parish is abundantly confirmed by the letters that poor people wrote back to their settlements. An outstanding collection of such letters is T. Sokoll (ed.), *Essex Pauper Letters, 1731–1837* (Oxford, 2001).

utmost extent of her voyages had been about *two and a half miles!'*. He added that

the *facilities*, which now exist of *moving human bodies from place to place*, are amongst the *curses* of the country, the destroyers of industry, of morals, and, of course, of happiness. It is a great error to suppose, that people are rendered stupid by remaining always in the same place. This was a very acute woman, and as well behaved as need to be.[18]

George Eliot in *Felix Holt* wrote of the shepherd whose 'solar system was the parish', and she elaborated extensively on this theme in *Silas Marner*, where she described how 'superstition clung easily round every person or thing that was at all un-wonted', especially attaching itself to outsiders like pedlars, knife-grinders, or a wandering weaver like Silas. Many writers and witnesses described very localised senses of place and loy-alty.[19] Indeed, one of the thoughts that attracted John Constable to paint Willy Lot's cottage – the house depicted in *The Haywain* – was that its occupant had lived there all his life.

Certainly to the rural labouring poor the parish boundaries mattered. One need only read John Clare's poetry and prose to

---

[18] W. Cobbett, *Rural Rides* (1830, Harmondsworth, 1975), pp. 291–2 (his italics). I am not suggesting that such immobility was normal or common, for that would be contrary to significant evidence on migration. Nevertheless, many commentators documented it, and it was repeatedly discussed in the poor law reform literature of *c.* 1795–1834, and indeed thereafter. Cobbett was much less disparaging of such local attachment than some of his radical contemporaries. See the excellent discussion in I. Dyck, 'Local attachments, national identities and world citizenship in the thought of Thomas Paine', *History Workshop Journal*, 35 (1993).

[19] Eliot, *Felix Holt* (1866, Harmondsworth, 1975), p. 76; Eliot, *Silas Marner*, pp. 51–2; *Sixth Report from the Select Committee on Settlement, and Poor Removal*, XI (1847), p. 266: 'they are so much attached to the localities where they have been living, that you can hardly drive them out of a parish to any distance . . . There is a very great indisposition on the part of our labourers to leave their parish to seek work elsewhere; and in fact it is a thing generally known, that they will not do it . . . The very nature of the work that they carry out, and their habits of life, all operate against it.' This was a statement from Essex, and there were many similar comments throughout the 1847 Reports. Counter-examples tended to come from northern England, especially Northumberland. Rather later, see R. L. Gales, *Studies in Arcady, and Other Essays from a Country Parsonage*, vol. I (London, n.d., *c.* 1912), p. 40 ('for many of them . . . the outside world does not exist'), pp. 42, 64, 104–5. Even on a small island like Guernsey, another parish was looked upon 'as quite another part of the world'. J. Stevens Cox (ed.), *Guernsey Folklore: Recorded in the Summer of 1882* (1971, St Peter Port, 1986), p. 12, originally published by 'A. P. A.' in *The Antiquary* (November 1882). For discussion of rural localism in a later period, see H. Newby, *The Deferential Worker* (1977, Harmondsworth, 1979), pp. 74, 261–2.

sense this. He migrated locally in search of work, usually within a radius of about six miles around his Northamptonshire parish of Helpston, and he was highly literate. Yet he still referred to the area and people outside his parish as being 'out of the world', 'the world's end', beyond 'the brink of the world', 'out of my knowledge', 'the inhabitants of new countrys', 'another country', 'a foreign land to me'.[20] One recalls so many intensely detailed local maps (relating for example to enclosure, tithes, or rating), including some Ordnance Survey maps until 1872,[21] on which, at the parish boundary, nothing was shown beyond, the parish-maintained roads simply seeming to terminate as dead-ends, as if dropping off the edge of the world. Indeed, many roads or tracks *did* terminate at the parish edge, notably in the open-field village, their function being only for access to parish fields from a nucleated settlement. Such terminating radii, like a fallen immobile spokeful wheel rimmed by cramped felloes – and my meaning moves close to similar sounding words – intensified the feeling of the parish as a closed circumferential world. We do not construct maps like that now. The parish boundaries were usually intimately known by the poor, who were often consulted by clergy,[22] by JPs, Tithe or Enclosure Commissioners when they were conducting tithe apportionment surveys or arbitrating boundary matters.[23] Parish boundaries

---

[20] E. Robinson (ed.), *John Clare's Autobiographical Writings* (1983, Oxford, 1986), pp. 34, 58, 63, 67. Out of his parish, 'I even was foolish enough to think the suns course was alterd and that it rose in the west and sat in the east.' *Ibid.*, p. 63. On Clare, see in particular J. Barrell, *The Idea of Landscape and the Sense of Place, 1730–1840: An Approach to the Poetry of John Clare* (Cambridge, 1972), esp. ch. 3. Compare Eliot, *Silas Marner*, p. 51, on how to rural inhabitants 'the world outside their own direct experience was a region of vagueness and mystery'.

[21] D. Smith, *Maps and Plans for the Local Historian and Collector* (London, 1988), pp. 105, 110, discussing the OS 25 inch maps produced as parish plans for about fifteen counties. In Ordnance Survey work, the importance of the parish boundary often significantly lessened in the later nineteenth and early twentieth centuries. See G. Messenger, *The Ordnance Survey One-Inch Map of England and Wales. Third Edition (Large Sheet Series). A Descriptive and Cartographical Monograph* (London, 1988), pp. 9, 235, 237, 239–40.

[22] R. Wells (ed.), *Victorian Village: The Diaries of the Reverend John Coker Egerton of Burwash, 1857–1888* (Stroud, 1992), 16 August 1857, p. 27: 'met a man who chaperoned me shewed me the boundaries of the parish wh. are intricate. His name was Budd.'

[23] For examples of hotly fought boundary disputes accompanying enclosure, involving intervening commons, road closures, costly examination of witnesses, and enmities between lords of manors, see Notts. County Record Office (CRO), DD.SK 217/1

also had much bearing on pauper settlement, militia balloting, the duties of constables, vital registration, burial entitlement, liability for tithe, church and poor rates, the limits of commons and wastes, access to fuel, rights of way or the responsibility to repair roads or bridges.[24]

All of these matters had implications for the village poor. When the surveyors and 'meresmen' (boundary men) of the Ordnance Survey were doing their work, they frequently recruited and paid agricultural labourers for advice about precise boundary locations and markers.[25] Indeed, such labourers often served as meresmen, signing (or when illiterate making their mark) in the boundary remark books of the Ordnance Survey after the Ordnance Survey Act in 1841.[26] Elderly inhabitants' memories (going back to their childhood experiences on parish Rogationtide perambulations) were often crucial in the resolution of boundary disputes, as they were for checking the accuracy of estate maps and issues of tithe liability.[27] Such people of humble status were commonly active in perambulations, partly to prevent encroachments on commons or wastes.[28] They were strongly encouraged by the Anglican Church, which

---

(between Ollerton and Walesby over an area of land that was an alder holt), or the fence breaking affecting Basford against Nottingham, or Lenton against Radford: *Nottingham Journal*, 9 November 1799 and 25 May 1793. I am grateful to Madge Brown for these references.

[24] See e.g. Wells, *Victorian Village*, pp. 275–6, for a dispute between parishes over the repair of a bridge.

[25] J. H. Andrews, *A Paper Landscape: The Ordnance Survey in Nineteenth-century Ireland* (Oxford, 1975), pp. 62, 320–1; C. Cox, 'Parish boundary markers and the decline of parish authority: a 19th-century Gloucestershire study', *The Local Historian*, 18 (1988), p. 58.

[26] T. Owen and E. Pilbeam, *Ordnance Survey: Map Makers to Britain since 1791* (London, 1992), p. 39; Cox, 'Parish boundary markers', p. 37.

[27] B. Bushaway, *By Rite: Custom, Ceremony and Community in England, 1700–1880* (London, 1982), pp. 84, 86; Reay, *Microhistories*, p. 239.

[28] J. C. Cox, *Churchwardens Accounts from the Fourteenth Century to the Close of the Seventeenth Century* (London, 1913), p. 90; D. Underdown, *Revel, Riot and Rebellion: Popular Politics and Culture in England, 1603–1660* (Oxford, 1985), pp. 90–1; Thompson, *Customs in Common*, pp. 117–19. In many parishes, the custom of perambulation declined after Parliamentary enclosure, partly because the cartographic and related documentation at the end of that process made such activity less necessary, and partly because ambiguities about boundaries on open, common, moor or waste land were less contentious when such land had been enclosed. Bushaway, *By Rite*, pp. 25, 87–8: 'although the labouring poor persisted in its actions in many places well into the nineteenth century'.

had a vested interest in parochial exclusivity, and played a coordinating and sometimes funding role in perambulations.[29] This wide participation was especially true before perambulation became a minority pursuit (or a revived custom in altered form) among historically minded clerical associates, as it often did in the later nineteenth and early twentieth centuries. Perambulation (or 'bannering', 'hunting the borough', 'processioning', 'ganging') was also significantly called 'possessioning' or 'possessing'.[30] It was one of many forms of marching being practised during the eighteenth and nineteenth centuries, almost all of which served to reinforce a clear sense of the limits and boundaries of parochial space, creating a subjective map that served as 'the collective memory of the community'.[31]

---

[29] Bushaway, *By Rite*, pp. 84, 273. The lord of the manor would also sometimes finance food, drink, payments for hole digging, etc., during perambulations, and their costs could also be defrayed against the poor rate. Anglican clergy especially disliked evangelical and Nonconformist propensities to override parochial boundaries in their preaching. See Revd E. F. Synnott, *Five Years' Hell in a Country Parish* (London, 1920), p. 101; R. Brown, *Church and State in Modern Britain, 1700–1850* (London, 1991), p. 428. In at least one case (involving Earls Barton and Castle Ashby in Northamptonshire), a dispute between two clergymen over rights to baptise and marry certain parishioners (1756–63) led to threatened prosecutions, and aggravated or caused a long-running feud that overflowed into boundary issues and matters of pauper settlement for at least the next fifty years. I am grateful to Christine Vialls for this information. For similar reasons, disputes could often accompany the creation of new parishes in the nineteenth century, as under the 1843 New Parishes Act (6 & 7 Vic., c. 37), or the 1844 and 1856 Acts (7 & 8 Vic., c. 94; 19 & 20 Vic., c. 104), passed to facilitate this. For example, P. Howell, 'Church and chapel in Wales', in C. Brooks and A. Saint (eds.), *The Victorian Church: Architecture and Society* (Manchester, 1995), p. 121, on ill-feeling between Llanelwedd and Cwmbach Llechryd (Brecons.) after a new church was built in 1886.

[30] Bushaway, *By Rite*, p. 83; S. Farrell, 'The chaining of the countryside: an evaluation of Parliamentary enclosure with reference to three Northamptonshire parishes' (MA dissertation, Centre for English Local History, University of Leicester, 1997), p. 52 n. 124, citing an example of twenty-six 'Persons who went Possessing', their names listed in the parish register of Great Addington (Northants.) in a note dated 30 May 1703. Such a list was clearly thought to be of future use to the parish. Other such processions included skimmingtons, the activities of plough Monday, mummers and wassailing at Christmas, the activities of St Thomas' and St Valentine's days, the marching of Sunday school children, or of friendly societies on club-walking day and other local clubs, the Shrove Tuesday activities, harvest workers appealing for largess, and so on.

[31] Bushaway, *By Rite*, p. 84. It is also worth noting that in Norfolk, threshing machinery was dragged to parish boundaries, in acts of exclusion. J. E. Archer, *'By a Flash and a Scare': Arson, Animal Maiming, and Poaching in East Anglia, 1815–1870* (Oxford, 1990), p. 80. Even as late as the mid-twentieth century, one could find evidence that 'the precise location of the parish boundary is very widely known and a very real difference is recognized between the people who live on either side of it, even when

The rural working poor, so often conservative in their local outlooks, were attentive to parish boundaries partly because those boundaries affected their legal settlements, upon which their rights to poor relief and other benefits depended. The parish was the unit of poor law responsibility. Many legal disputes over pauper settlement involved judgements about boundaries. It had to be decided in which parish certain houses (or even parts of houses) were located, where a person had been a servant, or an apprentice, or rented property, and so on. These matters conferred legal settlement, which was absolutely central to a poor person's identity and security. The labouring poor were frequently active in the 'informal' resolution of boundary disputes, contesting any movement of boundary markers. They took seriously Deuteronomy, 19: 14 – 'Cursed is he who removeth his neighbour's landmark.' Such disputes could be especially prevalent in areas lacking natural features to define boundaries, like the chalk downlands or Ashdown Forest.[32] Parish and Forest boundary stones surviving into the twentieth century were, for example, especially numerous in and around the Forest of Dean, to judge from their recording by the Ordnance Survey – as in a topographically complex, much subdivided and semi-wooded Dean area such as Pope's Hill. Parochialisation came relatively late within the central extra-parochial area of the Forest of Dean, in the 1840s. Yet parish attachment in this and the surrounding areas was also manifested by farm wagons being painted in parish colours, as for example at Westbury upon Severn.[33] Inter-community enmity between youths in this Forest persisted well into the twentieth century.[34] Forest perambulation was long-established. In countless regions beyond this, parish perambulations frequently

the actual distance is a matter of a few yards . . . the accompanying distinctions applied to non-members are very apparent in attitudes towards "offcomers"'. M. W. Williams, *The Sociology of an English Village: Gosforth* (London, 1956), p. 168.

[32] J. H. Bettey, *Church and Parish: An Introduction for Local Historians* (London, 1987), pp. 97–8, mentioning the case of Stratton *versus* Charminster (Dors.).

[33] See the wagon from this parish displayed and interpreted at the Dean Heritage Centre (at Soudley, near Cinderford).

[34] My personal observation after a year of working in a Forest of Dean sawmill, 1971–2; and see D. Potter, *The Changing Forest: Life in the Forest of Dean Today* (London, 1962), pp. 100, 128.

brought skirmishes with rival groups from surrounding parishes.[35]

As notoriously in the Forest of Dean, inhabitants also acted to protect local resources against 'foreigners', outsiders, out-townsmen, squatters or the depredatory poor of surrounding parishes, enforcing by-laws regulating who had a right to communal resources. Scalford in Leicestershire, for example, had regulations governing gravel land and 'herbidge' arising from it, which laid down that 'the said lands shall not be let to any person not belonging to the said Parish of Scalford'.[36] It was very typical in that respect. Local industries, like coal and iron-ore mining in the Forest of Dean, were frequently controlled by long-established clannish regulations to restrict 'encroachments' by 'foreigners' within clearly understood local bounds, and there is no doubt about the intensity of antagonistic feelings when 'foreigners' moved in to work within those boundaries.[37] Parishioners' access to poor law benefits and other resources – such as employment, poor housing, parish charities, alms-houses, the parish medical practitioner, seasonal doleings, soup kitchens, commons, wood, furze and other fuel, bracken, reeds, sedge, wildfowl, sheep-washing pits, gleaning, lane and verge grazing, etc. – was usually contingent upon their residence and work within clearly ascertained local boundaries, which often limited their eligibility.[38] Even molecatchers were only paid for

---

[35] Bushaway, *By Rite*, p. 86; B. Le Messurier, 'Recreation', in C. Gill (ed.), *Dartmoor: A New Study* (1970, Newton Abbot, 1977), pp. 227–8. The accounts of perambulations often record such disputes. See e.g. *The Parish Registers of Oldswinford, Worcestershire*, vol. III: *1719–1735* (Stourbridge Historical and Archaeological Society, Birmingham, 1973, trans. C. J. Voyce and A. Page), pp. 101–2, on such a dispute recorded in 1733 between Kinfayre and Oldswinford.

[36] Leics. CRO, DE 3091/88 (27 March 1799).

[37] H. G. Nicholls, *Nicholls's Forest of Dean: An Historical and Descriptive Account, and Iron Making in the Olden Times* (1858 and 1866; Dawlish, 1966), pp. 49, 52, 62, 68–73, 110–12, 116, 120, 123, 145, 151, 234, 237; C. Fisher, *Custom, Work and Market Capitalism: The Forest of Dean Colliers, 1788–1888* (London, 1981), pp. xi, 6–7, 46–9. A 'foreigner' in the Forest of Dean usually meant someone who had been born outside the Hundred of St Briavels, and 'resentment of foreigners was a potent factor in riots that occurred over commoning rights in 1831', and against incoming 'foreign' capitalists involved in coal mining. N. M. Herbert (ed.), *A History of the County of Gloucester*, vol. V: *Bledisloe Hundred, St. Briavels Hundred, The Forest of Dean* (Victoria County History, Oxford, 1996), pp. 329–33, 362.

[38] For an example of plebeian action against an interloper pilfering and cutting wood in a parish, see Ayres, *Paupers and Pig Killers*, p. 24. For regulations 'That the poor of this

moles caught 'within the parish boundaries',[39] which raised issues for moles which paralleled the more serious ones concerning the parochial rating liability of coalmines. Other more surface or aerial forms of hunting were also liable to boundary restrictions. There were countless reasons why the poor needed to familiarise themselves with and preserve parish boundaries.

This sense of boundary and of parochial difference was fortified over a long period by many cultural and legal considerations. There was an enduring proclivity towards popular abuse or rivalry between people from different parishes. In Scotland, this was famously outlined by Robert Chambers, when he wrote that:

There is a nationality in districts as well as in countries: nay, the people living on different sides of a streamlet, or of the same hill, sometimes entertain prejudices against each other, not less virulent than those of the inhabitants of the different sides of the British Channel or the Pyrenees. This has given rise . . . to an infinite number of phrases, expressive of vituperation, obloquy, or contempt, which are applied to the inhabitants of various places by those whose lot it is to reside in the immediate vicinity.[40]

Such attitudes existed and took many forms in England and Wales. In the earliest periods they may even have influenced place names, some of which became established in usage. There

---

parish, and not the poor of other parishes, be allowed to enter our fields to glean', see Leics. CRO, DE 829/86 (Bottesford vestry book, 2 August 1832). On restricted access to parish sheep-pits and wash dykes, with higher costs for non-parishioners, see Leics. CRO, DE 3018/2 (Ab Kettleby vestry book, 14 May 1889); Leics. CRO, DE 829/87 (Bottesford vestry book, 1 June 1865). For two-year residential restrictions in Seagrave (Leics.) to qualify for 'lane money' (from letting herbage in 'charity lanes' and 'general lanes', which was given to 107 people at 2s. 4d. each, and was not permitted to anyone who left the parish), see Leics. CRO, DE 5851/1 (4 April, 24 March and 28 March 1895). In earlier periods, legal settlement would often determine eligibility to such parochial benefits. See for example J. M. Neeson, *Commoners: Common Right, Enclosure and Social Change in England, 1700–1820* (Cambridge, 1993), pp. 175–6, discussing furze cutting being restricted to the settled poor at Raunds (Northants.) in 1740, or access to stone and gravel being restricted to parishioners.
[39] Leics. CRO, DE 3018/2 (Ab Kettleby vestry book, 14 May 1889).
[40] R. Chambers, *Popular Rhymes, Fireside Stories, and Amusements of Scotland* (Edinburgh, 1842), pp. 123–4, cited in R. M. Dorson, *The British Folklorists: A History* (London, 1968), p. 131. To similar effect, on Scotland, see S. Johnson, *A Journey to the Western Islands of Scotland* (1775, London, The Abbey Classics edn, n.d., intro. by J. Freeman), p. 68: 'Thus every Highlander can talk of his ancestors, and recount the outrages which they suffered from the wicked inhabitants of the next valley.'

was for example the derogatory Taddiport in Devon, meaning 'toad town', which was probably first referred to as such in the thirteenth century.[41] By extension of such naming, there was a well-heeled assemblage of localised insult. This continued over many centuries, and indeed in some regards it persists today. 'Oi can't read, and oi can't write, but oi can drive a trac-tor', chant the Chelsea football fans to infuriate their rival Ipswich supporters. This is a modern urban equivalent of a kind of inter-village rivalry and abuse that ran rampant in the past. People from other parishes were often held to be ugly, idle, uncouth, unnatural or immoral. Stressing the key role of the parish, as *cymdogaeth* (a neighbourhood),[42] as well as an administrative and cultural unit, D. Parry-Jones wrote of his Teifiside parish in rural Carmarthenshire in the later nineteenth century that

the local loyalties of previous generations and their dislike of 'foreign-ers' had led them to coin a nickname for their neighbours, invariably of a sarcastic and abusive character, such as cats, donkeys, dogs, cowards, sheep-stealers and so forth. In fair or festival, the hurling of one of these epithets at a group of youths from another parish was enough to start a vicious fight, in which fists, feet and sticks would be used.[43]

This language of 'foreigner' extended widely across rural England and Wales. In Hampshire, W. H. Hudson wrote about 'the effect of that enmity or suspicion with which the stranger, or "foreigner", as he is called, is often regarded in rural districts. The person from another county, or from a distance, unrelated

---

[41] I am grateful to Harold Fox for this information. Other possible examples of contemptuous naming include Thorpe Thewles (immoral), Full Sutton (dirty), or Stratton Strawless. K. Cameron, *English Place Names* (London, 1996), p. 105. On inter-village church architectural rivalry of the medieval period, see J. C. Cox and C. B. Ford, *The Parish Churches of England* (1935, London, 1937), p. 93.

[42] 'Cymdogaeth was something that was very real, something very old, embracing, intimate, to which one had a very profound sense of belonging.' D. Parry-Jones, *My Own Folk* (Llandysul, 1972), p. 64.

[43] *Ibid.*, pp. 65–6, and see p. 89 on the naming of one community as the *Cyndrwynin* – the dog-nosed. On p. 66 he also cites T. Gwynn Jones, *Welsh Folklore and Folk-custom* (London, 1930), p. 31, on these insults: 'the application to the inhabitants of certain districts of animal names is of totemistic origin. The habit seems to be general throughout Wales.' A linked interpretation of this would be to suggest that people from other places were *ipso facto* identified as animals, and thus as beyond the bounds of humanity. In both England and Wales, the Irish were sometimes so described, and people from other parishes could be equated with rats.

to any one in the community, is always a foreigner, and the foreign taint may descend to the children.'[44] In a village, as Ronald Blythe wrote of East Anglia, a 'foreigner' came from five miles down the road[45] – 'make no bones about it, six miles from us it is all another country'.[46] 'How Suffolk used to suspect the "foreigner"', exclaimed Adrian Bell.[47]

Rupert Brooke made much of the tradition of inter-village misanthropy in 'The Old Vicarage, Grantchester', when, in a poem indeed so quintessentially English, he compared 'the lovely hamlet Grantchester' with the places around it:

> For Cambridge people rarely smile,
> Being urban, squat, and packed with guile;
> And Royston men in the far South
> Are black and fierce and strange of mouth;
> At Over they fling oaths at one,

[44] W. H. Hudson, *Hampshire Days* (1903, Oxford, 1980), p. 184. It is interesting to note that Hudson also argued that 'the gentry, the landowners, and the wealthy residents generally, are always in a sense foreigners . . . he is never racially one with the peasant . . . His parents and his grandparents and his ancestors for centuries have been mixing their blood with the blood of outsiders. It is well always to bear this in mind, and . . . to see the carriage people, the gentry, and the important ones generally as though one saw them not, or saw them as shadows, and to fix the attention on those who in face and carriage and dress proclaim themselves true natives and children of the soil.' *Ibid.*, pp. 175–6.

[45] R. Blythe, *Divine Landscapes* (Harmondsworth, 1986), p. 21; H. Williamson, *The Phasian Bird* (1948, Woodbridge, 1984), pp. 103, 105, 108; A. Morrison, *Cunning Murrell: A Tale of Witchcraft and Smuggling* (1900, Ipswich, 1977), p. 29. To similar effect, see F. Thompson, *Lark Rise to Candleford* (1939, Harmondsworth, 1976), p. 69; C. H. Warren, *The Land is Yours* (1943, London, 1948), pp. 33–4, 142. For such use of the word 'foreign' in Scotland (Ayr.) to describe someone from outside the parish, see J. Galt, *Annals of the Parish; or the Chronicle of Dalmailing during the Ministry of the Rev. Micah Balwhidder* (1821, Oxford, 1986), pp. 95, 230, and pp. 5–7, 14 for an account of the pastor being violently reviled as an outsider. For such usage of the term 'foreigner' in Wales, see M. Humphreys, *The Crisis of Community: Montgomeryshire, 1680–1815* (Cardiff, 1996), p. 133, where the quotation from 1730 refers to tenants from outside the locality. The term 'foreign unions' referred to other poor law unions; as for example in *Select Committee on Poor Removal*, XII (1879), p. 38. The word 'foreigner' was also used by artisans against those who were under-qualified to practise, and who were undercutting, their trade. For an example, see J. Hollingshead, *Ragged London in 1861* (1861, London, 1986), pp. 14–15.

[46] R. Blythe, *Word from Wormingford: A Parish Year* (1997, Harmondsworth, 1998), p. 136.

[47] A. Bell, *The Budding Morrow* (London, 1946), pp. 86–7. In the same book, he wrote of harvesting and the war effort: 'It is something fresh, I think, for the old countryman to be credited with more than a parish loyalty' (p. 134). See also L. Rider Haggard (ed.), *I Walked by Night: Being the Life and History of the King of the Norfolk Poachers* (1935, Oxford, 1982), p. 28, on children from two different Norfolk villages going to the same school, and so always fighting each other.

And worse than oaths at Trumpington,
And Ditton girls are mean and dirty,
And there's none in Harston under thirty,
And folks in Shelford and those parts
Have twisted lips and twisted hearts,
And Barton men make Cockney rhymes,
And Coton's full of nameless crimes,
And things are done you'd not believe
At Madingley, on Christmas Eve.
Strong men have run for miles and miles,
When one from Cherry Hinton smiles;
Strong men have blanched, and shot their wives,
Rather than send them to St. Ives;
Strong men have cried like babes, bydam,
To hear what happened at Babraham.
But Grantchester! ah, Grantchester!
There's peace and holy quiet there,
Great clouds along pacific skies,
And men and women with straight eyes,
Lithe children lovelier than a dream . . .
In Grantchester their skins are white;
They bathe by day, they bathe by night;
The women there do all they ought;
The men observe the Rules of Thought.

Clearly, the inhabitants of Grantchester were whiter than white, without twisted lips – at least in those days. An arch poem like this built upon a large backlog of local prejudice, and very many local rhymes and examples of folklore and *blason populaire* could be added to suggest how widespread and deeply rooted local sentiments like these were. Local taunts, wrote Katharine Briggs, comprise 'a particularly large class [of folklore] in England'.[48] The 'noodle tale', the Gotham-type story, about a village of fools, or even about whole areas of fools (Borrowdale, the Fens, Whittingham Vale), or towns of fools (Cambridge), are rife in English folklore. Many of the stories told were easily transferable and were applied to many different villages: places which apparently try to wall in the cuckoo to keep springtime; or attempt to rake in the moon from a pond; or send out a boat to pick up floating millstones; or whip a hake through the town

---

[48] K. M. Briggs, *A Dictionary of British Folk-tales in the English Language, Part A, Folk Narratives*, vol. II (Bloomington, 1970), p. 3.

to stop its voracious brethren from playing havoc with the pilchard shoals; or are terrified of crabs found on land; or read letters upside down; or buy red herrings to stock a horse-pond; or who revenge themselves against eels by dumping them in a pond to drown them; or which put fish-nets around their town to catch the smallpox and then drown it at sea; or throw sparrows from the church tower to kill them; or shut the toll-gate to keep the wind out; or try to entice the cock down from the steeple by throwing corn into the churchyard; or destroy a windmill to ensure that there is sufficient wind to turn the remaining one; or forget to put windows in their church, and so carry the light into it in hampers; or dig a hole in which to bury the heap of earth thrown up when they sank a well;[49] or endeavour to get a bull out of a field by lifting it over the gate.[50]

These kinds of taunts or insulting local proverbs were legion. Most were recorded, and clearly still had hard currency, in the nineteenth century.[51] Some persisted into the twentieth century. While some of the most famous were particularly directed at certain places – like Gotham, or Ebrington ('the Gotham of the Cotswolds'),[52] or Folkeston (an anagram for Kent Fools) – far more parishes were targeted. Of Cornwall, for example,

[49] This example, and some other such fool stories, go back a long time, and can be found in other countries too. They were adapted to local circumstances and dislikes in England. On digging a hole to put earth in, see S. Thompson, *The Folktale* (1946, Berkeley, 1977), p. 192.

[50] These examples are from Briggs, *Dictionary of British Folk-tales in the English Language, Part A, Folk Narratives*, pp. 11–13, 24–7, 35, 43–4, 51–3, 55, 74, 86–9, 197, 233–4, 256, 262, 348–61. There are many more in this volume. For further such cases, see K. M. Briggs, *British Folk Tales and Legends: A Sampler* (London, 1977), pp. 51–65; J. A. Halliwell, *The Merry Tales of the Wise Men of Gotham* (London, 1840); W. A. Clouston, *The Book of Noodles: Stories of Simpletons; or, Fools and their Follies* (London, 1888); E. Welsford, *The Fool, his Social and Literary History* (1935, Gloucester, Mass., 1966); F. Grose, *A Provincial Glossary, with a Collection of Local Proverbs, and Popular Superstitions* (1787, Menston, 1968), n.p., under Notts.; A. Bell, *Men and the Fields* (London, 1939), pp. 26–7, for an example against the people of Polstead (Suff.) being unable to tell the time, taken as 'a proverb with them here'. Many examples of insults against Burwash are mentioned in Wells (ed.), *Victorian Village*, e.g. pp. 149, 234: 'a great deal of chaff about Burwash as an unknown place supposed to be peopled by higglers & fair cart people'; 'bad vulgar language was called "Burwash Grammar"'.

[51] An extensive collection of these can be found in G. F. Northall, *English Folk Rhymes: A Collection of Traditional Verses Relating to Places, Persons, Customs, and Superstitions* (London, 1892).

[52] Briggs, *Dictionary of British Folk-tales in the English Language, Part A, Folk Narratives*, p. 362.

M. A. Courtney wrote: 'In fact, of nearly all the parishes in the county some joke is current in the neighbouring villages.'[53] A poem by the people of Burrington (mid-Devon) about their neighbours in the hamlet of Week went as follows:

> Out to Week beneath the trees,
> Barley bread and vinid cheese,
> Risty bacon as tough as a thong,
> That's how Week boys git along.[54]

Among the places treated in a comparable spirit, we find the couplet (attributed to Shakespeare) about 'Piping Pebworth and Drunken Bidford'.[55] Or there is the reference to villages in south Warwickshire: 'Idlicote on the Hill, Whatcote Downderry, Beggarly Oxhill, Lousy Fulready, Yawning Yettington [Ettington], Peeping Pillarton [Pillerton], and one-eyed Marston.'[56] The latter reminds us of Thomas Hardy's description of Kingsbere-sub-Greenhill in *Tess of the d'Urbervilles*: 'a little one-eyed, blinking sort o' place'.[57] Francis Grose recorded many of these in his *Provincial Glossary*. A Suffolk example was 'Beccles for a puritan, Bungey for the poor, Halesworth for a drunkard, and Bilborough for a whore.'[58] Ipswich was 'a town without inhabitants, a river without water, streets without names, where asses wear boots'. This description was said to originate in a report from the Duke of Buckingham to Charles II.[59] Many local taunts addressed sexual matters, imputing infidelity, or suggesting that a place's women were prostitutes: 'An old man who weds a

---

[53] M. A. Courtney, *Folklore and Legends of Cornwall* (1890, Exeter, 1989), p. 107.

[54] R. Staines, *The Old Farm: A History of Farming Life in the West Country* (Exeter, 1990), p. 53. I am grateful to Harold Fox for this reference. Vinid (veined) cheese was old cheese with green cracks in the surface. Risty (rusty) bacon was bacon streaked brown from an incomplete cure.

[55] A fuller version was given in the *Times* (23 June 1934), p. 13, col. D. 'Haunted Hillboro and Hungry Grafton, Piping Pebworth and Dancing Marston, Dodging Exhall and Papist Wixford, Beggarly Broom and Drunken Bidford.'

[56] B. Smith, *The Village of Oxhill and the Church of Saint Lawrence* (Oxhill, 1971), p. 2.

[57] T. Hardy, *Tess of the d'Urbervilles* (1891, London, 1982), p. 37. 'A one-eyed place' was in fact a common slur. See e.g. Wells, *Victorian Village*, p. 191; H. E. Bates, *Love for Lydia* (1952, Harmondsworth, 1977), p. 138.

[58] Grose, *Provincial Glossary*, p. R3 (this work is oddly paginated). Or, in Leicestershire, there was: 'Sutton for mutton, Broughton for beef, Littlethorpe for pretty girls, Cosby for thieves, Whetstone's a dirty place, and Cosby's no better, But if you want a pretty girl, go to Littlethorpe to get her.' I am grateful to Mike Thompson for this information, obtained from his Littlethorpe girlfriend about fifty years ago.

[59] *Ibid.*, p. R3.

buxom young maiden, biddeth fair to become a freeman of Buckingham.'[60] 'Braintree for the pure, and Bocking for the poor; Cogshall for the jeering town, and Kelvedon for the whore.'[61] 'There are more whores in Hose, than honest women in Long Clawson.'[62] 'Sutton for mutton, Cashalton for beeves, Epsom for whores, and Ewel for thieves.'[63] As in modern ethnic or religious conflicts, or in gypsy–'*gorgio*' confrontations,[64] or indeed in Rupert Brooke, there was a long tradition of impugning the sexual purity of women from the other side or place – different moral potentialities within persons being split between two groups. In Lincolnshire, certain villages were said to be notorious for incest, or for characteristics (e.g. limps or squints) attributed to such behaviour.[65] This was a prejudice that some parishes in the Fens especially suffered from. Other sayings related to idleness, like 'Long, lazey, louzy Lewisham';[66] or to incompetence, 'Like Banbury tinkers, that in mending one hole make three';[67] or to stupidity: 'You were born at Hog's-Norton' – 'a village, whose inhabitants, it seems, formerly, were so rustical in their behaviour, that borish and clownish people are said to be born at Hog's-Norton'.[68] As shown above, some villages were

---

[60] *Ibid.*, p. L3. Accusations of shrewness among women of certain places were also found, such as 'Stretton on the street, where the shrews meet'. A. R. Traylen (comp.), *Dialect Customs and Derivations in Rutland* (Stamford, 1989), p. 24. There were also charges of excessive gossip, as at 'Tit tattling Teigh'. *Ibid.*, p. 24.

[61] Grose, *Provincial Glossary*, n.p., under Essex. On Coggeshall, local insults and other foolish places to jeer at, see 'Rural wit', in G. R. Warren (ed.), *The Contented Countryman: the Best of C. Henry Warren* (Stroud, 1991), pp. 103–8. 'When they saw the grass growing on their church tower [the Coggeshall men] hoisted up a cow to graze on it.' *Ibid.*, p. 104.

[62] Grose, *Provincial Glossary*, n.p., under Leics.: 'Hose and Long Clawson are neighbouring villages . . . the entendre lies in the word Hose, which here is meant to signify stockings, so that the assertion is, that there are more whores who wear stockings, than there are honest women dwelling in Long Clawson.'

[63] *Ibid.*, n.p., under Surr. Another version was 'Sutton for mutton, Tamworth for beef, Walsall for bandy-legs, "Brum" for a thief.' *Times* (25 June 1934), p. 15, col. E. By 1934, the contributor of this rhyme to the *Times* had come to the conclusion that it was 'unnecessarily libellous'.

[64] J. Okely, *The Traveller-Gypsies* (1983, Cambridge, 1984), pp. 201–14. The '*gorgio*' means the non-gypsy: that 'other' in the fundamental division of traveller–gypsy culture.

[65] M. Sutton, *We Didn't Know Aught: A Study of Sexuality, Superstition and Death in Women's Lives in Lincolnshire during the 1930s, '40s and '50s* (Stamford, 1992), p. 106.

[66] Grose, *Provincial Glossary*, n.p., under Kent.

[67] *Ibid.*, n.p., under Oxfordshire.

[68] *Ibid.*, n.p., under Oxfordshire, although the village referred to may be one of the Nortons in Leicestershire. Through confusions of the words Hogh, High and Hogs,

accused of drunkenness: 'Clunbury, Clunford, Clungunford and Clun, are the drunkenest places under the sun.'[69] Other places were accused of being inarticulate, gutteral or dissonant in speech. An example of this was the 'Carlton Wharlers', who apparently spoke in 'an ill-favoured, untunable, and harsh manner', 'labouring under a kind of *wharling*'. This reminds us of the localism of dialect and vocabulary.[70] Some sayings jibed at poverty: 'Bedworth-beggars',[71] or 'You are in the highway to Needham.'[72] One that dated from 1845 was 'Andover picks the bone.'[73] Others imputed dishonesty: of a man who had broken a promise, it could be said that 'You are a man of Duresley.'[74] Or we find in Leicestershire that 'At Great Glen there are more great dogs than honest men.'[75] Accusations of dirt or smell were made in some local rhymes, such as: 'Brill on the hill, Oakley in the hole, Dirty Ickford, and stinking Worminghall.'[76] Or there were taunts about insignificance. In south Leicestershire villages people talked of 'going to Huncote, to see what's there'. Other villages were targeted for probable topographical reasons: 'Wotton under Wever, where God comes never': about which Grose commented that this 'is a black dismal place near the Morelands in Staffordshire, covered by hills from the chearing rays of the sun'.[77]

---

the saying may have lent itself to the more generalised term Hodge, to caricature the nineteenth-century farm labourer.

[69] *Times*, 'Village rhymes' (22 June 1934), p. 15, col. D, recollecting this from 'many years ago'. Another example was 'Sleepy Ilsley, drunken people, Got a church without a steeple, And what is more, to their disgrace, They've got a clock without a face.' *Times* (25 June 1934), p. 15, col. E.

[70] C. J. Billson (ed.), *County Folk-lore. Printed Extracts, No. 3. Leicestershire and Rutland* (London, 1895), p. 152; J. Nichols, *The History of the Antiquities of the County of Leicester*, vol. II, pt II (1798, Wakefield, 1971), p. 544. For very many examples of Rutland village vocabulary and sayings, which were esoteric to outsiders, see Traylen (comp.), *Dialect Customs and Derivations in Rutland*, pp. 3–20. Such distinctive vocabulary and dialect could be documented for every British district, frequently changing over short distances. Local rhymes often made play with these variations in pronunciation, sometimes to ridicule them.

[71] Grose, *Provincial Glossary*, n.p., under Leics.

[72] *Ibid.*, n.p., under Suff.

[73] *Times* (23 June 1934), p. 13, col. D; N. Longmate, *The Workhouse* (1974), pp. 119–35.

[74] Grose, *Provincial Glossary*, p. N1.

[75] *Ibid.*, p. O3.

[76] F. W. Bateson, *Brill: A Short History* (The Brill Society, Buckinghamshire, 1966), p. 1.

[77] Grose, *Provincial Glossary*, p. R2.

Many taunts were directed against London. In these Tyburn, cockneys, knaves, ruffians, fish markets, ladies of pleasure, and imputations of venereal disease put in a regular appearance, confirming the worst suspicions of William Cobbett or John Clare. Indeed, we should not forget either that *within* London there were many local hostilities between different areas, often between small congeries of streets. Here parish boundaries may have been less instrumental than in non-metropolitan regions, although this awaits research. These urban 'tribal' antagonisms (described as such by Mayhew, Dickens, Hollingshead, Booth, Morrison, Zangwill, Jack London and many others) probably coincided more frequently with divisions relating to class (e.g. East and West End), ethnicity (e.g. Jew and Gentile), or British place of origin, than I am documenting for rural areas.

Beyond all the species of taunts were the local legends of places associated with the devil, or with witchcraft, or affected by curses. This genre could take us into a very extensive area of folklore, most of it revealing dislike, fear or abhorrence of another place. It was after all to exonerate a parish from a similar genus of evil repute that R. D. Blackmore created his legendary narrator in *Lorna Doone* – 'John Ridd, of the parish of Oare, in the county of Somerset' – to 'write for the clearing of our parish from ill-fame and calumny'.[78] In less fictional life a parochial reputation of such a kind preoccupied many parishes and their inhabitants. In some areas the sites of boundary stones were supposed to be haunted by ghosts, and the references sometimes call into mind the idea of an *abyss* there.[79] Over much of the Pennines, prominent features on remote parts of township boundaries were named 'Black' in some form: Black Hill, Black Dyke, Black Haw or Black Moss, to take examples of ancient boundary spots around Malham.[80] In any topographical analysis of local legend and 'the haunted places',[81] boundaries of fear

---

[78] R. D. Blackmore, *Lorna Doone: A Romance of Exmoor* (1869, Regent Classics edn, n.d.), p. 7.

[79] For example, in Guernsey several boundary stones were haunted by the *Tchi-Co*, the '*Dog of Death*', also known as *le chien bodu*, from the Gaulish word *bodu*, which means the abyss, referring to the mythological dog of Hades. J. H. L'Amy, *Jersey Folk Lore* (1927, St Helier, 1983), p. 167.

[80] A. Raistrick, *Malham and Malham Moor* (Lancaster, 1947), p. 78.

[81] Robinson (ed.), *John Clare's Autobiographical Writings*, p. 60.

and tolerance and the role of local xenophobia would assume a prominent place. The topographies of the dishonouring folktale, of evil legend, of the haunted story, with all their abysmal stalking grounds, remain to be studied. John Clare, by his own account muttering to himself in abject fear as he walked to Maxey, a parish two miles away from Helpston, felt himself assailed and terrified by 'ghosts and hobgoblings . . . as I passed those awful places'.[82] 'Thin death like shadows and gobblings with sorcer eyes were continually shaping in the darkness from my haunted imagination.'[83] The feared domains were death-like and life-threatening.

Life and beauty nestled in Clare's own parish, amidst his own parochial ecology. This was true, for example, of the birds Clare was so fond of,[84] whose migration was disputed by contemporaries. Indeed, the culturally habituated manners of anthropomorphist thinking left many people feeling dubious that creatures might move elsewhere. It is significant that many naturalists in the eighteenth and early nineteenth century so resisted the idea of bird migration. Gilbert White referred to 'our birds', or the 'parish birds', 'that belong to this place' – and (rather like a parish constable searching for vagrants) he stripped thatch, grubbed bushes, and searched church towers and pools and streams to detect where they hibernated, perhaps (he thought) in 'secret dormitories'. He accepted that some birds migrated, albeit in the human sense of going on a journey from a place, but he would have been incredulous to learn that 'his' swallows were in south Africa. One needs to stress a possessive parochial consciousness and loyalty to understand why such mistakes were made, why parish searches for 'torpid birds' were made, even by such an acute and interesting observer as this, for whom tortoises, carp, harvest mice, water rats, slugs and snails conformed much more closely to 'expected' behaviour. White described Selborne as 'the secret, private parish inside each one of us' – the parish as mental paradigm – and Richard Mabey has written perceptively of this clergyman's 'wilful

---

[82] *Ibid.*, pp. 8–9, 60.   [83] *Ibid.*, 146.
[84] John Clare, *Bird Poems* (London, 1980); E. Robinson and R. Fitter (eds.), *John Clare's Birds* (Oxford, 1982).

parochialism' and his 'single-minded commitment to his native village'.[85]

A rougher vein of evidence was presented by Joseph Lawson, when he reminisced about the townships near Leeds and Bradford in his *Progress in Pudsey* (1887). It was, apparently, a common remark that '"Yeadon was the last place God made, and that He made it out of the refuse", – or what we should now call "shoddy".'[86] Another insult in this area was to say to someone: 'Go to Pudsey!'[87] He depicted a very stark and often violent picture of such local xenophobic attitudes fifty or sixty years previously. 'Every village at that day formed a clan against other villages', he wrote.

When villagers met each other at the various feasts or at other gatherings, the various Pudsey clans would combine against outsiders . . . and deserve the appellation of 'Pudsey Blacks' . . . The Pudseyites were a bold and sturdy lot, and being more numerous than others were, would not be so easy to conquer by rude physical force, though we remember a case where they were overpowered by numbers, and many nearly killed, one being killed outright.[88]

He remembered how 'Pudsey has often been charged with pelting and otherwise insulting strangers.' However, he added, this 'was too common not only in Pudsey, but in most of the surrounding villages as well'.[89] Lawson wrote of 'narrow local prejudices, forming a kind of clanship'.[90] This was true even within villages:

If a person, especially a young man, went to reside from one part of a village to another [Lawson is probably writing here about townships within a large parish], he was looked upon as a kind of foreigner or interloper, who had no right there. We have known persons

[85] G. White, *The Natural History of Selborne* (1788–9, Harmondsworth, 1987), e.g. pp. 208, 242, 246, 270, 280. *Ibid.*, pp. viii, xi–xii, xvi–xvii; R. Mabey, *Gilbert White* (1986, London, 1999), pp. 13, 49, 98, 104, 113, 115, 127, 166, 172; T. Dadswell, *The Selborne Pioneer: Gilbert White as Naturalist and Scientist: A Re-examination* (Aldershot, 2003), pp. 35–45.

[86] J. Lawson, *Progress in Pudsey* (1887, Firle, 1978), p. 79.

[87] *Ibid.*, p. 80.

[88] *Ibid.*, pp. 75–6.

[89] *Ibid.*, p. 75. An atmosphere of antagonistic violence and stone throwing at strangers was depicted for the Black Country in F. Brett Young, *Far Forest* (London, 1936), pp. 4, 25–31.

[90] Lawson, *Progress in Pudsey*, p. 74.

both insulted and assaulted for a long time till they got initiated or naturalised.[91]

The Lutheran pastor from Berlin, Karl Moritz, visiting England in 1782, rapidly found that 'a traveller on foot in this country seems to be considered as a sort of wild man or an out-of-the-way being who is stared at, pitied, suspected, and shunned by everybody who meets him'. He was 'hissed at so much that he walked on into the night'.[92] As William Shenstone had written in his poem 'The School-Mistress':

> Those saunt'ring on the green, with jocund leer
> Salute the stranger passing on his way.[93]

Local xenophobes with bones to pick, rather than bosom friendship to share – the early Methodist itinerant preachers were well acquainted with them. So were the Primitive Methodist preachers in the early nineteenth century, who were very frequently attacked.[94] Many of them recorded experiences like that of John Garner, in the village of Sowe near Coventry:

I necessitated to expose myself to the malicious rage of wicked men, who furiously drove me out of the village with stones, rotten eggs, sludge, or whatever else came to hand . . . After being shamefully beaten with their hands, feet and other weapons, I was dragged to a

---

[91] *Ibid.*, p. 75.

[92] M. Jebb, *Walkers* (London, 1986), p. 23, and see pp. 24, 32, 60, 61, 63.

[93] W. Shenstone, 'The school-mistress', in D. Davie (ed.), *The Late Augustans: Longer Poems of the Later Eighteenth Century* (London, 1958), p. 12, stanza 32. The poem was written between 1737 and 1748.

[94] K. D. M. Snell, *Church and Chapel in the North Midlands: Religious Observance in the Nineteenth Century* (Leicester, 1991), pp. 71–2 (n. 9), for many references to violence against incoming Methodist preachers; D. Eastwood, *Government and Community in the English Provinces, 1700–1870* (London, 1997), p. 33; J. Ede, N. Virgoe and T. Williamson, *Halls of Zion: Chapels and Meeting-Houses in Norfolk* (Norwich, 1994), p. 10; H. D. Rack, *Reasonable Enthusiast: John Wesley and the Rise of Methodism* (1989, London, 1992), pp. 223, 270–81; E. R. Wickham, *Church and People in an Industrial City* (1957, London, 1969), pp. 51–2; D. Hey, *Yorkshire from AD 1000* (London, 1986), p. 208; J. Cooper, '"A fine field for usefulness": Primitive Methodism in the Saffron Walden Circuit, 1839–1900', *Family and Community History*, 5 (2002), pp. 48–50. Such violence extended to other religious incomers, for example people engaged in home missionary work, or members of the Salvation Army, or the Church Army, which was often seen as interfering with the parochial system. Wilson Carlile (the founder of the latter organisation) spent six months in hospital after one assault on him. K. S. Inglis, *Churches and the Working Classes in Victorian England* (London, 1963), pp. 44–5. There were religious, or anti-religious, sentiments lurking behind cases like this; but local xenophobic attitudes were clearly manifest too.

pond, and the enraged mob seemed anxious to gratify their cruelty, by witnessing the death of one of their fellow creatures.[95]

As for the Irish – perhaps included among 'Our brethren 'neath the western sky' in Victorian hymnology[96] – 'They were mobbed with sods, etc., and all kinds of bad and threatening language was used to them . . . The people were saturated with the spirit of hate.' Lawson continued, 'If a man employed an Irishman, he was looked upon by many as a kind of traitor to his country.'[97] Anti-Irish sentiments of this kind, as with anti-French feeling, could be documented for very many English and Welsh regions, especially before the 1860s.[98] In south Wales, when sea captains brought Irish people over as 'human ballast' in their returning coal ships,

there is generally an appearance of dissatisfaction in the port when these Irish arrive; the lower kind of people get around, and they use no measured terms of severity and taunt towards the captain for bringing such numbers over . . . [H]e has . . . the jeers and sneers of the people on shore . . . They say that these people are coming to eat them up; that they are poor enough themselves, and they believe that they will be made poorer than they are through their coming.[99]

To avoid such antipathy, the Irish were commonly off-loaded on mud flats and coastline a few miles outside Newport. In East

---

[95] Revd W. Garner, *The Life of Mr John Garner, Senior, One of the Early Ministers of the Primitive Methodist Connexion, and Original Deed Poll Member of the Conference* (London, 1856), pp. 32–3. In a similar way, Samuel Atterby reminisced about how local crowds 'not unseldom gave him a shower of stones or filth for his pains'. J. Simpson, *Memoir of the Life, Labours, Character and Death of Samuel Atterby, Primitive Methodist Minister* (London, 1849), p. 32. I am most grateful to Delia Garratt for these references.

[96] *Hymns Ancient and Modern, Revised* (1861, Norwich, 1995), p. 22.

[97] Lawson, *Progress in Pudsey*, pp. 82–3. Some Irish urban communities themselves acted violently against outsiders, for example against evangelical missions. See H. D. Rack, 'Domestic visitations: a chapter in early nineteenth century evangelism', *Journal of Ecclesiastical History*, 22 (1973), p. 369.

[98] For example, L. P. Curtis, *Anglo-Saxons and Celts: A Study of Anti-Irish Prejudice in Victorian Britain* (Bridgeport, Conn., 1968); L. P. Curtis, *Apes and Angels: The Irishman in Victorian Literature* (Newton Abbot, 1971); 'A grave digger's diary, 1763–1831', in J. W. Robertson Scott (ed.), *The Countryman Book: A Selection of Articles and Illustrations from The Countryman* (London, 1948), p. 160, entry for August 1824, on a mob of thirty men attacking the Irish with cudgels. Its unknown author appears to be from a village in Bedfordshire.

[99] *Report from the Select Committee on Poor Removal*, XVII (1854), evidence of James Salter (relieving officer, Newport Union), p. 493. The Irish were said to be carried as ship ballast, on coal ships as a return cargo: evidence of Evan David (chairman of the Cardiff board of guardians) on Cardiff, Swansea and Newport, *ibid.*, p. 480.

Anglia, there were frequent fights against the Irish, scythes *versus* sickles, resulting in fatalities. One source reported that the Irish 'all desired to be locked up at night safe from the English'.[100] And the antipathy to 'blackleg' labour (the term itself had Irish famine connotations), and the extreme violence often used against any form of such labour,[101] was part of an associated range of anti-'foreigner' attitudes about which books can be written. John Archer referred to 'all the xenophobic, sectarian and racist baggage' of the London crowd – people who came to the metropolis from all parts of the country.[102] Such broader anti-outsider subjects, whether relating to labour disputes or popular *mentalité*, put into context but go beyond my concentration upon inter-parish xenophobia.[103]

---

[100] D. H. Morgan, *Harvesters and Harvesting, 1840–1900: A Study of the Rural Proletariat* (1982), p. 79, and see all ch. 5; Archer, 'By a Flash and a Scare', pp. 14, 97.

[101] Extreme vitamin C deficiency causes a 'blackening' of the legs, the latter noticed by witnesses of the Irish Famine. For examples of anti-blackleg violence, see R. Colls, *The Collier's Rant: Song and Culture in the Industrial Village* (London, 1977), pp. 104–5, 107–9, 118.

[102] J. E. Archer, *Social Unrest and Popular Protest in England, 1780–1840* (Cambridge, 2000), p. 59.

[103] I am also not extending discussion to opposition against incoming tenants to vacant farms, which was frequent in Wales – see D. J. V. Jones, *Rebecca's Children: A Study of Rural Society, Crime and Protest* (Oxford, 1989), pp. 286–8 – and hostility to many other classes of 'outsider'. These included coloured people, some Anglican clergy (notably high ritualists, e.g. in Brighton, St George's in the East, Pimlico, East Grinstead, Exeter, etc.), evangelical city 'missionaries' (e.g. in many parts of London), Catholics, Quakers, Methodists, Jews, non-resident landlords, toll-pike keepers, bailiffs, game-keepers, police, Poor Law Commissioners, relieving officers and guardians, press gangs, excise officers, eviction agents, election campaigners, gypsies, drovers, vag-rants (there was a long, legally backed tradition of apprehending vagrants, with much further action before 1795 against newcomers felt 'likely to be chargeable'), pregnant single women, and so on. All these relate closely to my theme of local xenophobia, and can be heavily documented. On earlier comparable themes, see S. Hindle, 'Exclusion crises: poverty, migration and parochial responsibility in Eng-lish rural communities, c. 1560–1660', *Rural History*, 7 (1996); S. Hindle, *On the Parish? The Micro-politics of Poor Relief in Rural England, c. 1550–1750* (Oxford, 2004), ch. 5: 'Exclusion'. Hindle's scholarly discussions are invaluable on the early modern background to my theme here.

As a study of popular *mentalité*, one could extend coverage to types of exclusory folk practice, such as hunting the wren on St Stephen's day, or Devil-excluding rituals and behaviour (e.g. 'clipping the church' on Shrove Tuesday night, to create an endless magical chain and drive out the Devil, stressing consecrated ground – which by mental extension could entail a comparable status for the whole parish, *vis-à-vis* the external world), or 'cupping of the church' and placing flowers on graves in July (the congregation surrounding the church holding hands, singing 'We love the place O God'), or child encirclement games – 'Round and round the village . . .

Much of the local rivalry and dislike of other places found particular expression in football and cricket matches between parishes. Elias Owen, D. Parry-Jones and other Welsh commentators wrote of how loyalty to the parish was reinforced above all by the annual wakes (the *gwylmabsant*) and by football games 'played between neighbouring parishes, the two church doors often serving as goals'.[104] Such football matches were often violent expressions of inter-parochial dislike.[105] Even cricket was sometimes associated with 'uproar, confusion, and even fighting'.[106] These occasions were frequently condemned by Methodists and other Nonconformists.[107] By the late nineteenth century these sports were a more institutionalised, rule-controlled, manifestation of local competitive feelings and antagonisms, although even in the 1880s, around Aldershot, cricket matches were said to increase 'the intense dislike and contempt felt for neighbouring villages'.[108] Rivalry took many

As we have done before' (a widely documented game, with a circle of children representing a village, probably inspired by boundary perambulation).
[104] Parry-Jones, *My Own Folk*, p. 66.
[105] Lawson, *Progress in Pudsey*, p. 77; T. M. Owen, *The Customs and Traditions of Wales* (Cardiff, 1991), pp. 91–3; Revd H. B. Kendall, *The Origin and History of the Primitive Methodist Church* (London, n.d., *c.* 1905), p. 179; R. W. Malcolmson, *Popular Recreations in English Society, 1700–1850* (Cambridge, 1973), pp. 83–4. In parts of Lancashire, 'township plays against township, with irons fixed in front of their heavy clogs', quoted in D. Underdown, 'Regional cultures? Local variations in popular culture during the early modern period', in T. Harris (ed.), *Popular Culture in England, c. 1500–1850* (London, 1995), p. 38. West Cornish hurling too was 'a contest between whole parishes', often violent like 'a pitched battle'. *Ibid.*, pp. 38–9. See E. H. Hall, *A Description of Caernarvonshire (1809–1811)* (Caernarvon, 1952), p. 317, on football matches between parishes as 'something very like a pitched battle'. Other parishes staged seasonal (Shrove Tuesday) cock fights against each other, e.g. Nuneaton *versus* Bedworth: see M. Aldis, 'One man's Nuneaton, 1810–1845' (Centre for English Local History, University of Leicester, MA dissertation, 1992), p. 93, on such fights in 1819, citing Anon. [probably John Astley], *A Memoranda of the Daily Happenings in Nuneaton*, vol. 1 (Nuneaton Public Library), p. 34.
[106] Lawson, *Progress in Pudsey*, pp. 81–2. Another such occasion was the bottle-kicking competition between Hallaton and Medbourne in east Leicestershire, which was often accompanied by fighting.
[107] A. D. Rees, *Life in a Welsh Countryside: A Social Study of Llanfihangel yng Ngwynfa* (1950, Cardiff, 1996), pp. 133–5; Hall, *Description of Caernarvonshire*, p. 321; Owen, *Customs and Traditions of Wales*, p. 91.
[108] C. Garbett, *The Claims of the Church of England* (1947, London, 1948), p. 212. Between 1824 and 1832, even as gentle an author as Mary Russell Mitford could describe a cricket match between villages in which 'each attacks the other for honour'; in which the rival village were 'braggers born, a whole parish of gasconaders'; discussing 'the

even rowdier forms. Village 'heroes', 'champions' or 'best men' would engage in pugilistic combat against their neighbouring equivalents.[109] These fights often took place at annual feasts, or at remoter but significant sites on the parish boundary, cheered on by rival inhabitants of the parishes concerned, who might themselves join in. Fair grounds or even markets could also provide venues for fights of this sort, in which localised xenophobia was often a strong undercurrent and motive. Roughs from another village would invite themselves to feasts, dances or fairs to pick fights with the host village.[110] 'It was customary for the pugilists of all the villages to visit each other's feasts, and in many cases with the avowed object of meeting other pugilists there', wrote Joseph Lawson.[111] Richard Jefferies described the 'boisterous brutality of the hamlets'.[112] Here, as elsewhere, it is as well to remember that 'custom' could involve plebeian groups habitually attacking each other, and that there is no special reason to associate custom with class alignments.

Faction fighting, usually involving youths and young men, was extremely common between parishes, and in some places it had become a seasonal tradition. This is well discussed in John Stevenson's book on popular disturbances between 1700

---

regular native forces'; 'the genuine and hearty sympathy of belonging to a parish . . . Give me a parochial patriot, a man who loves his parish!'; and of 'desertion! Here was treachery! Here was treachery against that goodly state, our parish!' when someone abandoned the parish to play elsewhere; how a player had 'crossed the boundaries of his old parish, and actually belonged to us', alongside other issues of cross-class eligibility, which she stressed. See her *Our Village* (1824–32, Oxford, 1982), pp. 96–105, an account of Three Mile Cross, then a small and straggling village near Reading. On the football club as 'a symbol of village prestige and unity in the face of the outside world', see R. Frankenberg, *Village on the Border: A Social Study of Religion, Politics and Football in a North Wales Community* (London, 1957), pp. 152–4.

[109] For example, A. Howkins, *Whitsun in 19th Century Oxfordshire* (Oxford, 1973), p. 17.

[110] *Ibid.*, pp. 41–2, giving the example of antagonism between Garsington and Baldon; A. Howkins, *Poor Labouring Men: Rural Radicalism in Norfolk, 1870–1923* (London, 1985), p. 33; R. Russell, *From Cock-fighting to Chapel Building: Changes in Popular Culture in Eighteenth and Nineteenth Century Lincolnshire* (Sleaford, 2002), pp. 11–12, on 'strangers' acting in disorderly fashion at the Sibsey feast, 1824.

[111] Lawson, *Progress in Pudsey*, p. 76; R. Jefferies, 'The future of country society', in his *Landscape and Labour*, ed. J. Pearson (Bradford-on-Avon, 1979), p. 72, initially published in *New Quarterly* (July 1877). On the pugilistic popular culture of this period, see Malcolmson, *Popular Recreations in English Society*, pp. 42–3, 145–6; I. Dyck, 'From "Rabble" to "Chopsticks": the radicalism of William Cobbett', *Albion*, 21 (1989), pp. 61–4.

[112] Jefferies, 'The future of country society', p. 92.

and 1870.[113] He noted many regional and almost routine examples of this fighting, in which people were often severely injured or even killed. Such faction fights expressed 'an intense localism'.[114] Among his examples were animosities between Redruth and Gwennap in Cornwall; the 'brawl-cum-football match' at Shrovetide between the Derby parishes of All Saint's and St Peter's; the parish contests at Alnwick (Northumberland); and other fights between 'up-town' and 'down-town' parties from different places.[115] The latter phenomenon, dividing men by their residence in the town, could be found as far north as Kirkwall in Orkney.[116] Other cases were the fighting between Bruton and Batcombe in Somerset,[117] between Bala and Llangollen,[118] between the youths of Llechryd and Cardigan (local newspapers reporting the results),[119] between St Anne's and St Giles in London (featuring annual stick fights, which involved deaths),[120] or between Coneyhurst Hill in Ewhurst and Rudgwick over the Sussex border. The latter dispute had a rival terminology of 'Kaffirs' (i.e. Cavaliers) and 'Roundheads' ricochetting down from Civil War clashes, and its imperial (Bantu) vocabulary was superimposed in the late nineteenth century.[121] Then there were the fights between mobs from

[113] J. Stevenson, *Popular Disturbances in England, 1700–1870* (London, 1979), pp. 51–2.

[114] *Ibid.*, p. 51.

[115] *Kicking and Screaming*, BBC2 (16 October 1995); G. Findler, *Folk Lore of the Lake Counties* (Clapham, Yorks., 1968), pp. 58–60; and for a rural Irish equivalent, C. McGlinchey, *The Last of the Name* (Belfast, 1986), p. 74.

[116] Wojtas, 'History gives us combat and cuisine for the festive season', *Times Higher* (24 December 2004), p. 9.

[117] Underdown, 'Regional cultures?', p. 35.

[118] G. Borrow, *Wild Wales* (1862, London, 1970), pp. 257–9: his informant 'swears by Bala and abuses Llangollen, and calls its people drunkards, just as a Spaniard exalts his own village and vituperates the next and its inhabitants'.

[119] Jones, *Rebecca's Children*, p. 179.

[120] M. D. George, *London Life in the Eighteenth Century* (1925, Harmondsworth, 1976), p. 272. In London, as in other cities and towns, gangs drawn even from particular streets would often fight each other, adapting to urban areas the intense localism of the countryside. H. McLeod, *Class and Religion in the Late Victorian City* (London, 1974), p. 103, on Bethnal Green. Such urban localism and antagonism between groups of streets as 'tribal areas', 'an extremely local life', with boundaries apparently based on the urban parish, persisted in some towns into the mid-twentieth century. R. Hoggart, *The Uses of Literacy* (London, 1957), pp. 52–3.

[121] G. Jekyll, *Old West Surrey: Some Notes and Memories* (1904, Chichester, 1999), p. 189. Inter-county hostility was also an issue here. It is worth noting the terminology recorded by Jekyll, which was intended as insult and conflated recent south African

Walsall and Darlaston (vividly described by John Wesley, who found himself dramatically swept up by them),[122] between Sheringham and Cromer,[123] or Hadleigh and Leigh on Sea,[124] between some of the villages of north and south Gower,[125] between the city of Durham and surrounding pit villages, between Berry and Yorkley in the Forest of Dean,[126] or between Clovelly and Appledore on the north Devon coast.[127] Indeed, many fishing towns and villages had long-standing rivalries against each other.[128] For example, the novels of Leo Walmsley on the English north-east fishing communities are full of discussion of local xenophobia against people from other places, and these novels explicitly claimed authenticity for what they described.[129] Speaking of parish wakes, in the Rhuthun district of Wales, one observer recorded of the 1780s that

history with that of England in the seventeenth century. This may suggest that even the internationalism of the Empire had done little to mitigate the parochial (or county) rivalries at stake here. High levels of local patriotism, however expressed – a nationality in parishes – could often coincide with and buttress national patriotism. On survivals in a different area of 'an intense local patriotism . . . attachment to a particular community', which of course is not necessarily linked to local xenophobia, see T. Brennan, E. W. Cooney and H. Pollins, *Social Change in South-west Wales* (London, 1954), pp. 6–7, 97, 99.

[122] J. Wesley, *The Journal of John Wesley, 1735–1790*, ed. N. Ratcliff (London, 1940), 20 October 1743, p. 156; J. Capon, *John and Charles Wesley: The Preacher and the Poet* (London, 1988), pp. 11–16.

[123] I am grateful to David Parry for information about this case.

[124] Morrison, *Cunning Murrell*, pp. 52–4, who described the 'customary fight' between men from these two places.

[125] I refer to memories in my Welsh mother's family, from north Gower, against the more English southern half of the peninsula. Even today, blood group mapping shows this north–south divide through Gower.

[126] Potter, *Changing Forest*, p. 100.

[127] S. Ellis, *Down a Cobbled Street: The Story of Clovelly* (Bideford, 1987), p. 30. 'Great jealousy existed between villages then' (c. 1918).

[128] For example, see Jones, *Rebecca's Children*, p. 11, on antagonism between Carmarthen and Ferryside fishermen.

[129] See for example L. Walmsley, *Phantom Lobster* (1933, Harmondsworth, 1948), pp. 9, 13, 16 ('if you were not pure "Bramblewick", you were regarded as a foreigner and an outlaw, and anybody's game. In every fight the odds were so adjusted that I should be beaten . . . there was always some stout patriot to step in and finish me off'), pp. 19–20 ('an active and remorseless hostility', driving them back to where they came from; 'a spirit of enduring enmity'), p. 21 ('an intense pride . . . in themselves, and in their place'), p. 22 (pelting outsiders with 'balls of wet clay or fish-guts'), p. 24 ('Most of these "foreigners" . . . made a speedy escape'), p. 30 ('Wherever you turned for sympathy or support you would find that enmity'), p. 68 ('the old enmity, the unyielding hatred of the "foreigner", in the very way they looked at you when they spoke, with a humourless smile, and a hard twinkle in their eyes, which at its kindest

The young men of the surrounding parishes would assemble all their force and visit the wake; and towards the evening, when the liquours had begun to operate upon their senses, the men of one parish would easily be provoked to quarrel with those of another, and both would turn out, and the encounter would commence with clubs, sticks and stones, in a most furious manner; the parties would break each other's lines, and then would ensue a desperate confusion. I have even seen females enter the list in defence of their brothers, and even in the middle of rivers, scuffle and contend with robust men.[130]

As Parry-Jones later added, 'The existence of rival gangs [from different parishes] having a go at each other is nothing new in Wales, nor in England either.'[131] A similar view was expressed by S. G. Kendall: 'since feuds often existed between neighbouring villages in those days these fights were sometimes glorified into heavy punishments, often meted out to some parochial representative who dared to stand up for his parish and principles'.[132]

There was a persistent effort to muzzle or prohibit this kind of behaviour in the nineteenth century by some working-class leaders, as well as by middle- and upper-class interests. Methodist or other Nonconformist groups played an important role here. Yet, despite some notable reforming successes, inter-village and inter-town fighting could often linger on well into the twentieth century. H. E. Bates recalled this for Northamptonshire in his autobiography. He described 'when gangs of

seemed to convey a contemptuous pity'). Walmsley's 'Author's note' claimed that 'This book is the record of an actual experience', describing 'real' people.
[130] Cited in Owen, *Customs and Traditions of Wales*, 93.
[131] Parry-Jones, *My Own Folk*, p. 66. For vivid descriptions of xenophobia in Wales directed against himself, the English, or people from other parts of Wales, with accompanying statements, movements and implicitly violent, almost dance-like gestures, see Borrow, *Wild Wales*, pp. 365, 371–4, 386–8, 434–5, 437, 477, 485. On the Rebecca riots driving all English residents away from Troedyraur, such that all services were subsequently held in Welsh, see W. T. R. Pryce, 'Welsh and English in Wales, 1750–1971: a spatial analysis based on the linguistic affiliations of parochial communities', *Bulletin of the Board of Celtic Studies*, 28 (1978), p. 17. There is considerable evidence on Welsh opposition to what was sometimes called 'the English invasion'; and on English prejudice against the Welsh – for example, see P. Morgan, 'From long knives to blue books', in R. R. Davies, R. A. Griffiths, I. G. Jones, and K. O. Morgan (eds.), *Welsh Society and Nationhood: Historical Essays Presented to Glanmor Williams* (Cardiff, 1984); or J. Davies, *A History of Wales* (1990, Harmondsworth, 1993), p. 513, on the insulting of Welsh soldiers by English officers during the First World War.
[132] Parry-Jones, *My Own Folk*, p. 67; S. G. Kendall, *Farming Memoirs of a West Country Yeoman* (London, 1944), p. 19.

louts brawled in small possessive warfare . . . between township and township, when men out of crude bravado rolled from one town to another, beating up rival gangs, rough-housing outside ever-open pubs and inventing strange labels of contempt for rival towns' – labels like 'Hock-and-Dough' for Wellingborough, 'Hair-and-Teeth' for Raunds, or 'Yow-Yows' for Irthlingborough.[133] Such fighting never reached the extremes found in late nineteenth- and early twentieth-century Russia, where 'deep historical enmities between villages' could erupt in fights involving well over a thousand people, with much loss of life.[134] Even so, inter-parish hostility and violence was very widespread indeed in rural and small-town England and Wales.

Many conflicts between villages persisted over centuries, even if they were less characterised by open fighting. Their contexts and preconditions varied greatly. One well-documented example was that between the Thriplow 'Royalists' and the Fowlmere 'Roundheads' in Cambridgeshire. As the terms indicate, this feud went back to the Civil War, rather like that between Ewhurst and Rudgwick mentioned above.

In the 17th century, the main division in Fowlmere seems to have been between the Royalist Lord of the Manor and Rector and almost the entire remainder of the village who were Puritans . . . Thus to this day, people in the formerly Royalist Thriplow, a mere mile away, can speak dismissively of the Fowlmere 'Roundheads'. Perhaps this also explains why worshippers at Fowlmere Parish Church still regard Thriplow as more 'high church' . . . while Fowlmere Chapel is at times stronger than the parish church, and Thriplow has lost its chapel.[135]

Inter-parochial hostilities also revealed themselves in opposition to youths entering a parish to court local women. Lawson commented on this 'narrow local prejudice in the matter of courtship'.[136] He wrote of how a man coming in to court a

[133] H. E. Bates, *The Vanished World: An Autobiography of Childhood and Youth* (1969, London, 1987), p. 39. 'Hair and teeth' was also a Fenland jibe: 'E's all 'air and teeth like a Ramsey man.' S. Marshall, *Fenland Chronicle* (1967, Harmondsworth, 1998), p. 9.

[134] S. P. Frank, *Crime, Cultural Conflict, and Justice in Rural Russia, 1856–1914* (Berkeley, 1999), pp. 156–8.

[135] A. S. Ahmed and J. B. Mynors, 'Fowlmere: Roundheads, Rambo and rivalry in an English village today', *Anthropology Today*, 10, no. 5 (October 1994), pp. 3–8. On similar inter-village feuding, see also P. Wright, *The Village that Died for England: The Strange Story of Tyneham* (1995, London, 1996), p. 143.

[136] Lawson, *Progress in Pudsey*, p. 75.

woman 'is looked upon as an interloper by the young men there, and as a poacher on their preserves, and is often badly treated. Many have to give up in despair, after being covered with mud, and suffering much bodily harm.'[137] Local women themselves were said to torment a man who courted elsewhere, being 'up in arms against such cosmopolitanism'.[138] George Ewart Evans added much further comment on his areas of East Anglia. Discussing the 'negative side of the closeness of the old village community', he wrote of how it was

parochial in the worst sense of the word. The people who lived in the next parish were strangers, even 'foreigners'; and were treated as such in all dealings with them. Ordinary commerce was sometimes inevitable, but any intimacy was frowned upon: to be married to one of them was almost a crime. An old lady in the parish of Needham Market recalled her young days when she was rash enough to walk out with a man from the next parish. Her father's command, although ultimately ineffective, was direct enough: 'You must not do it! I can't have a daughter o' mine a-courting one o' those owd Creeting *jackdaws*.' Creeting is a village less than half a mile away, at the other side of the river.[139]

---

[137] *Ibid.*, p. 30.

[138] *Ibid.*, p. 30. Or see Findler, *Folk Lore of the Lake Counties*, p. 11: 'The young man who left his village or town to seek a bride was considered to be nothing more than an outlaw against the rules of decency'; chapter 4 of this book, on rural societies and geographical marital endogamy. Popular sayings represented the same sentiment – for example, 'Better wed over the mixen, than over the moor', in Grose, *Provincial Glossary*, n.p., under 'Cheshire'.

[139] G. E. Evans, *Ask the Fellows Who Cut the Hay* (1956, London, 1962), p. 239 (original italics). Evans continued with another story to illustrate 'this intense parochialism': about the grandfather of an elderly man who left his parish only once, to visit a place five or six miles away, and who upon returning remarked 'Thank God I'm back in good owd England!'. He never left again. *Ibid.*, p. 239. In his autobiography Evans described how the first physical education class he ran for young men in rural Cambridgeshire broke up, because he had put together people from three proximate villages. They said: 'We are not going to spend the rest of the evening with *foreigners*.' This, he wrote, 'was my first lesson in inter-village rivalry that was so intense fifty years ago'. Eventually 'this intense parochialism died a natural death' in his Sawston area, its passing aided by the village college. G. E. Evans, *The Strength of the Hills: An Autobiography* (1983, London, 1985), pp. 105–6 (his italics). Evans outlined the direction of change: 'this stage of inbred isolationism' of 'the old traditional unit of the parish', which was prone to judge a man 'by the stock he stems from' (Evans, *Ask the Fellows*, pp. 208, 238–9), was fast declining in favour of larger units, a change that he felt was much accelerated by the pace of farm mechanisation. Even so, he described 'the true village community' as 'that vague yet organic brotherhood that functions, as it were, underground and keeps its identity through all changes short of the most drastic social organization' (*ibid.*, p. 208).

In folklore and fable, jackdaws were associated with bad luck, heathenism, evil, ill health, imminent death, sorrow, excess chatter, vanity, roguery, quarrels, thieving, as well as the arrival of rain. The word 'daw' was used synonymously with knave to mean someone held in low esteem, with connotations of stupidity.[140] These were characteristics that were repeatedly found in the accusatory schema of local xenophobia.

A high (and rising) proportion of marriages in rural parishes in the eighteenth and early nineteenth centuries were between partners who were both parochially resident. It was not till the mid- or late nineteenth century that this considerable degree of geographical marital endogamy began to decline noticeably.[141] The rural exodus, and the arrival of the bicycle in the 1880s, played a major role in this.[142] Yet even in the twentieth century, from as far apart as Elmdon in Essex, to Staithes in North Yorkshire, to Llanfihangel yng Ngwynfa in north Montgomeryshire, one finds abundant evidence of outsiders, intent on courting and perhaps 'stealing' local girls, being trailed and set upon by local youths, beaten up, pelted with mud and stones, their horses or bicycles being incapacitated.[143] Laura Knight wrote of Staithes that 'It was only a short while since no marriage outside their own village was allowed; a few years earlier, any strange man coming to court a girl was stoned out of the place.'[144] Exton in Rutland was said to be 'so self-centred it was unbelievable. You didn't want to know a stranger . . . They couldn't bear any strangers in the village. And as to outsiders

---

[140] F. Greenoak, *British Birds: Their Folklore, Names and Literature* (London, 1997), pp. 190–1; I. Opie and M. Tatem (eds.), *A Dictionary of Superstitions* (Oxford, 1989), p. 215; K. Thomas, *Man and the Natural World: Changing Attitudes in England, 1500–1800* (1983, Harmondsworth, 1984), p. 78; J. C. Chadwick, *Folklore and Witchcraft in Dorset and Wiltshire* (Lyme Regis, n.d.), p. 17; Revd R. H. Barham, 'The Jackdaw of Rheims', in *The Ingoldsby Legends* (London, 1840).

[141] See chapter 4 of this book. Averaging sixty-nine rural parishes across very diverse regions, by the 1830s just over 70 per cent of all marriages were parochially endogamous.

[142] P. J. Perry, 'Working-class isolation and mobility in rural Dorset, 1837–1936: a study of marriage distances', *Transactions of the Institute of British Geographers*, 46 (1969), pp. 115–35.

[143] M. Strathern, *Kinship at the Core: An Anthropology of Elmdon, a Village in North-west Essex in the Nineteen-sixties* (Cambridge, 1981), pp. 176–9; Rees, *Life in a Welsh Countryside*, pp. 83–4, 135.

[144] Dame L. Knight, *Oil Paint and Grease Paint: The Autobiography of Laura Knight*, vol. 1 (1936, Harmondsworth, 1941), p. 95.

courting Exton girls, it was courting death. They used to put bedsteads across Empingham Road just to stop people coming up.' 'It's got a terrible name, whether its true or not, for being inbred, for incest, for everything.'[145] Strathern argued for Elmdon in Essex that as a manifestation of local ideas of belonging and entitlement, a possessive attitude towards local women was historically prevalent. There were many attempts to exclude suitors who were not 'Elmdoners'. As she observed, signs of village solidarity like this could endure despite population mobility.[146] Much the same was true, she argued, with regard to parish housing and employment. Such a concept of 'core' Elmdoners, felt to have a prior claim in these matters, was particularly noticeable among the working classes. They held on to their local perquisites all the more strongly because of the frequent sense that they had little such opportunity elsewhere.

This perception of limited goods available locally, to be defended against interlopers, was a very common attitude indeed in previous centuries, especially among poorer inhabitants.[147]

---

[145] N. Duckers and H. Davies, *A Place in the Country: Social Change in Rural England* (Harmondsworth, 1990), p. 3. 'There are whispers of witchcraft and evil deeds, that they "boil goats' heads" in Exton . . . that the school children are subnormal.' *Ibid.*, pp. 3–5. Most of this talk, of course, falls into the category of scurrilous slander, in this case against a picturesque estate village that was *ipso facto* precautionary about admitting newcomers.

[146] Strathern, *Kinship at the Core*, p. 179. As someone whose early research on migration was supervised by E. A. Wrigley at the Cambridge Group for the History of Population and Social Structure, I am well aware of the extent of local mobility in the past, which I have stressed in print. Personal mobility in the eighteenth and nineteenth centuries seems not to have undermined strong senses of local allegiance and belonging. Indeed, legal concepts of 'home' and belonging were conditioned by that mobility. John Clare, one the most celebrated exponents of an intense sense of local belonging, was also a labouring migrant whose mobility took him as far afield as London, Holywell (north of Stamford), Market Deeping and Peterborough, and villages within that area much nearer his own fen-edge parish of Helpston. See Robinson (ed.), *John Clare's Autobiographical Writings*, pp. xx–xxi, for a map. Many of the parochial antagonisms discussed here in fact derived from the ways in which such migration was handled. Even so, one of the priorities at present is to reconcile more fully the demographic evidence of considerable migration, with the cultural evidence of localised xenophobia and belonging. For example, more attention might be paid to the internally expulsive dynamics of the parish. Demographic work should not foreclose the cultural research, and the two should be rendered compatible. This agenda is complicated by the different and sometimes almost unmatchable types of evidence (demographic *versus* literary) documenting these phenomena.

[147] For anthropological discussion of ideas of 'limited good' (signs of which can be found in our subject matter), see G. M. Foster, 'Peasant society and the image of

It was fundamental to resource allocation under the old poor law, when settled 'insiders' could be treated with generosity in many regions, while incipient or actual paupers from elsewhere were victimised or cold-shouldered. One also finds such attitudes manifest in the stinting of commons in the open-field village, and in other manorial regulations governing entitlement and usage, in access to 'parish' housing, in gleaning entitlement, in rules about who was eligible for certain charities, and in the presumptions about who had priority for employment. Indeed, so-called 'moral economy' actions like food rioting, to stop grain being taken out of the locality, had long been posited on these perceptions of 'limited good'. Resistance against outsiders being employed was also very strong, and was often associated with intimidation.[148] In the 1830s, J. M. White drew a distinction, with reference to settlements at parish level, between 'Foreign and Native poor'. In doing this he put the accent on a common line of discrimination, a boundary within people's minds.[149] For most of the eighteenth and nineteenth centuries, the payment of parish rates by parish employers brought with it the overwhelming presumption that those who were legally settled in the parish ought to be given precedence in employment. Any ratepayer who employed outsiders, and by so doing threw locally settled poor on to the poor rate, disadvantaged the entire parish, ratepaying and labouring classes alike. In one perhaps extreme case, that of St Faith's and Horsford (just north of Norwich), it was said that 'the farmers there would hardly dare to employ a stranger'.[150] Quite typically, though, the

---

the limited good', *American Anthropologist*, 67 (1965); and his 'The anatomy of envy: a study in symbolic behaviour', *Current Anthropology*, 13 (1972). As a feature of popular *mentalité*, the concept of limited good is curiously parallel to the theory of the wages fund in classical political economy.

[148] For example, D. H. Morgan, 'The place of harvesters in nineteenth-century village life', in R. Samuel (ed.), *Village Life and Labour* (London, 1975), p. 38; M. Reed, 'Social change and social conflict in nineteenth century England: a comment', in M. Reed and R. Wells (eds.), *Class, Conflict and Protest in the English Countryside, 1700–1880* (London, 1990), p. 107; Jones, *Rebecca's Children*, pp. 65, 111: 'all non-parish workers were resented by the village community'; local families 'were incensed when outsiders came into the parish to harvest or make road repairs'.

[149] J. M. White, *Parochial Settlements: An Obstruction to Poor Law Reform* (London, 1835), p. 16.

[150] *Fifth Report from the Select Committee on Settlement, and Poor Removal*, 11 (1847), p. 48.

inhabitants of one Leicestershire village agreed in 1835 that 'We the undersigned inhabitants of Bottesford, agree not to employ any laborers who do not belong to this parish or any whose settlement there may be any doubt of.'[151]

This was a policy which came very much to the fore in the century after about 1750, with its rising poor relief expenditure and problems of rural poverty. The experience of rising poor relief was shared by almost all rural areas, although labour shortages in some of the industrial hinterlands made such a consideration less important there. Such rising relief expenditures, dwindling access to commons and unenclosed land as enclosure proceeded, rising population, often high unemployment, food shortages, near-famine prices, and the legal liability to maintain settled paupers, drew ever greater attention to the parish as a crucial administrative, economic and apparently moral unit upon which the poor depended, while also reinforcing the need to protect scarce parish resources. All these factors probably aggravated parochial xenophobia. Twenty-two years of Napoleonic war-time pressures and anti-foreigner rhetoric, plus a perception and fear of more people on the move – labourers, tramping artisans, vagrants, militias, ex-soldiers and so on – may well have had the same effect. I have pointed elsewhere to 'the rapidity of local authorities' action against those felt to be a potential encumbrance on the rates', taken partly through the settlement laws.[152] The agricultural

---

[151] Leics. CRO, DE 829/86 (Bottesford vestry book, 8 October 1835); Sir E. W. Head, 'The law of settlement', *Edinburgh Review*, 87 (April 1848), p. 459: 'the farmers in the agricultural districts have become thoroughly imbued with the principle that the parish to which a man belongs, and not his ability to work, is the first point to be considered'; *Sixth Report from the Select Committee on Settlement, and Poor Removal* (1847), p. 262: 'it is so in every parish; it is tacitly understood so by the parishioners, that they shall employ the persons resident in their parishes, and belonging to their parishes, in preference to others, because they are interested in doing so . . . it is generally understood so, and it is a principle generally acted upon'; *Fourth Report from the Select Committee on Settlement, and Poor Removal*, xi (1847), p. 84. As the Revd David Davies put it, 'For it is manifest that our laws consider all the inhabitants of a parish as forming one large family, the higher and richer part of which is bound to provide employment and subsistence for the lower and labouring part.' *Case of the Labourers in Husbandry* (Bath, 1795), p. 38.

[152] K. D. M. Snell, *Annals of the Labouring Poor: Social Change and Agrarian England, 1660–1900* (Cambridge, 1985), pp. 17–18. One historian misconstrued my meaning here, taking statements describing post-1795 settlement law practice as covering in the

depression after 1815, and its attendant poor law and unemployment problems, ensured that a similar climate persisted for
another three decades in many midland and southern parishes.
If one bears this context in mind, a strong presumption could be
held for inter-parochial rivalries and forms of exclusion intensi-
fying over this period, especially in the southern half of England
during early industrialisation after about 1780.

One aspect of this was the high number of settlement disputes
at Quarter Sessions from the late eighteenth century, which
inevitably accompanied escalating prices, rising relief expenditures, increasing sums spent on poor removals, and growing
problems of rural structural and seasonal unemployment.[153]
Settlement disputes between parishes continued at a heightened
level during the early nineteenth-century rural depression. Most
of these disputes were localised, reflecting the predominant
patterns of migration – they were often between very proximate
parishes. They were very costly, given the expenses incurred on
solicitors, court fees, finding witnesses, journeys, maintenance
of the fought-over paupers, and so on. They often rose to over
£20 per case, sometimes well over £50. The average costs grew
considerably between about 1760 and 1810.[154] Such legal con-
frontation was a common experience for parishes over this
period. Even the smallest rural parishes could become embroiled in such a dispute every few years; while for the more
populous parishes it was a more frequent event. A whole parish

same terms all the eighteenth century, so the passage is slightly reworded in my
'Agricultural seasonal unemployment, the standard of living, and women's work,
1690–1860', in P. Sharpe (ed.), *Women's Work: The English Experience, 1650–1914*
(London, 1998), pp. 74–5. See also chapter 3 of this book, and my 'Settlement, poor
law and the rural historian: new approaches and opportunities', *Rural History*, 3
(1992), pp. 145–72. The close relation between the settlement and poor laws meant
that issues of parish settlement became more prominent and disputatious during
periods of rising pauperism, as from the late eighteenth century.

[153] On rising sums spent on removals, as percentages of total sums assessed and relief
expenditures, 1776–1815 (from about 2 per cent to about 6 per cent), see Anon.,
'Inquiries with respect to the progress and state of pauperism in England since the
reign of Queen Elizabeth', *Edinburgh Review* (May 1828), p. 325. For an example of
steep rises in disputes, in this case for Oxfordshire from *c.* 1810, see B. K. Song,
'Agrarian policies on pauper settlement and migration, Oxfordshire 1750–1834',
Continuity and Change, 13 (1998), p. 368, fig. 1.

[154] C. M. Vialls, 'The laws of settlement: their impact on the poor inhabitants of the
Daventry area of Northamptonshire, 1750–1834' (Ph.D., University of Leicester,
1999), pp. 367–70, 375–6, 379.

could be involved in a case: the ratepayers would have an immediate pecuniary interest in its conduct and outcome; while the poor themselves would be implicated as witnesses, and as people whose interests were at stake as recipients of parish money, or as residents in parish housing, and who had their own views on the legal and moral issues involved. These disputes would frequently unite the settled poor with the principal ratepayers of a parish, just as efforts to prevent settlements being gained could do (by hindering yearly service, preventing illegitimate births in the parish by women settled elsewhere, or by driving out some newcomers). All rural classes could find themselves consulting and making similar witness statements in court. Any local resident 'belonging' to the opposing parish in a legal dispute could face resentment from inhabitants. Church bells were sometimes rung to celebrate victory in a settlement court case, just as they were rung to celebrate national victories like Waterloo or the capture of Quebec.[155] Such ringing would often be audible to the rival parish,[156] much as triumphal bonfires were visible to parishes all around Egdon Heath.[157] Local bell chimes were widely known and associated with each parish. We saw earlier how the insults of *blason populaire* made play with the cock on the church tower. A cock on a church weather-vane stood for vigilance. Church cocks, like parish maypoles or garlands in an earlier period,[158] were sometimes audaciously stolen as trophies by altitudinous heroes

---

[155] For example, see G. Hannah (ed.), *The Deserted Village: The Diary of an Oxfordshire Rector, James Newton, of Nuneham Courtenay, 1736–86* (Stroud, 1992), p. 65.

[156] For an example of this in 1843, see Jones, *Rebecca's Children*, p. 118.

[157] T. Hardy, *The Return of the Native* (1878, London, 1971), pp. 22, 35. Such ritual fires – e.g. at Halloween, 5 November, May Eve or Midsummer – were partly intended to ward off baneful external influences, often associated with liminal and thus vulnerable turning points in the year, when the known gave way to the unknown. (They were lit in some urban areas too, such as Haslingden (Lancs.), by rival street districts, which competed against each other in fire sizes, and stole from each other's fire stacks.) In folkloric terms, one might speak of a (regionally varied) calendrical cycle of local vulnerability, which also related to socio-economic aspects of the parish (e.g. the seasonality of farm servant arrivals and departures).

[158] R. Hutton, *The Rise and Fall of Merry England: The Ritual Year, 1400–1700* (1994, Oxford, 1996), p. 142; Owen, *Customs and Traditions of Wales*, pp. 71–2; D. Dymond, 'God's disputed acre', *Journal of Ecclesiastical History*, 50 (1999), pp. 487–8, on outsiders capturing other parishes' garlands, rioting and fighting in churchyards, and disrupting church services, dancing sports, may-games: 'quarrelling, ready to murder one another'.

from a rival parish. In the case of a settlement victory, with the bells ringing, the cock crowed from on high.

Many contemporaries observed that the settlement laws and their effects had 'a direct tendency to create an ill-feeling between parishes'.[159] Indeed, this was one of the compelling arguments in favour of union or national poor law settlement, which in effect won through respectively in 1865 and 1948. Richard Burn, later quoted in agreement by the Poor Law Commissioner Sir George Nicholls, wrote that the settlement laws 'led to a greater quantity of litigation and hostile divisions than any other law on the statute-book'.[160] One historian has commented that settlement 'battles between parishes were pursued with all the bitterness and ruthlessness of tribal warfare'.[161] Another wrote

---

[159] *First Report from the Select Committee on Settlement, and Poor Removal* (1847), pp. 61, 65; *Second and Third Reports from the Select Committee on Settlement, and Poor Removal*, XI (1847), p. 2; *Report of George Coode to the Poor Law Board on the Law of Settlement and Removal of the Poor*, XXVI (1851), p. 276; *Report from the Select Committee on Irremovable Poor*, XVII (1860), p. 62; R. Pashley, *Pauperism and Poor Laws* (London, 1852), p. 327, quoting the clerk to the Southwell Union (Notts.) in 1850 on 'much bad feeling between parish and parish'. A further factor, which also aggravated parochial antagonisms, was the 'open' and 'close' parish divide – closely tied up with the settlement laws – and their labour-market consequences. There were many long-term hostile repercussions here, which continued even with the irremovability legislation of the period after 1846 (9 & 10 Vic., c. 66), when open parishes were resentfully paying for many labourers of nearby close parishes.

[160] Sir G. Nicholls, *A History of the English Poor Law, in Connection with the State of the Country and the Condition of the People*, vol. II (1854, London, 1898), p. 211.

[161] B. Osborne, *Justices of the Peace, 1361–1848* (Shaftesbury, 1960), p. 188. During the old poor law, it was possible for JPs to support a parish with levies from other parishes within the hundred or even county (under 43 Eliz., c. 2), but such mutual aid between parishes was extremely rare. Sir G. Nicholls, *A History of the English Poor Law*, vol. I (1854, London, 1904), p. 191; E. Trotter, *Seventeenth Century Life in the Country Parish, with Special Reference to Local Government* (Cambridge, 1919), p. 73. Examples of coordinated poor law administration across parishes can be found: the workhouse or joint-parish house building under 9 Geo. I, c. 7 (1722) or subsequent private Acts, especially in London; the incorporated hundreds of Norfolk and Suffolk which began to be formed from 1756; the incorporation of the Isle of Wight parishes from 1771 (11 Geo. III, c. 43); the Gilbert unions formed under 22 Geo. III, c. 83; non-resident relief payment, which required cooperation between parishes or townships, once the main issue of a pauper's settlement had been resolved, a system that appears to have expanded in the late eighteenth century, and may well have existed long before then; or there was provision for the insane (who, *ipso facto*, lost parochial retention). I have only ever found one example of two parishes agreeing to share relief costs for a disputed pauper, for an elderly woman not likely to live long, and they had to draw up a legal agreement to achieve that (Beds. CRO, P48/16/1). Up to 1834 any such cooperation was normally eclipsed by parochial independency. Even from 1834, only one union (Docking, Norf.) took up the option in the Poor Law Amendment Act of

about 'the perpetual war of parish against parish which the Law of Settlement had long created as a sort of national sport'.[162] Thomas Mackay discussed the 'weapons of offence in the "dirty warfare" which went on perennially between the 15,000 parishes into which the country was divided'.[163] The Medical Officer of Health of North-West Cheshire, Dr J. B. Yeoman, when he penned his history of the Wirrall Union in the early twentieth century, spoke of how 'For a couple of centuries a battle raged, between parishes, on the subject of the chargeability of the poor.'[164] And when E. J. Lidbetter looked back, in the early 1930s, at the past history of settlement disputes, he reflected that 'the days of the gladiatorial contests of settlement officers are, happily, ended'.[165]

There were good reasons for this rather martial descriptive language. Settlement had been a highly disputatious matter throughout the seventeeth and eighteenth centuries. Attempts in the seventeenth century to exclude poor people who would be burdensome to parochial poor rates, charities and other resources underlay what Steve Hindle called 'the extraordinary

---

the union becoming the unit of settlement, which helped to diminish inter-parochial disputes there. J. Caird, *English Agriculture in 1850–51* (1852, Farnborough, 1968), p. 176. Intrinsic to anti-alliance motivation was an aversion to anything that might increase the parish poor rate. J. J. and A. J. Bagley, *The English Poor Law* (London, 1966), p. 30. Under the new poor law, some parishes even objected to being in the same union as another, 'most frequently a neighbouring one, against which some feeling of anger or jealousy existed'. Nicholls, *History of the English Poor Law*, vol. II, p. 292. And when parishes joined in some form of administrative union, either before or after 1834, a high level of self-interest continued, with persistent tensions between them.

[162] J. R. Poynter, *Society and Pauperism: English Ideas on Poor Relief, 1795–1834* (London, 1969), p. xxi.

[163] T. Mackay, *A History of the English Poor Law*, vol. III: *From 1834 to the Present Time* (1854, London, 1900), p. 345, or see p. 346, citing George Coode on 15,535 parishes and townships as 'direct antagonists each of every other', and on 'interparochial warfare'. Similar language, 'of warfare between the parishes', is used in J. Johnston, 'The management of the poor law in seven parishes of western Lincolnshire, 1790–1834', *East Midland Historian*, 8 (1998), p. 15.

[164] J. B. Yeoman, *Some Poor History and the Wirrall Union* (n.d., c. 1919–29, Birkenhead, 1965), p. 8.

[165] E. J. Lidbetter, *Settlement and Removal* (London, n.d., c. 1932), p. iii. 'The tendency of all modern movements in matters relating to public administration is towards an abandonment of the spirit of parochialism in which the law of settlement originated and developed.' *Ibid.*, p. iv; see also Nicholls, *History of the English Poor Law*, vol. II, p. 433, on parish 'antagonism'.

hostility of social relations between parishes'.[166] Coming on
top of such long-term conditions, the unprecedented number
and cost of inter-parochial settlement disputes from the late
eighteenth century (with rising parish relief expenditures and
considerable personal mobility) pitted parish against parish,
and augmented complex legal and cultural patterns of exclusion
or acceptability.[167] Such legal disputes themselves often triggered a pattern of tit-for-tat legal reprisals, and other action to
hinder settlements, particularly under the old poor law, as parishes revenged themselves against their adversaries in future
years. In fact, some nearby parishes engaged in a sequence of
arguments over responsibility for paupers that was opportunistic and virtually endemic. This bore witness to overseers' sense
of parochial honour and responsibility. Such litigious behaviour
tended to subside as a result of more coordinated administrative, financial and eventual irremovability arrangements in the
unions of the new poor law, arrangements which dated mainly
from 1846–54.[168] Around the same time, some of the London
unions, such as the Strand union, began to take steps with
regard to settlement policies to try 'to avoid litigation' and establish a 'friendly and rational intercourse between unions and

---

[166] Hindle, *On the Parish?*, p. 353; and on late seventeenth-century settlement disputes
causing 'great inter-parochial bitterness' see J. Broad, *Transforming English Rural
Society: The Verneys and the Claydons, 1600–1820* (Cambridge, 2004), p. 168.

[167] Another indication of inter-parish cooperation diminishing at this time was the
system of briefs, which declined markedly in the late eighteenth century, and ceased
in 1828. N. J. G. Pounds, *A History of the English Parish: The Culture of Religion from
Augustine to Victoria* (Cambridge, 2000), pp. 269–70; W. A. Bewes, *Church Briefs, or,
Royal Warrants for Collections for Charitable Objects* (London, 1896). Briefs were a weak
counter-example to an argument for parochial xenophobia. They were read from
pulpits and used to help rebuild churches elsewhere, or to relieve sufferers outside
the parish from fires, floods or other calamities. They had been organised by the
enactment of 4 & 5 Anne, c. 14, subsequently regulated by the Lord Chancellor's
directions in 1755 and 1804, and abolished by 9 Geo. IV, c. 42. The sums voted by
parishes were often exceptionally small, as little as 2d. as a fixed sum, and there was
much neglect or avoidance of the system by churchwardens and incumbents.
M. H. Port, *Six Hundred New Churches: The Church Building Commission, 1818–1856*
(London, 1961), p. 6.

[168] In particular, after an angry flurry of settlement litigation during the early years of
the new poor law, such litigation was reduced after 1848 by the operation of 11 & 12
Vic., c. 31; 11 & 12 Vic., c. 110; and 14 & 15 Vic., c. 105. These Acts diminished the
legal repercussions of small inaccuracies in settlement documentation, and allowed
settlement cases to be submitted by consent to the Poor Law Board for less expensive
and acrimonious arbitration than had hitherto occurred.

parishes'.[169] Nevertheless, very many thousands of removals still occurred across the country every year, throughout the nineteenth century, and many of them were disputed.[170] And boards of guardians of different unions were often criticised, as for example by Helen Bosanquet, for 'a curious, jealous narrowness . . . which makes them unwilling to co-operate . . . with each other'. The 'average guardian . . . does not like to be mixed up with the neighbours [other parishes in the union] at all. It is quite impossible . . . to get over that prejudice.'[171] One can see, therefore, why so many poor law unions resisted interference by a London poor law authority. As in Huddersfield in 1844, there was a 'deeply rooted antipathy amongst the ratepayers against strangers being appointed to intermeddle with their own parochial affairs, which extends to every class of society'.[172]

Even so, the new poor law was often criticised because it was said to have 'weakened local attachment, and destroyed local respect'.[173] One way it did this was by setting in place further administrative machinery that began to transcend the parish and the vestry. It thus played a significant part in reducing parochial xenophobia, at the same time as it slackened local attachments, further contributing to the ambiguous judgements that the new poor law invites. Assessment of that law also needs to be informed by the view that its de-localising and harsh

[169] 'Resolutions passed at a meeting of the board of guardians of the Strand union', *Official Circulars of Public Documents and Information: Directed by the Poor Law Commissioners to be Printed, Chiefly for the Use of the Members and Permanent Officers of Boards of Guardians, under the Poor Law Amendment Act*, vol. vi (9 December 1845), p. 14.

[170] For example, there were 13,867 removal orders in 1849, affecting about 40,000 people. Nicholls, *History of the English Poor Law*, vol. ii, p. 435.

[171] H. Bosanquet, *The Poor Law Report of 1909* (1909, London, 1911), pp. 154, 162; and see D. Ashforth, 'Settlement and removal in urban areas: Bradford, 1834–71', in M. E. Rose (ed.), *The Poor and the City: The English Poor Law in its Urban Context, 1834–1914* (Leicester, 1985), pp. 85–6, on unions in the 1840s and 50s not cooperating over non-resident relief.

[172] The chairman of the Huddersfield board of guardians, cited in F. Driver, *Power and Pauperism: The Workhouse System, 1834–1884* (Cambridge, 1993), pp. 140–1.

[173] Sir G. Crewe, *A Word for the Poor, and Against the Present Poor Law* (London, 1843), p. 10. The intensity of localist sentiment, and the distrust of centralisation, were major obstacles that the new poor law had to surmount. For example, there was intense opposition in some rural areas – 'where xenophobia ran high' – to the idea of bringing in outsiders such as ex-London policemen or NCOs to serve as relieving officers. For discussion of this 'entrenched particularism' and hostility to outsiders, see P. Harling, 'The power of persuasion: central authority, local bureaucracy and the New Poor Law', *English Historical Review*, 107 (1992), pp. 45–9.

agenda, even though only partially implemented (see chapter 5), probably did more than any other measure to quicken the emergence of class consciousness among the rural poor.[174] By late 1838 the anti-poor law movement had fed into Chartism, and in some regions that influenced rural labourers, even though Chartism was more associated with urban and manufacturing areas.[175] Emerging working-class consciousness was not necessarily contingent upon an erosion of parochial xenophobia – but in this case a fundamental poor law reform of questionable moral value conduced strongly to both ends. Both that class consciousness, and the centralising agenda and administrative frameworks of the new poor law, acted in ways that were detrimental to local attachment, bringing to the fore issues, alliances and purposes which necessarily transcended localism.

Other barriers had accompanied and were aggravated by the disputations situation affecting legal settlement, especially before 1834. Among these were the issues of boundary maintenance, disputes over inter-commoning and animal trespass, opposition to parochial inter-marriage, reluctance to employ outsiders, arguments over poor payment or non-resident relief, and local traditions of mutual insult and fighting. Such issues often compounded each other. There was, for example, a strong disinclination to inter-marry between some Leicestershire parishes often in settlement disputes with each other. In some cases here, deeper historical antagonisms or differences underlay

---

[174] Snell, *Annals of the Labouring Poor*, pp. 114–37.

[175] See the geography of Chartist associations, 1839–40, mapped in J. Langton and R. J. Morris (eds.), *Atlas of Industrializing Britain, 1780–1914* (London, 1986), p. 188, showing that such associations were concentrated in parts of the north midlands, in industrial areas of Lancashire and Yorkshire, and around Tyneside. London was another centre of Chartist activity. The low-wage, southern and midland arable regions, and the large regional swathe of Parliamentary enclosure encompassing open-field arable, had negligible Chartist representation using this measure. Chartist interest can certainly be found in the countryside, or nearby market towns, and one appreciates both the bitterness and vulnerability of many rural workers to victimisation, and their potential interest in the Land Plan – but the evidence for Chartism among agricultural workers is fairly scanty. D. Thompson, *The Chartists: Popular Politics in the Industrial Revolution* (1984, Aldershot, 1986), pp. 173–9; H. Fearn, 'Chartism in Suffolk', in A. Briggs (ed.), *Chartist Studies* (London, 1962); Archer, '*By a Flash and a Scare*', p. 106; R. Wells, 'Southern Chartism', *Rural History*, 2:1 (1991), pointing out that farm workers were the largest single sector of the working-class population, and doing much to reveal the weakness of southern agrarian Chartism.

the combined indications of distrust and non-cooperation. Some of these inter-parochial aversions in Leicestershire lasted into the twentieth century, although other nearby parishes were regarded as amicable or tolerable. Successive efforts to rationalise local boundaries in the nineteenth century – for example, to make parish and borough boundaries coterminous – or to join parishes together (to facilitate local rating, or reduce the numbers of officers and elections of guardians), had to encounter what W. G. Lumley in 1873 called 'the feeling of antagonism' between parishes. He commented that such uniting of parishes was not 'a very palatable thing'.[176] When the Local Government (England and Wales) Bill was presented on 21 March 1893, its clauses allowing smaller parishes to be diluted, out-voted or absorbed by larger adjoining parishes evoked intense opposition throughout the country, as parishes baulked and cold-shouldered each other. Gladstone was no enemy to parish revivalism, and he ensured that these schemes were heavily modified in the second reading of the bill, to placate the intense feelings that had been stirred up.

Whatever their many possible causes, my main intention here is to stress the importance of such local antagonisms and rivalries, and their often long-standing nature. In overlooking them, historians are not appreciating some of the main instincts and counter-alignments affecting rural societies in the eighteenth and nineteenth centuries. We do not at present know how far such attitudes were shared across local social hierarchies. The presumption is that the culture of local xenophobia was strongest among the more vulnerable groups in rural parishes, whether paupers, labourers, artisans, small tenants or freeholders, who were together a majority of inhabitants. Advanced education, travel, wider social horizons and geographical exogamy were more prevalent among higher ranks and orders. Some of their ideas of community were certainly not parochial, and their senses of place may often have transcended the parish. However, there were some reasons for local xenophobic views

---

[176] William G. Lumley, QC, one of the most impressive authorities on local boundaries and poor law administration, was the Assistant Secretary and Counsel to the Local Government Department. I cite his evidence here in the *Report from the Select Committee on Boundaries of Parishes, Unions, and Counties*, VIII (1873), p. 17.

to spread upwards socially, when one considers the self-interest of ratepayers, the nature of many vestries, the farmers who utilised commons, or some clerical motives and parish-centred preserves noticeable in the Anglican Church. Overseers often received their marching orders from higher up the social scale. Local antagonisms, in which the labouring poor were deeply involved, often had higher social involvement, allying people from very different ranks and orders. As such, they had significant repercussions for the hesitant emergence of working-class consciousness in the countryside, and they suggest instead the continuing hold of very local loyalties and interests well into the nineteenth century.

The development of religious gatherings and organisations across parishes, notably through the structures of Methodism, was a major factor in bringing hitherto antagonistic parishes together.[177] Methodism is often given importance by labour historians because of the organisational and leadership qualities it developed among poorer people. This is indisputable among denominations like the Primitive Methodists or Bible Christians. Of perhaps greater significance, however, is the fact that Methodism (unlike most of the Anglican Church) encouraged extra-parochial allegiances, and thus fostered conditions in which broader levels of social consciousness could occur. It did this by its breaking down of disputatious localism, partly via its flexible circuit structures,[178] its stress on an extended society of shared belief, and through the open, outward-going nature of its Arminian rather than Calvinist theology – as was true of Wesleyan Methodism and most of its English offshoots. To Wesley, the divine laws of salvation applied to *everyone* with no regard to parish or place. It was the spiritual links and shared aspirations between people that mattered, not the parochial ones – and so to him a 'community of believers' could not be bounded by parish. Time and again, Wesley's *Journal* reads as the triumph of welcome and openness, over xenophobia and

---

[177] Parry-Jones, *My Own Folk*, pp. 65–7.
[178] On Methodist circuits, see R. W. Ambler, 'Preachers and the plan: patterns of activity in early Primitive Methodism', *Proceedings of the Wesley Historical Society*, 46 (1987–8), pp. 21–31; D. Garratt, 'Primitive Methodist circuits in the English–Welsh borderland', *Rural History*, 14 (2003).

closedness: 'I look upon all the world as my parish.'[179] It takes an understanding of local xenophobia to appreciate the full originality, charisma and decisiveness of Wesley's contribution to expanding the area of local consciousness and sympathy. For linguistic and theological reasons (the latter stemming mainly from the split between Arminian and Calvinistic Methodism), such Wesleyan openness may have been more pronounced in England than in the heartlands of Welsh Calvinistic Methodism. The latter also coincided with the strongest Welsh language areas.[180] Some of these directions of change had been presaged in elements of Old Dissent. This was most notable among the Quakers – whose intrusions and beliefs had earlier made them such a prime target of parochial xenophobia, persistently documented in George Fox's *Journal* and their books of sufferings. Countless of those 'sufferings' originated in their cross-parish perambulations (and sometimes their behaviour reinforced people's views of outsiders). They became famed for altruistic charitable work, as for example during the Irish Famine.[181] Yet the *scale* of Wesley's and the Methodist contribution was certainly unprecedented. It was to be an important influence in helping to assuage xenophobic outlooks, complementing the staged decline of the parish as an administrative and cultural entity, and the slowly emerging effects of wider class consciousness.

The general direction of change in the countryside is usually said to have been from hierarchical social orders based upon the parish and locality, to social classes experienced at regional and eventually national levels. This transition had certainly not taken place by the late eighteenth century. In some northern and

[179] N. Curnock (ed.), *John Wesley's Journal* (London, 1903), 11 June 1739. Despite Wesley's openness, it should be noted that many chapel communities were rather exclusive, calling themselves 'the elect', 'the people of God', 'the dear people' and so on. Such a language could be extra-parochially open, embracing people at a distance, but it might also be selective and closed. Such attitudes long persisted among Wesley's followers, and were also found among other Nonconformist denominations.

[180] On Welsh Calvinistic Methodism, see K. D. M. Snell and P. S. Ell, *Rival Jerusalems: The Geography of Victorian Religion* (Cambridge, 2000), esp. pp. 154–9. On the Welsh language regions, *Y Fro Gymraeg*, see J. Aitchison and H. Carter, 'Rural Wales and the Welsh language', *Rural History*, 2 (1991).

[181] J. L. Nickalls (ed.), *The Journal of George Fox* (1694, Philadelphia, 1997), e.g. pp. 42–5, 218–19, 226–7, writing about stone throwing and considerable violence against him as he visited many different places. On the Quakers and the Famine, see A. Somerville, *Letters from Ireland during the Famine of 1847* (Dublin, 1994), pp. 50, 64.

western rural areas, including parts of Wales, where 'family-and-farm history' (to use a Norwegian term) might sometimes be preferred to a stress on class, one may question whether it had occurred a century later, or even whether it ever occurred.[182] The general change was facilitated by the reduced administrative and cultural purpose of the parish in the nineteenth century, notably with the new poor law, and the Union Chargeability Act of 1865, which did much to lessen the 'rivalry between parishes in the same union'.[183] Many other factors were involved here, as notions of parish autonomy gave way to the political economy of free market and exchange, as the civil and ecclesiastical functions of the parish separated, as the parish waned administratively and as a moral and religious ideal, and as the technology of transport was revolutionised after the 1830s. Captain Swing and other protest movements of the early nineteenth century saw people from different parishes congregating together in combined actions,[184] although by no means all parishes in the affected regions were involved, and some Swing letters attacked farmers for employing 'strangers' and Irishmen. Many farmers and landowners blamed 'strangers' for Swing itself.[185] This early expression of rural collective action was to be repeated in a more organised form in the later nineteenth-century agricultural unions. Other kinds of collective protest or organisation were developing among the rural poor over this period. These included localised unions like that at Tolpuddle, friendly societies, trade organisations among rural artisans, anti-new poor law agitation, gatherings against tollgates and other grievances in south and mid-Wales, solidarities of labourers collected for seasonal work, anti-Irish protests, spontaneous strikes among railway navvies,

---

[182] I. G. Jones, *Communities: Essays in the Social History of Victorian Wales* (Llandysul, 1987), p. 224: 'in the country "middle-class" or "working-class" were concepts utterly foreign to and contradictory of the fundamental concept of a unitary society'.

[183] 28 & 29 Vic., c. 79. The quotation is from Richard Jones, chairman of the Holyhead Union, in the *Report from the Select Committee on Irremovable Poor*, XVII (1860), p. 87.

[184] E. J. Hobsbawm and G. Rudé, *Captain Swing* (1969, Harmondsworth, 1973), pp. 89–92.

[185] M. James, 'The Swing project – protest and unrest, 1830–1832', *Centre for Local History Studies, Newsletter*, 7 (Kingston University, December 2003), pp. 4–5. Indeed, strangers and foreigners were often blamed for Swing in the answers to Rural Queries for the 1832–4 Poor Law Commission.

or (during the earlier inflationary years between 1794 and 1813) market-focused protests against high prices and related issues. These, and many other protest movements, have been excellently documented by historians. However, even in these examples (as with lone protests like arson, animal maiming, or anonymous letter writing) one should point to many actions, clubs or causes which were grounded in the parish or local community. The organisational effort lay in transcending parochial or very small groups, with their local prejudices and hesitancies, and bringing them together at a wider level. This was true of many early parish friendly societies (especially before the rise of the affiliated orders in the 1830s and 40s),[186] burial and clothing clubs, harvest strikes, religious confederations among the poor, and indeed of the many highly localised, small-scale agricultural trade unions that Joseph Arch, George Edwards and others finally, in the railway age, put together to form the National Agricultural Labourers' Union.

---

[186] The growth of affiliated unities, with their headquarters, districts and lodges, notably from the 1830s, helped to enlarge a sense of extra-parochial allegiance and belonging among the poor. Some of these unities (like the Manchester Unity of Oddfellows, the Hearts of Oak, or the Foresters) had large numbers of lodges and members by mid-century. Their growth was encouraged by the move from local to national registration of friendly societies (10 Geo. IV, c. 56). However, their precursors were very local, rarely with over 100 club men. Such localism had been compounded by legislation against corresponding societies and seditious meetings. In some agricultural counties parish societies heavily outnumbered the affiliated lodges. Hobsbawm and Rudé, *Captain Swing*, pp. 45–6. This could remain true well after the mid-nineteenth century. Howkins, *Whitsun*, pp. 41–2, 67–8. Their organisation, annual club days and club walkings (successors of the Whitsun Ales) were often coordinated at parish level by village gentlemen and clergy, with whom the club men dined after 'an appropriate discourse from the pulpit'. On these village friendly societies, see W. Barnes, 'Associations', in C. Wrigley (ed.), *William Barnes, the Dorset Poet* (1988, Wimborne, 1990), pp. 228–9, originally in *Dorset County Chronicle* (24 December 1829); Howkins, *Whitsun*; D. R. Mills, *Lord and Peasant in Nineteenth-century Britain* (London, 1980), pp. 52–3, 59–60, 127; P. H. J. H. Gosden, *The Friendly Societies in England, 1815–1875* (Manchester, 1961), pp. 7–8, 17–25. Village club walking developed especially in the late eighteenth century. The clubs had elaborate regalia, banners, rosettes, ribbons, flags, staves and so on, the meaning of some emblems being secretive. J. H. Bettey, *Church and Parish: A Guide for Local Historians* (London, 1987), pp. 64–5; Howkins, *Whitsun*, ill. 2; M. D. Fuller, *West Country Friendly Societies* (Lingfield, Surrey, 1964), plates III, IX–XVI. Club days brought people back to their 'home' villages from surrounding areas. By 1803 there were nearly 10,000 'friendly societies', most of them independent and highly localised, some of them no doubt being disguised trade unions. Even in the later era of the large affiliated orders, the small village societies and local lodges remained key rural associations expressing strong senses of belonging, local working identity, and pride in place.

One should not minimise the significance of these forms of collectivisation in the countryside, nor the extreme bitterness of many rural protests, nor question the historiography justly dedicated to them. Local ties and social obligations did not, in the long term, usually prevail over class; although in later periods a populist parochialism could still often reassert itself, and a strong distrust of strangers remained common.[187] After all, Thomas Paine ('citizen of the world') had been scornful of such English local attachments, 'prejudices', or parochial cultural identities, particularly in the countryside, attacking them as a liability in the development of a radical political outlook.[188] We have seen that these attachments persisted long after Paine's death in 1809. Rather later, the outsiders Karl Marx and Friedrich Engels believed that 'The working men have no country',[189] but the indications are that working men thought themselves to have intense and preclusive ties to local areas, expressed in the many ways that I have outlined. They relinquished these with great reluctance, knowing how insecure they might otherwise be. That parochial sightedness had indeed been a major factor inhibiting broader class feeling, just as it had often confined the expression of humanitarianism. With regard to debates about counter-radical tendencies in the early nineteenth century, it was as significant as the possible securities and 'insurance against unrest' of the old poor law,[190] with which it was closely associated, or the oft-presumed conservative, detractive

---

[187] Williams, *Sociology of an English Village*, p. 151. These were matters that surfaced again as late as the war-time evacuation between 1939 and 1944, with some evacuees from cities such as Coventry, London or Ipswich recalling much rural prejudice against them, shown in gang attacks, stone throwing, school bullying, insults ('London scum') and related behaviour. Some evacuees felt like going to 'a foreign country'. In this case, and by this later period, class sentiments were often combined with the prejudices of localism. C. Ward-Langman, 'The effects of evacuation on Leicestershire: an oral history' (MA dissertation, Centre for English Local History, University of Leicester, 2002), pp. 12–13, 51.

[188] Dyck, 'Local attachments, national identities and world citizenship'.

[189] K. Marx and F. Engels, *The Communist Manifesto* (1848, Harmondsworth, 1975), p. 102.

[190] P. Solar, 'Poor relief and English economic development before the industrial revolution', *Economic History Review*, 48 (1995), pp. 1, 6, 9, 17; Snell, *Annals of the Labouring Poor*, ch. 3; E. Halévy, *A History of the English People in the Nineteenth Century: England in 1815* (1913, London, 1970), p. 379, who I quote above on the role of the poor rate in avoiding 'an agrarian revolution'.

tendencies of Wesleyan Methodism.[191] Many achievements of the larger popular protests or reform movements lay in surmounting an intrinsically parish-centred view of rural society: one in which a parish was often set in rivalry with and distrust of other parishes and their inhabitants; in which inter-parochial hostilities could be deep-rooted, and may even have intensified after *c.* 1780; in which social concerns were often literally parochial, especially among the poorer classes. John Clare was a striking and fluent example of this, a labouring man with plenty of experience of working elsewhere, but whose social, emotional and political life was strongly centred upon 'the parish state' of Helpston.[192] In his writing, published from 1820, there was a deeply felt division between 'the poor' and 'the idly great'. He dwelt vividly on the abuses of power by over-seers, the vestry and the landed classes, notably with regard to enclosure. His sympathies were always for the ill-used and the defenceless, whether human or animal. Yet his resentments were contained within a very local milieu. The local concerns and intimate attachments expressed by Clare were such a dom-inant feature of his poetry and prose that it is hard to see them as compatible evidence for 'class' in the usual, generalised under-standing of that word. Clare was attached to *place* (and to an anachronistic understanding of how people should behave within it) much more than to class. We surely see here a fervent parochial consciousness now brimming over with indignation, having reluctantly to discount the parish as a basis for moral relations, stepping out to a broader faith in the judgement and

---

[191] Halévy, *History of the English People: England in 1815*, pp. 387–440, using Methodism as 'the key to . . . explain . . . the extraordinary stability which English society was destined to enjoy throughout a period of revolution and crises' (*ibid.*, p. 387); Thompson, *Making of the English Working Class*, ch. 11. I have discussed Methodism as one of the ways in which parish-centredness was circumvented, and so it is worth stressing how Wesleyan Methodism came in this hesitant and politically reassuring form. Much more radical perspectives developed among some of its break-away denominations, notably the Primitive Methodists.

[192] Robinson (ed.), *John Clare's Autobiographical Writings*, pp. 104–5. The term 'state' to describe a parish was quite common; for example, used by George Crabbe, in book 2 of 'The Village', line 5, in his *Tales, 1812, and Other Selected Poems*, ed. H. Mills (Cambridge, 1967), p. 10, 'through all the little state'; or by Jefferies, *Landscape and Labour*, pp. 72–4: 'a rural parish . . . forms of itself a miniature state'.

action of what he called 'the common people'.[193] In short, the growth of a broader rural working-class consciousness was gradual, delayed – more delayed than E. P. Thompson's great humanity and creditable internationalist hopes led him to envisage – and one of the major stumbling blocks that it had to surmount was the culture of local xenophobia.

---

[193] 'The common people' is a frequent term in Clare's writing. See e.g. Robinson (ed.), *John Clare's Autobiographical Writings*, p. 147.

CHAPTER 3

Settlement, parochial belonging and entitlement

Settlement is that right which a parishioner becoming impotent or poor has of claiming relief from the funds raised by means of the poor's rate, by virtue of the social relationship or connection which subsists between him and the other members of the parish. This right is always acquired in that parish or place in which parishioners have acquired their last legal settlement.[1]

The whole experience of the poor law shows, with what a degree of selfishness parishes deal with those upon whom they look as strangers to themselves; they have never hesitated to condemn a man to the worst evils if he was a charge to them and they could remove him. There has been no want of vigour on the part of parishes in dealing with those classes of poor whom they did not recognise as their own.[2]

'Anybody can have roots if they want them', I said.
'Human beings are like strawberry plants.'[3]

INTRODUCTION

The Revd Anthony Huxtable was rector of Sutton Waldron, near Shaftesbury in Dorset. He was a poor law guardian, one of the more regular attendants at board meetings. He was also a farmer, with a farm of about 100 acres on the high chalk down-land, bordering upon the Vale of Blackmore. In May 1847 he was called before the Select Committee on Settlement and Poor Removal. His evidence underlined the importance of the laws of settlement to the poor, and also discussed people's local

---

[1] J. Shaw, *The Parochial Lawyer; or, Churchwarden and Overseer's Guide and Assistant* (1829, London, 1833), p. 178.
[2] *Select Committee on Poor Removal*, XIII (1854–5), p. 206.
[3] E. Humphreys, *A Man's Estate* (London, 1957), p. 252.

attachments in Dorset. Among the questions asked him was whether he thought it desirable to abolish the settlement laws, by which people became eligible for poor relief through 'belonging' to particular parishes. His reply was most revealing. He felt that any such repeal might enlarge the sphere of labourers' work and broaden horizons. 'On the other hand', he said,

the objection that presented itself to me was this, whether it would not loosen that interest which landlords now feel with regard to their parishioners, and dissolve those ties which bind persons brought up in a certain place, the remains perhaps of the feudal system, at all events local attachment, whether a national settlement would not tend entirely to abolish that. I have not come to a satisfactory result.

'Do you not think', asked Charles Buller, the chairman of the Committee, 'from your experience as a clergyman and a resident, that these ties operate to a very beneficial extent upon the poor?'

I think in their heart of hearts they do very much think of their parish. I had a letter the other day from a poor person who has not been in Sutton for 30 years, and it was marked with the strongest sentiment of parochial attachment. The feeling they have is, that it is their home; go where they will they have a home. With regard to the churchyard, I have been rebuilding the church, and in the churchyard, pulling down the old church, the materials have been scattered about very much, and I have seen the poor people trying to clear away the rubbish to see where their relations were lying . . . I do say that I cannot fancy any body of men of such high moral conduct, considering their sinister circumstances, their dwellings, and other things, as the Dorsetshire labourers; you never hear them complain. I think that is owing to the parochial system, parochial attachments . . . There is a deep feeling about their native place, and they do feel a strong attachment to it.[4]

These themes of parochial home and attachment, and the effects of settlement law upon belonging and the exclusion of outsiders, are the concerns of this chapter. Historians of settlement have written about its administration, its impact upon English and Welsh migration and industrialisation (the system did not extend to Scotland or Ireland, although Scotland had a weaker and different practice), its effects upon 'open' and 'close'

---

[4] *Sixth Report from the Select Committee on Settlement, and Poor Removal*, XI (1847), pp. 151–2, 159.

parishes, the connections between the settlement and poor laws, and the evidential uses for settlement records.[5] For many years, the huge deposits of settlement papers (mainly examinations, removal orders, and settlement certificates) were used to study mobility and urban migrants. The examinations preceding pauper removal have lent themselves to research on the labouring poor, as they document past events and current situations affecting poor people's lives: parental background, birth, migration, apprenticeship, past and present employment (or the lack of it), yearly wages, renting or ownership of property, leaving home, marriage or cohabitation, family lives, paternal settlement, illegitimacy, literacy, and so on, bearing essentially upon where settlement had been gained.[6] Like contemporaries, almost all historians have highlighted the fundamental connections between settlement and the poor law, while being well aware of the influences of settlement upon migration and exclusion.[7] In addition, there has been growing awareness of

---

[5] The best introductions to the laws of settlement by historians are J. S. Taylor, 'The impact of pauper settlement, 1691–1834', *Past and Present*, 73 (1976); and in particular his fine book *Poverty, Migration, and Settlement in the Industrial Revolution: Sojourners' Narratives* (Palo Alto, Calif., 1989). On early modern (pre-1662) settlement practice, see R. Burn, *The History of the Poor Laws, with Observations* (London, 1764), pp. 106–19; P. Styles, 'The evolution of the law of settlement', *University of Birmingham Historical Journal*, 9 (1963–4); S. J. Wright, 'Sojourners and lodgers in a provincial town: the evidence from eighteenth-century Ludlow', *Urban History Yearbook* (1990); S. Hindle, *On the Parish? The Micro-Politics of Poor Relief in Rural England, c. 1550–1750* (Oxford, 2004), pp. 306–25, 403–5, 431–2.

[6] K. D. M. Snell, *Annals of the Labouring Poor: Social Change and Agrarian England, 1660–1900* (Cambridge, 1985).

[7] Alongside the above historiographical references, see in particular D. Marshall, *The English Poor in the Eighteenth Century: A Study in Social and Administrative History* (London, 1926); S. Webb and B. Webb, *English Local Government: English Poor Law History, Part 1: The Old Poor Law* (London, 1927), ch. 5; E. M. Hampson, 'Settlement and removal in Cambridgeshire, 1662–1834', *Cambridge Historical Journal*, 2 (1926–8); A. Redford, *Labour Migration in England, 1800–1850* (1964, Manchester, 1976), esp. ch. 5; D. Mills, 'The geographical effects of the laws of settlement in Nottinghamshire: an analysis of Francis Howell's report, 1848', in his (ed.), *English Rural Communities: The Impact of a Specialised Economy* (London, 1973); M. E. Rose, 'Settlement, removal and the new poor law', in D. Fraser (ed.), *The New Poor Law in the Nineteenth Century* (London, 1976); D. Ashforth, 'Settlement and removal in urban areas: Bradford, 1834–71', in M. E. Rose (ed.), *The Poor Law and the City: The English Poor Law in its Urban Context, 1834–1914* (Leicester, 1985); B. Stapleton, 'Migration in pre-industrial southern England: the case of Odiham', *Southern History*, 10 (1988); K. D. M. Snell, 'Pauper settlement and the right to poor relief in England and Wales', *Continuity and Change*, 6 (1991); J. S. Taylor, 'A different kind of Speenhamland: nonresident relief in the Industrial

settlement correspondence, notably the letters from the poor
to their parishes of settlement seeking poor relief or other necessities. A few historians have used and published these
letters, giving a further 'voice' to the poor, and showing what
these people thought about the many interconnections between
settlement, poverty and the poor law.[8]

In this chapter my concern is with the social and cultural
questions of how settlement related to ideas of 'home' and
'belonging', how settlement led to perceived differences between local inhabitants, how it set up graded insider–outsider
divisions, and how it contributed to exclude certain people. The
Revd Huxtable stressed belonging to the parish as 'home', and
such terms were used persistently in correspondence. This was
true of the poor's letters to their 'home' parishes, or of how the
poor were discussed by the officers who dealt with them and
tried to make the parishes they belonged to pay for them.
'Belonging' and 'home' were everyday administrative terms.
This suggests some key questions, which also have much relevance to modern themes of community and belonging. What
was the nature of local 'belonging' under the settlement laws?
How important was such 'belonging' to the poor, or indeed to
inhabitants from higher social classes? What were the perceived

Revolution', *Journal of British Studies*, 30 (1991); K. D. M. Snell, 'Settlement, poor law and
the rural historian: new approaches and opportunities', *Rural History*, 3 (1992); R. Wells,
'Migration, the law and parochial policy in eighteenth- and early nineteenth-century
southern England', *Southern History*, 15 (1993); C. Vialls, 'The laws of settlement: their
impact on the poor inhabitants of the Daventry area of Northamptonshire, 1750–1834'
(Ph.D., University of Leicester, 1998); L. R. Charlesworth, 'Salutary and humane law: a
legal history of the law of settlement and removals, c. 1795–1865' (Ph.D., University of
Manchester, 1998); B. K. Song, 'Agrarian policies on pauper settlement and migration,
Oxfordshire 1750–1834', *Continuity and Change*, 13 (1998); B. K. Song, 'Landed interest,
local government, and the labour market in England, 1750–1850', *Economic History
Review*, 51 (1998). Contemporaries defined and spoke of the settlement and poor laws
together as 'the law for the relief of the poor', and the consensus among historians on
settlement is that there was a very close link between settlement and the poor laws.

[8] J. S. Taylor, 'Voices in the crowd: the Kirkby Lonsdale township letters, 1809–36', in
T. Hitchcock, P. King and P. Sharpe (eds.), *Chronicling Poverty: The Voices and Strategies
of the English Poor, 1640–1840* (Basingstoke, 1997); T. Sokoll, 'Old age in poverty: the
record of Essex pauper letters, 1780–1834', in Hitchcock *et al.* (eds), *Chronicling Poverty*;
T. Sokoll, 'Negotiating a living: Essex pauper letters from London, 1800–1834', *Inter-
national Review of Social History*, 45 (2000); and, most outstandingly, T. Sokoll (ed.),
Essex Pauper Letters, 1731–1837 (Oxford, 2001). An important forthcoming book is
S. King, A. Tomkins and T. Nutt (eds.), *Narratives of the Poor in the Long Eighteenth
Century* (London, 2006).

entitlements that flowed from being settled in a parish or township? The social history of settlement and belonging throws up some paradoxical questions which in international terms were almost unique to England and Wales: how 'moveable' was the idea of belonging, as connected to one's legal settlement; and how did people combine strong local attachments with insider–outsider divisions, when such 'eligibility to belong' was transferable if they obtained a settlement elsewhere? How did these subjects change over time, during the phased reforms of the settlement and poor laws, and how did cultural ideas of attachment and belonging alter alongside the legal reforms? What were the implications for 'community' of these changes? What were the adverse features of this system, for example the selective exclusion of the poor? And in the modern world, as so many discuss nostalgically or prescriptively the idea of 'community', or study their 'roots', are there any lessons for us when we look back at the very long history of settlement and belonging between 1662 and 1948?

The settlement laws have been ably outlined elsewhere, and there is little need here for a detailed account of their legal essentials.[9] Briefly, 'settlement' was the eligibility to receive poor relief in a parish or township where one had gained that status. One of many similar definitions heads this chapter. Following legislation in 1662, 1685, 1691, 1697–8, and some other lesser Acts, one could gain, or earn, one's settlement in a number of ways: by birth for an illegitimate person;[10] by marriage for a woman, who thereby lost her maiden settlement and now belonged to her husband's settlement; by serving a public annual office *in* the parish (it did not have to be strictly a *parish* office);[11] by payment of parish rates; by renting property with

---

[9] Beyond the literature referenced above, useful summaries of settlement legislation were by W. G. Lumley (the Assistant Secretary to the Poor Law Commission), in *Second and Third Reports from the Select Committee on Settlement, and Poor Removal*, XI (1847), pp. 9–12; and the barrister G. A. R. Fitz-Gerald, in the *Select Committee on Poor Removal*, XII (1879), pp. 1–5, 171.

[10] Although from 1834 illegitimate children took the settlement of their mother. 4 & 5 Wm IV, c. 76, s. 71.

[11] R. Burn, *The Justice of the Peace and Parish Officer* (London, 1814), vol. IV, pp. 568–72, 790. Unless otherwise stated, the 1814 five-volume edition of Burn is cited below and elsewhere in this book.

a combined annual value of £10 or more; by yearly service for a full year while unmarried; by serving a legal indentured apprenticeship and residing in the parish for forty days during one's term; by owning estate in the parish; and, if none of these applied, one took one's paternal settlement. (From 1876, if paternal settlement was problematic to ascertain, then birthplace was used instead, so limiting derivative settlements.[12]) These were the 'heads' of settlement. One's last gained settlement superseded any earlier ones. The 1662 Act had empowered overseers and justices to remove to their last settlement people who were chargeable or likely to become so, from 'parishes into which they have migrated, for the purpose of finding work or employment'.[13] From 1795, only those who were actually chargeable (with certain exceptions) could be removed. Parallel to this were many vagrancy Acts developing earlier legislation, notably in 1740, 1744, 1822, 1824, which allowed punishment for a range of vagrancy offences and removal to one's settlement. The main contribution to settlement law of the new poor law in 1834 was to abolish settlement by yearly hiring and by office-holding, and that Act also qualified settlement by estate and renting. Thereafter, the main modification was the introduction of 'irremovability' legislation in 1846–7, 1861, 1865 and 1876, permitting one to be 'irremovable' if one had resided for a certain period in a parish. Many further Acts covered the Irish, Scots, people from the Channel Islands and so on. The system was perpetuated in the twentieth century, though administered in different ways and by new authorities. It was finally abolished by the National Assistance Act of 1948, which in effect created for welfare purposes what the Revd Huxtable had spoken of a century earlier as 'a national settlement'. This brief outline simplifies a very complex legal situation, and most of the 'heads' were qualified in various ways and times, but it depicts in simple brushstrokes the legal form of the system. Further nuances, details, and changes will appear below.

---

[12] 39 & 40 Vic., c. 61, s. 35; A. F. Vulliamy, *The Law of Settlement and Removal of Paupers* (1895, London, 1906), p. 21.
[13] Shaw, *Parochial Lawyer*, p. 193.

IDEAS OF HOME AND BELONGING AMONG THE POOR

A language of 'home', in relation to the parish of settlement, infuses the correspondence over settlement conducted by the poor and overseers. William King, for example, wrote back to Braintree from London in 1834: 'Perhaps Sir I May have to Coum Home and tis a Pleaseing Reflection Mixed with Humble thankfulness that I have Ever Such an Asylum My old Birth Place till then Sirs I Must Beg and Rely on your United feelings of Kindness and Help.'[14] Samuel Hearsum wrote from St Marylebone to Chelmsford in 1824, about how he might have to apply 'to Marylebone Parish to Pass me home', by way of removal, as he was in great distress. A representative of the parish vestry had visited him in London, and had written back to Chelmsford saying that 'I think 1s. pr week would prevent him from coming home.'[15] In other words, this parish language of 'home' was shared by others higher in the social scale, and it was routinely used by overseers. The overseer of Falmer, for example, writing to the overseers of Worth, discussed the state of a pauper and commented that 'he should go home to his Parish'.[16]

Charlotte May, writing from Brighton to the overseer at Worth in April 1820, complained that

I am Still Reman in this Deplorable Stat Extremely ill unable to do anything for Myself and famyly and that Wretched husband has not been near me to bring me one farthing Since last Saturday fortnight. I [would] not have trouble you if I had the means to have brought myself and famyly home have not any Other home. Please to Send means to come home or arange some plan you think Mos Advisable.

She signed her letter 'your Unfortunate parisoner Charlotte May'. She feared being designated a vagrant.[17] Davey and Susannah Rising wrote from Halstead (Essex) to the Chelmsford overseers in 1824, telling them that they were in distress, and asking for money to be sent them: 'and if you most wordy Gentellmen Do not think proper to Answer our needy Request we must Be

---

[14] Sokoll (ed.), *Essex Pauper Letters*, p. 149.
[15] *Ibid.*, pp. 178–9.
[16] N. Pilbeam and I. Nelson (eds.), *Poor Law Records of Mid Sussex, 1601–1835* (Lewes, 2000), p. 380.
[17] *Ibid.*, p. 379.

Brought home For wheare no money Can Be Earnt no Living Cannot Be had'.[18] William Webb in Ipswich wrote to Braintree to say that 'The Kellsey Peop[le] are now expecting me home . . . you must do as you Please aboaut sending me home.'[19] Thomas and Ann Cooper in Woolwich (Kent) wrote to the overseer in Chelmsford in 1825, pointing out that Thomas was very ill and out of work, 'and in a decline and we must come home for we have nothing here to subsist upon'. They wanted to know whether they should apply to Woolwich parish 'to be past [passed] home' with their four children, or whether their parish would send them some money to enable them to come home of their own accord.[20] Ann Hitchcock wrote from Feering (Essex) to the churchwardens and overseers of Braintree in 1823:

Gentlemen if I am to Come Home you must let me know for I may as Well come as stop hear to be starved for my Boys cannot get no work so how am I to do But if I come home you will have to buy me Goodes for if I have to come home my Creators Will tak my goodes and chatels for money due To them.[21]

'Home' was thus a term of parish attachment, a notion of legal entitlement, a welfare security, a concept that people carried in their minds when they left it. The parish 'home' was an entity that they could return to in hard times, or obtain relief from, even when they were living many miles away.

An explicit language of 'belonging' was also very prominent in pauper letters. Jacob Brown wrote to Great Bardfield to let them know that Laindon-cum-Basildon was 'agoon to bring me and my wife and seven children home to bardfield', even though 'i always will stand by it that i belong to the parish of landon and nother'.[22] Contested settlements like this were commonplace, and caused much worry for those among the poor who were unclear about their legal settlement, and could find themselves at the centre of disputes between different parishes.

---

[18] Sokoll (ed.), *Essex Pauper Letters*, pp. 179–80.
[19] *Ibid.*, p. 117.
[20] *Ibid.*, p. 214.
[21] *Ibid.*, p. 101.
[22] *Ibid.*, p. 100. Many more writers in this collection use this language of 'home' parish.

Samuel Spooner wrote in 1828 from Norwich to the overseer of Braintree that 'On account of the scarcity to work I am obliged to apply to the parish to which I belong . . . we are in extreme distress.'[23] Some months later he wrote again, pointing out that his allowance was insufficient, and so he had caused his family 'to be forwarded to the parish they belong [to]'.[24] William King pointed out to the overseer in Braintree that 'we Do Not Blong to Bethnal Green', and continued: 'I Humbly Beg the Gentlemen to Remember there old Townsman.'[25] Others wrote repeatedly about 'My Parrish', conveying the same sentiment and legal attachment.[26] This language of 'belonging' was also used much higher in the social scale. It was, for example, routinely used by legal counsel in settlement cases, as by Mr Burnaby in Leicester in 1819: 'His son of course belongs to you and you must provide for him accordingly.'[27]

THE POOR'S KNOWLEDGE OF SETTLEMENT

As one would expect of a subject that bore so directly upon their lives, the poor often had a close understanding of legal settlement. They needed to be sure that they had gained a settlement, and they needed to know how to do that. They sometimes wished to obtain a settlement elsewhere, or indeed to avoid one in certain places, and so they had to plan how to attain such ends. Settlement and belonging was not something beyond their control or manipulation. Charles Varley wrote in his autobiography about how

My greatest worry was that we had no settlement . . . neither could we gain a settlement, as we were married; therefore . . . we might perish for want. Whereupon I was determined to go to be a farmer's servant for one year: in order to gain a settlement, my wife and I were to part for that year, and then to meet as strangers, and to be married in the parish church where I had served my year. Upon our affairs being thus settled, I bought a suit of strong servant-like clothes, and took my way into the country; when I had got about ten miles from

---

[23] *Ibid.*, p. 105. [24] *Ibid.*, p. 110.
[25] *Ibid.*, p. 116. [26] *Ibid.*, pp. 112, 116.
[27] Leics. CRO, 17 D 64/F/231 (21 May 1819).

London I hired to a farmer, for a year, and served it faithfully, at the end of which we were married in the parish church.[28]

Settlement as gained by yearly hiring was possible only for unmarried people, and so we see here how Varley manoeuvred around the law. When conventional yearly hiring went into decline in many regions in East Anglia and the south-east – often being supplanted in the early nineteenth century by other terms and arrangements – the ways in which settlement could subsequently be denied to hired single people raised ill-feeling. The labouring poor knew very well how and why this was being done: to deny them any entitlements to poor relief in the parish where they had worked, to control their 'belonging', and to restrict their options.

Sometimes in pauper letters one sees mention of aspirations to gain a settlement in a certain place, often where one resided, and once more knowledge of the law and of one's options are revealed. For example, the shoemaker William King, writing in 1828 to Braintree from Bethnal Green (an urban district where it was hard to gain a settlement), commented on how: 'I Long for the time to take a House and Pay So Much for it for a Twelve Month as May Make Me a Parrisoner in London.' In such writing one is also seeing the pauper holding out an incentive to the parish of settlement: in effect saying, give me non-resident relief, and I may soon belong elsewhere, and I know how I might achieve that; but if I remove back to my settlement, then there is no chance of that occurring, and then you will have to look after me and my family.[29] In some cases, whether one calls distant payments from one's parish 'non-resident relief', or recurrent bribes to stay away, is a moot point.[30] More confidential views are seen in correspondence between poor men and their wives. For example, Daniel Rust wrote to his wife Sarah in 1825, saying: 'the Pore men tell me that this is a verry good Parrish and that

---

[28] C. Varley, *The Modern Farmer's Guide, by a Real Farmer* (Glasgow, 1768), pp. xxv–xxvi.
[29] Sokoll (ed.), *Essex Pauper Letters*, p. 112.
[30] Some contemporaries viewed such non-resident payments virtually as bribes to parish poor to stay away. For example, see the Report from Joseph Richardson, the Assistant Commissioner for Northamptonshire, *Report from His Majesty's Commissioners for Inquiring into the Administration and Practical Operation of the Poor Laws. Appendix (A). Reports of Assistant Commissioners, Part 1*, XXVIII (1834), p. 397 A.

thay Pay thare Pore men with famelys 3 shillings pr day and if i should be so Luckey i will trie and settle my self thare'.[31] William Trudget wrote to Steeple Bumpstead in 1817 about his son, who had a bad leg, asking for the large sum of £12 as an apprenticeship premium to a shoemaker, and saying fairly persuasively that 'if he is Bound to an apprentice it will settle him so that he will be no more Expence to Your parish'.[32] His letter started with a dire account of just how bad that leg was, and what a long-term condition it was, to make it clear to the parish officers what the financial consequences of denying the apprenticeship premium would be. While he was writing, he also drew attention to his daughter as well, who had fits, and after a fall could not get out of bed, thus increasing the pressure on his home parish's officers. He would have known that many such officers frequently tried to apprentice children out of their parishes, to displace their settlements elsewhere.

In these examples, one sees paupers not only showing legal knowledge, but also being aware of how parish officers would think within the law, and taking logical as well as emotional steps to manipulate their decisions accordingly. James Ebenezer Bicheno grumbled in 1817 that 'no one inexperienced in the business would credit the dexterous craft and the practical knowledge of the law, which the poor possess on points relating to themselves. It is a part of the business of their lives, and they often make a proficiency that turns to profitable account.'[33] In some cases the poor even read legal texts like Richard Burn's *Justice of the Peace and Parish Officer*, saving up to buy such manuals, so as to familiarise themselves with their legal rights or alternatives.[34] They may often have interpreted the law incorrectly, but then (on a subject as complicated as settlement) so did parish officers and legal authorities. Pauper letters often commented on how they had obtained their settlement, showing close knowledge of the system. Joseph Wright, for example,

---

[31] Sokoll (ed.), *Essex Pauper Letters*, p. 211.
[32] *Ibid.*, p. 155.
[33] J. E. Bicheno, *An Inquiry into the Nature of Benevolence: Chiefly with a View to Elucidate the Principles of the Poor Laws, and to Show their Immoral Tendency* (London, 1817), p. 140.
[34] *Select Committee on the Poor Law Amendment Act*, XVIII (1837–8), pt III, p. 197; Snell, *Annals of the Labouring Poor*, p. 115.

wrote to a parish officer in Steeple Bumpstead in 1816, pointing out that 'I gain a settlement by living with the Revd Stewart two years', which was a year beyond what was necessary.[35] First-person statements in settlement examinations (which occur most in first drafts of the documents) often convey a sense that the pauper was reciting his or her statement with a precise purpose in mind, although one can never be sure to what extent such words were being put into their mouths by justices, or parish or petty-session clerks. In a few sequential settlement examinations, one finds variations between what was mentioned in different examinations, it becoming clear that important biographical information had been omitted earlier, probably through selective memory of the examinee, because such information produced a settlement result that s/he did not favour. Examinees might, for example, wish to avoid going back to a settlement that was ungenerous, or where they owed money, or where they had abandoned a spouse, or where they had committed bigamy or another offence, and to that end they might 'forget' their last and legally operative settlement, in effect opting for an earlier one in the selective evidence that they gave. Alteration of evidence was also occasionally complained of when a case came before Quarter Sessions, and that often originated in a pauper's awareness of the law and willingness to manipulate it. Of course, a pauper could be charged legally for providing false information relating to settlement. Yet given the complex law, any such person could always feign ignorance of legal significance, deferring to the superior knowledge of the people judging him.

Where immediate gain was apparent, however, the poor 'kept up with the latest enactments of the Poor Law and tenaciously invoked its clauses' in their encounters with local officials.[36] This was true over a long period. One sees it, for example, in the way that they resisted badging in the 1690s, using 'their detailed knowledge of the law to avoid it wherever possible',[37] in their assertion of their rights regarding allowances to soldiers'

---

[35] Sokoll (ed.), *Essex Pauper Letters*, p. 154.
[36] S. Koven, *Slumming: Sexual and Social Politics in Victorian London* (Princeton, 2004), p. 33.
[37] Hindle, *On the Parish?*, p. 444.

or militiamen's wives and families,[38] in their knowledge of irremovability law – 'Yes, I think it is thoroughly understood by
them'[39] – through to the way that they insisted upon their
'rights' under the Metropolitan Houseless Poor Acts of 1864–5,
obliging London guardians to provide food and lodging for all
destitute wayfarers regardless of their character and settlement.[40] Of the Irish too, it was said that 'generally speaking,
they know the law as well as our poor law officers do'.[41]

SETTLEMENT AND BELONGING, *c.* 1690 – *c.* 1795

The ways of obtaining a settlement, and the insider–outsider
divisions that the settlement laws enshrined, inevitably led to
clear-cut differentiation of people at local level according to their
settlement status. These differences had real meaning in the
past, and were crucially important to people, in a way that we
now find hard to appreciate. One way of thinking about such
divisions of people is shown diagrammatically in the 'T' shaped
emphasis of figure 3.1. (Many people project their town, university, political, national, sexual, or other identities on 'T' shirts
in the modern world, rather like some paupers badged with
their parish's first letter in the seventeenth and eighteenth centuries,[42] or animals branded with their parish's brand, so let us

---

[38] An example of a detailed letter from a soldier insisting on such rights, citing the
relevant Act of Parliament, showing knowledge of the required documentation and
witnesses, of the dates of entitlement, and threatening proceedings 'According to
Law', is in Leics. CRO, 17 D 64/F/230 (9 July 1813).

[39] *Select Committee on Irremovable Poor*, VII (1859), pp. 82–3 (evidence of Thomas Bushfield,
chairman of the Whitechapel guardians).'It is difficult to obtain any information from
them [the poor] that will enable you to administer the law, except in the way that they
like best . . . [there is] a great disposition when a poor person comes before the Board,
to dress up a case in such a way as exactly suits their convenience . . . There are very
many cases of that kind.' *Ibid.*, p. 83.

[40] Koven, *Slumming*, p. 33.

[41] *Select Committee on Irremovable Poor*, XVII (1860), p. 124, evidence of the clerk to the
guardians of St Saviour's, Southwark.

[42] An interesting feature of parish belonging, on which see S. Hindle, 'Dependency,
shame and belonging: badging the deserving poor, *c.* 1550–1750', *Cultural and Social
History*, 1 (2004); Hindle, *On the Parish?*, esp. pp. 433–45; Burn, *History of the Poor Laws*,
p. 119. In the early nineteenth century, pauper possessions could also be marked or
branded by a parish, and seen as thenceforth belonging to that parish, with a view
to later sale by overseers seeking reimbursement. (For similar earlier practice, see
Hindle, 'Power, poor relief, and social relations', p. 94.) Most parishes had their own

Parish and Belonging

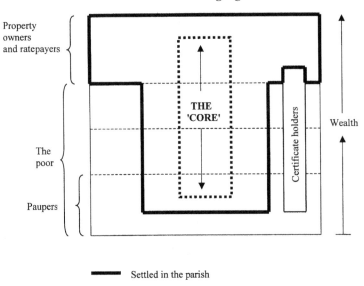

Figure 3.1   Settlement and belonging in an eighteenth-century parish.

adopt that shape diagrammatically for the purposes here. It also has connotations of 'the parish body', which are appropriate here.) This figure purports to depict an archetypical single parish's inhabitants by one criterion, that of settlement. All parish residents are within the square, while all *settled* residents are within the bold 'T' shape. The figure represents the situation as it would broadly have been in each of thousands of parishes through most of the eighteenth century, and in some respects into the early nineteenth century. It will be compared below with another figure, which will show how the situation regarding settlement categories of belonging compared in *c.* 1870. The respective shapes and sizes of the boxes and divisions in the figure may be taken to approximate roughly to the numbers of people falling within them, and while this would have varied considerably by locality and type of parish, the figure attempts, through demographic and poor law knowledge, to make its

brand, used for animals, which was another sign of parochial distinctiveness. For example, at Denton (Northants.), it was of a hunter's horn. D. Hall, *The Open Fields of Northamptonshire* (Northampton, 1995), pp. 30–3.

interior shapes represent quite general experience, especially in rural and market-town parishes.

For the purpose of this figure, the discussion of belonging in mid-twentieth-century villages in Marilyn Strathern's book *Kinship at the Core* has been adopted, by using her concept of 'core' belonging, loosely to indicate a section of the parish inhabitants who felt themselves quintessentially to 'belong' to the 'real' parish.[43] This phraseology is not contemporary, having been formulated later by anthropologists working 'at home', and it has also been used by some rural sociologists. A great variety of other regional words were used at the time, whether having connotations of social rank or not, such as 'the neighbours', 'the parish', 'the principal inhabitants', 'our townsmen', 'in-townsmen', 'our deserving poor', and so on. As in Strathern's work, the word 'core' is used here in a loose and permeable sense, not liable to objective verification (and thus it is shown figuratively within dotted lines), because it comes close to unifying contemporary notions about settlement and super-added criteria relevant to belonging and associated precedence. In this earlier period these 'core' inhabitants would have been legally settled, and they also had further claims to belong, relating for example to kinship, property, length of association, moral standing, and so on, which I will mention below. It is worth noting that, in the eighteenth century, many of the parish poor may be thought of as being in such a 'core' group. After all, these were vulnerable people who had particular reasons to establish and broadcast their parish connections, for their own security. They could not usually construct safeguards in other ways, such as through property ownership or personal capital accumulation. Many more people in modern Britain benefit from the latter forms of security, which have in some ways reduced the need for strong senses of local belonging of the kinds that characterised the eighteenth and nineteenth centuries. We saw in chapter 2 that the contemporary poor often exercised their ideas of local

---

[43] M. Strathern, *Kinship at the Core: An Anthropology of Elmdon, a Village in North-west Essex in the Nineteen-sixties* (Cambridge, 1981). See also her 'The place of kinship: kin, class and village status in Elmdon, Essex', and her 'The village as an idea: constructs of village-ness in Elmdon, Essex', both in A. P. Cohen (ed.), *Belonging: Identity and Social Organisation in British Rural Cultures* (Manchester, 1982).

belonging in xenophobic ways, and were among the most vola-
tile and hot-blooded in sentiments and selective actions against
'outsiders'.

In figure 3.1, the wealth of inhabitants rises upwards according to where they are situated within the strata of the figure,
as shown on the right hand axis. Towards the top of the
figure, one has the property owners, £10+ tenants, and ratepayers. These would gain a settlement by virtue of their property, or by renting over £10 value per annum, or by payment of
parish or township rates,[44] and so all such people are shown as
being legally settled in this parish. The useful contemporary
phrase 'principal inhabitants' described many within this group.
Further down the figure, among the poor, many would not be
settled in the parish, never having been able (or perhaps wishing) to gain a settlement there – this would vary considerably
by parish – and so these are outside the 'T' shaped zone of
settled people. The 'poor' were, in this period and economy, a
large section of the parish population,[45] and the property-
owning, £10 renting and ratepaying classes were relatively small
by comparison. (In all these matters, the figurative ratios between such groups varied by parish and region.) Many of these
poor were settled elsewhere, but resided locally. One did not
of course have to live in one's place of legal settlement, and
many did not, although if one became a pauper one could be
obliged to do so through the process of removal (or threatened
removal) under the settlement laws, or as a condition of relief.[46]

[44] From various dates in the early to mid-eighteenth century, national or county taxes
(e.g. window or house tax, or the county rate), and highway or scavenger taxes (see
Geo. I, c. 7, s. 6), were held not to confer parish settlement. In other words, only
payment of poor and church rates produced a settlement, as they were parish levies.
35 Geo. III, c. 101 (1795), abolished settlement by paying public taxes for a tenement
not of the yearly value of £10.

[45] I am well aware that a lengthy and complex article could be written on varying
definitions of 'the poor'; but for the sake of clarity of exposition here, in connection
with figures 3.1 and 3.2, I am using the term here simply to mean those who were not
rated to the poor rate. This is in contradistinction to 'the ratepaying classes', another
term frequently used by contemporaries. For some other purposes, I would adopt
more subtle and wider definitions.

[46] Besides parish policies controlling where one might receive poor relief (which, with
non-resident relief, are little researched in this early period), the main provision
linking residence and settlement was (from March 1723) that nobody could obtain a
settlement by buying an estate of less than £30 value unless s/he lived on it, the

'Belonging' via settlement, in that sense, could thus become a restrictive condition, governing one's location because of on-going pauperism. Yet parochial belonging did not normally tie one to one's parish, just as ethnicities are de-coupled from locality and not necessarily constrained to any specific territory or polity in the modern world. However, unlike modern ethnicity, in the eighteenth century one could alter one's settlement with relative ease. It follows, therefore, that many people settled in this parish were resident elsewhere, in situations of what we might call 'parochial pluralism' to describe the assortment of insiders and outsiders residing in any parish. Those non-resident but settled people had more of a claim on this parish, and probably felt that they 'belonged' there to a greater degree, than did many of the poor who resided in the parish, but had no settlement in it. As seen in many pauper letters, in England and Wales one did not have to reside in a place to believe that one belonged to it, or to know that one belonged to it in a much more legally secure way than many who lived there. These paradoxes were intrinsic to the ways in which the settlement laws interacted with a capitalist labour market.

Towards the bottom of figure 3.1, one finds the strata of paupers, that is those in receipt of parish relief. These were of course a sub-set of 'the poor', and in the eighteenth century were typically quite a large proportion of the poor. Indeed, by the late eighteenth century they were a significant proportion of the entire parish population, and remained so into the early nineteenth century, particularly in the low-waged agrarian south of England, where they often grew as a proportion. Some of them were settled elsewhere, but were residing in this parish. These had occasional or regular non-resident relief from their

<hr />

'settlement' in this case being forfeited without residence. See 9 Geo. I, c. 7, s. 5; M. Nolan, *A Treatise of the Laws for the Relief and Settlement of the Poor*, 2 vols. (1805, London, 1808), vol. i, pp. 543, 569; Burn, *Justice of the Peace*, vol. iv, pp. 540–62; 'Eighth Report of George Taylor on Settlement', *Report from His Majesty's Commissioners for Inquiring into the Administration and Practical Operation of the Poor Laws*, xxxvii (1834), Appendix C, p. 123 c. One can very occasionally find examples of a parish refusing to allow anyone to live there unless they were settled, but this was extremely rare. This could even occur in the mid-nineteenth century; see *Norfolk News* (31 October 1863): 'They won't let anybody live at H[eydon] unless they belong to the parish.' I am grateful to Robert Lee for this reference.

parishes of settlement. Others among them were settled in the parish, and so came within the emphasised 'settled' area of the figure. Among the settled paupers, some thought of themselves as having special claims upon 'their' parish, and we may loosely take them as being among the 'core' inhabitants, by virtue of long-established relations with the parish and its most permanent parishioners. These people among the very poor may well have thought of themselves as 'belonging' to the parish with an intensity that matched that of property owners much higher in the social scale, even though the reasons for their senses of belonging differed in many ways from those who owned property and who dominated local office-holding. By comparison with the poor, there were some among those property owners and higher-status groups who held property in other parishes, as well as in this parish, and so that sense of multiple proprietorial belonging tended to dilute their idea of belonging distinctly to this parish. Seasonal social movement involving places like Richmond, Bath, Brighton or London had a similar effect. In this period, wealth or class did not very strongly affect one's sense of parish belonging, even though relatively high proportions among the wealthier ranks of parish society were legally settled. So the 'core' element has been shown in the figure as a vertical rectangle rather than a downward pointing triangle. This became much less applicable by the later nineteenth century, as we will see, because of the later move to wealthier local societies, the corollary of which was ideas of belonging coming to be linked more strongly to property ownership or association.

An element in many parishes is shown to the right of the figure: that is, the settlement certificate holders. Someone with a certificate was widely referred to as 'a certificate man' – and the gendering here was not inadvertent, as women rarely had certificates. Such people were settled in other parishes, but lived as 'sojourners' in this one, by token of their certificate. In most parishes many people resided without a certificate from their 'home' parish. Historians debate how efficacious or widespread the certificate system was, and at least one has much exaggerated its importance. In fact, the 1795 Settlement Act commented that the certificate system had been 'very ineffectual', and in the face of prevailing levels of migration that verdict by knowledgeable contemporaries was certainly correct.[47] Furthermore, aggregations of certificates show the system in steep decline from the 1750s.[48] There were proposals to abolish them in the mid-eighteenth century.[49] Parishes varied greatly in asking for or issuing certificates (many refused to give them), and record survival across the country makes it impossible to judge this issue properly. Yet many parishes before the mid-eighteenth century asked for certificates from at least some of their resident, non-settled poor, especially from those who they thought were most vulnerable. A certificate to some extent guarded against both the person and family gaining a settlement (via some of the legal 'heads' of settlement),[50] and against that person creating servant or apprentice settlements through his employing behaviour.[51] It thus helped to 'save the parish harmless'. Such a document was issued by a parish of settlement to another named parish, and it did not have general applicability beyond that, for example if a migrant moved on. It could be issued by request of a receiving parish's officers or the certificate holder, and it guaranteed to take that person back or provide for him if he became chargeable.[52] Before 1795, in a period when poorer people could be removed if they were thought 'likely to be chargeable', a certificate normally prevented removal until chargeability occurred. It could thus be in the interests of both a poor migrant, and the parish of residence, to obtain a certificate.

---

[47] 35 Geo. III, c. 101. Only one pre-census listing of inhabitants shows certificate holders, that for the fairly small village of Barlborough (Derb.) in 1792. Of 146 householders, 115 were settled there, 26 were settled elsewhere, 5 were uncertain, and there were about 25 servants and lodgers whose settlements were unstated. However, this was the site of Barlborough Hall, a large Elizabethan mansion, the seat of the Rodeses, and was a restrictive parish in some senses, which may help explain why the listing and its choice of information came into being. So one cannot know how typical such figures were.

[48] For example, see the impressive chart in Vialls, 'Laws of settlement', Appendix 7, p. 381, showing steep falls in the numbers of certificates granted to men in Northamptonshire from the 1750s. (In any period, almost negligible numbers were granted to women, and they were also falling from the 1750s.) Record survival chances would, of course, predispose to greater survival in later decades, and so this result is almost certainly reliable. My own unpublished tabulations of certificates issued per annum across southern, midland and western English counties produces much the same picture.

[49] For example, Burn, *History of the Poor Laws*, pp. 235–6, 284.

[50] 9 & 10 Wm III, c. 11.

[51] 12 Anne, c. 18, s. 2.

[52] Burn, *Justice of the Peace*, vol. IV, pp. 592–3.

However, it was much less obviously in the interests of the parish of settlement to grant one.

Most migrants almost certainly did not carry a certificate, for this was a mobile society, certificates were fairly costly, were cumbersome to obtain as they usually required overseers', churchwardens' and JPs' signatures, and 'great numbers of parishes' refused to give them,[53] because they contributed to tie the certificate-person to the issuing parish and also made that parish liable for removal costs. Surviving gender ratios of certificates make it obvious that very few female migrants can ever have had one. The very large majority of settlement examinations of migrants never mentioned certificates, even though certificates were very compelling legal evidence of settlement and would have been mentioned if given. So the certificate-less inhabitants are shown as a miscellaneous and sizeable group outside the main boxed areas of figure 3.1, and of course below the better-off ranks who had little need of certificates, or whose certificates were annulled by virtue of them gaining a property- or rent-based settlement.[54] The people without certificates were the most vulnerable to removal, but they were also the people who were most likely to gain settlements, and thus become legally absorbed into the parish and entitled to its poor law benefits. Without a certificate, they lacked the partly preventative barrier

[53] For example, Sir F. M. Eden, *The State of the Poor*, 3 vols. (1797, Bristol, 2001), repeatedly documents parishes that refused to give settlement certificates. See e.g. vol. III, pp. 735, 825, 859, 874; W. Greaves, *Reasons for Introducing a Law, to Prevent Unnecessary and Vexatious Removals of the Poor* (Cambridge, 1775), reprinted (and incorrectly referenced) as an excerpt in G. Coode, *Report of George Coode Esq. to the Poor Law Board on the Law of Settlement and Removal of the Poor*, XXVI (1851), p. 319 ('great numbers of parishes will not give certificates'); Styles, 'Evolution of the law of settlement', p. 51. Furthermore, JPs could refuse to sign certificates, thus invalidating them, and they could do so if they felt that the system was being used to inhibit settlements. As a solicitor for Priors Marston (Northants.) said in 1782, 'the courts have always leaned in favour of settlement and uniformly have ordered that they should be favoured as much as may be'. Quoted in Vialls, 'Laws of settlement', pp. 214–15.

[54] Even if one had a certificate, one could gain a settlement by estate, or renting a tenement of over £10 value per annum and living in it, or serving an annual office, but one would not gain a settlement solely by being rated for a property worth under £10 per annum, so some among the upper strata of figure 3.1 with settlement certificates would remain unsettled in the parish. 8 & 9 Wm III, c. 30 (1697); 9 & 10 Wm III, c. 11 (1698); Burn, *Justice of the Peace*, vol. IV, pp. 554–9, 591, 619; Styles, 'Evolution of the law of settlement', p. 52.

to attaining a settlement that a certificate provided. In fact, there were probably also differences in moral standing between those with and those without certificates.[55] The certificate holders were discussed as such among parish inhabitants. The advantages or disadvantages for the parish or for the certificate holder of having a certificate were widely known and were subjects of normal conversation. (After all, if a person hired himself to such a person, or served the certificate man as an apprentice, s/he would not gain a settlement – but then that person might already have a settlement elsewhere that s/he did not wish to lose, and many other such motives occurred.) Certificate holders were not necessarily only poor people, given the legal bearings of a certificate (although there was no point in requiring a certificate from someone who would own property or rent over £10 per annum) – and so an elongated rectangle represents them in figure 3.1.

These 'sojourners' (a common word for them) were a form of 'registered outsider resident among us', to invent a phrase. They were immune from removal until actually chargeable, but separate from others insofar as they did not 'belong' to the parish. They clearly belonged to another named parish or township, being 'floaters', 'out-township poor' or 'out-parishioners' from those places, and they were seen as such. Their certificates were usually held by the parish overseers and often carefully stored in the parish chest.[56] Some certificate holders managed to keep their own certificate, occasionally handing it down through the generations rather like a family heirloom. Such a document or other evidence of settlement gained utility in the nineteenth century, when later generations increasingly found it hard to

---

[55] T. Mackay, *A History of the English Poor Law*, vol. III: *From 1834 to the Present Time* (1854, London, 1900), p. 343, agreeing with George Coode, thought that 'chief parishioners' 'naturally were disinclined to grant certificates to good workmen, and only too eager to grant them to the idle and indisciplined', or 'the most worthless or mischievous inhabitants'. (This issue could be argued in a number of ways, as certificates lessened the chance of a settlement being gained elsewhere, and so might be given to migrants one wished to retain as settled in one's own parish.) Sir G. Coode's views are best seen in *Report of George Coode, Esq. to the Poor Law Board on the Law of Settlement and Removal of the Poor*, XXVI (1851); see p. 253 on certificates being given to disreputable people.

[56] In some cases, parish officers would not part with a certificate, such was their desire to safeguard it in their own interests. For an example of this, see W. E. Tate, *The Parish Chest: A Study of the Records of Parochial Administration in England* (1946, Cambridge, 1960), p. 202.

obtain a settlement in their own right compared to most poor
people in the eighteenth century (during the heyday of traditional yearly hiring and indentured apprenticeship). During
the nineteenth century ever larger proportions of people therefore took their paternal settlement.[57] Certificates were sometimes produced going back many decades to attest to that
settlement. As from 1795, most people could not be removed
until they were actually chargeable, and so much of the *raison
d'être* of certificates became redundant. One can still find them
very occasionally being issued thereafter; they were mentioned
in a few subsequent Acts of Parliament;[58] and they remained
compelling legal evidence of where a person was settled. However, their use had almost certainly been declining even in the
second half of the eighteenth century, and they were of negligible importance after 1795. Parish officers could still certify
that someone belonged to them, and much of the law relating
to certificates continued, but it was no longer necessary to
grant certificates to prevent removal of the non-chargeable
poor.[59] One should therefore think of this legal category of
'resident-outsiders' in figure 3.1 as fading away after 1795.[60]

Of course, settlement as a form of belonging had greatest
relevance for those who were vulnerable to poor relief dependency, and settlement was universally defined as the right to poor

[57] See the graphs and discussion in Snell, *Annals of the Labouring Poor*, pp. 77–81. About
15 per cent of settlement examinees had failed to gain an independent settlement in
the mid-eighteenth century (and so took paternal settlement), and that rose to about
70 per cent in the 1860s. This was a trend among the poor, most apparent after 1795. It
was less pronounced more widely, as the increased accessibility in the nineteenth
century of settlement by renting and property (for those who would not generally be
examined) counter-balanced this to some degree.

[58] 51 Geo. III, c. 80; 54 Geo. III, c. 170; 1 & 2 Geo. IV, c. 32.

[59] Burn, *Justice of the Peace*, vol. IV, p. 590. Certificates also had some continuing utility if
one returned and again became chargeable to a parish of removal, thus helping one to
avoid a vagrancy offence, although one very rarely finds them issued after 1795. *Ibid.*,
pp. 700–2. They were used this way before 1795 as well, to permit non-vagrant return
to a removing parish (see the 1744 Vagrancy Act, 17 Geo. II, c. 5). In such cases, it was
clearly the very poor and indigent who were benefiting from them. Sir G. Nicholls,
*A History of the English Poor Law, in Connection with the State of the Country and the
Condition of the People*, vol. II (1854, New York, 1967), pp. 196–7.

[60] By 1857, Henry Hodgson claimed that 'certificates have now become obsolete'. H. J.
Hodgson, *Steer's Parish Law, Being a Digest of the Law relating to the Civil and Ecclesi-
astical Government of Parishes; Friendly Societies, etc., and the Relief, Settlement, and
Removal of the Poor* (1830, London, 1857), p. 761.

relief in a parish.[61] 'High' poor rates (*c.* 1780–1840) kept this point very much in mind. The inter-linked concepts of settlement and belonging had greatest applicability to 'the poor', or 'the labouring poor', however locally or regionally defined. However, everyone (aside from certain national immigrants) had a settlement, and in this period one never knew who might sink to parish-dependent poverty through old age, illness, disability, insanity, fire, bankruptcy, unemployment and so on. Friendly societies and mutual assurance clubs existed, increasingly so from the later eighteenth century, but adequate insurance was usually outside the realms of the parish poor.

Just as some people living in this hypothetical parish belonged outside it, so many people belonging to this parish were resident elsewhere. They had settlements in this parish, and so they 'belonged' there, arguably with much more connection for the purposes of poor relief than many resident people who were settled somewhere else. Some of the latter would have been resident for very many years, but lacking a settlement they could be removed, especially if they became chargeable. In this respect, every parish had a clear sense of its 'own' resident/ settled inhabitants, and, unfortunately, a rather less clear sense of its own non-resident/settled inhabitants, or its own 'out-parishioners'. People were also spoken of as 'our poor', or 'the poor of the parish', and these could include people who were known about and living elsewhere. Some of those might be in receipt of non-resident relief. The parish's image of who 'belonged' thus excluded certain residents, but flowed *beyond* the parish, to encompass people in the country (or the world) who 'belonged' to it. Later sociologists invented terms like 'belonging or community without propinquity', something that they variously associated with 'modernisation' or 'postmodernism' – but in fact one sees this phenomenon long before, notably with this feature of the settlement laws.

Property owners, ratepayers, or parish officers had views about how many people ought to belong, how they should earn their settlements, and what restrictions (if any) ought to be

---

[61] Snell, 'Pauper settlement and the right to poor relief', pp. 377–9, and see n. 1 above. Such a definition does not of course mean that the settled poor had a legal right to poor relief upon demand, even if they sometimes believed that.

practised against extra people belonging. They had an eye on how many belonged already, where they might be, and how vulnerable they were. Yet it was very difficult to have a clear picture of how many people belonged to one's parish, when so many of one's settled poor resided elsewhere, and were able in a variety of ways to gain settlements in other parishes, about which one had little knowledge. Despite the utility of gossip and hear-say, outside the ambit of one's parish this was an 'information-poor' society. Reliable information was often parochially confined: the contrast between the intense fulsome detail of what was known about *within* the parish, and what was not known about *outside* the parish, was enormous. The modern world has, in some regards, reversed that situation.

This contrasting awareness had considerable cultural significance in the eighteenth and much of the nineteenth centuries. Word of mouth, correspondence, occasional demands for relief, kin connections, village talk, information from external carriers and others, and some censuses of the poor, all assisted knowledge of who living elsewhere still belonged. That knowledge was always imperfect. Certainly, in the minds of overseers, there could be a sense of palpable relief or achievement when it became known that certain individuals had apparently gained a settlement elsewhere. Some parish actions (like out-apprenticeship,[62] and other more 'corrupt' methods) could be intent on achieving that. Some parishes took decisions to restrict subsequent settlements, knowing that they were vulnerable to abnormally high and unwelcome returns from settled poor, even if that knowledge was necessarily highly inadequate, and rarely documented in any register.[63] In some cases, targeted

---

[62] Mackay, *History of the English Poor Law*, p. 346: 'not as a legitimate means of giving the young person chargeable to the parish a fair start in life, but as a means of getting rid of legal responsibility for their maintenance'. This was a frequent point, although one that need not be exaggerated.

[63] Dunstable (Beds.) kept a record of persons with certificates (probably who they had given certificates to). Such lists of non-resident 'belonging' poor seem not often to have been kept, and prevailing demography made this difficult. On Dunstable's 1769 list of 140 names headed 'Certificates', see Webb and Webb, *English Poor Law History*, p. 338. Other parishes kept records of those living among them who were settled elsewhere. For example, 'A list of Persons now living in the Parish of Brinkley, not belonging to the Parish', Cambs. CRO, P16/12 (Brinkley Parish Meeting Minute Book, March 1850, also giving the names of their parishes).

restrictions on settlement occurred, trying to stop people from certain unpopular parishes gaining a settlement in one's own parish. Settlement disputes at Quarter Sessions aggravated this selectively xenophobic tendency. In periods of trade recession, rural parishes in the midlands, the north, and around some southern cities like Norwich or London, often faced sizeable numbers of returnees, coming back to 'their' parishes for relief. This caused much ill-feeling, and it was a major factor in the introduction of irremovability legislation from 1846. That legislation forced industrial towns in particular to pay for the poor who had been five years in continuous urban residence, as well as making them responsible for recently widowed women and many people who were chargeable because of accident or sickness.[64] We shall see that the 1846–76 irremovability legislation slowly departed from earlier concepts of 'belonging but not residing'. However, such 'non-resident belonging' was fundamental to most of the long period of poor law settlement, and was a crucial feature of parish or township 'belonging'.

Figure 3.1 could be adapted to different circumstances in a number of ways, and much local evidence and changing contexts of pauperism would justify that.[65] For example, some parishes routinely asked poorer incomers other than servants and apprentices for certificates, especially up to the mid-eighteenth century, while other parishes never did. Villages at the extremes of a 'closed' or 'open' spectrum would look quite different in terms of such a diagrammatic scheme. 'Close' parishes often had more belonging to them than resided in them; typically their proportions of inhabitants who were resident but settled elsewhere would be quite small. The opposite was normally true of 'open' parishes: these would have large proportions of inhabitants who were resident but not settled.[66] The

---

[64] 9 & 10 Vic., c. 66. Under this so-called 'Five Years Act', magistrates could remove a person resident for under five years and suffering from sickness or an accident, but only if it was deemed that the person would be permanently disabled as a result.

[65] A parallel diagrammatical model of settlement administrative categories, showing the administrative groupings subject to varying procedures and types of settlement document, and discussing other category differences, is in my 'Settlement, poor law and the rural historian', pp. 146–57. One could combine both diagrams, but that would make for extremely sophisticated presentation.

[66] G. White, *Parochial Settlements: An Obstruction to Poor Law Reform* (London, 1835), p. 16. White was an acute observer, a close friend of Nassau Senior, and his comment is

proportions of village populations who were legally settled
where they lived varied considerably. These are fundamental
matters for comparative community history. Yet we currently
know little about the respective sizes of groups of ratepayers,
'the poor', and paupers, of the 'native' and 'foreign' poor; nor
about how such groups' relative sizes affected parish policies on
settlement and poor law administration; nor about how these
consideratons changed over time; nor about how they varied by
parish, region and local economy.

Above all, it must be stressed that figure 3.1 is a framework or
archetypical 'model' that describes the situation *only* with
regard to legal settlement. Many other criteria relating to ideas
of belonging were superimposed on to these divisions, bearing
upon people's senses of where they belonged, and why. Some
of these are explored as themes in other chapters of this book.
Such criteria differed enormously by parish, region, social rank,
occupation, gender, and legal efficacy, so much so that it would
be unwise to attempt a fuller discussion of them here. They
would in some cases conduce to legal settlement, but not necessarily so. Among these other criteria were: parental settlement;
maiden settlement; birth; previous settlements (which might
resurrect if one's last settlement was legally invalidated, or
'forgotten'); marriage; kinship and ancestry, or that of their
spouse; property ownership or tenancy, and the type and duration of tenancy; labouring and/or property status; a person's
occupation and its links to skills, resources or trade organisation
in the locality (e.g. 'free miners' or quarry workers in the Forest
of Dean,[67] or members of guilds and companies in gildated

highly relevant here: 'The intermixture of what, with reference to settlements, may be
called Foreign and Native poor, extends more or less over the whole kingdom; and it
would be a matter beyond curiosity or mere interest, to ascertain with accuracy what
the true state of this species of pauper statistics may be, for it becomes a question of
paramount importance, when considered with reference to the broad principle of
Poor Laws, and the taxation consequent upon them.' *Ibid.*, p. 16. This 'intermixture'
was also fundamental to community identities and history. His plea was not much
taken up by others, to produce the statistics he wanted (going beyond those who were
paupers). This was no doubt largely because of the great difficulties in ascertaining
reliable contrasting figures on settlement status, and because of the public effects of
producing and publishing them.

[67] Forest of Dean 'free miners' gained that status through birth to a free-miner father, in
the Hundred of St Briavels, and by working for a year and a day in a mine there.
H. G. Nicholls, *Nicholls's Forest of Dean: An Historical and Descriptive Account, and Iron*

towns); considerations bearing upon whether the person was deemed to be deserving or undeserving, and depending upon who was making that judgement; length of settlement; length of residence; location and duration of work (for example on an estate, shipyard, in a mine); British or other country of origin (usually affecting Irish or Scottish people); parish office-holding and other services rendered; religious affiliations and offices held; speaking the dialect of the district; having valued local skills and knowledge, and so on.

Some of these other notions might precede legal settlement in the subjective ways in which they tied a person to locality or parish. Yet without legal settlement a person could be removed in some circumstances, notably when falling upon hard times, and so it was important to attain a settlement. Before the introduction of irremovability legislation in 1846, there was no point in proclaiming indignantly, to (let us say hypothetically) a Folkestone vestry or petty sessions deciding whether to remove you to Carlisle, that you 'belonged' to Folkestone because your wife came from there, because you had also been born there, lived and worked there sixty years, rented a small property there for decades, had children, many relatives and countless friends there, and so on, because if all that life story had not produced a legal settlement in Folkestone you could still be removed with your wife to Carlisle, if your settlement was deemed to be there, and even if you were 'entire strangers' there.[68]

In other words, compared with other criteria the concept of legal settlement was relatively clear-cut, despite all its legal

---

Making in the Olden Times (1858 and 1866, Dawlish, 1966), p. 120. This definition (from 1834) was similar over a long period, but it was contested in fine detail and one can find slightly different versions, in some cases also extending to Dean stone-quarry workers. As a *very* rough figure, about 1,000 Dean miners felt themselves to be so eligible in the 1830s. One can see the similarity of these local quasi-legal criteria to certain 'heads' of legal settlement, but clearly they were not the same, and one might even conceive of some 'free miners' being removable from the area under the settlement laws.

[68] Wording from James Corder, clerk to the Birmingham guardians, *Select Committee on Irremovable Poor*, XVII (1860), p. 68; or see Alfred Moore's evidence on p. 137: 'I have known a removal from our township [Leeds] to Cornwall, where none of them had resided for generations . . . I have known cases of settlement obtained by hiring and service, 70 or 80 years ago, where the parties being removed have known nothing about the place.'

difficulties and implications for local practice. It placed people
within the central 'T' section of figure 3.1. Yet of those settled
people, some would clearly be felt (or feel themselves, which
might be a different matter) to 'belong' to a far greater degree
than others. After all, one could gain a settlement in a parish by
marrying one of its men, never having even been to that settlement oneself, or by serving a final forty days there as an apprentice to a travelling master, while others with settlements had
lived there all their lives. I have therefore adapted the idea of
'core' belonging to help identify people with extra socio-moral
claims to belong, and the extra-settlement criteria listed above
further identified 'core' people and families, augmenting ideas
of belonging that derived from legal settlement. In some cases,
those criteria would overlap with settlement, and indeed create
it (for example, marriage, property ownership, tenancies over
£10 per annum, public office-holding, or payment of parish
rates). Yet many of these criteria were contested in various ways,
with regard to how effective they were in conveying (or convincing others about) a sense of belonging and entitlement, and
what such entitlements ought to be. The poor felt that they had a
'right' to poor relief in their 'home' parish, but, as Steve Hindle
has pointed out, that supposed 'right' might be questioned
by parish officers or others, even for those who were legally
settled.[69] Local inhabitants would have different perspectives on
these issues, and the conflicts and motives did not necessarily
emerge in the clear-cut way of this analytical discussion. In
many cases they certainly did so. One thinks of arguments over
entitlements to employment, housing, charities, seasonal doles,
marital partners, gleaning, fuel, fallen timber, wildfowl, and
many other such matters, where ideas of precedence based upon
parish belonging and whether one was considered a 'foreigner'
were crucial. (Such themes have been discussed in chapter 2
on the culture of local xenophobia.) Many other disputes would
be swayed in various ways because of the issues discussed here.
Such criteria and perspectives obviously varied so much across
different regions and types of parishes and townships that
they cannot be dealt with schematically in the diagrammatic

---

[69] Hindle, *On the Parish?*, esp. pp. 398–432.

way of figure 3.1, although that figure serves as a malleable template for further research.

In England and Wales we therefore had a system of 'belonging' that (i) put great stress upon it as a concept, attaching crucial importance to it in legal terms and in matters of welfare entitlement; (ii) that allowed people to transfer their 'belonging' through obtaining subsequent settlements, each eclipsing the earlier one, taking people away from their families, and from parishes where (for whatever other reasons) they might be felt, or feel themselves, to belong; (iii) that could be used or manipulated as a barrier to migration or settlement as well as a system of attraction, absorption, belonging, and arguable entitlement; (iv) that, unlike many 'peasant' societies, allowed people to 'belong' to a place where they did not live and had not lived for many years (and in the cases of many wives or descendants, had never lived at all); and (v) was fully compatible with a long-standing capitalist market economy and with high levels of labour mobility, proving that capitalism was not inimical to strong ideas of belonging. Indeed, as a system of pre-migration reassurance, settlement may even have conduced to mobility: contemporaries could migrate elsewhere in the security that if they fell upon hard times they would normally be cared for and removed back 'home'.[70] Much migration might not otherwise have taken place.

One should extend that latter point further. It was a paradoxical fact that the legal disputes over settlement, the travelling to ascertain legal and biographical details, the search for witnesses to settlement having been gained elsewhere, the trips to see lawyers, the delivery of subpoenas, the trips to Quarter Sessions to conduct disputes, the movement of people by parish officials and contractors under removal and vagrant orders, the need to obtain costs, and so on, all tended on the one hand to widen people's geographical horizons, but also to deepen a sense of

---

[70] In 1834, for example, it was said that labourers 'change [their services] more frequently than formerly, and impute it to the indulgence of the Poor Laws, which afford them a refuge in their own parish, when they fail in adventuring elsewhere'. *Report from His Majesty's Commissioners for Inquiring into the Administration and Practical Operation of the Poor Laws, Appendix (B.1.). Answers to Rural Queries, part IV*, xxxiii (1834), p. 183 d. Reply of Thomas Carr, overseer of Prittlewell (Essex).

their local belonging, and to reinforce the identity, pride and independent reputation of the parish. Overseers' and constables' accounts, and lists of settlement costs, are full of details of trips and travel expenses incurred in connection with settlement.[71] Furthermore, Sir Frederick Eden grumbled, 'parish officers are by no means economical travellers'.[72] One only has to read the accounts of settlement disputes and of the picaresque horse-riding search for evidence to find these conclusions reinforced. That process of seeking evidence, with the oral testimonies, the head-scratching among oldest inhabitants, the parish-register and parish-chest record searching, enquiries to parish lawyers, and the like, with its incidental findings, strongly reinforced notions of local belonging while inadvertently contributing to local history and bolstering parish identity. Every settlement case was a rehearsal of parish history and remembrance. The reminiscence was not about elite family history, heraldry or landed title – on the contrary, it was mundane, relating to the common people. For example, the overseer of Chewton Mendip in Somerset wrote to his opposite number in Daventry in 1841 saying that: 'Having examined some of the oldest and most intelligent inhabitants, they have never heard the name here, and having likewise referred to the Parish Registers, I find there never was any entry of the surname Eales.'[73] Such statements, whether true or otherwise, are routinely encountered in settlement cases. One can imagine the hours of parish conversation and gossip underpinning them, elderly witnesses being constantly plumbed, a community history being recounted, a plan of recollection being formulated. In all its social depth and ramifications, therefore, settlement backed up and gave social, legal and cultural justification to our central theme of transferable local belonging. Furthermore, parochial pride, self-assertiveness, a sense of the parish standing alone and with repute, were all augmented by the settlement laws and their legal appurtenances.

---

[71] Such lengthy itemisation is often encountered. For example, Derb. CRO, D1642 A/PO 3–102 (Microfilm 90, Calow overseers' accounts, costs in the removal of William Davinson, 27 November–19 January 1772–3).
[72] Eden, *State of the Poor*, vol. III, p. 809.
[73] Northants. CRO, D7997, cited in Vialls, 'Laws of settlement', pp. 288–9.

A quotation from the famous Welsh novelist Emyr Humphreys, one of those with which this chapter started, has special relevance to the operation of settlement and the culture associated with it, even though it was written in the mid-twentieth century and without the settlement laws in mind: '"Anybody can have roots if they want them", I said. "Human beings are like strawberry plants."'[74] People could migrate, obtain another settlement, even one far away, set down 'roots' there, gain entitlements or precedence there, and do the same again and again, as could their children and members of their families. In fact, almost everyone *did have roots* in this system. One could not deny oneself a legal settlement altogether; the 'heads' of settlement were such that it was impossible to do that, except for national immigrants or by emigration from England and Wales. However, even for emigrants the settlement would reinstate itself reassuringly if the person returned, and in that sense nothing had been lost. The picaresque accounts that one reads in settlement examinations often extend thousands of miles beyond British shores. Using the analogy of plants with rooting stems that run along the ground, therefore, some of the main historical issues about settlement and its effects are how comparatively numerous were the 'runners', and for what purposes; how lengthy, long-lasting, and significant were those runners; what else in cultural and economic terms influenced or opposed them; how single-ended were they; how did they vary across, accommodate to, and take root in different soils (parishes or regions); how and why did the extending or colonising nature of this plant change over time; and what were the international connotations of mentalities bred within this system? After all, the local parish system discussed here was also a foundation for the invasive British empire, spreading English as the dominant language around the world, and the nature of the connections invites enquiry. It seems likely that the taken-for-granted culture of local transferable, capitalistic 'belonging' outlined here was an influence upon that expansion, and that the forces which selectively excluded some people from many parishes were also a contributory factor.

---

[74] Humphreys, *Man's Estate*, p. 252.

Speaking anthropologically and comparatively, this was a 'shallow' (non-peasant, non-feudal, non-tribal) but distinctive sense of belonging – perhaps only Japan under the Tokugawa shogunate (1603–1868) and post-1731 Prussia had something closely similar in legal terms, both of them much more repressive, and those societies were radically different in other regards.[75] This was a sense of belonging that was legally enshrined in England and Wales, that conferred legal rights and practical benefits which were internationally unique, that guaranteed the long-term survival and indeed popularity of settlement among many people, whether rich or poor (different ranks in society saw its respective advantages to themselves), and that laid the foundations of 'the welfare state' long before most historians date that development. Adam Smith and other early political economists made well-known statements attacking the settlement system, but it did not survive for over 300 years without good reason. Well into the twentieth century, strong and politically persuasive arguments were being made for its retention.[76]

Furthermore, while the English and Welsh labouring classes protested against a great deal during industrialisation, there is no recorded protest by them against settlement *as a system*, whatever they may have thought about the hardship of individual cases, and whatever the agendas of political economists or higher-class reformers who, in wishing to abolish settlement, sometimes also asserted that it was disliked by the poor.[77] Even

---

[75] Many other societies restricted 'settlement' in a conventional sense, hindering people entering, placing controls on where they could live, and so on. For example, in Sweden an Act of 1788 permitted parishes to control their boundaries against an influx of workers who might become a local charge, selecting those who they wished to accept. P. Aronsson, 'Swedish rural society and political culture: the eighteenth- and nineteenth-century experience', *Rural History*, 3 (1992), p. 48. In Switzerland, there were tight restrictions on settlement in lowland areas, and hence much of the population tended to gravitate to the mountains and hills, where industry often came to be located. I am grateful to Sidney Pollard for the latter point.

[76] As in the Majority Report of the Royal Commission on the Poor Laws (1909), or as embodied in unemployment and poor law legislation of the inter-war period. Indeed, even as late as the mid-1980s, some older magistrates in English south coast resort towns were recalling settlement, and urging its revival, to prevent people from elsewhere sleeping on their beaches!

[77] For example, Nicholls, *History of the English Poor Law*, vol. II, p. 407. However, it is likely that many of the more permanent Irish immigrants disliked the system, even

Adam Smith reluctantly conceded, from his Scottish desk, that 'it has never been the object of any general popular clamour', complaining (like Marx later) about 'the common people of England . . . so jealous of their liberty, but like the common people of most other countries never rightly understanding wherein it consists'.[78] Others, by comparison, were less quick to denounce 'false consciousness'. These included Robert Pashley, who spoke of how judges used to consider settlement 'as a peculiar privilege of the poor'.[79] Witnesses to the 1832–4 Poor Law Commission spoke of how the poor viewed settlements as being their 'heir-looms, or their freeholds'.[80] As Nathaniel Alexander (a guardian of Epsom) explained: 'they think the parochial settlement is a property which exists for them when their old age drives them to the necessity of giving up labour; then it is a kind of property that they fall back upon. I think that is the feeling all over the country.'[81] He also

though (with clever manipulation) it often gave Irish harvesters free passage home to Ireland, and was therefore favoured by those workers. A. O'Dowd, *Spalpeens and Tattie Hokers: History and Folklore of the Irish Migratory Agricultural Worker in Ireland and Britain* (Dublin, 1991), pp. 3–4, 23, 273–6. Non-recognition of marriages in Catholic chapels also 'bastardised' most Irish children, rendering those infants settled where they were born, which was a further problem. For much of our period, one could remove their married parents back to Ireland, but not their children so born as 'bastards' in England and Wales. *Report from His Majesty's Commissioners on the Administration and Practical Operation of the Poor Laws. Appendix (B.2.). Part IV. Answers to Town Queries with Indices*, XXXVI (1834); see complaints against this on pp. 151 i, 225 i. Settlement illegitimacy stipulations must have been widely resented among the English and Welsh poor as well, for often taking children above the age of nurture from their mothers to their birthplace settlements. One can think of other features of settlement law that were resented by the poor (e.g. its handling of non-married consensual unions), and many policies and effects that stemmed from settlement (e.g. 'open'–'close' divisions, cottage destruction, and walking long distances to work). In making difficult generalisations about the labouring poor's attitude to the system as a whole, I do not wish to deny that removal was frequently resented by the family being removed, and one can very occasionally find dramatic examples of that.

[78] A. Smith, *The Wealth of Nations* (1776, Harmondsworth, 1977), p. 245. Karl Marx's overwrought verdict was that the 'Laws of Settlement . . . had upon the English landworkers the same effect that the Edict of the Tartar Boris Godunoff in 1587 had on the Russian peasantry'. K. Marx, *Capital*, 2 vols. (1867, London, 1972), vol. II, p. 801, wording that presumably he congratulated himself upon, as out-doing Smith's language of poor men feeling 'most cruelly oppressed' by settlement. In fact, perhaps as a German and a Scotsman unfamiliar with the system, neither showed much knowledge of it.

[79] R. Pashley, *Pauperism and Poor Laws* (London, 1852), p. 268.

[80] S. G. Checkland and E. O. A. Checkland (eds.), *The Poor Law Report of 1834* (1834, Harmondsworth, 1973), p. 249.

[81] *Sixth Report of the Select Committee on Settlement, and Poor Removal*, XI (1847), p. 217.

associated this with access to parochial charities, which enhanced the sense of parish belonging, and to 'the kindly feeling
which now exists in parishes' towards the settled poor. Sir James
Graham commented that the lower classes 'attach great importance to obtaining either a settlement, or an equivalent for a
settlement [irremovability status], and have a great fear of
parting with it'.[82] It is no surprise, therefore, that the radicals
or Chartists of the early and mid-nineteenth century seem not to
have attacked settlement. The rural protests between 1790 and
1850 also seem never to have condemned it, even though the
participants censured many other features of the poor law, and
through their poverty were very familiar with settlement. On the
contrary, as we have seen from their letters, the English and
Welsh poor usually adopted settlement as fundamental to their
senses of local belonging and entitlements, to their ideas of
'home'. They often acted to enforce prerogatives and ideas
stemming from it, buttressing parish identities, and it was
deeply embedded in popular attitudes.

SETTLEMENT AND BELONGING, *c.* 1795 – *c.* 1876

The question that arises now is how did this system change
during the nineteenth century? How did categories of belonging
via settlement compare by the later nineteenth century with
what we have been discussing earlier? Figure 3.1 can be supplemented by another interpretative diagram (see figure 3.2), showing settlement categories of belonging as they would broadly
have been in an archetypical parish by about 1870. The comparison highlights important changes in the theme of settlement and
belonging, and shows differences of emphasis that become clear
when presented in this visual way. Between 1795 and 1846 the
main changes involving settlement were, first, the ending in
1795 of the ability to remove people under the 1662 Act who
were 'likely to become chargeable' (with a few exceptions).[83]

---

[82] *Second and Third Reports from the Select Committee on Settlement, and Poor Removal*, xi
   (1847), p. 19.
[83] 35 Geo. III, c. 101. Some single pregnant women, or unmarried women with child
   (depending upon their employment status), could still be removed while not chargeable (that was repealed by 4 & 5 Wm IV, c. 76, s. 69). Other exceptions were felons,

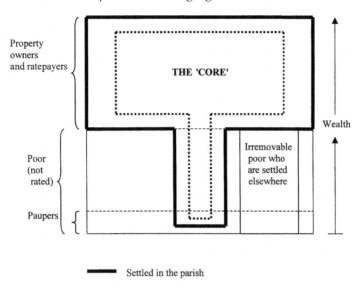

Figure 3.2   Settlement and belonging in a parish in *c.* 1870.

That 1795 Act was passed as ever greater numbers came on to the parish and thus the settlement laws during the food price crises of the mid-1790s. Secondly, in 1834 there were the prospective repeals of yearly hiring, office-serving, and apprenticeship to the sea service or to a fisherman as 'heads' of settlement, some slight restrictions of settlement via purchasing or renting a tenement, and by estate, and changes to settlement conditions affecting illegitimate children.[84] The abolition of yearly service as a 'head' (the main settlement reform in 1834) was intended to revive the institution of yearly service that contemporaries saw as having been in decline in many southern counties. They blamed that decline on employers hiring for lesser periods

---

vagrants, and 'reputed thieves' or people of ill repute. Shaw, *Parochial Lawyer*, pp. 191, 201; J. F. Archbold, *The Poor Law, Comprising the Whole of the Law of Relief, Settlement, and Removal of the Poor, Together with the Law relating to the Poor Rate* (1853, London, 1872), pp. 590–1. In addition, rating as a head of settlement was now only to involve rents of £10 or more. One could obtain a settlement anyway through renting £10 per annum, so rating effectively became redundant as a 'head' of settlement, even though not repealed. Burn, *Justice of the Peace*, vol. IV, p. 589.

[84] By the Poor Law Amendment Act, 4 & 5 Wm IV, c. 76. The person occupying rented premises must have been assessed to the poor rate and paid it, for one year. Hodgson, *Steer's Parish Law*, p. 681. See also Vulliamy, *Law of Settlement*, p. 2.

to avoid settlements being gained, or even almost discarding yearly service altogether in some counties in favour of day or weekly labourers – which created problems of youth unemployment as married men had labour-market precedence.[85] In other ways too, as we shall see, many parish officers and ratepayers were increasingly inclined to hinder settlements from the 1780s onwards, as the burden of pauperism and relief expenditure rose dramatically then and in subsequent decades, when the country came close to a major Malthusian crisis.

After 1834, the major development was the introduction of 'irremovability', which occurred sequentially in 1846–7, 1861, 1865 and 1876. A person became irremovable to his settlement after five years' continuous residence in another place (1846–7),[86] then three years (1861),[87] and then one year (1865).[88] Finally, in 1876, residence and irremovability (three years' residence in one parish without receiving relief) came to confer a settlement (1876), creating 'a pure residential settlement for the first time', as the barrister Gerald Fitz-Gerald put it to one Select Committee.[89] (He was seemingly unaware of practice before

---

[85] On the regional decline of farm servants, and important regional differences in survival, see D. E. Williams, 'Payment of farm servants in the Towy valley, 1774–1869', *Journal of the Royal Welsh Agricultural Society*, 29 (1960); A. Kussmaul, *Servants in Husbandry in Early Modern England* (Cambridge, 1981), ch. 6; Snell, *Annals of the Labouring Poor*, ch. 2; B. M. Short, 'The decline of living-in servants in the transition to capitalist farming: a critique of the Sussex evidence', *Sussex Archaeological Collections*, 122 (1984); M. Reed, 'Indoor farm service in 19th-century Sussex: some criticisms of a critique', *Sussex Archaeological Collections*, 123 (1985), and the rejoinder there by Short; S. Caunce, 'Twentieth-century farm servants: the horselads of the East Riding of Yorkshire', *Agricultural History Review*, 39 (1991); S. Caunce, *Amongst Farm Horses* (Stroud, 1991); G. Moses, 'Rustic and rude: hiring fairs and their critics in East Yorkshire, *c.* 1850–75', *Rural History*, 7 (1996); S. Caunce, 'Farm servants and the development of capitalism in English agriculture', *Agricultural History Review*, 45 (1997); G. Moses, 'Proletarian labourers? East Riding farm servants *c.* 1850–75', *Agricultural History Review*, 47 (1999); A. J. Gritt, 'The census and the servant: a reassessment of the decline and distribution of farm service in early nineteenth-century England', *Economic History Review*, 53 (2000). There are a few indications among contemporaries that the 1834 abolition of yearly service as a 'head' of settlement led to slight recurrence of such hiring in some regions. For example, *Seventh and Eighth Reports from the Select Committee on Settlement, and Poor Removal*, XI (1847), p. 11, on Oxfordshire.

[86] 9 & 10 Vic., c. 66; 10 & 11 Vic., c. 110; and see 11 & 12 Vic., c. 110.

[87] 24 & 25 Vic., c. 55.

[88] 28 & 29 Vic., c. 79.

[89] Report from the *Select Committee on Poor Removal*, XII (1879), p. 3. The 1876 Act was the Divided Parishes and Poor Law Amendment Act, 39 & 40 Vic., c. 61.

1662, or of forty day residential settlements from 1662 to 1685.)[90] Irremovability was, especially prior to 1876, a different legal concept to settlement, and so one could be irremovable in one place (commonly a town one had migrated to), yet settled in another parish, either by having gained a settlement there in one's own right, or, increasingly among the poor in the nineteenth century, by virtue of paternal settlement. One significance of irremovability, of course, was that it served to reduce the importance of settlement, even though the latter concept survived, was reinforced in twentieth-century inter-war legislation, such as the Poor Law Act of 1930,[91] and indeed lasted right through to the National Assistance Act in 1948, which might be said to have created a national settlement.[92]

Figure 3.2 tries to capture the main elements of the system in c. 1870, following most of these changes. It shows interesting

[90] Earlier English and Welsh practice, while a complicated subject, had commonly involved birth or three-year residence. It is perhaps curious that 200 years of legal wrangling and enormous expense had by the 1860s in some ways returned the system to what it was before 1662. It is worth comparing the much less developed practice of Scotland. In that country, residence (where the poor 'have had their most common resort', or 'have most haunted' for the previous three years) had also been a requirement for parochial relief, although parentage, marriage or birth also made one eligible. A. Dunlop, *Parochial Law* (Edinburgh, 1841), pp. 375–90. The residence in Scotland did not have to be constant, but was rather the 'most common resort . . . his headquarters, as it were'. This was a weaker understanding of 'residence' than in England under the irremovability legislation. Many English overseers would probably have grimly appreciated the Scottish term 'haunting' in connection with pauper 'headquarters'. See also 8 & 9 Vic., c. 83 (1845), developing Scottish settlement, also summarised by Edward Willoby in *Select Committee on Poor Removal*, XIII (1855), p. 60. The Channel Islands had complex settlement regulations, on which see R.-M. Crossan, 'Guernsey, 1814–1914: migration in a modernising society' (Ph.D., University of Leicester, 2005). By comparison, Ireland had no settlement system.

[91] In the early twentieth century, see *The Minority Report of the Poor Law Commission. Part 1. The Break-up of the Poor Law* (London, 1909), pp. 401–5. On inter-war settlement, see E. J. Lidbetter, *Settlement and Removal* (London, 1932). As he pointed out, even in 1930 irremovability was still distinct from settlement, settlement by residence being a consequence of irremovability. *Ibid.*, pp. 11–12. On the continuity of the earlier 'heads' of settlement in the 1930 Act (marriage, parentage, residence, estate, apprenticeship, renting, payment of rates or taxes, etc.), see *ibid.*, pp. 41–3.

[92] 11 & 12 Geo. VI, c. 29. National settlement involved a national poor rate, which to many in the nineteenth century entailed the 'abolition of all local chargeability', which they thought 'would be absolutely ruinous'. See, for example, Mackay, *History of the English Poor Law*, pp. 355, 361–2; White, *Parochial Settlements*, p. 24; or see White's evidence in *Second and Third Reports from the Select Committee on Settlement, and Poor Removal*, XI (1847), p. 8. They argued this for reasons of financial prudence and accountability, public trust, and local obligation and attachment.

and significant shifts compared with figure 3.1. The decline in many regions of eligible yearly service and legally indentured apprenticeship, at least as institutions that conferred settlement,[93] had reduced the capacity of the poor to gain settlements in their own right. Whereas in the early eighteenth century, yearly servants had routinely gained a sequence of settlements, through their full yearly hirings from about the age of fourteen, by the mid-nineteenth century very many had never gained a settlement for themselves. They therefore took their father's settlement (unless they were married women, in which case they took their husband's settlement, which was increasingly that of his father or grandfather). The decline in some trades of indentured apprenticeships, noticeable from the mid-later eighteenth century as occupational 'job training' often took over without proper indentures, was also problematical for settlement.[94] Increasingly, therefore, more of the poor were residing in parishes where they were not settled. Their settlements came to bear less proximity to their recent employment locations. The major reductions in pauperism (falling poor expenditure per head of population, and a falling ratio of paupers to population) after the 1820s also contributed to this.[95]

Figure 3.2 accordingly shows a shrinkage in the lower half and width of the 'T' shape representing the settled inhabitants of this 'typical' parish as compared with figure 3.1. There are few statistics on this matter, but it is highly likely that by 1870 a smaller proportion of the lower classes were resident in their

---

[93] Yearly service continued in many regions, as I have pointed out elsewhere (*Annals of the Labouring Poor*, pp. 96–7), notably in the west and north, and in some areas of the south, but it often did so with small modifications, or with application to married people, making it ineligible for settlement. Historians who rightly point to such continuance often do not notice the precise links between service and settlement, and see how 'survival' of service in some areas was of a modified form of 'service' that (unlike its early modern equivalents) frequently did not impart settlement. With these problems in mind, and with resurrection in view, traditional yearly service was abolished as a 'head' of settlement in 1834. Among other results, that abolition tended 'to relieve the rich parishes at the expense of the poor [parishes]', badly affecting poorer unions like Fulham in London. *Select Committee on Irremovable Poor*, VII (1859), p. 13.

[94] K. D. M. Snell, 'The apprenticeship system in British history: the fragmentation of a cultural institution', *History of Education*, 25 (1996); Snell, *Annals of the Labouring Poor*, ch. 5.

[95] See figures 5.1 and 5.3, pp. 213, 216.

settlements compared with the eighteenth century.[96] Irremovability legislation from 1846 in effect acknowledged that, and major reductions in pauperism also indicate it. The proportion of the parish inhabitants that we should define as 'poor', and (for the sake of this discussion) as not being ratepayers, has also diminished compared with figure 3.1. This owed most to economic growth and considerable increases in *per capita* income, that were apparent to almost all commentators by 1870. The numbers of inhabitants who could be rated had grown considerably in many parishes by 1870, given the extension and well-being of manufacturing, retail, service, farming and other employment.[97] Rateable property and property values had grown. The landed area over which the rate could be levied had also expanded, through enclosure, drainage, cultivation of wastes, legal reforms and judicial interpretation. This relatively wider spreading of the poor rate, with lower poor expenditure per head of population compared with the 1790s to the 1830s,[98] and the gradual 'settling-down' of the new poor law after

---

[96] Figures on this issue are hard to come by, and vary greatly. The Poor Law Commission in 1832–4 asked towns 'What proportion of the labouring poor in your parish do you believe to be non-parishioners?' *Report from His Majesty's Commissioners on the Administration and Practical Operation of the Poor Laws. Appendix (B.2.). Part IV. Answers to Town Queries with Indices*, XXXVI (1834), query 42. This was seemingly taken to mean 'not having a settlement in the parish' (e.g. p. 154 i). 'A half' was the most common reply, and 'a third', 'two-thirds', 'a quarter' were very frequent replies. Some town parishes stated higher fractions than these. In St Benedict (Mdx), 'The whole of the labouring poor are non-parishioners.' *Ibid.*, p. 116 i. Later, more than three-quarters of the settled poor in the City of London union were said to be non-resident in their parishes of settlement. *First Report from the Select Committee on Settlement, and Poor Removal*, XI (1847), p. 19. See also *Second and Third Reports from the Select Committee on Settlement, and Poor Removal*, XI (1847), pp. 16–17: 'the great mass of the labouring classes are not living in the parish in which they are settled . . . the very great amount of non-resident relief shows that very strongly'. One might expect such proportions in rural parishes to have been lower than in towns, but see *ibid.*, p. 20, suggesting little difference between urban and rural parishes in this, because of 'the great difficulty in acquiring a settlement'. A contemporary table in White, *Parochial Settlements*, pp. 12–13, for the Blything Hundred in Suffolk (forty-six parishes incorporated together from the mid-1760s, and so perhaps not representative), indicates that 3,737 out of 12,531 residential poor were not settled (30 per cent).

[97] On the expansion of many such employments in the countryside in the nineteenth century, see especially E. A. Wrigley, 'Men on the land and men in the countryside: employment in agriculture in early-nineteenth-century England', in L. Bonfield, R. M. Smith and K. Wrightson (eds.), *The World We Have Gained: Histories of Population and Social Structure* (Oxford, 1986).

[98] See figure 5.1, p. 213.

the Andover scandal, were reasons why the poor law was becoming slightly less of a bone of public contention, as compared
with the heated debates and reform proposals earlier. The dwindling numbers and proportions of paupers, very apparent by
1870, due largely to economic growth and the deterrent new
poor law, are also shown in figure 3.2. While paupers had
comprised very sizeable proportions of some parish populations
in the very late eighteenth and early nineteenth centuries, they
were by comparison normally a marginalised and minor group
in 1870.

Figure 3.2 shows the effects of these developments in its deep-
ening of the span of 'property owners and ratepayers', and its
narrowing in settled poor. Immediately one senses that something remarkable has occurred affecting 'belonging' via settlement. There has been a major shift from the large numbers of
settled and thus 'belonging' poor (figure 3.1), who had numerically dominated many parishes in the decades of high pauperism (*c.* 1790–1840), when they had asserted their pre-emptive
'rights', posing a threat and obliging certain types of behaviour
from the upper ranks in parish society. That had given way to a
situation, by 1870, in which the 'poor' were numerically less
significant among those claiming through settlement to 'belong'.
The paupers were even less significant, having become (courtesy of the new poor law) highly marginalised and socially
disparaged, if not despised. The new poor law continued out-
door relief to most paupers, as we will see in chapter 5. Yet some
paupers who 'belonged' now found themselves excluded and
placed elsewhere, in the union workhouse. The poor were
eclipsed in figure 3.2 by the ratepaying classes, and it was now
those relatively well-to-do classes – not the poor – who dominated the 'belonging-via-settlement' inhabitants in parish society.

The social meaning and nexus of parish 'belonging' had thus
shifted. It had become more and more *difficult* for the poor to
gain settlements where they lived, and *easier* for slightly better-
off inhabitants to do so. This was largely because yearly service
had been abolished as a 'head' of settlement, while the other
'heads' of settlement had remained much the same. £10 renting
and property owning were now more accessible than earlier,
especially £10 renting in urban environments. The socio-
economic milieu of the law had changed, rendering the law

more specifically anachronistic to the poor. Such anachronism had been quietly and favourably received by many in the propertied classes who wished to resist extra settlements, and whose views were becoming more marked by middle-class sentiments and disdain. By contrast, many among the poor claimed that it was now impossible for them to gain a settlement. They were, so to speak, becoming cold-shouldered and by-passed through the deliberate failure to reform the law properly, and by middling to small-scale propertied interests who found that the remaining 'heads' of settlement suited their interests perfectly.

Renting above £10 and property ownership had greatly increased in significance as 'heads' of settlement, with trends in the local economy lifting ever more people to acquire settlements by those means. Rating *per se* had in effect been abolished as a head of settlement in 1795,[99] and this allowed new poor law administrators deliberately to extend ratepaying down the social scale, encouraging the rating of poorer people, partly to spread the rate, and partly in recognition of the widening scope of potential rating. It was argued that this deliberately brought about wider disparagement of pauperism. The loosely defined 'core' element in figure 3.2 has now much altered, and is shown expanded sideways within the enlarged property-owning and renting inhabitants, ceasing to be a multi-ranked rectangle of social depth (as in figure 3.1). It now only narrowly reached down into the poorer classes of parish society. Some among those poor still laid strong claims to 'belong' via settlement, ancestry, long association, employment, and other connected means, much as their more numerous equivalents had done fifty to a hundred years earlier (and they remained numerous in many southern parishes into the 1830s, 1840s, and sometimes after then). They laid claim for similar reasons of self-interest, insurance and emotion as their forebears. Further, because of the increasing frequency of inherited, paternal settlement (which was most pronounced among them, being much less true for higher classes) they felt even more cause to do so. Yet by 1870 they were reducing as a residential parish group, and in

[99] From 1795 only those renting £10 or more could gain a settlement by paying parish rates, and they already had a settlement by renting.

agricultural regions depopulation was weakening them still further. In the nineteenth century, and in enclosed parishes, the poor also found it hard (sometimes increasingly hard) to gain a foothold in a parish through property owning. Enclosure had closed off many forms of squatting, encroachment, and upward avenues of social advance through use of commons and wastes. By comparison, the propertied and £10 tenants had become the most numerically dominant and assertive portion of inhabitants who 'belonged' by settlement. In most English rural parishes these were no longer a relatively small elite. Such people already felt assured that they 'belonged' for reasons beyond legal settlement, because ownership, a stake in parish property, and paying significant local rates strongly enhanced their sense of belonging, producing such an effect for ever larger numbers of middle- and lower-middle-class people, as well as for the better-off among the skilled working class.

In other words, thinking through the issues of settlement and belonging, and without wishing to exaggerate the chronological contrast, we should conceive of some class or social shift in emphasis among those who resided and 'belonged' by settlement. The transition was from assertive proletarian majorities regularly prone to pauperism and claiming their old poor law parish 'rights' under the settlement laws, being elbowed aside numerically by more propertied or rated inhabitants, who 'belonged' by virtue of their lower-middle- or middle-class propertied attributes. These naturally accepted settlement as yet another badge of their belonging, precedence, local attachment, and pride in place, even if they believed (unlike many among the poor) that they would never require poor relief. They were classes that were often key players in parish administration, especially from the 1830s. One thinks, for example, of their roles in the new poor law, as parish office-holders of continuing importance (as we will see in chapter 6 on overseers), in the Church of England at parish level among those who remained Anglican, or in the circles of religious Nonconformity. In chapter 8 we will find such classes numerously asserting themselves to be 'of this parish' on their gravestones in the mid- and late nineteenth century. Issues about belonging and the continued vitality of parish life in the second half of the nineteenth century thus need to focus especially upon these middling classes, and on the connections between 'belonging' and property.

The other main development shown in figure 3.2 can be seen in the lower right hand side of that figure. These were the 'irremovable poor', following the 1846 and subsequent legislation.[100] In this figure, they bear some slight resemblance to the certificate holders of an earlier era: both were irremovable in some circumstances; both were settled elsewhere; but there was otherwise no linkage or continuity between the two groups. A sizeable gap of half a century of legal and poor law practice separated them, and in administrative terms they were quite different. The irremovable poor could not now be removed to their parish or township of settlement, and unlike the eighteenth-century certificate holders this was the case even when they were chargeable, although they retained their settlement as a legal entitlement. They came to assume ever larger predominance among parish populations from the mid-nineteenth century. Ever more people became irremovable, as the length of residence required for that status diminished through successive Acts of Parliament. Further related Acts affected those from outside Wales and England, notably the Irish residing in Welsh and English towns and cities. Irremovability generated endless legal argument. It brought with it predictable ambivalences, and sometimes ideas of dual or 'multiple' belonging. Did one 'belong' to one's settlement, or to one's parish of irremovability? Where (it was now asked) was one entitled to parish charities?[101] One could now legally 'belong' to two places, especially if one was poor, albeit in different ways. There was no consensus about which place should assume predominance in people's minds. W. D. Salter, the clerk to

---

[100] This concept was felt to be new at the time, but there was in fact some precedent for it after 1662. While the term was not used, one could be 'irremovable' in the past in certain circumstances, but not gain a settlement. Earlier examples would be a servant in employment, but who in due course did not serve out the year, or an illegitimate child with its mother for nurture, or a certificate person, or (from 1723) a person residing on a purchased property under £30 in value. By such residence these people were irremovable, but they would not have gained a settlement. Other than with regard to certificates, I have not made any slight adjustments to figure 3.1 to take account of such cases.

[101] *First Report from the Select Committee on Settlement, and Poor Removal*, XI (1847), pp. 13, 61, 65.

the Fulham union, was asked by a Select Committee in 1859: 'They feel a certain comfort in belonging to the parish?—Yes; they feel that that is their home, as they call it; their place of settlement, although it is not so.'[102] In this case, Salter was talking about the place where the poor had gained five-year irremovability under the 1846 Act. He believed that 'their home' was their settlement, not the parish from which they had become irremovable. Others interpreted the situation the other way, highlighting the place of irremovability. There seems not to have been any class predilection to construe this issue one way or the other.

In any parish, where many people knew each other, rival forms of 'belonging' now became even more complicated than hitherto. As implicit in the divisions in the bottom half of figure 3.2, these were issues that were most contentious among the poor, rather than between classes. Leaving aside many cultural and status divisions within 'the poor', which were very important – and arguably becoming more so with the growth of Nonconformity, and as ideas of respectability and the stigma of pauperism gathered pace – there were now three essential divisions *vis-à-vis* belonging: the settled, the irremovable, and those who were neither. Then there were the paupers, similarly divided.

Further, as a separate and significant group in popular mentalities at this time, there were the Irish: aspiring to achieve irremovability, sometimes lodged in urban ghettos which they were apprehensive about quitting, as that might undermine their irremovability. If one gained irremovability, and then moved to reside elsewhere, that irremovable status ceased to have legal effect.[103] One could then be removed back to one's settlement, and lacking a settlement one could be removed to Ireland, a country of which many Irish had Famine memories untouched by nostalgia. Some Irish were removed back to Ireland after thirty to fifty-five years' residence in England: 'a gross act of inhumanity and hardship', commented one member of a Select Committee.[104]

---

[102] *Select Committee on Irremovable Poor*, VII (1859), p. 10.
[103] *Ibid.*, p. 10.
[104] *Select Committee on Poor Removal*, XII (1879), p. 33.

The concept of irremovability, and its practice between 1846 and 1865, thus conduced to urban ghettos, ethnic cohesion, and non-integration. It was a paradox of irremovability legislation, that it was introduced into a poor law system ostensibly designed to expedite labour mobility, to enforce political economy; but it had the effect in many urban areas of making the poor wary of moving out of the towns, in case they lost their irremovable status. For example, it was said by T. Bushfield (chairman of the Whitechapel guardians), about the Spitalfields silk weavers, that the law of settlement

makes these people cling to their own localities, where they consider that they have a perfect right to go and ask for relief. We have many charities in the parish of Spitalfields, and the people object to leave, indeed they will not leave the parish, they consider that they lose a right by leaving it . . . with respect to the poor themselves where they feel that they have what they call a legitimate claim, they will hang there and remain there.[105]

A move from one urban parish to another broke one's irremovability, and this was a problem in towns where there were many small parishes.[106] It was also an issue in slum clearances. Even so, the urban irremovable poor grew ever larger as a category, and British rural depopulation occurred like a ratchet mechanism, with urban irremovability hindering the chances of rural return. This set England and Wales apart from many European countries. After all, the 1846 Act had been passed to restrict the urban poor returning to their rural settlements in times of trade depression. The Irish in particular were often thought to adopt such stick-in-the-tenement urban attitudes, understandably because of their vulnerability to removal back to Ireland.[107] It could be argued that this residential consolidation of the urban poor fostered the growth of an urban working class. Yet settlement practice, with its insider–outsider divisions and notions of rival belonging and benefits, persistently disposed against a unified working class. We shall also see

---

[105] *Select Committee on Irremovable Poor*, VII (1859), p. 82.
[106] *Select Committee on Poor Removal*, XVII (1854), p. 449, evidence of John Harrop, clerk to the Manchester guardians.
[107] *Select Committee on Irremovable Poor*, VII (1859), pp. 10–11.

this in subsequent chapters. Indeed, if conscious motivation on this subject among law-makers was involved, which is questionable, settlement reform could hardly have been better designed to disuniting ends, while it also united the enlarging propertied classes, as shown in figure 3.2.

As a matter for everyday conversation – 'where do you belong?' – the settled poor were usually aware of who shared their own status, of the non-settled and irremovable poor, and of the aspirant poor who lacked either claim. Some among the latter sought to establish irremovability for themselves, just as did the Irish, and sometimes suffered great hardship in doing so. This was because in order to gain irremovability, the normal interpretation was that one had to be continuously resident for the required period without claiming poor relief. That fitted well with the deterrent principles of the new poor law. Settlement was persistently supported in the eighteenth and nineteenth centuries as a deterrence against poor relief applications, which is one reason why it survived so long.[108] Countless relief applications were abandoned when it became clear that a removal would ensue.[109] Many in the ratepaying classes, sometimes informed or assisted by the local poor, sought to prevent people becoming irremovable, mainly to protect the poor rates, because they knew that people could then claim relief without fear of removal. People were sometimes removed after four years' residence, to stop five years being obtained.

Avoiding irremovability was a recurrent theme in urban landlord policy, just as avoiding settlements had earlier been in rural English landlord policy. Thus we see re-run, from the 1840s, the older debates about exclusion and the formation or perpetuation of 'open'–'close' parishes, but now in novel legal ways, and usually in urban contexts. For on top of *settlement* and its prevention – motives that continued – one now also had

---

[108] 'The poor will put up with a considerable privation, if they have anything to keep them in a particular locality, rather than subject themselves to the chance of removal.' *First Report from the Select Committee on Settlement, and Poor Removal*, xi (1847), p. 37.

[109] *Report from His Majesty's Commissioners on the Administration and Practical Operation of the Poor Laws. Appendix (B.2.). Part IV. Answers to Town Queries with Indices*, xxxvi (1834), pp. 164 i, 174 i, 175 i (fear of removal also being used to keep people diligent and the Irish 'in order'); *Select Committee on Irremovable Poor*, xvii (1860), p. 64, evidence of James Corder, clerk to the Birmingham guardians.

irremovability and its prevention. Issues of discrimination and precedence inevitably arose as to entitlement, both within and between groups of the English poor, and between the poor by British country of origin. Who belonged most, and how, and why? How should the respective groups be treated? Inevitably, in any system of parish and local entitlement, that took ratepayers' resources, and which external people laid claim to so as to diminish or dilute the local benefits, questions of local self-protection and exclusion arose. These were linked to ideas of insiders and belonging in complex ways, and the resulting processes and struggles perpetuated ideas of local belonging, enhancing solidarity among those who belonged. 'Excluding the poor', and how that was done, will therefore take up the remainder of this chapter, while issues of policy 'discrimination' will be considered in chapter 5 on out-relief and the new poor law.

EXCLUDING THE POOR

It is well known that the division between 'open' and 'close' parishes owed a great deal to the settlement laws. Historians have much debated such parish classifications, providing real insights into the comparative nature of rural communities.[110]

---

[110] Among the literature on 'open' and 'close' parishes is D. Mills, 'English villages in the eighteenth and nineteenth centuries: a sociological approach', *Amateur Historian*, 6 (1963–5); A. Everitt, *The Pattern of Rural Dissent: The Nineteenth Century* (Leicester, 1972); B. A. Holderness, '"Open" and "close" parishes in England in the eighteenth and nineteenth centuries', *Agricultural History Review*, 20 (1972); G. Darley, *Villages of Vision* (London, 1975); D. Mills, 'The geographical effects of the laws of settlement in Nottinghamshire: an analysis of Francis Howell's report, 1848', in his (ed.), *English Rural Communities: The Impact of a Specialised Economy* (London, 1978); D. Mills, *Lord and Peasant in Nineteenth-century Britain* (London, 1980); M. A. Havinden, 'The model village', in G. E. Mingay (ed.), *The Victorian Countryside*, vol. II (London, 1981); D. Mills and B. M. Short, 'Social change and social conflict in nineteenth-century England: the use of the open–closed village model', *Journal of Peasant Studies*, 10 (1983), also in M. Reed and R. Wells (eds.), *Class, Conflict and Protest in the English Countryside, 1700–1880* (London, 1990); T. Williamson and L. Bellamy, *Property and Landscape: A Social History of Land Ownership and the English Countryside* (London, 1987), esp. pp. 161–4; S. Banks, 'Nineteenth-century scandal or twentieth-century model? A new look at "open" and "close" parishes', *Economic History Review*, 41 (1988); Snell, 'Settlement, poor law and the rural historian'; C. Rawding, 'Society and place in nineteenth-century north Lincolnshire', *Rural History*, 3 (1992); D. Spencer, 'Reformulating the "closed" parish thesis: associations, interests, and interaction', *Journal of Historical Geography*, 26 (2000); K. D. M. Snell and P. S. Ell, *Rival Jerusalems:*

Questions have arisen about whether 'open'–'close' divisions of rural parishes may be applied as a predictive model to anticipate related features of parish life (such as religion, landownership, the local labour market, poor law policy, population growth, or housing controls), and many historians have pointed to the majority of parishes that lay towards the middle of an 'open'–'close' spectrum. Even so, nobody disputes that some parishes operated the settlement laws fairly ruthlessly, excluding many outsiders, inhibiting their settlements, and so protecting parish or township poor rates and other resources. Many other parishes, and perhaps most rural ones in the eighteenth century, operated in a selective manner, often targeting newly arrived non-settled poor who were paupers or whose predicaments showed them to be very close to poor law dependency. My account thus far has concentrated upon characteristics that were largely shared across parishes, taking 'archetypical' features, and dealing with categories of 'belonging' as judged through the settlement laws. Although no one should underestimate the diversity of parishes, we have seen from two broad diagrammatic models how such categories changed over time. The discussion can now turn to practices of 'excluding the poor'. We need to observe how barriers could be erected against vulnerable parochial incomers, so as to limit those who might gain settlements or irremovability status, or alternatively, in more 'open' parishes, to accept certain outsiders and allow them to settle, and thus to concede or encourage industrial or other expansion in the parochial economy.

The certification system has been partially discussed above. Before 1795, asking for a certificate was one way to hinder a person's settlement, although it was never a firm guarantee that the person would not gain one. Among newly arrived people in a parish, only the poorer or indigent newcomers would be asked to obtain one, as others could void a certificate by obtaining a

The Geography of Victorian Religion (Cambridge, 2000), ch. 11, and see the references there. Among contemporary reports, see *Select Committee on Settlement and Poor Removal*, VIII, XI (1847); *Report of George Coode to the Poor Law Board on the Law of Settlement and Removal of the Poor*, XXVI (1851); *Select Committee on Irremovable Poor*, VII (1859); *Report on the Employment of Women and Children in Agriculture*, XVII (1867–8); *Report on the Employment of Children, Young Persons, and Women in Agriculture*, XIII (1868–9).

settlement by estate, or by contracting to rent a tenement worth £10 or more per annum.[111] That involved a rent of 3–4 s. a week, or less in some cases, the kind of sum that a poor artisan or better-off labourer might pay in the later eighteenth century. Parishes operating such a policy, and looking out for arrivals of vulnerable people, were usually very prompt in asking for a certificate.[112] This was because the certificate would thenceforth help to save them from settlements being gained by the person, his dependants or any servant or apprentice. Some migrants, knowing where they were moving to, asked and obtained certificates from their home parish before leaving, and carried them with them, delivering them to the overseer, but this was probably very rare, especially after the mid-eighteenth century. Some others were asked to obtain a certificate if they became chargeable, or looked likely to become so, to avoid removal to their settlement. This was probably the most common reason for certificates. These documents then sometimes facilitated the payment of non-resident relief from the settlement to the place of residence. Recent poor law historiography has demonstrated how important this non-resident relief was under the old poor law.[113] Indeed, it aided labour mobility to districts of emerging

---

[111] Until 1819, the property had to be *worth* £10 per annum. A rent of under that might still deliver a settlement if the property's value was deemed to be £10. A tenancy contract was sufficient, and one did not have to pay such a rent for a full year. From 1819 (59 Geo. III, c. 50), which was too late to have relevance to certificates, the tenement had to be occupied for a whole year, and the sum actually paid was crucial.

[112] This pre-1795 aspect of settlement was stressed by N. Landau, 'The laws of settlement and surveillance of immigration in eighteenth-century Kent', *Continuity and Change*, 3 (1988). I have myself emphasised 'the rapidity of local authorities' action against those felt to be a potential encumbrance on the rates'. Snell, *Annals of the Labouring Poor*, p. 18; reprinted with further clarification as 'Agricultural seasonal unemployment, the standard of living, and women's work, 1690–1860', in P. Sharpe (ed.), *Women's Work: The English Experience, 1650–1914* (London, 1998), pp. 74–5. However, in this and similar articles, it seems to me that Landau exaggerated the 'monitoring' effectiveness of settlement, the use of certificates, and the significance of the 1795 Act, and was incorrect in treating settlement as outside and detached from the poor law, a subject that she hardly mentioned. By contrast, *all* contemporaries and other historians stress the crucial and defining connections between settlement and the poor law. A balanced outline and diagram of poor law and supervisory options is in my 'Settlement, poor law and the rural historian', pp. 146–60.

[113] Taylor, 'A different kind of Speenhamland'; J. S. Taylor, '"Set down in a large manufacturing town": sojourning poor in early nineteenth-century Manchester', *Manchester Region History Review*, 3 (1989); Taylor, 'Voices in the crowd'; Sokoll (ed.), *Essex Pauper Letters*; Sokoll, 'Negotiating a living'; S. King, '"It is impossible

industrialisation, being a hidden welfare subsidy from rural parishes to industrial ones, even sometimes within the same union. That form of rural–urban subsidy continued long after 1795 into the new poor law, when it was legitimated under certain conditions.[114] It then persisted into the post-1846 era of irremovability, for example as subsidies to those who lacked irremovable status. It was in the interests of parishes to grant it to their absent paupers, and even to conceal it (as receipt of relief could interrupt irremovability), so as to facilitate settled people becoming irremovable elsewhere.[115]

Parishes did not *have* to grant a certificate to anyone. As we have seen, many, perhaps most, refused to do so. They were motivated by the thought that it would tend legally to attach that person or some of his descendants to them for longer than might be necessary, sometimes indeed for over a century.[116] It would supply evidence of settlement with them in any inter-parish dispute at Quarter Sessions, and such disputes were very numerous throughout the eighteenth and nineteenth centuries. Yet such parishes might not wish to lose certain individuals. They might for that reason refuse a certificate to skilled artisans or others desiring to move, even though that would not stop

---

for our Vestry to judge his case into perfection from here": managing the distance dimensions of poor relief, 1800–1840', *Rural History*, 16 (2005).

[114] From 1834 no relief was meant to be given to anyone not residing in a parish of the union, unless that person was receiving such relief when the union was formed, in which case there was to be enquiry about whether it should be continued. In other words, the Poor Law Amendment Act acknowledged non-resident relief and agreed to it in certain circumstances, and so warranted its continuance. The 1834 Report had shown this practice to be widespread, and in some cases extreme. For example, St Andrew by the Wardrobe (Mdx) replied to the Town Queries by saying that 'Nearly the whole of the poor relieved by this parish live out of it; perhaps not more than four reside in the parish.' *Report from His Majesty's Commissioners on the Administration and Practical Operation of the Poor Laws. Appendix (B.2.). Part IV. Answers to Town Queries with Indices*, XXXVI (1834), p. 114 i. Subsequently, many poor law unions had large registers documenting non-resident relief, showing it being given to many people, seemingly regardless of personal precedent before 1834.

[115] It should be noted that some commentators saw the 1846–7 Acts as reducing non-resident relief, and putting the poor more at risk of being removed, mainly because parishes where the poor resided (though settled elsewhere) saw non-resident relief as a means whereby such poor might gain irremovability. *First Report from the Select Committee on Settlement, and Poor Removal*, XI (1847), p. 7; *Second and Third Reports from the Select Committee on Settlement, and Poor Removal*, XI (1847), p. 15.

[116] In one legal brief in the Daventry Collection, a certificate dated 1737 was used as evidence in a settlement case of 1843. Vialls, 'Laws of settlement', pp. 220–5.

their migration, and being certificate-less might even make it easier for them to gain a settlement elsewhere. Such artisans with parish settlement had almost certainly been apprenticed locally, thus often gaining their settlement, and so this also involved keeping people the parish had trained. Through much of the eighteenth and nineteenth centuries, certain trades (blacksmith, cordwainer, tailor, wheelwright, thatcher, butcher, baker, etc.) were indispensable to almost every parish, and in many ways parishes needed to be skill-subsistent. So a parish could try to hold on to useful individuals, who it had trained, even though such people might leave regardless of such attitudes.[117]

A certificate or its refusal, in other words, could serve many ends, encompassing diverse parish policies: as a partial barrier to settlement; as a hindrance to a favoured parishioner gaining a settlement elsewhere; as an excuse to remove someone; as a marker of a particular kind of 'outsider–insider' or 'sojourner'; as indicating someone who (denied or lacking a certificate) was an 'outsider' eligible for 'insider' status via easier settlement attainment; as a partial security against the risk of vagrancy charges being brought; as a ticket of 'belonging'; as a family heirloom attesting to paternal belonging; as a way of differentiating separate internal groups of the poor; as a policy indicator of parish ties to favoured other parishes in the region. Its refusal could be a sign of dislike for certain parishes, or a way of extracting non-resident relief, and thus of allowing outsiders or sojourners to remain resident, or could signal other motives. There were many further possibilities. We can thus see how complex a 'game' this was, designed and locally adapted by law-makers in the later seventeenth century, who were attuned to sophisticated political or social game-playing, with multiple motives being possible. Furthermore, settlement was played out through independently minded justices, parish officers,

---

[117] One can think of many parallels in motivation affecting training, transferable skills, reference writing and retainment policy among modern employers, although it would be anachronistic to do so. While a certificate was not a 'reference' in any modern sense, the decision on whether to grant one could involve some comparable personal judgements. On such issues and comparisons affecting skilled training over time, see my 'The apprenticeship system in British history', and the more modern references there, especially G. Becker, *Human Capital: A Theoretical and Empirical Analysis, with Special Reference to Education* (New York, 1964).

migrants and paupers – all the pieces on this local game board could move independently, of their own volition.

The roles of the paupers and poor people also need to be stressed. For, contrary to some accounts, migrants and paupers were not passive pawns shifted, blocked, monitored or sacrificed, in predictable uni-directional ways, by politicised chess-playing JPs or parish officers. As their letters 'home' indicate, poor people *themselves* had varied leeway for action, movement, selective recall, or moral and economic pressure. Many of them behaved in a wilful and determined way, fixed on their supposed 'rights', and were sometimes hardly amenable to control or persuasion by any authorities.[118] They felt themselves to be justified by their own notions of the law, by their own 'moral economy of belonging'.[119] All this had a crucial bearing upon how, where, and why people 'belonged', and the complex motivations that resulted. Such 'belonging' occurred within the legal frameworks, as well as within the context of other socio-economic, kinship and cultural considerations. These framed and nestled the nature of local attachment, and affected how people were perceived (and perceived themselves) in terms of insider–outsider divisions and sub-groups of belonging.

The formal way to eject the poor was by a removal order, through the powers granted in 1662 and subsequently. Up to 1795, a parish or township could remove anyone who was likely to be chargeable, or was actually chargeable. To be chargeable meant being a burden involving formal payment by the overseer from the rates.[120] 'Casual' relief was not included

---

[118] For one example among many, see the case in 1831 of Elizabeth Harbour in Brighton, determined to return to Worth, regardless of any persuasion to the contrary. Pilbeam and Nelson (eds.), *Poor Law Records of Mid Sussex*, p. 383.

[119] Compare E. P. Thompson's disinclination to allow his concept of the 'moral economy' to be extended to the poor law and settlement, in his *Customs in Common* (1991, Harmondsworth, 1993), pp. 339–40. In fact, his concept of 'moral economy' would have been considerably strengthened if he had been more receptive on this issue, and I would still advocate its extension to popular understandings of settlement, the poor law and belonging. However, as we saw in chapter 2, concepts of local belonging and settlement do not fit easily with Thompson's insistence on the role of class, which is presumably why he had to define his moral economy so narrowly. A 'moral economy' that integrated stronger senses of local belonging, while being entirely compatible with contemporary evidence 'from below', would clearly have weakened Thompson's arguments on the making of the working class.

[120] Nolan, *Treatise of the Laws* (1808 edn), pp. 195–7; H. Davey, *Poor Law Settlement (Local Chargeability) and Removal* (1908, London, 1925), p. 6; J. F. Symonds, J. Scholefield and

here.[121] From 1795 only those actually chargeable could be removed, although pregnant women (and some vagrant cases)
were deemed to be in that category, regardless of whether
overseers had paid them anything (such was the perceived
vulnerability of those women).[122] 'Likely to be chargeable'
meant having a strong probability of that.[123] Before 1795 one
could not, for example, remove those renting to a combined £10
yearly value (they only had to *contract* to pay it, for whether it
was actually paid or not was immaterial), servants or those
contracted in employment, apprentices, soldiers, militiamen,
certificated members of friendly societies, office-holders, anybody paying public taxes or levies of any sort, and property or
'tenement' owners, however small. Furthermore, there was a
very wide definition indeed of 'tenement' which applied here.
'Anything is a tenement which is a profit out of the land.'[124] 'It
signifies any thing that may be *holden*.'[125] This included any
freehold, copyhold or leasehold interest by-law or purchase,[126]
offices, rents, a franchise, an advowson, a peerage, a right of
common, a mine, market toll, tithe, grass of a meadow, a fishery
or a stake in one, a cattle-gate in a stinted pasture, the right to
depasture cattle on a common, the rent of a cow, or anything
involving a mortgage, having an equitable interest, having a
right to property by descent, and so on. All this covered any
interest 'in a tenement of *ever so little value*'.[127] In fact, contemporaries spoke of the settlement laws as dealing with those
making 'a vagrant intrusion into a parish in which the party
has nothing of *his own*'.[128] Furthermore, before 1819 such
a 'tenement' did not have to be in one's own parish of

G. R. Hill, *The Law of Settlement and Removal, with a Collection of Statutes* (1882, London,
1903), p. 3; Taylor, *Poverty, Migration, and Settlement*, p. 21.

[121] There are legal and technical reasons for doubting how real the documentary distinction in removal orders was between 'likely to be chargeable' and actually chargeable, partly because the only necessity to state a person as actually chargeable was in
cases of certification, and other cases may have gone into *pro forma* default.

[122] Archbold, *The Poor Law*, p. 590.

[123] Burn, *Justice of the Peace* (1764 edn), vol. III, p. 123; Burn, *Justice of the Peace* (1814 edn),
vol. IV, p. 687.

[124] Nolan, *Treatise of the Laws* (1808 edn), vol. I, pp. 498, 503.

[125] *Ibid.*, p. 497 (his italics).

[126] *Ibid.*, pp. 492–8.

[127] *Ibid.*, pp. 549–50 (his italics).

[128] *Ibid.*, pp. 287, 493, 549–50, 563, and vol. II, pp. 2, 92.

residence;[129] it could be outside it, indeed, a long distance away, and thus difficult for parish officers to disprove.

Legal circumstances, local economies and customs brought into view many options here. The settlement stipulations make it plain that only the very poor and vulnerable would be removable as 'likely to be chargeable': those without any contract of service, employment or apprenticeship, or any stake definable as a 'tenement' in or outside the parish economy. No doubt some viable and independent labourers were unnecessarily removed as 'likely to be chargeable', and cases are known where the person objected to this. Yet a strong indication of the agrarian seasonality of unemployment emerges from examinations and removal orders (the documents are mutually reinforcing on this),[130] and this seasonal unemployment is confirmed by patterns of overseers' seasonal expenditure, by farm and estate accounts, and by contemporary comment on the vulnerable poor and practices of removal. Settlement was well attuned to regional circumstances, to the varied employment contracts for single and married people in skilled or unskilled occupations – yearly contracts in many artisan trades were eligible for settlement – to local apprenticeship traditions, to the differences in what was understood as a 'tenement', and to local forms of tenure, common right, renting, and so on.

In these respects, 'belonging' via settlement was not a condition legally imposed from on high to a national uniform standard, prescribing a set of general strict criteria. The legislation and judicial interpretations of the 'heads' of settlement were flexible, hugely elaborated in legal manuals, and adapted to local conditions. 'Belonging' in this system meant to belong to a very local unit – the parish or township – and for a century or more after 1662 it usually meant to belong via local usage, conditions and criteria. Much of the legal disputation involved questions of how local criteria fitted into the national legal framework, and such disputes sometimes involved parishes operating with certain presumptions, and challenging the local

---

[129] Such arrangements *vis-à-vis* renting for £10 were tightened up by 59 Geo. III, c. 50 (1819).
[130] Snell, *Annals of the Labouring Poor*, pp. 19–22, 147–59.

usage and legal inferences of other parishes. One senses this in the multiple understandings of 'tenement' indicated above. Such local usage and conditions are evident in thousands of settlement examinations from different regions. How one might gain effective 'irremovability' or a settlement could vary greatly, from, let us say, a fisherman in Hastings who owned a net-mending shed, to a 'free' coalminer in the Forest of Dean with a stake in a coal 'gale' or with the right to graze sheep in the Forest, to a livery-servant spending most time in Bath, to an apprentice to a migratory brush-maker who had served forty days of her term in a certain place, to a sempstress sub-tenanting a few rooms in St Martin-in-the-Fields, to a shepherd in the Westmorland hills with the right to depasture twenty sheep of his own, and so on, through infinite occupational and district possibilities. Whatever one's local circumstances – and they were often very local, customary and distinctive – legal conditions were such as normally to allow them to be slotted into and gain one eligibility under the settlement laws, in many cases preventing one's removal and gaining one a settlement. This was especially so before the laws became more anachronistic to the changing circumstances and new economic conditions of the poor in the nineteenth century.

Anyone who fulfilled these criteria and was not chargeable could refuse to be examined as to settlement, and, unless there was obvious doubt about their claims, few overseers would force the issue further. They would be wasting their time and putting their parish to unnecessary expense by doing so. For some eighteenth-century incomers, overseers might well try to obtain a certificate, but here they had to act very quickly because in many of these cases the person would gain a settlement in forty days. (Indeed, that was true of any incomer between 1662 and 1685, when one could gain a settlement simply by forty days' residency.) Taking an examination with a view to trying to extract a certificate, which sometimes happened, needed to be done promptly upon arrival. After all, a person's family members, servant or apprentice(s) might otherwise gain their own settlements.[131] An apprentice only had to serve forty days

---

[131] Nolan, *Treatise of the Laws* (1808 edn), vol. I, pp. 286–7.

in a parish to achieve that, and other major categories were also exempt from the post-1685 need to publish notice so as to achieve settlement after forty days.[132] In cases of indigence, occasional relief recipiency, non-resident relief and so on, the process of examination, removal and/or certification was again quite urgent upon a poor person's arrival, especially as a claim to settlement might subsequently be made on the basis of relief having been given, which was sometimes taken as an acknowledgement of settlement. However, if the person was not immediately chargeable or needing casual relief, and lacked dependants who might gain a settlement within forty days, such settlement business could be conducted in slacker seasons, when unemployment rose, and so when personal circumstances worsened.[133]

The examination as to settlement commonly took place at petty sessions before two justices, although one often finds it before one justice, which was legally acceptable in cases of illness, infirmity, old age, when it was risky to move someone, for upland townships where justices were less available, or for draft examinations.[134] One justice could act in vagrancy cases (against which there could be no Quarter Sessions appeal), increasing the chances of a vagrancy charge in certain areas. Many people could be accused of begging, or otherwise contravening vagrancy legislation – some were even incited to

---

[132] *Ibid.*, pp. 202–3, vol. II, p. 10.

[133] One occasionally finds examination and removal of groups of people at the same time, which is only to be expected after the harvest or other work-intensive periods. Irish harvest workers, for example, were sometimes removed as groups after the harvest, as they sometimes pooled their resources, sent them back to Ireland with one person, and then declared themselves in need of relief. C. J. Ribton-Turner, *A History of Vagrants and Vagrancy, and Beggars and Begging* (London, 1887), ch. 12, esp. pp. 282ff. Examination and removal of groups was, however, considered to be 'highly scandalous' by contemporaries, and their horrified reaction to it makes clear that it was a rare occurrence outside larger towns. Anon., 'Inquiries with respect to the progress and state of pauperism in England since the reign of Queen Elizabeth', *Edinburgh Review* (May 1828), p. 314, citing Mr Whitworth in the 28 April 1773 debate in the House of Commons on vexatious removals. Most rural parishes in fact experienced only about one to two removals each year. The numbers were often much larger in urban parishes.

[134] Of seventy examinations for Painswick (Gloucestershire), to take a published example, seventeen were signed by a single justice. Styles, 'Evolution of the law of settlement', p. 59 n. 89. For other examples, see Taylor, *Poverty, Migration, and Settlement*, pp. 43, 74.

beg – and were then removed as vagrants to their settlement.[135] Some people were given relief after 1795 deliberately to allow them to be removed. Many options were open to the parish. It could remove the pauper,[136] as is clear from countless removal orders signed on the same day as the examination. Notice of removal did not have to occur in the eighteenth century, and many parishes said during disputes that they never gave it. A period of twenty-one days' notice was insisted upon from 1834, reinforced in 1848, allowing the receiving parish time to appeal against the removal.[137] The examination and removal order could trigger a formal removal; or the pauper could move voluntarily, either back to the settlement, or elsewhere; or the parish of settlement could issue a certificate to allow the person to remain where s/he was; and/or there could be non-resident relief paid by the settlement, an agreement being entered into for that. Non-resident relief became very common in the late eighteenth century, and throughout the nineteenth century, and some historians (including myself) suspect that it was frequent much earlier, even though evidence has rarely survived for it. Non-resident relief was noted in Cambridgeshire as early as 1619, with a settlement certificate in one case (for 1690) 'offering to remove or "defray the charge" . . . obviously issued with the same principle in the background'. 'By the beginning of the

---

[135] Vagrancy legislation during this period made it possible to class the following as types of 'vagrant': ill-disposed persons in public places, unlicensed persons dealing in lottery tickets, beggars, 'lewd women' with an illegitimate child, those concealing a birth or abandoning a child, gypsy pretenders, anyone leaving or threatening to leave their family, those refusing to work, fortune tellers, unlicensed pedlars, unauthorised strolling players, persons obtaining money under false pretences, prostitutes, nightwalkers, alms gatherers, stage players, gamblers in an unlawful game, those refusing to maintain themselves, those returning after removal, suspected thieves, weapon carriers under suspicion, poachers or presumed poachers found in woods or parks with an instrument to trap game, or escaped prisoners. Others could be added. In other words, it was often possible to use vagrancy legislation to target indigent, vulnerable or morally dubious people who fell outside the possibility of action under the settlement laws, or who it was easiest to deal with as vagrants.

[136] The subjects of all removal cases in the eighteenth and nineteenth centuries – whether chargeable or likely to be chargeable – were termed 'paupers' by contemporaries. The instructions in the removal order addressed to the overseers of another parish always addressed and treated the removed persons as a charge upon the poor laws. A removal order was in every case an order of maintenance. Nolan, *Treatise of the Laws* (1808 edn), vol. ii, pp. 70–1, 214, 229, 575.

[137] 4 & 5 Wm IV, c. 76, s. 79; 11 & 12 Vic., c. 31.

eighteenth century the system [non-resident relief] was common in all parts' of Cambridgeshire, although relief to 'non-residents' expanded notably in the later eighteenth century.[138] In many cases non-resident relief accompanied settlement certification.

When a removal was appealed to Quarter Sessions, the costs to each parish could rise enormously. Many contemporaries, like James Shaw, complained about 'endless and expensive litigation on the subject of settlement and removal of the poor'.[139] If a parish did not challenge a removal, then its effect was binding upon it. Indeed, a duplicate order was meant to be deposited with the clerk of the peace as a record of settlement when there was no appeal against it.[140] Appeals to Quarter Sessions could also be made by removed persons, as well as by receiving parishes.[141] Almost all parishes had lawyers they turned to for advice in settlement disputes. While most legal papers have long since been destroyed, their survival for some legal practices is absolutely huge, and their numbers mean that these remain largely uncatalogued.[142] They are testimony to the intensity of parish settlement disputes, to their cost, and to the incidence of such confrontations, which often took up a third to a half of Quarter Session business in the eighteenth and early nineteenth centuries. Appeals were held by the Sessions for the county where the removing parish was. Some historians have written about how 'the battles between parishes were pursued with all the bitterness and ruthlessness of tribal warfare', even between very proximate parishes.[143] Network analysis of the patterns of settlement disputes between parishes, using court order

---

[138] Hampson, 'Settlement and removal in Cambridgeshire', p. 287. Or see Styles, 'Evolution of the law of settlement', pp. 62–3, on non-resident relief occurring between Alcester and Claverdon (Warws.) in 1693.

[139] Shaw, *Parochial Lawyer*, p. 179.

[140] Nolan, *Treatise of the Laws* (1808 edn), vol. II, pp. 26, 91, 327.

[141] *Ibid.*, p. 244; Shaw, *Parochial Lawyer*, p. 205; Burn, *Justice of the Peace*, vol. IV, p. 708.

[142] I consulted some of these collections for *Annals of the Labouring Poor*, but they often have massive numbers of documents which remain largely unresearched. A good example is the so-called 'Daventry Collection', in Northants. CRO, much of it uncatalogued because of its enormous size, including many barristers' briefs on settlement cases, and partially studied by Christine Vialls for her 'Laws of settlement'. It is even clear from surviving case papers in solicitors' collections, such as the Daventry collection, that the same legal practice sometimes acted for both parishes in a dispute.

[143] B. Osborne, *Justices of the Peace, 1361–1848* (Shaftesbury, 1960), p. 188, and see my chapter 2, pp. 66–71.

books, suggests that recriminations between parishes were self-perpetuating, seemingly leading to reprisals, accentuating distrust, and probably affecting parochial inter-marriage and other dealings of a cultural and economic nature. The sums spent on disputes rose in the later eighteenth and early nineteenth centuries, expediting demands for reform. Some arrangements of the new poor law alleviated this, but significant numbers of disputes between parishes, and then between unions, remained a feature into the twentieth century.

The physical removal itself has not been studied by historians. Removals of people under the vagrancy laws, and of those under settlement law, varied in certain respects. The costs of removal were normally borne by the parish of settlement in the early nineteenth century.[144] Earlier, a certificating parish had to reimburse costs of removal.[145] The overseer was meant to convey the removed person, at least until 1814 when another person could be employed to do this.[146] Overseers (or paid assistant overseers) often continued themselves to undertake the journeys associated with a removal, which were usually local, although they could sometimes be over long distances. In some cases this business was done by parish constables. The pauper(s) had to be maintained over this period, lodged, fed and cared for *en route*. There were complaints of overseers dumping removed persons at parish boundaries, and then returning home, of people being removed while ill (notably before 1795), of deaths on the journey, of sexual molestation, of bribery by overseers to removed paupers urging them to abscond, of refusals to accommodate paupers upon arrival, and other such problems. Much of that behaviour by overseers was illegal, and so one should not assume that it was frequent. Contractors were often employed to convey people, notably in nineteenth-century towns, and some had significant businesses dealing with vagrants. They often took people a limited distance, and then delivered them to other contractors, being allowed stipulated sums per day for maintenance of a vagrant. Many vagrants left their contractors *en route*, no doubt often by mutual

---

[144] Shaw, *Parochial Lawyer*, p. 203.
[145] 3 Geo. III, c. 29.
[146] 54 Geo. III, c. 170, s. 10.

agreement.[147] Some vagrants were given a 'walking pass' and left to make their own way, supposedly back home. (Even a monkey was once given a walking pass.)[148] Constables often conveyed vagrants in rural parishes, normally taking them to parish boundaries or delivering them to the constable of the adjoining parish, and so on to their settlement. Under the new poor law, much more formalised arrangements were put in place, although the affairs of parish settlement remained matters for overseers long after 1834, as we will see in chapter 6. Arrangements for removing the Irish and other people from outside England and Wales were complex, of much interest, and altered over time, but they are of less relevance here.

These formal features of removal are highly visible in the legal records, giving some historians the impression that legal methods predominated. However, it would be wrong to assume that resistance to 'outsiders' usually took place via the settlement or vagrancy laws. Much less expensive and more immediate methods were to hand. All parishes, and the poor themselves, would wish to avoid legal methods if possible. Most people, threatened with removal, would quietly move on if they could, leaving the more destitute or highly vulnerable to be dealt with under the settlement or vagrancy laws. Even when removal orders were drawn up, many of them never took place, because people just moved voluntarily. One also finds overseers pushing people into other parishes without legal warrant, especially in the eighteenth century.[149] Furthermore, this was a society in which the resolution of conflicts by threats or fighting was commonplace, and the autobiographical writings of Samuel Bamford, Joseph Lawson, Parry-Jones and others leave us in no doubt that the cultures of the labouring poor over a long period extolled pugilism and force. We considered some features of this in a previous chapter on local xenophobia. Such force was often used against unwelcome people to shift them. People with

---

[147] *Select Committee on the Laws relating to Vagrants*, IV (1821), p. 71, and see the vagrant contractor Thomas Davis, and other witnesses, to this Committee.

[148] *Ibid.*, p. 103. 'Passes' were used especially for ex-vagrants, ex-soldiers or mariners, or people not wishing to be construed as vagrants, notably in the eighteenth century.

[149] For an example of this from Bingley (Yorks.) in 1759, see J. W. Ely, 'The eighteenth-century poor laws in the West Riding of Yorkshire', *American Journal of Legal History*, 30 (1986), p. 21.

smallpox or other illnesses, for example, were often discharged for that reason by employers during a service contract, and might be illegally cast out of a parish against their wishes. The parish officers of Neithrop (Oxon.) found in 1777 that one of Elizabeth Butler's five children had smallpox. They went to her house, and

> threatened that if she refused to open the Door and consent to have herself, family and Goods immediately removed from thence to Wormleighton [from where she had recently been removed, but the order had since been quashed] they would break the Door open and throw her Goods into the Street and take and leave her in Bourton or some other open Field and that if she returned to see after her Goods, they would whip her or send her to Bridewell.

They then took the family and their goods to the open fields of Fenny Compton, threw their goods out of the wagon, damaging some of them, and left the family in the open air 'to shift for themselves'. A solicitor subsequently complained of 'this most cruel and barbarous treatment of Pauper and her family'.[150] The inhabitants of Wormleighton, where the family then went, were of course also put at risk of catching smallpox by these actions.

Many outsiders like this family, who were felt to threaten the poor rates, inhabitants' health, or the local social order, or who were disliked locally, were ejected through violence or the threat of it. Parish crowd or gang actions were sometimes acquiesced in, or even encouraged by, local authorities, including in some cases by the Anglican Church. Many of the stoned or pond-immersed Primitive Methodist preachers attested to this, like the Quakers before them.[151] Various Acts of Parliament alluded to such behaviour as substitutes for legal settlement action, and tried to stop it, but it continued well into the nineteenth century. In some of these cases, it was because the person being ejected fell outside the ambit of the settlement laws that s/he was targeted in this way. Yet force was often used as an ancillary method against those who were eligible for legal removal. The

---

[150] The case is discussed in Vialls, 'Laws of settlement', pp. 256–61. The children were aged between three and thirteen. The papers are at Northants. CRO, D5960.

[151] For violence against Methodists, see the many references in K. D. M. Snell, *Church and Chapel in the North Midlands: Religious Observance in the Nineteenth Century* (Leicester, 1991), pp. 71–2.

unmarried postmistress of Stalybridge (Lancs.), for example, was pregnant in 1824, 'and by force, which was used, they tore her out of her house, and removed her forcibly against her will, and she resisting . . . the overseers . . . exceeded in their violence the requisite strength'.[152] Some people like this were ejected by force to expedite the legal process. This could especially affect pregnant single women, who might be manhandled across parish boundaries to prevent them giving birth in a parish, even after swearing to the putative father who then had to pay towards lying-in and subsequent expenses. Until 1834, an illegitimate person took the settlement of the parish in which s/he was 'dropped', as some legal wording euphemistically described the reality of birth. Robert Southey protested that 'even women in the very pains of labour have been driven out, and have perished by the way-side, because the birthplace of the child would be its parish'. He also complained 'of wretches in the last stage of disease having been hurried away in an open cart upon straw, and dying upon the road', so that parishes could escape the costs of their burial.[153] Thomas Paine echoed this concern, when he outlined his own scheme of tax-based universal insurance, one in which 'The dying poor will not be dragged from place to place to breathe their last, as a reprisal of parish upon parish.'[154] Parish officers were often involved in illegal ejection, assisted by others. A Nottinghamshire example of this was Mary Mann of Hickling, who died in 1720 after

she had been barbarously and unnaturally carried from Hickling to the Red Lodge by the Constables and other officers of Hickling a distance

---

[152] *Sixth Report from the Select Committee on Settlement, and Poor Removal*, XI (1847), p. 112, evidence of Henry Coppock, a Stockport solicitor and clerk to the Stockport guardians.

[153] R. Southey, *Letters from England* (1807, Gloucester, 1984), p. 143. An earlier (1654), less coercive, example was noted by the clerk of Doncaster corporation: 'Given to Susan Stockham, being at her time, and ready to labore, to get shutt of her, 1s', and 4d. more to carry her to the next parish. D. Hey, *Yorkshire from AD 1000* (Harlow, 1986), p. 210. On 'attempts to remove pregnant single women near childbirth from their parishes', see L. Bradley, 'Derbyshire quarter session rolls: poor law removal orders', *Derbyshire Miscellany*, 6 (1972), p. 106.

[154] M. Conway (ed.), *The Writings of Thomas Paine*, 4 vols. (London, 1906), vol. II, pp. 501–2, quoted in G. Stedman Jones, *An End to Poverty? A Historical Debate* (London, 2004), p. 25. Paine also complained about the removal of widows immediately after their husbands' deaths, 'like culprits and criminals', which certainly occurred, despite various Acts which aimed to restrict it.

of at least seven miles in the most severe weather within a fortnight of her confinement and that she was in such a weak state that she had to be held up by two persons whilst she was being examined and that as the result of such usage she died.[155]

One might think here that 'such usage' also extends to justices who insisted that a woman in this state must be standing when examined before them.

As such cases show, many parishes were prepared to 'get people out' by almost any means. Richard Jefferies later told of the eviction of unmarried mothers and parents on some estates, and that was also an option, one that lent itself to moral control.[156] Richard Burn, James Shaw and others complained of many methods of ejection being illegal, or extra-legal, affecting pregnant women, sick or infirm people, poor children, and others.[157] Overseers were liable to fines for some actions, but they could readily tip the wink to certain other people in the parish, who would have little problem in achieving the desired result. Earlier tricks of renting or buying minor property for the parish poor in other parishes, so as to out-settle them, had over a long period been deemed inadmissible.[158] The new poor law tightened up further on this with its controls over overseers, showing awareness of many earlier practices, some of which certainly persisted. Another method involved the marrying-out of women who were burdensome, pregnant, or risky to the parish, ensuring that they gained a settlement elsewhere via their husband. For example, the incumbent of Morley (Derb.)

---

[155] K. Tweedale Meaby (ed.), *Nottinghamshire: Extracts from the County Records of the Eighteenth Century* (Nottingham, 1947), p. 126; Shaw, *Parochial Lawyer*, p. 211, on how overseers may be indicted for getting a single woman far advanced in pregnancy out of their parish. See also L. A. Botelho, *Old Age and the English Poor Law, 1500–1700* (Woodbridge, 2004), p. 64.

[156] R. Jefferies, *The Dewy Morn* (London, 1884).

[157] Burn, *Justice of the Peace*, vol. IV, pp. 186–7; Shaw, *Parochial Lawyer*, pp. 160–1. Acts in 1795 and 1809 led to the formal removal of sick people being suspended (*ibid.*, pp. 688–98), and allowed examination by one justice (which one can find long before). Yet when a parish presumed that there would be such delay, they had additional incentive to remove people by other means, especially if a pauper suffered from an infectious illness.

[158] For an example of this in Anglesey, involving the parishes of Lleckgwynfarwydd and Rhodygeidio, the former buying land and building cottages in the latter for its poor, and thus making them irremovable there, see *First Report from the Select Committee on Settlement, and Poor Removal*, XI (1847), p. 52.

wrote rather indignantly in his marriage register in May 1782 about the marriage of William Chambers and Sarah Kirkman: 'This is a Wedding procured by the Parish of Heanor by giving a sum of money to this man to marry her. She being a disorderly woman who had brought some illegitimate children, this old man almost superannuated and had applied for relief, he being too old to support himself.'[159] There seems to be much evidence of overseers forcing a marriage, usually with settlement in mind.[160] Some couples were legally removed shortly after their marriages, and could even be examined as to settlement on the same day. This could be because they were or had been paupers, or (before 1795) because they seemed about to become so, or because the couple had been cajoled into marriage by the parish, or because the man did not willingly marry and his desertion was likely, or because of the possibility of bigamy, which one sometimes finds in settlement cases, usually when a man's wives were sent to (and met in!) their husband's settlement.[161] In bigamous cases (which could occur 'in good faith' if someone believed a spouse to be dead), any children born to the marriage were illegitimate, and settled where they were born, and the risk of that could motivate removal.

[159] Ll. L. Simpson (ed.), *Derbyshire Parish Registers. Marriages*, vol. XIII (London, 1914), p. 132 (9 May 1782).
[160] For example, the Revd James Woodforde wrote on 22 November 1768: 'I married Tom Burge of Ansford to Charity Andrews of C. Cary by License this morning. The Parish of Cary made him marry her, and he came handbolted to Church for fear of running away, and the Parish of Cary was at all expense of bringing them to, I recd of Mr. Andrew Russ the overseer of the Poor of Cary for it o. 10. 6.' Revd J. Woodforde, *The Diary of a Country Parson, 1758–1802* (1929, Oxford, 1979), p. 54. Further compelled marriages are on p. 164 (22 September 1780), and p. 295 (25 January 1787): 'The Man was a long time before he could be prevailed on to marry her when in the Church Yard; and at the Altar behaved very unbecoming . . . It is very disagreeable to me to marry such persons.' On overseers bringing about marriages, commonly motivated by settlement, see also Revd J. Skinner, *Journal of a Somerset Rector, 1803–1834* (1930, Oxford, 1985), pp. 63–4 (6 April 1811), the man demanding two guineas from the overseers to marry a pregnant woman. See also G. Crabbe, 'The parish register', in *The Poems of George Crabbe*, vol. 1 (Cambridge, 1907), p. 184, on youthful marriage forced by warrant.
[161] On bigamy, see S. Colwell, 'The incidence of bigamy in eighteenth and nineteenth-century England', *Family History*, 11 (1980); Taylor, *Poverty, Migration, and Settlement*, p. 44; P. Sharpe, 'Bigamy among the labouring poor in Essex, 1754–1857', *The Local Historian*, 24 (1994); G. Frost, 'Bigamy and cohabitation in Victorian England', *Journal of Family History*, 22 (1997).

Many parishes took precautions against settlements being gained by other methods than certificates. Sureties or indemnity bonds were sometimes required to safeguard the parish against the settlement of 'poor strangers' or 'foreigners', the latter term meaning people from other parishes. This was common in the seventeenth century, and most historians have associated it with the early modern period, but it continued long after then. One finds it, for example, in Corbridge or Morpeth in the mid-eighteenth century, or Thorpe Langton (Leics.) or Garstang (Lancs.) in the early nineteenth century. In some cases, as in Hexham or Barnard Castle, there were by-laws governing these matters. Provisions for fines if one created settlements were quite common, and these might even cover settlements gained by servants or apprentices.[162] Owners and occupiers might (to take an example from Muker in upper Swaledale, lasting from 1780 into the 1830s) draw up agreements not to rent to any new tenants who lacked a settlement in the parish, unless the rent was to be over £50 per annum, and not to let to anyone who already had a rent of under £10, to prevent them from attaining that figure. Penalties were imposed for failure to observe this, in this case of £100.[163] Leases sometimes stipulated such conditions, the tenant guaranteeing to safeguard the parish in his or her employing or sub-letting behaviour, for example in the

---

[162] On these issues, see especially Hindle, *On the Parish?*, ch. 5 on 'Exclusion'; S. Hindle, 'A sense of place? Becoming and belonging in the rural parish, 1550–1650', in A. Shepard and P. J. Withington (eds.), *Communities in Early Modern England* (Manchester, 2000), pp. 100–5; Hindle, 'Power, poor relief, and social relations', pp. 88–90; P. Rushton, 'The poor law, the parish and the community in north-east England, 1600–1800', *Northern History*, 25 (1989), pp. 140–1; J. Broad, *Transforming English Rural Society: The Verneys and the Claydons, 1600–1820* (Cambridge, 2004), pp. 164–8; Eden, *The State of the Poor*, vol. III, pp. 743–4; Webb and Webb, *English Poor Law History*, p. 338. See also Leics. CRO, DE 1699/48 (Thorpe Langton, 5 December 1810): bond involving the overseers and a framework knitter to prevent settlements being gained by servants and apprentices, to the value of £80, which also bound his heirs, executors and administrators. Steve King informs me of such practice in Garstang, especially involving people like lodging house keepers. For a 1773 agreement in Moulton (Northants.) not to take an apprentice or servant who would gain a settlement, see Vialls, 'Laws of settlement', p. 321. In some cases, servants were required to reside in an adjoining parish, for a part of the year, to avoid settlement. *Ibid.*, p. 322, for an example of that arranged by a farmer in Winwick (Northants.).

[163] C. S. Hallas, 'Yeomen and peasants? Landownership patterns in the North Yorkshire Pennines, *c.* 1770–1900', *Rural History*, 9 (1998), p. 170.

taking of lodgers.[164] Bonds might also be demanded from those paternally responsible for an illegitimate child (including the man's father), to indemnify the parish where the woman wished to give birth, which was often her father's parish, and which would through birth become the settlement of the child.[165] Throughout this period, there were occasional enquiries in some parishes to identify poor strangers without a settlement, as occurred for example in Newland in the Forest of Dean (Glos.) in 1750 and 1755, and these often accompanied periodical efforts to tighten up on poor law administration.[166]

With regard to yearly service, under the settlement laws one had to be hired for a *full* year, while *unmarried*, on a continuous contract, and receive the full year's wages, to gain a settlement. One or two days less than a year, let alone other periods, would make the hiring legally ineligible for settlement. That is what often happened. One can find many examples of restrictions against servants and lodgers gaining settlements in any period. Yet towards the later eighteenth century, the practice of hiring servants for less than a full year became increasingly common, notably in southern England, and this developed further in the early nineteenth century. 'No man will hire either labourer or servant for a year from another parish', wrote the Revd G. Glover of Southrepps, who was describing a problem that was especially acute in his county of Norfolk.[167] Settlement examinations document growing numbers of fifty-one-week hirings, sackings a few days short of the year, permissions to attend statute fairs a day or so before the year ended, seemingly generous permission to attend other local fairs, refusals to hire until a certain number of days after Michaelmas Day, permission to visit one's 'friends' (a word for relatives in this period) being used to discount settlement, unpaid absences for mothering Sunday, employer's consent to marry during the year, slight

---

[164] Controls over the taking of lodgers and inmates had also been enacted by 31 Eliz., c. 7 (1588–9), because of the possible chargeability of such people. This Act was certainly being occasionally enforced into the early eighteenth century, but was repealed by 15 Geo. III, c. 32 (1774–5).

[165] An example of this is Leics. CRO, DE 2417/30 (23 August 1782), the agreement being between Glaston and Seaton in Rutland, and the bond being £40.

[166] N. M. Herbert (ed.), *A History of the County of Gloucester*, vol. v: *Bledisloe Hundred, St. Briavels Hundred, The Forest of Dean* (Victoria County History, Oxford, 1996), p. 222.

[167] Revd G. Glover, *Observations on the Present State of Pauperism in England* (London, 1817), p. 392.

deductions in yearly wages to 'prove' non-completion of the year, or swapping of masters during the year or for the last week of service.[168] These and other methods were all deployed to hinder settlements. In some western and northern regions 'traditional' yearly hiring became regularised into a period a few days short of a year, and in many southern counties (notably in East Anglia) it tended to become displaced by much shorter terms, especially when servants were hired from other parishes. Many contemporaries complained of the results, such as a witness from West Rainham (Norf.) who commented that 'Servants, under the existing law, can scarcely meet with a situation out of their own Parish.'[169] Thomas Estcourt MP (an ex-president of the Poor Law Board) later explained that 'the common evasion was to take servants for 51 weeks'.[170] These changes, and the 1834 abolition of yearly hiring as a 'head' of settlement, much reduced the accessibility of settlement for the poor. That 1834 abolition was intended to revive yearly hiring in the south; but, paradoxically, it made it much harder to gain settlements in regions where the institution had continued. In 1859, H. B. Farnall (the Poor Law Inspector for the Metropolitan District), speaking about 'servants and people of that class', said

---

[168] For examples of such practice, see E. Bott, *A Collection of Decisions of the Court of King's Bench upon the Poor's Laws, down to the Present Time* (London, 1773), p. 303, and see *ibid.*, pp. 265–315, on settlement by hiring generally, documenting many further ways to avoid settlement being gained by yearly service; Checkland and Checkland (eds.), *Poor Law Report of 1834*, pp. 245–6. On the decline of yearly service in many south-eastern regions of England, partly to evade settlements, see Kussmaul, *Servants in Husbandry*, ch. 6; Snell, *Annals of the Labouring Poor*, ch. 2. These two books are not denying the important survival of long-term contractual service in many regions, which their data clearly show. Interestingly, in much more recent times some European employers have offered women 51 week, or 364 day, contracts, to avoid the two-year consecutive service terms that would allow maternity leave and pay.

[169] *Report from His Majesty's Commissioners for Inquiring into the Administration and Practical Operation of the Poor Laws, Appendix (B.1.). Answers to Rural Queries, part IV*, XXXIII (1834), p. 319 d. Reply of Thomas Brown, churchwarden and overseer. Many of these rural answers made similar comments.

[170] *Select Committee on Irremovable Poor*, XVII (1860), p. 407, and see *ibid.*, pp. 313–14; 'Eighth Report of George Taylor on Settlement', *Report from His Majesty's Commissioners for Inquiring into the Administration and Practical Operation of the Poor Laws*, XXXVII (1834), Appendix C, p. 120 c; G. Jekyll, *Old West Surrey: Some Notes and Memories* (1904, Chichester, 1999), p. 185, on an elderly woman's memories about hirings for two days less than a year. Reducing one's poor and related expenditure via these means carried benefits for a parish into the new poor law, as it lowered the parish's 'averages': the parish contributions towards union finance based on relative pauperism.

that 'The modes of gaining a settlement which the poor now have are extremely few. They have been broken down and abolished, and there is very great difficulty in poor people getting a settlement at all.'[171]

Something comparable but of less significance occurred with apprenticeship. Settlement examinations often document a seven-year apprenticeship having been terminated too early, or the indentures being 'lost' or ripped up, or apprentice, master or mistress deserting each other (masters sometimes abandoned an apprentice, for example to avoid debts, or to take the premium without undertaking the training, or to escape an apprentice with an infectious illness). The apprentice might be sent on journeys to break required terms of parochial residence, or fabricated charges might be made against him or her, or other conditions not met, to render the apprenticeship ineligible for settlement. Further conditions could be stipulated in the indenture or 'clubbing-out' agreement which, when unfulfilled, might stop any settlement being gained. Disputes at Quarter Sessions often touch on these matters, and they were discussed by Nolan, Burrow, Nelson, Bott, Burn, Steer and others in their legal manuals. As with sub-yearly hiring, much of this practice was intended to hinder settlement, notably during the five or so decades of growing relief expenditures after about 1780. In fact, and by comparison with service, the law inclined in favour of apprentice settlements, perhaps because a skilled worker was less likely to become chargeable in the future than a servant or labourer. Despite evasive methods, shorter apprentice terms usually imparted settlement, so long as they were made by proper indenture and there was residence for forty days.[172]

Another method was out-apprenticeship from the parish. This was becoming more difficult to achieve in the early nineteenth century, with a view to settlement, because it was being

---

[171] *Select Committee on Irremovable Poor*, VII (1859), p. 124. Settlement was mainly derived from parents now, he claimed. *Ibid.*, p. 126. Or see the remark from the Revd Mark Coxon (chairman of the Wirral union): 'It is a most difficult thing now for a poor man to gain a settlement.' *Select Committee on Irremovable Poor*, XVII (1860), p. 77.

[172] *Select Committee on Poor Removal*, XII (1879), p. 2; Nolan, *Treatise of the Laws* (1808 edn), vol. I, p. 448.

subverted legally, and other parishes were so alert to it.[173] Parish and charity apprenticeships dealt with the most vulnerable local poor, and such apprenticeships conferred settlement. In some areas there was coercion upon masters to take apprentices, with fines for refusal, but overseers lacked powers outside their own parish. Apprenticeship involved paying premiums to masters or mistresses, and those taking an apprentice had to weigh the pecuniary advantage to themselves of the premium and labour services, against the censure from parishioners if they created an unwanted settlement. One of the reasons for the apprentice-ship of girls was that it gained them external settlements, just like boys, and this helped to preserve their apprenticeship into the nineteenth century, even if female apprenticeships were often to sweated needlework trades, housewifery and other such employment.[174] Overseers were also active in putting orphans and poor children out to service, and before 1834 there were presumptions of parochial gains if they could place them out-side the parish, especially into situations where a settlement might be obtained. Some parish indentures even stipulated that the receiving parish should ensure that the young person gain a settlement. A further method of ejection was assisted emigra-tion, sometimes termed 'shovelling out paupers'.[175] By the early nineteenth century and beyond, parish emigration schemes de-veloped apace, as a way of reducing the poor rates and reducing settlements, and a very large number of pamphleteers on the poor law advocated this. It was prominently broached in one of the queries from the 1832–4 Poor Law Commission.[176] Letters

---

[173] In addition, an Act in 1844 (7 & 8 Vic., c. 101, s. 12) restricted the gaining of settlements by parish apprentices.

[174] On female apprenticeship, see Snell, *Annals of the Labouring Poor*, ch. 6.

[175] H. J. M. Johnston, *British Emigration Policy, 1815–30: 'Shovelling Out Paupers'* (Oxford, 1972); Snell, *Annals of the Labouring Poor*, pp. 9–14; R. Haines, '"Shovelling out paupers"? Parish-assisted emigration from England to Australia, 1834–1847', in E. Richards (ed.), *Poor Australian Immigrants in the Nineteenth Century* (Canberra, 1991); G. Howells, '"For I was tired of England Sir", English pauper emigrant strategies, 1834–60', *Social History*, 23 (1998); G. Howells, 'Emigration and the new poor law: the Norfolk emigration fever of 1836', *Rural History*, 11 (2000); G. Howells, '"On account of their disreputable characters": parish-assisted emigration from rural England, 1834–1860', *History*, 88, no. 292 (2003).

[176] *Report from His Majesty's Commissioners for Inquiring into the Administration and Prac-tical Operation of the Poor Laws. Appendix (B.1.). Answers to Rural Queries, Part V*, xxxiv

from emigrants back 'home' were often read in churches and
published locally. Assisted emigration or regional migration
was also taken up in a variety of ways under the new poor
law, and it had the backing of leading political economists,
who were much concerned with surplus labour in southern
England.

Renting £10 per annum was another frequent way to gain a
settlement, although less applicable than service or apprenticeship. About 5–20 per cent of people in settlement examinations
had normally gained a settlement through renting in the eighteenth and early nineteenth centuries. That figure would of
course be higher among those not examined as to settlement,
and who were never chargeable. One possible effect here was to
turn that 'head' of settlement into a form of rent control.[177]
Urban parishes in particular often tried to keep rents below that
sum, and to hope in questionable cases that the yearly value of
such property was not challenged. (It was the annual market
value of the property that conferred a settlement, not necessarily
the actual rent paid, although the latter was usually sufficient
for legal purposes.) Furthermore, that £10 did not have to be
for a single property. So parish officers and landowners were
often thwarted as people rented small different properties (and
types of immovable property like a messuage, a dwelling house,
part of an orchard, a rabbit warren, and so on) from various
landlords, each landlord having incomplete knowledge of what
others were doing – and thus an incomer could accrue total
rent in excess of £10. Over much of this period, one could pay
some rents *outside* the parish, and if the total rents amounted
to £10 one gained a settlement in the parish of residence. Coordination between landlords was easier in 'close' parishes compared with 'open' ones, the latter usually having a multiplicity
of owners. Another 'head' of settlement, public office-serving,
could more readily be reserved for those who were already settled in the parish, and so one rarely finds people gaining a
settlement that way.[178] Someone valued in the community, but

---

(1834), query 46, part of the query being whether a person assisted to emigrate
  should thereby lose his settlement. (Many parishes answered affirmatively to that.)
[177] An effect first noticed by Taylor, *Poverty, Migration, and Settlement*, p. 135.
[178] Tate, *The Parish Chest*, p. 32; Vialls, 'Laws of settlement', p. 270.

still lacking a settlement, could be absorbed by appointing him to such an office, and that was virtually a deliberate act of legal assimilation.

Just as settlement had led to many controls and restrictions, whether legal or otherwise, to safeguard parochial ratepayers, so post-1846 irremovability had a similar result. The motives here were *either* to stop the requisite period of residence for irremovability being attained, *or* to make an already irremovable person leave so that his settlement in practical effect revived. There were also cases where a parish wanted to remove a sick man, so as not to have his wife irremovable with them for a year after his death. It was always difficult for vestry clerks and others to judge how long people had resided, especially in the relative anonymity of towns and cities, and so it was harder to prevent irremovability in towns than in rural parishes. It was also not always clear legally what amounted to a break in residence, which would negate irremovability, and there was much argument over that.[179] There were many efforts made to interrupt residence, to eject people who were irremovable, or to deny irremovability to dependants of a man after his death. In towns, even a move from one side of a street to another could negate irremovability, if the parish boundary ran down the road.[180] 'They do every thing they can to force an irremovable person out of the parish', commented Edward Gulson, the Assistant Poor Law Commissioner, who was familiar with Radnorshire, Glamorganshire, Carmarthenshire, and a large swathe of English midland and south-western counties.[181] The clerk to the Birmingham guardians reported that 'even the agricultural labourers are impeded in their efforts to acquire five years' residence'.[182] The Revd J. N. Dalton, speaking about Rutland and Buckinghamshire 'open' and 'close' villages, claimed that

---

[179] See for example *Second and Third Reports from the Select Committee on Settlement, and Poor Removal*, xi (1847), pp. 13–14.

[180] *Select Committee on Poor Removal*, xiii (1855), pp. 284–5, discussing this in Maidenhead and Chester. On this in London, see *Select Committee on Irremovable Poor*, vii (1859), p. 37.

[181] *Second and Third Reports from the Select Committee on Settlement, and Poor Removal*, xi (1847), p. 38.

[182] *Select Committee on Irremovable Poor*, xvii (1860), p. 56.

When a man has been in a parish for four years they try to make an excuse to get rid of him so as to prevent his stopping five years. It was only a few days ago that I heard of a very trivial objection which was raised to a man in order to get him out of a parish, so that he might not become one of their irremovable poor.[183]

Or the Rector of Willingham (Lincs.) complained that owners of cottages were sometimes pressured by the principal farmers 'to give notice to all those who have not gained settlements by five years' residence, to quit their houses next Lady-day'.[184]

What rankled with many observers of irremovability practice was that often the best labourers were subject to this kind of pressure, people who had shown initiative in moving away from their 'home' parishes. George Ludbrooke, for example,

a good labourer, who has been in the employ of one master for 14 years, received notice to leave the parish where he resided 'his master having removed', so that he was resident there only one year; and for fear that this man and his family should become chargeable, the most extreme measures were made use of to compel him to leave the parish, 'such as taking the doors and windows from the cottage, etc.' After struggling with casual work for several weeks, he was at length obliged to apply to the guardians for an admission to this workhouse [Keninghall, for the Guiltcross union, Norfolk], where himself, wife and two children are at present chargeable to North Lopham.[185]

There were countless other examples of such practice in the Parliamentary reports on irremovability and settlement after 1846. Many of these emanated from agrarian regions where 'open' and 'close' divisions had become notorious – East Anglia, Lincolnshire, but stretching up to Northumberland[186] – and these might be seen as an on-going regional tendency. Examples were also given of obstruction in urban areas, indeed in

---

[183] *Ibid.*, p. 293. This witness thought that the older system of parish settlement was preferable to the system of five-year irremovability.

[184] *First Report from the Select Committee on Settlement, and Poor Removal*, XI (1847), p. 39.

[185] *Second and Third Reports from the Select Committee on Settlement, and Poor Removal*, XI (1847), p. 36 (letter dated 23 February 1847). For another example, the lay-off after four and a half years of one of the best shepherds in Dorset – as 'it is a rule in our parish not to allow any man to become irremovable' – see *Select Committee on Poor Removal*, XIII (1855), p. 288. 'Nothing is more common at boards of guardians in the West of England than to hear the guardians saying, "This man must be removed out of the parish before long, or else he will acquire irremovability."' *Ibid.* To similar effect, see *Select Committee on Irremovable Poor*, VII (1859), pp. 23–4.

[186] *Sixth Report from the Select Committee on Settlement, and Poor Removal*, XI (1847), p. 319.

industrial and northern cities. The mind-set of hindering settlements thus carried over readily into public thinking about irremovability, with many similar actions, dismissals, evictions, interrupted employment, restrictive tenancies and so on being used to debar people from becoming irremovable.

Cottage destruction was a further way of ejecting and keeping poor people out. There were many accusations of such practice, and counter-claims made for its benefits, or concerning its morality, or impact upon housing improvement, emparking, model village creation, and new parish formation. It was discussed in relation to enclosure, rural slum clearance, game-law enforcement, 'moral improvement', tenant care, cottage design, sanitation, convenience or inconvenience in the labour market, and so on. All the debates about 'open' and 'close' parishes, not my focus here, came into view. The settlement and poor laws were very prominent in all these issues, and many commentators claimed that cottage destruction was influenced by the settlement laws. Landlords, it was said, 'take good care to prevent settlements being gained. They pull down cottages, or forbid their erection', and the charge was repeatedly made.[187] The English and Welsh debates about eviction and cottage destruction were coloured to some degree by Irish and Scottish experiences, where housing destruction and eviction were much more widespread and contentious.[188] Charges were also made that tenant eviction was occasionally due to religious or political allegiances, for example in Cardiganshire and Carmarthenshire after the 1868 election.[189] The vulnerability of the labouring poor to be turned out of their cottages at short notice was also a complaint.[190] Some of these English debates featured in well-known

[187] White, *Parochial Settlements*, p. 8.
[188] At the peak of Irish evictions, between 1846 and 1853, at least 70,000 families were ejected, much of this being wholesale 'clearance' and cottage destruction. W. E. Vaughan, *Landlords and Tenants in Mid-Victorian Ireland, 1848–1904* (Oxford, 1994), pp. 21–31, 235–6; A. Somerville, *Letters from Ireland during the Famine of 1847* (Dublin, 1994), pp. 131–3, 190–205.
[189] R. J. Colyer, 'The gentry and the county in nineteenth-century Cardiganshire', *Welsh History Review*, 10 (1981), pp. 514–16. For an English example of politically motivated tenant eviction, see E. A. Smith, 'Earl Fitzwilliam and Malton: a proprietary borough in the early nineteenth century', *English Historical Review*, 80 (1965), p. 62.
[190] See for example J. Collings, *The Colonization of Rural Britain: A Complete Scheme for the Regeneration of British Rural Life*, 2 vols. (London, 1914), vol. II, pp. 533–5; F. E. Green,

novels, such as *Middlemarch*, *Yeast*, *North and South*, or *Sybil*.
Accusations of cottage dereliction and poor ejection were also
prominent in critiques of enclosure, as in Oliver Goldsmith's
'The deserted village', and such ejection became a major theme
in Marxist interpretation.

There is no doubt that cottage destruction occurred, sometimes for unscrupulous pecuniary reasons to the local disadvantage of parishioners, while in other cases it had obvious
benefits.[191] Village clearances, and in some cases re-location
(even to a different parish), occurred for example at Holkham
(Norf.) in 1734, or at More Crichel (Dors.) in the mid-eighteenth
century (where villagers were moved to a new village called
Newtown, which conveniently was in another parish, that
of Witchampton).[192] Movement of people occurred at East
Lulworth between 1773–85 so as to extend the park walls of
Lulworth Castle, or at Milton Abbas from 1786, for the sake
of an emparked lake. Parts of Lockinge village were removed
in 1860 from around the church and manor house, to give the
latter more privacy from what Lady Wantage called 'farm sheds,

---

The Tyranny of the Countryside (London, 1913); M. Freeman, *Social Investigation and Rural England, 1870–1914* (Woodbridge, 2003), pp. 98–9, 161.

[191] For examples of cottage destruction, or refusals to repair them and letting them fall derelict, as linked to settlement law, see Anon., 'Inquiries with respect to the progress and state of pauperism in England since the reign of Queen Elizabeth', *Edinburgh Review* (May 1828), pp. 312–13 (also citing on this Thomas Alcock in 1752, and Arthur Young in 1770); Checkland and Checkland, *Poor Law Report of 1834*, pp. 248–9; *Report from His Majesty's Commissioners on the Administration and Practical Operation of the Poor Laws. Appendix (B.2.). Part IV. Answers to Town Queries with Indices*, XXXVI (1834), p. 238 i; *First Report from the Select Committee on Settlement, and Poor Removal*, XI (1847), pp. 39–40, 65; Sir E. Head, 'The law of settlement', *Edinburgh Review*, 87 (April 1848), p. 455; J. Caird, *English Agriculture in 1850–51* (1852, Farnborough, 1968), p. 95; *Select Committee on Poor Removal*, XIII (1855), p. 285 (evidence of Edward Gulson); *Select Committee on Irremovable Poor*, XVII (1860), p. 293; W. Hasbach, *A History of the English Agricultural Labourer* (London, 1908), p. 400; B. Inglis, *Poverty and the Industrial Revolution* (1971, London, 1972), p. 394; C. Taylor, *The Cambridgeshire Landscape: Cambridgeshire and the Southern Fens* (London, 1973), pp. 164–5; R. Samuel (ed.), *Village Life and Labour* (London, 1975), pp. 14–15; Rose, 'Settlement, removal and the new poor law', pp. 35–8; D. Roberts, *Paternalism in Early Victorian England* (London, 1979), pp. 37, 119–21; J. Burnett, *A Social History of Housing, 1815–1985* (1980, London, 1986), ch. 5; G. E. Mingay, 'The rural slum', in S. M. Gaskell (ed.), *Slums* (Leicester, 1990), p. 115. Cottage destruction is often mentioned in the official censuses (e.g. for Oakley (Suff.) in 1831).

[192] M. J. Flame, 'All the common rules of social life: the reconstruction of social and political identities by the Dorset gentry, c. 1790–c. 1834' (Ph.D., University of Warwick, 1997), p. 151.

muck yards and hovels'.[193] At Holdenby (Northants.), part of the village was removed and replaced by *parterres* and terraces, and as Tom Williamson points out there, and in connection with other villages like Houghton (Norf.), many removals of cottages or whole settlements took place from the 1720s to make way for parks.[194] In Northamptonshire between 1720 and 1850, at least eight villages were moved and about twenty-five were altered to allow emparking.[195] These developments do not necessarily warrant indignation: the older cottages were often replaced by estate housing, showing many signs of estate pride, and there were usually sanitary improvements. The Milton Abbas displacement was judged to have been 'no doubt a good exchange, which could be called despotism tempered with benevolence'.[196] In most such cases, a desire to improve the aesthetic, social, and economic features of estates lay behind the dislodgment or destruction of cottages. Sometimes this was accompanied by selective ejection of poor persons felt to be a nuisance, a threat to game, a moral discredit, and through possibly acquired settlements a charge on the poor rates.

However, one needs to ask why these significant but relatively small-scale removals did not lead to the turmoil and suffering associated with mass ejections and cottage destruction in Scotland and Ireland. Despite English debates about 'open' and 'close' parishes and the motive forces behind them, the dramatic evictions *of whole communities* in Scotland and Ireland were on a completely different scale to anything that can be documented in post-Restoration England and Wales. There were important differences in topography, demography, local political systems, landlordism, the economics of farming, and so on, that underlay some differences. Yet it seems to me that a

---

[193] M. Havinden, *Estate Villages Revisited: A Second, Up-dated Edition of a Study of the Oxfordshire (Formerly Berkshire) Villages of Ardington and Lockinge* (1966, Reading, 1999), pp. 68–9. Nuneham Courtenay (Oxon.) after 1759 is another example of village movement and rebuilding, to make way for Lord Harcourt's park extension.

[194] T. Williamson, *Polite Landscapes: Parks and Gardens in Georgian England* (Stroud, 1995), pp. 22, 57–8, 77, 103–4, 113–14. See also Darley, *Villages of Vision*, on model and estate villages.

[195] Williamson, *Polite Landscapes*, pp. 103–4; T. Williamson, *The Transformation of Rural England: Farming and the Landscape, 1700–1870* (Exeter, 2002), p. 45.

[196] G. Grigson, *Wessex* (London, 1951), p. 54.

crucial factor has never been noticed. Scotland and Ireland did not have the settlement and poor laws.[197] People in them who were displaced by landlord acts, with their roofs torn off, their walls and doors battered in, were truly banished: they were wholly ejected from their homelands, forced to migrate long distances elsewhere, in great suffering and starvation, in search of completely new livelihoods. This could never happen on any significant scale in post-medieval England and Wales, even at the hands of the same landlords whose behaviour was so condemned in Ireland or Scotland. That was because of the English and Welsh settlement and poor laws. The Welsh or English poor *had* to be rehoused, usually in the same parish, occasionally on the same estate if a landlord's propertied influence over-spread parish boundaries. A landlord might try to move a village, or destroy housing, but its poor had immediate legal recall: they simply claimed their settlement rights, while the parishes they had been pushed out to also acted legally to remove them back. The ejecting landlord would be compelled under the settlement and poor laws to receive them back, to house and maintain them, regardless of his destructive 'clearance'. One could not clear away English and Welsh poor, sweeping them to the seashores, forcing them to colonise America, Canada or New Zealand, or move to English cities, driving the remainder into violent fraternities and nationalist movements, when they were parochially settled. They *had* to be rehoused in their parish of settlement. If their livelihood was destroyed, for example through enclosure, they had to be maintained on the parish rates. It was therefore hardly rational for a Duke of Sutherland to operate in England as he did in Scotland. He would be creating extra expense for himself and his ratepaying tenants, cutting off his nose to spite his face, burning his houses to annoy his neighbours. Villages were removed by their lords in the fifteenth and sixteenth centuries, as part of a process of rural depopulation for which there is both written evidence, and the testimony of the sites of abandoned villages. Yet it was, possibly above all other considerations, because of the settlement laws that any such landlord policy in England and Wales

---

[197] Ireland had no such law; on Scotland see n. 90 above.

was futile and senseless from the early modern period, even though landlords often had the motivation – a motivation that took its ugly courses in Ireland and Scotland, but had to stay its hand in the two countries where the Settlement Acts so influenced policy and practice.

CONCLUSION

Eligibility to 'belong' was thus framed to a considerable degree by the settlement and poor laws, and was conditioned by socio-economic contexts. When belonging had such direct consequences for welfare entitlement, relief expenditure and ratepayers, and when those ratepayers faced depression – as did many southern farmers and farming-dependent trades after 1815 – vestries and overseers often did all that they could to restrict new people coming to belong. Shortages of labour in the north allowed more hospitable acceptance of new settlements. Yearly service in various forms also survived much more in the agrarian north of England, in Wales, and in small-farm pastoral areas where it was closely embedded in the structures and labour-exchange customs of farming. Paradoxically, the labour-market effects of industrialisation, which occurred so often in pastoral regions, facilitated the survival of something close to traditional yearly hiring in industrial hinterlands. Throughout the nineteenth century, most farm workers could shift their locale of belonging comparatively readily in the north and in Wales, if they wished to, subject to local cultural acceptance. Some counties, such as Northumberland, with distinctive hiring customs, were well known for this.[198] Even so, as from 1834 such hirings no longer conferred settlements, and they had never done so for married people. In many agricultural regions of the south, with low wages, surplus workers and stagnant labour markets, more and more labouring people belonged to their paternal settlement, even if they did not live there, having failed to gain independent settlements. In this way, high relief expenditures

---

[198] *Sixth Report from the Select Committee on Settlement, and Poor Removal*, XI (1847), p. 319. 'They migrate over the whole of [Northumberland]; they have no local attachment whatever.' Such a statement, pertaining here to married farm servants, was very rarely made of any other English county at that date.

and the rural depression of the 1810s to 1830s consolidated the 'rootedness' and inter-generational ideas of belonging of many among the poor. This fostered proletarian communities whose senses of local belonging and memory were reinforced by the fact that increasing numbers belonged to the same parishes as their parents or even grandparents. Such a social phenomenon had been much less prevalent at the time of the vigorous statute fairs and easily obtained full-year services in the early eighteenth century. In many regions it augmented and sometimes inflamed a culture of exclusion and of local xenophobia. It took the railway boom, the new poor law, rural trade unions, and widespread agrarian out-migration and emigration gradually to allow a break-out from these conditions.

We have seen how important settlement was in the shifting social composition and internal precedences of parishes, especially village and market-town parishes, over the eighteenth and nineteenth centuries. The changing accessibility of settlement, and the shifts in how it was obtained – from a stress on service and apprenticeship, to an emphasis on propertied eligibility – highlight some key points about how communities changed, and about how people felt that they 'belonged' to them. Belonging is a concept in which personal rivalry and ideas of rights and precedence loom large. The changes over time, encapsulated in the contrasts shown between figures 3.1 and 3.2, and the long-term survival of settlement, indicate that industrial capitalism was certainly not inimical to belonging. On the contrary, lacking 'peasant' stability, extensive kinship reliance, and agrarian rootedness, such a society called for prescribed welfare systems, and with parochial administration those systems necessitated settlement laws, which imparted strong legal backing to ideas of convertible 'belonging'.

However, industrialising society decisively altered social balances in the composition of residents who belonged locally, and how they did so. Settlements had been generated rapidly and in volume during the eighteenth century. Any parish then was full of poor people who felt that they belonged, and who, by 1795–1801, asserted their rights of belonging in their clamour for poor relief. Such people numerically dominated very many parishes. However, by the later nineteenth century, one belonged and resided in a parish much more by virtue of property there, whether rented or owned. Many among the poor, by comparison, 'belonged' but did not reside. The logic of settlement change suggests that better-off people had come to dominate concepts of 'core belonging', and increasingly regarded the poor as locally marginal to their parish, resident but often belonging elsewhere, except for a narrow core of eligible and sometimes 'deserving' poor whose ancestors had belonged in the parish, and whose settlements they had inherited. This marginalisation was heightened by a further thought. Some less favoured poor, even though they 'belonged' to the parish, now found that their settlements did not stop them being excluded in a new-fangled way – by being relegated to a union workhouse *outside* their parish. Out-relief predominated during the new poor law – as we will see later – but use of the workhouse amounted to unprecedented exclusion *by virtue of being a pauper*, which had hitherto been a contradiction in terms. Paupers had previously, in poor law theory, come back to the place where they belonged, unless, in rare cases, they were sentenced to houses of correction. These long-term changes were, of course, congruent with the growth of class society, with the Victorian emphasis upon property and its entitlements, with an equation between belonging and adjudged merit, with rural labouring out-migration, with growing extra-parochial loyalties of many religious and secular kinds, and with the political-economist principles of the new poor law.

'The place of settlement is the place to which a person "belongs". *To* such a place he may be removed; *from* such a place he may not be removed', wrote E. J. Lidbetter as late as 1932, in a book intended as 'a handbook for public assistance officers'.[199] W. Nelson, Richard Burn or other such authorities two or more centuries earlier would have accepted such a statement, and might have been reassured to learn of its date. Thus, in certain regards, many principles of the law had not changed even by Lidbetter's period of the Great Slump, mass unemployment, the hunger marches and the household means test. The total repeal of settlement had been advocated by many before 1834. Indeed, that had been one of the main instigations to poor

---

[199] Lidbetter, *Settlement and Removal*, p. 39 (his italics).

law reform then. It is all the more remarkable, therefore, that by the end of March 1930 the guardians, unions and 'workhouses' had come and ostensibly gone,[200] and *still* settlement continued intact. It was to out-live the new poor law by nearly two decades. There was active readiness to reform much else, and so this survival really bears witness to the remarkable utility of settlement law, to its cultural importance, and to the crucial ideas of belonging, local responsibility and accountability that it embodied. Whether anything of equivalent social significance replaced it (or should have replaced it) is debatable. Wider political developments, gradual de-territorialisation, globalisation and population fluidity now make that ever less likely.

This chapter has stressed how central and integrated the theme of belonging was to the settlement laws over the previous centuries. Because those laws have so often been discussed narrowly in their legal and administrative aspects, as an historical narration of recondite legal change, my discussion has focused differently, largely on what those laws meant in community and cultural terms. I have also given a more favourable verdict on them than some historians, or indeed some contemporaries. For the settlement laws were absolutely fundamental to welfare provision, and were shaped by the demands of a highly localised, relatively benevolent, and rate-dependent poor law system. For good or ill, they marked communities in terms of insiders and outsiders. They separated inhabitants by differential status of 'belonging', and arguably their intrinsic localism was a counter-balance to class conflict. These laws divided the parishioners of one parish or township from those of others. They inscribed a continuing culture of selective exclusion, and we have seen that they reinforced a culture of local xenophobia. Yet they also proved flexible and adaptable to local and regional circumstances, even if they had some problems in adapting to change over time. They encouraged pride in place, strong local loyalty, and a firm sense of 'home' and belonging. Developing from and using the Anglican parish, the settlement system delivered and nestled a Christian welfare system that was

---

[200] The Local Government Act, 1929, 19 & 20 Geo. V, c. 17, and the 1930 Poor Law Act, 20 & 21 Geo. V, c. 17, abolished 642 unions and boards of guardians, while 'workhouses' (where the buildings survived) became 'public assistance institutions'.

benevolent and encompassing when seen in international terms, one whose mini-statehoods laid expectations and groundwork for the broader welfare state of the twentieth century. Its bureaucracy, internal arrangements and appeal procedures were probably no worse or cumbersome than those of any other formal and encompassing welfare system. For the poor these laws allowed transferable 'roots', and imparted a belief in 'rights' and securities in one's 'home' parish or township. They fostered unique kinds of adoptive or manoeuvrable belonging, in which even the poor themselves had some choice and control over where and how they 'belonged'. Because of its faith in local society, its belief in Christian rate-aided welfare, and its erstwhile recognition of the need to 'belong', English and Welsh society found the settlement laws indispensable for an extraordinarily long time.

CHAPTER 4

Rural societies and their marriage patterns

Better wed over the mixen, than over the moor.[1]

The young man who left his village or town to seek a bride was considered to be nothing more than an outlaw against the rules of decency.[2]

'Of this parish', I say, reading the banns. The future bride who, although resident here for years has made a courteous first visit to the church in order to hear them, starts at this mention of her parochiality. She had not seen herself so localized . . . Beneficially, we are united on paper and in our hearts, but not parochially. Who can be? It is asking too much . . . At the same time we know our place – especially those who have driven ten or more miles to it – and an inexpressible happiness fills us as our own tree-held tower looms at the end of the lane . . . Now we have those who are 'of this parish' without knowing it.[3]

I

Marriage choices reveal a great deal about local horizons, and where people felt that they belonged. In this chapter, I wish to explore features of marriage, and to track changes in parochial endogamy and exogamy. By those terms I respectively mean marriage with both partners from the parish, and marriage to someone from outside the parish. Despite the huge growth of demographic studies in England over recent decades – something that has been less true of Wales – little attention has been

---

[1] F. Grose, *A Provincial Glossary, with a Collection of Local Proverbs and Popular Superstitions* (1787, Menston, Yorks., 1968), n.p., under 'Cheshire'.
[2] G. Findler, *Folk Lore of the Lake Counties* (Clapham, Yorks., 1968), p. 11.
[3] R. Blythe, *Word from Wormingford: A Parish Year* (1997, Harmondsworth, 1998), pp. 78–9.

paid to these aspects of marital behaviour. Yet they have considerable cultural and social importance, are relevant to key issues in anthropology, and clearly bear upon historical demography. My interests relate primarily to rural and community history. The neglect of such study is despite the information in parish registers about residence upon marriage. In addition, it is usually argued that nuptiality and fertility were the main determinants of demographic trends in England.[4] England's leading historical demographer has written that 'Marriage could be said to have been in the past the great valve which regulated population change.'[5] Given the demographic importance of female marriage age and of the proportions of women marrying, research has focused upon those topics, and upon the determinants, customs, and social history of marriage, producing a thriving field of investigation, yet one that needs to be augmented by study of parochial endogamy.

A further reason for pursuing this is the relevance of geographical endogamy to research on local cultural regions and their distinctiveness. Many areas of the country were noticeably more endogamous than others, as we shall see. The reasons for this might include population size or density, sizes of parishes, regional topography, local xenophobia or custom, or poor law administration, employment priorities and the settlement laws. Both the significance of this subject for the persistence of local cultures, and the demographic and economic importance of this cultural variation, remain unappreciated. It was also the case that marriage customs varied by region, in little fathomed ways. For example, it is frequently said that there was a custom in England for weddings to take place in the wife's parish ('uxorilocal' weddings), but for her then to move to her husband's parish.[6] Yet almost no research has measured the extent

---

[4] See in particular E. A. Wrigley and R. S. Schofield, *The Population History of England, 1541–1871: A Reconstruction* (London, 1981); and E. A. Wrigley, R. S. Davies, J. E. Oeppen and R. S. Schofield, *English Population History from Family Reconstitution, 1580–1837* (Cambridge, 1997).

[5] E. A. Wrigley, 'Small-scale but not parochial: the work of the Cambridge Group for the History of Population and Social Structure', *Family and Community History*, 1 (1998), p. 29.

[6] E. A. Wrigley, 'Clandestine marriage in Tetbury in the late 17th century', *Local Population Studies*, 10 (Spring, 1973), p. 16; E. A. Wrigley, 'A note on the life-time mobility of married women in a parish population in the later eighteenth century', in M. Drake (ed.),

of this, or changes in it. Nor has there been consideration of the regional variety that underlay it, or of the alternative practice of 'virilocal' weddings: of marriage taking place in the husband's parish.[7]

Analysis of geographical endogamy or exogamy also brings one to studies of migration, which have flourished in recent decades. Included here have been analyses of 'marriage horizons' and distances between spouses' residences. The results have underlined the predominantly local nature of marriage. In particular, considerable light has been shed on marital horizons after 1837, during the crucial period of rural depopulation. There have been pioneering articles by Peel, Constant, and Perry.[8] The pattern of change they uncovered, identified for certain districts only, was one in which often high levels of parochial endogamy and restricted marriage horizons declined rapidly from some point between about 1830 and 1880.[9] This was closely connected with out-migration from the land. Constant found that in an adjoining area of Northamptonshire and Huntingdonshire, in the century after 1754, the average distance

---

Population Studies from Parish Registers (Matlock, 1982), p. 117; E. A. Wrigley, 'The effect of migration on the estimation of marriage age in family reconstitution studies', *Population Studies*, 48 (1994), pp. 88, 95, 96; M. Strathern, *Kinship at the Core: An Anthropology of Elmdon, a Village in North-west Essex in the Nineteen-sixties* (Cambridge, 1981), p. 237; J. Robin, *Elmdon: Continuity and Change in a North-west Essex Village, 1861–1964* (Cambridge, 1980), p. 27.

[7] In this discussion, 'marriage' and 'wedding' will be used as synonymous terms. With regard to the terms 'uxorilocal', 'virilocal', 'endogamy' and 'exogamy', there is slightly different (and often varying) usage in the anthropological literature, and I ask for forbearance among anthropologists for my terminological reapplications here. A brief summary of changing usage of the term 'exogamy' within anthropology may be found in S. Wolfram, *In-laws and Outlaws: Kinship and Marriage in England* (New York, 1987), pp. 169–80.

[8] R. F. Peel, 'Local intermarriage and the stability of rural population in the English Midlands', *Geography*, 27 (1942), pp. 22–30; A. Constant, 'The geographical background of inter-village population movements in Northamptonshire and Huntingdonshire, 1754–1943', *Geography*, 33 (1948), pp. 78–88; P. J. Perry, 'Working-class isolation and mobility in rural Dorset, 1837–1936: a study of marriage distances', *Transactions of the Institute of British Geographers*, 46 (1969), pp. 115–35. See also B. Maltby, 'Easingwold marriage horizons', in Drake (ed.), *Population Studies*, pp. 113–14, on localised marriage patterns; D. Mills and J. Mills, 'Rural mobility in the Victorian censuses: experience with a micro-computer program', *The Local Historian*, 18 (1988).

[9] See also Strathern, *Kinship at the Core*, p. 293 n. 41, on the decline in endogamous (Elmdon–Elmdon) marriages registered in Elmdon church. These comprised 84 per cent of all marriages in 1813–22, falling to 74 per cent (1843–52), 50 per cent (1873–82), 19 per cent (1943–52), and 12 per cent (1953–62).

between spouses was very small indeed, being only a few miles. Marriage distances grew from about 1850, a consequence in particular of the railway, which re-oriented the outlook of parish inhabitants. Constant noted the persisting effects of physical barriers and 'local prejudice' as influencing marriage networks. He also indicated that marriage distances may enlarge or contract over time, and that there is no reason to suppose a linear historical increase in such horizons.[10]

In an important article covering twenty-seven west Dorset parishes, between 1837 and 1936, Perry revealed that change away from localism and high parochial endogamy occurred strikingly among the labouring poor from the mid-1880s.[11] He excluded many better-off classes to allow concentration upon the labouring population, and was thus able to show the decline of their 'isolation' within the countryside from about that time. This resulted from the effects of broader education and literacy, extra-parish school friendships, declining population and so lesser self-containment of villages, rising living standards, falling working hours, the railway, the widening of courtship areas (beyond about four miles) after the coming of the affordable Stanley safety bicycle from 1885, and the erosion of some features of local custom and prejudice. Although he omitted from his analysis higher classes and occupations, whose average marriage distances would have been greater than those for the labouring poor, a memorable feature of his study was how very isolated and endogamous the rural poor were prior to the 1880s. It would hardly be possible to find higher levels of endogamy than those obtaining at the start of his study – about 80 per cent of marriages then being intra-parochial. This raised previously unasked but important questions about whether those high levels had been long-established prior to 1837.

It is worth highlighting additional findings from the few other related studies. Millard, analysing marriages for Stony Stratford (Bucks.), discovered that there was an 'apparent retrenchment of marriage horizons' between 1794 and 1833.[12] He felt that this

[10] Constant, 'Geographical background', pp. 80–5.
[11] Perry, 'Working-class isolation', pp. 130–3. I have re-presented his interesting findings in figure 4.8 of this chapter.
[12] J. Millard, 'A new approach to the study of marriage horizons', in Drake (ed.), *Population Studies*, p. 161.

might be related to falling real wages and to aspects of poor law administration. A similar explanation, involving the settlement and poor laws, was advanced by Eversley, when he pointed to evidence for rising parochial endogamy in the eighteenth century.[13] In his study of Bickenhill (Warws.), Skipp argued for a shift towards very largely local marriages in the period 1758–1847, away from marriages involving greater distances between spouses which had been common earlier, when many spouses were from such places as Coventry, Birmingham, Solihull and Coleshill.[14] In an interesting study of seventeen Shropshire parishes, Sogner found that a tendency for both partners to come from the same parish became more pronounced over 1711–60, most notably between 1711–20 and 1751–60.[15] Hunter's work on the estate village of Haynes (Beds.) showed extra-parochial marriages falling considerably as a percentage of all marriages between 1754 and 1833, with few changes in their distances.[16] Yasumoto uncovered something similar in Methley and York, and there were hints of this in Estabrook's work on Bristol and nearby Olveston.[17] The evidence for changes in this direction – towards increasing geographical endogamy after the mid-eighteenth century – is as yet scanty, but it has been building up in a surprising and suggestive way. This is most tantalising,

---

[13] D. E. C. Eversley, 'Exploitation of Anglican parish registers by aggregative analysis', in E. A. Wrigley (ed.), *An Introduction to English Historical Demography* (London, 1966), p. 64. 'There is little', he added, 'in the English sociological literature about the pattern of marriages in the geographical or sociological sense' (*ibid.*, p. 94 n. 42), a point that still remains valid. D. E. C. Eversley, 'A survey of population in an area of Worcestershire from 1660 to 1850 on the basis of parish registers', in D. V. Glass and D. E. C. Eversley (eds.), *Population in History: Essays in Historical Demography* (1965, London, 1974), analysed fifteen parishes around Bromsgrove in north Worcestershire, and was able 'to state quite clearly that marriages between partners of different parishes were actually more frequent in the eighteenth century than in the early nineteenth century' (p. 412). His figures after *c.* 1800 gave much higher percentages of 'home' marriages than hitherto, especially in large parishes. He argued that 'Greater freedom of movement cannot therefore have contributed to increase of population by providing more scope for marriage.' *Ibid.*, p. 413.

[14] V. H. T. Skipp, *Discovering Bickenhill* (Birmingham, 1963), p. 39.

[15] S. Sogner, 'Aspects of the demographic situation in 17 parishes in Shropshire, 1711–1760', *Population Studies*, 17 (1963), pp. 132–3.

[16] A. Hunter, 'Marriage horizons and seasonality: a comparison', *Local Population Studies*, 35 (1985), pp. 38–40.

[17] M. Yasumoto, *Industrialisation, Urbanisation and Demographic Change in England* (Nagoya, 1994), pp. 72–3; C. B. Estabrook, *Urbane and Rustic England: Cultural Ties and Social Spheres in the Provinces, 1660–1780* (Manchester, 1998), pp. 94, 97, 99.

for if these hints from local studies were more widely applicable, they would demonstrate an accentuation of parochial endogamy during English industrialisation, when few historians would expect to find this occurring. The implications of this might well include some tightening and closure in parish senses of belonging over this period, at least when considered via this cultural and demographic theme.

II

As this distillation of earlier findings suggests, my concern here is with geographical marital endogamy and exogamy using the historical parish as the basis of study. In other words, I am not considering endogamy within status groups (so-called 'homogamy'), or within occupations,[18] or religious denominational endogamy,[19] or kinship endogamy as studied by many anthropologists. Nor am I considering 'marriage horizons' as conventionally measured, since it is usual to find short distances between spouses' residences, especially among the labouring poor.[20] Given the fundamental importance of the parish as the

---

[18] Significant occupational endogamy can be found, for example in fishing villages, among agricultural labourers, weavers, framework knitters, lead and coal miners. (This could also involve parochial endogamy, as some lower-class workers had more marriage options locally than higher-status people seeking a bride of equivalent social standing.) Such endogamy was sometimes related to the need for reciprocal skills between partners and high output from family economies, as in cottage textile trades. With agricultural labourers, there could be a kind of default endogamy, women from other occupational families preferring not to marry into such a low-waged group, as with women in some regions of twentieth-century Ireland. Yet England almost never attained the levels of occupational endogamy often found in parts of the Ivory Coast, or China, or among the Masai, or in India where caste was so intimately tied to occupation. See also J. R. Gillis, *For Better, For Worse: British Marriages, 1600 to the Present* (1985, Oxford, 1988), pp. 116–18.

[19] That existed to some extent. The best British examples, comparable to the South Dakota Hutterites, were the sixteenth-century Familists, the Quakers, and to a lesser extent some General Baptists in the early eighteenth century. Some of the Methodist denominations (such as the Primitive Methodists) inclined towards denomination endogamy in certain times and places. There was usually a tendency for people to marry partners of the same denomination.

[20] Sogner, 'Aspects of the demographic situation', pp. 131–3; Skipp, *Discovering Bickenhill*, pp. 39–40; B. Maltby, 'Easingwold marriage horizons', *Local Population Studies*, 2 (1969), also in Drake (ed.), *Population Studies*, pp. 113–16; J. R. Cole, 'Marriage horizons in east Kent, 1620–1640' (unpublished essay deposited in the Centre for English Local History, University of Leicester, 1977); Millard, 'A new approach', also in Drake (ed.), *Population Studies*; G. A. Harrison and A. J. Boyce, 'Migration, exchange, and the

local unit of administration, and of its northern township equivalents in many cases, it will be the unit of analysis here. This importance of the parish is universally recognised in historiography dealing with such diverse subjects as the Anglican Church, registration of vital events, boundary maintenance, highways, enclosure, the militia, local charities, the poor law and legal settlement, or many facets of folklore, the cultural calendar and local politics. The centrality of the parish to local life and identity is indisputable. Such a stress here has the benefit of relying upon a local sense of place that was subjectively and administratively very real indeed to contemporaries, and it will serve us best for the analytical purpose in hand.

To explore these issues more extensively, 18,442 marriages were analysed from the published registers of sixty-nine parishes, scattered across eight counties.[21] These comprise rural parishes in Derbyshire, Dorset, Lancashire, Leicestershire, Norfolk, Northumberland, Oxfordshire and Sussex. They are listed in Appendix 4.1, alongside the documented years used for calculations. Their locations are shown in figure 4.1, from which it will be apparent that I have picked clusters of parishes in disparate English regions, to check for national homogeneity, or to allow any possible regional patterns to emerge. Rural parishes rather than larger market towns were chosen so as to dilate earlier historiographical findings, and to give this study a rural coherence which it would lack if a fuller range of parishes across the whole rural–urban spectrum was used. However, a diversity of rural settlements in very differing regions was deliberately chosen, from places such as Snoring Parva in Norfolk or Wootton Fitzpaine in Dorset, to Urswick in Lancashire or Edlingham in Northumberland. Considerable variation in population size and acreage existed across such places, their 1841 populations ranging between 59 and 1,433. With regard to the

---

genetic structure of populations', in G. A. Harrison and A. J. Boyce (eds.), *The Structure of Human Populations* (Oxford, 1972), p. 133.

[21] The places studied are listed in Appendix 4.1, at the end of this chapter. Calculations were conducted on a parochial basis from Anglican registers. A very large majority of these places are parishes. In a few cases, the place was a township or chapelry within a parish, having its own Anglican register. To ensure consistency, calculations for such places were still made on a parochial rather than township basis, a township register being treated here as a geographically unrepresentative sample of all marriages in that parish. The published registers analysed are listed in Appendix 4.2.

Figure 4.1   Places providing registers.

religious complexion of these places, and its possible influences upon courtship, marriage or registration, 58 per cent of them had a Nonconformist or Catholic chapel at some point during the nineteenth century. This is close to the figure that one might expect (51 per cent) from analysing such English rural parishes in the 1851 Census of Religious Worship.[22] Allowing for some additional chapels documented in other and later sources consulted, it is very closely representative. There were no Quaker meeting houses, with the potential to register marriages separately. Given the expansion of 'Old Dissent' from the mid-eighteenth century, only a few old dissenting places of worship could have existed in these places a century earlier. Religious dissent would have had little effect upon marriage registration, especially after Lord Hardwicke's 1753 Act. Nonconformity mainly affected baptism and burial registration.[23] Further tests suggest that the cultural repercussions of Nonconformity had little influence on my calculations of endogamy.[24] I started this

[22] The latter 'expected' figure is calculated from 1,726 English rural parishes with populations under 1,500 in 1851, using the enumerators' returns to the 1851 Census of Religious Worship. These data are outlined in K. D. M. Snell and P. S. Ell, *Rival Jerusalems: The Geography of Victorian Religion* (Cambridge, 2000). After 1837, a range of sources (the Census of Religious Worship, nineteenth-century county directories and the 1874 edition of Wilson's *Imperial Gazetteer*) showed a Catholic chapel (or school) in Eastwell, Melling, and Pyrton; an Independent chapel in Ardingly, Cocking, Piddletown, Rampisham, South Creake, and Stoke Abbot; a Baptist chapel in East Stower Gilmorton, Knipton, Morley, Queniborough, Smalley, and Standlake; a Wesleyan Methodist chapel in Bothal, Breadsall, Chickerell, Downham, East Stower, Elvaston, Hanborough, Holme Hale, Houghton on the Hill, Morley, Pennington, Piddletown, Swithland, Syderstone, Thurmaston, and Whalton; and a Primitive Methodist chapel in Chickerell, East Barsham, Helhoughton, Holme by the Sea, Holme Hale, Horningtoft, Northmoor, Pyrton, Queniborough, Runham, South Creake, Snoring Magna, Snoring Parva, Standlake, and Syderstone. There were also unspecified dissenting chapels at Birstall and Stoke Abbot. Most of these were built after 1801, and many of them after 1837 (when my analysis of marriage ends), although their later building may hint at earlier congregations.

[23] From the operation of that Act in 1754, until the start of civil registration of marriages in 1837, 'the Church of England had a monopoly of legally valid marriages and a legal duty to administer them, with the exception of the marriages of Jews, Quakers, and members of the royal family'. Wrigley and Schofield, *Population History*, pp. 29, 73; Wrigley, Davies, Oeppen and Schofield, *English Population History from Family Reconstitution*, pp. 87–91; Wrigley, 'Clandestine marriage in Tetbury', p. 20.

[24] My interest here relates not to the adequacy of marriage registration, but to the possibility that some Nonconformists had different senses of place to Anglicans. Methodist circuits traversed the Anglican (or non-evangelically led) parish, and the various layers of Methodist organisation could open up different prospects of potential marriage partners. This might separate some Nonconformist courtship and marriage horizons from those of Anglicans. This should be borne in mind, and might be expected

study from 1700, because some of the parish registers provided inadequate documentation of residence in the later seventeenth century.[25] Given the introduction of civil registration in 1837, and the work done by others on the post-1837 period, the research ended at that date, the main interest here being in the lesser studied eighteenth and early nineteenth centuries. We will, however, consider trends after 1837 from published data in due course.

It is necessary to clarify what was meant in parish registers when a person was said to be 'of' this, or another, parish. It was a very common statement indeed, becoming general after Hardwicke's 1753 Act, although widely found before then as well. The phrase 'of this parish' is found on countless gravestones too, although changing in frequency over time, something dealt with in the final chapter. The meaning of this information in registers has often seemed unclear. Historians have wondered whether 'of this parish' meant that the person was legally settled there, or was 'from' there in some loosely understood sense, or was born there, had parents or a guardian resident there, or was resident there in the short or long term.[26] One could, of course, 'belong' to a place (or to different places) in manifold ways, and ideas about 'belonging' were complex in the past, given the permutations of legal settlement, 'irremovability' status, and related legal and customary entitlements. However, Hardwicke's Act and contemporary discussions were very clear about what 'of this parish' meant, and it is worth dwelling upon this meaning.

Hardwicke's Act laid down that

all banns of matrimony shall be published in an audible manner in the parish church, or in some public chapel . . . of or belonging to such

---

to conduce to rising exogamy over time, as Nonconformity expanded. However, removing the parishes with the most nineteenth-century dissenting chapels had little effect on the county trends shown here, and the parishes where Nonconformity was strongest had similar trends in endogamy to other parishes. This inclines me to believe that religious dissent is not an important issue for these marriage calculations.

[25] In some cases, this inadequacy continued into the early eighteenth century. Yearly data were analysed manually on plots distinguishing the four possible types of marriage, and in no case did analysis of a register begin until I was confident that information was being supplied on this matter. Some sub-periods have been omitted for the same reason. (See below, n. 51.) The years used are shown in Appendix 4.1.

[26] Among other discussions, see A. J. Pain and M. T. Smith, 'Do marriage horizons accurately measure migration? A test case from Stanhope parish, County Durham', *Local Population Studies*, 33 (1984).

parish or chapelry wherein the persons to be married shall dwell . . . upon three *Sundays* preceding the solemnization of marriage, during the time of morning service, or of evening service . . . and whensoever it shall happen that the persons to be married shall dwell in different parishes or chapelries, the banns shall in like manner be published in the church or chapel belonging to such parish or chapelry wherein each of the said persons shall dwell . . . the marriage shall be solemnized in one of the parish churches or chapels where such banns have been published, and in no other place whatsoever.[27]

(In such cases of dual parishes, the Act was neutral on which parish should hold the wedding.) No clergyman was obliged to publish banns unless the persons to be married, seven days before such publication of banns, delivered to him notice in writing stating 'the house or houses of their respective abodes within such parish, chapelry or extraparochial place as aforesaid, and of the time during which they have dwelt, inhabited or lodged in such house or houses respectively'.[28] With regard to residence, this therefore *implied* a week's notice plus three weeks for the calling of banns. Further, no licence for marriage was to be granted to solemnise any marriage in any other church or chapel than that belonging to the parish or chapelry 'within which the usual place of abode of one of the persons to be married shall have been for the space of four weeks immediately before the granting of such licence'. There was further reference in the Act to 'the usual place of abode of one of the parties'.[29] The wording 'of this Parish', or 'of the Parish of . . .', was specified as the form for the entry.[30]

Throughout Hardwicke's Act, it was abundantly clear that residency was meant. No alternative was even hinted at.[31] This should not surprise us, for such intent was common long before

---

[27] An Act for the Better Preventing of Clandestine Marriages, 26 Geo. II, c. 33, s. 1 (italics in original).

[28] *Ibid.*, s. II.

[29] *Ibid.*, s. x. The other stipulations of the Act (e.g. about under-age marriages, and the marriages of Quakers and Jews) do not bear on this issue. Hardwicke's Act became operative from 25 March 1754. It brought about a situation in which the residency requirements for marriage were tighter than those for baptism or burial.

[30] *Ibid.*, s. xv.

[31] For excellent discussion of residency requirements and practice under the Act, see R. B. Outhwaite, *Clandestine Marriage in England, 1500–1850* (London, 1995), pp. 80–4, 87, 98, 113, 116, 135–7.

1753. Canons 62 and 102 concerning regular church marriage had stated that marriage should be in the parish of residence of the bride.[32] Marriage was also supposed to be in place of residence under marriage licences.[33] Reforming efforts by the lower clergy in Convocation in 1714–15 had included an attempt to ensure that licences should allow marriage only in the place of residence of one of the couple, and efforts to bring this about had continued thereafter.[34] Such efforts may not have been very successful,[35] but the point here is that the presumed option had long involved *residence*, not any other concept such as birth, or place of legal settlement under the post-1662 settlement laws. From 25 March 1754, and allowing for occasional evasion of Hardwicke's Act or local circumstances such as the temporary closure of a church for repair, queries over the status of a chapelry, or the handling of extra-parochial places,[36] there can generally speaking be little further doubt about what was intended.

Some contemporaries added comments to parish-register entries to clarify their own meaning. It is possible to find clear explanatory phrases such as 'himself of this parish by residence',[37] or 'residing in this parish',[38] or 'both servants in this parish',[39] or 'one of our antient and prinple [*sic*] farmers',[40] or

---

[32] L. Stone, *Road to Divorce: England, 1530–1987* (Oxford, 1990), pp. 66, 97; Outhwaite, *Clandestine Marriage*, pp. 8–9; R. B. Outhwaite, 'Sweetapple of Fledborough and clandestine marriage in eighteenth century Nottinghamshire', *Transactions of the Thoroton Society of Nottinghamshire* (1990), pp. 40–2.

[33] Outhwaite, *Clandestine Marriage*, p. 9. In some places, many licences broke the rules about residency. See *ibid.*, pp. 35, 47–8, 66, and his 'Sweetapple of Fledborough', pp. 40–2.

[34] Stone, *Road to Divorce*, pp. 110, 116–17, 121. On problems affecting the residency stipulations of the 1753 Act, especially in city parishes, see *ibid.*, pp. 129, 135. On residency and marriage in this pre-1754 period, see Outhwaite, *Clandestine Marriage*, pp. 9, 11–12, 15–16.

[35] Stone, *Road to Divorce*, p. 100, and see below, figure 4.2.

[36] Hardwicke's Act (s. 1) laid down that when both or either of the persons to be married 'shall dwell' in an extra-parochial place, lacking a church or chapel where banns were normally published, then the banns were to be published in a church or chapel for a parish or chapelry adjoining the extra-parochial place, and the clergyman publishing the banns should proceed as if either of the persons to be married 'dwelt' in that adjoining parish.

[37] Simpson (ed.), *Derbyshire Parish Registers*, Smalley, 29 November 1789, p. 151.

[38] *Ibid.*, Elvaston, 29 October 1794, p. 106.

[39] J. F. Haswell (trans.), *The Parish Registers of Brougham, 1645–1812* (Penrith, 1943), p. 45.

[40] Wood (ed.), *Registers of Long Houghton* (Northumberland), 21 October 1710, p. 82.

'dter to the antient race of that name here',[41] 'of an old race here',[42] or 'native of Norton'.[43] Specific mention of residency, which is found before 1754 as well as afterwards, indicates an understanding similar to that found in Hardwicke's Act, and it is probable that in the other examples quoted above the person was also resident.

In a few cases an entry can be more ambiguous, as in the case of 'George Turner, a mariner, an inhabitant of no parish',[44] or 'William Hutton, a travlar, of no parish'.[45] Examples such as these can perhaps be taken as not locally resident. Thomas Sutton was said to be 'of Ashborne, but now of Kedleston'.[46] Samuel Merry was 'residing in this parish, but of the parish of Kidlington'.[47] William Wood was 'of Hugnaston, residing in this parish'.[48] In these cases residence seems apparent, but something else was being alluded to. In some instances, clearer allusions were made to legal settlement status, and this was most probably the case where a person was referred to as 'a sojourner', or the couple were said to be 'both sojourners'.[49] In such cases it is almost certain that the person so labelled was parochially resident, but legally settled elsewhere, perhaps with a settlement certificate, for that often meant a 'sojourner' in the eighteenth century. This is more explicit in the case of 'William Morgan, certificated to this par. from the par. of Dry Sandford, and Residing in Yarnton'.[50] However, I have found

---

[41] *Ibid.*, 16 June 1719, p. 85.

[42] *Ibid.*, 5 July 1726, p. 87.

[43] An example cited in Pain and Smith, 'Do marriage horizons accurately measure migration?', p. 45.

[44] Wood (ed.), *Registers of Long Houghton* (Northumberland), 1 December 1771, p. 98.

[45] *Ibid.*, 7 September 1779, p. 100.

[46] Simpson (ed.), *Derbyshire Parish Registers*, p. 180 (Kedleston, Derb.), 1 January 1763. It is my impression that estate or 'closed' villages (like this one) were often more observant in the wording used.

[47] Phillimore and Oldfield (eds.), *Oxfordshire Parish Registers*, Yarnton, 1815, p. 151. For some similar but much earlier examples, from the Diocese of Canterbury between 1475 and 1600, see D. O'Hara, *Courtship and Constraint: Rethinking the Making of Marriage in Tudor England* (Manchester, 2000), p. 125.

[48] Simpson (ed.), *Derbyshire Parish Registers*, Elvaston, 29 October 1794, p. 106.

[49] See for example *ibid.*, p. 180 (Kedleston, Derb.), 26 August 1765. One may also very occasionally find 'lodgers in the parish', as in Yarnton (1809), in Phillimore and Oldfield (eds.), *Oxfordshire Parish Registers*, p. 150.

[50] Phillimore and Oldfield (eds.), *Oxfordshire Parish Registers*, Yarnton, 1821, p. 152.

such reference to legal settlement status in only a handful of cases out of over 18,000 marriages. With regard to legal settlement, one does not find the attendant entries that one would expect if this was the main issue prior to Hardwicke's Act. Mention of a certificate (probably a settlement certificate) is very rare indeed, which is perhaps yet another reason why one should not exaggerate their usage. Further, if settlement was being referred to one would expect more often to see further qualifications made or mentioned (forty days' residency, certificates, rent paid, paternal settlement and so on). These are virtually always lacking in marriage registers.

While it is possible to dwell on interesting examples in the hope of general illumination, most entries in registers are plainer and simply state 'of this parish' or 'of [place]'. Standardisation of entry improves from 1754, as prescribed by the new Act, but there is unlikely to have been much difference in the *meaning* of such wording before and after 1754. I did not use entries when such reference to place was lacking in a register over a substantial number of years. Such periods sometimes coincide with particular clergymen's incumbencies. There are periods (mainly before 1754) when it is necessary to drop marriages from analysis because no information was being given.[51] However, for the (published) registers analysed here, I was struck by how

---

[51] The years used for analysis of parishes are shown in Appendix 4.1. The data from each register were inspected on yearly dot-type plots, in which the four possible types of marriage were visually distinguished, and periods of ten or more years with no mention of external places were generally excluded. When graphically shown, periods of omitted residential entries usually stand out very clearly against the running patterns for each parish. In my sixty-nine parishes, such periods affect twelve registers (mainly in Leicestershire, Dorset, and Norfolk), usually in the early eighteenth century. Excluding such parishes does not alter the findings (county graphs including them and excluding them were almost identical) and the omitted periods have no influence. Periods omitted because external residency was not being registered are indicated in Appendix 4.1. In normal periods, when people were being regularly entered as resident in another place, names with no residential wording were interpreted as being 'of this parish'. In an era in which insider–outsider divisions, however defined, were crucial to so much of parochial life, when the clergy were intimately involved with vestry administration, and when such register entries were often used as a leading avenue of enquiry in settlement cases and disputes, I suspect that these entries are really quite reliable. I have, however, used published registers, which are often of higher quality than unpublished ones, and careful scrutiny of the quality of the register is an essential prior condition for this kind of research, as for other demographic purposes.

good these details generally were both before and after 1754. Given the unequivocal wording of Hardwicke's Act, and the generally reinforcing nature of the more explicit register entries, the strong presumption is that residence was almost always meant by contemporaries. This may have been anything from long-term residence, amounting to family ties of considerable longevity, down to quite short-term residence, such as a period of recent service or brief employment. It is necessary to stress this possible residential variation. Such evidence does not necessarily tell us anything very certain about mobility, or where a person 'came from': one person may have been resident in a parish all his/her life, while another may have led a highly picaresque rambling existence before recently becoming resident. Both such cases would normally and simply be said to be 'of this parish', a phrase that cannot be taken to imply geographical stability. One needs therefore to be very careful indeed in generalising about trends in residential stability, or labour mobility, from parish-register material. Many familial, cultural and other factors influenced where vital events were registered, and the registration of those events may be a poor indicator of the nature of migration. It is possible that residence upon marriage better reflects adult residence than registration of baptisms and burials, given many customs affecting baptism or burial;[52] but marriage itself was also a custom-influenced and positioned event,[53] and clearly there are grounds for caution in extrapolations from findings about geographical endogamy. These points are inescapable, notably in a society with so many servants, apprentices, and other mobile people, and they may vitiate some incautious studies of migration using marriage registers. Even so, limitations and caveats of similar kinds are inherent in all sources which partially document personal mobility in the past, and they should not prevent research into geographical endogamy using the enormous quantity of parish-register evidence.

---

[52] And see above, n. 29.
[53] See my 'Parish registration and the study of labour mobility', *Local Population Studies*, 33 (1984), pp. 29–43, on custom-related mobility for registration of vital events.

III

For present analytical and presentational purposes, and to aid analysis of change over time, marriages may be categorised as follows:

A – All registered marriages in a parish.[54]

F – 'Foreign' marriages, where both partners are resident elsewhere.[55]

B – Bride-as-outsider marriages (the bride being resident elsewhere).

G – Groom-as-outsider marriages (the groom being resident elsewhere).

E – 'Endogamous' marriages, where both partners are resident in the parish of marriage.

Developing from these categories, for present purposes I shall define 'uxorilocal' marriages as those weddings taking place in the wife's parish of residence, in which the husband may or may not be resident elsewhere. (These comprise categories G plus E.) 'Virilocal' marriages are those taking place in the husband's parish of residence, in which the wife may or may not be resident elsewhere (categories B plus E). 'Exogamous' marriages comprise categories F, B and G. For some analytical purposes, however, it may be desirable to exclude 'foreign' marriages from that exogamous category, and this would entail taking only B plus G.[56] Changes in marriage behaviour over time may manifest themselves in shifts in the relative numbers of any of

---

[54] I included all registered marriages by banns or licence, that took place in the church or chapel documented by the Anglican register. Banns without a subsequent marriage, and mention of banns or licences for marriages elsewhere, were ignored. Five of the Northumberland registers (for Hebburn, Edlingham, Whalton, Longhoughton and Ingram) also gave entries (from 1754) for banns called in these places of worship for which the marriages were solemnised elsewhere. Dual calling of banns was required under Hardwicke's Act (section 1) when the persons to be married 'shall dwell in divers parishes or chapelries'. These Northumberland entries were usually for locally resident men who were marrying in another place, and I have excluded them from my calculations. No other registers supplied this information.

[55] The term 'foreign' marriages was used by contemporaries in the eighteenth century to describe such marriages, and that usage is adopted here.

[56] For example, one might wish to calculate exogamous marriages over time as a percentage of all marriages excluding foreign marriages: $((B + G) / (A - F)) \times 100$.

these five categories. I hope to illuminate these shifts between 1700 and 1837.

When I began to explore this subject, I anticipated finding a decline in endogamy over this key early period of industrialisation, and an opening up of rural marriage patterns. I envisaged an argument that linked rising exogamy with greater migration, associated with industrialisation and large-scale military mobilisation, some presumed relaxation of the settlement laws, agricultural innovation and regional specialisation, greater reliance upon solely wage-dependent labour, expansion of cottage industry and its supply and marketing networks, the effects of extra-parochial Nonconformist organisation, and other related matters. There were many indications in the historiography and theoretical literature that would support such expectations. The corollary, which I anticipated, would have been some loosening of the ties of belonging as a result of the enormously significant changes in English society over this period.

However, the findings were quite contrary to this. The results were unexpected and remarkably consistent across the diverse range of parishes. To display them, the parish figures for each county have been combined, and expressed by decade.[57] It is helpful to start with 'foreign' marriages, where both partners were resident outside the parish. The dramatic changes here are shown in figure 4.2. All counties show the same major reduction in 'foreign' marriages, to very low percentages of all marriages after 1754. One sees the very considerable proportion of such marriages before Hardwicke's Act, usually comprising between 10 and 30 per cent of all marriages. In some individual parishes the figures can be much higher. Hardwicke's Act, designed to restrict clandestine marriage by imposing tighter controls (with severe penalties) over residency requirements and the marriage of minors, shows itself to have been highly effective over all counties. Some 'foreign' marriages were found after 1754, but they were very few; and they were probably often the result of considerations such as the temporary closure of churches,[58] or

---

[57] This was done for analytical convenience, to distinguish counties as a guide to regions, and to avoid small number problems of the kind common in family reconstitutions.

[58] In 1830 marriages were allowed in nearby churches if a church was in disrepair or abandoned for demolition, and this certainly occurred earlier. See 11 Geo. IV, c. 18.

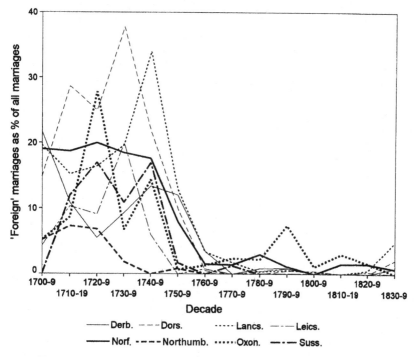

Figure 4.2   'Foreign' marriages as a percentage of all marriages.

absentee clergy, necessitating marriage in a place where neither partner was normally resident. Such marriages were rare after 1754, and the parish data indicate that this change came about swiftly following the Act.

In some cases registers contain entries resembling that for Chickerell, Dorset: 'Here end all Foreign Marriages.'[59] It is worth stressing the very large numbers of 'foreign' marriages conducted in some parishes before 1754, which was tantamount to a local clerical industry in some places. Of the chosen sixty-nine parishes, Askerswell (1719–53), Urswick (1723–48), Downham (c. 1724–54), Halton (1727–54), Tatham (1706–37), Swithland (1721–34), Syderstone (1729–54), North Barsham (1700–20), Tatterford (1743–53), Snoring Parva (1723–39), Edlingham (1710–22), and Alton Pancras (1700–18) all showed sizeable numbers of such marriages in the years indicated. Such marriage business

[59] Phillimore and Nevill (eds.), *Dorset Parish Registers*, Chickerell, 9 March 1754, p. 46.

and venues were very widespread, with competitive fees.[60] Foreign marriages, Anglican registration and fees draw attention to clerical incumbency, income, and the economic history of the Church of England. As Adair remarked about the Diocese of Ely in the seventeenth century, some ecclesiastical authorities probably saw clandestine marriage as 'a nice little earner'.[61] Connections between these subjects remain largely neglected by church historians and demographers. The practice was not one that was growing inexorably until 1754, for peaks often occurred some time before then, and some parishes show very little sign of it. In others, however, the large numbers indicate that certain clergy were deliberately supplementing their often inadequate income with fees from 'foreign' marriages, which they were clearly keen to conduct. High proportions of foreign marriages were associated with low values of ecclesiastical livings, markedly so in some of the Dorset and Derbyshire parishes. Scanty clerical income was a significant problem for many smaller benefices. The foundation of Queen Anne's Bounty in 1704 aimed to augment such income, but it was very slow and long term in effect. Gains in the clergy's economic position in parishes enclosed by Parliamentary Act had yet to occur. In addition, clerical non-residency was more of a problem at this time than later; and for many couples this would have necessitated marriage in places where they were non-resident. Presumably many of these marriages were 'clandestine', as perceived by Hardwicke's Act and by modern social historians – but the issue is not only a matter of demand from couples intent on surreptitious marriage. The use and abuse of the licence system also needs to be considered, as well as the supply of clerical services and competitive fees. Inadequate incomes often underlay clerical absenteeism, and until 1754 'foreign' marriages were one possible remedy for the clergy, so strikingly shown here.

---

[60] Some chapels or venues became notorious for such marriages. In my chosen counties a well-known example was Peak Forest near Chapel-en-le-Frith in north Derbyshire: an extra-parochial chapel apart from normal episcopal jurisdiction, and famous for runaway marriages – so much so that it had a separate register for them, entitled 'Foreign Marriages'. For some time these averaged about sixty a year, bringing in around £100 per annum for the minister. T. L. Tudor and E. C. Williams, *Derbyshire* (1903, London, 1950), p. 140.

[61] R. Adair, *Courtship, Illegitimacy and Marriage in Early Modern England* (Manchester, 1996), p. 141.

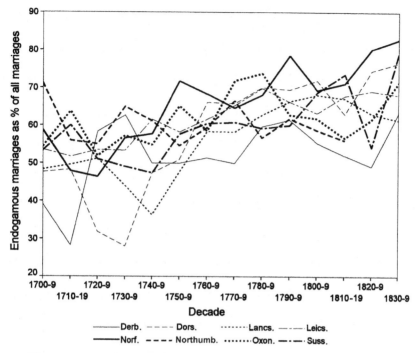

Figure 4.3   Endogamous marriages as a percentage of all marriages.

The most significant long-term change cannot be adduced as easily to Lord Hardwicke. This was the rise in endogamous marriages (category E: where both partners were from the same parish). This is shown in figure 4.3, where endogamous marriages are expressed as a percentage of all marriages. This is perhaps the most surprising finding. The change was from between approximately 45–60 per cent endogamy, rising to about 60–80 per cent. It was a consistent and steady rise across all these varied counties. (The converse of this was a long-term decline in exogamous marriages as a percentage of all marriages: from some 40–60 per cent, down to approximately 20–40 per cent.) As a development during the heyday of early industrialisation, it will be contrary to many historical expectations, although it is a change that accords well with initial suggestions in the historiography, as cited earlier. Hardwicke's Act seems to have been less instrumental here, for its date marks no sharp break: the change was certainly under way well before 1753, and it continued thereafter. This shift to very high levels of endogamy by the 1830s (when more than 80 per cent of all marriages in some parishes were endogamous) is very surprising. It lays the groundwork for the subsequent decline in endogamy from such high levels which was documented from various points after the mid-nineteenth century, by authors including Constant, Perry and Peel. We will see that later. Contrary to some presumptions, the high level of endogamy in the early to mid-nineteenth century was *not* a long-standing historical condition, stretching timelessly and unchangeably into the pre-industrial past. Like many other demographic phenomena, it had been subject to noticeable change earlier, and in particular the rise shown here between 1700 and 1837.

We have seen that Hardwicke's Act curtailed the numbers of 'foreign' marriages. This affects the total marriages from which these percentages have been calculated, and thus may tend to lessen the predominance of endogamous marriages before 1754. Figure 4.4 tests for this effect, by combining all sixty-nine parishes, and expressing endogamous marriages as a percentage of all marriages minus foreign ones.[62] This is shown alongside the combined percentages (all parishes) for all marriages, calculated as in figure 4.3. It will be seen that the trend is diminished when foreign marriages are eliminated, but that the overall movement is still unmistakably upward over the long term.

One of the types of marriage listed above was the 'bride-as-outsider' category, with the wedding taking place in the groom's parish of residence. These marriages are shown in figure 4.5, as a percentage of all marriages.[63] The movement was downwards here, as a long-term change, not very obviously tied to Hardwicke, with quite marked declines for the parishes in some counties, such as Norfolk, Dorset, or Northumberland.[64] In other words, it was becoming less and less common to find

---

[62] That is, using the marriage categories above: $(E/(A-F)) \times 100$.

[63] The removal of foreign marriages from the total marriages tends slightly to accentuate the downward trend, but has very little other effect.

[64] Here, as elsewhere, too much heed should not be paid to short-run fluctuations of the data, for these are largely attributable to the data sizes for these parishes, and if further data were added for more parishes such fluctuations would tend to be smoothed out. The overall patterns of change would probably be little affected.

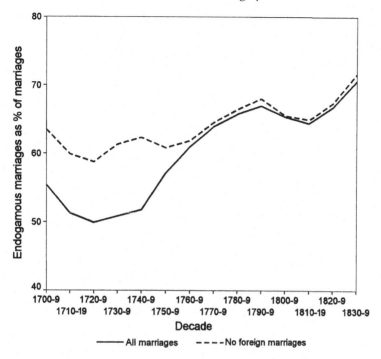

Figure 4.4   Endogamous marriages as a percentage of marriages (all counties).

'bride-as-outsider' marriages. Secondly, and associated with this, it can be shown that 'bride-as-outsider' marriages were diminishing markedly relative to 'groom-as-outsider' marriages. Taking all sixty-nine parishes together, there were about three groom-as-outsider marriages to every one bride-as-outsider marriage in the early eighteenth century. This ratio had moved to about 7:1 by the early nineteenth century, the change being especially concentrated between 1750 and 1770. Indeed, in the combined parishes of some counties, this ratio moved from about 3:1 to well over 10:1. In the Northumberland parishes, it went from about 1:1 in 1700–9, to around 20:1 between 1790 and 1819. There were steep rises also in Norfolk and Sussex, although in these three counties these ratios were declining from about 1800 (Sussex) or 1810 (Northumberland and Norfolk). In such cases one wonders about the effects of war-time mobilisation and de-mobilisation on male residence. Over the entire

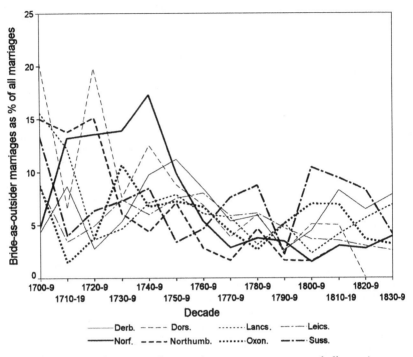

Figure 4.5 Bride-as-outsider marriages as a percentage of all marriages.

period, the trend of this ratio was strikingly upward in every county.

Another way to address these changes is to consider 'uxorilocal' marriages, defined here as weddings where the bride was resident in her parish of marriage (marriage categories G plus E). The trend here is shown in figure 4.6. Much of this encompasses the upward movement of endogamy (category E), and it was a development mainly in the mid-eighteenth century, presumably closely related to Hardwicke's Act. One also sees here a growing uniformity of practice over time and regions. From the 1760s, about 95 per cent of all marriages were of this type. As an historical generalisation, it would, of course, be an exaggeration to say that uxorilocal weddings were the norm, particularly in the early eighteenth century. However, 'giving away the bride' in her own parish, usually followed by neolocal residence in the groom's (increasingly identical) parish, was

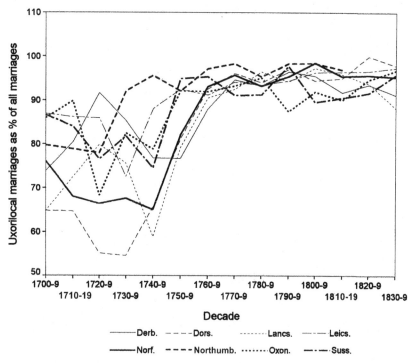

Figure 4.6   Uxorilocal marriages as a percentage of all marriages.

seemingly becoming more common.[65] Going further, some readers may already be trying to detect regional contrasts in the data for these different counties. No doubt further quantitative research would help to document local and regional

[65] Where the spousal parishes were different, this change may point to higher valuation of men and less reluctance to lose women, although the anthropological literature is uncertain about this implication. However, a rising trend of endogamy would counteract this, the women not being lost to their community. A further matter to consider is that throughout this period a wife took her husband's settlement, 'belonging' to it even if she had never been there. This had implications for her post-marital residence. With the later eighteenth- and early nineteenth-century rising relief expenditure, this could more frequently involve adverse reactions to 'foreign' married women, legally imposed upon a community that did not know them. It is therefore possible (assuming frequent synonymity of legal settlement and residence after marriage) that geographical endogamy, and thus a growing identity between maiden settlements and those of grooms (i.e. a continuity of maiden to marital legal settlement), would help to obviate the difficulties or hostility which some newly wed women might otherwise have faced during a period of high relief costs.

differences in practice (for instance in uxorilocal weddings), and would lay the groundwork for a more refined exploration of regional differences, which might also incorporate regional literary evidence. There is, after all, massive and surprisingly untapped potential for such work in English and Welsh parish registers.

IV

To develop the analysis further, and as an aid to explanation, further tests were conducted to see what factors were associated with high endogamy. The results showed that parish population size, and population density, were positively associated with high percentages of total marriages being endogamous.[66] The larger the settlement, the higher the percentage of endogamous marriages. The point here is that marriage partners could be found more easily in larger or more densely settled parishes, whereas residents in smaller parishes more commonly had to seek partners resident elsewhere.[67] This has been suggested by French data,[68] and is certainly true for these English

---

[66] Using parishes as the units of analysis, the Pearson correlation coefficient between total population (1841) and the percentage of marriages that were endogamous (for each parish over its documented period) was 0.386 ($p = .003$). Very similar results were obtained with 1811 and 1831 population totals, and with Spearman (rank) correlation. The equivalent Pearson coefficient using population per square kilometre in 1831 was 0.425 ($p = .001$). In other words, in bivariate analyses such a variable explains about 15 to 18 per cent of the variability in parochial endogamy, measured (with due precaution) as a percentage. In regression equations, population size and population density used together produce values for R squared of about 0.24 ($F = .000$). If all 'foreign' marriages are eliminated from consideration, percentages of endogamous marriages are re-calculated from the resulting totals, and these procedures are repeated, the results are little altered. All findings were re-examined with this precaution in mind, but the results differed very little from those reported here.

[67] See also D. Bryant, 'Demographic trends in south Devon in the mid-nineteenth century', in K. J. Gregory and W. L. D. Ravenhill (eds.), *Exeter Essays in Geography in Honour of Arthur Davies* (Exeter, 1971), p. 133, who argues that larger parishes had more stable populations. I do not wholly agree with this as a deduction from Bryant's data.

[68] J.-L. Flandrin, *Families in Former Times: Kinship, Household and Sexuality* (1976, Cambridge, 1979), pp. 34–5, 47, on villages in the Vallage, suggesting that the larger the village, the higher the endogamy. In very small villages, the percentages could be as low as 31 to 34. In others they rose to over 70 per cent, up to 93 per cent, sometimes associated with violence against outsiders trying to court village women (also found in England and Wales). In some mountain villages, topographical conditions could compound this and induce 'startlingly high' figures, which led to very dense kinship

parishes.[69] It can also be demonstrated for other and earlier English data.[70] Additional factors positively associated with endogamy were the population growth rate (1811–41), average numbers of marriages per annum, the proportions of families

ties. The English changes towards higher endogamy would also intensify village kin ties and produce high surname densities (which certainly was true of some Norfolk parishes). Richard Jefferies, writing about Wiltshire, commented on high levels of village inter-marriage in the early to mid-nineteenth century, and on how 'some hamlets, and even small towns, seem once to have been almost all related. The same clan name was met with at every step. Even now this may be found among the farmers; in some districts, seven or eight farms are held by men of the same name and descent. But this, too, is fast passing away, as the young men grow dissatisfied with work like that of the labourer, and seek their fortune in towns or abroad. The feudal and local spirit is all but dead.' R. Jefferies, 'The future of country society', in his *Landscape and Labour*, ed. J. Pearson (Bradford-on-Avon, 1979), p. 95, initially published in *New Quarterly* (July 1877). Such kin ties would have had many implications for community formation and consciousness. They could also have conduced to lower marriage ages through more, and more certain, courtship opportunities. S. King, 'English historical demography and the nuptiality conundrum: new perspectives', *Historical Social Research*, 23 (1998), p. 150. Such densities would have enhanced the roles of relatives and 'friends', facilitating contacts based on trust and knowledge, providing more local support for young couples, and so on. (I use the term 'friends' in the sense of the English labouring poor: to denote both 'family' and closely linked people, whether they be kin or those in close upbrought or dependent alliance.)

[69] It is a historical paradox that the most 'closed' or 'estate' parishes had to bring in many outsiders to marry (because of their 'closed' nature and small populations), while the more 'open' or populous parishes could rely more upon their own populations for partners. Thus for marriage an 'open' parish could be more 'closed' than a 'closed' one – while a 'closed' parish had to be 'open'. Such an effect was contrary to the nature of 'closed' parishes. Labour shortages in 'closed' parishes may also have conduced to similar ends, and temporary incoming labour was a way in which potential partners resident elsewhere might be met. Of my sixty-nine parishes, Kedleston, Helhoughton, Hanborough, and Langton Herring had property held 'in one hand', and Breadsall, Elvaston, East Stower, Rampisham, Swyre, Downham, Birstall, Eastwell, Queniborough, East Barsham, North Barsham, Holme by the Sea, Toftrees, Bothal, Edlingham, Ingram, Longhoughton, Pyrton, and Cocking had property held 'in a few hands'. I use here the landownership classifications of J. M. Wilson (ed.), *The Imperial Gazetteer*, 6 vols. (Edinburgh, n.d., *c.* 1872), favourably assessed as evidence in Snell and Ell, *Rival Jerusalems*, Appendix E, pp. 440–8. This distribution of the sixty-nine parishes into categories of landownership, as judged from this source, is exactly representative of broader patterns for the most 'closed' parishes (5.8 per cent), and shows less parishes than expected being 'in a few hands' (28 per cent, as compared with an expected 54 per cent). See *ibid.*, table 7.2, p. 225.

[70] A. Mitson, 'The significance of kinship networks in the seventeenth century: south-west Nottinghamshire', in C. Phythian-Adams (ed.), *Societies, Cultures and Kinship, 1580–1850: Cultural Provinces and English Local History* (Leicester, 1993), pp. 60, 74; C. Phythian-Adams, *Re-thinking English Local History* (Leicester, 1987), p. 35; O'Hara, *Courtship and Constraint*, pp. 123, 132–3, 135–7. I have re-analysed Mitson's figures for eleven parishes (1561–1710) along the lines of my presentation, using an unweighted mean of her population totals from five sources (1603–1743). They show much the same positive relationship (Pearson's r = 0.599) between population size and parochial endogamy as do my parishes. Curiously, their positive scatter is parallel

engaged in trade (1831), measures of religious denominational diversity (calculated from the 1851 Religious Census),[71] the value of parochial property, values of the clerical living,[72] and average per annum poor relief (1832–6). Property values *per capita*, and the proportion of families engaged in agriculture (1831), were negatively correlated with endogamy. The sex ratio was (perhaps surprisingly) irrelevant. In other words, the more these rural parishes leaned towards 'urban' characteristics, judged by such measures, the higher their percentages of endogamous marriages. All these results follow predictably from the influence of population size and density, and in statistical tests these two variables take precedence in explaining the relative ease, or difficulty, experienced by people in finding marriage partners resident in their own parish. There must have been many further cultural and social variables having influence here, most of them less amenable to statistical exploration. At present their precise roles are largely hidden from historians.

It is possible to extend this analysis, and to shed interesting light on a further regional dimension, by considering the distribution that emerges when parish endogamy percentages are plotted against population size. Figure 4.7 shows this, using parish populations in 1841, the counties of each parish being symbolically distinguished, and a lowess curve fitted.[73] The

to, but noticeably below, a linear trend for my (later) data, suggesting significantly *lower* endogamy (about 20 per cent lower) for any given population size in 1561–1710 compared with 1700–1837. (Any poorer registration earlier would produce the loss of some information about differential residency, and so would predispose to seemingly higher endogamy at earlier dates.) If this is a valid evidential and historical finding, it has very interesting implications indeed for the structure of communities and kinship densities over time, and it may suggest a longer-term rise in endogamy commencing well before 1700. It is also necessary to consider the possibility of even earlier cycles, and I have in mind the downward shift in endogamous *courtships* documented by O'Hara for Kentish parishes (1475–1594), in her *Courtship and Constraint*, pp. 127–9. As with Mitson, however, O'Hara's mean figure of 47 per cent of courtship cases being co-resident parochially (if translated into 'endogamous marriages') is well below the later figures from my work. This throws into sharp relief the very high parochial endogamy of the period *c.* 1780–1840.

[71] For further discussion of such measures, see Snell and Ell, *Rival Jerusalems*, Appendix C, esp. pp. 436–7.

[72] The latter two variables are from Wilson (ed.), *Imperial Gazetteer*, and are only loosely dependable as they are not contemporaneous with the marriage data.

[73] A few places of non-parochial character were omitted from this scattergram. On the lowess curve, see M. J. Norusis, *SPSS for Windows: Base System User's Guide, Release 6.0* (Chicago, 1993), pp. 558, 645–6.

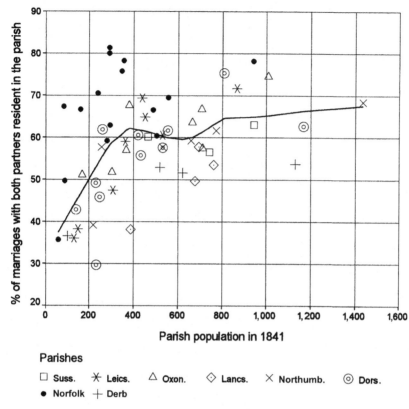

Figure 4.7 Parochial endogamy and population size.

tendency for endogamy to rise steeply up to a population of nearly 400, and then to level off, should be noted. This shows the threshold population size needed to stabilise endogamous practice. Very similar results are obtained with 1811 and 1831 population data, or with earlier measures involving average marriages per year or decade, or with population density as the independent variable.[74] The logical coherence of these

[74] With population density, endogamy rises (to about 63 per cent), stabilising when a level of approximately 50 people per square kilometre is reached. Something comparable is also found when acreage is used as the independent variable: the lowess curve rising sharply to a parish acreage of about 1,800, and then almost completely levelling off at 55–63 per cent endogamy.

findings is also reassuring for such use of residency data from parish registers.

Interesting regional characteristics are also immediately apparent from figure 4.7. The most conspicuous is the case of Norfolk, whose rural inhabitants in the past have indeed sometimes been described, for various reasons, as having rather 'stay-at-home' proclivities. One hesitates to reinforce such stereotypes, but it happens to be true that of all these parishes those in Norfolk show very much the highest endogamy relative to population size.[75] In general they are situated together in figure 4.7 well above the parishes of other counties, all being on or above the fitted line, in positions higher than their population sizes would warrant. The rural parishes of Dorset come somewhat lower in the endogamy stakes, but endogamy was still relatively high there – as one would expect from Perry's striking findings on working-class rural isolation in that county.[76] Parishes in Oxfordshire also feature high endogamy. At the other extreme, certain parishes in Derbyshire and Lancashire reveal levels of endogamy which are the lowest relative to population. These were more industrial, higher waged counties, ones in which farm service persisted in relatively unchanged forms compared with the low-wage rural south, and in which the numbers leaving their parishes of birth were higher than in the south. We should thus envisage courtship patterns which had become rather different across these regions. Furthermore, figure 4.7 clearly shows low-wage counties as having higher endogamy than high-wage ones. The indications are that higher levels of indigenous mobility, associated with the survival of service, and with proximate cottage and factory industrialisation (the pull of which helped farm service to survive in midland and northern regions), may have had a significant effect upon these geographical marriage patterns, differentiating the Derbyshire and Lancashire parishes from those in Norfolk, Dorset, Oxfordshire, and some other agricultural and southern areas. In other words, high endogamy appears to be linked to the decline of service (an institution that had structured high

---

[75] The same is true in relation to population density (people per square kilometre in 1831).
[76] Perry, 'Working-class isolation'.

youth mobility), relatively stagnant labour markets, low wages, high structural and seasonal unemployment, and perhaps resulting plebeian cultures that were hostile to interloping competitors. On the other hand, 'low' endogamy or 'high' exogamy obtained where such adverse conditions were less pronounced – that is, in the rural midlands and north.

It is always interesting to combine quantitative research with literary description, and the high endogamy of the rural Norfolk parishes invites further comment. Norfolk, like Dorset, was notorious for very low wages, high poor law dependency, and associated problems of surplus labour. Such conditions fostered sentiments that were protective of local resources for the labouring poor, and probably induced further resistance against outsiders seen to be rivals for local work, welfare, and wives. This may have heightened endogamous tendencies within these parishes. There was certainly considerable mobility. Yet in rural Norfolk from the late eighteenth century it may have involved longer-distance movement away from home in search of work (to Norwich or the East Anglian towns, London, or further afield), rather than to immediately surrounding parishes which shared surplus labour and poor law problems, and from which one might otherwise expect most marriage partners to come. Many commentators remarked upon fixity and stolid tendencies among Norfolk labourers. Very few people in Norfolk took up the assisted migration schemes under the new poor law, many fewer than in Suffolk. The Reverend C. D. Brereton (of Little Massingham, Norf.), one of the most perceptive of poor law pamphleteers, wrote in the 1820s of how

The marriages among the peasantry are now very much confined to their respective villages, or villages immediately adjoining each other. The close intermarriage of near relatives . . . is of course more frequent. We have in this parish four old men, none of whom are natives of this village . . . This is the case of the oldest inhabitants in the adjoining villages . . . they migrated in early life, in quest of employment and improvement. Whereas now . . . where they have been born, there they usually (to use the common phrase) belong; and there they seem to think they are to . . . exist and die.[77]

---

[77] Revd C. D. Brereton, *A Practical Enquiry into the Number, Means of Employment and Wages of Agricultural Labourers* (Norwich, 1824), pp. 33–4.

Immobility was even sometimes encouraged as parish policy or cultural practice. Rider Haggard, for example, commented that 'I have noticed all my life that Bradenham people cling very much to their own village.' He noted that farms to let were generally taken 'by a native and not by a foreigner'.[78] He also quoted from a printed parish form for Necton (as used in the 1830s), which spoke of the need 'to encourage those who do marry to marry those women who belong to their own village'. The aim of this was apparently to reduce 'the superabundant population', being part of a larger attempt to restrain marriage, which included rewards and penalties respectively for late and early marriage.[79] George Edwards, the Norfolk agricultural unionist, wrote about how 'there was a good bit of clannishness' about workers in rural Norfolk, and observed that 'they did not like people coming from other parts of the county to work in their district'.[80] A. G. Street in the early twentieth century wrote of how 'Norfolk's farming community . . . does not approve of interlopers from other parts . . . it would take at least three generations before one really belonged.'[81] Similar evidence could be provided for rural Dorset, although it is slightly weaker than for Norfolk. For example, a commentator in 1847 spoke of how 'In Dorsetshire we very much vegetate where we are born, and live very close indeed.'[82] Such comment should not be endorsed in any simple way, and I have sceptically discussed crude stereotypes of 'Hodge' elsewhere.[83] Even so, it is of much interest that the quantitative findings here, from a source undoubtedly open to some interpretative ambiguity in connection with migration, should reinforce such literary comment.

---

[78] H. Rider Haggard, *Rural England*, 2 vols. (London, 1906), vol. ii, p. 502.

[79] *Ibid.*, pp. 502–3. I have not found elsewhere such explicit instruction to marry women from the same parish. (Necton and East and West Bradenham are in central Norfolk, between Swaffham and East Dereham.)

[80] G. Edwards, *From Crow-Scaring to Westminster* (London, 1922), p. 28.

[81] A. G. Street, *In His Own Country* (London, 1950), p. 168, extracted from his *Country Calendar* (London, 1935).

[82] *Sixth Report from the Select Committee on Settlement, and Poor Removal*, xi (1847), p. 157.

[83] K. D. M. Snell, *Annals of the Labouring Poor: Social Change and Agrarian England, 1660–1900* (Cambridge, 1985), pp. 1–15.

V

There is no doubt that Hardwicke's Act explains some of the changes discussed here, notably the sharp decline in 'foreign' marriages. That 1753 Act certainly brought marital behaviour under tighter control.[84] In this case, the change was swift, dramatic, and permanent, perhaps more so than many demographic studies have indicated, although it is possible that consensual unions became more numerous as a consequence. The Act also presumably returned the marriages of some inhabitant couples (defined as 'foreign' elsewhere, and perhaps marrying in towns where licence surrogates were likely to live) back to their own parishes. It would in effect have augmented the endogamy rate in their home parishes. Furthermore, the Act seems to have strengthened the custom of uxorilocal weddings. Even so, many of the changes documented here were gradual and long term, beginning well before the mid-eighteenth century, and continuing long afterwards, and with regard to them the role of this Act seems less certain. The rise in endogamy was one such long-run trend, and so probably needs explanations beyond Lord Hardwicke.

There are evidential issues here, concerning improvements in parish registration and specification of residence, and the possibility that such improvements may have contributed to the patterns of apparent change shown. A number of points may be made in this connection. All data and graphs were analysed with and without the inclusion of 'foreign' marriages, and where their omission made a significant difference readers have been alerted to this. Any such improvement would have been sudden, commencing with the introduction of Hardwicke Act registers.[85] Yet this does not seem noticeable in the steady, century-long shift to higher endogamy. It may be that better documentation of residence, or perhaps a clearer understanding

[84] On the effectiveness of the Act, see also Outhwaite, 'Sweetapple of Fledborough, pp. 36, 45. The ramifications of the Act for marriage within propertied elites are discussed in D. Lemmings, 'Marriage and the law in the eighteenth century: Hardwicke's Marriage Act of 1753', *Historical Journal*, 39 (1996).

[85] Some of the parishes studied showed this introduction, older style registers being abandoned from 1753/4 and replaced by new ones, sometimes with comment by incumbents to mark the replacement.

among contemporaries that it was *residence* rather than any other concept that should be entered in registers, would have tended to increase the likelihood of extra-parochial residence being noticed after 1753 than before. Yet, as noted above, it seems clear that incumbents had long before adopted residence as the ruling presumption. In addition, any such documentary changes would probably induce an apparent shift to higher *exogamy* (i.e. partners resident in different parishes being more commonly noted), rather than higher endogamy. It would thus work against the rising trend of endogamy documented here. While such possibilities cannot be ruled out, notably after 1753, it seems more likely that the apparent trends reflect something real historically. Furthermore, if 'residency' entries in registers were fickle, random, and of little documentary value, we would surely not be finding the very clear-cut and intelligible relationships between endogamy and population size that were revealed in figure 4.7.

Accordingly, I shall proceed on the assumption that we are indeed witnessing something that was historically substantive, and which calls for an explanation in demographic and socio-economic terms. This is uncharted territory, with no historiographical signposts, and so what follows is a tentative suggestion of causation. Future historians will be able to refine or extend this account, for such work invites many comparative possibilities. The degree of endogamy certainly varied between parishes and regions, as we have seen, and I have covered only rural parishes. Yet the major changes appear to have been shared by very disparate regions. We therefore need to think about possible causes that were quite widespread.

The number of marriages in every decade was rising steadily in these parishes, as it was more widely. There is no doubt that most of these places were growing in population. Given the relationship between population size and endogamy, the rising population of settlements would itself tend to engender higher endogamy, making it easier to find partners within the parish. This must be part of the explanation. Yet this 'mechanical' explanation seems insufficient by itself, for the following reasons. First, the sixty-nine parishes were divided into sub-groups, and those eight parishes experiencing population decline between 1811 and 1841 were analysed separately.[86] While this is not a reliable guide to their eighteenth-century demography, it was nevertheless the case that these eight parishes also experienced significant rises in endogamy, much as did the entire group of parishes. Secondly, such a mechanical explanation would mainly affect the smallest parishes, with populations under about 400. At larger population sizes, further increase in population appears to have little association with higher endogamy (see figure 4.7). Endogamy (without foreign marriages) in these parishes rises from about 60 per cent to about 70 per cent (1700–1837). Extrapolation from figure 4.7 suggests that it would have taken a doubling of population size in the smallest twenty-eight parishes to achieve this (and such a doubling certainly did not occur for all small rural parishes).[87] Even when allowing for eighteenth-century growth, about half the parishes would probably be little affected by this cause.[88] It is therefore necessary to suggest additional causes.

From various points after the mid-eighteenth century, poor law expenditure also began to grow in almost all regions, usually accelerating very sharply in the 1790s and early nineteenth century. Real *per capita* expenditure on the poor also usually rose, especially from about 1813 in the south and south midlands. Very large numbers of the labouring classes became more reliant upon the poor law, and that law permeated local labour markets. This brought the labouring poor more often into touch with the settlement laws, as parishes ascertained their settlements with a view to their removal or the claiming of non-resident relief for them. Huge numbers were being examined

---

[86] Cassington, Eastwell, Edlingham, Halton, Kedleston, Tatterford, Toftrees and Whalton.

[87] Given the well-known problems with earlier sources, it is hard to arrive at satisfactory population figures for the early eighteenth century. The Cambridge Group's 404 parishes, as used by Wrigley and Schofield, *Population History*, include only three of my sixty-nine parishes. These are Ardingly, Cowfold and Standlake. Analysis of their vital events, using appropriate crude birth rates, suggests that their respective populations between 1700 and 1812 went from about 316 to 468 (Ardingly), 203 to 653 (Cowfold), and 622 to 493 (Standlake). In other words, one should not assume that such rural parishes shared national growth patterns. I am grateful to Ros Davies for these calculations using the Cambridge Group's data.

[88] The use of average numbers of marriages per annum for the early eighteenth and early nineteenth centuries produced very similar lowess curves to figure 4.7, and also suggested that over half these parishes would be largely unaffected by this 'mechanical' effect.

and removed to their settlements from the later eighteenth century. This was above all a southern situation,[89] but very many northern parishes also experienced such problems. The poor of course associated strongly with their parishes of legal settlement. Such parishes were where they 'belonged', as many letters from them said,[90] and legal settlement – defined by all contemporaries as the right to poor relief – was their final recourse and safeguard. The two most common means to gain a settlement, farm service and indentured apprenticeship, were changing away from their traditional legal forms in many areas from the mid-eighteenth century, making it harder to gain legal settlements in one's own right, enlarging the proportions who therefore took paternal settlements, and perhaps discouraging movement away from home parishes. As we have seen in chapter 3, legal settlement was something that landowners and employers (as ratepayers) were often keen to restrict, especially when relief expenditure rose sharply.[91] This legal framework, and this context of rising relief costs, provided the perfect breeding ground for intensified forms of local xenophobia: against interlopers, 'foreigners', outsiders who might threaten to usurp portions of the 'limited good' available to 'core' and settled parochial inhabitants.[92] This theme was developed in chapter 2. There had, of course, always been efforts to restrict access to communal resources, by manorial court action, local by-laws, settlement law, crowd action, and many other means. Yet issues

---

[89] For example, see B. Stapleton, 'Inherited poverty and life-cycle poverty: Odiham, Hampshire, 1650–1850', *Social History*, 18 (1993), pp. 352–4, where he also notes a significant decline (comparing 1800–49 with 1650–99) in the proportions receiving poor relief who had not been baptised in Odiham.

[90] See chapter 3, pp. 87–91. For an excellent collection of pauper letters, see T. Sokoll (ed.), *Essex Pauper Letters, 1731–1837* (Oxford, 2001).

[91] See also Snell, *Annals of the Labouring Poor*, pp. 69–84, 234–9, 334–43, on the regional decline of farm service and traditional apprenticeship, notable in many parts of southern England, and the resultant growth of the proportions who failed to gain a settlement in their own right. Those changes conduced to inter-generational continuity in parishes, and thus may be related to the rising trends in endogamy outlined here. The points I made there about changing social relations and senses of community (*ibid.*, pp. 334–43) are augmented by these complementary findings on endogamy.

[92] The discussion here derives partly from the anthropological theories of 'limited good' associated with G. M. Foster, 'Peasant society and the image of the limited good', *American Anthropologist*, 67 (1965); his 'The anatomy of envy: a study in symbolic behavior', *Current Anthropology*, 13 (1972); and Strathern's ideas of 'core' belonging, outlined in her *Kinship at the Core*.

of entitlement, and access to and exclusion from resources, became extremely acute in many rural parishes over this period. Among the examples were disputed rights to traditional forms of employment, agitation over soaring prices in years such as 1795–6, 1799–1801, or 1809–12, low wages, poor law and charity administration, reduced access to remaining commons and wastes, gleaning, the controversy over enclosure as a form of discipline and exclusion, let alone the violence against Irish harvesters, Luddism, the destruction of threshing machinery, and many other protests (e.g. 'Bread or Blood' in 1816, Captain Swing in 1830–1) that were defensive of employment. Many of these were set against the recurring and extended background of European wars. As Wrigley has pointed out, the country was on the verge of a Malthusian crisis, and, as he and Schofield have shown, it was not by any means yet clear that productivity gains would be sufficient to avert this.[93] Most labouring people in the countryside were aware of acute competition for limited resources and means of livelihood.

Such near-famine conditions and high parish dependency probably consolidated local rivalries, aggravated attempts to stop settlements being gained, and in many rural areas induced hostility to interlopers who were felt to detract from local well-being. The labouring poor faced with these crises are often described as coming to see themselves more in class terms; but these social perceptions were still chained to conservative expectation and sanguine ideas of parochial administration.[94] John Clare's *The Parish: A Satire*, to take one among many examples, was intensely bounded locally, vehement though its social grievances were.[95] Through much of rural England, a broader labouring sense of union gained fuller expression only in the 1870s, bringing together labour unions which had often hitherto

[93] E. A. Wrigley, *People, Cities and Wealth: The Transformation of Traditional Society* (Oxford, 1987), pp. 234–41; E. A. Wrigley, *Continuity, Chance and Change: The Character of the Industrial Revolution in England* (1988, Cambridge, 1990), pp. 60–7; Wrigley and Schofield, *Population History*, chs. 10–11.

[94] K. D. M. Snell, 'Deferential bitterness: the social outlook of the rural proletariat in eighteenth- and nineteenth-century England and Wales', in M. Bush (ed.), *Social Orders and Social Classes in Europe since 1500: Studies in Social Stratification* (Harlow, 1992), pp. 177–81.

[95] John Clare, *The Parish: A Satire* (written 1820–7, Harmondsworth, 1986).

been extremely localised.[96] Against this background of localised identification, compounded by many local rivalries,[97] a growing suspicion of extra-parochial outsiders coming in to marry was to be anticipated.

In the rural conditions of the late eighteenth and early nineteenth centuries, it is therefore not surprising to find parochial endogamy becoming more frequent. For women had long been seen as a 'local perquisite', and their courtship by outsiders often met with misgivings or even violence. Contemporaries remarked upon this, as they also did in France, and such views have been widely documented in later community studies touching upon notions of 'core' belonging.[98] Suspicion of interlopers, particularly newly married men coming in to reside from elsewhere,[99] was another corollary of the socio-economic conditions increasingly pressing upon the rural poor after the mid-eighteenth century. Among the sixty-nine parishes studied here, parochial endogamy was at its most extreme in rural parishes in Norfolk and Dorset, and to a slightly lesser extent in Oxfordshire and Sussex. While some of these rural areas may, for a variety of reasons, have been culturally inclined to

---

[96] N. Scotland, *Methodism and the Revolt of the Field* (Gloucester, 1981), p. 12.

[97] See chapter 2. Parochial rivalries and antagonisms were widespread across the country, fuelled by many prejudices. They periodically flared into youth-group factional violence. There is little evidence that early industrialisation diminished these local hostilities, and it may well have aggravated them.

[98] Strathern, *Kinship at the Core*, pp. 170–1, 176–9, on 'stealing women'; G. E. Evans, *Ask the Fellows Who Cut the Hay* (1956, London, 1969), p. 239; J. Lawson, *Progress in Pudsey* (1887, Firle, 1978), pp. 74–83; A. D. Rees, *Life in a Welsh Countryside: A Social Study of Llanfihangel yng Ngwynfa* (1950, Cardiff, 1996), pp. 83–4; J. Stevenson, *Popular Disturbances in England, 1700–1870* (London, 1979), pp. 51–2. Women themselves sometimes objected to the exogamous courting behaviour of men from their parish. For example, the women of Ravenstonedale (Cumbria), who 'have for many years past been much injured and abused by the illegal practice of our neighbouring parishioners', issued a proclamation in 1776 to all single men of their parish, telling them that they would be made to pay a fine or imprisoned if they married a woman from another parish. Findler, *Folk Lore of the Lake Counties*, p. 11.

[99] Brides who married in their own parishes and came to live in their husbands' parishes were perhaps more readily tolerated, as they were less threatening to parochial resources. In addition, many parish authorities during this period were eager to marry their local women to men from elsewhere, as this removed those women from parochial responsibility and risk (wives took their husbands' settlements under settlement law, and illegitimate children took their place of birth as settlement: a settled and pregnant single woman could not be removed anywhere). These considerations may underlie reinforced 'customs' of uxorilocal weddings and virilocal marital residence during this period, although it is too early yet to give this a regional underpinning.

such behaviour, these were counties with among the lowest wages, worst living standards, and highest relief expenditures in England. They were also counties where there had been considerable decline of farm service in the later eighteenth and early nineteenth centuries – that was especially true of Norfolk – and this, like their low real wages, set them apart from many other counties in the north and midlands, where mobile farm service among the unmarried usually persisted, where rural wages were much higher, and where the levels of endogamy were significantly lower (see figure 4.7).

Linking my findings to those of Perry, Constant, and Peel for the later nineteenth century, it therefore seems that rural endogamy peaked in the most adverse period of rural living standards: from about 1770 to 1840. This occurred in all regions, but it was most extreme in the rural south. In all likelihood, those threatening living conditions intensified parochial resistance against outsiders among single labouring men seeking brides.[100] Southern rural labour markets and poor law administrations especially disadvantaged single men, for married men had precedence for employment among employers who were also ratepayers. This was a factor where yearly service went into decline. In addition, solidarity among such men was likely to have been more apparent in larger, more supposedly 'open' parishes. Xenophobic parochial factionalism in such contexts, probably buttressed by 'high' kin densities, thus augmented 'mechanical' explanations of rising endogamy as linked to settlement size, which I have outlined.

The later nineteenth-century decline in endogamy can be well seen in Perry's evidence for twenty-seven rural Dorset parishes. I have re-presented those findings graphically in figure 4.8. They document a region where high endogamy was especially

---

[100] Social tensions were probably not eased by a situation in which parish poor law authorities – well versed in Malthus and illegitimacy fears – were rather differently disposed than single men towards unmarried women, seeing them as potential burdens (or suppliers of burdens) on the parish poor rates, and having every wish to see such women married out. In such social tensions over marriage, the rising endogamy of the period may suggest that in this rural arena, if in few others, the interests of the early nineteenth-century labouring poor predominated. Here, as with the causes of rising endogamy and its implications for the changing composition of communities, one sees further links connecting historical demography with the historiography of the labouring classes.

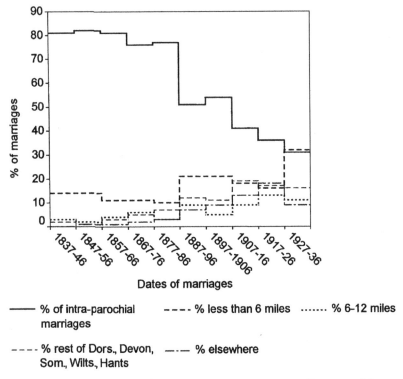

Figure 4.8   Parochial endogamy in twenty-seven west Dorset parishes,
1837–1936.

characteristic, and relatively persistent. Yet this general trend
was widely shared by other rural regions. One can see in the
figure the high endogamy that my own findings also indicated,
but then dramatic plummeting of endogamy from the 1880s, as
the Stanley safety bicycle, the railway, and other factors connected with the rural exodus widened courtship horizons. These
changes were indeed momentous, but we now know that they
did not occur from a long-standing and constant 'high' background level over previous centuries. As is now clear, the century
and a half earlier had also seen changes of great consequence,
putting in place the situation from which the late nineteenth-
century decline of endogamy occurred. It took the rising rural
standard of living, broadened horizons and declining village

populations after the mid-nineteenth century to weaken such endogamy and its associated attitudes in most parishes, to reassert a greater outwardness of rural marital behaviour as found in the early eighteenth century, and then, during the twentieth century, to reduce such extreme levels of rural endogamy to something of an historico-anthropological curiosity.

Let me end with contrasted examples of literary evidence, from very different periods, which sum up this later transition, and shed further light on the theme of belonging as seen through courtship and marriage. One always needs to be extremely cautious when reading about supposed generational changes. Nevertheless, caution spurs curiosity, and these statements contain some truth as broad generalisations, reflecting shifts that are now apparent in the quantitative evidence. I earlier quoted a Norfolk clergyman, the Reverend C. D. Brereton, writing in the 1820s from Little Massingham on the once mobile elderly men, non-native to his parish, whom he contrasted with the more endogamous, stay-at-home tendencies of the younger generation, whose 'marriages [are] very much confined to their respective villages'.[101] Now let us move forward a century or so, and compare the courting youth of a later period. By the close of the inter-war period in the twentieth century, the rural commentator and broadcaster F. G. Thomas was writing in *The Changing Village* about older 'ghetto-like' rural inhabitants who 'show very little desire to move. They seem almost as immobile as their parents . . . they will tell heroic tales of journeys in their youth in a cart drawn by a donkey.' By contrast, he wrote, 'A new mobile generation is in the country . . . infatuated by mobility. The pedal cycle, the motor bike and pillion seat, are increasing . . . They go "courting" outside the village.'[102] As T. S. Eliot put it in a passage that prefaces this book:

> . . . every son would have his motor cycle,
> And daughters ride away on casual pillions.[103]

[101] See n. 77 above.
[102] F. G. Thomas, *The Changing Village: An Essay on Rural Reconstruction* (1939, London, 1945), pp. 19–20.
[103] T. S. Eliot, 'Choruses from "The Rock"', II (1934), in his *Collected Poems, 1909–1962* (London, 1974), p. 168.

Places supplying registers for analysis of marriage

All are parishes except where indicated. Contemporary spellings have been used below. I have indicated any periods omitted because information about external residency was absent (see nn. 25 and 51). Any other non-documented years lack registers or entries.

	Years documented for endogamy
Derbyshire (total marriages: 1,395)	
Breadsall	1700–1837
Elvaston	1702–4, 1720–1837
Kedleston	1702–1836
Morley	1700–1837
Smalley (chapelry in Morley)	1702–1837
Dorset (total marriages: 2,006)	
Alton Pancras	1700–1812
Askerswell	1700–1810
Chickerell	1723–1812
East Stower	1710–1812
Fleet	1702–53
Langton Herring	1731–1812 (1700–30 omitted as residency not given)
Piddletown	1700–1812
Rampisham	1709–41
Stoke Abbot	1700–19, 1740–1837 (1720–39 omitted as residency not given)
Swyre	1702–56, 1811–37 (1757–1810 omitted as residency not given)
Wootton Fitzpaine	1700–10, 1728–1812
Lancashire (total marriages: 3,478)	
Blawith (in parish of Ulverstone)	1730–1837
Downham (chapelry in Whalley)	1700–1837
Halton	1727–1837

Appendix (*cont.*)

	Years documented for endogamy
Lowick (chapelry in parish of Ulverstone)	1727–30, 1757–1801, 1813–37 (1802–12 omitted as residency not given)
Melling (in Halsall parish)	1701–1837
Pennington	1700–1837
Seathwaite (in Kirkby Ireleth parish)	1737–1837
Tatham	1704–1837
Urswick	1700–1837
Leicestershire (total marriages: 2,678)	
Birstall	1706–9, 1760–1837 (1710–59 omitted as residency not given)
Burrough on the Hill	1703–1837
Eastwell	1722–1832
Gilmorton	1701–1837
Houghton on the Hill	1711–31, 1753–1836 (1700–10 and 1732–52 omitted as residency not given)
Keyham	1703–1836
Knipton	1700–1837
Queniborough	1720–1836 (1700–19 omitted as residency not given)
Swithland	1700–1837
Thurmaston	1721–1837
Wartnaby	1700–1837
Norfolk (total marriages: 3,260)	
East Barsham	1702–1835
Helhoughton	1700–1836
Holme by the Sea	1705–1811
Holme Hale	1700–1837
Horningtoft	1701–1834
North Barsham	1700–20, 1740–1837 (1721–39 omitted as residency not given)
Runham	1700–1812
Snoring Magna	1700–1837
Snoring Parva	1700–1837
South Creake	1727–1837

Appendix *(cont.)*

	Years documented for endogamy
Syderstone	1700–1837
Tatterford	1700–5, 1721–1837 (1706–20 omitted as residency not given)
Tattersett	1755–1836
Thursford	1700–1837
Toftrees	1757–1834
Northumberland (total marriages: 2,372)	
Alnham	1705–1812
Bothal	1700–1812
Edlingham	1700–1812
Hebburn (chapelry in	1755–1812
Bothal parish)	(1700–54 omitted as residency not given)
Ingram	1700–1812
Longhoughton	1700–1812
Whalton	1730–1812
Oxfordshire (total marriages: 2,419)	
Cassington	1700–1837
Crowell	1700–25, 1760–1836 (1740–59 omitted as residency not given)
Hanborough	1755–1837
Northmoor	1700–1837
Pyrton	1701–1836
Standlake	1700–1837
Stanton Harcourt	1721–1838
Yarnton	1706–1836
Sussex (total marriages: 834)	
Ardingly	1724–1812
Cocking	1711–1837 (1700–10 omitted as residency not given)
Cowfold	1700–1812
Total places: 69	

Published parish registers analysed

Alcock, A. and Alcock, E. (eds.), *The Registers of the Parish Church of Halton, 1727–1837* (Newport, Salop., 1987), for Halton.

Blagg, T. M. (ed.), *Leicestershire Parish Registers. Marriages*, vol. IX (London, 1913), for Swithland.

Brierley, H. (ed.), *The Registers of Tatham, 1558–1812*, Lancashire Parish Register Society, vol. 59 (Preston, 1922), for Tatham.

Challen, W. H. (trans.), *The Parish Register of Cocking, Sussex, 1558–1837* (London, 1927), for Cocking.

Clark, J., Walker, S. R. M. and Jones, A. C. J. (eds.), *The Registers of the Parish of Seathwaite*, Lancashire Parish Register Society, vol. 127: *Furness Registers* (Newport, 1988), for Seathwaite.

Dickinson, R. (ed.), *The Registers of the Chapel of Blawith in the Parish of Ulverston* (Preston, 1954), for Blawith.

The Registers of the Chapel of Lowick in the Parish of Ulverston (Preston, 1954), for Lowick.

The Register of Pennington, Lancashire Parish Register Society, vol. 127: *Furness Registers* (Newport, 1988), for Pennington.

Dukinfield Astley, H. J. (ed.), *Norfolk Parish Registers. Marriages*, vol. VIII (London, 1914), for Helhoughton, Horningtoft, South Creake and Syderstone.

Elliott, E. K. (ed.), *Leicestershire Parish Registers. Marriages*, vol. X (London, 1913), for Birstall, Houghton on the Hill and Thurmaston.

Godman, P. S. (ed.), *The Parish Register of Cowfold, Sussex, 1558–1812* (London, 1916), for Cowfold.

Harrington, D. W., Knipe, W. D., Jones, A. C. J., Benson, S. M. and Dunn, G. S. (trans.), *The Register of the Parish of Urswick, 1696–1837* (Leyland, 1992), for Urswick.

Leech, E. B. (trans.), *The Register of Tatham Fells Church (Church of the Good Shepherd), 1745–1837* (Preston, 1940), for Tatham.

The Register of Tatham Church (S. James the Less), 1813–1837 (Preston, 1940), for Tatham.

Loden, G. W. E. (ed.), *The Parish Registers of Ardingly, Sussex, 1558–1812* (London, 1913), for Ardingly.

Nall, Revd W. (trans.), *The Registers of Alnham, in the County of Northumberland* (Sunderland, 1907), for Alnham.

Phillimore, W. P. W. (ed.), *Norfolk Parish Registers. Marriages*, vol. V (London, 1910), for Holme by the Sea, Holme Hale and Runham.

Phillimore, W. P. W. (ed.), *Oxfordshire Parish Registers. Marriages*, vol. I (London, 1909), for Crowell and Pyrton.

Phillimore, W. P. W. and Blagg, T. M. (eds.), *Leicestershire Parish Registers. Marriages*, vol. v (London, 1911), for Burrough on the Hill, Gilmorton and Knipton.

    Norfolk Parish Registers. Marriages, vol. vi (London, 1912), for East Barsham, North Barsham, Snoring Magna, Snoring Parva, Tatterford, Tattersett, Thursford and Toftrees.

Phillimore, W. P. W. and Hartopp, H. (eds.), *Leicestershire Parish Registers. Marriages*, vol. vii (London, 1912), for Keyham.

Phillimore, W. P. W. and Nevill, E. R. (eds.), *Dorset Parish Registers. Marriages*, vols. vi, vii (London, 1914), for Alton Pancras, Askerwell, Chickerell, East Stower, Fleet, Langton Herring, Piddletown, Rampisham, Stoke Abbot, Swyre and Wootton Fitzpaine.

Phillimore, W. P. W. and Oldfield, W. J. (eds.), *Oxfordshire Parish Registers. Marriages*, vol. ii (London, 1910), for Cassington, Hanborough, Northmoor, Standlake, Stanton Harcourt and Yarnton.

Phillimore, W. P. W. and Randall, T. (eds.), *Leicestershire Parish Registers. Marriages*, vol. vi (London, 1911), for Eastwell, Queniborough and Wartnaby.

Price, W. B. (ed.), *The Register of the Parish Church of St. Leonard, Downham, 1605–1837* (Leyland, 1979), for Downham.

Simpson, Ll. L. (ed.), *Derbyshire Parish Registers. Marriages*, vol. xiii (London, 1914), for Breadsall, Elvaston, Kedleston, Morley and Smalley.

Walker, Revd J. (trans.) and Wood, H. M. (ed.), *The Registers of Whalton, in the County of Northumberland* (Sunderland, 1909), for Whalton.

Williams, T. (ed.), *The Registers of Melling Chapel in the Parish of Halsall, 1607–1837* (Leyland, 1969), for Melling.

Wood, H. M. (ed.), *The Registers of Bothal with Hebburn (Bothal), in the County of Northumberland* (Sunderland, 1901), for Bothal.

    The Registers of Bothal with Hebburn (Hebburn), in the County of Northumberland (Sunderland, 1901), for Hebburn.

    The Registers of Edlingham, in the County of Northumberland (Sunderland, 1903), for Edlingham.

    The Registers of Ingram, in the County of Northumberland (Sunderland, 1903), for Ingram.

    The Registers of Long Houghton, in the County of Northumberland (Newcastle-upon-Tyne, 1926), for Longhoughton.

CHAPTER 5

'A cruel kindness': parish out-door relief and the new poor law

Of all the many controversies which have been fought upon Poor Law questions the most persistent and irreconcilable has been that upon the respective merits of 'indoor' and 'outdoor' relief.[1]

It has always seemed to me a grievous error in the national economy to shut people within workhouse walls because they sought employment and could not get it . . . To me it has seemed cruel, terribly cruel, to take the aged and infirm from the cottages they have laboured to keep above their heads, and which they have sanctified with their affections, and shut them up in the workhouse, drilling them in their old days under the discipline of a barrack-yard . . . terribly cruel to break up 'the old house at home' of an old couple whose eyes see 'home' written in every corner of it.[2]

For every one in-door pauper, there are, on the average, more than twelve out-door. Such is the result of the endeavour so severely made, by the administrators of the Poor Law Amendment Act, for some time after its passing in 1834, to make the workhouse the only place of relief for the poor![3]

INTRODUCTION

At first glance, the title of this chapter might be thought self-contradictory. We are so accustomed to associate the new poor law with the union workhouse, both in popular and academic discussions, that a consideration here of out-relief in people's own homes and parishes after 1834 might seem a misplaced emphasis. After all, everyone knows that the new poor law set up unions of parishes, centrally administered in each case by

[1] H. Bosanquet, *The Poor Law Report of 1909* (1909, London, 1911), p. 168.
[2] A. Somerville, *The Whistler at the Plough* (1852, London, 1989), pp. xiv, 257–9.
[3] R. Pashley, *Pauperism and Poor Laws* (London, 1852), pp. 12–13.

regularly meeting boards of guardians, and that the administrative focus of each union was its workhouse. That building
varied greatly in terms of architecture and size; but it was commonly large, prominent, intimidating, often built on the edges
of a significant town. It was internally subdivided to cater for
classifications of paupers and vagrants. It was run by its own
staff of master, mistress, porters, school master or mistress,
nurses, chaplain and others, with an extensive budget and expenses, and it often had hundreds of inmates, many of whom
helped in its operation. Some of the urban workhouses, especially by the 1880s, were huge institutions, comprising extensive
conglomerations of buildings that covered many acres, as for
example in Liverpool. The deterrent workhouse was crucial to
'the principles of 1834'. Its conditions were in theory 'less eligible' than those experienced by the lowest day labourers
outside. It incorporated work such as stone-breaking, oakum-
picking, grinding corn, pounding bones (which was prohibited
from November 1845), wood cutting, teazing hair and coconut
fibre (to make bedding or twine), sandknocking,[4] beating
carpets, making mats, house cleaning and so on. It had dietaries
which were deliberately spartan and unappealing. All this was
fundamental to the 1834 Poor Law Amendment Act – probably
the most important legislative Act of the nineteenth century –
and an Act that remained in force for almost a century until it
was itself overturned by the 1929 Local Government Act and
the subsequent legislation which ended administration by the
guardians, set up Public Assistance Committees, revised the
rating system, and transferred poor law administration from
the unions to the County and County Borough Councils.

It is hardly surprising, therefore, that so much literature and
historiography has been dedicated to the workhouse.[5] The

---

[4] 'Sandknocking' was pounding down sand from a stone. The sand was sold for
cleaning floors, by inmates who would go out as 'sand-travellers'. This was a workhouse test at Rochdale. J. Cole, *Down Poorhouse Lane: The Diary of a Rochdale Workhouse*
(1984, Littleborough, 1994), p. 40.

[5] Among a very large literature, see M. A. Crowther, *The Workhouse System, 1834–1929:
The History of an English Social Institution* (London, 1983); P. Wood, *Poverty and the
Workhouse in Victorian Britain* (Stroud, 1991); F. Driver, *Power and Pauperism: The
Workhouse System, 1834–1884* (Cambridge, 1993). An exceptional website dedicated to
the workhouse is at *www.workhouses.org.uk*.

intense dislike of that institution – whether named 'the bastille', 'union', or 'spike' – among the working classes and many others led to an enormous contemporary popular and official literature discussing, attacking, enquiring into or defending its administration and poor law roles. The evidence leaves one in no doubt about the importance which contemporaries attached to the workhouse, whether that evidence be the Annual Reports of the Poor Law Commission, the Poor Law Board from 1847, and the Local Government Board from 1871, a long succession of Parliamentary Committees, the Special and General Orders of the central authorities, the campaigning literature for and against the new poor law, in all its subsequent stages of administration, the literature of Chartism and other popular reforming movements, a formidable body of published personal testimony, poor law pamphleteering, journalistic coverage, fictional literature, and many other publications, or much later oral history.

Furthermore, among surviving records of the new poor law, one usually finds that workhouse records are most prominent. This is generally true, but especially so of the largest urban workhouses, which have come to dominate many historical perspectives. These workhouse records included the minutes of the boards of guardians – who often met in a room in the workhouse – the admission and discharge registers, in-door relief lists, purchases, dietary tables, provisioning accounts, punishment books, master's journals and day books, medical officer's reports, and so on. In many cases, it was specifically the workhouse records that were considered worthy of archival protection. Other records (for example, out-door relief lists, abstracts, and distribution forms,[6] application and report books or ledgers, receipt and expenditure books, as filled in by relieving officers for their relief districts, or letter books containing letters from paupers seeking out-relief) have frequently been

---

[6] Relieving officers' weekly out-relief lists, in particular, have not survived well as records of the new poor law. For examples, see Salop. CRO, PL 5/105–122 (Cleobury Mortimer union); Norf. CRO, C/GP 13/841 (Kings Lynn union), and for the Aylsham union: C/P 1/145–217 (Aylsham district), C/P 1/218–85 (Eynsford district), and C/P 1/286–91 (Oulton district); Northants. CRO, PL 1/501–7 (Brackley union); Centre for Kentish Studies (Maidstone), G/AE/R/O/1–28 (East Ashford union), and G/AW/R/O/1–4 (West Ashford union).

thrown away by local government officials and archivists, who have themselves obviously been swayed by a view of the central significance of the workhouse. Even in the records kept by the central authority, workhouse documentation is much more fulsome than that about out-door relief, partly because the central authority had fairly limited powers over out-relief policy.[7] As one poor law historian has rightly commented, 'Little attention was paid to paupers on out-door relief and little information is available about the conditions under which they lived.'[8]

Accordingly, if all such emphases upon the workhouse are correct, one would certainly believe that the 1834 Act and subsequent administration marked a fundamental watershed: away from parochial localism and domiciliary forms of out-door relief, to relief being provided in workhouses which for a majority of paupers were at a distance from their home places, to which they travelled for in-door maintenance. For the poor, such an emphasis would suggest that 1834 was a major transition from parish-based poor relief to workhouse relief, in places where a large majority of them did not belong. An early reassessment of pauper cases after 1834, and the putting of many into the new workhouses, contributed to this impression. These considerations must have scored the idea into the minds even of those not receiving poor relief that their various places of settlement, belonging, or habitation were no longer where they would be relieved. This carried dire implications for their local connections, senses of community, pride in place, feelings for neighbours and local ties. It also implied that the ways in which local inhabitants had hitherto developed such associations and entitlements (through work, kinship, ratepaying, parish office-holding, loyalty to place and people) were irrelevant to fundamental life-cycle assistance, as felt by vulnerable people, who often faced severe economic circumstances which were hard to prepare for, given prevailing wage levels. Such a transition to the workhouse as the outlet for relief, rather than the parish or township, would have driven home to the labouring poor the conclusion that (what they believed to be) their traditional

---

[7] These points are also made in two excellent studies of the workhouse, by Crowther, *Workhouse System*, p. 7; and Driver, *Power and Pauperism*, p. 48.
[8] T. Thomas, *Poor Relief in Merthyr Tydfil Union in Victorian Times* (Cardiff, 1992), p. 28.

entitlements to residential welfare in their own parishes, as based upon ideas of earned local right, were now terminally ruptured and bankrupt. If this was the case, then we would have to consider 1834 as an extremely significant watershed in connection with belonging and local attachment.

However, despite the contemporary and historiographical floodlights pointed at the workhouse, I wish to argue for a different emphasis here. This will be done through an extension to the new poor law of the issues of parish and belonging – that is, by shifting the terms of reference and frequent dichotomies of much new poor law historiography, and addressing that subject through the terms and questions of this book. In other words, this is a chapter about the new poor law and how it may have accommodated, influenced or developed senses of belonging and the responsibility of parishes. There were many regional differences, and diverse local–central tensions, both of which will be stressed. Yet it appears to me that the dominant feature of welfare provision under the new poor law remained that of out-door or domiciliary relief, to people who still normally resided and felt themselves to belong in their own parishes. Indeed, so important was this out-door relief that in many regions it completely eclipsed the workhouse, and in almost all regions, and in most periods, it was far more important than the workhouse. The workhouse was certainly an instrument of moral and disciplinary control, necessitating close historical research – a feared and shameful institution that deterred many people (particularly the able-bodied) from applying for relief. It was undoubtedly a fundamental feature of the new welfare system. However, its functions, administration and conception altered considerably over time, and varied greatly by region and local economies. It was poorly adapted to the circumstances of pauperism, frequently inadequate as a response to unemployment, rather expensive, impractical and, despite the underlying utilitarian calculus, it was sometimes quite irrational as a method to relieve poverty-stricken people. It was even unpopular among many overseers, relieving officers, guardians and other poor law officials. When we delve into the records of the new poor law a different picture emerges from that usually accepted by historians and the public: one that sidelines relief in the workhouse – while acknowledging the workhouse's notorious deterrent role – and one that highlights domiciliary, parish or township relief as the dominant practice, indeed all the way through to the late 1920s and beyond.[9]

The new poor law was not a fixed entity, any more than it was standardised across regions. Its emphases altered noticeably. We need briefly to outline some of these changing features and to correct some misapprehensions. These trends can then set the scene for more detailed analysis of the regionality and types of out-relief in people's parishes, and other less chronological themes, which are the main concerns of this chapter.

Poor law expenditure per head of population over the long term, as shown in figure 5.1, had risen considerably after the 1770s.[10] From low levels then of about 4s. per head, this measure rose to peaks during the 1795–1812 high-price years and the high rural unemployment years of 1813–20, up to about 13s. per head. It fell markedly thereafter through to the late 1830s, from when it ranged rather unexceptionally at around 5–7s. per head for the rest of the nineteenth century. It rose into the twentieth century, and was to rise very strikingly indeed in the inter-war period, up to about 25s. per head in 1927, in the immediate aftermath of the coal dispute and the General Strike. Historians are not usually aware that the 1834 enactment intersected *the end of a fall* in this measure, one that had commenced from about 1817. By 1836–7, when the new poor law began to be seriously implemented, poor law expenditure per head of

---

[9] For other emphases on out-door relief after 1834, see M. E. Rose, 'The allowance system under the New Poor Law', *Economic History Review*, 19 (1966); A. Digby, 'The labour market and the continuity of social policy after 1834: the case of the eastern counties', *Economic History Review*, 28 (1975); Thomas, *Poor Relief in Merthyr Tydfil*, pp. 22–5; A. Kidd, *State, Society and the Poor in Nineteenth-century England* (Basingstoke, 1999), p. 34; S. King, *Poverty and Welfare in England, 1700–1850: A Regional Perspective* (Manchester, 2000), pp. 243, 249.

[10] Data are for England and Wales, from Sir G. Nicholls, *A History of the English Poor Law, in connection with the State of the Country and the Condition of the people*, vol. II (1854, New York, 1967), pp. 437–8; K. Williams, *From Pauperism to Poverty* (London, 1981), pp. 169–72. Further figures, not presented here, are in F. W. Purdy, 'The statistics of English poor rate before and since the passing of the Poor Law Amendment Act', *Journal of the Statistical Society*, 23 (1860), p. 316, and *Fifth Annual Report of the Local Government Board, 1875–76* (London, 1876), p. 282.

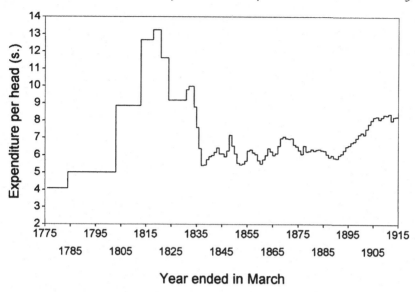

Figure 5.1 Poor expenditure per head of population (s.), 1775–1915.

population had already returned to the relatively unproblematical levels which had obtained in the mid-1780s, and was indeed already at about the lowest level (5s. 5d.) that it was *ever* to reach in the nineteenth century. If contemporaries had seen such a chart in 1834, it is extremely unlikely that the new poor law would have been enacted.

A comparable measure is total relief expenditure, and this is shown in figure 5.2.[11] Again one sees that 1835–7 were years of exceptionally low expenditure, the lowest indeed of the nineteenth century, such costs in the mid-1830s having been falling very noticeably from their early nineteenth-century peaks. For all the rhetoric of urgency that accompanied it, the new poor law in fact came into operation during years when the costs of pauperism were remarkably low. As can be seen from these two figures, there is little warrant to a contemporary view that this enactment successfully curbed unbridled runaway expenditure on feckless paupers. In fact, the main declines in

[11] Data are for England and Wales, from Williams, *From Pauperism to Poverty*, pp. 158–62.

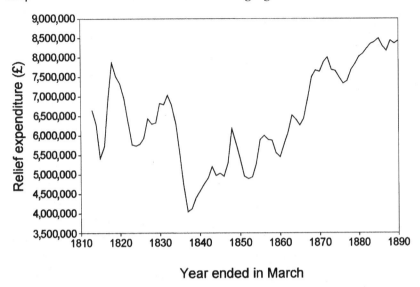

Figure 5.2   Relief expenditure (£), 1810–90.

expenditure per head of population had already occurred under the old poor law, and stayed fairly constant thereafter; while total expenditure rose in a sustained manner throughout the period of the new poor law, by 1870 reaching the kinds of levels that had obtained in the 'worst' years of the old poor law.

The new poor law, therefore, should not be seen as a reform that successfully cut in and curtailed increasing rates of poor expenditure per head of population, or total expenditure on the poor, as so often claimed by its contemporary advocates. In fact, the law and its early implementation came at the end of a fall in poor law expenditure per head, and in total expenditure, and can hardly be said to have instigated those changes. Without the 1834 Act and the costs of building and equipping workhouses, it is even likely that expenditure would have continued to decline in 1834–40.

These long-term shifts in poor law expenditure were heavily dependent upon the earlier Malthusian relationship between population and resources. Poor law expenditure per head of population reached a crisis long before the 1834 Act; it was subsiding as population pressure on resources slackened after the Napoleonic Wars, and as the British economy shifted to ever higher and more impressive levels of industrial and agricultural productivity. Such productivity growth in agriculture was betokened by the declining agricultural prices from *c.* 1813, despite the rapid demographic growth rates of 1800–30, and this deflation was thereafter broadly to characterise the nineteenth century. Seen in this way, the new poor law was (rather like the Revd Thomas Malthus) responding to a national problem which was fading at its moment of legislative enactment. To say this is not to suggest that many difficulties of social order, rural surplus population, regional unemployment, wage subsidies, work discipline and the like were absent in the mid-1830s – many contemporaries were quite certain about those problems – but it is to propose that claims made for the contribution of the new poor law in cutting expenditure were over-played by its advocates. It is also to suggest that the subsequent history of the new poor law, with its large increases of total expenditure throughout the nineteenth century, and with its huge levels of out-door relief running so contrary to its intent, can only be explained with some regard to this relatively innocuous situation at its inception.

The decline in pauperism expressed as a long-term rate of paupers per 1,000 population may be seen in figure 5.3.[12] Data on the numbers of paupers are unavailable before 1840, but expenditure patterns suggest that there were over a million paupers in England and Wales in 1803: about one ninth of the population. In the mid-1840s paupers were probably about one eleventh of the population. By mid-century, they were about one eighteenth of the population, in 1870 about one twenty-third, and by 1920 about one fiftieth. Such broad fractions are also subject to qualifications (made below) about the growth from the later nineteenth century of alternative forms of 'public assistance', which took many people off the poor law. The second half of the nineteenth century (apart from 1863–4) also witnessed a fall in adult able-bodied paupers as a percentage of total paupers, a statistic which had been falling over the longer term.[13] The able-bodied also declined as a percentage of

---

[12] Data are for England and Wales, from *ibid.*, pp. 158–62.
[13] Calculated from figures for England in the *Fifth Annual Report of the Local Government Board, 1875–76*, p. xv.

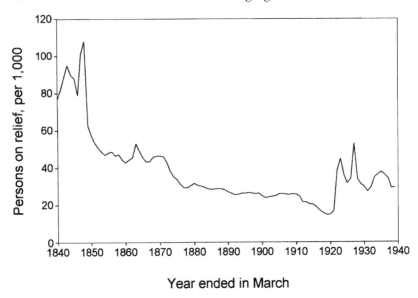

Figure 5.3   Persons on relief, per 1,000 population, 1840–1940.

workhouse inmates: from about 38 per cent in 1842, to about 15 per cent in 1860, and they were rarely above that for the rest of the century.

Many contemporaries believed that these trends were caused by the deterrent character of the new poor law, and especially its workhouses, as well as being due to the buoyant Victorian economy, and to more efficient charity organisation from 1869, with much influence from the Charity Organisation Society. The declines led some commentators, such as Henry Fawcett or Thomas Mackay, to think that one could realistically aim for the abolition of out-door relief and even the entire poor law system.[14] Such sentiments were voiced much earlier (for different reasons) by the Revd Thomas Malthus. Leaving aside the

---

[14] H. Fawcett, *Pauperism, its Causes and Remedies* (1871, Bristol, 1996), pp. 24, 41, 49–50; T. Mackay, *A History of the English Poor Law*, vol. III: *From 1834 to the Present Time* (1854, London, 1900), chs. 22–3. Mackay, always extolling the personal responsibility of the individual, wrote in favour of 'that monumental document' of 1834, and against 'that terrible engine of destruction, an ill-administered system of out-door relief', which he felt was given 'too readily and without sufficient inquiry', and which conduced to the 'stall-fed comfort of the out-door pauper'. *Ibid.*, pp. 521, 534, 574, 598, 600.

temporary upturn around 1863–4 (due to the cotton famine induced by the American Civil War), and another around 1868–71, after the peaks in the first half of the nineteenth century there was progressive decline in the numbers and rates of poor law defined pauperism, to historically low levels relative to population by the early twentieth century. That was then severely reversed by the economic history of the inter-war period. Even so, this country did not see a return to the rates of poor law dependent pauperism of the period of incipient Malthusian crisis, industrialisation and economic readjustment from 1790 into the 1840s.

Figure 5.4 shows the long-term changes affecting the numbers of people on in-door and out-door relief in England and Wales in the hundred years between 1840 and 1940.[15] As in some previous and subsequent graphs, the data have been extended beyond 1929, to show continuities into the 1930s, continuities which are to be expected in view of the out-door emphases of relief under the new poor law which are argued for here. The huge preponderance of out-door relief under the new poor law is very evident. In no single year did in-door relief numbers ever

---

[15] Data are from Williams, *From Pauperism to Poverty*, pp. 158–62, and (as with figures 5.1–5.3) are subject to the qualifications and discontinuities in their composition which he outlines on pp. 156–7, 163–8. Comparable but differently constructed figures are in Mackay, *A History of the English Poor Law*, pp. 603–4, but the overall pattern is common to all such series. The poor law figures are normally averages for 1 January of the stated year and 1 July the preceding year (from 1849 onwards). They are thus seasonal 'snapshots' which heavily under-represent the 'real' totals; and they do not *equally* under-represent those fuller totals. This is because much out-relief was more temporary in nature than workhouse relief, which had a somewhat longer average duration. This was due to differing balances of pauper types in each group, to the more desperate or hopeless paupers going into the workhouse, and it was also related to the more time-consuming procedures of workhouse admission and administration. Robert Pashley, in his impressive *Pauperism and Poor Laws*, pp. 36–7, felt that out-door figures needed to be multiplied by a factor of about 3.5 to approximate to the 'real' figures, while in-door figures needed to be multiplied by 3 to represent the true totals. (Virtually all contemporaries felt that some such adjustment was necessary, although regional and chronological variations were far too great to allow agreement on the multipliers.) In other words, the official figures for pauper numbers *underestimate* out-door relief compared to in-door relief. If we had full annual figures for everyone who received such relief, rather than counts at only two points in each year, the real disparity between the numbers of paupers receiving the two types of relief would be even higher, with out-relief assuming even greater numerical predominance. In so far as an argument (as made here) for the dominance of out-relief in the parishes is so strong in any case, even though the official figures are biased against such an argument, I have not adjusted those figures to deal with these points.

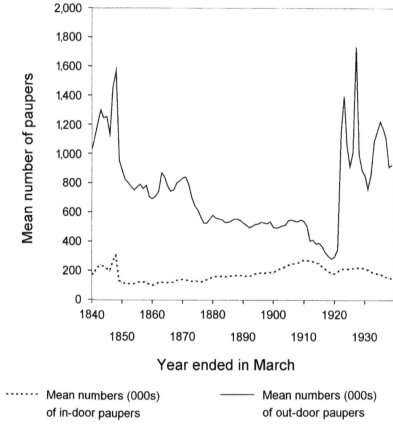

Figure 5.4   Mean numbers on in-door and out-door relief, 1840–1940.

exceed those on out-door relief. Average annual out-door relief recipients ranged between 1.5 and 7.9 times higher than in-door relief recipients. Out-door relief numbers over this entire period, as a yearly average, were 4.4 times greater than in-door relief numbers. If one were to take into account the many public assistance forms of out-relief that developed from the later nineteenth century and into the twentieth century, which contemporaries knew had in effect expanded even further the scope of out-door relief (and which cannot be shown in the figure here), the prevalence of 'out-relief' would become all the more striking.

Out-relief over short periods fluctuated more than in-door relief, as can be seen in figure 5.4. In-door relief was certainly subject to seasonal and yearly cycles, and the seasonal component is something that the January and July poor law returns show quite well. Yet the relative stability of in-door relief compared with out-relief is apparent. In part, this was due to the constraints upon space within workhouses and the costs of expanding workhouse sizes. It was also owing to the longer-term categories of 'pauper' (the elderly, insane or mentally defective, orphans, the chronically sick) who were often maintained in workhouse buildings. The volatility of out-relief, the reasons for that, and the stratagems that underlay that form of assistance, comprise *the* dynamic component of new poor law history: it was out-relief that changed most markedly over time, that was usually most costly, and that was overwhelmingly the most common experience for paupers.

In-door relief was gradually expanding from 1851 until 1910, and out-relief tended to decline until 1919. There are complicated reasons for this. Prominent among these were enlarging workhouse sizes, especially in larger towns and cities, with higher numbers of salaried workhouse staff and a desire to use them; greater provision of specialised workhouse wards (vagrant wards, children's wards, infirmaries, venereal disease wards, etc.); the use of reformed and less deterrent workhouses as in effect old people's homes, hospices for the chronically ill, or temporary orphanages; efforts after c. 1869 to impose 'the principles of 1834' and to apply the workhouse test more rigorously; the relatively full employment of able-bodied people during the Victorian period, such that pauper composition shifted more towards the non-able-bodied; and other related considerations. These factors, affecting the two lines of figure 5.4, need not engage us in detail here.

None of these developments lead us to doubt the general emphasis upon out-relief. Figure 5.5 shows out-relief numbers between 1840 and 1939 as a changing percentage of total in-door and out-door relief recipients combined (excluding relief to casuals and the insane).[16] It demonstrates that out-door relief recipients fluctuated between 60 and 89 per cent of all relief

[16] Figures calculated from Williams, *From Pauperism to Poverty*, pp. 158–62.

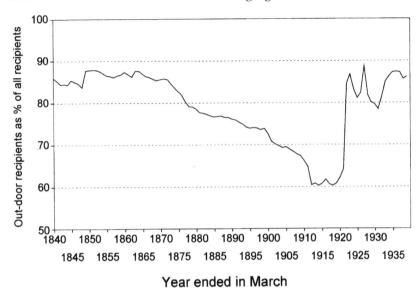

Figure 5.5 Out-relief recipients as a percentage of all relief recipients, 1840–1939.

recipients (they averaged at 79 per cent). There was a sustained decline from about 1872 until 1919, when the stress on out-relief reverted to the percentages which had obtained in the 1840s, 1850s and 1860s. Logarithmic transformations show that the most dramatic decline was between 1899 and 1912. There were further attempts to tighten up the granting of out-relief during those years. This occurred notably in the Relief Regulations Order of 1911, which deemed all expenditure on out-door relief to the able-bodied to be illegal, and required such cases to be reported to the Ministry of Health. This Order was in fact widely evaded, by reporting cases wholesale, by auditors' surcharges not being enforced, and through use of the Metropolitan Common Poor Fund in London. More importantly, these were years in which there was growing public expenditure and expanding non-poor law 'public assistance' under separate legislation.[17] Examples of this were the Unemployed Workmen's Act

---

[17] 'Public assistance' was defined by Geoffrey Drage as 'all beneficiary assistance from rates and taxes, whether maintenance or treatment, for which the recipient does not pay or only pays a portion'. *Public Assistance* (London, 1930), p. 138. Drage was urging

(1905), the Education Acts, the Children's Act (1908), the Acts relating to Reformatory and Industrial Schools, the Inebriates Acts, the Public Health Acts (in connection with hospitals, disease, maternity and child welfare), the hospitals and improved sanatoriums provided by local authorities, the Housing of the Working Classes Acts, old age pensions (1908), national insurance (1911), the Lunacy Acts, and so on. These major developments, with their late nineteenth-century precedents, in effect took many 'paupers' off the poor law, and increased welfare expenditures under separate 'public assistance' headings. Old age pensions, for example, were often coldly referred to by their critics as 'out-door relief under a different name'. In 1891, poor law expenditure was about 84 per cent of all expenditure on 'direct public assistance'. By 1928, that had fallen to about 17 per cent, because of the rise of so many other components of public assistance, such as those mentioned above, and with the major addition of war pensions.[18] The 1929–32 slump, and the peak of unemployment in 1932, did not see huge increases in poor relief, because the major rises then were in unemployment benefits. Such enactments and shifting heads of expenditure underlay the decline in out-relief expenditure percentages from the late nineteenth century onwards. No arguments about welfare expenditure can be persuasive if they fail to take account of the various means by which what had hitherto been poor law expenditure was increasingly paid through different channels. Indeed, the accountancy and category shifts accompanying the 1870–1914 social legislation were so enormous that one has to be extremely wary when making any statements about movements in welfare and poor relief expenditure and explaining them with reference to the poor law.

If the new poor law is conceived in the conventional way, as being in practice a workhouse-based system of welfare delivery – which is clearly a questionable generalisation – then judged within poor law accounting and administration its heyday was

---

considerable retrenchment of such expenditure, including that on post-1908 pensions, and I adopt his definition without sharing his political intent.

[18] Figures calculated from the so-called 'Drage Return', in *ibid.*, pp. 378–9; see also 'Rating reform. New Bill in the Commons. Health Minister on the scheme', *Times* (14 May 1925), p. 16, col. E.

paradoxically in the years between 1910 and 1918. (See figure 5.5.) That period saw the lowest percentage levels of out-relief under the new poor law, although (as indicated above) this was largely owing to the growth of other forms of public assistance. Even these years were short-lived; they still saw out-relief percentages of over 60 per cent; and they clearly do not characterise the new poor law as a whole. Seen in the light of figures for in- and out-door relief, that new poor law system might broadly be portrayed in its first four decades as continuous from the old poor law's high use of out-relief; and then from about 1871 as a system trying harder to lower such relief, but never achieving anything remotely approaching what had been envisaged by many proponents in 1834; and then, in the 1890s through (in relatively few cases) to immediately after the First World War, generally giving up on such restrictive endeavours and allowing out-door relief to expand again.

In the twentieth century, the numbers of out-door 'paupers' rose considerably, markedly so with growing unemployment in the 1920s, when as earlier (and now under the Ministry of Health) there was much variation in local policy, and in the scales of out-door relief which were adopted. This was to be expected, given the large disparities in the levels of distress across different regions. The numbers of able-bodied people in workhouses in the inter-war period declined, out-door relief came to be given more readily to the elderly, and the deterrent utility of the workhouse became increasingly a scorned policy option of the past. This was despite many efforts to revive workhouse deterrence, as in the Report of the Unemployment Insurance Committee (the Blanesburgh Report) of 1927. There were also many unsuccessful efforts to stress that out-door relief for the able-bodied without a labour test remained technically illegal, or at least required central warrant. The new poor law was now terminally ruptured, at least as a system masquerading in the livery of 1834. A growing democratisation of relief administration, the issue of relief policy and generosity in local elections with socially enlarged franchises, the decline of property qualifications for guardians, and the election of women guardians were coupled to shifts in public opinion, which became more sympathetic to the elderly, the unemployed, children in poverty, the war-wounded or widowed, and other such groups.

These people would frequently have been stamped as 'paupers' in the nineteenth century, albeit treated with an eye to their supposed moral worth. Even so, out-relief, its means-tested forms, and its use during industrial disputes (as in 1918–21, the 1923 dock strike, and the General Strike) were still hotly debated.[19] Certainly more generous out-relief usually came to be paid than in the nineteenth century – although there were localised exceptions to this, especially during trade disputes and in places like Lichfield, Nuneaton, Foleshill or Westbury on Severn. In some areas, curtailment of out-relief was used as a strike-breaking weapon, as in the nineteenth century. It was supported as such by many politicians, including Neville Chamberlain. In other regions, out-relief assumed historically generous proportions that horrified diehard exponents of the seeming 'principles of 1834'. Attempts by the Ministry of Health to control out-relief expenditure in strongly Labour unions, and the numbers of people receiving it – above all in places like Bedwellty, Chester-le-Street, Gateshead, Bermondsey, West Ham or Poplar – became major political issues after 1918 and throughout the 1920s.

We will return to these points relating to long-term trends and the nature of the new poor law in due course. They are introduced here to realign arguments about the inception of the new poor law, and as context for an examination of out-door relief after 1834. Obviously out-door relief cannot be considered in isolation from workhouse relief. Yet out-relief was so important that it should become the central focus of new poor law studies.

OUT-DOOR RELIEF DIFFERENCES IN THE NATIONAL DIVISIONS

One of the most striking aspects of nineteenth-century out-door relief was its regional variety. This was commented upon by the

---

[19] On disputes about the role of out-door relief during industrial disputes, see Thomas, *Poor Relief in Merthyr Tydfil*, pp. 121–31; P. Ryan, 'The Poor Law in 1926', in M. Morris (ed.), *The General Strike* (1976, London, 1980), pp. 358–78. On the influential 'Merthyr Tydfil judgement' of 1900, laying down a legal interpretation against poor relief to able-bodied men during a strike, see *ibid.*, pp. 361–2. Poplar and many other Labour-dominated boards of guardians (notably in East London and the mining districts) ignored this judgement in the 1920s, commonly giving out-relief to dockers and other men on strike.

Local Government Board, which wrote in a Circular of 1871 about 'a great diversity of practice in the administration of out-door relief'.[20] That Circular, like others before and after it, wished to constrict and standardise the administration of such relief, but it was very ineffective in achieving that. When examining the regional features of out-relief, one also notices how extensive it often was. To analyse this and show it cartographically, I have chosen union expenditure from the *Fifth Annual Report of the Local Government Board, 1875–76*.[21] The *Report* supplied data for the year ending at Lady Day (25 March) 1875. This is a mid-point in the history of the new poor law, and one that captures the effects of the tightening up on relief in the late 1860s and 1870s. It will be seen from the graphs shown above that this date is about as representative of the financial history of the new poor law as it is possible to be, for it is neither a year of very low nor high expenditure. There had also probably been more regional standardisation of relief practices by this date than was true of the initial decades after 1834, although one should not overstate that. During earlier decades, the use of out-relief was higher than it was by 1875, because *inter alia* of the widespread public resistance to the new poor law, the enduring traditions of the old poor law, the difficulties of acceptance faced by the Poor Law Commission and then the Poor Law Board, the lack of powers in the central authority to compel unions to provide workhouse accommodation,[22] and the reluctance of unions to spend money building or expanding workhouses.

Let us first consider patterns of expenditure in the eleven poor law divisions of the country. The dark bar lines of figure 5.6 show out-relief in those divisions as a percentage of the totals of in- and out-door relief (1874–5).[23] Great regional variation is

---

[20] 'Circular on Outdoor Relief' (2 Dec. 1871), cited in E. J. Evans (ed.), *Social Policy, 1830–1914: Individualism, Collectivism and the Origins of the Welfare State* (London, 1978), p. 151.

[21] *Fifth Annual Report of the Local Government Board, 1875–76*, pp. 218–71.

[22] *Select Committee on Poor Removal*, XIII (1854–5), p. 221.

[23] Figures are from the *Fifth Annual Report of the Local Government Board, 1875–76*, p. 203. Total relief for this chart is taken as the sum of in-maintenance and out-relief (i.e. it does not include the costs of lunatics, workhouse loans, salaries and rations of officers, and other miscellaneous expenses).

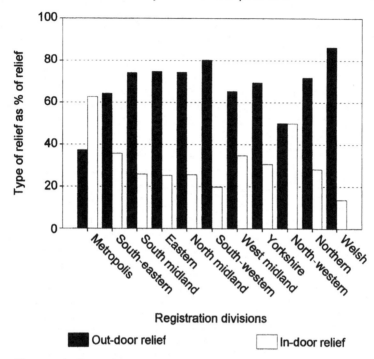

Figure 5.6   In- and out-door relief as a percentage of relief, 1874–5.

immediately apparent. The metropolis made much lower use of out-relief than the other regions. London was followed by the north-western division, giving half its relief in this form. All the other divisions gave well over half their relief as out-door relief, commonly over 70 per cent. The south-western division, and most markedly the Welsh division, gave over four-fifths of their relief as out-door relief. Wales indeed gave 86 per cent of its relief as out-door relief. In doing that, it set itself very markedly apart from the metropolis and the north-western division, although there were plenty of other English divisions with patterns of out-relief which were not far behind Wales. Among those divisions, it was only in the metropolis that in-door relief was more important than out-relief, and in this case the workhouse was certainly more significant. In many other divisions, workhouse relief was about a third to a half of expenditure on out-relief.

Most unions were subdivided into two to five *districts*, each under a separate relieving officer. In the English rural midlands, for example, such districts usually comprised about five to fifteen parishes each. For out-relief purposes (and indeed in assessing paupers generally), these districts and their pay or relief stations were crucial administrative units, with a more local disposition than was implied by *union* administration.[24] The Out-door Relief Regulation Order in December 1852 laid down that half of the weekly out-door relief to the able-bodied should be given in kind (i.e. fuel, food and other such articles), normally by the district relieving officers at their relief stations. Among the intentions here were to avert money payments in aid of wages, to deter applicants, and to allay suspicions that relief was being spent in morally undesirable ways. Figure 5.7 examines the breakdown of relief in money and kind in 1875, again by the poor law divisions.[25] It is fairly representative of the returns on this to the Local Government Board. At the most, only about a fifth of relief was being given in kind, in the metropolis, southeastern and the eastern divisions. In all other divisions, the proportion was smaller than that, usually very much smaller. In the northern English divisions, the proportions given in kind were a tiny fraction of the whole. Wales once more departed from the official expectation, but six English divisions were very similar to Wales, some of them giving even lower proportions of relief in kind. Payments in kind were attacked by pauper recipients (who preferred the convenience and liberty of money), and in many cases they were even condemned by relieving officers and other officials, who found such goods inconvenient, time-consuming to negotiate with suppliers, hard to transport and store, difficult to preserve, and who were subject to bitter accusations when the goods were uneatable, sub-standard or over-valued.[26] Forms of payment in kind that

---

[24] On pay stations, see G. Cuttle, *The Legacy of the Rural Guardians* (Cambridge, 1934), pp. 55–6.

[25] Data are from the *Fifth Annual Report of the Local Government Board, 1875–76*, p. 290. These returns cover all such out-relief, not relief only to the able-bodied; and so the chart is intended to show regional variations, rather than to demonstrate how far regulations were being observed.

[26] For example, *Royal Commission on the Aged Poor*, xiv (1895), p. 350, for accusations of poor flour being given as out-relief in Norfolk unions.

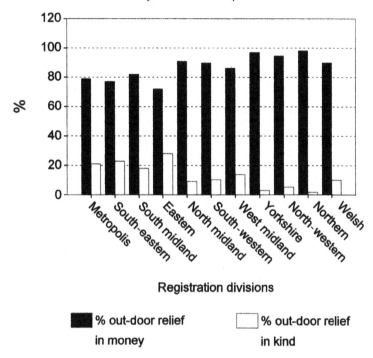

Figure 5.7   Out-door relief as a percentage in money and kind, half-year to Michaelmas 1875.

utilised tickets, redeemable in local shops (in ways similar to truck systems), were equally unpopular, partly because they left paupers vulnerable to deception and unsound pricing. In some unions, different categories of pauper were ordered varying proportions of relief in kind. It was evident to all administrators that regulations governing relief in kind were frequently by-passed. Many unions (for example in Lancashire) only gave out-relief in money.[27] Not only was the new poor law marked by very high dependency upon out-door relief, but its regulations

[27] R. Boyson, 'The new poor law in north-east Lancashire, 1834–71', *Transactions of the Lancashire and Cheshire Antiquarian Society*, 70 (1960), pp. 41–2.

with regard to the nature of that out-relief were flouted in unions throughout the country.

THE UNION CARTOGRAPHY OF OUT-DOOR RELIEF, AND RURAL—URBAN DIFFERENCES

Expenditure on out-door relief as a percentage of the combined costs of workhouse in-maintenance and out-relief is mapped in figure 5.8, for the year ending Lady Day 1875. In-door and out-door relief of course comprise the bulk of poor law costs.[28] For the year ending Lady Day 1875, across England and Wales, 65 per cent of combined in- and out-door relief expenditure was out-door relief.[29] Figure 5.8 shows 'black spots', as it were, from the perspective of an official in the Local Government Board trying to assert the supposed 'principles of 1834', by restricting out-relief. The darkest areas are the unions with highest percentage out-relief expenditures.

One can see immediately that there were great regional differences. Wales, large parts of Lincolnshire, Norfolk, the

---

[28] These main headings exclude lunatics in asylums or licensed houses, workhouse or other loans repaid and interest on them, salaries, rations and superannuation of poor law officers, including sums repaid by Her Majesty's Treasury, other expenses connected with poor relief (these headings were the other elements in 'total relief to the poor'), and items deemed by the Local Goverment Board to be unconnected with poor relief, which comprised: legal proceedings, payments for county, borough or police rates; payments by overseers to highway boards; contributions by overseers to the rural sanitary authority for general expenses; contributions by overseers to the school board (if any); payments on account of the Registration Act; fees to clergymen and registrars; outlay for stationery; vaccination fees; expenses allowed in respect of Parliamentary or municipal registration; costs of jury lists; payments under the Parochial Assessment Act and Union Assessment Committee Acts; medical relief; loans under orders of the Local Goverment Board; and any sums expended for any other purposes.

[29] *Fifth Annual Report of the Local Government Board, 1875–76*, pp. 207, 214, or see p. 288 for half-yearly figures. In-maintenance and out-door relief comprised 61 per cent of 'total relief to the poor', other costs connected with poor relief (see n. 28) being the remainder. If out-relief expenditure is analysed and mapped as a percentage of 'total relief to the poor', a very similar result emerges to figure 5.8, the possible percentage measures being very tightly correlated indeed, with no outliers. These figures are representative of the period for which data have been mapped here. The out-door figures as percentages of in- and out-relief are slightly lower than was the case for 1866–74, when such a percentage was falling (see *ibid.*, p. 207), thus working against my argument for the dominance of out-relief as the essential characteristic of the new poor law. The position of 1874–5 within longer-term trends affecting the new poor law will be apparent from my opening discussion.

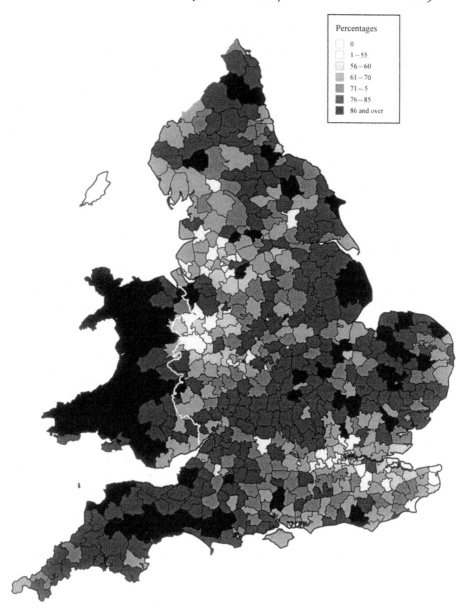

Figure 5.8 Out-door relief as a percentage of in- and out-relief, year ending Lady Day 1875.

south-west, some unions in the north-east, parts of the south midlands, and other scattered unions, gave very high proportions of their relief as out-door relief, in many cases well over 80 per cent. In Wales these figures were extremely high, usually above 90 per cent, and outside Monmouthshire and Cardiff virtually always over 80 per cent. Of the thirty unions with the highest percentage out-relief in England and Wales, twenty-four of them were in Wales: unions such as Tregaron, Bala, Aberayron, Holyhead, Llanrwst, Ffestiniog, Pwllheli, Cardigan, Caernarvon, Machynlleth and many others. Wales emerges almost as a different welfare country in these regards, in much the same way as it emerges as almost a separate country in terms of its mid-nineteenth-century religious geography.[30]

Featuring highly among the English unions with very high out-relief percentages were Todmorden, West Ward (Westmld.), Honiton, Dorchester, Rothbury, Morpeth, Mildenhall, Beaminster, Axbridge, St Thomas, and Louth (all over 90 per cent). Marginally lower (in descending order) were unions such as Swaffham, Chard, Okehampton, Tiverton, Blandford, Wayland, Crediton, Biggleswade, Thrapston, Bridlington, Spilsby, Freebridge Lynn, Smallburgh, Walsingham (which had a long-standing reputation as a generous union in this regard, said by contemporaries to be linked to its royal connections), Axminster, Thingoe, Peterborough, Brixworth (its later ruthless reputation merely for workhouse relief yet to be acquired), Depwade, Westbury, or Barnstaple. It will be seen that many of these very heavily out-relieving English unions were in the south-west, or in Lincolnshire, with others scattered elsewhere, such as in East Anglia and adjacent areas of the south-east midlands, as indicated in figure 5.8.

At the other extreme were those unions which gave relatively low proportions of their relief out-door. These appear as the lighter shaded unions in figure 5.8. There were three main regional centres of this policy: in and around London, in Shropshire, and in south Lancashire and adjoining parts of Derbyshire and the West Riding. The unions giving under 35 per cent of relief

[30] K. D. M. Snell and P. S. Ell, *Rival Jerusalems: The Geography of Victorian Religion* (Cambridge, 2000).

out-doors were Whitechapel (10 per cent), ranging upwards through Strand, Hampstead, St Giles, Bethnal Green, Westminster, Richmond, Shoreditch, Chelsea, Stepney, St George in the East, Hoo, Preston, Manchester, Atcham, Kensington, St Saviours Southwark, Aston, St Marylebone, Oldham, St Georges, Mile End Old Town, Holborn, Liverpool, and Oxford (35 per cent).[31] The region of low out-relief in and around the metropolis extended quite widely out to unions such as Hoo, Medway, Maidstone, Sevenoaks, Easthampstead, Eton, Edmonton, Barnet, or Windsor. Beyond these areas, other geographically large unions on the map showing low out-relief include Faringdon, Bath, York, Sedbergh, and, to a slightly lesser extent, unions around the Kentish coast, in the Fens, in the urban north-east, and many towns which appear as very small light areas on the map. In some regions there were dramatic variations between relief policies, with 'high' and 'low' out-relief areas being in very close proximity to each other – this was true, for example, in northern parts of Sussex, or from Middlesex into Hertfordshire, or north Lancashire, and it appears most dramatically where the Shropshire unions abutted the Welsh border, where a deep cultural clash in poor relief practices is as evident as the language and religious divides were to contemporaries.

Many urban unions shared the London pattern of relative parsimony in out-relief provision, although not usually in such an accentuated way as in and near the metropolis. It is worth listing a number of these low out-relief urban unions, because such practice in Victorian towns and cities, where the poor were relatively unknown to administrators, suggests that rural–urban differences, and accompanying contrasted knowledge of the poor in different environments, were important keys to the issue of in- and out-door relief. Some of these unions had earlier been strongly anti-new poor law, with significant Chartist presence. (The percentage of poor relief which was out-door is shown here in brackets.) Among the 'low' out-relief urban unions were Preston (27), Manchester (28), Aston (32), Oldham (32), Liverpool (33), Oxford (35), Ashton under Lyne (38), Derby

[31] In comparison with Oxford's very low 35 per cent, Cambridge gave 80 per cent of its relief as out-door relief.

(40), Reading (41), Toxteth Park (43), Salford (43), Birmingham (46), York (46), Bolton (48), West Derby (48), Warrington (50), Bath (51), Bradford (51), Coventry (52), Hull (52), Stoke on Trent (53), Maidstone (54), Nottingham (55), Macclesfield (55), Bury (56), Bristol (56), Leicester (56), Brighton (58), Wolverhampton (58), Sunderland (59), and Newcastle on Tyne (60). Among the market-town/rural unions giving low out-relief were Sedbergh (41), Faringdon (50), Eastry (50), Ellesmere (51), Romney Marsh (54), Oswestry (56), and Whittlesey (57). These more rural unions were often in Kent or the home counties, or in Shropshire. However, there were very few largely rural unions with low out-relief percentages, and the very large majority of such unions were giving much higher proportions of relief outside the workhouse.

There were plainly many scattered English unions that were trying to enforce the workhouse test to the extent that they appear among unions with low out-door relief. Yet one is struck above all by the relatively 'low' percentages of out-relief in many urban unions, especially in and around London, some parts of the English midlands, and in south Lancashire. In these regions the light areas in figure 5.8 call to mind the geography of Victorian population density and urbanisation. One should not exaggerate the association of urbanisation with low proportions of out-door relief, because this quantitative relationship was strongly found in some regions and rather less so in others, and was statistically non-linear. The relief policies of urban unions were also often swayed by political and administrative attitudes towards the new poor law of the region in which they were situated. Yet only Cambridge among the highly urbanised unions (measured by population per square kilometre) was giving over 75 per cent of its relief as out-relief, and so sharing that poor relief characteristic with 298 other unions which had much lower population densities. Exeter, Bury St Edmunds, Norwich, Sheffield and Dudley gave over 70 per cent out-relief, being towns among 397 other more rural unions doing this. In other words, urban unions (showing high population densities) were very rare indeed among those making extensive use of out-relief. However, unions with very high population densities massively predominated at the other end of the scale, among those which gave *low* percentages of relief outside the workhouse. Overall, and speaking statistically, there was a clear inverse relationship between urbanisation/population density and percentages of relief given as out-door relief – that is, the most urban unions tended to make more use of the workhouse.[32]

The low out-relief administrations, led by Whitechapel, thus tended to be highly urbanised. In the case of London and its proximate unions they were much under the influence of the Local Government Board and its centralised predecessors. In the nature of their relief, they were very far removed in policy and geography from unions like Tregaron, or the other Welsh unions, or many of the high out-relief English unions, especially in regions such as the south-west, Lincolnshire, Northumberland, and so on. Such quantitative differences are one indication of the very real variations in union relief practices, affecting countless thousands of relief-dependent people across the country. The map shows that huge regional variations characterised mid-Victorian poor relief, and reveals how the Poor Law Commission, the Poor Law Board, or the Local Government Board, as successive administrations, had failed through central control, legislative interpretation, instruction and General Orders to bring about a system of regulated and standardised relief across the localities of England and Wales. Disparate poor relief practices had been a feature of the old poor law at parish level, which the 1832–4 Poor Law Commission and the new poor law had aimed to curtail. Yet such a policy had unquestionably failed by 1875 to standardise regional poor relief practices on this most basic measure of out-door as compared with in-door relief. In some ways, these quantitative differences affecting relief at union level in 1875 were almost as eye-catching as anything that can be pointed to by way of parish or regional difference under the old poor law.[33]

When one speaks of 'high' and 'low' percentages of relief dispensed as out-door relief, one needs to note carefully the

---

[32] The Pearson correlation coefficient was −.517 (significance = .000). In other words, 27 per cent of the variation in the out-relief measure can be explained statistically by population density.

[33] For similar stress on local diversity under the new poor law, see A. Digby, 'Recent developments in the study of the English poor law', *The Local Historian*, 12 (1977), pp. 206–8.

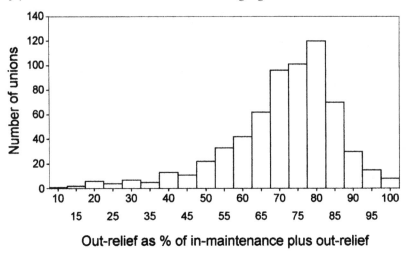

Out-relief as % of in-maintenance plus out-relief

Figure 5.9   Histogram of the percentage of relief that was out-relief, year ending Lady Day 1875.

figures involved. Certainly, some of the percentages, such as for Whitechapel and other London unions, were low by any standards. Yet the very large majority (over nine-tenths) of these 650 unions were giving 50 per cent or more of their relief outside the workhouse. The distribution of this measure – the percentage of relief which was out-door – is shown in figure 5.9. The overwhelming stress upon out-relief is again obvious from this histogram. In the left hand tail of the chart one finds unions in London, some other cities and towns, and a few other unions such as Richmond, Hoo, Atcham, Gravesend, Hursley, Sedbergh, Medway and so on. However, the data are heavily distributed around the higher values, and far over to the right hand side of the chart one finds the Welsh unions. The large majority of unions lay between the cultural and administrative extremes of London on the one hand, and Wales on the other – and their figures were usually closer to Wales than to London. The unweighted union average was 71 per cent, and the median percentage was 74. The range for these data was a huge 90 (from 10 to 100 per cent), again demonstrating the great regional extremes of new poor law relief practice.[34]

[34] The standard deviation for these figures was 15.1. The skewness was −1.14.

THE POOR LAW GENERAL ORDERS

At this point, we need to go back to the central poor law authorities, and consider in detail the rules laid down for different periods and unions governing out-door relief. It is obvious that the salient character of new poor law administration was out-door relief. Both in terms of expenditures and numbers of paupers involved, that was much more important than workhouse relief. This was true throughout the nineteenth century, despite some tightening up on out-door relief from about 1870.

The new poor law is often discussed as though it 'abolished' out-door relief and insisted that all relief should be in the workhouse. In fact, the 1834 'Act for the Amendment and Better Administration of the Laws Relating to the Poor in England and Wales', which is normally called the New Poor Law,[35] did not lay down such absolute rules. It was especially concerned to hinder out-door relief to able-bodied adults; but in a number of sections it made open reference to the continued possibility of out-relief, while also giving the Poor Law Commissioners powers to declare what individuals or classes of people might receive such relief in their parishes.[36] In the Act, out-relief to infirm adults or the elderly who were unable to work was accepted, if the person to be relieved so desired it.[37] Under that Act, and particularly in all the subsequent official Circulars and Orders, which in countless ways eclipsed the 1834 Act, the

---

[35] Note the disjunction in names for 4 & 5 Wm IV, c. 76. 'The New Poor Law', especially if thus capitalised, has definitive and total connotations of reformation: in effect, a new law, a new system, a new start is signalled. The proper legal title of the Act, however, which I use in the text above, signals amendment, and improved administration, of existing laws. To some degree, its opponents wished to capitalise on what they saw as its dramatic break with the past – *un faux pas vers bastilles* – while some of its proponents wanted to portray it as continuing and modifying past enactments, and even as returning to the principles of 1601. Other proponents, proud of what they had done in breaking with the recent decades of the old poor law, were content with the phraseology and capitalisation of 'The New Poor Law'. The very language of description, applied to naming of the Act itself, embodied debates about its novelty or continuity which were so strident at the time, and which have repeatedly appeared in the historiography ever since. My preference and practice here, in line with my stress on the dominance of out-door relief, is a compromise: to refer to the Act as the new poor law, in lower case!

[36] 4 & 5 Wm IV, c. 76, ss. 26–7, 52, 54; J. F. Archbold, *The Act for the Amendment of the Poor Laws, with a Practical Introduction* (London, 1839), pp. 4, 20.

[37] *Ibid.*, p. 21, or in the 1834 Act, s. 27.

many exceptions were so numerous that one can readily see why out-relief predominated. This is best shown by outlining fairly persistent features of a few of the General and Consolidated Orders, some of the most notable of which were issued in 1836, 1841, 1842, 1844, 1845, 1847, 1852, 1905 and 1911. These were a major way in which the Act was implemented. The character of the new poor law was essentially defined by the General Orders of 1836–52.

An important example was the Out-door Relief General Prohibitory Order of 1 January 1845.[38] That Order was issued to 477 named unions, that is to a large majority of all unions. It was still in force in 1914. It laid down the principle that able-bodied adults were to be relieved in the workhouse with their families. 'Able-bodied' was in effect defined in 1848 by clarifying what was meant by non-able-bodied: those who are 'sick, [or] have met with an accident, or are labouring under bodily or mental infirmity',[39] although questions of definition persisted throughout the new poor law, and indeed thereafter.[40] However, the injunction applying even to the *able-bodied* was followed by a long list of exceptions. Those exceptions included cases judged to be of 'sudden and urgent necessity', and such a judgement respecting many paupers was widely made thereafter.[41] Another exception was where relief was needed because of 'sickness, accident, or bodily or mental infirmity affecting such person, or any of his or her family'. Such cases could be very widely interpreted indeed, given nineteenth-century levels of infirmity. Other exceptions were cases involving burial expenses

---

[38] 'Out-door Relief General Prohibitory Order', *Official Circulars of Public Documents and Information: Directed by the Poor Law Commissioners to be Printed, Chiefly for the Use of the Members and Permanent Officers of Boards of Guardians, under the Poor Law Amendment Act*, vol. v (1 January 1845), esp. pp. 9–16. (The editions used here, initially published in 1840–51, were the New York, 1970 reprint editions, bound as two volumes for the initial vols. I–VI, and vols. VII–X. These are hereafter cited as *Official Circulars*.) This 1845 Order and its accompanying 'Instructional Letter as to the General Prohibitory Order' (21 December 1844), *ibid.*, pp. 12–16, rescinded and slightly amended the General Order of 2 August 1841.

[39] 'Definition of the term "able-bodied"', *Official Circulars*, vol. VII (17 April 1848), pp. 227–8.

[40] W. Ivor Jennings, *The Poor Law Code, Being the Poor Law Act, 1930, and the Poor Law Orders now in Force* (London, 1930), p. 45.

[41] 'Instructional letter as to the General Prohibitory Order', *Official Circulars*, vol. v (21 December 1844), p. 12.

of anyone in the family; cases during the first six months of widowhood; cases of widowhood with one or more legitimate children, where the widow was not able to earn her livelihood, and who had had no illegitimate child since being widowed; where a woman's husband was in gaol or in an institution for safe custody, in which case the woman was to be treated as though she was a widow; with regard to the wife or children of any man in the Forces, where 'great latitude' was given to guardians;[42] where an able-bodied husband did not live in the union, but the wife and child(ren) did (there were many variations on themes of non-residency in later regulations, which were usually permissory of out-door or non-resident relief); and a variety of other circumstances in which the pauper did not reside in the union. Superimposed upon all such exceptions to the main theme that able-bodied adults should be not relieved out-doors were some injunctions that out-relief 'must' be paid in some cases, as for example where a woman without her husband had children under the age of nurture and needed relief specifically for them.[43]

Non-resident relief to paupers residing away from their settlements had been an important feature of the old poor law, especially with regard to relief sent to urban districts.[44] It was

---

[42] *Ibid.*, p. 13; and see the Amended Prohibitory Order of 1840, which included a similar wide list of exceptions to the rules applying to the able-bodied. 'Relief – prohibition of, out of the workhouse, to able-bodied and non-resident paupers', *Official Circulars*, vol. I (25 September 1840), pp. 104–10.

[43] 'Instructional letter as to the General Prohibitory Order', *Official Circulars*, vol. V (21 December 1844), p. 13.

[44] On non-resident relief before 1834, see A. Redford, *Labour Migration in England, 1800–1850* (1964, Manchester, 1976), pp. 91–2; J. S. Taylor, 'A different kind of Speenhamland: nonresident relief in the Industrial Revolution', *Journal of British Studies*, 30 (1991); King, *Poverty and Welfare in England*, pp. 186–8, 238–9; T. Sokoll, 'Negotiating a living: Essex pauper letters from London, 1800–1834', *International Review of Social History*, 45 (2000), p. 24; N. Pilbeam and I. Nelson (eds.), *Poor Law Records of Mid Sussex, 1601–1835* (Lewes, 2001), pp. 379–80, 382, 384; T. Sokoll (ed.), *Essex Pauper Letters, 1731–1837* (Oxford, 2001), pp. 10–17 (on p. 17 he gives percentages of 17–26 for paupers residing elsewhere for seven Essex parishes, 1820–32). People being examined as to settlement under the old poor law often mentioned non-resident relief as seeming proof of their settlement in the place sending it. The practice was even mentioned in the 1831 population census: *Abstract of the Answers and Returns*, vol. I (1831), p. 498, note b: 'The decrease of Population (33 Persons) in the Parish of Stoke-Talmage [Oxfordshire] is occasioned by the non-residence of Pauper parishioners.' The resident population there was 107. In other words, about 24 per cent of the potential population here was away on non-resident relief, showing how extensive this system

intended to be largely banned from 1834, with Edwin Chadwick and George Nicholls in particular making strictures against it. Nicholls later claimed, when speaking about his earlier work in Southwell (Notts.), that 'This class of cases was peculiarly open to misrepresentation and abuse', a view which he carried over to his work on the Poor Law Commission.[45] Chadwick wrote of 'the frauds and evils which are incidental to non-resident relief'.[46] It was felt that parish ratepayers could not personally observe such distant paupers relieved at parish expense, and decide whether their relief should continue.[47] This was an argument under the new poor law (surprisingly made by Chadwick) which prioritised parish accountability and local knowledge. There were also legal and practical objections to a non-residential relief system which involved more than one board of guardians, which raised ambiguous issues of responsibility for relieving officers, practical problems of repayment and double accounting across unions, additional work for union clerks, and so on. Much distress was caused by trying to restrict it after 1834, for example in unions like Merthyr Tydfil or Brecon.[48] This move also strongly reinstated the role of the parish of settlement, and brought many people back to their settlements – contrary to some supposed ideological and market imperatives of the new poor law.

However, non-resident relief survived, whether between parishes or unions, despite attempts to restrict new cases,[49]

could sometimes be. J. M. White provided detailed statistics on this practice for forty-six incorporated Suffolk parishes in the Blything Hundred in *Report from His Majesty's Commissioners for Inquiring into the Administration and Practical Operation of the Poor Laws in England and Wales, Appendix C. Communications*, xxxvii (1834), pp. 233–5. In summary, exactly a third of the poor relief expenditure by these Suffolk parishes was to non-resident poor. These parishes, incorporated in 1764, rarely removed paupers between themselves, and so this fraction should be relatively high compared to non-incorporated parishes elsewhere. J. M. White was also a witness in the *Second and Third Reports from the Select Committee on Settlement, and Poor Removal*, xi (1847), pp. 1–8, 93–100, but he did not discuss changes in non-resident relief under the new poor law.

[45] Nicholls, *History of the English Poor Law*, vol. ii, p. 233, and see p. 298.

[46] 'Relief – prohibition of, out of the workhouse, to able-bodied and non-resident paupers', *Official Circulars*, vol. i (25 September 1840), p. 106.

[47] *Ibid.*, p. 106; 'Instructional letter as to the General Prohibitory Order', *Official Circulars*, vol. v (21 December 1844), p. 14, s. 13.

[48] Thomas, *Poor Relief in Merthyr Tydfil*, p. 148.

[49] 'Relief – prohibition of, out of the workhouse, to able-bodied and non-resident paupers', *Official Circulars*, vol. i (25 September 1840), pp. 106–7, and see the seven categories of exceptions to whom non-resident relief was allowed in the Amended

and was also regulated by the General Order of 1845.[50] In some unions the large non-resident relief ledgers show that it could be widespread, being accounted under 'non-settled poor relief', and 'non-resident poor'. Union clerks also had to provide auditors with parish-specific information on the numbers and sums involved in non-resident relief.[51] In the West Riding, for example, between 1839 and 1846, about 20 per cent of those relieved were non-resident paupers.[52] This was yet another feature of the new poor law which normally involved parochial out-relief being given, often at specified rates, and usually reimbursed by a parish or union on a quarterly basis. In Bradford and North Bierley, for example, 'non-resident relief was almost exclusively confined to outdoor relief' – here as elsewhere because workhouse relief raised too many practical and accounting complications to be sorted out between unions.[53] After 1846 there were many further cases of non-resident relief affecting people who were not yet irremovable. While the gradual reduction between 1846 and 1865 in the length of residence needed to acquire irremovability status tended to reduce non-resident relief, the system still remained widespread thereafter.[54]

Prohibitory Order at *ibid.*, pp. 108–9; 'Relief – prohibition of, out of the workhouse, to able-bodied and non-resident paupers', *Official Circulars*, vol. ii (14 October 1841), pp. 163–4; 'General Prohibitory Order', *Official Circulars*, vol. ii (14 October 1841), pp. 165–8.

[50] 'Non-resident relief – General Order', *Official Circulars*, vol. v (1 January 1845), pp. 5–8; 'Letter respecting the non-resident relief General Order', *Official Circulars*, vol. v (21 December 1844), pp. 8–9.

[51] 'Non-resident relief – General Order', *Official Circulars*, vol. v (1 January 1845), pp. 6–7.

[52] M. E. Rose, 'Settlement, removal and the new poor law', in D. Fraser (ed.), *The New Poor Law in the Nineteenth Century* (London, 1976), p. 36.

[53] D. Ashforth, 'Settlement and removal in urban areas: Bradford, 1834–71', in M. E. Rose (ed.), *The Poor and the City: The English Poor Law in its Urban Context, 1834–1914* (Leicester, 1985), p. 87.

[54] There has been little analysis of the extent and continuity of non-resident relief before and after 1834. For an example of a non-resident poor ledger, see Barrow on Soar union, Leics. CRO, G/2/9d/1 & 2 (1845–75). For non-settled poor ledgers, see Leics. CRO, G/7/9d/1 (Loughborough union, 1913–29), or Portsmouth City Records Office, 193A/1/8/2/1–4 (Portsea Island union, 1899–1933). For non-resident relief in Ashby de la Zouch union (Leics.), see Leics. CRO, G/1/57/1 (1840–2, e.g. 31 October 1842). See 'Out-door relief – General Prohibitory Order', in *Official Circulars*, vol. v (1 January 1841), pp. 13–14, prohibiting new cases of this sort; 'Undertaking to repay relief to non-resident paupers', *Official Circulars*, vol. viii (9 May, 22 May, 5 June 1849), pp. 72–3, with regard to the Frome and Wincanton unions (largely in Somerset);

The unions excluded from the 1845 General Order are shown in figure 5.10. Although that Order, like its predecessors, contained many loopholes permitting out-relief even to the able-bodied, the excluded unions had yet more leeway in this respect. Large areas of the north-west (in Cheshire, Lancashire, Westmorland, and into the West Riding), parts of the north-east, much of mid- and north Wales, many unions in and near to London, and many in Cornwall, were excluded. Various urban unions scattered throughout the country, but especially in the midlands, were also excluded. Given the numerous excepted categories of pauper, and the accompanying latitude in union policies, the usefulness of such excepted unions in explaining the geography of out-door relief is open to doubt. This and other maps exploring regional exceptions to General Orders are often revealing of local opposition to central policy (or central perceptions of such opposition), but do not go far to explain the regional patterns of out-door relief in figure 5.8. Nor does the geography of the permitted out-door labour test add much to the explanation. That is mapped in figure 5.11, for 31 December 1847.[55] Here one sees the labour test being applied in 130 unions, allowing out-door relief in return for work. This was notable in the south-west, parts of Wales, parts of the north-west, in and around London, but also in other unions throughout the country. The labour-test unions in Wales and the south-west do proximate to the regional pattern of later out-relief. Yet the geography of central regulation, shown in such ways, does not go far to explain proportions of regional expenditures given as

---

T. Smith, *The Old Poor Law and the New Poor Law Contrasted* (London, 1840), p. 22; K. H. Baker, 'General ledgers of boards of guardians', *Journal of the Society of Archivists*, 2 (1963), p. 368; M. E. Rose, 'The new poor law in an industrial area', in R. M. Hartwell (ed.), *The Industrial Revolution* (Oxford, 1970), p. 140; Rose, 'Settlement, removal and the new poor law', pp. 35–6; D. Ashforth, 'The urban poor law', in Fraser (ed.), *New Poor Law*, pp. 145–6; A. Digby, *Pauper Palaces* (London, 1978), pp. 133–4; Ashforth, 'Settlement and removal in urban areas', pp. 67, 71–6, 79–81, 83–7; K. D. M. Snell, *Annals of the Labouring Poor: Social Change and Agrarian England, 1660–1990* (Cambridge, 1985), pp. 123, 338; D. Englander, *Poverty and Poor Law Reform in Britain: From Chadwick to Booth, 1834–1914* (London, 1998), p. 15.

[55] This information is from S. Webb and B. Webb, *English Poor Law Policy* (1910, London, 1963), Appendix A, pp. 321–42: 'Memorandum from the Local Government Board as to the local authorities for poor law purposes and the out-relief orders in force at the end of the years 1847, 1871, 1906.' Further cartography of 'the geography of regulation' is in Driver, *Power and Pauperism*, pp. 47–53.

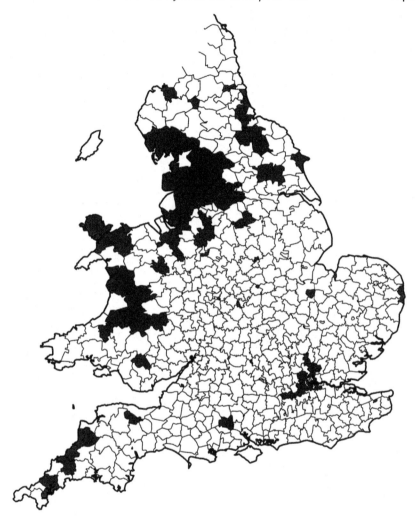

Figure 5.10   Unions excluded from the Out-door Relief Prohibitory Order,
1 January 1845.

out-relief. This suggests how easy it was to give out-relief through the loopholes in the legislation and General Orders, and undercuts the permissive significance of the excepted unions listed in the schedules of the General Orders.

The issue of rent payment had been a contentious one under the old poor law. After 1834, no rents were meant to be paid to

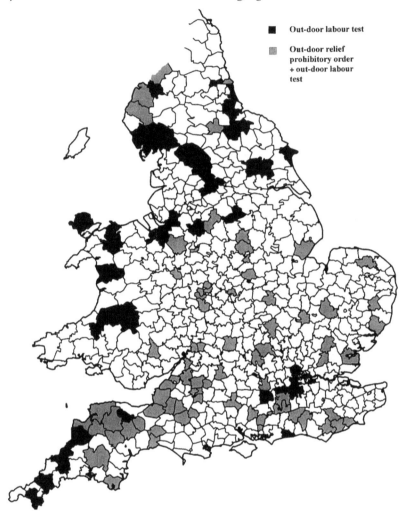

Figure 5.11   Unions applying an out-door labour test, 31 December 1847.

the able-bodied, nor were rent arrears to be paid, although any shelter that was needed for 'sudden and urgent necessity' could be paid by being included in the sum given to the pauper, which in practice could mean much money being given for the purposes of rent. If goods had been distrained for rent, guardians were permitted to replace them if really necessary, as with beds, bedding, and so on, perhaps out of the workhouse stores, and in some cases as a loan. The prime point about such thinking on rent was to avoid parish ratepayers or guardians paying the rent *directly*, as often occurred under the old poor law.[56] In cases like this, relief could now be offered as a loan, which occurred but was less common before 1834.[57] Indeed, the option of loans was strongly advanced in the 1834 Act, something which was to be regulated by the Commissioners. Advice about their terms and conditions, for many out-door purposes, appears frequently in new poor law official documentation.[58] The usual instruction in the General Orders was to avoid loans for purposes which would not warrant normal relief, but to suggest that loans might be given instead of such relief. The indirect payment of rent, therefore, whether in a prevaricating way via the pauper, or as such a loan, was yet another permitted exception which enlarged the scope of out-door relief.

These many exceptions were so encompassing as to defeat any widely applied principle that able-bodied adults should

---

[56] 'Instructional letter as to the General Prohibitory Order', *Official Circulars*, vol. v (21 December 1844), p. 11; and see 'Relief by purchase of a pauper's goods seized for rent', *Official Circulars*, vol. vi (23 May 1846), p. 95.

[57] During the old poor law loans were authorised under 59 Geo. III, c. 12, s. 29 (1819), although one can find earlier examples in overseers' records.

[58] 4 & 5 Wm IV, c. 76, ss. 58–9, which included provision to summon employers and reclaim such loans from wages, payable to overseers or guardians; 'General Prohibitory Order', *Official Circulars*, vol. ii (14 October 1841), p. 166; 'Repayment of cost of relief given to a pauper, who has become possessed of property', *Official Circulars*, vol. iv (1 July 1844), pp. 172–3; 'Instructional letter as to the General Prohibitory Order', *Official Circulars*, vol. v (21 December 1844), p. 15; 'Relief on loan – recovery of in county courts', *Official Circulars*, vol. vii (12 July 1847), p. 141; 'Loans – collection of repayments of', *Official Circulars*, vol. vii (15 September 1846), p. 151; 'Medical relief by way of loan', *Official Circulars*, vol. vii (13 December 1847), pp. 195–6; 'Proceedings for the recovery of relief by way of a loan', *Official Circulars*, vol. vii (19 October 1846), pp. 197–8; 'Relief by way of loan given to the wife, if recoverable from the husband', *Official Circulars*, vol. viii (19 September 1849), pp. 170–1; 'Relief – supplying beds, bedding, clothes etc., to out-door paupers', *Official Circulars*, vol. ix (8 April 1850), p. 108. Relief as a loan was often given to cover temporary incapacity. In Cardiff, for example, loans in the 1890s were repaid at 6d. or 1s. a week. All subsequent relief would be refused, save that in the workhouse, if someone did not repay them. The workhouse was thus used as a threat to coerce loan repayment. *Royal Commission on the Aged Poor*, xiv (1895), pp. 282–3. Young people in particular were offered loans in Cardiff. *Ibid.*, p. 291. Guardians could often reclaim loans by enforced sale of any pauper property. Leics. CRO, DE 1379/22/1 (Lutterworth union, 27 April 1893), regarding a male pauper accorded 3s. and 7 pints of milk weekly, as a loan, at Pailton (Warws.); 'Property of deceased pauper', *Official Circulars*, v (7 March 1845), pp. 108–9.

not be given domiciliary relief in their parishes. We will see that such domiciliary weekly costs per pauper were considerably lower than equivalent workhouse relief costs. In the hands of guardians who wished to minimise expenditure, who often had workhouses which were much too small to hold all their paupers, and who often dragged their feet in building or expanding workhouses, these many exceptions – notably the first two ('sudden and urgent necessity', and illness in the family) – rendered the workhouse potentially irrelevant for a majority of paupers. This is especially apparent when one considers, as we shall, the age and gender composition of pauperism. 'Sudden and urgent necessity' often led to repeated out-door relief for the able-bodied, as well as other classes of pauper, and often no labour test was required.[59] There was much subsequent deliberation on what was meant by 'sudden and urgent necessity', some of it of delightful legalistic and Dickensian nicety, as for example when necessity perhaps was sudden, but not urgent, or perhaps urgent, but not sudden.[60] The Poor Law Commissioners stated it to mean 'any case of destitution requiring instant relief'.[61] With regard to overseers ordering relief in cases of sudden and urgent necessity (which they were legally entitled to do),[62] the Poor Law Board thought in 1848 that there was little difficulty in seeing when that formulation applied.[63] Most unions took it to mean that the pauper urgently needed assistance. Therefore when overseers, relieving officers, or guardians chose to give out-door relief in such circumstances they could usually justify their actions, if they were requested to do so by an auditor or the Poor Law Board. Moreover, with regard to 'illness in the family', the clerk of the Kensington union probably spoke for almost all unions when he said that 'the rule is relaxed at once'.[64]

---

[59] Bosanquet, *Poor Law Report of 1909*, p. 108.
[60] Letter from the clerk of the Tewkesbury union, *Official Circulars*, vol. VIII (8 August 1849), p. 169.
[61] 'Instructional letter as to the General Prohibitory Order', *Official Circulars*, vol. V (21 December 1844), p. 12.
[62] 4 & 5 Wm IV, c. 76, s. 54.
[63] 'Payment of fees to medical officer for attendance on order of overseer', *Official Circulars*, vol. IX (15 February 1848), pp. 47–8.
[64] *Select Committee on Irremovable Poor*, VII (1859), p. 33.

Out-door relief, even to the able-bodied, was therefore accepted in a variety of ways by the General Orders of 1841–52. These Orders were long enduring, still being in effect in the early twentieth century, when they were updated by the 1911 Relief Regulation Order, which aimed (rather unsuccessfully in many areas) to consolidate and perpetuate the main principles of the 1841–52 Orders, to allow out-relief with labour testing in all unions, and to expand the use of case papers for applicants. The mid-nineteenth-century Orders allowed considerable discretion to boards of guardians regarding out-door relief. As Samuel Cornell of the Kensington union pointed out: 'I think the Committee will find that there are . . . some five, six, or seven circumstances, all or any of which, if they occur, would give the power of giving relief without compelling the man to go into the house, or forcing him into the stone-yard.'[65] The concern in these Orders was especially with able-bodied men. There were somewhat laxer rules for married women, and especially for widows with dependent children, and even more so for the non-able-bodied, aged or infirm, who had low prominence in the General Orders and for whom out-door relief could readily be granted.

Readers will probably have noticed, from the above discussion, that new poor law officials were urged to think in terms of refined categories and subdivisions of paupers. 'Types' of pauper and charity recipient had been variously defined and thought about in earlier centuries, and there was nothing new in that way of handling poverty and welfare. However, using and developing earlier precedents, the intensity of new poor law pauper sub-categorisation was unprecedented. The central authority wished to see policy decisions made with regard to such sub-categorisations, rather than being made on the basis of local knowledge of individuals. Close knowledge of the latter apparently had too many connotations of the parish and the old poor law. Workhouse children, for example, were subdivided in the 1840s by gender, and then into three age groups, and then into fifteen descriptive groups, making a possible ninety

---

[65] *Ibid.*, p. 33.

sub-groups.[66] Add to this all the multiple subdivisions of adults (by gender, age, mental and bodily health, nature of handicap, moral behaviour, vagrant habits, etc.), and one begins to appreciate the centralised pigeonholeing habit of mind trying to regulate the new poor law. This went well beyond anything found under the old poor law. The central authority never criticised any guardians for applying too fine a taxonomy of paupers. The categories themselves proved to be surprisingly durable and long-lasting, but they also embodied their own shifting moral charges and sanctioned imperatives. Usually policy adjustments focused on specific listed categories of pauper. Any one of such pauper groups, especially across its age range, might be subject to local or centrally directed policy changes, and specific policy changes affecting particular categories of poor were often targeted at named unions or groups of them. Such regional directedness indicates just how varied regional policies could be, as contrasted with those currently thought correct by the central authority. The huge volumes of official correspondence, Circulars, Special and General Orders underscore how important is an understanding of changes in category significance in new poor law studies. One of the traits of the eighteenth century had been its relative disinterest in making undue distinctions among those who belonged to the parish. Moral and personal judgements were abundantly made then, sometimes harshly, for example in many cases of illegitimacy. Yet belonging to the parish, a perceptively and inclusively Christian entity, tended to prioritise people as individuals rather than as categories. By contrast, under the new poor law, the historian must enter into the excessively distinction-prone mind of a Bentham acolyte, in which taxonomic inventiveness was a substitute for flexible empathetic understanding. That historian must adopt the thought processes natural to a well-disciplined and somewhat anti-social person sitting half-hidden behind a large, heavily

---

[66] See, for example, the Return to the Poor Law Board from the Mitford and Launditch Union, 18 March 1847, on workhouse children, in A. Reid, *The Union Workhouse: A Study Guide for Local Historians and Teachers* (1994, Chichester, 1998), p. 71. Categories of children include such groups as 'Children deserted by mother', 'Children whose residence in the Workhouse is caused by the bodily or mental infirmity of their Father or Mother', 'Illegitimate – their mothers not in the Workhouse', and so on, through fifteen such groups.

partitioned Victorian clerk's wooden desk, staring at all the multitude of partitions before him. Such partitioning, or moralistic cabinet-making, was one of the features that marked the new poor law off, rather superfluously, from a style of decision-making under the old poor law which was more indifferent to category distinctions, more knowledgeable of personal need, and for which moral blame or worth attached to the individual, rather than pertaining to that person by virtue of his or her specific categorisation. Of course, many boards of guardians continued to interest themselves closely in the morality and personal circumstances of individuals, to enquire into those, and to reject any central view that policy must be consistently applied within a pauper category. Out-door relief was often the result. Insofar as they operated like this, guardians' policies often represented a provincial rejection of the sophisticated classifications being urged on them centrally, and a persistence of earlier qualities of parish localism as against central canons urging uniformity of relief within categories – which often could not see the desk for the drawers – and which occasionally achieved that consistency of treatment per category at the expense of uniformity of relief practices generally and across classifications.

The rules of the two 1852 General Orders[67] represent fairly small category modifications of those of 1841–4; although such changes could have dramatic effects for individual paupers – especially widows, single women, and certain other definitionally refined groups – who might suddenly find themselves subject to altered policy because of some re-thinking about the significance of their category. In principle, the Orders were aimed especially against relief to men in aid of wages. However, they left open possibilities to work part of the week, and obtain relief for another part in which a man was unemployed.[68] Such

[67] The August 1852 Order triggered much protest, especially from northern English unions, and so was modified and slackened in December, allowing guardians more discretion over the non-able-bodied and over short-term relief to able-bodied applicants.

[68] In the Salford union, for example, out-door relief 'in aid of wages' was not allowed on the day when work took place, but was quite acceptable on the next day if the man was then unemployed. See the evidence of John Adamson (accountant and clerk of the Salford union), in *First Report from the Select Committee on Poor Relief*, x (1862), p. 33.

part-time work was the experience of many poor law claimants.
It was also easily amenable to claims of 'sudden and urgent
necessity'. The apparent danger of institutional interference
in the labour market was very much in the minds of those
who framed the 1841–52 Orders, although they were not able
to prevent that, and relief in aid of wages was very frequent
for widows, the elderly and the infirm. In addition, the Orders,
notably that of 1842, laid down that out-door relief could take
place to able-bodied poor in return for a labour test. Yet labour
tests were not defined in any Order, and their nature was left
to the guardians to decide. Those tests and the products which
resulted from them (chopped wood, broken stone, coconut fibre,
etc.) undercut the market in some regards, and the system was
often criticised for that.

Permission for out-door assistance after 1852 could be given
for many reasons. In countless instances, out-relief was permitted by Special Orders, Circulars or correspondence from
the Poor Law Commission, the Poor Law Board or the Local
Government Board, often as replies to union queries, which
supplied precedents that were sometimes formally publicised
to other unions. The cumulative, albeit oscillating, effects of
these, coming on top of what was already allowable, were very
considerable. They included, for example, providing clothing
to young people going into service.[69] The main point here was
not to pay for such clothing if they were already in service, or
if the father was in employment, as this was thought to amount
to a form of 'relief in aid of wages', which dredged up official
memories of the old poor law, and which could be tantamount
to providing institutional support for an employer paying low
wages to the father.[70] There was to be care that such assistance
in clothing did not place such children in a better situation than
the offspring of independent labourers.[71] Another case was

---

[69] 'Relief – clothing, etc., to young persons going into service', *Official Circulars*, vol. IX
(correspondence from 10 August to 27 September 1850), pp. 139–40; 'Relief in clothing
to a girl going into service – proceedings under the Vagrant Act against the father',
Official Circulars, vol. X (29 August 1851), p. 75.
[70] 'Relief of clothing for a young person in service', *Official Circulars*, vol. VIII (17 October
1849), p. 169.
[71] 'Relief – clothing, etc., to young persons going into service', *Official Circulars*, vol. IX
(21 August 1850), p. 139.

women deserted by their husbands, who had dependent children, where the husband was not in the union. Such women *had* to be given out-door relief if they demanded it.[72] There was the question of a widow who had an illegitimate child, after having had legitimate children. This was also held to be a potential exception to the General Prohibitory Order, and guardians could at their discretion grant such a woman out-door relief.[73] Guardians could give out-door relief to an illegitimate child when the mother was in service, if that child was not residing with its mother.[74] A woman whose husband had been transported could be treated as a widow, and guardians could then give her out-door relief if they saw fit.[75] The same applied to a woman whose husband was 'beyond the seas'.[76] Out-door relief, even for the able-bodied, could also be allowed prior to a pauper's removal to the parish of settlement.[77] With regard to the aged and infirm, the Poor Law Board repeatedly directed that there should be 'careful attention' to their needs.[78] These paupers were always eligible for out-door relief at the discretion of guardians, and high proportions of them received that. At the end of March, 1906, for example, 70 per cent of those aged over sixty were receiving relief 'in their own homes'.[79] Furthermore, if guardians accepted such people into the workhouse, they usually had to forgo the prospect of extracting sums in assistance from relatives, and this was a further motive to relieve them out-doors.

---

[72] 'Relief to a woman, with her children, whose husband has deserted her', *Official Circulars*, vol. IX (7 June 1850), pp. 88–9.

[73] 'Relief to a woman who has an illegitimate child', *Official Circulars*, vol. VII (6 January 1848), p. 228.

[74] 'Relief to an illegitimate child', *Official Circulars*, vol. VII (23 February 1848), p. 228.

[75] 'Relief to the children of a woman whose husband has been transported', *Official Circulars*, vol. X (29 May 1852), pp. 109–10; although see 'Relief – to an illegitimate child born since the transportation of the mother's husband', *Official Circulars*, vol. III (13 July 1843), pp. 139–40, on cases where such a woman subsequently had an 'illegitimate' child.

[76] 'Relief to the children of a woman whose husband is beyond the seas', *Official Circulars*, vol. X (11 September 1850), pp. 28–9.

[77] 'Removal – out-relief with a view to removal', *Official Circulars*, vol. III (25 January 1844), p. 192.

[78] 'Relief: in the agricultural districts, to able-bodied labourers during periods of the stoppage of work by continued frost or snow, or the inclemency of the weather', *Official Circulars*, vol. I (4 January 1837), p. 139, s. 30.

[79] Bosanquet, *Poor Law Report of 1909*, p. 56.

OUT-DOOR MEDICAL RELIEF

Medical relief was another pervasive form of out-relief after 1834. The Poor Law Report of 1834 had not paid much attention to such relief, despite its saliency in any period. It was only later that Edwin Chadwick showed greater awareness of the issue of sickness and its role in creating pauperism, and by then he had largely been removed from poor law administration. However, medical relief was not really intended to be part of the calculus of 'less eligibility' and the workhouse test, despite the fact that it was occasionally applied in that way. An enormous amount of medical relief took place in people's own homes. The poor law unions were divided up into districts for medical relief purposes, making assumptions about the maximum distance at which people might receive visits from, or visit, the medical officer for their district. About seven miles was considered the maximum distance in this respect, a figure that was adopted because it fitted Welsh circumstances, where the unions were often geographically larger than in England.[80] In English terms, 15,000 acres was considered the maximum for each medical officer (which would, for example, be roughly the size of about seven rural Leicestershire parishes); or, with urban unions in mind, a maximum population per district was envisaged of 15,000 people.[81] There was an average across the country of about four medical districts per union. In recommending practices for medical relief, the Poor Law Board was at pains to stress 'the wide differences between the circumstances of different unions, especially in regard of the density and character of the population'.[82] This led to some large differences in medical provision, particularly in the 1870s and 1880s. This point held for other forms of relief too, although the central authorities were slower to acknowledge that.

The medical arrangements followed logically from the rule that illness in the family was a criterion for out-door relief. It was

---

[80] 'Medical Order – maximum area and population of medical districts', *Official Circulars*, vol. II (12 April 1842), p. 252.

[81] *Ibid.*, p. 252.

[82] 'General Medical Order – instructional letter thereon', *Official Circulars*, vol. II (12 March 1842), p. 249.

recommended that regular visits be made by medical officers to sick poor persons in their own homes.[83] If parish overseers ordered medical relief, and duly reported it to the relieving officer, the guardians had to accept that, because this was held to constitute a form of relief through 'sudden and urgent necessity', which was, as we have seen, one of the criteria warranting out-door relief.[84] Even an able-bodied man, with someone ill in the family, could have out-door medical assistance if the guardians decided that he could not afford it himself.[85] The assumption in the 1842 General Medical Order, the General Consolidated Order of 24 July 1847 (which provided an administrative framework for medicine in workhouses, combining earlier regulations), and in subsequent Circulars was that out-door medical relief would be extremely frequent. This was clearly the case, although the total sums spent on medical care under the new poor law were often very small in relation to total relief. The small number of dispensaries that were set up in the metropolis after 1867 also presumed out-door patients.[86] Across the country, the usual practice was for medical tickets to be issued by guardians, usually for the aged, infirm, and the permanently sick and disabled, qualifying them for repeated visits and domiciliary medical attention.[87] Records of these medical visits were to be kept by the medical officers, separately itemised in every case, so as to allow them easily to be charged to the pauper's parish in due course, rather than to the union common fund.[88]

Under the old poor law, parishes had normally contracted with a local doctor to provide medical care for their paupers.

---

[83] 'Medical Order – substitutes for medical officers', *Official Circulars*, vol. ii (12 April 1842), p. 253; 'Medical officer – as to visiting the sick poor', *Official Circulars*, vol. v (3 April 1844), p. 60. This also extended to lunatics: 'Lunatic pauper. Duty of medical officer with regard to', *Official Circulars*, vol. vi (10 June 1846), p. 89.

[84] 'Medical relief. Payment of midwifery fee, where order given by overseers – medical tickets, how far available', *Official Circulars*, vol. vi (11 October 1845), p. 40.

[85] 'Medical relief', *Official Circulars*, vol. v (23 May 1845), pp. 88–9.

[86] Under the Metropolitan Poor Law Act, 30 Vic., c. 6.

[87] 'Medical Order – mode of obtaining medical relief by permanent paupers', *Official Circulars*, vol. ii (12 April 1842), p. 253; 'Medical relief. Payment of midwifery fee, where order given by overseers – medical tickets, how far available', *Official Circulars*, vol. vi (11 October 1845), p. 40.

[88] 'Medical Order – mode of charging fees payable under', *Official Circular*, vol. vi (2 March 1846), p. 55.

Under the new poor law, the parish was still responsible financially for such medical assistance, often delivered within the
parish boundaries rather than in the workhouse, particularly
in the early decades of the new poor law. Chadwick's own view
in 1840 was that ill people were probably best provided for
in workhouses, for reasons of cleanliness, appropriate food (as
ordered by the medical officer), and medical attention there,[89]
even though they comprised a category that could be given out-
door relief. The post-1860 expansion of workhouse infirmaries
facilitated this. Medical provision generally was another area
in which parochial accountability under the old poor law continued after 1834, albeit in more scrutinised audited forms, with
district planning in each union, and with the appointment and
remuneration of medical officers now a matter under the guardians rather than the overseers, even though overseers had to
pay for medical out-relief for their settled paupers.[90] In the later
nineteenth century, the idea of the workhouse infirmary as
virtually a poor man's hospital emerged, notably in populous
urban unions. In Birmingham, for example, the workhouse was
seen 'to a certain extent' as a 'state hospital'.[91] Those infirmaries
and sub-wards were often seen as suitable for giving birth in;[92]
or for treating smallpox, diptheria, fevers, 'the itch', those with
venereal disease, tuberculosis, and other such illnesses. They
also handled many of the insane or mentally handicapped,
either before or instead of their going into insane asylums.
A tendency gradually arose among the sick to view the infirmary in a different light from the rest of the workhouse, and for
them, at least, some of the abhorrence of the workhouse eased.

---

[89] 'Relief of destitution occasioned by disease; sanitary measures', *Official Circulars*, vol. 1 (10 November 1840), p. 119.

[90] Whether the standards of medical care fell after 1834 is debated by historians. Among a growing literature, see J. Stewart and S. King, 'Death in Llantrisant: Henry Williams and the New Poor Law in Wales', *Rural History*, 15 (2004); A. Hardy, *Health and Medicine in Britain since 1860* (Basingstoke, 2001); A. Digby, *Making a Medical Living: Doctors and Patients in the English Market for Medicine, 1720–1911* (Cambridge, 1994); M. A. Crowther, 'Paupers or patients? Obstacles to professionalization in the Poor Law Medical Service before 1914', *Journal of the History of Medicine and Allied Sciences*, 39 (1984); Crowther, *Workhouse System*; M. W. Flinn, 'Medical services under the New Poor Law', in Fraser (ed.), *The New Poor Law*.

[91] *Royal Commission on the Aged Poor*, xiv (1895), p. 172.

[92] 'Relief to single women during pregnancy', *Official Circulars*, vol. x (14 December 1850), p. 29, letter from the Keynsham union.

RURAL–URBAN DIFFERENCES AS EXPLANATION

We have seen that there were striking urban and rural differences in the incidence of out-relief. As Helen Bosanquet argued in 1909, whether a person gets out-door relief 'depends at present very largely upon whether he lives in the town or in the country, and upon what town or what part of the country he lives in. That is to say, it depends upon considerations which are largely irrelevant to the question of his needs.'[93] This was true throughout the period of the new poor law. It was true above all of the contrast in the nineteenth century between most London unions and averages for the rest of the country.

Robert Pashley found in his *Pauperism and Poor Laws* (1852) that the proportion of relief which is in-door is 'far greater' in London than elsewhere.[94] We have seen this to be true. Even so, Pashley observed that out-door relief in London was still about three times more prevalent than in-door relief, comprising about 75 per cent of relief in the capital, so the workhouse did not dominate relief in London.[95] He also thought that 'the proportion between the number of in-door and out-door poor varies greatly'.[96] Out-relief in the capital was especially pronounced in 'what may be called parishes of the working classes' (such as Shoreditch, Lambeth, Rotherhithe, or the East London union), where it was four times greater than in-door relief. It was less a feature of a 'wealthy and aristocratic parish' such as St George Hanover Square, St James Westminster, or St Martin-in-the-Fields, where in-door and out-door relief numbers were more balanced.[97]

The explanations for this London phenomenon are interesting, and as some of these explanations extend to urban contexts more generally they help to illuminate senses of local belonging as mediated through the poor law. A number of factors contributed to the special status of London as an area giving relatively 'low' levels of out-door relief, at least before some of the East

---

[93] Bosanquet, *Poor Law Report of 1909*, p. 49.
[94] Pashley, *Pauperism and Poor Laws*, p. 42, and see pp. 12, 36.
[95] *Ibid.*, pp. 37, 41.
[96] *Ibid.*, p. 42.
[97] *Ibid.*, pp. 41–2, and see his Appendix, p. 384.

End unions gained notoriety or renown for their out-relief policies in the early twentieth century.

As was often true of nineteenth-century towns, because of the age-specific nature of rural out-migration, and the problems of periodic metropolitan unemployment, there was a much higher proportion of adult able-bodied paupers in London than was usual in the country unions.[98] Workhouse relief was intended above all as a deterrent against able-bodied male paupers, and so it may best have served that purpose in cities like London. This is perhaps a paradox – after all, the workhouse test had been designed in 1832–4 with southern *rural* able-bodied pauperism mainly in mind. There is relatively little in the 1834 Poor Law Report about London pauperism. However, the subsequent extent of rural out-migration, from those agrarian regions of surplus labour, and thus the increasing transfer of that problem to the cities, had inadvertently resulted in this reapplication of the workhouse test to urban environments in particular, where it became adapted to deal with a displaced rural problem – a displacement, we might note, that itself owed something to the reception and impact in rural areas of the new poor law itself.

Much of the broader difference between urban and rural out-relief stemmed from contrasting knowledge of the poor among guardians, and this affected decisions as to whether the workhouse test should be applied. Henry Longley – an experienced Inspector of the Local Government Board who had served in western, eastern and metropolitan districts, and who took a dim and brooding view of out-door relief – found himself before a Select Committee in 1873 trying to rationalise parish, union and county boundaries. (That was a subject 'at present so complicated and unintelligible that very few people understand it'.)[99] While imparting his thoughts on that matter, he told them that the differences in poor relief between London and the country unions lay in the 'personal knowledge on the part of the guardians of the poor'.[100] He was asked:

---

[98] *Ibid.*, p. 42. On the nature of unemployment in London, see especially G. Stedman Jones, *Outcast London: A Study in the Relationship between Classes in Victorian Society* (1971, Harmondsworth, 1984).

[99] *Select Committee on Boundaries of Parishes, Unions, and Counties*, VIII (1873), p. 65. We return to that subject in chapter 7.

[100] *Ibid.*, p. 71.

'Have not the guardians in the country a large amount of personal knowledge of the poor, which is wanting in the guardians of the metropolis?'

'Yes, I think in some cases that is so. There are three or four unions or parishes in the metropolis in which the guardians have a surprising knowledge of the poor, considering the extent of the unions, but, as a rule, they have not anything like the knowledge which the country guardians have.'

'Not having that knowledge, they are obliged to use the workhouse as a test to prove the necessity of the applicant?'

'I think the effect of their want of knowledge is that they rely more upon the relieving officer than they otherwise would.'

'There is not the same inducements in country parishes at present to give indoor relief, as there might be if other reasons and arguments were brought to bear upon the guardians in their administration of relief?'

'The test becomes necessary in proportion to the ignorance of the administrators of relief.'[101]

This was clearly an important reason for the urban–rural differences in out-door relief. Indeed, the Poor Law Report in 1834, when discussing the situation in 'towns and, above all in the metropolis', had itself alluded to 'the difficulty of obtaining information where everybody is lost in the general crowd'.[102] The need for personal knowledge of the poor had in fact been one motive behind the permission for northern parishes to subdivide into township units with regard to settlement and poor relief in 1662.[103] However, as far as Henry Longley was concerned, ignorance of the poor among urban guardians was not a disadvantage; on the contrary, he thought that anything that conduced to in-door rather than out-door relief was beneficial. True to Chadwick's ideas and 'the principles of 1834', he felt that small and less populous areas had an 'evil influence', because they tended to pay out-relief.[104] In fact, this even disposed him to look favourably at the idea of *county* administration for some welfare matters.[105]

[101] *Ibid.*, p. 70.
[102] S. G. Checkland and E. O. A. Checkland (eds.), *The Poor Law Report of 1834* (1834, Harmondsworth, 1974), p. 231.
[103] 14 Car. II, c. 12.
[104] *Select Committee on Boundaries of Parishes, Unions, and Counties* (1873), p. 65.
[105] *Ibid.*, pp. 65–6.

Longley also discussed another factor that helps to explain the regional differences as mapped above. In London (after legislation in 1867 and 1870), a significant part of the workhouse costs were borne by the Metropolitan Common Poor Fund, and he pointed out that this had the potential to increase in-door relief compared with other regions.[106] About three-quarters of food and clothing for the in-door poor in London, plus officers' salaries, were paid from that metropolitan poor fund. Out-door relief was paid for by the parish.[107] This disposed to greater workhouse relief in the metropolis, as high in-door relief costs were spread more evenly across unions via that metropolitan fund, with the poorer unions benefitting from the high rateable values of other unions. These considerations favoured workhouse relief, as did the administrative proximity of the central authority. Working against such influences was the need for new workhouse buildings in London: 'the workhouse accommodation at present existing is insufficient'.[108] Nevertheless, Longley was well aware that metropolitan workhouse relief was much greater relative to out-relief than was generally true in the rest of the country,[109] and these considerations had clearly influenced that outcome.

THE SITUATION IN WALES

At the other extreme from London was Wales, where there were particularly high levels of out-door relief. Workhouse relief in Wales was very much a minority experience among paupers. Many commentators remarked upon this. It was evident in Parliamentary Returns in the mid-1840s, when far more able-bodied people in Wales were in receipt of out-door than in-door relief.[110] Much later, the Revd T. W. Fowle, while discussing 'The poor law in 1890', complained about how 'Wales is still the worst in respect of the proportion of out-relief.'[111] Fowle was the English rector of Islip (Oxon.), an ecclesiastical living worth

---

[106] *Ibid.*, p. 66.
[107] *Royal Commission on the Aged Poor*, XIV (1895), p. 129.
[108] *Select Committee on Boundaries of Parishes, Unions, and Counties* (1873), p. 67.
[109] *Ibid.*, p. 70.
[110] D. W. Howell, *Land and People in Nineteenth-century Wales* (London, 1977), p. 103.
[111] T. W. Fowle, *The Poor Law* (1881, London, 1893), p. 166.

£400 a year. His book was in a series on 'The English Citizen', and his announced purpose was 'to expound the mysteries of the English Poor Law'.[112] The fact that the Welsh were running their own justified versions of the poor law irritated him – one often finds such English-centred views of administration, expressing the view that policy deviancy in Wales needed to be corrected. A more positive statement about the dominance of out-relief in Wales came from John Davies, of Dyffryn (Mer.), who had been a guardian for Llanenddwyn in the Dolgelly union. He was asked 'Is the general feeling in your part of the world in favour of out-door relief, rather than in-door relief?' He replied: 'I should say the majority of the guardians have that feeling.' In fact 90 per cent of paupers in his union were out-door.[113] *The Imperial Gazetteer* in the mid-1870s remarkably commented on the two poor law unions of Anglesey and Holyhead: 'There is no workhouse, out-door relief being given in all cases.'[114] This contributed to the unusual structure of the new poor law in Anglesey, with some Anglesey parishes being in the Bangor and Carnarvon unions. The central authorities always had great difficulties in convincing people in Wales of the necessity of the new poor law. Indeed the Rebecca unrest in 1843 and thereafter was much influenced by opposition to the new Act's enforcement.[115] Writing letters in English to Welsh-speaking guardians may not have helped to persuade Welsh unions of their 'intransigence'. What one historian wrote of the Merthyr Tydfil union could be said, perhaps in a slightly different tone, of many other Welsh unions: 'Time and events proved the Merthyr Tydfil Board to be a stubborn, intractable body which clung tenaciously to the old ways of administering poor relief, often carrying out their heavy duties in a defiant and dilatory

---

[112] *Ibid.*, p. v; on his benefice, see *The Clergy List: Alphabetical List of Benefices* (London, 1896), p. 178.

[113] *Royal Commission on the Aged Poor*, xiv (1895), pp. 434–5.

[114] J. M. Wilson (ed.), *The Imperial Gazetteer*, 6 vols. (Edinburgh, n.d., *c.* 1872), vol. i, see under 'Anglesey'; *First Report from the Select Committee on Settlement, and Poor Removal*, xi (1847), p. 52: 'we have no union workhouse'; *Report from the Select Committee on Boundaries of Parishes, Unions, and Counties*, viii (1873), p. 49, on refusal to build a workhouse in the Anglesey union.

[115] D. J. V. Jones, *Rebecca's Children: A Study of Rural Society, Crime, and Protest* (Oxford, 1989), pp. 129–34, 334–5, 348–9.

manner.'[116] For many years people in Merthyr did not build a workhouse. For many years too they did not even elect guardians. Needless to say, out-relief in money remained the dominant practice here, as in the rest of Wales.

Some flavour of the problems faced by the Poor Law Commission in imposing its regulations upon the 'provinces', and most notably upon the 'province' of Wales, can be gained from a frustrated letter by Edwin Chadwick to the Lords Commissioners of Her Majesty's Treasury. Few historians can remain unmoved in the face of such Welsh off-hand indifference to Edwin Chadwick's directives from Somerset House, and in consideration of the great frustration such attitudes caused him.

Poor Law Commission Office, Somerset House, October 14, 1839.
The Commissioners take the occasion to notice, as within their own experience of the delivery of letters in remote and thinly populated districts, that letters containing notices and orders in the public service to the overseers of parishes in Wales, have been delayed for considerable periods, and on inquiry it has been found that it has not been the practice in such districts to deliver letters, but to allow them to remain in the window of the post-office, until, from some person seeing a letter in the window, the fact of the existence of such a letter came to the knowledge of the person to whom it was directed; and the Commissioners have had reason to believe that overseers or others, on seeing in the windows letters under the official frank, have concluded that the act of calling for them would involve some labour, and have purposely abstained from taking them. The Commissioners have therefore been advised that it is necessary to provide in such cases for the delivery of such letters by some special agency, and they have, in such cases where it appeared necessary to insure the delivery of a letter to an overseer, forwarded it to the clerk of the Union, with direction that it should be delivered by a relieving officer. In some instances these officers traverse their districts at regular intervals, and in places where the expense of the delivery would seriously outweigh the cost of providing a person to go on foot for the purpose. The Commissioners submit that it might be deserving of inquiry, whether the officers in such districts may not inform the postmaster of their ordinary routes, that he may avail himself of them, when special occasion arises, without any additional expense.
The Commissioners do not pretend to offer an opinion on the whole subject of the proposed change; they confine themselves to a request

---

[116] Thomas, *Relief in Merthyr Tydfil*, p. 22.

that the facts which they have indicated as coming within their own observation . . . may be submitted to their Lordships' consideration. (Signed) By order of the Board, E. Chadwick, *Secretary*.[117]

The image of his important unopened letters gathering dust in the windows of Rhayader or Llandrindod Wells must indeed have caused Chadwick many sleepless nights, before he hit upon this expedient involving the Lords Commissioners of Her Majesty's Treasury. In fact, many letters from parts of Wales to the poor law authorities in London were strident and assertive, protesting against interference and defending their own arrangements.[118] The Poor Law Board replied to such letters in its characteristically flat 'officially authorised' manner. The Welsh unions had no monopoly in the writing of such oppositional letters, for countless more were written from northern English unions such as Huddersfield, which was one of the unions reluctant to apply a workhouse test.[119] Even so, letters written from Welsh unions seem rarely to adopt the forelock-touching style of 'I beg to inform the Poor Law Commissioners that . . .', which is the phrasing that so often emanated from English unions.[120] As David Englander wrote, 'Welsh resistance to the workhouse principle was such that the abolition of out-door relief was too provocative to contemplate.'[121] This is not to say that Welsh poor relief was particularly generous. On the contrary, as it was said in 1847, 'There is no such thing as liberality in the relief of the poor in Wales.'[122] However, Welsh social relations were at odds with ideas of workhouse testing, especially in the Welsh countryside. John Thomas, the clerk to the Carnarvon union, commented that 'In Wales the frequency with which they go to chapels, and there meet each other, causes

---

[117] Letter from Edwin Chadwick to the Hon. E. J. Stanley etc., in *Official Circulars*, vol. I (14 October 1839), p. 16.

[118] For example, see 'Averages – on which the cost of relief charged on the common fund should be calculated', *Official Circulars*, vol. x (2 October 1851), p. 52, for an outspoken letter from the guardians and overseers of the poor of the parish of Bettws Gwerfil Goch (of the Corwen union).

[119] Driver, *Power and Pauperism*, pp. 141, 143.

[120] For example, Leics. CRO, G/1/57/1, Ashby de la Zouch union letter book (22 July 1840), p. 6.

[121] Englander, *Poverty and Poor Law Reform in Britain*, p. 29.

[122] Evidence of William Owen Stanley, MP, chairman of the Anglesey guardians, in *First Report from the Select Committee on Settlement, and Poor Removal*, XI (1847), p. 52.

them to become personally acquainted, and they [the poor and the guardians] become friendly . . . in consequence of meeting them so often when going to chapel and being members of the same religious communities, they become very friendly.' This led, in some people's minds, to a 'lavish administration of out-door relief', or at any rate, to a dependency upon out-relief for paupers which was very pronounced by comparison with much of England. The guardians in the Carnarvon union were also endeavouring to make the workhouse itself 'far more comfortable'. There was a fairly high rate of 'pauperism' in the population around Carnarvon, and Thomas was asked why this was so. He replied: 'I can only account for it in one way – that the guardians are kindly disposed, and that the paupers generally, though not exactly of their own class, often mix with them in their different chapels, and other small communities, and that the guardians want to extend their kindness to those whom they happen to know the best.' 'The poor become personally friendly with the guardians.'[123] This was a statement that applied to many rural Welsh unions. It was less descriptive of many English unions by the 1890s, where hostile class relations had often developed.

A high incidence of live-in farm servants, and low rateable values per head – which induced cost-concerned scepticism about the workhouse – also influenced rural Welsh poor law policy.[124] Out-relief to the elderly in the Carnarvon union was considered among recipients 'as their right'. It was almost seen as a pension among the poor, and the ethos of 'degration' which the English authorities wished to instil in paupers was little established in such an area.[125] These Welsh forms of poor relief were clearly embedded in the nature of Welsh communities, ancillary to very high religious Nonconformity and chapel-going, to a shared linguistic and moral culture, to kin inter-relations, to small farm livelihoods and a survival of servants in husbandry, with accompanying close employment relations – in short to a society which in rural and market-town areas was less class-divided than in England, and which (outside its heavy

---

[123] *Royal Commission on the Aged Poor*, XIV (1895), pp. 375–6, 379–80.
[124] *Ibid.*, p. 380.   [125] *Ibid.*, p. 381.

industrial areas) was prepared to resist any plunge towards such a centrist English model of human disaffinity.

The early insistence by the Poor Law Commission upon strict regulation and prohibition of out-relief to the able-bodied relaxed somewhat from the late 1840s. There were many reasons for this. Foremost among them was the scandal of the Andover workhouse in the mid-1840s, and the devastating use that critics of the new poor law ('the bone-gnawing system') made of the appalling evidence from the Andover enquiry.[126] The subsequent replacement in 1847 of the Poor Law Commission by the Poor Law Board, which was more closely overlooked by the government, and a desire to avoid subsequent mortification, made administrators wary of too rigorous a system. A consolidation of audit districts in 1844 and a marked reduction in the numbers of union auditors (from 454 to 52 auditors) probably made out-relief easier for guardians to dispense, despite the auditors' powers of surcharge and disallowance.[127] In the same Act, illegitimacy proceedings were taken out of the hands of the poor law authorities and turned into a civil matter between the parents. There were important changes affecting settlement with the introduction in 1846 and 1847 of legislation allowing the poor to become irremovable if they had resided in a parish for five years, the residential terms being cut to three years and then one year in 1861 and 1865. This may have led to greater leniency in allowing out-relief to the irremovable poor, because they were chargeable not to an individual parish, but to the entire union by having their costs paid out of the union common fund. Wayfarers were also now chargeable to that common fund.[128] An 1847 Act relaxed the separation of aged married couples in workhouses. This was pretty ineffective in altering internal workhouse accommodation, but it tended to increase out-relief to such couples 'as the number of separate sleeping

---

[126] I. Anstruther, *The Scandal of the Andover Workhouse* (1973, Gloucester, 1984).
[127] 7 & 8 Vic., c. 101.
[128] 11 & 12 Vic., c. 110.

apartments in any workhouse must of necessity be limited'.[129]
From 1848, the costs of workhouse teachers were taken in hand
by central government, which further relaxed guardians' purse
strings. The Orders affecting out-relief and labour tests in 1841–
52 built up clearer rules and precedents about the circumstances
that should apply when out-relief was given, rules which were
very frequently used to legitimise out-relief. There was also a
tendency for workhouse dietaries to improve. These were mainly small but significant signs that poor law administration was
relaxing in some respects during the mid-nineteenth century.
Above all, the buoyant early Victorian economy itself made
poor law questions and policy less pressing to contemporaries
than had been the case during previous decades, when there
had been a perpetual furore over poor relief.

THE 'CRUSADE' AGAINST OUT-DOOR RELIEF

In one of the fascinating about-turns that periodically mark poor
law and welfare administration, the period after about 1869
saw a reversal of this liberalising trend, with heavier insistence
on 'the principles of 1834'.[130] George Goschen became President
of the Poor Law Board in 1868, and issued a memorandum to
the London unions on 20 November 1869. In it he expressed
concern about increases in out-door relief (especially relief in
aid of wages), about 'indiscrimate distribution of charitable
funds' and 'double distribution of relief to the same persons'
by the poor law and charities. He sought ways of making the
most effective use of charitable funds and of marking out separate limits for poor relief and charity.[131] Such a view of problems
in poor law administration preoccupied the Local Government
Board from 1871, manned by personnel with a more doctrinaire

---

[129] 10 & 11 Vic., c. 109, which affected couples where both partners were over sixty years
old, and was enforced at the discretion of guardians. It was reinforced by a General
Consolidated Order making similar provision. The quotation above about the effects
of this on out-door relief is from Nicholls, *History of the English Poor Law*, vol. II, p. 387.

[130] Among the best discussions of this development are Webb and Webb, *English Poor
Law Policy*, chs. 3 and 4; Williams, *From Pauperism to Poverty*; M. MacKinnon, 'English
poor law policy and the crusade against outrelief', *Journal of Economc History*, 47
(1987).

[131] *Twenty Second Annual Report of the Poor Law Board* (1869–70), App. A, no. 4.

attitude towards out-relief than in the Poor Law Board, who came from a generation with little direct experience of the workhouse scandals of the 1830s and 1840s, and who felt that such scandals would not happen again with the auditing and central direction now in place. Like Goschen, they were also very worried by the rises in out-door relief during the 1860s, by the worsening economic situation at the end of that decade, notably in London, and by the way in which charity was rivalling or undercutting the poor law. These concerns were also manifest in the formation of the Charity Organisation Society (COS) in 1869, with its array of arguments for familial self-reliance and lower public assistance. The COS advocated close investigation of cases and carefully delivered remedies tailored to the personal needs of the 'deserving' poor. It wished to see greater control and coordination of 'indiscriminate' charity. Such priorities fitted well with the Local Government Board's agenda.

The so-called 'crusade' against out-relief which dates from this time was successful in a limited way, and the change in policy aroused much debate. We saw some of its effects in the graphs that introduced this chapter. Out-door paupers as a percentage of all paupers declined from about 87 to about 73 per cent by the end of the century, and this was the most perceptible result. The 'crusade' operated in part by highlighting categories of pauper which had hitherto usually been accorded out-relief, and advocating their redesignation as workhouse cases. Women suffered in this process, notably widows, married women who had been deserted, or single able-bodied women. There was greater effort to make relatives pay supportive contributions. Even so, the reduction in out-relief affected all categories of paupers, although that may not have been intended.[132]

The apparent decline in out-relief was, as we have seen, also caused by newer forms of public assistance starting to substitute for the poor law. Growth in national productivity and wealth throughout this period continued to be the main factor reducing pauperism. As the percentages show, very high levels of domiciliary out-relief persisted over the entire period. Furthermore,

---

[132] Williams, *From Pauperism to Poverty*, pp. 103–7.

reductions in the 1870s appear the more striking because they came from the abormally high 1860s levels. In fact, the 1850–1920 downward trend line of paupers per 1,000 population (see figure 5.3) was not much altered by the campaign against out-relief. Rising pauperism in the 1860s was counter-balanced by the decline in the 1870s, and the secular trend continued much the same through these fluctuations. The new poor law upward trend in relief expenditure was also little interrupted. (See figure 5.2.) In this wider picture, with these trends in mind, the national significance of the 1870s was that those years were a corrective for the 1860s, but arguably not a great deal more. One should not therefore exaggerate the effects of this campaign, although there were some largely rural unions – like Brixworth (Northants.), Bradfield (Berks.), or Atcham (Salop.), and urban unions like Manchester[133] – in which the curtailment was drastic, inducing much self-congratulation among guardians. In these unions the effects were thorough-going in the deep misery and ill-feeling they produced.[134]

There had earlier been fundamental difficulties in expanding workhouse relief. The Poor Law Board had never been able to compel the erection of workhouses, or their enlargement, and in the early decades of the new poor law guardians would often

---

[133] *Royal Commission on the Aged Poor*, XIV (1895), p. 267.

[134] On Brixworth, see the important articles by E. Hurren, 'Labourers are revolting: penalising the poor and a political reaction in the Brixworth Union, Northamptonshire, 1875–1885', *Rural History*, 11 (2000); her 'Agricultural trade unionism and a crusade against out-door relief: poor law politics in the Brixworth Union, Northamptonshire, 1870–1875', *Agricultural History Review*, 48 (2000); her 'Welfare-to-work schemes and a crusade against outdoor relief in the Brixworth Union, Northamptonshire, in the 1880s', *Family and Community History*, 4 (2001); and E. Hurren and S. King, 'Begging for a burial: form, function and conflict in nineteenth-century pauper burial', *Social History*, 30 (2005). In the Brixworth union, by 1890, the ratio of out-door to in-door paupers was 1:127. The ratio had been 1:12 in 1870, the main declines occurring in 1873, and the 1870s generally. Elderly labourers were forced into the workhouse. These changes were largely instigated by Earl Spencer on his Althorp estate. The situation only began to be reversed with the extension of the franchise to labourers, and the ejection of farmer guardians in the 1890s. A useful list of low out-door relief unions (using 1893 data) is given in Williams, *From Pauperism to Poverty*, pp. 104–5, which closely supports my figure 5.8 above. Yet it is not always clear whether these unions had heavily restricted such relief *after* 1870, or had had very low out-relief *before* then. Some of the city unions probably fell into the latter category. Others, such as Birmingham and Reading, seem to have restricted out-relief mainly in the 1880s.

'not listen to a proposition' to build or extend workhouses.[135] There had of course been much slowness in building them in some regions. Furthermore, many urban workhouses could not be enlarged because of the constraints and costs of space. John Bowring (clerk to the City of London union) spoke of how 'we are rather peculiarly situated; we have a very small area . . . every inch of ground is built upon – we can scarcely build anything more'. Three years later Bowring was making the same point: 'We cannot get any land . . . it is too valuable.'[136] Efforts to deal with this problem by increasing union sizes were attacked for taking away 'all local interest and local responsibility'.[137] And by enlarging the population catered for they aggravated the workhouse accommodation problem.

However, workhouses did tend to grow in size after about 1860, particularly from the late 1860s. From that date it was easier for guardians to borrow money for such building purposes, and union rateable values had been growing considerably over the mid-century years. Workhouses also became more sub-departmentalised internally, notably in many cities and towns. Authorised expenditure on workhouses was sustained thereafter at relatively high levels, and indeed grew considerably from about 1895.[138] For some cities, the architecturally improved workhouse even featured in middle-class notions of civic pride, although it hardly had any such resonance among the working classes, for whom it remained a detested building. In 1861 and 1865, the accounting for the union common fund had shifted from contributions based upon triannual parochial pauperism – the so-called 'averages' – to rateable values of parishes in the union. From 1865, there was no further pauper removal to and from parishes within unions, as union settlement in effect eclipsed parish settlement. In other words, during the 1860s unions could spend

---

[135] Richard Hall, metropolitan Poor Law Inspector, before the *Select Committee on Poor Removal*, XIII (1854–5), p. 123; *ibid.*, evidence of G. Poulett Scrope, pp. 89–90.

[136] *Select Committee on Irremovable Poor*, VII (1859), p. 62; *Third Report from the Select Committee on Poor Relief*, X (1862), p. 146. This union could not even get a building in the city to put people to work; it would cost £1,000–£2,000 per annum. *Ibid.*, pp. 146–7.

[137] *Select Committee on Irremovable Poor*, VII (1859), p. 65.

[138] Williams, *From Pauperism to Poverty*, p. 224.

more on workhouse enlargement with less resistance from individual guardians hoping to save their parish from additional expenditure, which had earlier been levied on them towards the union common fund as based upon their parochial pauper expenditure. That earlier system had spurred the protestation that 'Poverty pays for pauperism'; but this was less true from the 1860s. Spreading the levies across the union, on the basis of parish rateable values, led to re-thinking of policy and expenditure, and facilitated the 'crusade' against out-relief of the 1870s. Having been able to incur additional capital outlay on workhouses, the argument that guardians should use those facilities more intensively was often irresistible at board meetings.[139] Costs per head of workhouse provisioning were also falling with the general deflation of food prices, notably from the early 1870s – a consideration which had made workhouse adoption much more credible in 1834 than in, say, 1795–1818, and which probably favoured workhouse relief in earlier periods too.[140] And arguments that the workhouse was so repugnant that it could not be applied by Christian authorities were now less persuasive, given the improvements within workhouses.

The problems of limited 'house' capacity were understood by many paupers. Workhouses were often not full – indeed in many cases they were much under-utilised. Yet their internal departmentalisation meant that certain wards might be congested, while others were only partially occupied. The Liverpool workhouse in 1854, for example, had accommodation for 2,846, 'but we cannot avail ourselves of 500 vacancies, for this reason: our house is divided into departments' (e.g. the fever hospital, the wards for cutaneous diseases, etc.), 'so that we have apparently 500 vacancies, and yet have only a mere working

---

[139] Crowther, *Workhouse System*, pp. 58–9.
[140] One thinks of Knatchbull's Act in 1722 (9 Geo. I, c. 7), passed during a period of low prices, and a shift towards workhouse or poor house relief in some cities and regions thereafter. There may be a parallel here with the cycles of yearly (live-in) farm service, which prevailed when prices were low (notably in the early to mid-eighteenth century), but in many regions tended to decline in preference for non-board money wages during rising or high prices. (Snell, *Annals of the Labouring Poor*, ch. 2; A. Kussmaul, *Servants in Husbandry in Early Modern England* (Cambridge, 1981), ch. 6.) The balance between workhouse relief, and out-door relief, seems in very general terms to have been similarly influenced.

margin'.[141] By 1859, this workhouse had increased its capacity to 3,500, but presumably with the same problem.[142] It grew even more thereafter, to become a huge geographical complex by the time of aerial photographs. Other large workhouses had similar problems, such as the Birmingham workhouse which opened in 1852, which had 2,291 inmates and 86 staff, and cost £44,476.[143] The Marylebone workhouse could hold 1,852 people in 1859, but it had another problem – it was so crammed full that 'we have no means of properly applying the labour-test in that house; we have no room'.[144] Many workhouses in populous urban areas were much smaller than these, such as that for the East London union, which could hold 750–800 inmates in 1859,[145] down to workhouses like those for Rotherhithe or Lewisham, which could house 340 and 300 respectively.[146] And most workhouses were smaller still, often with capacities of 60–200, as for example in rural or market-town unions like Thrapston, Oundle, Uppingham, West Ward (Westmld.),[147] Carnarvon,[148] Dolgelly,[149] and so on, but still they were usually much subdivided. Their Benthamite compartmentalisation, which was so fundamental to the concept of workhouses under the new poor law, constricted further entry. In Liverpool, as a result, they often had to give out-door relief. They would have needed another workhouse with 3,000 places to do away with outrelief. Applicants frequently waited, if they could, until their union's workhouse was full before applying. They knew then

---

[141] Evidence of George Carr (master of the Liverpool workhouse), *Select Committee on Poor Removal*, XVII (1854), p. 401.

[142] *Select Committee on Irremovable Poor*, VII (1859), p. 154. The nearby workhouse for the Wirral union had a similar problem of under-capacity. *Select Committee on Irremovable Poor*, XVII (1860), p. 82.

[143] C. Upton and J. Fellows, 'Birmingham and its workhouses', *The Birmingham Historian* (1989), p. 2.

[144] *Select Committee on Irremovable Poor*, VII (1859), pp. 56, 60.

[145] *Ibid.*, p. 68.

[146] *First Report of the Select Committee on Poor Relief (England)*, IX (1861), p. 123.

[147] This workhouse, at Eamont Bridge, must have been one of the smallest operating, with about fifty-nine beds in the 1830s and 1840s, and only seventy-three in 1851. In some parishes in the union, the ratio of in- to out-door paupers was 1:20. See B. Tyson, 'The Mansion House, Eamont Bridge, Cumbria: a tercentenary history of its owners, occupiers and associations', *Transactions of the Ancient Monuments Society*, 31 (1987), pp. 158–63.

[148] *Royal Commission on the Aged Poor*, XIV (1895), p. 375.

[149] *Ibid.*, p. 431.

that they would almost be guaranteed out-door relief. This happened for example in Derby.[150] Or in Leicester, once people heard that the workhouse was full, there was 'an immense crowd of single persons immediately applying for relief'.[151] Edward Gulson, a Poor Law Inspector, complained in January 1840 that in Taunton there was 'an assemblage of from 150 to 200 able-bodied persons seeking relief. It was very evident . . . that they were aware that out-door relief had been given on the previous board day, and that they had reason to believe they could not be received into the workhouse.'[152]

Guardians faced with this situation had limited options. As John Darlington, the Bradford union clerk, said in 1855, 'our poor-house has been for a long while full; we have no alternative but to give them out-door relief . . . the workhouse is small'.[153] Paupers in Bradford knew when the house was full, and if they were settled locally or were irremovable they then applied. Of course, if they were removable, they were often much less inclined to apply, because removal was another 'test' against applicants, and served as a deterrent against them applying.[154] The Bradford union would have had to expand its workhouse 'enormously' to deal with the levels of pauperism.[155] Because of this problem of restricted capacity, there was a rapid turn around of inmates in some workhouses, as the 'workhouse test' was adopted for a week or so for many cases, and then the pauper was given out-relief, to make way for others to have the 'test' applied to them in this short-term manner. Paupers, having been 'tested', were then given out-door relief, albeit often with the on-going 'test' of labour in stone-yards or other venues. This occurred in Leicester, where 'parties who had proved their destitution by going into the house were, after having remained there a week or two, allowed to come out and work at the out-door labour test'.[156] The unions whose workhouses had not

---

[150] *Select Committee on Irremovable Poor*, XVII (1860), p. 20, evidence of John Lambert.
[151] *Ibid.*, p. 107, evidence of Benjamin Chamberlain, the union clerk.
[152] 'Relief – of able-bodied persons – workhouse accommodation', *Official Circulars*, vol. VIII (11 January 1840), pp. 63–4.
[153] *Select Committee on Poor Removal*, XIII (1854–5), pp. 80, 82, 86.
[154] *Select Committee on Irremovable Poor*, VII (1859), p. 125.
[155] *Select Committee on Poor Removal*, XIII (1854–5), pp. 80, 82, 86.
[156] *Select Committee on Irremovable Poor*, XVII (1860), p. 106. This had the additional advantage of paupers not having to sell their furniture. *Ibid.*, p. 106.

expanded in the 1860s and early 1870s had less policy flexibility, and could not adopt rigorous in-door relief practices. As always it remained considerably more expensive to maintain people indoors than in their own homes and parishes. Nevertheless, the expansion of workhouse accommodation from the 1860s made some of these earlier practical and financial objections to workhouse relief less compelling, and opened up greater possibilities of using the workhouse test in the way that Chadwick and others had earlier envisaged.

Changes in settlement law also exerted pressure on workhouse accommodation and out-relief policy. The reluctance to be removed to one's parish of settlement, and among the Irish the fear of being removed to Ireland,[157] had hitherto restrained applicants for relief. Removal was defended by many poor law officials for this reason. When changes in removal law were discussed at Select Committees, it was argued that ending powers of removal would necessitate larger workhouses.[158] The persistence of the settlement laws and powers of removal after 1834 is often remarked upon as if it was an anachronism that had survived contrary to the spirit of the new law. Yet as a deterrent, settlement and removal were indispensable to the

[157] William Cleaver, clerk of the West Derby union, spoke of how the Irish 'have stated that they would rather be in prison than go back to Ireland; and they have often told me themselves that they would rather die than remain in Ireland'. They told him that 'repeatedly'. *Select Committee on Poor Removal*, xvii (1854), p. 418. Andrew Doyle, a Poor Law Inspector, referred to 'the terror of removal' of the Irish, and of how they were 'appalled by the threat held over them'. *Select Committee on Poor Removal*, xiii (1854–5), pp. 188–9. See also *First Report from the Select Committee on Settlement, and Poor Removal*, xi (1847), p. 9, on how the Irish 'dreaded' being sent back to Ireland.

[158] *Select Committee on Poor Removal*, xvii (1854), p. 380, the Revd Augustus Campbell, rector of Liverpool: 'if the power of removal is taken away, we shall have to increase our workhouse accommodation enormously. We have already spent £160,000 in workhouse buildings. I believe that we shall have to enlarge them very considerably if we have to apply the workhouse test . . . I am anxious that that power [poor removal] should be retained as a precautionary measure, *in terrorem*, if I may venture to use the expression, preventing anything like abuse.' George Carr, master of the Liverpool parish workhouse, agreed. If it was impossible to remove, 'the workhouse would fail as a check upon the influx of Irish paupers . . . it would involve the necessity of a second workhouse, decidedly'. 'It would involve the necessity of increased accommodation?' – 'Yes.' *Ibid.*, p. 407. This is what happened subsequently in Liverpool. The city's workhouse became one of the largest establishments in the country. Liverpool was, for reasons of Irish immigration, an extreme case of the general impingement of settlement law reform upon urban workhouse building and strategy.

new poor law, which above all was a system predicated upon effective restricting tests to deter applicants. Removal may have been contrary to political economy, but it was an additional 'test' that was required because of the limited applicability of the workhouse test, especially where workhouses were too small, a situation that was usual. Removal was a 'test' that applied to non-settled or removable applicants only. It is important to notice that this test thus discriminated in favour of the local poor, and against 'outsiders': the latter faced this additional 'test' against their applications, while the local poor experienced fewer obstacles to obtaining local relief. John Harrup, clerk to the guardians in Manchester, commented that 'I do not think that we could retain the present system of administration of out-door relief if we had not the test of removal.'[159] The possibility of removal was, in that sense, a first deterrent hurdle against applications *from outsiders*, with labour tests and workhouse tests looming ahead as subsequent hurdles facing applicants. As such, removal was in the process of being lowered as a hurdle, or (for some) demolished. Five-year residence conferring irremovability was introduced in 1846, 1847 and 1848;[160] three-year irremovability came in 1861;[161] and one-year irremovability in 1865.[162] Irremovable paupers were a charge on the union common fund, rather than being charged to individual parishes. Under this legislation, people could apply for relief, and if they had been continuously resident for the required period they could not be removed.

We can thus see that a system of *three* tests (removal, the workhouse, and labour tests) for the non-settled/removable poor, and of *two* tests for the settled/irremovable poor (the workhouse, and labour tests), gave way gradually to a system only of workhouse testing and labour tests affecting the very large majority of applicants. This 'insider–outsider' difference in

---

[159] *Ibid.*, p. 448.
[160] 9 & 10 Vic., c. 66 (1846); 10 & 11 Vic., c. 110 (1847); confirmed by the Union Charges Act, 11 & 12 Vic., c. 110 (1848). In the 1846 Act, widows also became irremovable for twelve months immediately after the death of their husbands, and those applying for relief because of illness or accident were also irremovable, unless they were certified by magistrates to be permanently disabled.
[161] 24 & 25 Vic., c. 55.
[162] 28 & 29 Vic., c. 79 (the Union Chargeability Act).

'testing' strategies, linked to possible removal, which had hitherto favoured the local poor, broke down. The advantages of
'belonging' (via settlement or irremovability) became less apparent. The increasing inutility of removal as a deterrent meant
that other or more efficient kinds of labour testing had to be
substituted for it. This was one of the reasons why labour
testing, and the use of the workhouse itself, expanded in the
period after 1861–5.

From 1846, parishes where paupers were irremovable (commonly urban parishes, given the nature of Victorian migration)
could no longer apply for relief money from parishes of settlement for those who were irremovable, and so non-resident
relief diminished accordingly. This of course increased urban
expenditure on the poor, compared with the rural areas, and so
hardened urban guardians' resolve in applying the workhouse
test. The subsequent settlement Acts compounded that effect.
This was another reason for rural–urban differences in out-door
relief policy. These Acts were thought by many contemporaries
to increase applications for relief, the deterrence of removal
having been lost in cases of irremovability. Irremovable poor
became ever higher proportions of all paupers, as more residents gained that status. Their applications now either needed
to be restrained by the narrower range of methods – notably by a
more stringently applied workhouse test – or they had to be
granted relief, sometimes (and to maintain deterrent credibility)
in-doors. To have any chance of success, both options required
larger workhouses. The irremovable poor had less local and
legal ties than the parochially settled poor in the union, those
poor who the vicar of Steyning in Sussex called 'the original
poor', the 'original labouring population', those who 'have resided in the parish for a very long time'.[163] Such ties were frequently an argument made by a sympathetic guardian against
'offering the house', and applicants would often make their case
to 'their' guardian before the board meeting, while also asking
him to attend and ensure that they were well treated.[164] By

---

[163] *Select Committee on Irremovable Poor*, xvii (1860), p. 274, evidence of the Revd Thomas
Medland.
[164] *Select Committee on Irremovable Poor*, vii (1859), p. 127. According to H. B. Farnall (Poor
Law Inspector for the Metropolitan District), in agricultural parishes 'it is a common

comparison with the settled poor, the irremovable poor were relative outsiders, less well known, probably less prone to present themselves in this way, and they were unwelcome new charges usually to large urban unions. That could mean *very* low out-relief sums to them, or there could be less moral objections among guardians to offering them the workhouse. In either case, the intention often was to deter these applicants and make them leave town, thus breaking their irremovable status. We will assess these issues of discriminatory policy later. However relieved, these irremovable poor were in a way less visibly costly than parochially settled paupers, because, paid for by the union common fund, their expense was more diffused throughout the union. Some urban parishes could thus feel that rural parishes in the same union were contributing more to the workhouse poor, via these new funding arrangements for the irremovable poor.

In the guardians' politics of many semi-urban unions (which often had chronic rural–urban tensions), this was one way of getting even with rural parishes, who were increasingly released (in 1846–8, 1861, and 1865) from the burden of directly paying for their parochially settled poor, who now lived irremovably in town. The case of such paupers was, therefore, less likely than before to be taken up by sympathetic guardians. If rural guardians put forward compassionate arguments for their settled but more distantly resident paupers, there were urban guardians who could respond with heavy-hitting comment against out-relief, opportunistically making selective use of central directives. The fortunes of those directives were, as ever, played out in the contexts of the politics and accountancy of localism. Over this period, rural out-migration placed mounting burdens on urban parishes. These rural–urban accounting rivalries, affecting the irremovable poor in particular and the way that paupers were paid for, were always an influence upon how differently attached categories of pauper were dealt with. Rural

---

thing . . . for a poor person who is in want of relief to go to a certain guardian and ask him whether he is going to attend the next board; and if so, he hopes that he will see his case is attended to. They have great confidence in their guardians, and know them well.' If this was widely true, it must have conduced strongly towards out-relief being arranged.

pauperism over this period became urban poverty, through rural out-migration, and the nature of both forms of indigence altered. As far as most urban guardians were concerned, the poor were better contained in poverty than in pauperism. This was a view readily justified by the moral-economic argument that pauperism perpetuated poverty. The predominance of out-relief usually persisted, because most guardians thought it expedient to offer as many paupers as possible small sums as out-door relief, given the lower costs of that relief to the union, regardless of how those costs were accounted and defrayed, and because low-sum out-relief might also induce irremovable poor to move on. For some boards of guardians, however, a harder-headed attitude had come to stay, especially if they were persuaded by the workhouse deterrence arguments of the poor law theorists, and perturbed by the pace of the rural exodus.

The campaign against out-relief was much influenced by administrative developments in London. There were long-standing disparities of wealth and pauperism in the metropolis, between adjoining parishes, unions, and in general terms between the East and West Ends. In considering such disparities, one is sometimes tempted to apply the rural language of 'open' and 'close' parishes to the metropolis, such were the localised differences in labour supply, habitations and *per capita* wealth between, for example, some of the dockside parishes and nearby parishes where merchants and businessmen resided. The Metropolitan Poor Law Act of 1867, and Goschen's Amendment Act of 1870,[165] established and made use of the Metropolitan Common Poor Fund, which each union contributed to according to its rateable value. This was very significant for local taxation. Certain items of poor law expenditure became a charge across all the metropolis. And under the 1867 Act the Poor Law Board could add their own nominees to elected boards of guardians in London unions, making those boards particularly susceptible

---

[165] 30 Vic., c. 6, amended by 30 Vic., c. 6 and 33 & 34 Vic., c. 18. These Acts had been preceded by the Metropolitan Houseless Poor Act, 27 & 28 Vic., c. 116 (1864), a temporary Act made permanent by 28 & 29 Vic., c. 34 (1865). This provided for vagrant casual wards (as approved by the Poor Law Board) to be set up and funded by a common charge on London unions. These provided 'destitute wayfarers' in the metropolis with food and shelter regardless of their settlement and character.

to central influence. The common fund was used to set up isolation hospitals for infectious cases, infirmaries, mental asylums, out-door dispensaries, and to help pay for workhouse schooling. London unions were put into 'sick asylum districts' with their own hospitals. This did much to enhance hospital, infirmary and nursing provision in London, and related forms of in-door relief, although gross inadequacies remained.[166] Crucially for our purposes here, from 1870 the Metropolitan Common Poor Fund was used to pay a subsidy of 5½d. a day towards the costs of workhouse pauperism, while out-door relief was left as the one major burden still charged entirely to each poor law union. In other words, the taxation and accounting system had now shifted more towards favouring workhouse relief rather than out-door relief in London. Metropolitan parishes could therefore incur the higher costs of in-door relief without feeling that only their own ratepayers were paying for that, and the poorer parishes and unions now felt that their richer neighbours were contributing to alleviate their burdens. In addition, high out-door relief and unemployment in London in the late 1860s, affecting shipbuilders, weavers, dockers and other occupations, and a perception that generous and uncoordinated charities existed in London, had made the metropolitan authorities very amenable to policy changes that restricted out-relief.[167]

It was also true, as stressed by Henry Fawcett and others, that in London (as in other large cities) one could not easily distinguish the deserving from the undeserving, or be sure that someone was suffering from 'involuntary' poverty.[168] The impersonal scale of urban human relations made such knowledge of paupers improbable. There was, the argument ran, therefore all the more reason for in-door relief in such cities. In effect, the workhouse test was an administrative *mechanism* that substituted for the face-to-face knowledge of paupers that usually existed under the old poor law, or in many rural unions. It was of course a 'mechanism' that was appallingly blunt in discerning whether a person was 'deserving', because, cynically

---

[166] Wood, *Poverty and the Workhouse*, pp. 134–5.
[167] R. Humphreys, *Poor Relief and Charity, 1869–1945* (Basingstoke, 2001), pp. 10–11.
[168] H. Fawcett, *Pauperism, its Causes and Remedies* (1871, Bristol, 1978), pp. 43–4.

disposed towards human nature, it took no account of people's individual differences in character, pride, self-reliance and conscience. However, coupled with the principle of workhouse less eligibility, its attraction to early Victorian social technicians was that it did in theory allow real need, destitution and hunger to be distinguished from able-bodied 'loafing' idleness and dislike of work. Furthermore, it accomplished this via 'independent' paupers' own despairing choices. Paternalistic discernment might here be an irrelevance (although in fact that continued in a variety of forms under the new poor law). The machinery of the new poor law (despite having been designed for rural arable parishes) was especially adaptable to the impersonality and lack of human acquaintance of the large Victorian cities, even though the large scale and periodic nature of unemployment in those cities was poorly reconcilable with workhouse relief, mainly because of limits on how many people could be accommodated. We have seen in figure 5.8 the results of these developments, in the low out-relief of the London unions and many other large towns. These administrative innovations in London, and the need for poor law systems to adapt to chronic urbanisation as epitomised by the metropolis (or by Birmingham, Manchester, Liverpool and so on), were to have enormous implications for London and poor law history in the future.

Such administration was also to have implications for local senses of belonging. We can see here how the regionally varied breakdown of the parish, as a face-to-face local society, featuring individual knowledge and discernment with policy repercussions for paupers, manifested itself in differing in- and out-door relief systems. These were such that the large cities and towns went over most rapidly and thoroughly to in-door relief, mainly because of their guardians' ready ignorance of applicants; while the rural and more humanly scaled unions (with some notable exceptions, especially during the post-1879 agricultural depression) stayed with more reliance upon out-door relief. That out-relief was not a naive leap of faith on the part of gullible farmer guardians, even though the London-based central authority often revealingly thought it was, as is clear from much of its patronising and pedagogic correspondence with union clerks in the provinces. On the contrary, provincial rural out-relief was a corollary of such unions' greater appreciation of the circumstances of individual applicants, and (despite the low sums involved in out-relief) it showed a more sympathetic understanding of how paupers' needs could be met in domiciliary and traditional parochial terms. That was of course what the poor themselves so often pleaded for.

One is struck by the intense moral tone that permeates poor law discussion in the 1870s and 1880s. In author after author, there was a stated intention to make people self-reliant, prudent, provident, responsible for their own futures, to make them join friendly societies and other mutual clubs, and to encourage families to support their members. One can find this abundantly in earlier periods: throughout the old poor law, in pamphleteering during the later years of the old poor law, in the wording of Acts like Sturges Bourne's Select Vestries Act (1819),[169] and it was frequent in the Report of the 1832–4 Poor Law Commission. Yet in the early nineteenth century it usually comprised defensive statements against ideas of pauper 'right', coupled with quite generalised points about the need for gratitude, 'independence' and religious decorum among the labouring poor. By the later nineteenth century, with the added influence of the COS and its provincial branches, it had become more focused, more prone to make specific criticisms of individual paupers, just as the forms of working-class self-reliance and self-improvement themselves had become far more obvious, institutionalised and visible as providential options. The apparent rise in real incomes among the working classes augmented the argument that what was morally right (greater self-reliance) was now also affordable and practicable. Moralistic assessment of applicants, on a case-by-case basis by relieving officers and guardians, was normal. Choice of in-door or out-door relief was always 'very much guided by the character of an individual', as Lord Redesdale said in 1860.[170] Henry Coppock, the clerk to the Stockport union, spoke of how 'we never apply the workhouse test except we find that we have a worthless individual to deal with; then we find that the workhouse test is a valuable test, but it is never applied except in those cases'.

---

[169] 59 Geo. III, c. 12.
[170] *Select Committee on Irremovable Poor*, XVII (1860), p. 424. Lord Redesdale was chairman of the Shipton-on-Stour union (Warwickshire).

If the guardians think that the applicant 'is a skulking, idle man, they say he must have the test of the workhouse'.[171]

Such assessment of people's moral character, resulting in different relief outcomes, remained markedly true until the 1920s, when such criteria gave way to rather more objective and morally somewhat less intrusive judgements. In a variety of local ways, policy from the 1870s had come to expect certain standards of deportment, domiciliary abode, manners, and signs of self-reliance, and out-door relief was often openly conditional upon meeting such informal and 'deserving' criteria. The new poor law had become thoroughly impregnated with moralistic expectation and attitude. 'Deserving' and 'undeserving' judgements, labels, and methods of ascertainment, while always present in poor law history, had perhaps never had so much influence. Claimants thought to be the most obviously undeserving, such as vagrants, or mothers of illegitimate children, were especially penalised. Such moralism complemented the legalistic letter of the Official and Special Orders, or the Annual Reports of the Local Government Board, and permeated such documentation. It had a major influence upon whether out- or in-door relief was granted, as well as upon the sums given to out-relief recipients.

There were many notable examples of this moralism. Henry Fawcett, for example, realised in 1871 that 'the great proportion of paupers receive relief in some form or other at their own homes'. He knew that out-relief, which he critically called 'parochial relief' as though it was a throw-back to past localism, was in fact eight times more prevalent than in-door relief.[172] But rather than seeing this as buttressing the sanctity of the Victorian home, family, and local senses of attachment and belonging – which was one way his argument might have run – moralising prerogatives and financial expediency led him to stress indolence and self-indulgence as the results.[173] He believed that 'the direction of all poor law reform [was] by gradual degrees to

---

[171] *Select Committee on Irremovable Poor*, VII (1859), p. 148. The large majority of cases in the Stockport union received out-relief, including able-bodied men, although the clerk sometimes wrote to the Poor Law Board to confirm that.

[172] Fawcett, *Pauperism*, pp. 26, 47.

[173] *Ibid.*, p. 46.

discourage and ultimately to abolish out-door relief'.[174] This was to be done by the workhouse test. Rehearsing a series of common arguments, he held that out-relief discouraged relatives to look after each other. Out-relief, he claimed, lowered savings when people were in employment. It reduced motives to invest in annuities, or in friendly society membership, as potential members realised that they would diminish their claim on the rates by joining.[175] It produced 'mischievous results' everywhere.[176] The workhouse was needed to encourage thrift. The authorities could control relief in the workhouse much more easily, for there it might be likened to a steam engine 'which is completely subject to our direction'.[177] If it was impossible to prevent out-relief, then it would be preferable to abolish the poor law altogether.[178] The boarding-out of pauper children, which was another form of out-relief, was attacked by Fawcett as 'a demoralising influence', which might put them into a more eligible position than many labourers' children.[179] It might even be a motive to abandon one's children, or to have illegitimate children, and it certainly did not encourage providence. Fawcett was equally critical of small parish charities, whereby 'poor old decrepit creatures are induced in all weathers to drag their weary limbs to church, many of them being almost too lame to walk, and too deaf to hear'.[180] Scornful of most things parochial, Fawcett was however in favour of the parish as the unit for rating.[181] This was a common ambivalence at the time, which even Edwin Chadwick had shared. The seeming contradiction between admiring larger units of administration, while still favouring small units for rating, was explained by a belief that small units were conducive to closer scrutiny and economy of financial administration. Fawcett himself was blind – but fortunately as Professor of Political Economy at the University of Cambridge and a Fellow of Trinity Hall, his disability did not produce the penury that blindness did for many other people during the new poor law. Writing in 1870 at the start of the

---

[174] *Ibid.*, p. 24.
[177] *Ibid.*, p. 49.
[180] *Ibid.*, pp. 52–3.

[175] *Ibid.*, p. 39.
[178] *Ibid.*, p. 50.
[181] *Ibid.*, p. 68.

[176] *Ibid.*, pp. 32–4.
[179] *Ibid.*, pp. 79–81, 84, 86, 92.

'crusade' against out-relief, his views were very influential, and were shared by many other policy makers.

The 'crusade' against out-relief was most associated with the 1870s and 1880s, and it was largely over by the early 1890s. The extension of the franchise and the ending of plural voting and property qualifications for guardians, under the Local Government Act of 1894, helped to conclude such unpopular policy. Given their longer-term decline, rates of pauperism were now evidently very low compared with earlier national experience. There was growing appreciation of the involuntary nature of much able-bodied unemployment, and sympathy for the unemployed, notably during recent depressions. Local social surveys were increasing a sense of responsibility for the poor, and in the countryside the rural exodus was also affecting guardians' attitudes. Public works were assuming a greater role in relief, a development that is often dated from a Circular promoting them in 1886 from Joseph Chamberlain, the President of the Local Government Board. Relief under such schemes was extra-poor law in nature, partly to avoid 'respectable' workmen becoming habituated to poor law relief. Out-door relief regulations were relaxed in Circulars of 1895, 1896 and 1899, allowing such relief to be given more easily, especially to the deserving and the elderly. Indeed, the aged poor, and the limitations of current relief for them, were high in policy discussion by the mid-1890s. That prominence, and the findings of the Royal Commission on the Aged Poor of 1895, ensured that a strict 'dispauperisation' campaign to restrict relief to the workhouse had very limited on-going support.

TYPES OF LABOUR TEST

Some of the forms of labour test that were used under the new poor law have already been mentioned. Applicants were put to such work as a condition of domiciliary relief, whether in money or kind. That work would be a 'test' in a similar way that the workhouse, or the threat of removal, was a 'test' against unnecessary applications. H. B. Farnall, who in 1859 was the Poor Law Inspector for the Metropolitan District, spoke of such labour as 'a very good test, but not so good a one as the workhouse'. The men, he thought, should be 'made to work all day, and everyday, for that relief', rather than working a few days and spending the rest of the time unoccupied.[182] One can certainly find that latter approach adopted in some unions. The men would reside in their own homes and parishes, and would usually walk to a workplace to do an allotted work test, either everyday for fixed hours, or for particular days during the week. That fitted in with the casual and part-time nature of much work, for example in the building trades, or for occupations such as car-men, dockers, and general labourers. The labour test was usually coordinated by one or more task masters or 'Superintendents of Out-door Labour', who kept time, and measured the work performed. In the Strand union, the labour master oversaw the work done, and then 'he sends a certificate back to the relieving officer, stating the amount of labour done, and the time the man has been employed upon it'.[183] Some cities like Manchester, Birmingham and Liverpool built 'able-bodied test workhouses' in the 1890s, which were aimed to be especially deterrent, for example against tramps, and which offered a punitive form of poor relief conditional upon intense labour tests (large quantities of stone-breaking) under almost military discipline.[184] This approach was fairly rare. One often finds a presumption that the more deserving paupers would be offered out-door labour tests, while the less deserving would be 'offered the house'.[185] There was considerable scope under the new poor law for such moral discrimination between categories of relief recipients. These possibilities were often made quite explicit in central or guardians' regulations on in- and out-door relief, and they were put into effect via different types of labour testing.

Stone-breaking for men was one of the most common methods. It was allowed where an Outdoor Labour Test Order was in effect, and was frequently adopted. It was usually in a labour yard or in sheds that sometimes adjoined, or could even

---

[182] *Select Committee on Irremovable Poor*, VII (1859), p. 125.
[183] *Ibid.*, pp. 76–7.
[184] A. J. Kidd, '"Outcast Manchester": voluntary charity, poor relief and the casual poor, 1860–1905', in A. J. Kidd and K. W. Roberts (eds.), *City, Class and Culture: Studies of Social Policy and Cultural Production in Victorian Manchester* (Manchester, 1985), pp. 55–7.
[185] Kidd, 'Outcast Manchester', p. 55.

be in, the workhouse, while in other places it was further distant. In some unions, such as Thrapston in Northamptonshire in 1838, the work could take the form of digging and breaking stone from local pits, showing continuity from the old poor law.[186] More usually it consisted of stone-breaking in special yards. One can sometimes find details of rents paid by a union for stone-yards used for this purpose, while some unions owned their own premises. Many unions, like Liverpool, had a stone-yard 'situated near the workhouse, but forming no part of it'.[187] Here men would break stones at 'so much per tub, which is somewhere about a ton . . . We should give him that employment until he could get something better to do.'[188] Married men here could earn up to 1s. a day, single men up to 10d. A few men were employed measuring the stones. In Kensington, nine-tenths of able-bodied pauper men worked in the stone-yard. Stone-breaking here went back long before Kensington became a separate union.[189] Fulham had 'a large stone-yard connected with the establishment', in this case at the back of the workhouse. The majority of men were sent there, 'and according to the family of the man, they have so much relief, so much in money, and so many loaves of bread, according to whether the man is a single or a married man, or with two, three, four or five, or more children'.[190] The wife and children stayed 'in the cottage', by which was meant their London home.[191] The difficulty lay in providing work for very large numbers. In the Fulham stone-yard, it was said, 'their numbers are so great it is impossible for us to provide them with labour'.[192] 400–500 or more men would work in the stone-yard at any one time, notably during winter. If one multiplies such numbers by a notional family size, one sees how many were dependent upon such labour, and how far workhouse capacity fell short in such districts. Because of the scale of unemployment affecting brick-makers, market-gardeners and others, the 'workhouse test is

---

[186] On Thrapston, see E. Whelan, 'An examination of the continuity of poor relief between the old poor law and the new poor law: a study of the Oundle and Thrapston unions of Northamptonshire' (MA dissertation, Centre for English Local History, University of Leicester, 2004), pp. 50–1.
[187] *Select Committee on Irremovable Poor*, VII (1859), p. 155.
[188] *Ibid.*   [189] *Ibid.*, p. 21.   [190] *Ibid.*, p. 7.   [191] *Ibid.*, p. 15.
[192] *Ibid.*, p. 110.

utterly impossible of being acted upon in the Fulham Union . . .
the house is not one-fourth big enough to hold them'.[193] Stone-
breaking thus allowed guardians to by-pass problems of limited
capacity workhouses. The remuneration from stone-yard labour
in Fulham was 3s. 6d. plus six loaves a week, for a man, wife
and two children. The resulting penury in London can hardly
be imagined. This was 'far too low for anybody to work at that
[who] could get work elsewhere; it keeps life and soul together,
and that is all that anybody can say for it, and more than some
would say to it'.[194]

This kind of work raised special difficulties for men whose
normal occupations were sedentary and clerical, or who were in
delicate branches of the textile trades, like silk weaving or
some product specialisms of framework knitting, or in other
trades like tailoring, book-keeping, watch-making in London,
jet working in Whitby, and so on.[195] One can certainly find such
men being coerced into stone-breaking (they could be charged
before a magistrate under the 1824 Vagrancy Act for refusing),[196] despite the arduous conditions and effects on their
hands and physique. In some cases, such as tailors in Fulham,
they were made to break less stones than labourers, although
before 1853 the practice here had been to make everyone break
the same amount.[197] One can also find such men being put to
oakum-picking, street cleaning, rubbish clearance, or wood
chopping instead, if they were unable to perform heavy labour.
In Stockport, men were put to sweeping streets, a 'test' which
added to the shame of the pauper.[198] Mill hands in Salford were

---

[193] *Ibid.*, p. 9.
[194] *Ibid.*, p. 14, the view of W. D. Salter, clerk of the Fulham union. To similar effect, see
ibid., pp. 148–9.
[195] For a scathing attack by a Prestwich clergyman on silk weavers being put to farm
labour, see *First Report of the Select Committee on Poor Relief*, x (1862), pp. 105, 114–17:
'very unfair and very humiliating'.
[196] On this use of the vagrancy Acts, see 'Out-door labour test – Newcastle-upon-Tyne
union', *Official Circulars*, vol. III (31 July 1842), pp. 41–2. The clerk of that union
questioned the applicability to such stone-yard paupers of this legislation (notably
the 1824 Vagrancy Act, 5 Geo. IV, c. 83, s. 3), but the Poor Law Commissioners
defended its use, as relating to a man 'in part' able but neglecting to support his
family, i.e. by working at stone-breaking.
[197] *Select Committee on Irremovable Poor*, VII (1859), p. 8.
[198] *Ibid.*, pp. 148–9.

put to oakum if they were not strong enough to hammer stones.[199] The quantities of stones to be broken varied greatly, and there seems to have been little central attempt to regulate that. It was controlled by the guardians. Vagrants were also often made to break stones, prior to release from the vagrant ward and as a condition of a scanty morning meal. The stones in such cases often had to be broken down to sizes that could fit through a grill set in the side of their vagrant cell. One finds orders for stones in very many union accounts, and complaints were frequent that this form of labour test, whether in-door or out-door, did not make any profit for the guardians. Indeed, they usually made a significant loss with it, as they often admitted.[200] Nevertheless, stone-breaking was a very widespread labour test. The overall output across the country, over the entire span of the new poor law, must have been enormous, and must have made a very significant contribution to the road-building industry.

Chopping wood was another form of labour test. It was used quite frequently in rural unions, especially in the late nineteenth and early twentieth centuries. It was even adopted by some charitable societies, for example in Manchester around the turn of the century by the Salvation Army and by some churches, alongside other work such as sorting paper.[201] In the Leicester union, one possible form of labour test involved farm work on a 48 acre farm a mile out of town, although this raised problems in supervising the work, and the farm made a heavy loss.[202] In other regions, in the twentieth century, men could be put to work for the Forestry Commission, or employed at ditch digging, road making, levelling land and so on, or could be trained at government training and instructional centres.[203] Many councils involved in relief work had stone-yards, and they also put men to work on tasks such as road building.[204] This kind of

[199] *First Report from the Select Committee on Poor Relief*, x (1862), p. 38.
[200] *Select Committee on Irremovable Poor*, vii (1859), pp. 21–2. Evidence of Samuel Cornell, the clerk of Kensington parish.
[201] Kidd, 'Outcast Manchester', p. 64.
[202] Bosanquet, *Poor Law Report of 1909*, p. 107.
[203] C. M. Mowat, *Britain between the Wars, 1918–1940* (1955, London, 1968), p. 488.
[204] Kidd, 'Outcast Manchester', p. 64, on relief work conducted by Manchester City Council.

municipal involvement in public relief and labour testing expanded in the late nineteenth century and especially after the Unemployed Workmen's Act of 1905. Further examples of it will be discussed below.

Stone-yard work of course excluded women, but labour testing of women often occurred. It became more pronounced after December 1871, when a Circular forbade out-door relief to able-bodied women except on condition of a labour test. In theory, they were now placed on the same footing as able-bodied men. The work for women often involved oakum-picking and sorting hair, washing and laundry, scrubbing floors and stairways, cleaning, needlework, nursing, or looking after children. Women were sometimes put to such tasks in the workhouse, even though they were not resident there, and this was in effect a form of partial out-door relief. Women doing nursing work, for example, were often female paupers, partly because it was difficult to recruit 'respectable' nurses to work in such environments, or to pay them adequately.[205] Able-bodied women were often given out-door relief on condition that they worked in the workhouse a number of days every week, as for example in Merthyr Tydfil.[206] This partial in-door relief was an experience that some male paupers also shared, as in the Forehoe union (Norf.) in the 1870s, where labourers would present themselves at the workhouse in Wicklewood for a meal and then leave.[207] Pauper girls of school age often had to make clothes and knit stockings for workhouse inmates.[208] These 'tests' continued, although sometimes they became more refined and less repellent or tedious over time. Oakum-picking, probably one of the most mind-numbing forms of work ever invented – 'for I know not what insignificant use', Engels commented[209] – remained as a test well into the early

---

[205] On such pauper nursing before 1834, see S. Williams, 'Caring for the sick poor: poor law nurses in Bedfordshire, *c.* 1770–1834', in P. Lane, N. Raven and K. D. M. Snell (eds.), *Women, Work and Wages in England, 1600–1850* (Woodbridge, 2004).

[206] Thomas, *Poor Relief in Merthyr Tydfil*, p. 113.

[207] S. Pope, 'Norfolk's pauper palaces', *Suffolk and Norfolk Life*, 15, no. 164 (April 2003), p. 39.

[208] Leics. CRO, G/1/57/1 (Ashby de la Zouch letter book, 12 October 1841), p. 40.

[209] F. Engels, *The Condition of the Working Class in England* (1845, London, 1984), p. 312. The picked oakum was normally used for caulking boats and ships.

twentieth century, as workhouse photographs and oakum accounts indicate.[210]

A CASE STUDY OF BILLESDON

One way in which stone-breaking as task work operated can be seen in detail in the Billesdon union of east Leicestershire. This was geographically quite a large rural union, divided into four districts, comprising twenty-two parishes and eighteen townships, hamlets, liberties and chapelries. (The numbers of constituent parishes changed over time.) Some of its parishes, such as Newton Harcourt or Owston, were up to ten miles away from the workhouse, which was on a small hill overlooking the main street of Billesdon village. Its elected guardians were mainly farmers and graziers. The Out-door Relief Prohibitory Order (1844) was supposedly in force here. However, out-door relief was 78 per cent of combined in-door and out-door relief in 1874–5, making Billesdon fairly typical of English rural unions in that respect.[211] At any one time, for example in the 1840s, many (often a majority) of its parishes had no paupers in the workhouse. Some out-relief payments were partly in kind. For example, in 1839, the value of such kind payment was about 31–9 per cent of out-relief, which was a high proportion.[212] In a randomly chosen week ending 2 January 1892, it was 16 per cent.[213]

Faced in 1837 with growing applications from able-bodied men thrown out of work 'by the bad state of the Trade', the Billesdon board of guardians resolved upon the following regulations:

> 1st. That ablebodied single men, or women shd be sent to the workhouse to the number it would contain.
> 2nd. The aged and infirm to be relieved at home as usual.

---

[210] For example, Berks. CRO, G/Wi 13/1 (Windsor union); West Sussex Record Office, G3/41a (Cuckfield union).

[211] *Fifth Annual Report of the Local Government Board, 1875–76*, pp. 250–1.

[212] Leics. CRO, G/4/8a/1 (Billesdon Union Minutes, 31 May 1839), p. 399; G/4/8a/2 (Billesdon Union Minutes, 8 November 1839), p. 4.

[213] Leics. CRO, G/4/8a/7 (Billesdon Union Minutes, 1892), p. 171.

3rd. Ablebodied men with families to appear at the workhouse every morning and break the quantity of stones allotted, & to receive their board there & to be paid for the work done, half in kind, & half in money for the support of their families.

To be allowed ½ cwt (where the Pauper has to walk to the workhouse) for each mile above 2 from the workhouse.

No pay to be allowed until the work is done. Each Pauper to be allowed to leave as soon as it is finished.

The work to be apportioned by the workhouse Master into 3 parts.

Any Pauper being ½ an hour after his time or not performing the portion asigned before any Meal, to lose that Meal.[214]

Some of these Billesdon union paupers were walking distances of up to ten miles in all weather to get to the workhouse, there to perform their task work, running the risk of missing their workhouse meal, and then walking the same distance home after having broken their allotted weight of granite. They were doing this day after day while they were unemployed, a regimen which must soon have become exhausting.[215] Clearly a significant proportion of the 'task work' for some of the paupers was walking to and from the workhouse. Some of them were framework knitters, during a dreadful period for their trade. Contemporaries sometimes attacked labour tests for becoming habitual places of work for paupers, but it is hard to believe that this objection applied to the Billesdon system. The guardians' minutes do not usually specify the weight of granite to be broken, which was for the master to determine. In 1839 each pauper had to break five hundredweight of granite per day.[216] Payment for such work was two loaves and 1s. 3d. per week in 1839, while others were paid between 4d. and 6d. a day plus a

---

[214] Leics. CRO, G/4/8a/1 (Billesdon Union Minutes, 17 April 1837). An adapted version of this is also summarised in Leics. CRO, G/4/8a/2 (Billesdon union minutes, 10 January 1840), p. 31.

[215] Walking long distances to do a labour test was found elsewhere too. For example, able-bodied men put to work in reclaiming wasteland near Sheffield had to 'walk six miles in the morning, attend certain hours at the farm, and walk back to their families at night'. *First Report of the Select Committee on Poor Relief*, x (1862), p. 158.

[216] Leics. CRO, G/4/8a/2 (Billesdon Union Minute Book, 1839–44), p. 18.

few loaves per week if they had a wife and children to support.[217] This was well below external market rates. John Barnes, for example, was made to go to the workhouse and break stones 'according to his ability', and he was paid 6d. a day plus one loaf every other day.[218] The cost of relieving an adult in the Billesdon workhouse at this time was just over 3s. weekly,[219] and so this was both an incentive to give out-relief, and to constrain its value. In the 1850s and 1860s, the Billesdon guardians purchased granite for about 8s. 9d. per ton; and when broken they sold it for varying sums, usually about 8s. 3d. per ton.[220] So to judge from their stone account, it is almost inconceivable that they made any profit from it. Other Leicestershire unions, such as Blaby, had similar stone-breaking schemes. Variants of this method persisted in Billesdon throughout the new poor law, although by the early twentieth century chopping wood had usually been substituted, a labour test that until recently was remembered without relish by local inhabitants.[221] When the workhouse was finally demolished, in January 1935, some of the workmen employed on the demolition took special pleasure in their work, even though it had been used as a military hospital during the First World War.[222] Labour test schemes of this kind – and there were countless such schemes across the country, often involving quite different work loads – characterise the new poor law. Despite their centrality to the system, they have been little studied by historians, and we still know little about them, about how they compared regionally, and about how they changed over time.

THE RELATIVE COSTS OF IN-DOOR AND OUT-DOOR RELIEF

Workhouse relief was more costly than out-relief. The difference was often referred to by contemporaries, and it helped to

---

[217] *Ibid.*, pp. 18–19, 58.
[218] Leics. CRO, G/4/8a/1 (Billesdon Union Minute Book, 1839), p. 405.
[219] Leics. CRO, G/4/8a/2 (Billesdon Union Minute Book, 10 January 1840), p. 33.
[220] Leics. CRO, G/4/8a/4 (Billesdon Union Minute Book, 27 February 1862), p. 74, and many other references there to stone costs; Leics. CRO, DE 3325/1 (Billesdon Union Minute Book, 1857), pp. 77, 82.
[221] Oral testimony from Mr Stanley Mills, March 1988.
[222] *Ibid.*

persuade guardians that out-relief was preferable to the work-house. Table 5.1 gives ten examples of such costs. The sums are per person, probably all of them for adults, although it is just possible that children were included in a few figures. It must strongly be borne in mind that such figures are very hard to use, and to compare across unions, because one does not know exactly how they were calculated.[223] Their gender composition is also unclear. These or any other such figures must therefore be treated as indicative, despite being shown in decimal places. They give an impression of relative costs per head within each union. Figures have been chosen from 1854 to 1862 for chronological consistency, and one needs to bear in mind that such sums changed during the new poor law, especially in the twentieth century.

Despite the many caveats about such figures, a few points seem clear. Workhouse costs per pauper could be anything between 1.2 and 2.9 times higher than out-relief costs. In very general terms, they seem to have been about twice as high. As Nassau Senior admitted in 1862, 'in-door relief is so much more expensive than out-door relief'.[224] One should be wary of making regional comparisons from these data, as it is unclear from the sources exactly how figures were produced in different unions. Differences of practice certainly occurred across regions and unions – in some unions guardians refused out-relief, while in others relatively generous scales existed. These differences were true throughout the new poor law, and were much remarked upon.[225] Even within a union, there could be very sizeable disparities in relief sums by category of pauper.

---

[223] For example, in workhouse costs one does not usually know whether expenses like officers' salaries, heating, provisions, rent for the building, and so on are included. Nor does one always know whether the figures are for adults only. They usually exclude vagrants. It is unclear whether they include in-house lunatics. For out-relief, one does not usually know whether the sums are for cash payments, or represent the combined value of cash and kind payments. I suspect that most of these sums are money payments. Some were calculated at source on the basis of a week's expenditure; others were weekly averages based on yearly calculations, which *purport* to give the weekly costs per pauper; so there are difficulties relating to such calculations as well.

[224] *Ibid.*, p. 70.

[225] For example, see *Select Committee on Irremovable Poor*, VII (1859), pp. 130–1; *First Report from the Select Committee on Poor Relief (England)*, IX (1861), p. 119.

Table 5.1 *Relative costs of workhouse and out-door relief: weekly costs in (decimalised) shillings per person.*

Place	Date	In-door costs	Out-door costs	Ratio of in- to out-relief costs
'Manchester district' (46 unions)[a]	1854	2.12	1.37	1.5
Bradford union[b]	1854	3.10	1.54	2.0
Leeds township[c]	1854	2.10	1.60	1.3
Wigan union[d]	1854	2.41	1.17	2.1
Liverpool (West Derby union)[e]	1854	2.13	1.19	1.8
Manchester (Chorlton and Salford unions)[f]	1854	1.91	1.55	1.2
St Thomas' union, Exeter[g]	1857	2.58	1.50	1.7
'The metropolis'[h]				
All paupers	1861	4.04	1.37	2.9
Adult paupers	1861	6.00	4.00	1.5
City of London union[i]	1862	4.67	2.00	2.3
'A country union' (a general statement)[j]	1862	3.42	1.50	2.3

Notes:
[a] *Select Committee on Poor Removal*, XIII (1854–5), p. 328.
[b] *Ibid.*, p. 337.
[c] *Ibid.*, p. 338.
[d] *Ibid.*, p. 339.
[e] *Ibid.*, p. 340.
[f] *Ibid.*
[g] *Select Committee on Irremovable Poor*, VII (1859), p. 67.
[h] *First Report from the Select Committee on Poor Relief (England)*, IX (1861), p. 111.
[i] *Third Report from the Select Committee on Poor Relief*, X (1862), p. 147.
[j] *Ibid.*, pp. 147–8.

Contemporaries knew that costs in London workhouses were higher than elsewhere, because of higher provisioning expenses.[226] London's high costs of living also led to relatively large out-relief sums. Both points are borne out by the table. The London ratios between in- and out-door relief per head appear broadly representative of unions elsewhere.

[226] *Third Report from the Select Committee on Poor Relief*, X (1862), p. 147.

THE VALUE OF OUT-RELIEF PAYMENTS

These sums given as out-relief were hardly generous, even
allowing that they should be doubled for a married couple.
Helen Bosanquet wrote about the aged poor that 'many are
half-starved on an utterly inadequate allowance'.[227] This was a
frequent judgement. The Revd Augustus Campbell, Rector of
Liverpool, told a Select Committee in 1854 that 'it was the
practice to give a great deal of out-door relief' in Liverpool. They
were discussing whether this would attract more Irish to the
city. (Ireland offered negligible out-door relief at this time.)[228]
Campbell's views on this were as follows: 'To say the honest
truth, I do not think from what I have seen, that our out-door
relief is of a very splendid nature; I do not think that we give
anything very attractive in the way of food to the paupers out
of doors; I do not think it ought to be any great attraction to
them.'[229]

One should stress the importance of out-relief in people's
own parishes and homes under the new poor law, rather than
in extra-parochial institutions. Yet this needs to be accompanied
by a large caveat about the low sums paid. The out-payment
was not meant to be a merely nominal sum, such as a few pence
per week,[230] but it was often very low nevertheless. From an

---

[227] Bosanquet, *Poor Law Report of 1909*, pp. 7, 58.
[228] The Earl of Donoughmore, with experience of the Clogheen union, spoke of 'the
almost utter absence of out-door relief in Ireland'. In England in 1851–2 it was 57 per
cent of *all* relief however defined; in Ireland the equivalent figure was 0.6 per cent.
Select Committee on Poor Removal, xvii (1854), p. 159. Many categories of paupers who
were allowed out-relief in England were forbidden it in Ireland. The figures vary
according to sources and period. Irish out-door relief given as medical relief had
grown somewhat by 1860, contributing to some increase of out-relief in Ireland, to
about 6 per cent of paupers, but the essential contrast between the two countries
remained. *Select Committee on Iremovable Poor*, xvii (1860), pp. 266–8, evidence of
Alfred Power.
[229] *Select Committee on Poor Removal*, xvii (1854), p. 380. Other witnesses took a different
view, and believed that the relative generosity of English or Welsh relief, whether in-
door or out-door, attracted the Irish. See, for example, Evan David, chairman of the
Cardiff union, speaking of the attractions to the Irish of both the workhouse and out-
door relief in Cardiff. *Ibid.*, pp. 477–82. However, almost no one questioned the
lowness, in English and Welsh terms, of the sums given in out-relief, and those sums
appeared generous only in relation to the extreme destitution of the Irish migrants.
[230] 'Relief – justices not empowered to fix amounts of relief, under 4 & 5 Wm IV, c. 76,
s. 27', in *Official Circulars*, vol. iii (20 April 1843), p. 111.

early date during the new poor law, there were official worries that the sums given in out-relief might lead to extended illness or death by starvation, with adverse coroners' inquests and legal repercussions for relieving officers and guardians.[231] Following the death of a boy in the Axminster union 'through the want of the common necessaries of life', the Commissioners revealingly pointed out that 'death was an example of the dangers attendant upon any system of out-door relief, especially of partial relief, in aid of other means'.[232] This was in fact used by Edwin Chadwick as an argument for workhouse relief. As this suggests, out-door relief was rarely conceived as providing total sustenance and other expenses such as rent. The sums given at relieving officers' relief stations every week were usually intended to supplement other income and means, whether from charities, relatives, trade unions, sick and benefit clubs, work, tied housing, pensions from other sources, and so on. It was put to Nassau Senior in 1862 that

in 99 cases out of 100, whatever is given for out-door relief is very far short of the complete resources of out-door paupers, and is only a sum given in aid of other resources which the out-door paupers possess? . . . Is it not the fact . . . that full out-door maintenance is never given by Boards of Guardians?[233]

Having been so instrumental in the 1834 Poor Law Report, Senior was predictably keen in his reply to disassociate himself from this idea of relief being paid in aid of wages, but he found it very hard to deny this questioner's statement. In fact, as became evident during the sitting of the Royal Commission on the Aged Poor in 1895, a lack of any other resources, including work, was often a major reason for the workhouse being offered, because then it was obvious to guardians that the pauper would starve on the out-relief they would give. In 1900 and 1910, there were official Circulars which stressed that out-door relief should be

---

[231] 'Relief, out-door: dangers of its misapplication', *Official Circulars*, vol. I (10 November 1840), pp. 113–18. See also 'Relieving officers' duties', *Official Circulars*, vol. IV (29 January 1844), p. 95, on legal responsibility for 'fatal effects' to those in 'absolute distress' following relieving officers' decisions.

[232] 'Relief, out-door: dangers of its misapplication', *Official Circulars*, vol. I (10 November 1840), p. 115.

[233] *Third Report from the Select Committee on Poor Relief*, x (1862), p. 70.

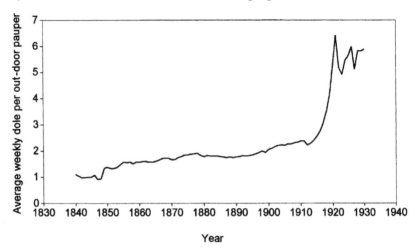

Figure 5.12   Average weekly dole (s.) per out-door pauper, 1840–1930.

'adequate' for carefully assessed individual requirements. This was one reason for the subsequent increases (see above, figure 5.12), which point quite dramatically to the inadequacy of earlier sums.

We saw in figure 5.7 that payments in kind were small, usually well under a fifth of the value of out-relief. Attempts to pay some relief in kind had led to rioting,[234] and was often impractical or burdensome to implement, and so that had usually been diminished to small payments in kind or none at all. Many guardians refused to put into effect the Poor Law Board's request for a third of relief to be given in kind, and faced with threatened resignations the central Board usually gave way on this issue.[235] Other 'payments' in kind, in the form of clothing, tools, bedding, and so on, were a fraught subject for the central authorities. They wanted to avoid them, but were occasionally obliged to accept their necessity, even though they 'cannot recognise' them 'as being a legal or proper mode of affording

---

[234] See for example J. P. D. Dunbabin, *Rural Discontent in Nineteenth-century Britain* (London, 1974), pp. 37–8.
[235] Thomas, *Poor Relief in Merthyr Tydfil*, pp. 148–9.

relief'.[236] Payments of relief in kind, where this was practised, resulted in lowered monetary sums paid in out-relief. They had a similar effect to subsidies obtained from relatives in support of paupers, which also reduced apparent monetary sums in out-relief. Many unions were paying relief partially in kind well into the twentieth century, even though its value was often very small. For the historian, this (and the issues associated with table 5.1) complicate inter-union or chronological comparisons of monetary sums paid in out-relief, because one often has little knowledge of the payments in kind, of how they changed over time, and because it is hard to value the latter.

One needs to appreciate such matters before one can interpret the very low weekly out-relief sums which are found in nineteenth-century records. Those figures were commonly in the region of 9d. to 6s. per adult, and rarely above that. George Nicholls wrote of how the sums were usually between 1s. and 6s., with small allowances in kind.[237] However, such higher possible amounts were quite unusual in the mid-nineteenth century, when the normal sums were between 1s. and 2s.

Let us take some examples of these payments. In the Bradford union in 1854–5, relief comprised about 1s. 6d. per head for those with families, while single adults received about 2s.[238] There was much local variation, influenced by the wealth of each union, and the customary practices of the region in which the union was situated. In the Salford union, 2s. 6d. in money and an equivalent figure in kind (coupled to labour tests) was a common sum in the early 1860s.[239] In the East London union, 'in our poverty', they gave about 1s. 6d. plus two loaves; but in the City of London union they gave about 4s. and two loaves.[240] St George's Hanover Square in the late 1850s, for example, was much more generous in its out-relief than St George's in the East. Some City parishes gave as much as 5s. 6d. per head to out-door paupers, which was nearly double the sums given by

[236] 'Relief – supplying beds, bedding, clothes etc., to out-door paupers', *Official Circulars*, vol. IX (8 April 1850), p. 108.

[237] Nicholls, *History of the English Poor Law*, vol. II, p. 379.

[238] *Select Committee on Poor Removal*, XIII (1854–5), p. 80.

[239] *First Report from the Select Committee on Poor Relief*, X (1862), pp. 30–1, evidence of John Adamson, accountant and clerk.

[240] *Select Committee on Irremovable Poor*, VII (1859), p. 69.

other London unions.[241] There is 'a great variation in the amount of relief given to the out-door paupers in different places', as one witness said in 1861.[242] The sums were allocated entirely at the discretion of the guardians. Justices could order that certain paupers be relieved out-doors, but they no longer had any powers to fix the amounts paid as out-relief.[243] Nor could such sums be controlled by the Poor Law Board, which had negligible powers in this respect.[244] Sums like these were for each adult. What were in effect 'head' or child 'allowances' could also be added to all these sums, which varied as a proportion of the adult sum (usually about a third or half of it). The early years of the new poor law had often seen such child allowances cut, for they were a key part of the Malthusian critique of the old poor law – but of necessity they re-emerged and continued to be paid in most unions throughout the new poor law. In other words, an entire family with four children, in a union in the 1850s which gave about 1s. 6d. per adult, might receive a weekly figure of 5s. to 6s.

Most commentators were aware that sums like these were too small to live upon. Many witnesses and writers attacked them for that reason. The Revd Charles Carr, chaplain to Stepney union, complained that in many cases 'the relief, for instance to old paupers, is inadequate to support life'. They might have other means, or access to charity, but he thought that they often did not. The guardians, he said, in giving sums like 1s. 6d., 'do not profess to give out-door relief sufficient to sustain life'.[245] Henry Selfe, a magistrate at the Thames Police Office, said that he would 'certainly rejoice to see a more liberal administration of out-door relief by the guardians and their officers'.[246] The workhouse or labour test was 'wholly unfit' to be applied to 'a vast number of those who are as destitute and as deserving [as many] . . . in the east of London', where 'the most deserving poor never go near the poorhouse; they would not do it; they would sooner die'. If guardians offered a decent woman the

---

[241] *Ibid.*, pp. 130–1.
[242] *First Report from the Select Committee on Poor Relief (England)*, IX (1861), p. 111.
[243] 'Relief – justices not empowered to fix amounts of relief, under 4 & 5 Wm IV, c. 76, s. 27', *Official Circulars*, vol. III (20 April 1843), p. 111.
[244] *First Report from the Select Committee on Poor Relief (England)*, IX (1861), p. 111.
[245] *Ibid.*, p. 150.   [246] *Ibid.*, p. 164.

workhouse, rather than such out-relief, this would in effect be 'a positive refusal of relief', given that there are workhouses in east London 'which no decent woman would enter'.[247] In other words, the workhouse forced many people to accept extremely low out-relief. Others did not complain 'of what is called the inadequate amount of out-door relief', because, while agreeing that such sums were so low as to 'debilitate' a working man and not put him into a condition to return to work, they considered it 'a wise arrangement that out-door relief should be so inadequate as to be a constant stimulus to the person receiving it to maintain himself'.[248] This was a way of thinking about incentives that was clearly at odds with the earlier requirement under the new poor law to avoid any relief in aid of wages.

The average weekly dole (in shillings) per out-door pauper had been rising in the nineteenth century, notably from the late 1840s. This is seen in figure 5.12.[249] The average money dole between 1840 and 1900 increased from about 1s. to about 2s., and deflation over much of that period augmented the real value of this increase. It was also central policy in some periods, such as the 1870s, to encourage slightly larger out-relief sums, in the paradoxical hope that this would make in-door relief appear to guardians less costly by comparison, and thus promote the use of the workhouse.

That increase in the nineteenth century was of some significance, but it was as little compared with what happened in the twentieth century, with dramatic increases in the value of out-door relief during and after the First World War. One should bear in mind that out-relief in the 1920s was hardly considered generous. Prices in the 1920s were about 1.4 times higher than they were in the 1860s, but weekly out-relief was about 3.7 times higher. There is no need to explore here the real value of such changing sums in finer detail. In short, between 1840 and 1900, average out-relief roughly doubled, but between 1900 and 1930

---

[247] *Ibid.*, p. 164. The point that people would sooner die than enter a workhouse was often made. See for example *Royal Commission on the Aged Poor*, XIV (1895), p. 439, on the Dolgelly union, or p. 433 (same union) on a man drowning himself rather than enter the workhouse.

[248] *First Report from the Select Committee on Poor Relief (England)*, IX (1861), pp. 82–3, 86, the views of Edward Yardley, a magistrate in London.

[249] Data are from Williams, *From Pauperism to Poverty*, pp. 169–73.

it rose about threefold. The lowness of the sums given as out-door relief through much of the nineteenth century is readily apparent.

OUT-DOOR RELIEF AND KIN SUBSIDIES TO THE ELDERLY POOR

The elderly (contemporaries used that term for those aged above sixty or sixty-five) were always prominent among recipients of poor relief. That relief was usually given to healthy elderly people as out-door relief. Life expectancy was rising in the nineteenth century, especially in the countryside.[250] This contributed to make the issue of relief to the elderly an even more pressing one than had been the case under the old poor law. Helen Bosanquet wrote in 1909 of how

> in the country 'the parish' tends to be the most obvious source to which they can turn for help, and so much is this the case that in many places the parish allowance is looked upon as a right, to be claimed and granted as a matter of course, as an 'old age pension', and often irrespective of any real need . . . In rural districts in all parts of the country outdoor relief is practically regarded as an old-age pension. There is no reluctance in applying for relief, and it is not confined to destitute cases, but given to all comers of a certain age.[251]

Bosanquet's language of 'the parish', which continued to be used by many others, highlighted the extent to which such relief was home- and parish-connected. She was describing a system which existed long before the Old Age Pensions Act of 1908 – old age pensions (in her sense) had been given 'for years', as she said.[252] This meaning of the terms 'pensions' and 'pensioners' also went back a long time, to at least the early eighteenth century.[253]

---

[250] *Royal Commission on the Aged Poor*, XIV (1895), p. 256.

[251] Bosanquet, *Poor Law Report of 1909*, p. 47.

[252] *Ibid.*, p. 48.

[253] A 'pension' much earlier had a specific technical meaning as the annual sum paid by a church to a superior authority – an appropriated rectory would pay a pension to a bishop. It was later used in the provisions for maimed soldiers or servicemen of the late sixteenth century, echoing some earlier usage for retired servants. It was hardly ever used in seventeenth-century overseers' accounts ('weekly pay' or 'collectioner' being the usual term), but it became common from the early eighteenth century to encompass its usual nineteenth-century meaning (an out-door relief sum, usually but

When one looks at individual unions, one finds widespread out-relief to the elderly, but much variety of local policies. Dr Henry Paine, chairman of the guardians in Cardiff, commented that 'We rarely give an order for admission to the workhouse to any above 60, except under special circumstances.' In Cardiff those circumstances were sickness, poor financial conduct of the applicant, or 'where the applicant was living in wretched apartments totally unfit for habitation'. Such living conditions and the behaviour of applicants was enquired into by the relieving officer, often with working-class neighbours giving information. There were subsequent surprise visits, 'to see if the applicant is conducting himself in such a way as would commend itself to the board'. Henry Paine 'never found that there was any difficulty in getting information as to past or present conduct'. Neighbourhood gossip usually assisted relieving officers and guardians in their role as social judges, or whenever they felt the call within themselves to restructure moral life. Those elderly poor who had been temperate, industrious, 'and have lived a creditable life', could receive out-door relief. Those who had not behaved as they ought could be offered the 'house'. They were in effect removed from the parish community, or de-localised. Such policy was 'our custom on every relief day'.[254] This was common practice much more widely, beyond Cardiff, and was described by many witnesses in 1895.

To be thought 'deserving' was thus (in modern theoretical terms) the 'social capital' of the poor – those who lacked other forms of capital – and this was a reputation that some of them felt that they needed to preserve *both* with their neighbours (who could behave as informants), *and* with the officials of the poor law. For this was a welfare system that (unlike more modern ones) did not undermine social capital, but, on the contrary,

---

not always to an elderly person). I am grateful to Christopher Dyer and Steve Hindle for advice on this point.

[254] *Royal Commission on the Aged Poor*, XIV (1895), pp. 272, 281, 283–4. The workhouse in Cardiff at this time could accommodate about 900 people, but it usually contained much less than that. *Ibid.*, p. 291. The attention that was paid in Cardiff to general living arrangements of the elderly was true elsewhere too, as for example in Birmingham. Aged people living in unwholesome surroundings were often denied out-relief in that city. *Ibid.*, p. 162.

actively promoted it among the poor, and established it as a *parochial* reputation, rather than a class-specific, union, or simply official/bureaucratic one. (It arguably promoted repute among some unpaid guardians and overseers as well, giving them motives as office-holders, enhancing their status among people from a similar social standing as themselves, and conveying extra credence or social repute from below if they appreciated ideas of respectability among the poor, which they could show by giving out-relief when the appropriate neighbourhood criteria were met.) The continuing very local practice of the post-1834 welfare system allowed the poor law to manipulate or recognise repute in this way, and to help construct the community bases of social capital or reputation, something that would be almost inconceivable with the larger scales of administration after 1948, and perhaps earlier in the twentieth century. Once again, one needs to stress the local, parochial continuities of the new poor law, and their relation to one's community reputation, to understand these considerations and this dimension of the new poor law.

In many cases, the 'deserving', parochially maintained poor seem to have been those who were currently economically active and useful. We should therefore also think of this policy as implementing a utilitarian concept of belonging and parochial retention. Those who were economically undesirable could be seen as 'immoral' in capitalistic terms, regardless of past contributions. They included many elderly people, who might well be banished from their community if they could earn nothing – in other words, if they could not subsist on the meagre out-relief. That out-relief was thus in effect a utilitarian 'test', a way of forcing the elderly and others to work. The policy was thought by the Cardiff guardians to have the multiple advantages of controlling behaviour, inculcating provident living, while also making the workhouse all the more undesirable and 'less eligible', as a place of resort for people deemed by informants and poor law officials to be morally dubious or worthless. The workhouse was a place of moral scrutiny; its inhabitants included many who could not be trusted morally outside. Removed from their parish outside, married couples were then usually removed from each other inside the workhouse. The 'deserving' poor were another matter. Those who were morally valued stayed in the parish, together as a family, and were not removed from a 'respectable' to a shamed environment. Francis John Beavan, a member of the Cardiff Corporation, argued that these 'decent' poor should not receive a sum which is 'pauper relief', but should be given 5s. each, perhaps in almshouses if necessary, rather than in the workhouse. He spoke of how they tried not to ask people over sixty years of age to come into the workhouse, 'unless he or she be entirely without friends [a term that often meant close relatives], or we know that he or she is leading a dissolute life'.[255]

We can therefore see here the unfortunate link between those without local relatives, and those thought to be dissolute – both conditions could result in the same outcome: the workhouse. It is also deeply ironic that the new poor law, as a Malthusian and political-economy measure, while embroiled in a work ethic and in community understandings of repute, had in fact inculcated strong motives to have children, in the hope that they would not migrate away, would look after one in old age, keep one out of the workhouse, and help one to remain in one's parish. It was elderly *childless* people, or those with children who had migrated in search of better conditions (migration that was approved of by the political economists and poor law authorities), who were most likely to suffer the degradation, shame and marital separation of the workhouse. Political economists, overshadowed by Malthus, had in fact put in place a poor law system which, in these regards, worked against many of their own intentions.

In the Carnarvon union, about 800 people aged over sixty were on out-door relief in August 1890, while only thirteen of the same age group were in-door paupers.[256] Remarkable figures like these underscore just how hugely prevalent out-relief could be in Wales, including to the elderly. The out-door sums here tended to be between 1s. 6d. and 4s. per person, the amount rising with age, and with the declining likelihood that the person could also earn some money. It was presumed here in the 1890s that such a person could live on 5s. 3d., and the intention of the guardians was to make up to that sum.

---

[255] *Ibid.*, pp. 287–8.   [256] *Ibid.*, p. 373.

In the Carnarvon union such assistance in aid of earnings was taken as commonplace for those aged sixty to sixty-five, and in many cases beyond that age too. When a member of the 1895 Commission questioned that 'they have no power to grant relief to able-bodied people out of the workhouse?', John Thomas (Carnarvon's union clerk) simply replied 'But they do so.' In fact, they did that even though the out-door relief prohibitory order was in force in this union.[257] The recipients were often ageing agricultural labourers, general labourers, quarry-workers, and so on.

John Davies, of Dyffryn (Mer.), who had been a guardian for Llanenddwyn in the Dolgelly union, discussed sums of between 5s. to 7s. disbursed as out-relief to the elderly in his area of Wales in the 1890s.[258] If they needed care and nursing out-doors, sums above 5s. were often given.[259] These would seem to be relatively generous amounts. Even in high-cost London, to take St Pancras as an example, out-door relief sums were commonly 2s. 6d. to 4s. – which they 'do not consider . . . nearly sufficient to keep a person alone'. The elderly people here had to eke out a living by doing further work, such as needlework, charring, washing, odd jobs, or by assistance from close relatives. Asked whether relief in aid of earnings was 'a strict application of the Poor Law', the clerk replied 'Well, no . . . we do not apply the Poor Law very strictly in St. Pancras.'[260] In 1909 Helen Bosanquet cited one witness before the Royal Commission on the Poor Laws and the Unemployed who claimed (even at that late date) that the sums involved in agricultural districts were commonly 1s. 6d. to 2s. 6d. per person.[261] This supports what we saw in figure 5.12. A little earlier, in the Wimborne union in Dorset (a union that gave about 90 per cent of its relief out-doors), 2s. 6d. was the usual out-door relief to the aged, or 4s. 6d. to an elderly couple combined. This was felt to be 'entirely inadequate'.[262] Such out-relief to elderly paupers was said by witnesses to be 'starving them',[263] which was a frequent

[257] *Ibid.*, p. 377.   [258] *Ibid.*, p. 430.
[259] *Ibid.*, p. 439.   [260] *Ibid.*, pp. 124, 129.
[261] Bosanquet, *Poor Law Report of 1909*, p. 48.
[262] *Royal Commission on the Aged Poor*, XIV (1895), p. 244.
[263] *Ibid.*, p. 255.

statement.[264] In fact, the members of the 1895 Royal Commission persistently tried (and failed) to understand how elderly people could live on the kinds of sums that they found prevailing.[265] The result in some infamous unions was fairly evident. Sidney Ward, a labourer from Brixworth (Northants.), explained that 'there is a good many would have been living to-day if it had not been for the policy of the Board'.[266] All of them had been 'respectable, well-conducted people'. The Revd J. Frome Wilkinson, who was rector of Kilvington (Notts.) and a guardian in the Newark union, commented that many aged poor had been 'done to death by a semi-starvation process . . . they have not lived out the full term of their natural lives in consequence of want of nourishment, and of the imperfect food which they have received in their old age'. He described this as 'a cruel kindess, that of inadequate out-relief', a phrasing which lends itself to the title of this chapter.[267]

The extent to which kin assisted the elderly affects any calculation of out-relief 'pensions' under the new poor law, and it has many further ramifications for the history of welfare and the family.[268] One finds many regional practices on this after 1834. In Cardiff, relatives were called upon to help support the elderly, and the Cardiff union had a special collector who marshalled such work, and the repayment of loans.[269] In

---

[264] *Ibid.*, pp. 813, 842.

[265] For example, *ibid.*, p. 320.

[266] *Royal Commission on the Aged Poor*, xv (1895), p. 845.

[267] *Royal Commission on the Aged Poor*, xiv (1895), pp. 306, 318–19, 324. This was the author of *Mutual Thrift* (London, 1891). One is reminded of Sir Frederic Eden's comment on the old poor law, that there is 'among many of the Poor, a degree of pride; who, though they would willingly receive an unjust allowance at their own dwellings, would scorn the relief afforded by the parish work-house'. Sir F. M. Eden, *The State of the Poor*, 3 vols. (1797, Bristol, 2001), vol. iii, p. 809.

[268] For discussion on the new poor law period, see D. Thomson, 'The decline of social welfare: falling state support for the elderly since early Victorian times', *Ageing and Society*, 4 (1984); D. Thomson, '"I am not my father's keeper": families and the elderly in nineteenth-century England', *Law and History Review*, 2 (1984); J. Robin, 'Family care of the elderly in a nineteenth-century Devonshire parish', *Ageing and Society*, 4 (1984); D. Thomson, 'The welfare of the elderly in the past: a family or community responsibility?', in M. Pelling and R. M. Smith (eds.), *Life, Death, and the Elderly: Historical Perspectives* (London, 1991); P. Thane, 'Old people and their families in the English past', in M. Daunton (ed.), *Charity, Self-interest and Welfare in the English Past* (New York, 1996); P. Thane, *Old Age in English History: Past Experiences, Present Issues* (2000, Oxford, 2002), pp. 167–8, 179–80.

[269] *Royal Commission on the Aged Poor*, xiv (1895), pp. 282–3.

Birmingham, the superintendent of the out-door relief department commented that 'in all the cases where out-door relief is
given, I do not know a single case where out-door relief is the
only income'.[270] One source of other income was from relatives
who were legally liable to pay, and who were taken before a
magistrate if they refused. This allowed the guardians to give
low sums in out-relief, of about 2s. to 3s. The assistance from
relatives was enforced by offering the elderly the workhouse,
and so bringing pressure to bear via familial and public opinion.[271] Low out-door relief sums and the workhouse had thus
been adapted to implement other purposes, namely to compel
assistance from relatives. In other less urban Welsh unions,
enforced support from kin may have been less common. One
of the reasons for this, as for example in the Forden union in
Montgomeryshire, was that there were many yearly servants in
husbandry. These frequently lived in with their employers and
were paid to a considerable extent in kind. Money wages were
very low and intermittent. As a result they did not have much
money with which to help their parents, rather like their earlier
counterparts under the old poor law in south-eastern England.
Even 'labourers' often chose to have their food in the farmhouse,
and so take lower wages, which had the same result.[272] This was
one reason why, in a union such as Carnarvon, the guardians
'rarely' imposed the law against children of aged parents, and
'very very few' cases went to justices on this issue.[273]

In many areas, notably in some of the English low-wage
agricultural regions, rural labourers objected strongly to being
made to pay contributions to the relief of their aged parents,
because of their own low earnings. Poor law commentators
often protested about sons 'keeping out of the way', or parents
saying that they did not know about 'the whereabouts of a son,

---

[270] *Ibid.*, p. 163.
[271] *Ibid.*, p. 171.
[272] *Royal Commission on the Aged Poor*, xv (1895), pp. 901, 906, evidence of William Disley,
a labourer from Berriew, Montgomeryshire. One would expect to find a similar result
in English unions where farm service survived as an institution, most notably in the
more pastoral and small-farm regions of northern and western England.
[273] *Royal Commission on the Aged Poor*, xiv (1895), pp. 374–5. Here and elsewhere in
discussing Wales I use the place names and spellings from my sources, which are
usually English renditions.

that they have not heard of him for years'.[274] Unlike some contemporaries, one should not deduce anything about familial affection among the labouring classes from such behaviour, because poor law policy necessitated such responses, whether true or otherwise. George Edwards, the agricultural union leader from Aylmerton, Norfolk, took up these issues before the 1895 Royal Commission on the Aged Poor. (His parish was in the North Erpingham union, and he spoke also about the South Erpingham and Henstead unions.) He pointed out that such terms of out-relief involved long walks to see the relieving officer, rough and 'uncivil' treatment by such officers who were sometimes 'complete bullies', long delays in obtaining relief, and extremely low sums (6d. to 2s. 6d.) being awarded as out-relief to people who were 'in the greatest destitution, my Lord'. The out-door relieved poor were 'terribly pinched', and in some cases there was 'absolute starvation'. In Norfolk the 'aged people have a great liking to remain in their own village in which they have worked and lived, and brought up their families', and these villages were often 'a great many miles' from the nearest workhouse, and too far away for the elderly to be regularly visited by their relatives and friends. 'They have a great repulsive feeling against going into the workhouse', and so these arrangements of low relief and contributions from kin were often felt to be their only option.[275]

In the Wimborne union in Dorset, according to Robert Elcock (a builder and guardian), orders were frequently made by guardians and magistrates against children to repay relief given to their parents. Such children (in such a low-wage area) often could not pay these sums. On the other hand, if they were ratepayers they especially resented this policy.[276] If a parent lived with a son, the out-relief could be lowered to make the son look after the elderly parent. Thus, instead of awarding 4s. 6d., the guardians would award 3s. This had the advantage

---

[274] This example of such wording is taken from T. Mackay, *The English Poor: A Sketch of their Social and Economic History* (London, 1889), pp. 211–12.

[275] *Royal Commission on the Aged Poor*, XIV (1895), pp. 344–52. See also G. Edwards, *From Crow-Scaring to Westminster* (London, 1922), esp. pp. 22–3, 69, on how as a Norfolk labourer he looked after his mother and mother-in-law, and on the extreme meanness of out-relief.

[276] *Royal Commission on the Aged Poor*, XIV (1895), pp. 244–5.

(to the guardians) of saving the relieving officer from trying to
collect the son's contribution. This method of indirect enforced
kin payment was said to be 'the custom that is prevailing very
generally in our own union . . . It is an easier way for the
guardians to do it.'[277] In many cases, this meant that out-relief
sums were down to about 1s. 6d. for the elderly, depending
upon the view taken of the pauper, and taken separately of
the son, by guardians. If a guardian thought highly of the son,
and spoke up accordingly, the relief given to his parents might
be higher. It was therefore not only the parents' moral standing
that affected such decisions.

A further issue in this Dorset union in 1895 was rural depopulation, which, markedly unlike in 1834, 'is a thing certainly not
to be desired in these days'.[278] Some people believed that the
rural exodus was accentuated by taking elderly people from
their home parishes to a workhouse up to sixteen miles away.
The sons of these elderly people,

> when they see what the ending of the life, so to speak, of their parents
> is, that they have to end their days in the workhouse, simply say to
> themselves, and carry it out in practice: 'We will not stay to end our
> days in the way that our parents have done.' The consequence is that
> the whole of the hale and hearty migrate from the villages, and go to
> fill our already overcrowded towns.[279]

The fact that the out-relief 'is so meagre', and impossible to
live on, also induced them to leave the countryside.[280] Their
higher urban wages helped them to assist their parents, or the
move made it more difficult for the guardians 'to discover their
whereabouts' and enforce filiation orders on them. The guardians in the Wimborne union were 'sometimes composed of a
class of individuals who, I am sorry to say, have not much true
sympathy with the working man'.[281] Robert Elcock blamed such
policies for some of the depopulation of rural Dorset, even
though (as we have seen) 'it is in the towns rather than in the
country that we find the sterner administration of the Poor
Law'.[282] He objected strongly to the elderly 'being transported
into a workhouse, as they have been in the past, away from their

---

[277] *Ibid.*, pp. 248, 256.   [278] *Ibid.*, p. 249.   [279] *Ibid.*, and see p. 254.
[280] *Ibid.*   [281] *Ibid.*   [282] *Ibid.*, pp. 250–1.

own villages, their own homes, their own houses'.[283] He felt that relief in people's own homes, without such duress involving kin, would help to obviate the problems of the rural exodus.

Out-relief sums thus varied considerably with local policies and conditions, just as they were also affected by decisions governing payments in kind. Relatives' contributions could in effect make out-relief even cheaper (to the guardians) than workhouse relief, and so could increase the proportions of paupers on out-relief. Perhaps ironically, relatives' assistance was especially keenly insisted upon in the 'crusade' period of the 1870s and 1880s. One needs to caution, therefore, against any assumption that high percentages of out-relief (whether of expenditure, or numbers of paupers) necessarily equated to 'generosity' of relief administration. Out-relief was very often given in a benevolent spirit and with scepticism towards the utility of the workhouse; and it was perceived by paupers as the 'generous' and humane option, even when low amounts were granted. It requited senses of personal moral value. It recognised the strength of local attachment and senses of belonging. Yet it also exploited those feelings of belonging, for guardians knew those feelings to be so strong as to suppress pauper indignation at the low relief sums. Out-relief could also be given with Wimborne motives in mind: as the cheapest policy, and to elicit payments from kin, payments which were extolled by the central authorities, and which had long precedent back to the Act of Elizabeth in 1601, but which could undermine or contradict the central authority's resolve on the need for the workhouse test. After all, once an elderly pauper was in the main workhouse, it was difficult and very unusual to elicit any contributory payment from relatives.[284] And the move could well be irreversible, especially if furniture was sold and the home was broken up or lost. These were yet further downsides to workhouse-oriented policy, which local guardians in the provinces often seemed more aware of than the central authority.

---

[283] *Ibid.*, p. 252.
[284] In some unions, close relatives did sometimes pay a contribution towards infirmary costs.

THE CATEGORIES OF OUT-DOOR AND IN-DOOR RELIEF

The abundance of Poor Law Reports and statistics in the nineteenth century clearly shows the categories of pauper relieved out-doors and in the workhouse. This is a subject which could be explored in much comparative detail, across regions, unions, and through time, and related in interesting ways to regional cultural, demographic and economic circumstances. It is not the intention to do that here. Yet it is useful in general terms to consider who received out-door relief, and how they compared with the paupers who were relieved in workhouses. Perhaps the best way to do this is to show (in table 5.2) a tabulation of in- and out-door paupers, in the form of an Official Circular produced by the Poor Law Board covering 595 unions in January 1851. The classificatory headings are themselves revealing, and, while the return does not give an age breakdown of paupers, some telling conclusions emerge.

The table shows the high proportion of all paupers who were relieved out-doors (87.3 per cent). This is what we would expect. Among the workhouse inmates, adult males and females were roughly equal in number, but women were about 70 per cent of all adult out-door paupers. Despite the consternation in 1832–4 over male able-bodied pauperism, women almost always out-numbered men as recipients of poor relief. Sir George Nicholls provided figures for 1852–3 which showed that women were about 75 per cent of all adult able-bodied paupers. They were about 70 per cent of adult in-door paupers at that time, and about 76 per cent of adult out-door paupers.[285] Their vulnerability in the job market, the vicissitudes of family circumstances, desertion by husbands, poverty and ill-health induced by children, the penalties of illegitimacy, longer female life expectancy, and other such reasons underlay this. The higher predominance of women among out-relief recipients, which was especially notable among the elderly, and the greater likelihood that elderly men would be in workhouses,[286]

---

[285] Nicholls, *History of the English Poor Law*, vol. II, p. 425.
[286] *Royal Commission on the Aged Poor*, XIV (1895), pp. 124, 267, or 308, for data showing this for St Pancras, Manchester and Newark.

Table 5.2 *Out-door and in-door paupers relieved on 1 January 1851 (595 unions, England and Wales).*

OUT-DOOR PAUPERS	N.	% of out-door paupers
ABLE-BODIED, OR FAMILIES OF ABLE-BODIED		
Adult males (married or single), relieved because of sudden & urgent necessity	200	0.0
Adult males (married or single), relieved because of their own sickness, accident, or infirmity	19,799	2.7
Adult males, relieved on account of sickness, accident or infirmity of any in the family, or of a funeral	7,489	1.0
Adult males (married or single), relieved because of want of work or other causes	5,347	0.7
Families of adult males (as above) resident with the father		
Wives	26,399	3.6
Children under 16	78,356	10.8
Widows	50,628	7.0
Children under 16 dependent on widows	123,413	17.0
Single women without children	6,385	0.9
Illegitimate children and their mothers		
Mothers	3,703	0.5
Children	5,862	0.8
Families relieved on account of parent being in jail		
Wives	1,910	0.3
Children	5,427	0.7
Families of soldiers, sailors and marines		
Wives	544	0.1
Children	1,124	0.2
Resident families of other non-resident males relieved		
Wives	3,359	0.5
Children	8,538	1.2
NOT ABLE-BODIED		
Males	102,453	14.1
Females	212,160	29.2
Children under 16 relieved with parents	35,467	4.9
Orphans or other children under 16 relieved without parents	17,230	2.4
LUNATICS, INSANE PERSONS, AND IDIOTS		
Males	4,233	0.6
Females	4,827	0.7
Children under 16	257	0.0
VAGRANTS RELIEVED OUT OF THE WORKHOUSE	2,220	0.3
TOTAL RELIEVED OUT OF THE WORKHOUSE	727,330	100.2

Table 5.2. (*cont.*)

IN-DOOR PAUPERS	N.	% of in-door paupers
ABLE-BODIED AND THEIR CHILDREN		
Adults – married couples		
Males	1,396	1.3
Females	1,506	1.4
Other males	6,958	6.6
Other females	11,877	11.3
Children under 16, of able-bodied inmates		
Illegitimate children	7,470	7.1
Other children	10,350	9.8
NOT ABLE-BODIED		
Adults – married couples		
Males	1,205	1.1
Females	1,116	1.1
Other males	19,082	18.1
Other females	13,261	12.6
Children under 16, of parents not able-bodied, being inmates		
Illegitimate children	1,087	1.0
Other children	2,071	2.0
Orphans, or other children under 16, relieved without parents	21,812	20.7
LUNATICS, INSANE PERSONS, AND IDIOTS		
Males	2,143	2.0
Females	2,648	2.5
Children under 16	238	0.2
VAGRANTS RELIEVED IN THE WORKHOUSE	1,170	1.1
TOTAL RELIEVED IN THE WORKHOUSE	105,390	99.9
TOTAL RELIEVED IN-DOOR AND OUT-DOOR	832,720	
PERCENTAGE OF ALL PAUPERS RELIEVED IN-DOOR		12.7
PERCENTAGE OF ALL PAUPERS RELIEVED OUT-DOOR		87.3

Source: 'Comparative statement of the number of paupers of all classes, in receipt of relief', *Official Circulars*, vol. x, no. 45 (January 1851), pp. 14–16.

was explained by contemporaries with reference to the worn-out nature of many aged labouring men, the greater readiness of kin to look after elderly women rather than men, the assistance which such women could offer to those with young families, and the possibilities for elderly women to earn small sums by needlework, charring, washing and so on. There were probably regionally varied cultural and kinship dispositions affecting this as well, which more detailed comparative research would reveal.[287]

A number of other important features emerge. Children aged under sixteen were about 38 per cent of all out-door paupers, and about 41 per cent of workhouse paupers. These are extremely high figures, and they show how significant child pauperism was. The deterrent principles of the workhouse and the 1834 Act appear either highly effective (in keeping adults away) or cruelly misplaced when one sees such figures for children. In the workhouses, 21 per cent of paupers were in effect 'orphans'. The other major group in this table was adults who were 'not able-bodied'. These were 43 per cent of all the out-door paupers, or 45 per cent if one includes 'lunatics, the insane, and idiots'. The latter category made up nearly 5 per cent of in-door paupers. If one takes a wide definition of the term 'not able-bodied' (to include the official category and the sick, accident-prone, lunatics, idiots, and their families), they were over half of both in-door and out-door paupers. By contrast, in January 1851 able-bodied men made up 0.7 per cent of out-door paupers, and 1.3 per cent of in-door paupers.

These patterns were fairly typical of the new poor law, leaving aside periods of industrial depression. Women, the elderly, children, disabled, non-able bodied, lunatics or idiots were the vast bulk of paupers. Out-door paupers relieved in their parishes were somewhat more likely to be female, widows, not able-bodied, and were less likely to be orphans, or mothers with their illegitimate children. Children were a high proportion among both in- and out-door paupers, although little regionally comparative analysis has been conducted on them. While the rhetoric of less eligibility and deterrence persisted in many quarters throughout the new poor law, commentators were also aware of these realities of pauperism. G. Poulett Scrope, for example, commented that 'the great bulk of our recipients of out-door relief consist of infirm persons past all work;

---

[287] In some regions, out-relief for elderly women was very characteristic indeed. John Davies, of Dyffryn (Mer.), an ex-guardian for Llanenddwyn (Dolgelly union), remarked upon how 'It is very seldom that you see an old woman in the workhouse', 'except they be weak-minded imbeciles'. He thought that this was true of workhouses generally in Wales. *Ibid.*, pp. 430–1.

occasionally widows and some of their families, and the sick poor, those who are reduced to destitution by sickness and require temporary relief'.[288] A witness speaking about the Birmingham union informed the 1895 Royal Commission that those aged over sixty years were 72 per cent of all their adult out-door poor.[289] In the Carnarvon union, it was said that 'We have very few paupers in the workhouse other than children, imbeciles and sick paupers.'[290] In the Dolgelly workhouse there were mainly old men, and young women 'that have been unfortunate'.[291] Those in the Wimborne workhouse were 'entirely unfitted for work'.[292] Examples of such statements could be endlessly multiplied. The unresolvable argument, of course, was about whether these categories would *always* encompass the large bulk of pauperism regardless of the legislative system adopted – a view which pointed towards a more humane system – or whether it was the *effectiveness* of the new poor law in deterring able-bodied applicants which had produced this result: a residue of inescapable pauperism comprising the most vulnerable in society, once the able-bodied had been deterred, which contrasted in a gratifying way with memories of southern agrarian pauperism in the latter decades of the old poor law.

DISCRIMINATION? THE SETTLED AND THE IRREMOVABLE

In 1846–8 major reforms took place in settlement law and welfare entitlement, with the introduction of five-year irremovability. Paupers could not be removed from a parish if they had resided in it continuously, without claiming relief, for five years. Widows became irremovable for a year following their widowhood. Those applying for relief because of illness or accident were also irremovable, unless this was such as to produce permanent disability. Irremovability was an additional status to legal settlement: it supplemented settlement rather than replacing it, but was a different concept, with fairly limited precedent in settlement law. The two legal statuses with their respective entitlements co-existed. Many paupers were settled

---

[288] *Select Committee on Poor Removal*, xiii (1854–5), p. 96.
[289] *Royal Commission on the Aged Poor*, xiv (1895), p. 163.
[290] *Ibid.*, p. 376.   [291] *Ibid.*, p. 431.   [292] *Ibid.*, p. 254.

elsewhere, but gained irremovability in their parish of residence. They were paid for out of the union common fund in the union where they resided. The legal change was, *inter alia*, a recognition of the difficulty in gaining settlements by the mid-nineteenth century, and of the problems that were associated with settlement through paternity, which had become so salient by that time, as certain traditional legal 'heads' of settlement became more inaccessible to the poor.[293]

More complex ideas of parish 'belonging' thus emerged after 1846: in any one place comprising those who were settled, and those who were irremovable. Unions distinguished settled, irremovable and non-settled poor in their accounts and minute books, accounted by parish, with further subdivisions relating to the type of relief given.[294] As we saw in chapter 3, in earlier periods many parishes took action to prevent settlements. Now some parishes or even unions tried to prevent people attaining irremovable status, and seized upon reasons like interrupted residence to exclude them from that. Movement to another parish was normally held to break one's irremovable status, especially if one gave up rented premises. Unlike legal settlement (which was a status carried with you), irremovability could easily be lost if somebody moved, and then legal settlement would revive and the person would become chargeable to his or her settlement, until gaining irremovable status again.

The exclusion or prevention of irremovability was less pressing than the need to hinder settlements had sometimes been. This was because the relief given to irremovable paupers was paid out of the union common fund, rather than being accounted directly to the parish of residence as happened with legally settled paupers. As this relief was shared across the union in this way, there was less motive to obstruct irremovable status than there had been to prevent settlement. Irremovability was also most frequently gained in the large towns. The concept had been introduced with urban areas in mind, to relieve rural

---

[293] See chapter 3 of this book; and Snell, *Annals of the Labouring Poor*, pp. 72–84.
[294] For example, see Billesdon union minute book, Leics. CRO, DE 3325/1 (week ending April 1856), or G/4/8a/4 (week ending 1 May 1861). Or see the parochial ledgers of the Lutterworth union, Leics. CRO, G/8/9c/1 (1848–52). In addition, non-resident poor were charged to their own unions. There were six such unions involved at this time in Billesdon, one as far away as Rugby.

parishes where migrants had come from and where they were still legally settled. In the towns, population density and anonymity made it relatively easy to claim five years' residence. There was no necessity to register one's arrival, and so this differed from some of the late seventeenth-century requirements. In rapidly growing towns, the irremovable poor became as numerous as the settled poor. Debates about settlement and poor removal came to focus heavily upon irremovability after 1846, as the concept was refined legally, as many practical problems became apparent, as the necessary residential terms were reduced, and as the relation between settlement and irremovability was gradually resolved.

With regard to out-relief practices, this question arises: how were the settled poor dealt with in comparison with the irremovable poor? As the irremovable poor were new and controversial additions to the union relief lists, who had hitherto been removed to (or paid for at a distance by) their parishes of settlement, was there a greater tendency to penalise them and thus oblige them to move away by offering them only the workhouse? Were other poor relief methods adopted to make them leave? Were there any differences in policy towards these two groups, which shed light upon ideas of belonging and entitlement, and the way these concepts were evolving?

The Poor Law Commissioners intended that there should be no discrimination between these different groups of paupers. In a letter of October 1846, they stressed that 'any difference in the treatment of the two classes of paupers settled and paupers simply irremovable, with reference to the nature, quantity, or quality of relief administered to them, cannot be too strongly censured, as not being warranted by law, and as being at variance with every principle of fairness'.[295] Nevertheless, some commentators certainly thought that there were differences. For example, John Bowring (the clerk to the City of London union, who had recently been clerk to St Thomas's union, near Exeter) believed that the irremovable poor

---

[295] This letter is cited by the Poor Law Commissioner G. C. Lewis, in the *First Report from the Select Committee on Settlement, and Poor Removal*, XI (1847), p. 2. However, Lewis was shortly to point out that the irremovable poor were prejudicially dealt with compared with the settled poor, and to say that this was a 'gross violation' by relieving officers. *Ibid.*, p. 7.

are rather sharply looked after [compared to the 'parochial poor'], and
. . . they are rather more screwed in the point of money . . . I think you
will find that, generally speaking, throughout the kingdom the irremovable poor are more screwed down than the settled poor; the
guardians do not like that class of poor upon them; and, strictly
speaking, probably the relief to the poor is better administered there,
as there is not that lavish expenditure upon them that there is upon the
settled poor.[296]

Very low sums given as out-relief to the irremovable poor were,
he thought, to try to make them break their irremovability status
and move on. (Or, to judge from his coffin-screwing language, to
bury them out of sight.) In his London union, he openly stated
of the irremovable poor that 'we want to drive them out if we
can'. At St Thomas's, Exeter, 'we say, "We will only give you 1s.
6d", and the man says, "I cannot live on that." "Very well, we
will give you no more."' In such thinking, the workhouse test
was not used, but extreme low out-relief was applied to these
ends, perhaps to greater effect than could be achieved by the
workhouse test. In some other unions, such as Bethnal Green,
the workhouse test was always applied to the irremovable poor,
again to try to make them leave.[297]

It can be difficult to distinguish in such terms within the
categories of out-door and in-door relief recipients, as relief
numbers or expenditure by settlement status were not usually
given in official returns. However, at least one return separated
relief to settled and irremovable poor. This was supplied in 1860
by the Poor Law Inspector John Lambert (who covered North
and East Yorkshire, Lincolnshire, much of Nottinghamshire,
and portions of Derbyshire, Huntingdonshire and Cambridgeshire). It detailed in-door and out-door relief for sixty-one
unions in those counties, distinguishing settled and irremovable
poor. From this it can be shown that unions giving high out-
door relief to their settled poor did the same for their irremovable poor.[298] And unions which were somewhat more reluctant

---

[296] *Select Committee on Irremovable Poor*, VII (1859), p. 67.
[297] *Ibid.*, pp. 67–8, 130.
[298] *Select Committee on the Irremovable Poor*, XVII (1860), Appendix No. 4, p. 455. Data were
for the half-year ended Michaelmas 1859. Figures were not supplied for two of his
sixty-one unions. The correlation coefficent across unions between (i) irremovable
out-relief as a percentage of irremovable relief, and (ii) settled poor out-door relief as

to give out-door relief were reluctant to give it to both categories of poor. A very large majority of these unions gave over 75 per cent out-door relief to both these categories of the poor. In some cases (Louth, St Neots, Spilsby, Stokesley) they gave over 90 per cent of all relief as out-door relief. A few were harsher in applying the workhouse test, across both categories. Even for the 'stricter' unions, however, total out-door relief was always over 63 per cent of all relief.[299]

In these unions somewhat higher proportions of out-door relief were given to the *irremovable* poor than to the settled poor. The settled poor received 81 per cent of their relief as out-door relief, while the irremovable poor received 88 per cent of their relief in that way. This was a characteristic of irremovability noticed by some others. The *settled* parish poor were still a parish charge, each parish paying into union funds in proportion to its costs (the so-called 'averages') for its own settled poor. The 'poorest' parishes, as measured by their burden of pauperism, paid the most. This funding mechanism grieved many of those poorer parishes, and they wanted it reformed. By contrast, the *irremovable* poor were charged to the union common fund, to which all parishes contributed, albeit in proportion to their settled poor charges. As some witnesses said, when guardians were dealing with irremovable poor they were less prone to enquire minutely into the circumstances. John Lambert himself believed that the irremovable poor were not so well investigated as the settled poor who were charged to the parish, and that guardians (as ratepayers in their parishes) were more interested in those settled poor.[300]

Parishes took steps to reduce their own poor, partly because that also reduced their 'averages', which then meant that they paid less towards the union common fund and the generality of irremovable poor in the union. There were a number of ways

a percentage of total settled poor relief, was 0.561. (In other words, the two headings were quite well correlated.) The total expenditure on the irremovable poor by this period, over fifty-five unions, was 22 per cent of settled and irremovable poor costs combined.

[299] The highly urbanised unions of Derby (63 per cent) and Nottingham (65 per cent) were conspicuous among the three unions giving the lowest proportions of their relief as out-relief.

[300] *Ibid.*, p. 6.

to achieve this. In some unions, such as the Malton or Thirsk unions in Yorkshire, parishes even levied a 'private' rate at parish level, so as to lower or discontinue their contributions to the union common fund.[301] This was a policy of parochial independency that worried the central authorities and their Poor Law Inspectors. Yet it was hard to detect, and indeed hard to prove legally as a fraud. Informal means to provide employment or relief for the settled poor within one's parish, and prevent their formal pauperism altogether, had the same effect, and were a beneficial by-product of the new poor law's accountancy systems. Such means included preference in parish employment, private rates, parish charities, the frequent relief via the highway rate,[302] relief from rents for letting parish lane verges, employment in parish stone and gravel pits, and so on. Long Ashton in Somerset, for example, employed men in their gravel pits.[303] In many parishes in the Louth union, men 'belonging to that parish' were often employed on parish roads, at 1s. a day, to save the parish costs of union relief. 'It relieves the ratepayers, to a considerable extent, of the expense of maintenance.' This was done by the parish surveyor, at the suggestion of the vestry.[304] Alverton (in the Newark union) let labourers have land and a cow, to stop them becoming a charge on the parish

---

[301] This policy was adopted in the Malton union (Yorks.), where seventeen parishes did it (in a union of sixty-five parishes) so as to lower their 'averages'. The money was paid direct to paupers as out-relief, thus by-passing the union. *Ibid.*, pp. 8–9. 'It is an exceedingly difficult thing to find out the particulars with regard to these private rates.' *Ibid.*, p. 9. Whenever he discovered them, Lambert added such sums to other 'normal' expenditures in making his calculations of the 'averages'. In one parish, income from the private rate exceeded the average formal expenditure. *Ibid.*, pp. 27–9, 446. Similar practices existed in the Thirsk union. *Ibid.*, p. 27. The policy fitted of course with an attitude of 'our parish or township first', because it was aimed *inter alia* to reduce payments to other parishes via the union common fund, and in this (as well as its out-relief dimension) it stemmed from an entirely traditional ethos of parish-centredness.

[302] Kirby Bellars in Leicestershire, for example, paid labourers 1s. per day for such work. Leics. CRO, DE 801/18 (14 January 1849, 22 February 1849, 31 March 1859). Bottesford vestry considered 'the Case of Laborers belonging to Bottesford Parish at present out of employment and the Propriety of requesting the Surveyor of the Belvoir Highway district to employ some of them for a time on the Highways of the Parish'. Leics. CRO, DE 829/87 (Bottesford vestry book, 28 January 1869). Such practices are very often documented in vestry books under the new poor law.

[303] Somerset CRO, D/P/1.ash (Long Ashton vestry minute book, 1844), 13 July 1869.

[304] *Select Committee on Irremovable Poor*, XVII (1860), p. 175.

and to ensure that the parish paid no 'averages' to the union.[305] Cotham (in the same union) ensured that if a labourer became chargeable he lost his cottage, which was let to him at a merely nominal rent, and this was another way to lower parish 'averages'.[306] Guardians sometimes wrote back to the parish overseers, recommending them to find work for their paupers, otherwise they would be admitted to the workhouse.[307] Some of these settled parish poor could thus be taken out of the union accounting system, leaving only a core of financial undesirables who often had to be relinquished to the workhouse. Such practices help to explain the differences in Lambert's figures for settled and irremovable poor. The whole union paid for the irremovable poor, not the parish of residence and irremovability, and so parish make-work schemes for the irremovable poor were less needed. Their costs were spread more widely. Parishes and their guardians knew that the direct accounting link between pauperism and the parish for irremovable paupers had been broken, a change that was reluctantly countenanced and much debated, partly because it was thought to dispose towards higher, 'irresponsible' expenditure when guardians were 'spending other people's money'. The latter issue was always a worry to contemporaries, especially in the early decades of the new poor law. It was a major argument for defending parish localism.

The 'parish' or settled poor were thus a separate accounting category from the irremovable poor until the Union Chargeability Act of 1865. These settled people were still directly chargeable to their settlement parishes. Relief to them had direct financial consequences for the parish, and (in raising the parish 'averages') also involved the parish in extra costs to the union's irremovable poor via the union common fund. There were no equivalent consequences with regard to the irremovable poor. Lambert's figures suggest that any remaining settled poor (after

---

[305] *Ibid.*, p. 209, evidence of James Ouzman, relieving officer for the northern district of the Newark union. The settled 'parish' poor in this union in 1860 cost about twice as much as the irremovable poor. *Ibid.*, pp. 210–11.

[306] *Ibid.*, pp. 209–10. Alverton and Cotham are a few miles south of Newark.

[307] For example, Leics. CRO, G/4/8a/2 (Billesdon Union Minutes, 6 March 1840), p. 52, the guardians writing to the Hungarton overseers, recommending them to find work for Samuel Bull and his wife in the parish, 'or they must send both to the workhouse'.

parish work and assistance schemes had kept some off relief) were most subject to enquiry, by guardians who were more likely to attend board meetings when a pauper from their own parish was due for discussion. There seems to have been a small tendency to apply the workhouse test more frequently to these residual 'parish' poor, particularly if they were not 'deserving', to try to keep them off parish rates. Offering the workhouse was a 'call-your-bluff'/'prove your destitution' policy by guardians, and it had in theory been intended that way. However, guardians were usually aware that its acceptance might be a 'call-your-bluff' reply by those settled paupers who knew that workhouse costs were high compared to meagre out-relief, and that guardians usually sought other methods. It is easy to appreciate what sorts of effects this bitter game of brinkmanship had on local social relations, particularly among the settled 'parish' poor. In practice, 'offering the house' always induced large numbers to go away without any relief whatever,[308] and they often returned unaided, vulnerable and resentful to their parishes. They had no rights of appeal. Considerations such as these impacted differently upon the motives and behaviour of settled and irremovable categories of poor. The separate treatment of settled and irremovable poor was not great within particular unions, and unions differed more as between themselves on whether they offered in- or out-relief, as Lambert's figures from 1859 also indicated. Nor are these findings inconsistent with the statement from John Bowring cited earlier, about how very low sums were offered as out-relief to the irremovable poor in the City of London union, and St Thomas' union near Exeter, to induce them to move away. Yet, however generous or mean the out-relief may have been, a tendency to give out-relief more readily to the irremovable poor certainly existed in Lambert's unions.

Paradoxically therefore, between 1846 and 1865 an accounting mechanism of the union and workhouse system may have led to some settled 'parish' paupers being treated more harshly – as most people deemed it – compared to the irremovable poor. Leaving aside the lunatics, sick, very young, and a very small

---

[308] *Select Committee on Irremovable Poor*, XVII (1860), pp. 179, 182.

number of institutionally adapted eccentrics (at least one of whom caused consternation by never wanting to leave the workhouse),[309] it is probably true to say that *any* out-door relief was normally considered preferable to the workhouse. The fact of 'belonging' to one's parish in the traditional way by settlement, often by now an inherited settlement, and so feeling more entitled to benevolence than the irremovable poor, predisposed such a person to be favoured by parish employers in various ways. This kept many off from the poor law. Some guardians, as parish employers, thought like this even while sitting at board meetings. Yet once people were before the board, which mostly comprised alien guardians, their status of 'belonging' to a parish often did not weigh that strongly against the logic of union accountancy, and may not have favoured them with a greater likelihood of receiving out-relief than the irremovable poor. Belonging via settlement to a parish was so strong a legal, financial, practical and moral consideration that it became integral to the accounting system of the new poor law. Yet, as so often in the nineteenth century – and as remains true today – motives flowed from accounting structures, swaying policy in unforeseen ways. Many rural parishes took steps to 'dispauperise' some among their own settled poor, to minimise their indirect payment for other parishes' irremovable poor. There were adverse consequences for some legally settled poor, even though they believed that they should be treated leniently. As specific *parish* rather than general union charges, the less desirable settled paupers in Lambert's unions seem to have been more prone to workhouse testing than those who had migrated away from their settlements, become irremovable, and who as common fund charges were more likely to receive out-relief. Those irremovable poor were also a growing proportion of all poor,[310] and so these were considerations that contributed to augment out-relief after 1846.

---

[309] 'Workhouse – a pauper refusing to leave workhouse may be compelled to do so', *Official Circulars*, vol. IX (31 October 1849), p. 112.

[310] *Select Committee on Irremovable Poor*, XVII (1860), pp. 56–8. The yearly figures given there by James Corder, the clerk for the parish of Birmingham, show this trend very clearly. In 1850–1 the irremovable non-settled poor accounted for 19 per cent of relief to Birmingham's poor. By 1859–60, that figure was 47 per cent. Or see *ibid.*, p. 116, on the two parishes in the Southwark union, where irremovable poor expenses more

DISCRIMINATION? THE IRISH, SCOTS AND ENGLISH

One of the persistent questions about English and Welsh out-door relief after 1834 was whether it acted as an incentive for the Irish to migrate in search of better welfare than they could obtain in Ireland. Would the Irish come over 'for the purpose of obtaining a better class of relief . . . rather than for employment?' asked Mr De Vere.[311] After all, in Ireland out-relief was miniscule compared to England and Wales. During debates on the Irish Poor Law Bill there had been strenuous efforts to prevent out-relief being allowed. The result was that 'in Ireland, out-door relief is almost at an end; there is scarcely any practically given at present'.[312] In one week in 1854, only £61 was given in out-relief for the whole of Ireland.[313] In some Irish unions in 1854–5, no out-relief whatever was given, whereas 83 per cent of paupers in England and Wales received out-relief.[314] Able-bodied out-relief in Ireland was only permitted by special order of the Poor Law Commissioners, but 'in England able-bodied poor are entitled to relief in or out of the workhouse everywhere'.[315] H. B. Farnall, a Poor Law Inspector covering Lancashire and the West Riding, spoke of how 'I firmly believe that a great number of poor Irish would come over for the sake of that relief alone.'[316] George Grey, assistant overseer of All Saints, Newcastle-upon-Tyne, argued that out-relief was a considerable attraction to the Irish. They 'were all told that they would obtain out-door relief if they came here'. They frequently told him that 'the amount of out-door relief given is much better here than in Ireland'. 'A great many' paupers (in fact about

---

than doubled in the 1850s. Such trends occurred in most urban areas, and indeed comparisons on this would tell one much about the compositional growth of nine-teenth-century towns.

[311] *Select Committee on Poor Removal*, XIII (1854–5), p. 109.

[312] *Ibid.*, p. 89, or see p. 106, on how it 'has been almost absolutely put an end to'; or Lord Monteagle on p. 148: 'in general terms . . . we have no out-door relief' in Ireland, or p. 227, with Edward Senior speaking to the same effect.

[313] *Ibid.*, p. 227.

[314] *Ibid.*, pp. 124, 127. See *ibid.*, p. 89, for more quantitative comparisons (for January 1853) between the two countries: about 1 per cent of paupers in Ireland received out-relief, but 87 per cent in England.

[315] *Ibid.*, p. 88, the quotation being from G. Poulett Scrope, MP.

[316] *Ibid.*, p. 261.

92 per cent) in his union received out-relief. 'We dreaded a considerable influx of Irish persons who would become paupers.' In the face of such fears the powers of removal were the main deterrent against their applications.[317] G. Poulett Scrope argued that to allow the Irish out-relief in England 'would scarcely be considered safe to English property', given that the Irish poor were 'so peculiarly attached to out-door relief'.[318] Even the English workhouses were considered by some to be a magnet for the Irish poor, given their 'very great superiority, greater liberality, in the character and amount of relief' over Irish workhouses.[319] There is some question over whether workhouses were considered so attractive, however, not least because in some districts orders of admission to the workhouse given to the Irish were 'torn up and trampled under foot on the spot'.[320] It was certainly the case that the Irish workhouses provided sustenance at starvation levels, with very low dietaries.[321] Edward Gulson (the Senior Inspector of the English Poor Law Board) thought in 1855 that the Irish would come over for English relief, given that 'about eight persons are relieved out of the workhouse for one who is relieved in', and on that workhouse relief he was clear that 'in-door relief in England is very different from in-door relief in Ireland'.[322] There was

[317] *Ibid.*, pp. 32–3, 40.
[318] *Ibid.*, pp. 88–9.
[319] *Ibid.*, p. 89. According to J. T. Ingham, a London magistrate, an English workhouse was 'an extremely comfortable and desirable residence' for the great majority of Irishmen during winter time, the difference from Irish workhouses being 'so great'. *Ibid.*, p. 168. Only fear of removal to Ireland held them back from applying. In Liverpool and elsewhere, admission of legally removable paupers to a workhouse often immediately triggered removal.
[320] *Ibid.*, p. 2, evidence of James Corder, clerk to the Birmingham guardians, who also remarkably claimed that of 3,000 Orders to the workhouse made to Irish people, not one was taken up.
[321] *Ibid.*, pp. 186–7, citing Coutill, County Cavan, as an example of this; *Select Committee on Irremovable Poor*, XVII (1860), pp. 150–1.
[322] *Select Committee on Poor Removal*, XIII (1854–5), pp. 280–1. Gulson had worked in Ireland as an Assistant Commissioner from 1838–47, having helped George Nicholls set up the Irish poor law. He was a firm believer in the workhouse test, who felt that the Irish workhouses were in many ways preferable to the English ones. In England, he complained, 'the Poor Law Board have no power, and the Poor Law Commissioners never had the power, of either ordering the building of a workhouse, or of laying down the plan for a workhouse if it was about to be built. English workhouses, therefore, are very imperfect and incomplete for the purpose for which they are intended, as compared with Irish; for in Ireland, the Poor Law Commissioners had

even a suspicion that some landlords in Ireland, and some Irish poor law authorities, were off-loading people by painting a glowing picture of the attractions of poor relief in England and Wales.[323]

These fears of poverty-stricken Irish, and the issues and implications of comparative generosity and out-door relief, dominated the questioning of many witnesses before Select Committee hearings on the laws of settlement and removal.[324] It was, as one would expect, an issue of particular concern in cities and towns where the Irish concentrated, such as Liverpool, Birkenhead, Preston, Chester, Manchester, Newport, Cardiff, London, Newcastle, Wolverhampton or Birmingham. Its importance to both central and regional authorities was such that the issue deeply affected questions about whether the poor law should be reformed, and whether stricter workhouse testing should take place. In Scotland, there was said to be no power to relieve able-bodied people.[325] However, the possible attractions of English relief to the Scottish poor was not much of a worry to English administrators, because they tended to believe that the Scots were much more provident and thrifty than the Irish – 'to the

---

the power, and exercised the power, of laying down the plans for the workhouses; they ordered them to be built; they supervised and built them themselves, and then called upon the ratepayers to pay the cost of the erections; the Irish workhouses are more complete than any workhouse I ever saw in England.' By contrast, in the south-west of England, several unions had only finally built workhouses within the past two years, and five were still being built, twenty years after 1834. Gulson had had to 'fight a battle' everywhere to get them built, and even then they could only contain about a tenth of the paupers relieved. Government control in Ireland facilitated the task; ratepayer control in England obstructed it. *Ibid.*, pp. 281–2, and see p. 290 on English workhouses being, in his view, 'more lax and more imperfect' than the much 'superior' Irish ones. The point about delayed workhouse building in the south-west of England was even more true of many northern English unions.

[323] *Select Committee on Poor Removal*, xiii (1854–5), p. 112.

[324] The parallels with modern issues of European Union enlargement, and the effects on welfare systems of in-migration from hitherto non-EU countries, are very striking: 'after all, as respects its influence upon the mind of a pauper, the real question is, what is the difference between the practical administration of the law and the facility of obtaining relief in the one country and in the other comparatively, and the amount of relief which he can obtain in one or the other; it is upon this the question turns as to whether you can safely admit the poor of one country almost without stint or limit to relief in the other country, if they find their way there'. *Ibid.*, p. 88. G. Poulett Scrope was even concerned that the disparate poor law regimes in England would lead to flows of paupers from 'in-door' to 'out-door' areas. *Ibid.*, p. 114.

[325] *Ibid.*, p. 88. This point is debateable.

honour of the people from Scotland' – and posed much less of a threat to English ratepayers and poor law resources.[326]

Given these worries about the Irish migrating in search of better welfare, and our concern with insider–outsider divisions, it is interesting to consider whether the Irish were discriminated against in English poor law practices. One would expect to find that. Yet many commentators denied any discrimination. G. Poulett Scrope spoke of how such different treatment, whether in workhouse diets or affecting whether someone received in- or out-door relief, would not be allowed in England, if both parties were equally destitute. 'It would be a most invidious distinction'.[327] Some administrators were also keen to point out, in connection with the housing of the Irish in English workhouses, that 'there is no sort of distinction between one nation, or part of one nation, and another'.[328] Evidence might be found for such segregation in some workhouses, but in a workhouse system fervently attached to the idea of subdivisions, such separation by country of origin seems not to have occurred.

This issue connected with out-relief can be investigated in a qualified way with figures for forty-six unions in the 'Manchester District', provided by the Poor Law Inspector H. B. Farnall to the *Select Committee on Poor Removal* of 1854–5. Numbers of indoor and out-door paupers were supplied, distinguishing Irish, Scottish and English. (The numbers of Welsh were not given, and these may have been subsumed in the English figures.)[329]

---

[326] *Report from His Majesty's Commissioners on the Administration and Practical Operation of the Poor Laws. Appendix (B.2.). Part IV. Answers to Town Queries with Indices*, xxxvi (1834), pp. 159 i, 160 i, being comments on Scottish 'prudence' from London parishes.

[327] *Select Committee on Poor Removal*, xiii (1854–5), p. 90.

[328] *Select Committee on Irremovable Poor*, vii (1859), p. 36, the view of William Best, clerk to the guardians at St Martin's-in-the-Fields.

[329] *Select Committee on Poor Removal*, xiii (1854–5), Appendix No. 5, pp. 326–7. Vagrants were not included. This analysis is subject to the proviso that many Irish and Scottish paupers without settlements or irremovable status could be removed from England, which would normally involve temporary workhouse orders. That might be thought to make them more prone to such orders. However, the same would be true of English paupers lacking such statuses where they applied for relief, and with no fear of being removed from their own country the English experienced possible removal as a lesser deterrent. Large numbers of Irish or Scots did not apply for relief until they had achieved five-year irremovable status under the 1846–8 settlement legislation, which applied here. The Irish were often said to suffer great hardship until they attained irremovable status. The English were less concerned about that. The costs of

Table 5.3   *In-door and out-door numbers relieved, by Irish, Scottish and English origin of paupers, in the 'Manchester District'.*

	In-door	Out-door	% out-door
Irish	3,025	10,915	78.3
Scottish	121	579	82.7
English	12,242	76,019	86.1
Total	15,388	87,513	85.0

Source: see n. 329.

Figures were given for the week ending 1 April 1854. This region lay within and included the unions of Lancaster, Settle, Skipton, Leeds, Wakefield, Barnsley, Sheffield, Stockport, Warrington, Liverpool, Ormskirk and Preston. It was the pre-eminent English reception area for Irish immigration.[330] Table 5.3 gives a breakdown of these figures. The leniency towards the English (86.1 per cent being given out-relief), slightly less so towards the Scottish, and even less so towards the Irish (78.3 per cent) can be seen. The bias is probably less than some would expect, but is visible nevertheless. Removal of the Irish to Ireland would normally involve a preparatory order for in-door relief, and this was probably contributing to their relatively low out-relief. The Scottish paupers were vulnerable to removal in much the same way, however, and yet were less affected. The very low numbers of Scottish paupers made them appear less of a problem, and there are many comments in Select Committee Reports about the Scots being less poor law dependent, and more thrifty, than the English and Irish. Some witnesses believed this to be a moral corollary of the less-developed poor law in Scotland. It is impossible to judge such matters from figures of the type published here, even though the Scottish figures are very low, because the whole populations in each union by country of

Irish removal were often higher than English removal, and thus acted as a relative disincentive to remove (via the workhouse). In short, procedural differences affecting relief and removal probably had a slight influence upon the respective in-door and out-door percentages discussed above, but that influence is impenetrable and was probably quite minor.

[330] Snell and Ell, *Rival Jerusalems*, pp. 173–84, esp. p. 176.

Table 5.4 *In-door and out-door numbers relieved, 1850, 1854 and 1855 (combined), by Irish, Scottish and English origin of paupers, in the Berwick-upon-Tweed union.*

	In-door	Out-door	% out-door
Irish	68	71	51.1
Scottish	53	191	78.3
English	110	954	89.7
Total	231	1,216	84.0

Source: see n. 332.

origin are unknown. Irish paupers in these unions were 13.5 per cent of all paupers.[331] This must have exceeded their proportion in the whole population, and there is every reason to believe that the Irish were more poverty-prone than the English in these unions, given the nature of Irish Famine emigration.

Similar calculations are possible for the Berwick-upon-Tweed union for 1850, 1854 and 1855 (years ending 25 March), covering paupers who were irremovable.[332] These are numbers of the irremovable poor, and so issues of procedure pending removal do not arise. Table 5.4 shows the figures combined for these three years. In the Berwick union there was a very clear gradiency of different treatment, with the Irish certainly worst placed, and the English best placed, with regard to access to out-door relief. Even the Scots, who were more numerous than the Irish this close to the Scottish border, were notably less likely than the English to be offered out-door relief. The Irish were much less likely to be offered out-relief, only about a half of them being given it. The Irish in this union were a tenth of all irremovable paupers.

Intriguingly, this Parliamentary Return on the Berwick union also gave the sums expended as out-relief and in-door relief for each group of paupers. This is rare information, which

---

[331] The incidence of Irish paupers in each union might have been expected to influence the likelihood of their receiving out-relief, but statistical analysis revealed that there was no relationship between these factors.

[332] *Select Committee on Poor Removal*, XIII (1854–5), Appendix No. 2, p. 310.

would be difficult to obtain from other sources on this scale. From these figures, it is possible to calculate out-relief per head for each national group. It is impossible to know the average duration of such relief, which affects the results, although there is no *a priori* reason to suppose significant difference in that. After all, these were all irremovable paupers in the Berwick-upon-Tweed union. Over these three years, the Irish received as out-relief £1.24 per head, the Scots £1.86 per head, and the English £2.64 per head.[333] These figures for *per capita* out-relief are readily compatible with the picture gleaned from the percentages of paupers offered out-relief. They suggest two levels of discriminatory practice in out-relief: regarding its offer (as compared to an order for the workhouse), and its relative generosity. The Irish on both measures came off the worst, and the English were the most favoured. Discrimination by guardians against the Scots was less apparent, but also seems to have occurred.

The above figures were for northern unions, where Irish immigration was a rancorous issue, and where anti-Irish feeling developed most strongly. The same 1854–5 Select Committee gave comparable figures for seventeen unions in Middlesex, two in Kent, ten in Surrey, and for ten parish areas in London which operated workhouses under local Acts. These figures were for the numbers of paupers relieved on 27 January 1855, by type of pauper and country of origin.[334] They are analysed in table 5.5.

---

[333] The equivalent sums for *workhouse* relief per pauper in the Berwick-upon-Tweed union (by country of origin) did not vary much: £1.67 for the Irish; £1.61 for the Scots; and £1.81 for the English. The English figures were still slightly higher. These figures are not comparable with the out-relief sums, because in-door and out-door relief tended to be for different durations. It was also harder to calculate workhouse relief costs per head (given workhouse overheads, medical care, differential diets ordered by the medical officer, etc.), and so the figures have lesser reliability than those for out-relief. *Ibid.*, p. 310.

[334] *Ibid.*, p. 134. The two Kent unions were Greenwich and Lewisham. The parishes under local Acts were St George Hanover Square, St Giles and St George Blooms-bury, St James Clerkenwell, St James Westminster, St Leonard Shoreditch, St Luke Middlesex, St Margaret and St John Westminster, St Mary Islington, St Pancras, and St Mary Newington. I have discounted figures for St Marylebone parish as they were incomplete.

Table 5.5   *In-door and out-door numbers relieved, 27 January 1855,*
by Irish, Scottish and 'Other' (i.e. very largely English) origin
of paupers, in London, Middlesex, Kent and Surrey unions,
and parishes with workhouses under local Acts.

	In-door	Out-door	% out-door
Irish	2,533	9,812	79.5
Scottish	99	168	62.9
'Other'	23,612	72,849	75.5
Total	26,244	82,829	75.9

Source: see n. 334.

In this region, in and proximate to the metropolis, the results were quite different from the northern unions. Here there was no detectable anti-Irish bias in the figures for paupers given out-relief. On the contrary, the Irish were favoured in this regard over the English and the Scots, being more likely to receive out-relief than the English, and much more likely to receive it than the Scots. About four-fifths of these unions/parishes said that it was their general practice to remove Irish and Scottish paupers.[335] Anti-Irish prejudice affecting poor relief practices, therefore, seems apparent in the northern unions, but not in and around London. This is despite the greater proclivity in the latter region to enforce the workhouse test than was generally true in the north. It may be that Irish labour was more valued in London; or that a stricter enforcement of the workhouse test encompassed higher proportions of paupers in the general metropolitan region regardless of their origins. It is also difficult to prove 'discrimination' from such sources, without more information on the issues of levels of aid and on possibly different union-specific criteria for the granting of aid. However, the suggestion here is that anti-Irish and Scottish discrimination in out-door relief practices appears to be regionally present in northern England, but cannot be demonstrated as universally true in England.

[335] *Ibid.*, p. 135.

OUT-RELIEF, PUBLIC WORKS AND UNEMPLOYMENT

In-door relief was being stressed more in the final decades of the nineteenth century, and yet the usual forms of relief remained out-door. Many government reports of the 1890s make this clear. One such report was from the *Select Committee on Distress from Want of Employment* in 1895. The winter of 1894–5 was severe, with many people laid off work. Out-door occupations such as urban and agricultural labourers, the building trades, tin-plate workers, fishermen, dock workers, quarrymen, brick-field workers, or cement workers became unemployed in large numbers. Circulars were sent out from the Local Government Board enquiring how local authorities were handling this unemployment. Replies were received from poor law officials and authorities organising public works for the unemployed, which had become an accepted policy option from the mid-1880s. The many replies from across the country reveal how widespread out-door expedients were in relieving this able-bodied distress. Once more they suggest that the workhouse was largely irrelevant for such classes of people.

In many unions or boroughs, unemployed men were put to work at this time in cleaning the streets, road mending, sweeping snow from roads and footpaths, and pavement making (for example, in Leek, Cardiff, Greenwich, Llandudno, Blackburn, Derby, York, Grimsby, Chichester, Deal, Folkestone, Wandsworth, Gravesend, Kendal, Poole or Fareham).[336] Stone-breaking, at out-door labour test yards under a taskmaster, was as usual a frequent expedient (for example, in Tenby, Wisbech, Bury St Edmunds, Hexham, Wandsworth, Hackney, Cardiff or Criccieth).[337] In Brighton they sifted coombe rock and broke flints.[338] In Hexham they broke whinstone (which the Council thought 'will not involve the stigma of pauperism').[339] In Wisbech they broke imported granite.[340] Some such places using a labour-test yard also resorted to oakum-picking as an option to stone-breaking for some men (for example, St Olave's

---

[336] *Second Report from the Select Committee on Distress from Want of Employment*, VII (1895), pp. 58, 59, 60, 67, 68, 71, 72, 73, 75, 89, 95, 96, 375, 414, 460.
[337] *Ibid.*, pp. 58, 66, 77, 80, 93, 385, 404, 460.
[338] *Ibid.*, p. 368.   [339] *Ibid.*, p. 93.   [340] *Ibid.*, p. 80.

union).[341] Many places put the unemployed men on to work
which enhanced public recreational facilities, such as parks, re-
creation fields, levelling playgrounds, cleaning municipal ponds
(for example, Banbury, Bath, Maidstone),[342] or in 'scavenging
work' and cleaning out gutters, courts and yards (as in Henley
on Thames).[343] Men were employed by the relief authorities in
pile-driving and fortifying sea defences in Penzance, Deal,
Tenby, or Brighton.[344] Less conventional practices could be
found in Hackney where there was 'exceptional distress' (here,
inter alia, they painted water carts and vans),[345] Brighton
(pulling down houses in a condemned area, and carrying water
to houses where the supplies had frozen),[346] Hoylake and West
Kirby (excavating and removing sand),[347] Llandudno (working
on the promenade extension),[348] Blackburn (painting under
bridges),[349] Derby (painting the Borough Asylum),[350] Beccles
(working on the marshes, cutting down trees and sawing
wood),[351] and Bury St Edmunds (painting inside the Corn Exchange).[352] At Romney Marsh they had almost wholly given
up and run out of options: this farming district was said to be
'in a state of hopeless bankruptcy'.[353] In almost all these districts, boroughs and unions, charity distributions were also very
common, taking the form of soup kitchens, food, coal and fuel
donations, special collections, agreements to find people work
temporarily, and the like, in some cases coordinated by local
branches of the Charity Organisation Society.

Amid such a variety of relief and labour-test methods, almost
no districts spoke of the workhouse as a focus of relief efforts.
Those that mentioned the workhouse, like Blandford in Dorset,
were usually more traditional market towns or rural areas
where unemployment was less of a problem. Even in Blandford,
however, it is obvious that there were difficulties in offering
the workhouse, and the guardians feared that those who refused
it might starve or come to serious harm: 'When direct out-relief
was refused, an order for the house was offered and made out,
but as there was little likelihood of the latter being accepted,
the Relieving Officer was directed to watch each case carefully.'

[341] *Ibid.*, pp. 479–80. [342] *Ibid.*, pp. 59, 64, 74. [343] *Ibid.*, p. 72.
[344] *Ibid.*, pp. 68, 75, 77, 368. [345] *Ibid.*, p. 385. [346] *Ibid.*, p. 368.
[347] *Ibid.*, p. 94. [348] *Ibid.*, p. 96. [349] *Ibid.*, p. 59.
[350] *Ibid.*, p. 60. [351] *Ibid.*, p. 65. [352] *Ibid.*, p. 66. [353] *Ibid.*, p. 384.

One of the main labour tests for out-door relief in Blandford consisted of shingle and gravel moving.[354] In the face of such hostility to the workhouse, the guardians and municipal authorities here, as elsewhere, had clearly been forced to offer able-bodied unemployed men slightly more humane and realistic alternatives, ones indeed that may remind us of the parish gravel pits of the old poor law.

CONCLUSION

One way of interpreting this picture of out-relief and the new poor law would be to suggest that it was the outcome of pragmatic, English provincial and Welsh common sense, morality, financial prudence and the enduring strength of parochial feeling, over utilitarian theorising, applied political economy and a faith in large, controlling and 'less eligible' institutions from the London poor law authority. However the contrast is worded, the tension between the two was certainly a major *leitmotif* of the new poor law, and over its duration the principle of out-relief in people's own parishes and homes triumphed. Out-relief and continued residence in one's own parish was *the* dominant mode of relief throughout the nineteenth century, despite sporadic efforts to reverse that, and out-relief became even more pronounced in the twentieth century. Even the so-called 'crusade against out-relief', after 1870, in fact had fairly limited success in reversing trends at national level, despite its undoubted local impact in some unions, and nationally it never brought out-relief down to a minority pauper experience. No one doubts the countless thousands who went into workhouses, nor how huge those buildings sometimes were, nor the crucial roles of those institutions – but if any argument is now made for workhouse supremacy in relief practice, as a general view across England and Wales, one needs to ask whether it is seeing the wood for the trees.

In part, it has to be reiterated, the regulations and legal details of the new poor law never insisted upon near total reliance upon workhouse relief, despite both pro- and anti-new poor law propaganda to that effect. One sees this realisation dawning on

[354] *Ibid.*, pp. 241, 461.

people fairly early during the new poor law. Alfred Austin (who was the Poor Law Inspector for central England, and then Yorkshire and Lancashire, before moving on to head the audit system) commented in response to questions:

—'I do not think you could reduce the out-door relief very materially in England.'

'Was not out-door relief prohibited upon the introduction of the Poor-law in England?'

—'Only to a certain class of paupers, the able-bodied.'

'And afterwards it was modified?'

—'I believe it was . . . I believe the prohibition was more extensive at first than it is now . . . the prohibition extends now merely to able-bodied paupers, with very considerable exceptions even in their case.'

'You would not recommend going back to that earlier stage?'

—'I think not; I do not think the public feeling in this country would permit it' . . .

'There has never been a state of things in this country anything like the exclusively in-door system of Irish relief?'

—'Nothing at all that I am aware of' . . .

'It would be impracticable?'

—'Yes, I think so; the public opinion being so clearly against it.'[355]

Similar points were made by countless other commentators. The Revd J. Frome Wilkinson (author of *Mutual Thrift* and a Newark guardian) remarked that

one of the great test points of the Act of 1834 is a failure, and the letter of the law is not carried out . . . It is interpreted in a spirit more humane than the letter of the law, and the expectations of the New Poor Law Commissioners have not been realised; that is to say, out-relief is the rule, not the exception.

There was no standard conception of what 'destitution' was across all the unions, or even across parishes in a union, and 'the result is, as we all know, that no uniform treatment under the Poor Law, as at present administered, is possible'.[356] Indeed,

---

[355] *Select Committee on Poor Removal*, XIII (1854–5), pp. 238–9.
[356] *Royal Commission on the Aged Poor*, XIV (1895), pp. 305, 307.

if the central authority had tried to lay down consistent and wider rules governing out-relief, taking account of its prevalence and the futility of trying to force guardians to behave otherwise, it would have signalled an unmistakable departure from 'the principles of 1834' – a departure which it was always shy of announcing, given the persuasiveness of the 1834 critique of the old poor law, the seeming logic of the 1834 Act, and the fact that such a departure might well cause even more people to ask why a central poor law authority was needed at all.

Nevertheless, from the early 1840s onwards there developed a growing and extensive array of enactments, regulations, Orders, minutes, Circulars, official letters, individual cases sanctioned by the central authority, sometimes aimed to limit out-relief, but in effect permitting it to a host of excepted categories. Surveying all this documentation, the Webbs were almost correct when they moaned that 'the extent, the variety, and the intricacy of the various sources are simply overwhelming'.[357] On the one hand, this could be highly confusing to local administrators and auditors. Claimants and paupers themselves, who often had a fair legal knowledge of their 'rights' under the old poor law, could sometimes find that the regulations of the new law were a fickle or closed book to them. Yet on the other hand, any board of guardians and its clerk, however they were motivated, did not have to search far to find plentiful warrant for parochial out-door relief. Strict-minded auditors often had to live with their doubts when faced with this kind of legitimate dexterity. After all, it was only the guardians' response to the pedantic legalism which they so often accused the Poor Law Board of.[358] In fact Charles Villiers, the President

[357] Webb and Webb, *English Poor Law Policy*, p. vii.
[358] See the attack by John Adamson (accountant and clerk of the Salford union) on the Poor Law Board's meddling in fine details and surcharging of guardians, in *First Report from the Select Committee on Poor Relief*, x (1862), pp. 31–2; or the similar condemnation by Henry Whitworth (clerk of Barton-upon-Irwell in Manchester) of prohibitory orders and auditors' disallowances and surcharging, which led to 'great dissatisfaction in the northern districts' (*ibid.*, pp. 61, 64–6, 68, 70, 75); or the Revd William Hutchinson (vice-chairman of the Prestwich guardians) condemning the 'frivolous and vexatious' surcharging by their auditor, the way he and the Poor Law Board tried to treat guardians as menials rather than as gentlemen, and the central authority's tendency to send out orders on matters about which it was ignorant. *Ibid.*, pp. 102–4, 110. As a result, it was hard to persuade educated guardians to serve, which would have disastrous consequences – this argument was also

of the Poor Law Board, was worried that some guardians, notably a blunt gentleman from Yorkshire, might not see any reason for his Board to exist at all.[359] Faced with such views, many job-conscious auditors came to work with a fairly open understanding that they did not have to disallow out-relief.[360] Ambiguity over the gendered definition of 'able-bodied' (which was not defined in the 1834 Act, and insufficiently defined later),[361] cases of 'sudden and urgent necessity', 'illness in the family', 'mental infirmity', and related new poor law concepts, permissive Circulars allowing labour tests, inadequate central specification of labour tests, and so on, were such as easily to permit out-relief, even in countless cases to able-bodied men. That relief was very often disbursed by parish guardians who did not partake of a strong faith in the workhouse test, who had local political motives, who in some environments were certainly intimidated,[362] and who usually saw it as their self-interested duty to lower costs by shifting from the workhouse to small-sum parish out-relief coupled with occasional work, test labour, and assistance orders upon relatives.

In the more extreme cases, delays in workhouse building were notorious. 'The creation of a workhouse system in Lancashire

made from Sheffield (*ibid.*, p. 149), and it was one which the central authority in this period could not prevail against.

[359] See the interview of Henry Crawshaw, chairman of the Sheffield union, in *ibid.*, pp. 155–7. Crawshaw stressed 'how much discretion the guardians have'. He probably had more important things to worry about than the Poor Law Board, given that his able-bodied inmates 'refused to work yesterday, and when several policemen were called in, they swore great oaths and set upon them with oakum, hitting the officers in the face. A large body of police were consequently sent down', and the 'awkward' inmates were 'nobbled on the head'. *Ibid.*, pp. 155–6. Oakum fights and nobbling on the head must have persuaded many guardians that out-relief was preferable.

[360] As Henry Potter, a guardian from the West London union, put it: 'we have continued to give out-door relief, although it is not the law; and the Poor Law Board, so long as I have been a guardian, namely, four years, have not attempted to instruct the auditor, as they have in some other cases, to disallow it'. *Second Report from the Select Committee on Poor Relief*, IX (1861), p. 27.

[361] Webb and Webb, *English Poor Law Policy*, pp. 22–3.

[362] On personal violence against guardians, firing of their property and maiming of their cattle, see 'Inquiry into incendiary fires', *Times* (4 July 1844). The *Times* reported that rural arson in many areas had become almost solely directed against poor law guardians. There was also intimidation against relieving officers and labour task masters. In Birmingham, 'many of the men threatened the lives of those who superintended them, and therefore they were almost obliged to relieve them as they wished'. *Select Committee on Irremovable Poor*, XVII (1860), p. 182.

largely proved to be a fiasco', wrote Eric Midwinter about the first thirty years of the system. That county took 'hardly one step towards an embargo on out-maintenance'. In fact, out-relief became more readily obtainable here. 'Lancashire was fundamentally untouched by the New Poor Law', so much so that this was an 'era of localism', notably from 1854.[363] Many other northern English unions gained reputations for intractable localism through the confrontational stance they adopted against central directives, and this occurred with many southern and midland unions too. Most of the Welsh unions did likewise, sometimes through a well-judged policy of dismissive indifference to important letters from the Secretary in Somerset House. Not all boards of guardians acted in this way; but the exceptions – Brixworth, Atcham, Manchester, many of the London unions – became well known or infamous, especially among the poor, because they acted against the general practice, operating policies (albeit sometimes for short periods) which set them aside from the administrative norms of out-door relief.

Even some of the more assiduous defenders of the workhouse test, such as Sir George Nicholls, were very frank about how in-door relief had been eclipsed numerically by out-relief in people's parishes. Nicholls – seen by some authorities as 'the founder of the new Poor Law' – provided abundant evidence to this effect.[364] He shuffled from one foot to another in regretting and bemoaning the preponderance of out-relief, while also using it as a defence against charges that the new poor law (which he had so influenced) was inhumane. He pointed out that under a quarter of relieved people were in workhouses in 1847, indeed down to about a sixth: 'a proportion the reverse of what was anticipated at the passing of the Amendment Act, 1834, when the extinction of out-relief was reckoned upon'.[365] Yet he still made the most of this, by writing that this was

---

[363] E. C. Midwinter, *Social Administration in Lancashire, 1830–60: Poor Law, Public Health and Police* (Manchester, 1969), pp. 49, 57–61, and see pp. 30–6, on the continuing strength of the townships and parishes, their control of amenities, the township affiliations of ratepayers, and the low attendance of guardians.

[364] Nicholls, *History of the English Poor Law*, vol. II, pp. 390–1. The quoted description of Nicholls is from Charles Villiers (President of the Poor Law Board, 1859–66), and it was endorsed by Thomas Mackay. See Mackay, *History of the English Poor Law*, vol. III, p. vi.

[365] Nicholls, *History of the English Poor Law*, vol. II, p. 391.

'a proof that the test was sparingly applied, and that the law was administered with great leniency'.[366] One might question the latter judgement today, even while stressing the predominance of out-relief, but the respective figures themselves are not in much doubt.

Given the opposition to the new poor law, and on-going dislike of its central principles, Welsh and English public opinion would have revolted against strict applications of the workhouse test. Putting stereotypes of hard-hearted Victorians aside – stereotypes which derive above all from an exaggerated stress upon workhouse history – this public opinion was always the chief reason why out-relief continued so extensively. It was repeatedly commented on by experts and witnesses on the poor law. The English poor law and its traditions of parish out-relief were, according to G. Poulett Scrope, 'a portion of the old established institutions of the country, having been on the statute book for 300 years', and public opinion was all the more sensitive on this issue as a result. The English poor, as Lord Naas said, 'have never been accustomed to an organized and extensive system of in-door relief'.[367] The issue was much less pronounced in Ireland, where (in the wording of G. Poulett Scrope) they have 'for centuries been habituated to something like an organized or licensed and universal mendicancy', with greater reliance there on charity.[368] When out-door relief was discussed by the Select Committees on Poor Removal in 1854 and 1855, looking at comparisons between relief systems in Ireland, Scotland and England, and the possible effects of out-relief in attracting migrants to England, William Smythe (the ex-Secretary to the Board of Supervision of the Poor in Scotland) commented that 'it would be utterly impossible to do away altogether with out-door relief, either in England or in Scotland; public opinion would not permit such a thing'.[369] Edward Gulson (the Senior Inspector of the Poor Law Board) saw the recent history of the poor law as follows: 'all legislation, and all practice, has been that of relaxation since the first few years

---

[366] *Ibid.*, p. 390.
[367] *Select Committee on Poor Removal*, XIII (1854–5), p. 96.
[368] *Ibid.*, p. 92.
[369] *Select Committee on Poor Removal*, XVII (1854), p. 255.

of the establishment of the English amended Poor Law, in consequence of public opinion being against a more stringent administration'. He felt that 'public opinion would be most violent' against in-door relief as the only option. He would have preferred to see the hard-nosed Irish system applied in England, but 'I look upon that as an impossibility.'[370] George Carr, the master of the Liverpool workhouse, remarked that 'I have no doubt that public opinion in Liverpool would be opposed to an exclusive system of in-door relief.'[371] The Poor Law Inspector in the Metropolitan District, Richard Hall, spoke of how 'an enormous proportion' of relief was given as out-relief. He believed that it would be 'impossible, on many grounds', to shift almost exclusively to in-door relief in London. This was because 'the feelings of the public would be entirely opposed to it'. The boards of guardians would not do it. He felt that it 'would be vain and totally unwise', indeed 'quite out of the question', to try and prohibit out-relief in London.[372] H. B. Farnall considered that 'popular opinion would be very averse' to strict out-relief prohibition.[373] 'I think it would be quite impossible and out of the question to put all those broken down or unemployed people into the workhouse.' In fact, 'The feeling of the public' would be wholly against abolishing out-door relief.[374] J. T. Ingham, a London magistrate, commented upon how 'there is a great deal of sympathy for the poor in England, which compels public bodies to adopt a more liberal system'.[375] 'Public opinion' in England, according to G. Poulett Scrope, was pretty uniform across manufacturing and rural areas on this issue, influencing guardians in much 'the same way everywhere'. It would not tolerate anything like the workhouse system in Ireland, nor anything like the refusal of out-relief in Ireland. That would be 'quite an absurdity'.[376]

On top of these considerations relating to humane Victorian public opinion, there was awareness that the workhouse test was quite inappropriate to many working conditions. For

---

[370] *Select Committee on Poor Removal*, XIII (1854–5), pp. 281–2.
[371] *Select Committee on Poor Removal*, XVII (1854), p. 401.
[372] *Select Committee on Poor Removal*, XIII (1854–5), pp. 123–4.
[373] *Ibid.*, p. 262.   [374] *Ibid.*, pp. 262–3.
[375] *Ibid.*, p. 169.   [376] *Ibid.*, pp. 89, 107, 111.

example, Andrew Doyle (Poor Law Inspector for north Wales, Shropshire, Cheshire, Staffordshire and Derbyshire) viewed that test as 'totally inapplicable' to mining area distress, as in Staffordshire, or to the Potteries, given the nature of unemployment in such regions.[377] Or in London, during a bad winter spell, huge numbers were laid off. The relieving officer of St George's in the East spoke about how 'we had 1,700 passed through the office in one afternoon', men like coal whippers, dock labourers, bricklayers' labourers, and others affected by hard frosts and adverse winds.[378] They were paid about 1s. to 2s. a day for working in the stone-yard, and given some bread if they had a family. Despite the Poor Law Board's worries over relief in aid of wages and similar practices, in effect the guardians eked out the employment and rates paid by the London Dock Company. Countless other examples could be given of similar occurrences, throughout the country.

Much of this chapter, therefore, provides evidence for considerable continuity between the old and new poor laws, and the on-going dominance of parochial localism in welfare provision. The parish remained the focus for people's lives, even when they were 'paupers'. In that regard, the new poor law probably did not much disrupt people's ideas of parochial belonging. The parish was far more important, and remained so for much longer, than most historians assume. It was put to the Revd Giles Daubeny of Lidyard Tregoz (in the Wootton Bassett and Cricklade union, Wiltshire), in 1860, that 'The parochial system [is] as much in existence as it was previously to the passing of the Poor Law Act?' He replied: 'Yes, quite; and much more clearly brought into action . . . I admire the parochial system now, which is the system of the poor law.'[379] He felt that this parochial focus tied in well with occupiers' interests, while they were much less concerned with the wider area of the union. Antipathy to the union and its hated workhouse ensured that very few people ever associated with the union as a geographical entity. The new poor law turned generations of working people and many ratepayers against centralisation.

---

[377] *Ibid.*, p. 173.
[378] *Select Committee on Irremovable Poor*, VII (1859), pp. 108–14.
[379] *Select Committee on Irremovable Poor*, XVII (1860), p. 436.

Indeed, in that paradoxical and negative sense the workhouse and the wider administration connected with it helped to perpetuate localism and a sense of belonging to the parish, for very many decades after 1834. Chadwick, Senior and their associates in 1834 did not anticipate this, and did not desire it. Yet if they had reflected upon people's feelings with more empathy, they might have realised that there could hardly be a stronger and more understandable reason for aversion to such a wider district, when its quintessential symbol was the workhouse.

Whether, in more general terms, one argues for 'continuity' or 'discontinuity' before and after 1834 is a matter of thematic emphasis, and indeed that debate *per se* has not been my main interest here. There can be little doubt that the new poor law represents fundamental administrative and perceived discontinuity in many respects: the roles of the central Commission and its successors; the creation of unions; the election of guardians; the extension of that franchise to women, long before the suffragettes;[380] the building of central workhouses with permanent staff; the fear and hatred of those workhouses, and their influence upon popular attitudes, politics, Chartism and the extension of working-class consciousness; the sales of many parish houses after 1835, partly to help fund the workhouse building programme; the effects of the new poor law on local labour markets; the relieving officers and their districts; union financing; the important audit and surcharge system; the medical arrangements, medical officer districts, and the handling of the insane in workhouses; the much more standardised documentation of the post-1834 era – all these matters should not be overlooked, gradually enforced though some of them were. Perhaps above all, the *mythology* of the union workhouse in popular consciousness, whether it related accurately to historically 'real' administration or not, was *itself* a subjective reality in people's minds. It was deliberately inculcated *both* by administrators keen to propagate 'less eligibility' and deterrence, *and* by the many fierce opponents of the new poor law. The poor

---

[380] And indeed the growing numbers of female guardians. S. King, '"We might be trusted": female poor law guardians and the development of the New Poor Law: the case of Bolton, England, 1880–1906', *International Review of Social History*, 49 (2004).

compared their feelings and understanding of the workhouse with their more favourable notions or remembrance of the old poor law, and so there developed comparative mythologies which themselves were striking features of discontinuity.

Nor should those features of the old poor law be unnoticed which dwindled immediately or gradually after 1834: some powers of overseers (but see the next chapter); the Speenhamland, roundsman, labour rate and other systems of relief; many earlier roles of justices; the changing ways in which illegitimacy was handled; the localised arrangements for relief in many districts, for example under Gilbert's Act or local Acts, even though these administrations often survived proudly intact for many years after 1834. Then there were the key innovations during the *longue durée* of the new poor law, such as the introduction in 1846 of irremovability in connection with settlement, or of union chargeability in 1865, or of the innovations in rating and funding practices, as in 1861 or 1865, the extremely important changes in central administration and political control, and so on. In general terms, I would not argue for continuity in the face of all this, and much more like it. Yet in one crucial area, which relates so closely to the theme of parochial belonging, there *was* continuity: the large majority of paupers continued to be relieved in their own homes and parishes. The workhouse was a threat and deterrence, usually a long walk away; and indeed it was all the more effective for being at a distance and thus alarming senses of local belonging. When receiving relief, public opinion ensured that the parish and its immediate neighbourhood usually remained the key setting. Nassau Senior, so instrumental in formulating the new poor law, at the very end of his life commented on it as follows: 'I believe that the intention of the law when it was passed was that out-door relief should be the exception, and that in-door relief should be the rule; but the administration of the law ever since the very beginning has been that out-door relief is the rule, and that in-door relief is the exception.'[381] As he closed his eyes, we see that his judgement was, at last, correct.

---

[381] *Third Report of the Select Committee on Poor Relief*, x (1862), p. 65.

CHAPTER 6

Nailed to the church door? Parish overseers and the new poor law[1]

The office of Overseer, which, at the time of its origin, simply involved the collection and expenditure of funds for the relief of the poor, is now rapidly becoming, from the effect of modern legislation, an office of considerable importance and responsibility.[1]

There are certain powers and duties . . . which still belong to the overseers of the several parishes, independently of the guardians. Such, for example, are the assessment of the poor-rates, and the removal of paupers to the parishes of their settlement. In incurring any legal expenses in matters of this kind, the overseers are under no obligation to consult the guardians, and the guardians have no power to control the overseers.[2]

The Webbs referred to the new poor law of 1834 as 'the strangulation of the parish', a view endorsed as dramatic but not unjust by W. E. Tate in his *The Parish Chest*.[3] Tate took the view that 'Eventually . . . the old parochial system was wound up by the Act of 1834.' So he ended his well-known book at that date.[4] The parish chest, it would seem, remained permanently padlocked and redundant from then on, eventually to be opened by local historians. It might have appeared, to a long-buried Thomas

---

[1] H. J. Davis and H. A. Owston, *Overseers' Manual, Showing their Duties, Liabilities, and Responsibilities* (London, 1864), preface.

[2] 'Powers of overseers', *Official Circulars of Public Documents and Information: Directed by the Poor Law Commissioners to be Printed, Chiefly for the Use of the Members and Permanent Officers of Boards of Guardians, under the Poor Law Amendment Act*, vol. v (29 July 1845), p. 108. (The editions used here, initially published in 1840–51, were the New York, 1970 reprint editions, bound as two volumes for the initial vols. I–VI, and vols. VII–X. These are hereafter cited as *Official Circulars*.)

[3] W. E. Tate, *The Parish Chest: A Study of the Records of Parochial Administration in England* (1946, Cambridge, 1960), pp. 11, 22. Tate gave no reference, but one such is S. Webb and B. Webb, *English Local Government: The Parish and the County* (1907, London, 1963), pp. 171–2.

[4] Tate, *Parish Chest*, p. 194.

Gray, that 1834 was a curfew which tolled the knell of parting days for the parish. Perhaps the overseer homeward plodded his weary way, leaving the world to darkness, and to the work-house – with the civil life of the parish, as it had been known over the past three centuries, shunted up a side-track, brusquely by-passed by the Victorian institutional and administrative in-novations. Parish administration, never very self-contained, seemingly became even less so after 1834.

There has accordingly been much research on the creation of unions, workhouses and their internal regimes, post-1834 cen-tralising tendencies, the politics of the London-based author-ities, and so on. Yet, as seen in chapter 5, normally between 70 and 90 per cent of poor relief under the new poor law continued to be domiciliary out-relief, given to people in their own homes and parishes. In many parts of the country over nine-tenths of relief was parochial out-relief – this was true of many poor law unions in regions as disparate as Wales, the south-west, East Anglia, the south midlands, Lincolnshire, Northumberland or Cumberland. The counter-parochial union workhouse was, when seen in proper perspective, a small minority experience for paupers, and one that found its heaviest use in large towns and cities rather than in the countryside and market towns. A set of questions follow from such conclusions, notably about the on-going vitality of parish life and administration after 1834.

Little has been written on this continuing role of the parish, and of belonging and responsibility to it, under the new poor law. In fact, through the work of some outstanding early modern historians, we probably know more about the life of the parish between 1500 and 1750 than we do about it between 1834 and 1930.[5] What happened to the overseers, or the church-wardens in their secular capacity? Is Charles Dickens' caricatur-ing term 'bumbledom' acceptable? How much administrative control did the parish have after 1834? Where did it exercise that control, and what possibilities for local initiative remained? What was the role of the parish vestry under the new poor law? I wish to explore one such issue here: the role of parish

---

[5] An excellent recent account is S. Hindle, *On the Parish? The Micro-Politics of Poor Relief in Rural England, c. 1550–1750* (Oxford, 2004).

overseers after 1834,[6] until their office was finally abolished –
which I was once surprised to find occurred almost a century
later, in 1927.[7] They had first been mentioned in legislation
back in 1572, over three and a half centuries earlier.[8] Parish overseers are significant in the context of this book, because they are
so central to the question of how far local autonomy, discretion
and control continued after 1834, and because, as voluntary
office-holders, they crystallise so many issues of belonging and
community. My stress will be upon the continued vigour of
the parish and its officers under the new poor law, on the
continuance of administrative localism, and of a strong sense
of community belonging, accountability and responsibility
throughout the nineteenth century.

There was a distinct seasonality to the administrative life of
overseers. They were appointed for a year, starting from 25
March. Immediately following that, they were to receive from
their predecessors any remaining balances, and all parish books,
deeds, papers, goods and chattels. Arrears had to be checked in
the *Overseers' Receipt and Payment Book*. They were to pay any
money or debts owing to the previous overseers. The transition
arrangements were much more demanding under the new poor
law than under the old. Shortly after the overseer's appointment, there was the auditing of accounts by the auditor for
the previous half-year. This became a serious occasion during
the nineteenth century. There were *seven* different types of accounting books kept by overseers at any one time under the new
poor law (I refer here to the early 1860s). In addition, there were

---

[6] 'The word "overseer" shall be construed to mean and include overseers of the poor,
churchwardens, so far as they are authorized or required by law to act in the management or relief of the poor, or in the collection or distribution of the poor-rate, assistant
overseer, or any other subordinate officer, whether paid or unpaid, in any parish or
union, who shall be employed therein in carrying this act or the laws for the relief
of the poor into execution.' See 4 & 5 Wm IV, c. 76, s. 109. For a similar extension of
the definition of overseers to churchwardens, see *Fifth Annual Report of the Local
Government Board, 1875–76* (London, 1876), p. 52.
[7] 15 & 16 Geo. V, c. 90 (the Rating and Valuation Act of 1925, effective from 1927). This
Act produced a single general district rate, simplified the earlier system inherited from
1601 and earlier, reduced the number of rating authorities from over 15,000 to under
2,000, and brought rating areas more into line with administrative areas.
[8] 14 Eliz., c. 5. Such officers had existed, albeit not in name, from 1536. See 27 Hen. VIII,
c. 25, where churchwardens were to be assisted by two others from the parish to collect
voluntary contributions for the poor.

three types of book which had to be kept by collectors of poor
rates. This was more extensive than under the old poor law.
These books covered such matters as rates, receipts, payments,
balance sheets, inventories of parish stock, money, goods and
effects, and so on. All these books had to match and balance each
other for accounting purposes.

Upon entry to office, overseers had to make a new rate. The
vestry might offer advice, but it had no legal powers over
overseers in the matter of rating.[9] These rating responsibilities
of overseers lasted until the mid-1920s, when *The Times* reported
that overseers were still the principal rating authority, 'the other
authorities making demands upon them for their expenses'.[10]
The rate needed to cover the sums required from the parish for
the poor law union, and it was allowed to go above that if the
overseers wished. After it was allowed by two justices, the rate
had to be made public, by being fixed to the principal doors of
all churches and chapels in the parish.[11] From 1844 the rate
books had to be made available for inspection and challenge
by any ratepayer, in a parish officer's house – information being
given about this to ratepayers on church and chapel doors.[12] It
was the overseers' task to proceed against those who did not pay
their rates within the tight period of seven days, for example by
distraint of goods. The overseers had to appear before justices
with the rate at any summons for non-payment, with proofs that
all formalities had been complied with.

Overseers were faced with countless difficulties and legal
issues in making rates. There were questions about whether
certain places could be rated, such as charity schools, churchyards, quarries, coal mines extending under two or more
parishes, markets, turnpikes, farm-houses, counting-houses,
brickfields, almshouses, fever hospitals, gas works, lighthouses,

---

[9] 'Vestry meetings – power in regard to making rates, etc.', *Official Circulars*, vol. VI
(16 January 1846), pp. 31–2.
[10] *Times* (14 May 1925), p. 9, col. b.
[11] Davis and Owston, *Overseers' Manual*, p. 23. There was contemporary dispute over
whether such notices had to be fixed to the doors of dissenting chapels as well as those
of Anglican churches. It was felt advisable to affix them on all churches and chapels to
avoid subsequent dispute. 'Publication of notices', *Official Circulars*, vol. VI (2 February
1846), p. 32.
[12] 'Summary of duties of guardians and their officers, and of overseers', *Official
Circulars*, vol. IV (30 September 1844), pp. 157–8.

lime-quarries and kilns, machinery, deer parks, register offices, canals, railway lines and stations, police stations, county lunatic asylums, and even workhouses. All these, and many more, had their complications. What for example should one do with a mill over the river Calder, the centre of which formed the boundary between Todmorden and Walsden, and Stansfield, where the head-quoit, dam and water-wheel were on one side?[13] How should one deal with the Revd G. G. Beadon, of Axbridge, who was exercised about whether he was rateable for the churchyard, 'in consideration of the grass, which was made into hay, and of the walnuts growing on a tree therein'. Various issues were raised for overseers here, as to whether the church-yard was held for the benefit of the parish, and whether the parson's occupation was for the benefit of the parish, or for his own benefit – about which there were mixed views – and whether the churchyard might be considered as glebe, in which case it would certainly be rateable.[14] How might one rate walnuts? More importantly, there were questions as to whether tolls, tithes, timber, commuted Easter offerings, rights of fishing and shooting, stock-in-trade, pier dues, and so on could be rated. There were many further questions, such as whether overseers could make two rates concurrently.[15] Another prob-lematical area was rates payable on assets which involved com-mercial confidentiality. After all, the valuations and rates were open to inspection. All such topics were subject to legal prece-dents and rules which overseers needed to understand.

The overseers had to provide a valuation list of all rated properties in their parish, with their annual values, in a specified form, for the union assessment committee. Such valuations were often made by surveyors, under instructions from overseers. Those valuations were not binding on overseers, who could still use their own judgement in making the poor rate.[16] A copy of

[13] 'Rating – of mill situate on river in two townships', *Official Circulars*, vol. vii (7 December 1846), p. 95.

[14] 'Rating – incumbent's liability to be assessed in respect to the churchyard', *Official Circulars*, vol. iii (11 August 1843), pp. 153–4.

[15] 'Poor's rate – right of overseers to make and collect two rates concurrently', *Official Circulars*, vol. iii (15 August 1843), p. 153.

[16] 'Valuation – power of overseers to depart from, in the making of rates', *Official Circulars*, vol. iv (16 October 1844), p. 175. For example, poor persons had to be listed

the valuation list had to be deposited in a proper place in the parish, and another copy delivered to the board of guardians. Public written notice had to be given of this deposited property valuation in the parish, which had to be put up on all church and chapel doors. There were persistent requirements that overseers put up such notices and information on church and chapel doors, and so it is worth mentioning that there was an average of over three churches and chapels in each parish in 1851. A tenth of parishes had over five of them, and about 5 per cent of parishes had over ten such ecclesiastical buildings.[17] In the seasoned hands of overseers newly invented drawing pins made a significant contribution to the whittling away of gothic doors.[18] Any complaints against the valuation list had to be received by the overseers, who could order a new valuation. The guardians could not order that.[19] In some parishes, notably urban ones, there could be hundreds of appeals. Notice had to be given (on church and chapel doors) of any meetings by the assessment committee to consider appeals against the valuation list. Changes to the valuation list needed to be re-presented to the parish, in the same manner. The lists had to be set before the justices. All these stages had fixed timetables and deadlines attached to them, with penalties upon overseers who failed to meet them. Some aspects of valuations were especially difficult, such as the gross and net annual values of tithes, which varied by year according to average prices of corn. Tithes and tithe commutation rent charges in fact raised extremely complicated issues in connection with rating.[20]

There were supplemental valuation lists which needed to be made, which covered property with changing rateable potential, or changing tenure, which might be liable to rates in different

---

who were exempt from paying to the poor rate. See for example Som. CRO, D/P/1. ash (9 October 1844).

[17] Figures calculated from the English and Welsh computerised data from the 1851 census of religious worship. See K. D. M. Snell and P. S. Ell, *Rival Jerusalems: The Geography of Victorian Religion* (Cambridge, 2000).

[18] Drawing pins were invented in name and as a mass-produced item in the mid–late 1850s, the first *OED* reference being for 1859. As a more convenient means for displaying public notices, their invention at this time is significant.

[19] *Select Committee on Irremovable Poor*, XVII (1860), p. 110.

[20] Davis and Owston, *Overseers' Manual*, pp. 39–40.

proportions, or which were prone to change in value for any reason. Appeals had to be directed to Quarter Sessions about any valuation list made or altered by the assessment committee which aggrieved the parish. Given the mathematics and principles of union funding, such grievances also involved the under-valuation of any *other* parish in the union, which thus raised one's own parish's contribution to union funds. Under the old poor law a parish's rate had been a matter for itself, with few external ramifications. However, under the new poor law overseers had to be concerned not simply with their own rates, but also with the way in which valuations and rates were made in other parishes in the union. This involved parish overseers having to give notice to the Quarter Sessions, the overseers of the other parish, and to the guardians of the union, when disputes about this were impending.[21]

When the rate had been made and collected, the overseers were the legal custodians of the money raised. They had to bank it themselves, and receive the interest. They were responsible for it, and the interest was their property. The same applied to the other money they collected, such as from the county rate or the highway rate. Very large sums indeed could thus pass through the hands of overseers every year. For example, in the Salford township over £20,000 from the poor rate was handled by the overseers annually in the early 1860s. They dealt with it as 'a private matter, they transfer it to a private banker as a banking account of their own . . . interest accrues upon their deposit'.[22]

The administration of relief to most paupers was of course generally appropriated from overseers by the new poor law, and taken over by the union guardians and their relieving officers, who overseers now had to liaise with.[23] However, overseers were empowered after 1834 to give relief 'in articles of absolute necessity, but not in money', and also to provide lodging, to people deemed to need it because of 'sudden and urgent necessity', whether the people requiring this lived in the parish or

---

[21] *Ibid.*, pp. 37–8.
[22] *First Report from the Select Committee on Poor Relief (England)*, x (1862), p. 29.
[23] 'Relief by overseers of sudden and urgent necessity: relative powers of medical and relieving officers in certain cases', *Official Circulars*, vol. III (9 November 1843), p. 156.

not.[24] Indeed, the Assistant Commissioner Alfred Power stressed this duty of overseers 'to incur any reasonable expense in providing lodging as well as other necessaries', underlining 'the true extent of their powers and responsibilities under the Poor Law Amendment Act'.[25] If overseers refused to give such relief they could be ordered to do so by any justice of the peace, who could also order them to give medical relief. Indeed, overseers themselves had powers to order the union or district medical officer to attend a case.[26]

Overseers also had to give relief to the 'casual poor' – that is, those who were not settled in the parish but who needed immediate temporary relief because of an accident or short-term circumstances. Leaving aside some vagrants and mendicants, casual poor were often irremovable, being only temporarily in the parish. They were seen legally as not coming under the terms of the 1662 Settlement Act; and there were regulations against parish officers moving them on.[27] They were therefore payable from the union common fund. Their relief needed to be paid by an overseer, who would then be refunded by a relieving officer.[28]

Overseers were thus not meant to give any relief except in cases of 'sudden and urgent necessity'. Compared with administration under the old poor law, this represented the largest withdrawal of powers from them through the 1834 Act. The magnitude of this change was equalled by the extra-parochial

---

[24] 4 & 5 Wm IV, c. 76, s. 54; J. F. Archbold, *The Act for the Amendment of the Poor Laws, with a Practical Introduction* (London, 1839), p. 19; W. A. Holdsworth, *The Handy Book of Parish Law* (n.d., c. 1859, London, c. 1872), pp. 194–5; Sir G. Nicholls, *A History of the English Poor Law, in Connection with the State of the Country and the Condition of the People*, vol. II (1854, New York, 1967), p. 379.

[25] 'Relief in cases of emergency – duties of medical and relieving officers and overseers in respect of', *Official Circulars*, vol. II (30 July 1842, citing in full a letter by Power written on 8 April 1842), p. 295.

[26] 'Medical relief – ordered by overseers, without reporting it to relieving officer', *Official Circulars*, vol. VI (6 February 1846), pp. 89–90; 'Medical relief – whether bound to attend, on the order of an assistant overseer, persons who are not destitute', *Official Circulars*, vol. VI (8 May 1846), p. 90.

[27] 'Circular to boards of guardians as to the illegal removal of casual paupers', *Official Circulars*, vol. II (13 February 1839), p. 222.

[28] Davis and Owston, *Overseers' Manual*, p. 79. The definition of 'casual poor' was much debated. See for example 'Casual poor – West Ham union', *Official Circulars*, vol. III (28 March 1842), pp. 43–4; 'Paupers – chargeability of', *Official Circulars*, vol. IV (8 June 1844), p. 120.

formation of unions, and the delegation of many responsibilities to the guardians and relieving officers. Supposedly non-urgent cases were to be referred to the district's relieving officer, with delays for some applicants before they could obtain any relief. However, a pauper could be admitted into a union workhouse by order of an overseer. Most cases of admission were by order of a relieving officer or board of guardians, but one can still find countless cases of overseers ordering this in admission registers.[29] The management of the workhouse lay with the board of guardians, but overseers could complain of the conduct of any workhouse master or officer, for example with regard to 'spirituous liquors', discipline, mistreatment and so on, and that could lead to fines, imprisonment, or dismissal of the officer.[30] Out-door relief to aged, infirm, or unable-to-work paupers could be ordered by two justices, via an overseer, but the relieving officer had to be told of this, and he would report the case to the guardians so that they could determine how much and what kind of relief should be given.[31]

It remained the task of overseers under the new poor law to proceed against people who were neglecting to maintain their families, and to obtain sums from relatives in support of poor persons. This was sometimes a duty performed by the clerk to the guardians, or the relieving officer, who acted here as an agent to the overseers.[32] The extent to which overseers acted in this way is not yet clear, and more commonly they found themselves negotiating with paupers and kin over property and support. In such negotiation, they aimed to promote a compliant sense of belonging and community. However, they could ask justices' permission to seize the property of any person liable to maintain others, and they could dispose of that property to recompense their parish for the costs of maintaining a wife or children.[33] The expenses of this process were payable by the

---

[29] For example, see Leics. CRO, G/1/60/3 (Ashby de la Zouch union admission and discharge register, 1843–4).

[30] 4 & 5 Wm IV, c. 76, s. 93; Archbold, *The Act for the Amendment of the Poor Laws*, p. 147.

[31] Davis and Owston, *Overseers' Manual*, pp. 97–8; Archbold, *The Act for the Amendment of the Poor Laws*, p. 19.

[32] Davis and Owston, *Overseers' Manual*, pp. 46–7.

[33] *Ibid.*, p. 84.

guardians, although it was a matter of discretion as to whether they should be paid from the union common fund, or by the parish. In this, the opinion of the Poor Law Board was sought. Petty sessions could grant orders of maintenance on anyone able to maintain their parents, children, or grandchildren, when any of them became chargeable – the costs of this were to be defrayed from the poor rates.[34]

Moving on to the settlement laws, it was the task of overseers to apply to justices for orders of removal against any chargeable pauper who was settled elsewhere, and had not become irremovable from their parish under the 1846–8 and 1861 irremovability legislation. As the Poor Law Commissioners stated in 1844: 'The removal of paupers is a matter within the province of the overseers, and not of the guardians.'[35] Indeed, if the union clerk was used for removal purposes by overseers, he had to be paid 'in the same way as any other solicitor would be'.[36] J. T. Ingham (a London magistrate) commented on such powers of overseers to the Select Committee on Poor Removal in 1855: 'If the removability is proved, and the parish officer insists upon the removal, you must remove the man.'[37] Such removals were very common in many regions. John Bowring (the clerk to the City of London union) remarked to the 1862 Select Committee on Poor Removal that 'as a board of Guardians we have nothing to do with the removals'; they were the responsibility of overseers. In the countryside, he said, 'in hundreds of parishes . . . they remove every poor person they possibly can'.[38] In fact, there were around 40,000 paupers removed annually in England

---

[34] Accordingly, records of such proceedings are not always to be found in union records, for they fell more properly under overseers' expenses, even under the new poor law. 59 Geo. III, c. 12, s. 26; 4 & 5 Wm IV, c. 76, s. 78. The law applied to relations by blood only, and to lawful rather than reputed parents or children. Davis and Owston, *Overseers' Manual*, p. 84.

[35] 'Professional remuneration to clerks', *Official Circulars*, vol. IV (16 April 1844), p. 117; 'Communications relating to the decision of the Court of Queen's Bench, in Reg. v. the Inhabitants of Christchurch', *Official Circulars*, VIII (15 February – 8 March 1849), pp. 34–8; 'Powers of overseers', *Official Circulars*, vol. V (29 July 1845), p. 108; A. C. Bauke, *The Poor Law Guardian: His Powers and Duties in the Right Execution of his Office* (London, 1862), p. 97.

[36] 'Professional remuneration to clerks', *Official Circulars*, vol. IV (16 April 1844), p. 117.

[37] *Report from the Select Committee on Poor Removal*, XIII (1855), p. 155.

[38] *Third Report of the Select Committee on Poor Removal*, X (1862), p. 148.

and Wales in the early 1840s, and that had fallen to the still substantial annual figure of about 12,000 by 1907.[39]

The overseers had to search out the settlement,[40] and they needed to give notice of chargeability and the grounds of removal to that supposed parish of settlement. They had to prosecute or defend appeals at Quarter Sessions against removal orders (as under the old poor law).[41] They had access to the pauper resident elsewhere when they were challenging a removal to their parish, and indeed they could take that pauper out of the removing parish for examination.[42] In the early decades after 1834, guardians did not have anything to do with settlement disputes at law.[43] In some cases, disputes could be conducted through the Poor Law Board, which from 1851 could act as a cheaper arbitrator; and so there was the necessary correspondence with that Board to defend the parish.[44] Overseers or assistant overseers usually had to convey removed paupers, and maintain paupers in transit, or make arrangements for this to be done. This was further business which had nothing to do with guardians.[45] Overseers had to receive paupers sent to their parish from elsewhere, as under the old poor law.[46] When removals were suspended to their parish, for example because of widowhood or ill-health, they were normally required to pay to the removing parish the costs of maintaining the pauper.[47] They had to claim and account for sums from other parishes owing in respect of paupers removed elsewhere.[48] In almost all

---

[39] D. Englander, *Poverty and Poor Law Reform in Britain: From Chadwick to Booth, 1834–1914* (London, 1998), p. 15; *The Minority Report of the Poor Law Commission. Part 1: The Break-up of the Poor Law* (London, 1909), p. 402.

[40] *Select Committee on Irremovable Poor*, XVII (1860), p. 205.

[41] Davis and Owston, *Overseers' Manual*, p. 69.

[42] 4 & 5 Wm IV, c. 76, s. 80.

[43] 'The costs of submitting a case, relative to a removal, to the Court of Queen's Bench cannot be paid from the common fund of the union', *Official Circulars*, vol. III (10 March 1843), p. 126.

[44] Davis and Owston, *Overseers' Manual*, pp. 51, 74; 14 & 15 Vic., c. 105.

[45] 'By whom the removal of paupers to their places of settlement is to be undertaken', *Official Circulars*, vol. IV (14 June 1844), p. 110; *Third Report from the Select Committee on Poor Relief*, X (1862), p. 148.

[46] They were not responsible for the removal of paupers to Ireland, Scotland, the Channel Islands or the Isle of Man, as these paupers were dealt with by the guardians of the union. Davis and Owston, *Overseers' Manual*, p. 71.

[47] *Ibid.*, p. 73.   [48] *Ibid.*, p. 47.

cases there were deadlines to be observed, notices to be given, statements of their case to be made – and failure to act by those deadlines would invalidate their case and often lead to penalties against overseers personally.

The 1865 Union Chargeability Act was meant to obviate the need for removals within a union, although for long afterwards one's settlement remained in a union parish.[49] From 1865 guardians applied for removal orders between unions, not the overseers. This was considered by one MP to be a move towards 'an abandonment of the parochial system'.[50] That was an argument heard in many contexts, from 1834 to as late as 1925 and beyond – much later than W. E. Tate allowed for – as for example during the passage of the 1876 Divided Parishes Act, which further simplified settlement law by allowing three years' residence to confer settlement.[51] This helped to free overseers of what an indignant Thomas Mackay called 'the waste of public money in absurd researches into the pedigree and antecedents of the pauper population'.[52] Mackay had little patience with the English and Welsh settlement laws, and evidently preferred the Scottish system.

Under the old poor law, every parish had its own housing stock. Much of that parish housing was sold off under a permissive Act in 1835, which was designed to facilitate the conveyance of workhouses and other property of parishes.[53] Nevertheless, many properties remained in the hands of parish officers in the form of houses, agricultural land, allotments, old poor law

---

[49] *The Minority Report of the Poor Law Commission. Part 1: The Break-up of the Poor Law* (London, 1909), p. 401.

[50] Cited in T. Mackay, *A History of the English Poor Law*, vol. III: *From 1834 to the Present Time; Being a Supplementary Volume to 'A History of the English Poor Law' by Sir George Nicholls* (1854, London, 1900), p. 363.

[51] 39 & 40 Vic., c. 61.

[52] Mackay, *History of the English Poor Law*, vol. III, p. 365.

[53] 5 & 6 Wm IV, c. 69. For examples of such sales, see Leics. CRO, DE 801/18 (Kirby Bellars vestry book, 6 April 1838), here involving nine poor houses and one coal house on the waste, value £80; or see *ibid.* (10 May 1839), for the sale of a further house; or Leics. CRO, DE 829/86 (Bottesford vestry book, 17 February 1836), ejecting the poor from such houses prior to selling them; or Leics. CRO, G/1/57/1 (Ashby union letter book, on sale of property at Heather, 25 September 1840), p. 6. An advantage of such sales to overseers was that they could then rate the houses, thus lowering the general rate. This motive, with the avoidance of maintenance costs, and the need to raise money for workhouse building and debt repayment, help explain why this Act was often acquiesced in at parish level.

workhouses,[54] and so on. Their details had to be entered in a special book, or *terrier*. Overseers had to obtain rents for them, and ensure that the rents on these cottages were in account.[55] They were responsible for making repairs to parish property, and for receiving and accounting for other income from parish investments, which had to be inventoried. In the early days of the workhouse, property such as furniture, utensils, clothes, garden crops, pigs, and so on was contributed to the workhouse by parishes. As in the West Ward union (Westmld.), these were itemised and a record was kept 'so that the overseers know which belong to their own parish'.[56] Some parish properties and investments were gradually taken over by the union guardians, although they were still credited to the parish in union accounts.[57] Countless such assets remained with the parish, as is also clear from vestry minutes, the Annual Reports of the Local Government Board, and even directories.[58] In this regard, the onus was still on the parish, on its enumerated property, on the idea of things belonging to it.

Some responsibility also remained with the overseers in affairs of illegitimacy. The earlier orders of filiation and punishment of parents ended with the 1834 Act, if we leave aside offences under the vagrancy Acts, and workhouse relief perceived or internally structured as a form of penalty. Overseers could still apply to Quarter Sessions for an order against the putative father to reimburse the parish for an illegitimate child's maintenance, and that order could extract money by distress and sale of goods or directly from the father's wages.[59] They

---

[54] The Cottingham (Yorks.) workhouse, for example, remained under the control of the overseers after 1834. J. Whitehouse, *Cottingham's Care of its Poor to 1834* (Cottingham, 1970), p. 4.

[55] 'Rents of tenements – neglect of overseers to collect – auditors' duty in such cases', *Official Circulars*, vol. II (3 January and 14 January 1842), p. 239; 'Overseers – duty of in reference to the rents of parish cottages', *Official Circulars*, IV (22 August 1844), p. 171; Leics. CRO, DE 829/86 (Bottesford vestry book, 28 March 1837).

[56] B. Tyson, 'The Mansion House, Eamont Bridge, Cumbria: a tercentenary history of its owners, occupiers and associations', *Transactions of the Ancient Monuments Society*, 31 (1987), p. 172 n. 44.

[57] Davis and Owston, *Overseers' Manual*, pp. 45–6.

[58] For example, Francis White's *History, Gazetteer, and Directory, of Norfolk and Norwich* (Sheffield, 1854), pp. 439–40, on parish cottages in Guist.

[59] 4 & 5 Wm IV, c. 76, ss. 69–76; Archbold, *The Act for the Amendment of the Poor Laws*, pp. 29, 120 n. 65. The sums were meant to support the child, not the mother, although

might do this, for example, if the father neglected his duty, or the mother died or was incapacitated. A woman's illegitimate children now had to be maintained by her husband if she married until they were sixteen years old, or until she died, regardless of their putative father.[60] This was partly intended to make such mothers seem less attractive as marriage partners than was (reportedly) the case under the old poor law, and thus to alter behaviour by indirect means. It was decided, however, that such children did not take their step-father's settlement, and their earlier settlement persisted (which for illegitimate children born after the 1834 Act was that of the mother).[61] It therefore fell to the overseers of that settlement to ensure that the step-father performed his duties with regard to such children, a task that could well exhaust their persistence and resources.[62] Following an Act in 1844 which took illegitimacy proceedings out of the hands of the poor law authorities, and turned them into a civil matter between the parents, overseers could no longer obtain an affiliation order against the father of an illegitimate child, and they were meant to abstain from interfering in applications for illegitimacy orders against the supposed father. From then the mother alone had to proceed through petty sessions against the alleged father for maintenance or other payments, and overseers were not thereafter meant to receive money for an illegitimate child under such an order.[63]

---

they were payable to the mother. Overseers also had legal powers to reclaim relief advanced as a loan. See 'Relief – proceedings for the recovery of relief by way of loan', *Official Circulars*, vol. VII (19 October 1846), pp. 197–8.

[60] 4 & 5 Wm IV, c. 76, s. 57.

[61] Archbold, *The Act for the Amendment of the Poor Laws*, p. 117. Illegitimate children born before 14 August 1834 took their place of birth as their settlement, and were not entitled to take settlement from their parents. Illegitimate children born after that date took their mother's settlement until they were sixteen years old. Their settlement then reverted to their place of birth, unless they had since gained another in their own right. Holdsworth, *Handy Book of Parish Law*, pp. 235–6.

[62] Archbold, *The Act for the Amendment of the Poor Laws*, pp. 100–2, n. 48.

[63] 7 & 8 Vic., c. 101, s. 7; Nicholls, *History of the English Poor Law*, vol. II, pp. 359–60 (Nicholls called this Act a 'Second Amendment Act', given its importance in this and other matters, *ibid.*, p. 365); 'Operation and construction of the Act – liabilities of persons relieved', *Official Circulars*, vol. IV (30 September 1844), pp. 149–51; *Report of the Committee on One-Parent Families* (Cmnd. 5629, HMSO, 1974), p. 119; D. J. V. Jones, *Rebecca's Children: A Study of Rural Society, Crime, and Protest* (Oxford, 1989), pp. 348–9.

Overseers' responsibilities extended to the burial of paupers. They had to make provision for any dead person found in the parish to be buried, taking care to keep within constraints placed upon the expenses of pauper burials. These burials under the new poor law, usually guided by overseers, were often conducted with more respect and decency than historians have hitherto appreciated.[64] As a rule, the costs of pauper burials were meant to be paid for by guardians.[65] If there was a parish burial board, the overseers had to pay from the rates any sums that the Board directed. In some cases, extra complications lay in the fact that the burial board and the parish were not co-extensive, and so such matters also had to be negotiated.[66] If a parish churchyard or burial ground had been closed, as increasingly happened, the maintenance of that area, with its walls, fences, and vaults, had to be paid for by the overseers.[67]

The binding of apprentices was considered to be a form of poor relief, as under the 1601 statute. Poor children were normally bound by the guardians and justices under the new poor law, for unionised parishes. However, overseers were intended to carry out the practical aspects of the apprenticing, and as such they remained very significant in the process, at least until 1844, when this role was curtailed (where a board of guardians existed).[68] They also retained some powers as far as apprenticeship to the sea service was concerned.[69] Guardians and overseers were also instructed to visit such apprentices, and servants bound from the parish, to check how they were being treated. Some such children were bound apprentice under the terms of

---

[64] As argued by E. Hurren and S. King, 'Begging for a burial: form, function and conflict in nineteenth-century pauper burial', *Social History*, 30 (2005).

[65] 7 & 8 Vic., c. 101, s. 31.

[66] Under 18 & 19 Vic., c. 128.

[67] Davis and Owston, *Overseers' Manual*, pp. 52, 58–9, 77–8.

[68] 'Apprenticing of pauper children – duty of overseers in regard to', *Official Circulars*, vol. III (9 August 1842), p. 3; 'Summary of duties of guardians and their officers, and of overseers', *Official Circulars*, vol. IV (30 September 1844), p. 157; 'Apprenticing poor children – notice to overseers not now necessary – construction of 7 & 8 Vic. c. 101, sec. 12', *Official Circulars*, vol. IV (5 November 1844), pp. 177–8; 'Apprenticing poor children – Order of Justices not now necessary – construction of 7 & 8 Vic. c. 101, sec. 12', *Official Circulars*, vol. IV (30 November 1844), pp. 178–9; 7 & 8 Vic. c. 101, s. 12.

[69] Davis and Owston, *Overseers' Manual*, pp. 95–6; 'Operation and construction of the Act – relief of the poor', *Official Circulars*, vol. IV (30 September 1844), p. 147.

parish charities, and overseers continued to have a major role in the receiving, disbursing and accounting of parish charitable funds.[70]

Defenders of the new poor law claimed that the election of guardians was a considerable advance in terms of local democracy. The electing constituency was in fact the largest of its period, comprising every ratepayer, including women – this was probably an electorate of over two million people by 1851. Elections were conducted by written papers, which was the first time this method had been used in local government. Such elections could be a fraught business, with plural voting according to rateable value, the questions of corporation, joint-stock company or other property, the gradual expansion of the franchise, and other issues of eligibility, let alone the innovations in voting method.[71] The Poor Law Commission also had powers to alter the voting arrangements in specific parishes,[72] which could aggravate the local complications dealt with by overseers. Before 26 March, the overseers in a *Register of Owners and Proxies* had to select every ratepayer who had been rated to the poor law for a whole year previously, and take note of other owners or nominated proxies who claimed the right to vote. Objections to the claims of owners were heard before the clerk to the guardians, notice of the time and place for this being fixed to church and chapel doors in the parish.[73] Overseers had to be present at such hearings, with their poor rate and other books, to answer any queries about eligibility to vote. After the election, a list of the elected guardians for the union or parish had to be put up 'at the usual place for affixing notices of parochial business in the parish'.[74]

Beyond the responsibilities and expenses relating to poor relief and the settlement laws, overseers had a large number of other responsibilities after 1834. They had to defray costs of perambulations of parish boundaries (commonly once every

---

[70] For example, Leics. CRO, G/7/148/1 (Belton overseers' accounts, 1901–25).
[71] Plural voting and some related arrangements were enacted by 4 & 5 Wm IV, c. 76, s. 50, replicating some earlier provisions under 58 Geo. III, c. 69.
[72] 4 & 5 Wm IV, c. 76, s. 51.
[73] Davis and Owston, *Overseers' Manual*, pp. 84–5.
[74] Ibid., p. 85.

three years), and indeed the setting up of boundary stones.[75] They had to levy sums for bath- and wash-houses for the parish (if it adopted the 1846 Act for Establishing Baths and Wash-houses for the Poor). They had similar responsibilities for librar-ies, museums, and lodging-houses, where these existed in their parishes.[76] Under the 'Act for Improving the Police in and near the Metropolis', overseers in the relevant parishes had to levy the whole of the police rate.[77] There were borough rates and watch rates, if the parish was partly inside and partly outside any borough not liable to county rates, or to county or district police rates. These usually involved a separate rate, like a poor rate, levied upon the part of the parish outside the borough, and a borough rate to be levied upon the part of the parish within it. Overseers were publicly accountable for the money, as with the poor rate. Similarly, for any parish that was partly within a borough, city, or corporate town, the overseers had to make out an alphabetical 'Burgess List' every year. Copies had to be made which were open for inspection. (There was a pen-alty of £50 for failing to make that list.) The overseers were also responsible in this connection for any adjoining extra-parochial places, which did not have overseers, but which had to be included for such rates.[78]

Another seasonal deadline facing overseers (to be done by 24 March every year) was the making out of a list of parish men (with details about them) who were qualified and could serve as parish constables. This had to be done following a vestry meeting of inhabitants. It had to include all resident men aged between twenty-five and fifty-five, rated to the poor or county rate, who were not exempt. Copies of this list had to be put up on the doors of all churches and chapels in the parish. Overseers also had to attend petty sessions with the list, answer questions on it, and when the constables had been chosen another visit to the doors of churches and chapels was required – to pin up the

---

[75] 7 & 8 Vic., c. 101, s. 60; 'Operation and construction of the Act – Poor rates – their assessment, collection and appropriation', *Official Circulars*, vol. IV (30 September 1844), p. 152; 'Parish – perambulation of boundary of', *Official Circulars*, vol. VI (1 August 1846), p. 106; Davis and Owston, *Overseers' Manual*, p. 51.
[76] Davis and Owston, *Overseers' Manual*, p. 52.
[77] 10 Geo. IV, c. 44, s. 20.
[78] Davis and Owston, *Overseers' Manual*, pp. 75–7.

names of those appointed. Furthermore, the costs incurred by a constable were payable from the poor rate by overseers.[79]

Then there were the returns that needed to be made to the committee for revisions of the county rate, returns which also had to give details about how the property had been assessed to find its annual value. The county rate was not assessed on a gross rent, but on a full and fair annual value. The poor rate under the Parochial Assessment Act (1836) was assessed upon net annual value. The overseers were thus confronted, or over-taxed, with two different principles for these rates, and for the county rate they had to add to the net rent the tenants' taxes and repairs.[80] The basis for the county rate had to be laid before a vestry in the parish. All ratepayers had a right to inspect it, and any appeals against it on behalf of the parish had to be made by an overseer to the Quarter Sessions. Once more, con-tention between parishes reared its head. The overseers had to ensure that the principles of their assessment to the county rate were the same as those for surrounding parishes, and that they were not paying through differential assessment a higher proportion of the county rate than other parishes. If the guard-ians failed to pay the rate to the county treasurer, the overseers had to do so instead, for their own goods were at risk from distress and sale by the justices.[81]

Compliance with the highway Acts was a further responsi-bility. Sums had to be paid from the parish poor rate to the highway board. Surveyors of highways could inspect the poor rates.[82] In some parishes, where highway rates had been levied for seven or more years before the 1862 Highway Act, the waywardens rather than overseers paid the contributions to the highway board. In the cases of 'highway parishes' – which did not maintain separately their own poor, and were not a poor law parish – the overseers of the poor law parish of which the highway parish formed a part were to act for the highway

---

[79] *Ibid.*, pp. 79–81.

[80] 'Rating – poor rate – county rates – Chertsey union', *Official Circulars*, vol. III (6 March 1843), p. 88; 55 Geo. III, c. 51.

[81] Davis and Owston, *Overseers' Manual*, pp. 81–3; 'Summary of duties of guardians and their officers, and of overseers', *Official Circulars*, vol. IV (30 September 1844), p. 158.

[82] 'Overseers – custody of rate-books', *Official Circulars*, vol. VII (31 October 1846), p. 151.

parish, levying a poor rate within it. In some cases, a highway parish formed part of two poor law parishes, and so implicated the overseers of both poor law parishes. Such circumstances predictably raised many difficulties, such as what property was eligible to be rated, by whom, and for what purpose, and what the spatial boundaries of rating were. Overseers had the same rights to levy rates for highway boards as for the poor law, and highway boards had to send a quarterly account of their expenditure to the overseers.[83]

The clerk of the peace sent out to overseers every year, on or before 20 July, a demand for a list of resident men who were able to serve on juries. There were many qualifications needed for such service, and very many exemptions (such as peers, judges, clergy, dissenting ministers, sergeants and barristers, solicitors, proctors, officers of court, coroners, gaolers, surgeons, chemists, officers of the army or navy, income tax or customs officers, high constables, policemen, or parish clerks). These all had to be considered by the overseers. Copies of these lists had to be printed. They had to be fixed to the doors of places of public worship for the first three weeks in September. The justices had to agree them in late September every year.[84]

By 10 June every year, clerks of the peace and borough clerks sent out instructions for the registering of voters for county and borough elections. Overseers and vestry clerks were responsible for returning the voters' lists, with the overseers facing fines of up to £500 for neglecting to do this.[85]

In many parishes, notably smaller and rural ones, which had not placed themselves under a local board of health after the 1848 Public Health Act, overseers were obliged to act against public nuisances containing anything that was offensive, such as foul sewers, drains, watercourses, insanitary wells, refuse pits, and so on. Acting with the churchwardens, they were to plan improvements, and put proposals before the ratepayers for their agreement. If they obtained that, they were then to carry out the suggested works, paying for them out of the poor rates.[86]

---

[83] Davis and Owston, *Overseers' Manual*, pp. 86–8.
[84] *Ibid.*, pp. 51, 88–90.   [85] *Ibid.*, pp. 51, 97.   [86] *Ibid.*, p. 96.

There were many other duties of, obligations upon, and costs payable by, overseers. These included dealing with any insane person 'at large within the parish',[87] about whom the overseer had to liaise with the relieving officer, justices, a physician or surgeon, and, if committed, the superintendent of an asylum. Many of the costs associated with the insane were covered by the union common fund, assuming that the parish was in a union.[88] Where the insane person's settlement was unclear, as was quite often the case, s/he was paid for by the county. Overseers also had a role in the appropriation of property belonging to the insane person, or in making claims on a spouse or relatives to contribute towards the insane person's institutional maintenance.

Then there were the costs of other proceedings before justices; the paying of allowances to discharged prisoners with passes;[89] parish legal consultations and related bills; the enforcement in some circumstances of the Vaccination Acts, payable from the poor rates;[90] buying for the parish copies of legal manuals, official circulars, and statutes; buying stationery; agreeing and making the contributions to the union common fund; appointing and paying salaries and expenses to assistant overseers or collectors, if there were any;[91] making journeys on parish business; removing paupers to the workhouse; dealing with the registration of newly born children who were abandoned in the parish;[92] making claims against recent employers of pauper

[87] *Ibid.*, p. 91.
[88] *Ibid.*, pp. 93–5. If the parish was not in a union, the powers of the overseers and clergyman were greater with regard to the insane, and they could even have such a person discharged from an asylum, as long as s/he was not dangerous. *Ibid.*, p. 94.
[89] *Ibid.*, p. 86.
[90] *Ibid.*, pp. 52, 98–9.
[91] Collectors could be appointed under 7 & 8 Vic., c. 101, ss. 61–2, to perform some of the duties of overseers. See Nicholls, *History of the English Poor Law*, vol. II, pp. 363–4; 'Keeping of accounts – separate parochial accounts', *Official Circulars*, VII (17 March 1847), pp. 83–5; Leics. CRO, DE 829/86 (Bottesford vestry book, 5 April 1836), for an example and the terms of a pre-1844 appointment. On assistant overseers, see 59 Geo. III, c. 12; S. G. Checkland and E. O. A. Checkland (eds.), *The Poor Law Report of 1834* (1834, Harmondsworth, 1974), p. 188 (reporting paid overseers in 3,249 parishes in 1831); Davis and Owston, *Overseers' Manual*, pp. 5–7; Holdsworth, *Handy Book of Parish Law*, pp. 197–9. See also Archbold, *The Act for the Amendment of the Poor Laws*, p. 20. In the nineteenth century, such officers were usually paid between £8 and £30 per annum.
[92] Davis and Owston, *Overseers' Manual*, p. 79.

artificers who had been paid in truck,[93] and so on. Where a vestry had adopted the 1833 Lighting and Watching Act, further levies for that purpose were necessary, which had to be kept separate from the poor rate.[94] The rate here also had to be made public, like the poor rate.[95] Some of these obligations could be lightened by one or more assistant overseers or collectors, nominated by the vestry, and appointed by two justices.[96] The central authority could insist on the appointment of a collector, if it thought necessary, in which case the guardians usually (local Acts aside) appointed that officer. There has been little research on these paid officers, and it is not clear how numerous or common they were, or in what regions or types of parish they were most used. They had to obey 'a majority' of the parish overseers. The overseer was still responsible and legally answerable for much of their activity, especially if it could be shown that they had not been vigilantly supervised.[97]

It is hard to find detailed breakdowns of expenditure spent directly by overseers which are immediately comparable with the sums spent by guardians. The many different heads of expenditure usually make this problematical, and in one real sense *all* expenditure by guardians was incurred by overseers, given the channels of funding. However, we do have something close to such a comparison for fifty-six townships of the Wirral union, in yearly summary for 1851–9, and in detail for the year ending March 1859. These detailed accounts cover almost all

---

[93] Under 1 & 2 Wm IV, c. 37, s. 7, overseers had the duty of proceeding against employers who over the previous three months had paid any newly pauperised artificer in truck. They could reclaim from that employer the wages which should have been properly paid in money, and use such sums to recompense the parish for any costs in relieving the person, any remainder going to the artificer. This expedient was strongly advocated by the Poor Law Commissioners and Edwin Chadwick, who seized upon it as a way to claim back parish expenditure from truck-using employers. 'Truck system – Circular to the clerks of boards of guardians', *Official Circulars* (30 January 1844), pp. 47–8.

[94] 3 & 4 Wm IV, c. 90; 'Duty of overseers under Lighting and Watching Act', *Official Circulars*, vol. VI (16 May 1846), p. 90; 'Whether duty of assistant-overseer to collect lighting rate', *Official Circulars*, vol. VI (19 May 1845 (*sic*) 1846), pp. 90–1.

[95] Davis and Owston, *Overseers' Manual*, p. 91.

[96] As under 59 Geo. III, c. 12, s. 7.

[97] Davis and Owston, *Overseers' Manual*, pp. 65, 104. An overseer could not simultaneously be an assistant overseer, mainly because the latter was a paid officer. 'Overseer not eligible for the office of assistant overseer', *Official Circulars*, IV (12 February 1844), p. 62.

expenditure, for whatever purpose.[98] Overall in the year 1858–9, the guardians spent £14,588 while the overseers spent £2,254. Between 1851 and 1859, the respective sums were £99,521 and £14,830. In other words, about 13 per cent of all expenditure accounted here was being spent directly by overseers. (Overseers spent about 14 per cent of expenditure immediately connected with poor relief, over the nine years.) There was in fact considerable variation between townships in the Wirral union, with overseers spending anything between 1 and 27 per cent of all expenditure. It is hard to know how the Wirral union compared with other unions, although this township variation was also true of the Bolton union.[99] The Wirral accounts suggest a union that was well organised, albeit one that had earlier received much Irish immigration, notably to Birkenhead. At township level, overseers' spending as a percentage of overseers' plus guardians' expenditure was weakly correlated with population density.[100] In other words, overseers may have played a relatively greater role in disbursing relief in the more urban townships or parishes, such as Birkenhead, Tranmere, or Liscard. This may suggest their special value as welfare officers where pressure was greatest on other union officials. In other words – using such a narrow gauge of the role of overseers – it might be wrong to suppose that overseers played the most prominent role in 'traditional', rural or market-town parishes, where perhaps continuities from the old poor law and 'high' out-door relief were more obvious. However, such local and regional administrative variations remain to be fathomed more deeply.

The Poor Law Commission was deeply suspicious of overseers. In its more sympathetic moods, it thought them liable to pauper intimidation, which certainly occurred.[101] Yet in general

---

[98] *Select Committee on Irremovable Poor*, XVII (1860), pp. 464–5.

[99] I am grateful to Steve King for this observation.

[100] Pearson's correlation coefficient was 0.388, sig. = .003, N. = 56.

[101] Checkland and Checkland (eds.), *Poor Law Report of 1834*, pp. 182, 232–3; Leics. CRO, DE 829/86 (Bottesford vestry book, 31 March 1834), taking steps 'for the mutual protection of property in consequence of malicious attacks to destroy that of the parish officers . . . That this Meeting view with detestation such cowardly attacks upon parish officers property in consequence of the faithful discharge of their duty. – think it expedient to use every exertion in their power to detect and put down the same'; P. Carter, 'Manifestations of enclosure resistance in Middlesex, 1656 to 1889: a study of common right assertion' (Ph.D., University of Middlesex, 1998), pp. 223–4.

it viewed them as prone to 'jobbing' behaviour, using their posts to maximise profits from their normal professions, whether as tradesmen, artisans or farmers; and it felt that their interests would sway decisions about relief.[102] This had been a rather strongly worded theme in the Poor Law Report of 1834.[103] The Commissioners repeatedly expressed this, one suspects echoing a stereotype of the old poor law, to 'defend' against 'defalcation', 'dishonest spirit and the facility for its gratification', 'embezzlement', 'defaults' and financially 'pernicious habits'. Apparently nothing less than 'a strict surveillance' of overseers was needed.[104] This thought obsessed Edwin Chadwick, and, coupled with influences of evangelical religion, it contributed to the unprecedented stress on auditing accounts that erupted into English and (less effectively) Welsh administration after 1834. Overseers bore the brunt of this. The auditor gave fourteen days' notice to overseers of his audit, advertising the fact in a local newspaper. All books had to be made up and balanced for the occasion. Public notice of the audit involved overseers in yet another trip to the churches and chapels, where the moral dimension of their roles was also meant to occur to them – and where the nineteenth-century buttressing of local office-holding by religious motives and education ought to occur to us. Overseers had to attend the audit, 'and every adjournment thereof'. Warrants of overseers' appointments had to be shown, 'for the satisfaction of the auditor'.[105] All accounts and vouchers had to be produced. Declarations had to be signed in their presence. Legal receipts for balances from previous overseers had to be presented. Forfeits of 40s. were payable by overseers for a long list of possible neglects, refusals, altered accounts, failure to allow rates to be inspected by ratepayers, failures to publish them by public notice, and so on, leading on to more serious

Under the administrative structures of the new poor law, overseers were more protected from intimidation, which was often now directed against guardians and relieving officers.

[102] Nicholls, *History of the English Poor Law*, vol. II, p. 245.
[103] Checkland and Checkland (eds.), *Poor Law Report of 1834*, pp. 180–90.
[104] Davis and Owston, *Overseers' Manual*, p. 65. Or see Nicholls, *History of the English Poor Law*, vol. II, pp. 245–7, 279.
[105] Davis and Owston, *Overseers' Manual*, p. 66.

penalties for perjury. The auditor could surcharge any parish officer for any deficiency, loss or unaccounted-for sum.[106]

In fact, one change from the old poor law was the multiplication of fines and penalties now placed upon overseers. These included fines of £2 for neglecting a warrant from a justice. There was a penalty of £5 for disobeying the orders of justices or guardians with regard to instructions from the Poor Law Board. The same fine applied for neglecting to list men eligible as constables. A fine of between £2 and £5 could be incurred for trying to make a poor person chargeable to another parish, or inducing any such person to leave their parish and become a charge elsewhere. There were financial penalties upon overseers for book-keeping inexactitude, neglect or non-compliance. A penalty of £100 could be incurred for providing for profit (in their own or another's name) any goods, materials or provisions for the workhouse, or for the parochial poor, or for being indirectly involved in such a contract. Nor could the overseer furnish anything, for his own profit, in the form of parochial relief to any person in the parish or union – the penalty here was £5. Anyone involved in contracts to supply goods or provisions for the poor could not become an overseer. (Indeed, pleading this was probably the best way to avoid the job.) Systems of 'farming' the poor, as sometimes found under the old poor law, had occasionally involved profit to the overseer, and clearly this aspect of such schemes had to end under the new poor law – although some types of 'farming' could survive, for example, with regard to the 'fostering' outside the workhouse of some orphan children. There were penalties upon overseers of up to £20 for wilfully wasting or purloining any goods belonging to a parish or union, with subsequent disqualification from office-holding. The same fine applied for failing to collect sufficient rates, or not paying those sums to the guardians.[107] Many items were now deemed to be illegal payments – churching women, killing birds, coroners' inquests, repairing parish pumps, refreshments while on duty, marrying paupers, and so on – and overseers had to be aware of those. Auditors could proceed

---

[106] *Ibid.*, pp. 66–7.
[107] 'Operation and construction of the Act – Poor rates – their assessment, collection and appropriation', *Official Circulars*, vol. IV (30 September 1844), p. 151.

against overseers for any such reasons, obtaining summary convictions before justices, and the justices had no powers to review the auditor's decision. Justices could convict overseers for misapplying parish funds, and could fine them treble the amount of misapplied money.[108] Overseers could be imprisoned for failing to hand over their books to their successors. Any fraudulent interference by them in the process of electing guardians carried severe penalties, with imprisonment for up to three months, with or without hard labour. In principle, an overseer was only culpable for his own practices, not for those of his associate overseer; but in some cases where there were two overseers in a parish the balance of blame was difficult to ascertain.

We need to remember that the office of overseer was an *unpaid* job. Indeed it could even be imposed on people against their will by justices. Overseers were also usually running their own private business or employment, keeping their own accounts, employing other people, and having lengthy working days. They were never allowed to charge for loss of their time when executing parish business. Nor were the benefits of office promising. As noticed above, there were strict safeguards after 1834 against any person in private business who benefited in any way from acting as an overseer. Making this office so regulated, so prone to penalty, so bereft of personal advantage, and reducing its powers, prestige and repute – indeed, even vilifying its holders, as in the 1834 Poor Law Report – conduced strongly to the subsequent extension of paid professional, non-local administrators in public welfare services. After all, it is hard to believe that people would voluntarily do such a time-consuming job on the post-1834 terms, as outlined above. The really remarkable fact is that, for a century across about 15,000 parishes, countless thousands – perhaps half a million people – did so.[109] That was testimony to the on-going strength of personal reputation and local community sentiment long after 1834,

---

[108] 'Recovery of balances from a defaulting overseer, who became insolvent', *Official Circulars*, vol. IV (27 June 1844), p. 103.
[109] There were 14,926 civil parishes in England and Wales in 1881, and 14,684 in 1891. *Census of England and Wales, 1891*, vol. IV: *General Report, with Summary Tables and Appendices*, p. 307. A civil parish was defined then as an area for which a separate poor rate can be made, and a separate overseer appointed.

which resisted the de-localising effects and costs of professional-isation. For this was in truth a voluntary participatory job, of a closely and advantageously local nature, 'serving' the local community, which eventually went to the wall because of distrustful and excessive demands being placed upon it. There may have been a gain in 'professionalism' as a result – and yet this change was in time to contribute to what, in the twentieth century, came to be widely seen as a decline of local knowledge and responsibility, neighbourly accountability, the importance of one's personal standing, and of participatory community spirit.

It is evident that overseers continued to play a vital role long after 1834. They must have agreed with the Board of the Billesdon union (Leics.) in 1862, when it resolved: 'That the time of the Overseers was already sufficiently taxed without having more duties thrown upon them.'[110] It is true that their scope for independent action on behalf of their parish, and the leeway allowed them, had been circumscribed by the new poor law and subsequent attempts at micro-management by the poor law authorities, who displaced some earlier roles of JPs and created many new ones for themselves. Nailing their many notices to the church door, badgered by paupers and their relatives, and dealing with guardians, relieving officers, auditors, local boards, justices, let alone the central authorities, weary overseers must often have wondered if they themselves were being nailed up. Yet many overseers went on to become guardians or relieving officers – there was much movement between these offices.[111] And the guardians relied upon overseers to finance the new poor law. Indeed, overseers' duties went much further than that, their office remaining an extremely arduous one throughout the nineteenth century.[112]

---

[110] Leics. CRO, G/4/8a/4 (Billesdon union minutes, 1861–6), p. 79.

[111] E. C. Midwinter, *Social Administration in Lancashire, 1830–60: Poor Law, Public Health and Police* (Manchester, 1969), pp. 32, 41–4, the 'salaried staff was, in the main, the old guard redressed'; E. Whelan, 'An examination of the continuity of poor relief between the old poor law and the new poor law: a study of the Oundle and Thrapston unions of Northamptonshire' (MA dissertation, Centre for English Local History, University of Leicester, 2004), p. 61; R. Howes, 'The Industrialisation of Wigston Magna' (MA dissertation, Victorian Studies Centre, University of Leicester, 2002), p. 70.

[112] My discussion here has concentrated upon the role of overseers in unionised parishes. Where parishes remained outside unions – and for some decades many did, because of regional opposition to the 1834 Act, or local Acts, or the survival of Gilbert unions – the role of overseers was arguably even greater, continuing very much as it

Overseers were finally abolished from April 1927, by the Rating and Valuation Act of 1925, alongside over 14,000 rating areas, their powers being transferred to county boroughs and rural districts.[113] The North-Western Association of Assessment Committees, whose meeting in March 1927 was reported on in *The Times*, featured a speech by Thomas White, of the West Derby union (Liverpool), who was about to become chairman of the Central Valuation Committee in London. Looking forward to his new job, Mr White nevertheless thought that

there ought to be an expression of regret that a great body of voluntary local administrators – namely, the overseers of the poor for England and Wales – would this week pass into history after an existence of centuries. In 14,000 local governing areas in this country the overseers would be extinguished, or appear in another guise, but the change meant the placing on the retired list of a vast army of men who had given unstinted and devoted service, who were leaving the rating and assessment business of this country in a highly satisfactory condition. That body of men ought not to be allowed to pass out of sight unhonoured and unsung.[114]

This statement elicited loud cheers from his audience.

---

had been in that area under the old poor law. In parishes not under guardians or a select vestry, the overseers had the whole management of the poor, although they were still under the control of the Poor Law Commissioners. Archbold, *The Act for the Amendment of the Poor Laws*, p. 19.

[113] 15 & 16 Geo. V, c. 90; 'Rating reform. The new valuation scheme', *Times* (4 May 1925), p. 11, col. A; 'Rating and poor law. Mr. N. Chamberlain on slum-clearing', *Times* (5 May 1925), p. 13, col. C; 'Rating reform. Municipal budgets and industry. Lord Derby's review', *Times* (6 May 1925), p. 10, col. A; 'The Rating Bill. Assessment Committee's criticism', *Times* (13 May 1925), p. 5, col. G; 'Rating reform. New Bill in the Commons. Health Minister on the scheme', *Times* (14 May 1925), p. 16, col. E; 'Rating Bill in committee. Overseers abolished', *Times* (12 June 1925), p. 13, col. F; 'Rating and valuation Bill. Sir Kingsley Wood's reply to Dorset guardians', *Times* (11 July 1925), p. 11, col. B; 'Poor law unions and Rating Bill. Certain clauses opposed', *Times* (21 November 1925), p. 7, col. E; 'New rating era. Transition in the north-west. Tribute to overseers', *Times* (29 March 1927), p. 9, col. A.

[114] 'New rating era. Transition in the north-west. Tribute to overseers', *Times* (29 March 1927), p. 9, col. A. There were also a small number of overseers who were women, and this had been permitted, but not encouraged, in the nineteenth century. See 'Eligibility of females to serve the office of overseer', *Official Circulars*, vol. VI (15 January 1846), pp. 19–20; 'Lady overseers of the poor', *Times* (30 April 1867), p. 12, col. E: 'the appointment of women to the office of parish overseer is not an unusual custom in country districts'. For interesting discussion of female guardians, see S. King, '"We might be trusted": female poor law guardians and the development of the new poor law: the case of Bolton, England, 1880–1906', *International Review of Social History*, 49 (2004), and his *Women, Welfare and Local Politics, 1880–1920* (Brighton, 2005).

CHAPTER 7

Three centuries of new parishes

*Looking back . . . upon England, as it was before the Reformation,
we find that . . . the religion of the country, by means of its forms
and ceremonies, was interwoven with the whole business of life . . .
The diseased growth of parishes frustrated the political as well as
the religious purposes of our old parochial system, if we may be
permitted to consider apart things which are, strictly speaking,
inseparable.*[1]

*Of late years, an abundant shower of curates has fallen upon the
north of England.*[2]

*The parochial system is, no doubt, a beautiful thing in theory, and
is of great value in small rural districts; but in the large town it is
a mere shadow and a name.*[3]

INTRODUCTION

The 1911 national census highlighted a remarkable fact. By that
date about 8,322 parishes in England and Wales (58 per cent of
the total) were not coterminous for civil and ecclesiastical purposes.[4] This phenomenon, which the census report emphasised

---

[1] R. Southey, in B. Coleman (ed.), *The Idea of the City in Nineteenth-century Britain*
(London, 1973), pp. 41–2.
[2] C. Brontë, *Shirley* (London, 1849), p. 1.
[3] Lord Shaftesbury, in *Hansard*, 3rd series, CXXXIX, 490ff, cited in O. J. Brose, *Church and
Parliament: The Reshaping of the Church of England, 1828–1860* (Stanford, 1959), pp. 205–6
n. 80.
[4] *Census of England and Wales, 1911. Area, Families or Separate Occupiers, and Population*,
vol. II: *Registration Areas*, p. iv, and vols. III–IV: *Parliamentary and Ecclesiastical Areas*, p. v.
The figures vary slightly in different sections of the census. In *ibid.*, vol. III: *Parliamentary Areas*, p. v, the Report refers to 'the differentiation between the area for ecclesiastical purposes and that for civil purposes which became so marked during the XIXth
century'. In *ibid.*, vol. II, p. iv, the Report also discusses how 'civil and ecclesiastical
parishes are coterminous only in a minority of instances'. By 1921, this situation was

as a matter of great concern, also raised apprehensions in earlier censuses.[5] It stood in contrast to the situation in the late eighteenth century or earlier, when the very large majority of parishes had been co-extensive for civil and ecclesiastical matters. At that earlier time, as throughout the medieval and early modern period, civil and religious affairs had been closely bonded together in parish life. Yet this was far less the case by 1911. Huge numbers of 'new' or reformulated parishes were created in the nineteenth century, often to form a parish or district for newly built churches. This process involved the separation of civil and ecclesiastical parishes and their functions, the 'parochialisation' of hitherto extra-parochial areas, and countless parish boundary changes, parish mergers, divisions and re-namings. This is an important subject which throws up many problems and insights for the historian. It bears on crucial changes affecting national life, including questions about the on-going vitality of nineteenth-century parishes, the nature of 'community' and belonging, issues of administrative efficiency, the separation of ecclesiastical and civil life, and the decline of religious influence.

Many of these changes affected so-called 'ancient' parishes,[6] while many involved 'ecclesiastical' or 'civil' parishes which

---

even more acute. See 'Ecclesiastical news: Bishop of Carlisle on church finance', *Times* (24 September 1924), p. 15, col. D.

[5] For example, *Census of England and Wales, 1871. Population Tables. Area, Houses, and Inhabitants*, vol. I: *Counties*, p. 72: 'No complete list of the Ecclesiastical Sub-divisions of the Country is published by the Privy Council, the Diocesan Registrars, or the Ecclesiastical Commissioners . . . the exact boundaries of these sub-divisions are often imperfectly known . . . Moreover, the precise designation or status of the several benefices, and the date of their formation, are points upon which there is often found to be some doubt.' The censuses struggled, with quite limited success, to come to terms with these relatively new divisions, the 1851, 1871, and 1891 censuses often contradicting or omitting details given in earlier censuses (e.g. on dates of ecclesiastical parish formation), being very incomplete in the information supplied, and frankly admitting the inadequacies of their printed information on these matters. The plea which the 1851 census 'ventured humbly to suggest' for 'the adoption of a uniform system of territorial divisions in Great Britain' went unheeded. *Census of England and Wales, 1851. Population Tables. Numbers of the Inhabitants*, vol. I: *Report*, p. lxxx.

[6] An ancient parish 'is generally understood to be a district or locality which is an entirety, both for ecclesiastical and for poor law or civil purposes, having its own church, its rector or vicar who receives the tithes, its churchwardens and overseers'. *Report from the Select Committee on Boundaries of Parishes, Unions, and Counties*, VIII (1873), p. 240.

had already been altered. Most parishes in the eighteenth century were 'ancient', that is they were both ecclesiastical and civil in function, the roles being inter-linked within the same territory. Under the old poor law, 'the ecclesiastical and the civil parishes were practically identical . . . and that state of things continued for a considerable length of time'.[7] (In fact, after the medieval period the introduction of poor law rating had probably done more than anything else to 'fix' parochial boundaries and other units.) Subsequent reforms were often dual-purpose, conducted for civil *and* ecclesiastical reasons. This means that it can be artificial or anachronistic to separate the processes of ecclesiastical and civil parish alteration, especially before the twentieth century. Indeed, many contemporaries used the term 'parish' vaguely, to mean either ancient, or civil, or ecclesiastical, or other legal categories of 'parish', and such vagueness can oblige similar usage among historians. Greater functional precision gradually emerged in the terminology – precision which would have been pointless to most people in the early modern period, and which resulted from later patterns of parochial change. In simple terms, an ecclesiastical parish was an area in which the incumbent had rights and responsibilities to residents; while a civil parish was one in which poor rates could be levied or an overseer appointed.[8] From the early seventeenth century, through to 1800 and beyond, one may conceive of a large majority of parishes having been essentially synonymous for civil and ecclesiastical matters, giving way to a situation, *c.* 1901, in which nearly half of these ancient parishes had civil and ecclesiastical functions which still coincided with each other. However, by the early twentieth century there was a huge separate group of 'ecclesiastical' parishes, while 'civil' parishes comprised another large group – the civil and the ecclesiastical miscellaneously overlapping – and many complex legal units and variously termed sub-entities existed. There were immensely complicated and regionally varied emphases and overlaps between all these. The administrative reforms of the first half of the twentieth century did little to simplify this situation, and often compounded it.

---

[7] *Ibid.*, p. 1.
[8] *Ibid.*, pp. 1–3; O. Chadwick, *The Victorian Church, Part II* (1970, London, 1980), p. 197.

In some ways, the growing separation of civil and ecclesiastical parishes reminds us of a situation that pre-dated the dissolution of the monasteries and the adaptation of the parish as the main unit of local administration from the 1540s. The Tudor period had seen the functions of parishes grow, as ecclesiastical units were used for new civil purposes, a change epitomised by the old poor law. In the eighteenth century, one is struck by the role of the parish vestries in lay affairs, by the bonds between secular and religious administration, by the dual roles of clergymen who also farmed, hunted, administered justice and the poor law, conducted vital registration, ran clothing clubs, penny banks, friendly societies, charities, and much more. One way to describe this was to say that the eighteenth-century church 'probably achieved a fuller integration of institutional, social, and religious forms than the English Church has had at any time before and since'.[9]

This was to change. By comparison, the nineteenth century was touched in many ways by medieval revivalism, and that occurred despite (or perhaps because of) industrialisation. Nineteenth-century interpretations of medieval architecture surround us today, its art and poetry were permeated with 'medieval' influences. This medieval church revivalism – with its raised altars, elevated and enlarged chancels, aisles to naves, pews facing the altar, high symbolism, ritualism, frequent eucharist, and diminished role for preaching and the pulpit – often necessitated new churches to carry such ideals into practice. Concepts of the clergy were swayed by the evangelical insistence upon a more 'spiritual', monastically austere priesthood, and by romantic or antiquarian medievalism. The Oxford Movement, the Cambridge Camden Society, *The Ecclesiologist*, and many other influential groups and publications elevated the clergy's spiritual role and the sacramental side of church life, argued for a refined and professionalised religious education, and even advocated clerical disengagement from secular affairs. Clerical magistrates, for example, declined steeply in number. The Oxford Movement's ideal of the clergy replaced

---

[9] R. E. Rodes, *Law and Modernization in the Church of England: Charles II to the Welfare State* (London, 1991), p. 78.

the Hanoverian relics. Parsons were dislodged by priests – James Woodforde gave way to Benjamin Armstrong.[10] An ecclesiastical parish appealed in principle to many who yearned to discard worldly secular roles. Such supposed 'medievalism' came alongside key administrative reforms, often conducted by Benthamite reformers who were disposed to keep the clergy out of civil management. The gradual parochial decoupling of the civil from the ecclesiastical, and the separation of local boundaries for secular and religious purposes, which was a key feature of this, departed noticeably from seventeenth- and eighteenth-century holistic, integrated presumptions of church life and civil administration.

These reforms sometimes influenced parish life in unpredicted ways. The parish was defended earlier as a moral ideal, as the basis for moral relations, symbolising Christian principles – but, however useful and realistic such a moral ideal may have been, it became far less credible when ecclesiastical and civil functions were separated. These religious–secular divisions were justified as clerical administrative and spiritual expedients, and often as civil reforms. In some ways they underline the vitality of the parish as a reconceivable and adaptable entity in the nineteenth century. Yet they disrupted relatively clear-cut, integrated units of local attachment, in which lay affairs had a spiritual overlay and shared personnel, in which economic relations had also to be defined as moral ones. They complicated and confused ideas of parish belonging, they undercut the parish as a moral ideal, and they splintered hitherto reciprocal and conjoint features of local life.

The most obvious exceptions to holistic, integrated parishes in earlier centuries were many outlying hamlets and townships in northern English counties, which had exercised powers confirmed to them in the 1662 Settlement Act to levy their own poor rates.[11] These were in practice civil, but not usually ecclesiastical, parishes, even though sometimes served by chapels of

---

[10] J. Woodforde, *The Diary of a Country Parson, 1758–1802* (1929, Oxford, 1978); H. B. J. Armstrong (ed.), *A Norfolk Diary: Passages from the Diary of the Rev. Benjamin John Armstrong, Vicar of East Dereham, 1850–88* (London, 1949); H. B. J. Armstrong (ed.), *Armstrong's Norfolk Diary: Further Passages from the Diary of the Reverend Benjamin John Armstrong, Vicar of East Dereham, 1850–1888* (London, 1963).

[11] 13 & 14 Car. II, c. 12.

ease. Townships had normally been defined much earlier by the nature of 'communal' farming, and they usually pre-dated parishes, which were a construct of the church. One can also find townships in southern, western and midland counties that had administrative roles akin to those further north. The 1662 Settlement Act explicitly allowed parochially subdivided township administration in northern counties, but it also referred to 'other counties', and so this was judicially permitted to apply elsewhere. In such cases of township administration parishes were often subdivided for civil purposes, but less commonly for ecclesiastical needs. This was because low-valued clerical endowments, problematical tithe returns and scanty fees from a scattered population worked against northern ecclesiastical division, ensuring that larger units were retained to provide a supposedly adequate living for the clergyman.

By contrast, in the nineteenth century, parishes were subdivided much more often for ecclesiastical purposes, notably via the Church Building and New Parishes Acts. Nineteenth-century ecclesiastical division of parishes was probably more pronounced than for civil parishes in earlier centuries – this seems highly likely at the national level, and was certainly true in the English south and midlands. In some nineteenth-century cases, newly formed ecclesiastical parishes (for example, in Sheffield) were roughly mapped on to pre-existing townships which in poor law terms had operated as civil parishes. In many other cases, ecclesiastical districts or parishes were formed as segments of a local area which had been, and continued as, an entire civil parish. Indeed, under the new poor law there was rather less motive to subdivide such a parish for civil purposes than was the case before 1834, because of the supra-parish layers of administration and finance in each poor law union, and the problems of coordinating that.

Civil parish subdivision and administration in the sixteenth, seventeenth and eighteenth centuries is largely unresearched at a national scale, going beyond a few local studies, much like ecclesiastical parish subdivision or merger is little researched for the nineteenth century.[12] The motivation, scale and overall

---

[12] There had been earlier attempts to reform parish structures, which went beyond many local Acts and initiatives. On parish unification or division, see 37 Hen. VIII,

geography of this remain obscure. As one moves into the nine-teenth century, the regional patterns of civil and religious ad-ministrative units have been little analysed. This is hardly surprising, crucial though the subject is. The early censuses, for example, say very little about the civil/poor law status of the various local units they record data for: the precincts, quar-ters, wards, liberties, villes, townships, boroughs, divisions, 'farms' (for example, St Helen, Berks.), 'priories' (for example, Sandleford, Berks.), chapelries, hamlets, tythings, villages, par-ishes, 'united parishes', extra-parochial places, detached parish parts, and so on. Even if the censuses had given more infor-mation about such statuses, in many cases one would still not know how temporary such status had been.[13] Parish subdivision into townships and chapelries, as recognised and legitimated by the 1662 Settlement Act, was certainly most common in nor-thern regions of scattered rather than nucleated settlement. Yet sometimes this seems to have been impermanent, opportunistic in response to poor law expediency and local property holding, for example to eliminate prior legal settlements via parish sub-division, which caused deliberate confusion in settlement-law arbitration.[14]

The new ecclesiastical parishes of the nineteenth century were formed in particular by the various new parish and related Acts especially after 1818, and by the authorities who created such new ecclesiastical parishes or districts (the Church Building Commissioners, the Ecclesiastical Commissioners, the

c.1; 17 Car. II, c. 3; 13 & 14 Car. II, c. 12. There had been debate in the 1621 Parliament and in the 1650s about the reformation of parish structures, and there was piecemeal rationalization of parishes under the Commonwealth and Protectorate in the wake of the Commonwealth survey, alterations that depended upon local initiatives. For discussion, see W. A. Shaw, *A History of the English Church during the Civil Wars and under the Commonwealth, 1640–1660*, vol. II (London, 1900). Among many pro-posals, there was even some talk in the 1650s about reconstructing parishes as similarly sized squares or rectangles, of four or six square miles, in a way (at micro-level) that appears to foreshadow the structures of subsequent American states, rather like an enclosed fenland landscape, or indeed some visual features of late seventeenth-century garden design.

[13] F. A. Youngs, *Guide to the Local Administrative Units of England*, vol. I: *Southern England* (London, 1979), and his *Guide to the Local Administrative Units of England*, vol. II: *Northern England* (London, 1991), while being extremely impressive and highly valuable, still omit many local units, administrative entities and changes in different periods.

[14] That process was contained by 7 & 8 Vic., c. 101, s. 21 (1844), which made it illegal to appoint overseers for any place not already having them.

bishops, or Parliament through local Acts). Their formation had a key influence upon church building programmes, the performance, reform and financing of the church, the status and incomes of the clergy, local administration and the role of the church in that administration, the framework for local education, and people's ideas of 'belonging' to a civil and religiously interconnected parish. These administrative reforms, coupled with the huge growth of private church building and benefaction, influenced parochial identity and tradition, and how the parochial system functioned.

The creation of new parishes could be via subdivision or merger of ancient parishes, by recently 'new' parishes or districts again being partitioned or altered, by adjustments to deal with extra-parochial places and detached parts of parishes, or by combinations of some or all of these processes. It affected many rural as well as urban areas, although its national geography has not hitherto been analysed. Its ecclesiastical dimension caused enormous numbers of clerically related disputes. These involved matters such as advowsons, boundaries, the rights of patrons, rectors and neighbouring incumbents, surplice fees, tithes, glebe land, external augmentation of clerical livings, church rates and repairs to churches, diocesan finances, endowments and funding of new churches, pew rights, burial grounds, parochial office-holding, parish charities, and other related subjects. There is an extensive and fascinating literature on new churches and their architects in the nineteenth century, notably by art and cultural historians. Yet the new parish creation that attended so many of them, and which often brought these churches into being, has been almost entirely neglected. So my discussion aims to shed further light on this subject, especially in connection with issues of parish and belonging. The main background questions to keep in mind – in the context of this book – are what does new parish formation tell us about the continuing vitality of the parish in the nineteenth century, and how did it affect local identities and senses of belonging?

EXTRA-PAROCHIAL PLACES

One needs initially to appreciate some of the oddities of parish structures that had come through into the early nineteenth century. Examples of this were the numerous extra-parochial places, and detached parts of parishes. A significant feature of new parish formation was the absorbing into parishes of many older extra-parochial places. Prior to 1858, these extra-parochial places were usually areas which historically made no provision for the poor, and which did not normally appoint overseers.[15] One could not 'belong' to them, for the purposes of poor law settlement, and one could not usually be removed to an extra-parochial place, even if one had done something there which would normally confer settlement elsewhere. They were also places where there was usually no church, no clergyman, no church rates, which were outside parochial jurisdiction and largely exempt from paying tithes. (The Crown had a *prima facie* right to extra-parochial tithes.)[16] In other words, in England and Wales these rather liminal places were interstices or anomalies in the parish system.[17] They were districts of 'unbelonging' in conventional parish terms, both for their inhabitants and for the places themselves; or they were places where one 'belonged' only by residence or property. In some instances they were places whose resources were customarily accessible because one belonged to certain places outside. They could be commons or ex-commons, forests or woodlands, undrained fenlands, poorly productive agriculturally, legally ambiguous and disconnected from local administration. They occasionally housed

---

[15] The new poor law authorities progressively extended the working definition of 'parish' to include extra-parochial places. Yet this was a definitional extension that they had to make explicit, and while it was in their interests to encroach in such a way, that understanding of the term was different to most earlier usage. For an example of this wide definition of 'parish' ('to include any place maintaining its own poor, whether parochial or extra-parochial'), see 'Non-resident relief – General Order', *Official Circulars of Public Documents and Information: Directed by the Poor Law Commissioners to be Printed, Chiefly for the Use of the Members and Permanent Officers of Boards of Guardians, under the Poor Law Amendment Act*, vol. v (1 January 1845), p. 12. (The editions used here, initially published in 1840–51, were the New York, 1970 reprint editions, bound as two volumes for the initial vols. i–vi, and vols. vii–x. These are hereafter cited as *Official Circulars*.) 'Extra-parochial', in such usage, still implied a place making no provision for paupers. Local administrative peculiarities were such that some extra-parochial places did make such provision before 1858, and even occasionally had their own overseers – but this was quite rare.

[16] R. J. P. Kain and H. C. Prince, *The Tithe Surveys of England and Wales* (Cambridge, 1985), p. 67.

[17] By comparison, there were no extra-parochial places in Scotland. A. Dunlop, *Parochial Law* (Edinburgh, 1841), p. 380.

inhabitants who were troublesome by repute, sometimes being districts that were irreligious, or places that were frequented by lay preachers and were venues for Nonconformist meetings.

Some of these were positioned on county boundaries, like Canwell in Staffordshire or Chute Forest in Wiltshire. The names of a few of these hint at their reputation, such as 'No Man's Heath' near the junction of Derbyshire, Leicestershire and Warwickshire, a place that was also on the edge of dioceses.[18] Or there was 'No Man's Land' on the Cheshire–Derbyshire border, or another so named in Wiltshire. Even more beguiling was the place of 'Nowhere', near Yarmouth (Norf.), a place of 484 acres, associated with 'fish-offices, manure-works, and the terminus of the Norwich and Yarmouth railway'.[19] Radical political gatherings were held in some extra-parochial places, bringing together people from different areas, taking advantage of weak policing and poor regulation. Some of the Chartist meetings around Leicester were held in extra-parochial Charnwood areas to the north-west of the city, where charismatic orators like Thomas Cooper stood on rocky outcrops to exhort large crowds. Yet the range of extra-parochial places and their social connections was very wide. Some 'hospitals' (the term could mean almshouses) were extra-parochial, like the medieval lepers' hospital and subsequent almshouses of Sherburn near Durham. By contrast, many extra-parochial places were elite or high-class in their social affiliation. These included emparked areas and gentry seats, depopulated villages, cathedral closes or precincts like Chichester, Canterbury, or Chester, religious establishments like abbeys and priories, castle grounds (such as Windsor or Chester Castles), most Oxbridge colleges, or the Inns of Court.[20]

---

[18] Youngs, *Guide to the Local Administrative Units of England*, vol. II, p. 81; J. M. Wilson (ed.), *The Imperial Gazetteer*, 6 vols. (Edinburgh, n.d., *c.* 1872), see 'No Man's Heath'.

[19] *Ibid.*, under 'Runham'; and see W. White, *History, Gazetteer and Directory of Norfolk* (Sheffield, 1883), p. 621. 'Nowhere' was also connected with the dean and chapter of Norwich, and with Acle. It is a matter of regret that 'Nowhere' does not appear to exist any more. It even has intimations of the 'non-places' in some postmodernist theory.

[20] The Inns of Court were historically extra-parochial. By 1873, it was said that 'The Inns of Court are parishes; but they have a special provision of exemption, which was rendered necessary in order that the Act [1868] with reference to extra parochial places should pass, because the members of the Inns of Court were excessively

For reasons of religious provision and social administration, there was pressure for extra-parochial places to be 'parochialised'. This meant either making them civil 'parishes' in their own right, or more akin to parishes, or joining them to parishes. After all, many of these places raised problems for local administrators, especially before legislation in 1857 and 1868 affecting their civil status.[21] Even after that many problems remained, and they were still usually termed 'extra-parochial'. There were many issues about church and clerical provision in such areas, and many ecclesiastical parishes were formed to deal with these. Then there were questions about how to support paupers in extra-parochial places.[22] The poor were said to suffer if they lived in such places, lacking a normal welfare system.[23] County funds were sometimes used for this. In other cases, adjoining

influential in the House of Commons, and they refused to allow the general Bill to pass, unless they obtained the exemption that they should never be placed in a union.' *Report from the Select Committee on Boundaries of Parishes, Unions, and Counties*, VIII (1873), p. 6.

[21] 20 Vic., c. 19 (An Act to Provide for the Relief of the Poor in Extra-parochial Places, 1857, effective from 1 January 1858). This Act effectively turned them into parishes for poor relief, poor rates, county police or borough rates, burial, removal of nuisances, registration of voters, and vital registration. If nobody suitable was available to be overseer, justices could appoint an overseer from an adjoining parish. The Poor Law Board, with the agreement of owners and occupiers in an extra-parochial place, could order that place to be added to a district administering the poor law under a local Act, if the guardians of that district agreed. A two-thirds majority of owners and occupiers of an extra-parochial place could cause its annexation to any parish, if the vestry of that parish agreed. 31 & 32 Vic., c. 122, s. 27 (effective from late 1868) laid down that for all civil purposes extra-parochial places were to be incorporated with the parish with which they had the longest common boundary. The sea shore was dealt with in a similar way. Everything was thereby 'brought within the area of rating'. *Report from the Select Committee on Boundaries of Parishes, Unions, and Counties*, VIII (1873), p. 5. However, extra-parochial places long continued after this legislation, raising issues for marriages and baptisms, and even having new types of places added. For example, army and air force stations could be deemed extra-parochial districts from 1868 and 1918.

[22] For an example concerning Haywood Forest in the Hereford union, see 'Relief – to a person residing in an extra-parochial place', *Official Circulars*, vol. V (13 August 1844), pp. 63–4. The guardians were instructed that they could not charge relief given to a destitute widow and her family residing in Haywood Forest to any parish, nor to the union common fund.

[23] *Report from the Select Committee on Boundaries of Parishes, Unions, and Counties*, VIII (1873), p. 4: 'in many cases the poor suffered very much. Some of these places were very thickly peopled; people had herded together there and congregated upon those spots, and when they were sick or disabled they were thrown upon the charity, as it were, of the adjoining parishes, and they suffered very much . . . Nothing could ever be done with them until the Statute the 20th Vict. c. 19 was passed.'

parishes had to contribute, as with parts of the Forest or Frith of Leicester.[24] A few 'extra-parochial places' (contrary to definition) even had overseers. Could justices appoint an overseer for an extra-parochial place?[25] (Justices were finally given powers to appoint overseers in them from 1858.) Where did one remove a pauper to who resided in an extra-parochial place? If a default settlement was claimed in an adjoining parish, or in a parish that supplanted an extra-parochial place, what was its legal validity? Under the new poor law, what contribution could an extra-parochial place make to union common funds, if it did not levy a poor rate? How might one extend the area of rating to include extra-parochial places, because that would spread the rate more thinly and thus benefit normal parishes? How might one rate extra-parochial places for the county rate? How should they pay fees for coroners? What were the obligations and entitlements of a JP who resided in an extra-parochial place (many such places were gentry seats), and did he have the right to sit *ex officio* on a board of guardians?[26] How should one deal with a situation where pregnant single women went to extra-parochial places to give birth, thus avoiding a parish settlement by birth for their children, and escaping other aspects of illegitimacy law? This occurred for example in the Forest of Dean,[27] or in an extra-parochial place (called Blockhouse) which 'was rather notorious in the city of Worcester . . . because it was a place where a vast number of illegitimate children were born . . . there were no overseers to follow the mothers, or the children, or the fathers'.[28] How should one register and charge fees for vital events in such places? Rents were abnormally high in some extra-parochial

---

[24] W. White, *History, Gazetteer, and Directory of Leicestershire, and the Small County of Rutland; together with the Adjacent Towns of Grantham and Stamford* (Sheffield, 1846), pp. 347, 530–1.

[25] Prior to 1858, it had been decided in court cases that overseers could be appointed for an extra-parochial place if it was a town or vill, but not otherwise. 'Overseers – for an extra-parochial place', *Official Circulars*, vol. IV (9 March 1844), p. 61.

[26] From 1844 a justice could sit *ex officio* on a board of guardians of a union or parish which had a boundary line with his extra-parochial place. 7 & 8 Vic., c. 101, s. 24.

[27] N. M. Herbert (ed.), *A History of the County of Gloucester*, vol. V: *Bledisloe Hundred, St. Briavels Hundred, The Forest of Dean* (Victoria County History, Oxford, 1996), p. 222.

[28] *Report from the Select Committee on Boundaries of Parishes, Unions, and Counties*, VIII (1873), p. 5.

places, such places being attractive to tenants because they did not usually levy a poor rate, a church rate, or pay tithe. This raised further economic questions or objections, relating to the price of land and property, the status of leases when parochial definitions changed, the unequal burden of maintaining the poor, the use of workhouses paid for by surrounding parishes but not by the extra-parochial place, the handling of irremovable or potentially irremovable poor (for example, the Irish in the Fens), the movement of labour from parishes to extra-parochial places on a daily working basis (an issue akin to open–close parish matters), and many other such issues.[29]

The creation of a new parish was often motivated by the proximity of one or more extra-parochial areas, and a new parish could also deal with other anomalies. Given these interconnections, it is worth considering the geography of extra-parochial places, before looking at the location of new parishes. Figure 7.1 shows this. I have constructed it from data on the ancient parishes of England and Wales held at the UK Data Archive,[30] J. M. Wilson's *Imperial Gazetteer* of c. 1872,[31] the decadal censuses, poor law returns and official reports, county directories, and details in some Acts of Parliament. This map plots 686 extra-parochial places, which are places I can discover to have been extra-parochial at some point in the nineteenth century. Most of them were long-standing in that status, at least until the civil changes of 1857–68. In a few cases their 'extra-parochial' status was in doubt among contemporaries, and was the subject of enquiry, topical avoidance, legal dispute or continuous ambiguity. For example, St Bartholomew, a tract contiguous to Sudbury, Suffolk, was 'held by some to be extra-parochial, by others to be within Sudbury borough'. Binbrook in Lincolnshire 'is held by some to include the hamlet of Orford, which others regard as extra-parochial'. The Tower of London 'claims to be extra-parochial, although we do not

---

[29] For examples of many of these problems in practice, see the complicated issues regarding the relations between Deeping Fen (an extra-parochial place) and Spalding, discussed in *Report from the Select Committee on Irremovable Poor*, XVII (1860), pp. 91–102.

[30] UK Data Archive (University of Essex): GIS of the Ancient Parishes of England and Wales, 1500–1850. Study number 4828.

[31] I am most grateful to Paul Ell for allowing me access to a recently created electronic version of the *Imperial Gazetteer*.

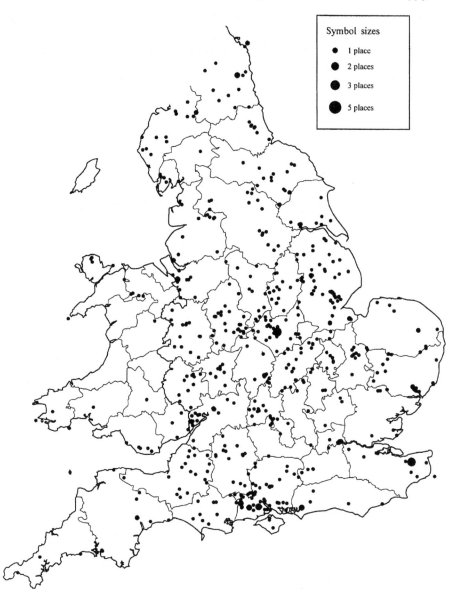

Figure 7.1   Extra-parochial places.

admit that it is so'.[32] A few places were perched in a mid-way status. For example, Haugh in Lincolnshire was 'an extra-parochial tract, but in some respects a parish'. The latter kind of ambiguity was in fact compounded by Victorian legislation.

All English counties had one or more extra-parochial places, but they were especially numerous in Hampshire, Lincolnshire, Leicestershire, Staffordshire, Nottinghamshire and Northamptonshire. The historical reasons for extra-parochial status were very varied indeed. In many cases, that status derived from royal forest or woodland situations.[33] This was true of many districts, seventeenth-century 'walks', 'lodges', and such named places, particularly in the New Forest (Hants.) and the Forest of Dean (Glos.), and also of Rockingham Forest (Northants.), Exmoor Forest (Devon), Groveley Wood (Wilts.), Melchet Park (Oxon.), Parkhurst (Isle of Wight), and the like. The royal status of many extra-parochial places is indicated by their place names: Kingsmark (Mon.), Kingsmarsh (Ches.), or King's Weir (Oxon.) are examples of this. Exmoor was subject to an Act passed in 1815, which 'ordained that the forest should be made a parish as soon as its population should so increase as to require a church; and that act took effect in 1856 . . . The church opened in 1857.'[34] Needwood in Staffordshire was used for royal hunting up until Charles I's reign. Like the Forest of Dean, it then underwent much alienation and disafforesting during and after the Civil Wars. It was extra-parochial until 1801, and was subsequently distributed among the parishes of Hanbury, Tatenhill, Tutbury, and Yoxhall. We will look in detail soon at the Forest of Dean, which is an excellent example of an extra-parochial royal forest, in this case being 'parochialised' from the early 1840s. Concentrations of extra-parochial places in the New Forest and the Forest of Dean are apparent in figure 7.1.

In some other cases, gentry or aristocratic seats and parks underlay the extra-parochial status: Althorp Park (Northants.), Belvoir (Leics.), Blenheim Park (Oxon.), Chatsworth (Derb.),

---

[32] *Report from the Select Committee on Boundaries of Parishes, Unions, and Counties*, VIII (1873), p. 5. Other quotations are from respective entries in Wilson (ed.), *Imperial Gazetteer*.

[33] For maps of medieval forests and crown lands, see O. Rackham, *The History of the Countryside* (1986, London, 1989), pp. 132–5.

[34] Wilson (ed.), *Imperial Gazetteer*, vol. II, under Exmoor.

Grace Dieu Park (Mon.), Markingfield Hall (Yorks.), and other places come to mind. Noseley in east Leicestershire, to take an example of about 1,300 acres, was extra-parochial because of the replacement of the parish church by the chapel at Noseley Hall in the fourteenth century.[35] The village was depopulated and emparked in the sixteenth century by the Hazlerigg family, fifty-three people being evicted, and there was total conversion to pasture by 1584. Noseley church was entirely demolished around 1549, leaving merely a fieldname – 'Churchyard' – to show where it had stood. ('The church is in ruins' is a statement that applied to a number of extra-parochial places.)[36] The parsonage was derelict in 1584. The Hall was the only house in Noseley in 1670. Deer were kept in the park, and formal gardens and two ornamental ponds were documented around the Hall in the early eighteenth century. Other ponds in Noseley have names like 'Woolpit', associated with sheep farming. Nearby in east Leicestershire, there was a good example of an extra-parochial place that was a religious establishment: Launde Abbey. Other examples of extra-parochialism which derived from religious institutions included Alnesbourn Priory (Suff.), Kirkham (Yorks.), Luffield Abbey (Bucks.), Malmesbury Abbey (Wilts.), or Ranton Abbey (Staffs.). Cathedral precincts, yards and so on were also usually extra-parochial.

Islands were often extra-parochial, such as Bardsey, Caldy, the Farne Islands, Lundy, Havergate, Puffin, or Skokholm. Some commons, or ex-commons, fell into the extra-parochial category – Alrewas Hays (Staffs.) was an example. There were many fenland or marsh areas which were extra-parochial, because of their limited habitation, late drainage and enclosure: Borough Fen, Byall Fen, Deeping Fen, Grunty Fen, Hale Fen, North Forty Foot Bank, Pelham's Lands, Rake's Farm, Rowland's Marsh, Welches Dam, West Fen, and others like these. In the Fens, marshy hollows without sediment, or old river beds like the Witham bed, often became extra-parochial, for these would take generations to dry out and were often not allocated upon enclosure. Or there were the Ferry Corner Plots which extended

---

[35] J. M. Lee and R. A. McKinley (eds.), *A History of the County of Leicester: Victoria County History*, vol. v: *Gartree Hundred* (Oxford, 1964), pp. 265–8.
[36] For example, Roosdown (Devon). Wilson (ed.), *Imperial Gazetteer*.

into Fosdyke Fen and Brothertoft.[37] Many districts in towns and cities were extra-parochial, like Blockhouse in Worcester, Castle Green in Carmarthen, Castle Inn and Christ's College in Brecon, or East Cliffe in Dover. Examples of castles which were extra-parochial included Chester, Lewes, Ludlow, the Tower of London, or Wallingford. Some institutions were in a similar position, as for example Bartholomew Hospital, comprising six acres on the south side of Sandwich (Kent), founded in the early twelfth century, which in 1871 'still exists, as an almshouse, with income of £766', and a population of fifty-one.[38] Other institutions occupying extra-parochial grounds were Norfolk County Jail, Lincoln Lunatic Asylum, Eastbridge Hospital in Canterbury, or St Cross Hospital near Winchester.

Beyond such categories, there were many extra-parochial places with their own miscellaneous reasons for such status. There was, for example, Rothley Temple (Leics.), which had once been the base for a commandery of Knights Templars. Most famously, there was Old Sarum (Wilts.) – William Cobbett's 'accursed hill'.[39] This was a decayed 'city' which sent two members to Parliament from the time of Edward I, until the 'rotten borough' was disfranchised by the Reform Act of 1832. John Constable drew it in 1829, and when David Lucas did a mezzotint based on that drawing, it was inscribed by re-using the words of St Paul: 'Here we have no continuing city.' In the 1870s it was 'represented by only remains of ditches and ramparts . . . now a dreary surface, partly under the plough, partly in a state of waste . . . The extra-parochial tract includes the quondam city, and bears the alternative name of Old Castle; but, in 1861, had only one house.'[40]

DETACHED PARTS OF PARISHES

Another feature of parish reorganisation involved detached parts of parishes. In many regions, parishes had detached external

---

[37] I am indebted to Betty Brammer for discussion of these areas.
[38] Wilson (ed.), *Imperial Gazetteer*.
[39] W. Cobbett, *Rural Rides* (1830, Harmondsworth, 2001), pp. xv–xvi, 37, 77, 121, 280, 297–8, 418, 455, 463.
[40] Wilson (ed.), *Imperial Gazetteer*.

areas, beyond intervening parishes, often some distance away. These were sometimes called 'foreign parts'. One finds many such examples in the Norfolk Broads, the Forest of Dean, Dartmoor, or Cumberland; indeed, there were examples in almost every county of such detached organisation. W. G. Lumley commented that 'This is one of the most remarkable matters, perhaps, which exist in our social or topographical arrangements . . . they exist all over the country . . . [they] create, of course, a considerable amount of inconvenience in the collection of the rates.'[41] Some of these involved exceptionally complex and much disputed boundaries, and some parishes had very many detached parts. For example, Welsh Hampton (Salop.) had about twenty-two detached parts lying to its south. Some parishes heavily comprised detached parts. Four constituent townships of Holme Cultram (Cumb.) contained 101 detached parts! Swinefleet (a township in the parish of Whitgift, West Riding of Yorkshire) comprised ninety-seven detached parts.[42] Some detached parts 'are really so intermixed that they cannot be described clearly in writing or language . . . the confusion is extraordinary . . . a mass of complex boundaries, and a perfect study to unravel'.[43] Detached parts could be urban as well: there was a detached part of Chelsea parish at Kensal New Town. The Crystal Palace stood on a detached part of Battersea parish.

In some cases, nobody knew how or why detached parts had come into existence. For example, when considering burial-board issues, it was said that 'the overseers of Measham [Leics.] cannot explain how this 12 acres came to belong to their Parish it is 6 miles distant from Measham in a direct line as the Crow flies and a portion of the County of Leicester and several other Parishes in Derbyshire intervenes between it and the Parish of

---

[41] *Report from the Select Committee on Boundaries of Parishes, Unions, and Counties*, VIII (1873), p. 6. They also caused major poor law problems where the links between parts crossed poor law union boundaries, because this 'serious evil' meant that the poor of a parish had to be dealt with by different unions' relieving officers. *Ibid.*, p. 7. See also 30 & 31 Vic., c. 106, s. 3, which partly covered poor relief in detached parts. New local government districts (e.g. sanitary districts) ran the risk of having boundaries which also crossed parish linkages of this kind.

[42] For these and many further such examples, see *Report from the Select Committee on Boundaries of Parishes, Unions, and Counties*, VIII (1873), pp. 40–2, 85, 241, 215–16.

[43] *Report from the Select Committee on Boundaries of Parishes, Unions, and Counties*, VIII (1873), pp. 41–2.

Measham'.[44] One can find cases where the detached part was over five miles from the centre of the parish it pertained to. Many detached parts owed their origins to separated portions of manors. Or they had become formed to deal with long-standing and conflictual zones of inter-commoning. Others were parts in forests, or former forests, which had provided parishes with fuel. Some were areas reclaimed from marshes or the sea, for example near Boston, allotted to certain parishes as detached parts. They may even have occasionally been rejected portions of a parish, practically adopted by another parish outside.[45] Their tithes were taken as though they were within the 'mother' parish.

In the Norfolk Broads there were many detached parts of parishes within the Halvergate 'triangle' of marshes, to the west of Yarmouth.[46] These areas of marsh were being exploited from an early medieval date. They were often some miles away from their parishes. They were used for sheep pasture, but also for salt pans as they were near the coast or on tidal creeks. Huge numbers of sheep were grazed on these marshes from the early medieval period, and their dung was taken 'upland' where it aided the fertility of arable land in the home parishes. Other resources here included reed, saw-sedge, osiers, some limited coppice-wood, rushes for floors and lights, thatch, coarse grass for fodder, and especially peat for fuel. In many regions, access to grazing grounds was an important feature of detached parishes, sometimes associated with transhumant pasturing. This was true of Dartmoor, Exmoor, the Lincolnshire marshes and fens, Charnwood, and countless other areas. In and around the Forest of Dean, parishes also used their detached areas to gain access to timber (which was partly needed for coal pits), wharfage space on the rivers Wye and Severn, coal and iron-ore mines, or mills in key locations, as well as sheep-grazing land. The Ordnance Survey provided widespread evidence of these

[44] Leics. CRO, DE 41/1/73 (1880, Measham burial district, response to the London Assurance Company).
[45] *Report from the Select Committee on Boundaries of Parishes, Unions, and Counties*, VIII (1873), p. 6.
[46] T. Williamson, *The Norfolk Broads: A Landscape History* (Manchester, 1997), pp. 42–7, 78–83.

detached parts across the country, attaching them cartographically by a line to the parish they belonged to. It allowed local people to inspect and query the sketch maps prior to publication, and made people more aware of detached parts. There were 15,416 'parishes or places' in England and Wales in 1871;[47] of these about 1,300 parishes had detached parts, and countless more if one includes the detached townships in northern English counties.

Detached portions were dealt with in a variety of ways during new parish creation. Many new ecclesiastical parishes incorporated them within their new boundaries, to make better spiritual provision for their inhabitants. For civil purposes they were often dealt with by the Poor Law Commission, and from late 1847 by the Poor Law Board, and civil adjustments could result in different boundaries than for the ecclesiastical parish. As with many extra-parochial places, and many other such reoriented areas of land, these detached places could find themselves outside any 'ancient' parish, inside a new ecclesiastical parish, and inside a different civil parish – and 'reforms' were themselves often 'reformed', exacerbating confusion as further parochial alterations were made. We will see examples of this shortly in the Forest of Dean. In the later nineteenth century the Local Government Board gained extra powers to alter parishes under the Divided Parishes Acts of 1876, 1879, and 1882. Under the 1882 Act, detached parts of extra-metropolitan parishes that were surrounded by another parish were to become part of that parish for civil matters, and if such a detachment had a population of over 300 it could become a distinct parish itself.[48] The Acts permitted detached parts to be joined with adjacent parishes, and dealt with the even greater anomaly of a detached part being in another county. Very many such cases were resolved in the 1880s, leading to many changes in parish boundaries. Even so, many of these detached parts survived into the twentieth century. The 1911 census listed them by county, and the 1921 census commented that 'Attention may be drawn to the large numbers of extra-parochial places and of detached

---

[47] *Report from the Select Committee on Boundaries of Parishes, Unions, and Counties,* VIII (1873), p. 239.
[48] 45 & 46 Vic., c. 58 (effective from 1883).

parts of ecclesiastical parishes that still exist.'[49] Many further boundary changes were thus required, often occurring in the 1930s, after the Local Government Act of 1929. Even as late as the 1980s, some detached parts of parishes were still being resolved.[50]

The phenomenon of detached parishes was thus one motive stimulating 'new' or altered parish formation, usually bringing detached parts into merger with adjacent parishes, rather than allowing them to remain separated from their earlier parish. It could stimulate both civil and ecclesiastical parish reform. This process of parish re-formation involving detached parts also suggests how local parish economies had been altering. Rather distant resources beyond the 'mother' parish, which were hitherto communally valuable and had sometimes caused local conflicts, were by the mid-nineteenth century (after Parliamentary enclosure) often wholly in private hands and thus legally inaccessible. Issues affecting tithe, glebe and clerical fees in connection with detached parts were also being resolved, for example by the Copyhold, Inclosure and Tithe Commission, who (if local landowners required it) had limited powers to redefine parish boundaries.[51] Detached parish links were being severed for financial, administrative and enumerative convenience, and this process was facilitated or accentuated as parishes became less self-reliant and more tied in to wider commercial and transport arrangements. Indeed, the Standing Orders governing railway construction necessitated greater clarity and simplicity of parish boundaries. The value of local resources found in detached portions also became relatively less important to the 'mother' parish's economy. This was partly because of transformed ways of making a living, and in some cases because those resources deteriorated through neglect, changing land use (e.g. shooting reserves, or recreational use), or

---

[49] *1911 Census of England and Wales. 1: Administrative Areas*, pp. 430ff; *Census of England and Wales, 1921. General Report with Appendices*, p. 33.

[50] K. P. Poole and B. Keith-Lucas, *Parish Government, 1894–1994* (London, 1994), pp. 213–14, on reform of detached parts of the Northumberland parishes of Allendale and West Allen in the mid-1980s.

[51] *Report from the Select Committee on Boundaries of Parishes, Unions, and Counties*, VIII (1873), pp. 86–8.

over-exploitation, which in the nineteenth and early twentieth centuries often affected coal or other mineral mines, coppice woodland, peat, reeds, osier beds and so on.

CHURCH REFORM, URBANISATION AND NEW PARISHES

Anomalies like the many extra-parochial places and detached parts were a chronic problem to civil and ecclesiastical administrators, which they tried to resolve by forming new parishes. With regard to ecclesiastical units, there were also many 'peculiars' which needed their status to be amended. There were nearly 300 of these 'peculiars' in 1832. These places were beyond diocesan jurisdiction – for example in matters of probate – having been assigned to another ecclesiastical person (the Crown, an archbishop, a bishop, dean, archdeacon, rector, etc.), and thus were different to extra-parochial places, while raising some similar problems. However, the greatest problems lay in the burgeoning growth of towns and cities. The nineteenth and early twentieth centuries saw dramatic rural out-migration and urbanisation, at a pace that exceeded any other European country. While about 65 per cent of the population had been resident in the countryside in 1801 (calculated for places with a population of under 10,000), by 1911 only 22 per cent was. The urban population had risen from 3 million to 28 million. Church seating in the towns was frequently inadequate. Deficiencies were especially apparent in London and the new industrial towns. Such seating was often in the form of reserved pews, which were inaccessible to poorer people. This deficiency was felt to be one cause of absence from church and irreligious habits among large sections of the working classes.

Many Victorian commentators felt that a population 'deprived of the corrective influence of morality and Christian principle, would contract habits and principles subversive of social order, and dangerous to the peace and welfare of the nation'.[52] They held it to be 'the moral duty of the state to

---

[52] J. C. Traill, *The New Parishes Acts, 1843, 1844, & 1856, with Notes and Observations, Explanatory of their Provisions* (London, 1857), pp. 18–19. Or see Revd Richard Yates, *The Church in Danger: A Statement of the Cause, and of the Probable Means of Averting that Danger* (London, 1815); E. Berens, *Church-Reform: By a Churchman* (London, 1828);

provide for the efficiency of the Church',[53] and to ensure that the church held the affection of the people. In the darker accounts, it was complained that 'a mass of heathenism has developed, and accumulated, and attained to such a magnitude and density in our large towns'.[54] There was an urgent need to bring the church into closer contact with urban dwellers, and to provide religious accommodation for them. Even by the end of the Napoleonic Wars, many contemporaries remarked on the towns about 'the state of spiritual destitution, as regards the Established Church', which was deemed (with some exaggeration) to be 'so appalling as to surpass description'.[55] Fear of urban radicalism compounded this concern. Over the coming decades it was hoped that church building, new parish formation, and many kinds of missioning and domestic visitation would help to deal with these problems.

It was hoped to restore the parochial system in many urban areas, such as Bethnal Green, and to recreate for urban districts the perceived benefits of the rural parish. This was to be a salient feature of nineteenth-century new parish formation in towns. 'We cannot deny the advantage of assimilating a town to a country parish', wrote the influential Thomas Chalmers. He advocated urban districts and visiting the poor, for purposes of spiritual and social welfare, views which he developed in the late 1810s and early 1820s in Tron parish, and the new parish of St John's in one of the poorest parts of Glasgow. Such practice was taken as having much wider applicability, especially by those connected with the evangelical movement, and was adopted by many bodies like the District Visiting Society. Chalmers wished to revive a feeling that a person's house be connected with its parish in the occupier's mind. However, the relation of the minister to his parish has 'to every moral, and to every civilising purpose, been nearly as good as broken up . . .

J. Walsh and S. Taylor, 'Introduction: the Church and Anglicanism in the "long" eighteenth century', in J. Walsh, C. Haydon and S. Taylor (eds.), *The Church of England, c. 1689 – c. 1833: From Toleration to Tractarianism* (Cambridge, 1993), pp. 18–19.

[53] Traill, *New Parishes Acts*, p. 19.

[54] T. Chalmers, *The Christian and Civic Economy of Large Towns* (Glasgow, 1821), cited in Coleman (ed.), *Idea of the City*, p. 42.

[55] Traill, *New Parishes Acts*, p. 20.

Every thing has been permitted to run at random; and, as a fruit of the utter disregard of the principle of locality, have the city clergyman and his people almost lost sight of each other.' The urban populations had outgrown the ecclesiastical system, and so had 'accumulated there into so many masses of practical heathenism'.[56] Church building, new parish creation, and the division of parishes into small districts, each under a deacon encouraging a local *esprit de corps*, were believed by Chalmers to be important means to remedy this. These should occur alongside voluntary district visiting, new schools, charity provision, improving the morale of incumbents, and so on, all such measures attempting to reconcile 'the principle of locality' to large cities.

There had been relatively little public church building in the eighteenth century compared with what occurred in the nineteenth century. Resource allocation during the Napoleonic Wars had also much delayed church building and parochial reformation, just as the wars had drawn many young men away from becoming clergy. Insofar as new urban churches had been built, they were often proprietary chapels, resting awkwardly as accessories to the parochial system. Many of these were erected between 1750 and 1830, often in new residential areas, catering to polite orders of society. In 1824, there were said to be 59 of them in London, and about 100 in London and its suburbs by the mid-1830s.[57] They charged high pew rents, and the poor were excluded. They tended to detract from parish affairs, and diverted congregations and income from parochial purposes. They had particular importance in evangelicalism, enabling the movement to find a place in many parishes where this would

---

[56] Chalmers, *Christian and Civic Economy*, cited in Coleman (ed.), *Idea of the City*, pp. 42–6; N. C. Masterman (ed.), *Chalmers on Charity: A Selection of Passages and Scenes to Illustrate the Social Teaching and Practical Work of Thomas Chalmers* (London, 1900). On Chalmers' influence, see D. M. Lewis, *Lighten their Darkness: The Evangelical Mission to Working-class London, 1828–1860* (Westport, Conn., 1986), pp. 35–8; H. D. Rack, 'Domestic visitations: a chapter in early nineteenth century evangelism', *Journal of Ecclesiastical History*, 24 (1973), pp. 359–60; D. E. H. Mole, 'The Victorian town parish: rural mission and urban mission', in D. Baker (ed.), *The Church in Town and Country-side* (Oxford, 1979), pp. 362–7; A. F. Young and E. T. Ashton, *British Social Work in the Nineteenth Century* (London, 1956), pp. 67–80.

[57] S. Baring-Gould, *The Evangelical Revival* (London, 1920), pp. 318–20, citing S. Leigh, *Leigh's New Picture of London* (London, 1824).

otherwise have been difficult.[58] Bishop Blomfield refused to allow any more proprietary chapels to be established in London.[59] Sabine Baring-Gould later judged many of them to have been put up by 'speculative pastors who hoped to attract a paying congregation'. Usually they were not consecrated, nor under the bishop, nor did they have districts attached to them. They relied heavily upon pew rents for their income, and some were in long-standing dispute with the parish rector. Rivalry over preaching was a common experience, for they often disregarded the still important principle that an Anglican clergyman should be pre-eminent, unchallenged, or at least courteously consulted, in his own parish. Baring-Gould thought the proprietary chapels were 'extremely ugly places of audition rather than worship'.[60] Many no longer exist. Whatever one's verdict on them, they were not designed with the poor in mind.

Among the priorities of church extension was the need to subdivide many large parishes, for reasons of population, acreage, and sometimes income – as for example in Leeds, Manchester, Liverpool, Sheffield, Bradford, St Marylebone, St George Hanover Square, St Pancras, and some other parishes in London.[61] Manchester had been only one parish, but by 1862 it had 'a vast number of parishes'.[62] Sheffield had only four churches in 1800, yet its population was already about 46,000. That population rose to 135,000 by 1851, by which time it had only eight churches. This situation in Sheffield changed quite dramatically in the second half of the century, when a further thirty churches were added, and many more were built in the twentieth century,

---

[58] On such 'entryism', see H. D. Rack, 'The providential moment: church building, Methodism and evangelical entryism in Manchester, 1788–1825', *Transactions of the Historic Society of Lancashire and Cheshire*, 141 (1992).

[59] P. J. Welch, 'Bishop Blomfield and church extension in London', *Journal of Ecclesiastical History*, 4 (1953), pp. 204, 210–11.

[60] Baring-Gould, *Evangelical Revival*, p. 320.

[61] Welch, 'Bishop Blomfield', pp. 203–4 (St Marylebone had a population of 75,624 as early as 1811, but could seat only 900 in church); P. Virgin, *The Church in an Age of Negligence: Ecclesiastical Structure and Problems of Church Reform, 1700–1840* (Cambridge, 1989), p. 34; J. H. Overton, *The English Church in the Nineteenth Century, 1800–1833* (London, 1894), pp. 145–7; F. W. Cornish, *The English Church in the Nineteenth Century, Part I* (1910, London, 1933), pp. 77–8. Throughout George III's reign, only about ten churches were built in London. *Ibid.*, p. 77.

[62] *First Report of the Select Committee on Poor Relief*, x (1862), p. 113.

mainly to cater for suburbanisation.[63] Dr W. F. Hook, the vicar of Leeds, faced with a population of over 150,000, advocated that his parish be subdivided into twenty-one vicarages, with their own churches and parsonages. He gave up £400 of his annual income and most of his living for this purpose, which came about through the Leeds Vicarage Act in 1844.

Other parishes faced the opposite problem: they were so small that they needed to be combined with others. This was true of a plethora of minute parishes in cities like London, Cambridge, Canterbury, Oxford, Lincoln, York, Bristol or Norwich. In the 1790s there were thirty-two parishes in Norwich, nineteen in Lincoln, eighteen in Bristol, sixteen in Colchester, and nine in Chester.[64] In such towns the complications can readily be imagined. York had about thirty parishes in the mid-nineteenth century: 'one street is in three parishes . . . another street is in four parishes, and Goodram-gate, another street, is in five parishes'.[65] In Lincoln, the different parishes ran 'into different portions of streets, so that it is next to impossible to know the boundaries . . . the houses on one side are in one parish, and the houses on the opposite side [are] in another parish . . . there are five or six parishes in one street'.[66] At least 153 parish vestries operated in London in the early nineteenth century.[67] As late as 1862 in the London City poor law union there were ninety-eight civil parishes, which made an average of only four acres per parish.[68]

---

[63] D. E. W. Harrison, 'The churches', in D. L. Linton (ed.), *Sheffield and its Region* (Sheffield, 1956), pp. 198–200; A. B. Webster, *Joshua Watson, the Story of a Layman, 1771–1855* (London, 1954), p. 60.

[64] Sir F. Eden, *The State of the Poor*, 3 vols. (1797, Bristol, 2001), vol. II, pp. 33, 177, 191, 416–17, 479. On numbers of parishes in such towns in the medieval period, see N. J. G. Pounds, *A History of the English Parish: The Culture of Religion from Augustine to Victoria* (Cambridge, 2000), pp. 122–3, 126–7, 130, 132. Plague and population change affected these numbers of parishes, notably in the late Middle Ages; but they remained more steady from the mid-seventeenth century, and even after the great fire of London the parish structure was mainly kept.

[65] *Report from the Select Committee on Irremovable Poor*, XVII (1860), pp. 3–4.

[66] *Ibid.*, pp. 203–5. On such a situation in Stamford, see A. Rogers, 'Parish boundaries and urban history: two case studies', *Journal of the British Archaeological Association*, 35 (1972), p. 61. Tithe for particular yardlands or parts of town fields was paid to individual churches, thus complicating matters still further in towns like Stamford or Cambridge. *Ibid.*, pp. 49–50; D. Hall, *The Open Fields of Northamptonshire* (Northampton, 1995), p. 110.

[67] S. Wise, *The Italian Boy: Murder and Grave-Robbery in 1830s London* (London, 2004), p. 78.

[68] *Third Report of the Select Committee on Poor Relief*, X (1862), p. 140.

The problems of parish size and church provision were not confined to the large towns or manufacturing districts, but existed in rural areas too.[69] Many regions such as the Fens,[70] the Forest of Dean, or Northumberland were scantily provided with churches in the early nineteenth century. Parishes like Bywell St Andrews, Chillingham, Long Horsley or Earsdon in Northumberland were very expansive. A 'normal' midland rural parish, let us say in mid-nineteenth-century Leicestershire, averaged about 2,250 acres with a population of about 650. However, the fenland parish of Doddington comprised 38,240 acres. Prestbury in Cheshire had a population of 47,257 in 1831. Whalley in Lancashire had a population of 97,785, and stretched over 106,395 acres.[71] Such parishes were often heavily subdivided into townships and chapelries with complex local traditions affecting administration, and yet religious provision in them was often distant and inadequate. Openings were thus created for Nonconformists, who could readily establish places of worship in response to local demand, a situation that alarmed many in the established church.

There were many other matters needing reform, which were relevant to the issue of new parishes. Stipends for clergy, fee income and general values of clerical livings were grossly unequal and irregular,[72] necessitating the re-thinking of parochial areas and their corresponding incomes. Cathedral and collegiate revenues were excessively inflated by comparison. Some of the clergy had no theological or religious qualifications, being

---

[69] Traill, *New Parishes Acts*, p. 20. For regional average sizes of parishes, see A. D. Gilbert, *Religion and Society in Industrial England: Church, Chapel and Social Change, 1740–1914* (1976, London, 1984), pp. 98–101; Pounds, *History of the English Parish*, pp. 84–7.

[70] There was a Fen Church Building Act in 1812, under which six churches were built following recent drainage and enclosure in the Lincolnshire Fens: at Carrington (1816), Wildmore (1816), Langrick (1818), Midville (1819), Frithville (1821), and Eastville (1840, where another was built in the 1860s). R. W. Ambler, *Churches, Chapels and the Parish Communities of Lincolnshire, 1660–1900* (Lincoln, 2000), pp. 53, 59–60, 198; N. Pevsner, J. Harris, revised by N. Antram, *Lincolnshire* (1964, Harmondsworth, 1990), pp. 213, 267, 290, 424, 563, 798. These churches were 'utilitarian Georgian buildings' made of red and yellow brick. Recent drainage made these fen church livings extremely wealthy ones. Many more fen churches were restored under Bishop J. R. Woodford of Ely (1868–85) and Christopher Wordsworth of Lincoln (1869–85).

[71] On this parish, see M. F. Snape, *The Church of England in Industrialising Society: The Lancashire Parish of Whalley in the Eighteenth Century* (Woodbridge, 2003).

[72] Virgin, *Church in an Age of Negligence*, p. 34; K. D. M. Snell and P. S. Ell, *Rival Jerusalems: The Geography of Victorian Religion* (Cambridge, 2000), pp. 83–9.

sinecurists who were irrelevant to the spiritual and related needs of their parishes. Pluralism, non-residence (often due to inadequate clerical housing), misuse of patronage, and poor administration were widely condemned in the early nineteenth century, not least by heavily recruiting Nonconformist and politically radical groups. Every parish was full of vested interests, many of which were set tightly against any reform. Such a parochial situation, coupled with growing evidence of irreligion and public agitation over the state of the established church, stimulated what J. C. Traill referred to as the 'great and important work of parochial subdivision and Church extension'.[73]

THE CHURCH BUILDING ACTS AND NEW PARISHES

In 1818, a million pounds was set aside by Parliament to create new churches.[74] Over 600 new churches were built following this initiative. These churches have sometimes been dubbed 'Waterloo churches', although this is misleading as they were not intended as war memorials. The motivation behind their building was much influenced by the growth of Nonconformity, by threats to public order, by a need to expand church education, and by an awareness of regional or local inadequacies in the Anglican Church. Such limitations were most noticeable in London and newly industrialising areas, but other towns like Brighton or Bath were also conspicuous in this regard. The authority to create new churches was vested in the Commissioners for Building New Churches, appointed following the 1818 Act. Over twenty church building and related Acts were passed after 1818 to assist this programme.[75] The Commissioners were

---

[73] Traill, *New Parishes Acts*, p. 40. This author commented that it needed sixty to seventy new churches every year (each seating 1,000 people) to keep up with population increase in the early nineteenth century. *Ibid.*, p. 20. The need to 'divide and unite parishes as seems best' was an important feature in plans for church reform, like that submitted to Sir Robert Peel by Sidney Herbert. G. F. A. Best, *Temporal Pillars: Queen Anne's Bounty, the Ecclesiastical Commissioners, and the Church of England* (Cambridge, 1964), p. 290.

[74] 58 Geo. III, c. 45.

[75] The main statutes affecting new churches, new parishes and parochial reorganisation were: 58 Geo. III, c. 45; 59 Geo. III, c. 134; 3 Geo. IV, c. 72; 5 Geo. IV, c. 103; 7 & 8 Geo IV, c. 72; 9 Geo. IV, c. 42; 1 & 2 Wm IV, c. 38; 2 & 3 Wm IV, c. 61; 7 Wm IV & 1 Vic., c. 75; 1 & 2 Vic., c. 106 (the Church Pluralities Act); 1 & 2 Vic., c. 107; 2 & 3 Vic., c. 49; 3 & 4 Vic., c. 60;

to enquire into the state of parishes and extra-parochial places in England and Wales, to see where new churches were needed, and to cause them to be built with money voted by Parliament, or to assist such building with grants which augmented other subscriptions.

The Church Building Commissioners inclined towards funding churches with large seating capacities which were cheap for their size, skimping on superfluous decoration. The grant for any such church was not to exceed £20,000 in London (and less in the provinces). Such a sum was quite large compared to that needed for many rural or market-town churches, but in a city context this economy could produce rather unimpressive architectural results. The historian J. H. Overton referred to the churches built in the early nineteenth century as 'a puzzle and a despair to architects and clergymen . . . Unmitigated ugliness and hopeless inconvenience are their chief characteristic . . . either absolutely nondescript or sham Gothic.'[76] That was a rather harsh judgement, but at worse these churches did tend to be galleried auditorium boxes, either Grecian or broadly Gothic in style, the latter being used more often in

6 & 7 Vic., c. 37; 7 & 8 Vic., c. 56 (Banns and Marriages Act); 7 & 8 Vic., c. 61; 8 & 9 Vic., c. 70; 9 & 10 Vic., c. 68; 9 & 10 Vic., c. 88; 11 & 12 Vic., c. 37; 11 & 12 Vic., c. 71; 14 & 15 Vic., c. 97; 17 & 18 Vic., c. 14; 17 & 18 Vic., c. 32; 19 & 20 Vic., c. 55; 19 & 20 Vic., c. 104 (Lord Blandford's Act); 20 Vic., c. 19; 23 & 24 Vic., c. 142; 30 & 31 Vic., c. 106; 31 & 32 Vic., c. 122; 32 & 33 Vic., c. 63; 39 & 40 Vic., c. 61; 45 & 46 Vic., c. 58. One nineteenth-century authority wrote about these Acts: 'These are so complex and conflicting in their nature as to have defied all endeavours to arrange or classify them, or render them at all intelligible to the general reader. And all attempts even to consolidate them into one Act have failed, in consequence of the difficulty of finding any one with sufficient time and practical knowledge on the subject to undertake the management of such a bill in its progress through parliament.' Traill, *New Parishes Acts*, p. 22. 'I need not comment', one Judge remarked of the Church Building Acts, 'upon their obscurity; that is a matter of public notoriety.' Cited in C. F. Trower, *The Law of the Building of Churches, Parsonages, and Schools; and of the Divisions of Parishes and Places* (London, 1867), p. viii. Another authority spoke of them as 'ill-drawn and obscure, and extremely difficult to assign a meaning to, presenting a labyrinth of ambiguity'. Vice-Chancellor Kindersley, cited in *ibid.*, p. viii. See also M. H. Port, *Six Hundred New Churches: The Church Building Commission, 1818–1856* (London, 1961), p. 111. From 1943, new parishes and districts were created under the New Parishes Measure of that year (6 & 7 Geo. VI, No. 1), which repealed and largely re-enacted with amendments most of the previous New Parishes Acts from 1818 to 1884. J. T. Edgerley (ed.), *Ecclesiastical Law, Being a Reprint of the Title Ecclesiastical Law from Halsbury's Laws of England* (London, 1957, Church Assembly edn), pp. 138–45.
[76] Overton, *English Church*, pp. 155–6.

country districts.[77] Refinements and closer copying of Gothic, the style increasingly adopted among younger architects, were to come slightly later under the influence of Pugin, the 'rules' of the Camden Society,[78] the Oxford Architectural Society, and John Ruskin's arguments for perfectionism in workmanship, self-sacrifice in building, and high spiritual motive.[79] Church building as 'a labour of love' and 'for the sake of the spirit that would build them' was very commendable.[80] Yet new churches needed their own parishes, and the implications for parochial planning and subdivision of so many new churches were much less carefully considered. Contemporary architectural writers discussing ecclesiological styles seem hardly to have given parochial division a moment's thought, and that is also true of almost all historians of nineteenth-century architecture.

Grants were made on a fairly unsystematic regional basis to enable this church building, and these did not reflect local needs very well.[81] In fact the initiative often came from the dioceses or parishes where such churches were felt necessary, and many diocesan church building societies were formed. 'Love of local independency triumphed', and local committees usually handled the business.[82] Standardisation of design was common, and indeed often the cheapest way to proceed, and many southern or London-trained architects moved northwards to take advantage of opportunities, taking with them a tendency towards uniformity of design. However, among some of the more antiquarian inspired architects, provincial and local features were imitated and perpetuated. Among the groups assisting the Commissioners, and indeed overlapping with them, were the diocesan societies, and notably the 'Society for Promoting the Enlargement, Building and Repair of Anglican Churches and Chapels in England and Wales', founded in 1818 with very

---

[77] Port, *Six Hundred New Churches*, p. 81. It could perhaps be argued that the avoidance of refinement and extravagant decoration may have made such churches less off-putting to the poor.

[78] J. F. White, *The Cambridge Movement: The Ecclesiologists and the Gothic Revival* (Cambridge, 1962).

[79] Ruskin, *The Seven Lamps of Architecture* (1849, London, 1909), esp. pp. 28–51.

[80] *Ibid.*, pp. 47, 49.

[81] Port, *Six Hundred New Churches*, p. 33, and see his Appendix 8.1 on grants made by the Church Building Commission, 1818–56.

[82] *Ibid.*, p. 53.

strong backing, to 'remedy the deficiencies of places set aside for public worship in our towns and cities'.[83] This society gave grants in aid, stimulating private benefactions, and was found so valuable that it was incorporated by statute in 1828, becoming the Incorporated Church Building Society.[84]

This wave of church building brought with it the need to give such churches their own endowed districts or separate parishes. Before 1818 a Parliamentary Act was needed to alter parochial geography. From 1818 the Commissioners had powers to divide parishes, so as to provide new districts for new churches. At first, parishes with populations over 4,000, a fourth of which could not be accommodated, or where over 1,000 people lived more than four miles from the closest church, were the ones eligible for such reorganisation. Then a second Church Building Act in 1824 allowed grants to be made to many hamlets or chapelries (prevalent in large rural northern parishes) which did not qualify under the 1818 Act. Provision was made for purchasing land for a church and burial ground, and for parsonages with gardens to be built. The intention here was usually to divide parishes for ecclesiastical purposes, leaving them intact for civil matters.[85] In the 1824 Act, half a million pounds was voted for new churches by Parliament. This was in the face of Parliamentary opposition that aimed in part to defend the established parochial system from innovations in nominating ministers. However, Palmerston's view prevailed in favour of 'a community of sentiment' tending to 'the general tranquillity and happiness of a people', with all classes at a church, and the sum was voted through Parliament.[86] The parishes henceforward were to make out a case for a new church to the Commission, who would consider making grants. As Port wrote, these

---

[83] *Historic Churches Preservation Trust – Incorporated Church Building Society, Annual Report, 2000*, p. 1; Cornish, *English Church in the Nineteenth Century, Part I*, pp. 78–9.

[84] 9 Geo. IV, c. 42. Among the many other societies assisting such work were the Church Pastoral Aid Society (1836), the Additional Curates' Society (1836), the Church Building and Endowment Fund (1836), the Metropolis Churches' Fund (1836), and the London Diocesan Church Building Society (1854). Administration of the ICBS was taken over by the Historic Churches Preservation Trust in 1983.

[85] 58 Geo. III, c. 45, s. 31.

[86] Port, *Six Hundred New Churches*, p. 94, and see p. 128.

Acts contributed 'in breaking down the old rigid parochial system'.[87]

As from 1831 a new church could be given all parochial rights without the patron of the older one consenting.[88] Those who built and endowed it had the complete advowson (the right to present a clergyman to it). The criteria that now needed to be met before parish division could occur were that over 2,000 parishioners existed, with room for no more than a third of them in the existing church, or that there were over 300 parishioners living over two miles away from any existing church or chapel but less than a mile from the one to be erected.

The Church Building Commission spent and augmented funds totalling about three million pounds, and built 612 churches.[89] The powers of that Commission were transferred to the Ecclesiastical Commission from 1857.[90] There was much overlap of personnel across the two Commissions. The Ecclesiastical Commission had been founded in 1836, and its recommendations influenced many Parliamentary Acts. Charles Blomfield, Bishop of London in 1828–56, was a dominant presence on it, and his influence upon church extension was immense, for example in encouraging much private donation to the Metropolitan Churches Extension Fund which he set up. Blomfield was also a close friend of Edwin Chadwick, he had supported the new poor law in the House of Lords, and he even approved of the new law's illegitimacy provisions. Charles Murray, the Ecclesiastical Commission's Secretary, has been termed 'the church's Edwin Chadwick',[91] and there were indeed many parallels between Murray and Chadwick, and between the Ecclesiastical and Poor Law Commissions. Both had arisen following major Royal Commissions in the early 1830s, enquiring respectively into church revenues, and the administration of the poor laws. In contemporary thinking, one dealt with 'spiritual destitution', the other with 'pauper destitution'. Both Commissions experienced much opposition from anti-centralisation

---

[87] *Ibid.*, p. 35.
[88] 1 & 2 Wm IV, c. 38.
[89] Port, *Six Hundred New Churches*, p. 125.
[90] 19 & 20 Vic., c. 55.
[91] Best, *Temporal Pillars*, p. 302.

interests. The Ecclesiastical Commission assisted many thousands of parishes through its 'common fund' (another new poor law term), and its parochial and diocesan redistributive schemes resembled some of those which evolved under the new poor law. The Ecclesiastical Commission benefited from rising revenues from mid-century. Its grants were usually intended to supplement voluntary benefactions. As documented in its new benefice files, it was responsible for many alterations to parochial and diocesan structures, consolidations or subdivisions of parishes, endowment of churches, assigning districts to new churches which had sufficient endowments, supplementation of benefices and stipends, management and redistribution of church revenues, and other matters like reform of patronage, non-residence, plural benefice-holding, and encouragement of voluntary donations.

THE 'NEW PARISHES ACTS' OF 1843, 1844 AND 1856

In addition to the Church Building Acts, there were the 'New Parishes Acts' of 1843, 1844 and 1856.[92] These (particularly the 1843 Act) were very important in the organisational reform of the Church of England. They were a key element in church extension into 'divers parishes, chapelries, and districts of great extent, and containing a large population, wherein . . . the provision for public worship and for pastoral superintendence is insufficient for the spiritual wants of the inhabitants'.[93] As in 1818, these Acts were also partly motivated by concerns over popular unrest (now taking the form of Chartism and the Rebecca riots in west Wales), and its supposed links to inadequate ecclesiastical supervision.[94] This legislation gave the Ecclesiastical Commission authority to make new parishes out of highly populated areas. The schemes were to be ratified by Orders in Council, and a new district took effect from the date of such an Order. An existing or intended church in the new parish area was to be designated as the parish church. Indeed, a district

---

[92] 6 & 7 Vic., c. 37; 7 & 8 Vic., c. 94; extended by 19 & 20 Vic., c. 104.

[93] 6 & 7 Vic., c. 37, s. 9.

[94] K. A. Thompson, *Bureaucracy and Church Reform: The Organizational Response of the Church of England to Social Change, 1800–1965* (Oxford, 1970), p. 63.

could now be formed even though a church for it did not yet exist, which was an innovatory feature of the 1843 Act.[95] The minister would become the perpetual curate of such a parish, performing all the pastoral duties within it. A stipend was provided for him, and the value of the living had to be at least £150 per annum. The minister of such an incipient parish was urged to begin his work immediately, in a school room or other building; and the new district became a parish once a church had been built, from when it was no longer financially or legally subordinate to the old parish church. Each new parish then had complete parochial status, with parishioners who had an interest in managing their affairs, which were now separate from those of the initial parish. These Acts facilitated new parishes, by simplifying procedures for subdivision, and they eased difficulties over matters such as lay impropriators, or the compromised rights of adjacent parish clergy. Under this legislation, the patron and incumbent of the mother church had the right only to comment on the proposed changes, and the approval of the bishop was required. Many urban parishes were thus subdivided into districts, each with a church, creating a large number of new clerical livings. The 1843 Act was passed by Sir Robert Peel, who also made a substantial personal donation to the Commission, and so the districts formed under it were often known as 'Peel districts' or 'Peel parishes'.

TYPES OF PAROCHIAL DIVISION

A number of differently named divisions for ecclesiastical purposes were possible under the Church Building Acts. Many contemporaries were unaware of the precise differences between them, or defined 'parish' so as to encompass all such divisions,[96]

---

[95] Brose, *Church and Parliament*, p. 201. Under the 1818 Act, no district could be created without a church.

[96] For example, see H. J. Hodgson, *Steer's Parish Law, Being a Digest of the Law relating to the Civil and Ecclesiastical Government of Parishes: Friendly Societies, etc., and the Relief, Settlement, and Removal of the Poor* (1830, London, 1857), p. 20: 'The expression "parish, district, or place", means and includes any ancient or distinct and separate parish, district parish, chapelry, district chapelry, consolidated chapelry, or extra-parochial place.' Elsewhere in this work 'parish' was defined (following 15 & 16 Vic., c. 85, s. 52) as 'every place having separate overseers of the poor, and separately

and terminological confusion has sometimes resulted. Such confusion has sometimes made the divisions themselves appear needless or mystifying – thus the term 'new parish' is commonly used instead. The divisions themselves were often reorganised or renamed subsequently. Some places were shuffled between legal categories and definitions. However, the five main possibilities had legal and practical significance. They remind us that nothing was straightforward in nineteenth-century parochial structures. Attempts to reform eighteenth-century confusions and intricacies led to a situation that seemed untenably complicated and thus potentially disposable to many parishioners. It is perhaps surprising that Charles Dickens, once he had completed *Bleak House* in 1853, did not tackle this subject. These possible 'parochial' divisions were (i) *distinct and separate parishes*, (ii) *district parishes*, (iii) *consolidated chapelries*, (iv) *district chapelries* and (v) *particular* or *patronage districts*. These divisions stemmed from different Acts of Parliament. The processes of formation were broadly similar. All of them required a consecrated church or chapel before being fully constituted. They were formed by an Order in Council following representation from the Church Building or Ecclesiastical Commissioners.

Distinct and separate parishes were formed by dividing an older parish.[97] Consent of the bishop and patron was required. Tithes, glebe and other permanent endowments were separated and reallocated between the old and new parish. Initially, the new church was to remain as a chapel of ease serviced by a curate while the original incumbent held his post. This rapidly changed to a situation in which they became distinct benefices immediately after consecration, although the division took complete effect only when the existing incumbent left his post. From then, the new parish became a rectory, vicarage, donative or perpetual curacy – following whatever had been the case for the original church.

---

maintaining its own poor' (*ibid.*, p. 63). This was the common usage of the word, as for example used by the Poor Law Commission, e.g. their *An Official Circular of Public Documents and Information* (26 July 1847), Art. 224: 'any place maintaining its own poor, whether parochial or extra-parochial'.

[97] Under 58 Geo. III, c. 45, s. 16, and 1 & 2 Vic., c. 107, s. 12.

Only the consent of the bishop was needed for a *district parish*,[98] the tithes and permanent endowments not being affected. The churches became separate benefices upon consecration, but were also perpetual curacies, served by a licensed stipendiary curate appointed by the incumbent of the mother church.

A *consolidated chapelry* was normally created from adjoining parts of different parishes or extra-parochial places.[99] It required the consent of the bishop and patrons of the involved parishes. Tithes and permanent endowments of mother parishes were not affected by the change, although incumbents could annex tithes and endowments to the new church, or make other alterations to their livings to help endow the new church.[100] These chapelries were perpetual curacies, under episcopal jurisdiction, and the perpetual curate had all spiritual responsibilities in the district.

A *district chapelry* was created under the 1818 Act, and a number of later Acts.[101] These Acts gave the Church Building Commissioners powers to assign a district to a parochial chapel or chapel of ease. Tithes and endowments were not affected, but the incumbents could make contributions or endow some tithe payment to the new chapelry, which was to be served by a perpetual curate.

A *particular district*, or a *patronage district*, owed its origin to Acts in 1831 and 1851.[102] These permitted the Church Building Commissioners and/or the bishop to assign districts to churches that had been built and endowed by private persons. They could do this without the consent of the patron of an older church. However, any intention to build a church had to be notified to the incumbent and patron of the parish affected, and that patron could take precedence and act in the same manner if he agreed to fulfil the same proposed conditions of building and endowment. In the 1831 Act, before parish division could occur, criteria

[98] Formed under 58 Geo. III, c. 45, s. 21, and under 1 & 2 Vic., c. 107, s. 12.

[99] By 59 Geo. III, c. 134, s. 6; subsequently by 8 & 9 Vic., c. 70, s. 9, and 14 & 15 Vic., c. 97, ss. 19–20.

[100] Under 1 & 2 Wm IV, c. 42, s. 21, and 1 & 2 Vic., c. 107, s. 14.

[101] 59 Geo. III, c. 134, s. 16; 1 & 2 Vic., c. 107, s. 12; 2 & 3 Vic., c. 49, s. 3; 3 & 4 Vic., c. 60, s. 1; 11 & 12 Vic., c. 37, ss. 1 and 3.

[102] 1 & 2 Wm IV, c. 38, ss. 10–11; 14 & 15 Vic., c. 97, ss. 7, 14, 16 and 21.

had to be met as to the number of parishioners, and the room currently available for them. Such restrictions ended in 1851. Those who built and endowed a new church had the complete advowson of it. Tithes and other endowments were not affected by any such division, but the Commissioners needed an endowment before creating the new district. They usually required at least £1,000, or a rent charge of £40 per annum. The new living was to be a perpetual curacy. Marriages could take place in these churches only after the Church Building (Banns and Marriages) Act of 1844.[103]

As well as the Church Building Acts, there was the effect of the Pluralities Act of 1838.[104] This was partly aimed to deal with clergy who avoided the legislation against pluralism by claiming that their two benefices were united. It allowed the union of two benefices on certain conditions,[105] or the separation of others hitherto united, where such change was felt to be in the interests of religion. It also allowed the annexing to parishes or districts of tithings, hamlets, chapelries and extra-parochial places for ecclesiastical matters.

The 1843 Act transferred £600,000 in annuities from Queen Anne's Bounty to the Ecclesiastical Commissioners, to allow the latter to endow new districts. 200 such districts were immediately endowed in this way, being ones in which there were no consecrated churches or chapels in use.[106] A permanent endowment for the clergyman of at least £100 per annum was needed, and this would be raised to £150 once the district became a new parish. The transferred stock from Queen Anne's Bounty was gradually expended and diminished to achieve this. Once the new church was built, the district became a new parish with full parochial rights and all normal pastoral duties for its incumbent (a perpetual curate) to perform. He received all fees from this. The Crown and the diocesan bishop had the right (alternately) to present a clergyman to the living. This important Act was

---

[103] 7 & 8 Vic., c. 56.
[104] 1 & 2 Vic., c. 106.
[105] These were that the aggregate income was less than £500, and that the new benefice would not have more than 1,500 inhabitants when combined. The consent of both patrons was needed. The £500 limit was removed by the 1850 Pluralities Act (13 & 14 Vic., c. 98).
[106] Traill, *New Parishes Acts*, p. 28.

distinct from the activities of the Church Building Commissioners, and it was trusted or hoped that it would not interfere with their practices and parochial formations.

These Acts set in place what Victorian commentators optimistically referred to as the 'modern' parochial system, which they contrasted with the 'ancient' parochial system. It paralleled in some ways much earlier stages of medieval parochial subdivision, which had created subsequent parishes and churches. Or at least, that was how it was justified and viewed in the nineteenth century by many who had an eye to historical practice and who had to argue against ideas of the perpetuity and stability of parochial structures as established by long-term precedent. A view of historically *flexible* practice, rather than of the immutability of parish structures, was essential to justify the scale of changes in the nineteenth century, even though the relative stability of those structures over recent centuries was not in doubt. In an age of medieval antiquarianism, it sometimes demanded appeals to medieval practice to justify such changes. It was believed that the apparatus set up to create new parishes, or alter older ones, would be self-adjusting as circumstances changed (such as population distribution or town growth). Lord Blandford's New Parishes Act of 1856 helped to achieve this by relaxing requirements in the 1843 Act governing endowment levels, and removing some earlier restrictions upon new parish formation. Echoing the earlier 'Peel parishes', the results of this Act were sometimes known as 'Blandford parishes'. That Act gradually allowed all these new divisions to be converted into new parishes with the usual ecclesiastical rights and status.[107]

SUMMARY POINTS ABOUT ALL THE ACTS

The combined effect of this complex legislation was as follows. The Commissioners could divide any parish into two or more parishes for ecclesiastical matters, or carve off pieces of parishes for such purposes, or convert an extra-parochial place into a district parish. They needed the consent of the bishop, and they normally needed to apply to the patron of the church for

---

[107] 19 & 20 Vic., c. 104; Traill, *New Parishes Acts*, pp. 32–3, 38–9.

permission. Having secured such agreements, they were to bring their plans to the monarch in Council, outlining the new boundaries, and stating the subdivisions of glebe lands, tithes, moduses and other endowments, and the estimated fees,[108] oblations and other ecclesiastical dues for each division. The monarch could agree to the change, which would take full effect after the death or removal of the existing incumbent. Until the latter vacated office, the incumbent of a new division was often in a subordinate position *vis-à-vis* the existing one, in a district which often had a semi-parochial nature, and this affected his status in the eyes of his 'parishioners'.[109] Any permanent charges upon an incumbent, or upon the parish to be divided, could also be divided and allocated to the separate divisions that had been created.

Sizeable populations had often become settled at the edges of parishes, or in extra-parochial or detached places, frequently residing at an inconvenient distance from the nearest church. In view of this, the Commissioners were allowed to form these areas into separate districts, with a new name and with distinct boundaries. They could make grants or loans for building churches or chapels in them, and for burial grounds. These new districts were the *consolidated chapelries* mentioned above. These were given virtually the same rights to marry or bury people as separate parishes. To all extents and purposes, they were made benefices. Their incumbents could levy all the usual clerical fees, were under the bishop's jurisdiction, and were subject to all the laws governing churches, presentation to the living, and clerical office-holding.

The Commissioners could decide whether a new ecclesiastical division was to be a separate parish, or an ecclesiastical district, or whether an extra-parochial place was to become a parish or a chapelry. They could also convert a district chapelry into a separate parish, or further divide chapelries. A chapel of ease could be formed into a separate parish by the bishop if it lay at some distance from the parish church and if it was adequately

---

[108] Fees could be reserved to the original incumbent, until the next avoidance of his incumbency, or the bishop could award a compensation in lieu of them. 19 & 20 Vic., c. 104, ss. 11–12. They were an issue especially in parishes with low endowments.

[109] Traill, *New Parishes Acts*, pp. 35–6.

endowed to permit a reasonable stipend for the clergyman. Places like tithings, hamlets, chapelries and so on could also be annexed by Order of Council to neighbouring parishes or districts, if the bishop felt this necessary, rather than being made into separate ecclesiastical parishes. As in other proceedings, the permission of the patron was needed for this. Any new church formed for a parish or district was to be separate for all purposes of worship and in relation to all ecclesiastical duties, such as marriages, christenings, churchings, burials, and their registration, plus fees, oblations and offerings. The boundaries of the district or parish were always to be carefully delineated, publicised, and their precise details were to be enrolled in Chancery and in the registry of the diocese.

CHURCH BUILDING AND THE GEOGRAPHY OF NEW PARISHES

The scale of church building in the first half of the nineteenth century became apparent in the Religious Census of 1851, which enquired into the dates of church building. Something approaching a fifth of all Anglican churches had been constructed after 1801, most of these from the 1830s.[110] Probably well over £10 million had been spent on church building, and for the second half of the nineteenth century that figure was probably tripled. Very large numbers of further churches were built in the two decades after 1851. Between 1835 and 1875, as many as 3,765 new or rebuilt Anglican churches were consecrated.[111] That is a remarkable average of one every four days. Many of these churches required new or altered parishes. Church restoration was especially concentrated between 1856 and 1874. The numbers of clergy in England and Wales grew considerably (from about 14,500 in 1811, to nearly 25,000 in 1911),[112] as did the numbers of parsonages; both were further reflections of new

---

[110] *Census of Great Britain, 1851. Religious Worship. England and Wales*, LXXXIX (1853), pp. xl–xli. Exactitude is impossible because some churches mentioned no dates of construction in their returns to the census. See also Gilbert, *Religion and Society in Industrial England*, p. 130.

[111] C. Brooks, 'Introduction', in C. Brooks and A. Saint (eds.), *The Victorian Church: Architecture and Society* (Manchester, 1995), p. 9.

[112] Figures vary, depending largely upon the inclusion of Wales. I include Wales in the figures above. See Gilbert, *Religion and Society*, p. 28; Brooks, 'Introduction', in Brooks and Saint (eds.), *Victorian Church*, p. 10. (As an indication of subsequent decline,

parish creation and wider Anglican reforms, for example, to control pluralism. Inter-denominational competition, and competition between towns, marked many regions, and there were huge increases in numbers of churches and chapels as a result. For example, the Church of England built about 25 churches in Halifax in the nineteenth century, and by 1919 there were 104 churches and chapels there. Keighley had 50 churches and chapels by 1914. Many of these 'are magnificent sights'.[113] The historian Simon Green has written of 'a figurative orgy of construction around mid-century', as a national trend, 'slowing down to a gentler flow' towards the end of the century. He commented perceptively about how these many churches 'bear witness to a particular confidence . . . that is, to the Victorian notion of sacred progress measured in ecclesiastical bricks and mortar', and such description was widely applicable.[114]

Figure 7.2 shows where these new churches were built. This figure is an English map of the new saints' dedications of the eighteenth and nineteenth centuries, every new church of course having a saint's dedication. Those saints' dedications can therefore be used nationally to show where and when the new churches were built.[115] This source documents 3,765 new saints' dedications. New churches commonly entailed new parishes, and we will see the close match between these shortly. Apart from Monmouthshire and a few border parishes, this source on saints' dedications does not cover Wales (although we shall turn to another source that does shortly). The new dedications are also given a key on this map – to show whether a new dedication occurred in 1700–99, 1800–49, or 1850–99: numbered respectively 1, 2, or 3. The vast majority are of course

clergy numbers in 2005 were 9,404, with proposals being made to cut that to about 6,400. *Times* (8 June 2005), pp. 1–2.)

[113] S. J. D. Green, *Religion in the Age of Decline: Organisation and Experience in Industrial Yorkshire, 1870–1920* (Cambridge, 1996), pp. 87–90, 94, 111, 113.

[114] *Ibid.*, pp. 89–91. On church building in large, industrialising parishes, see also E. T. Davies, *Religion and the Industrial Revolution in South Wales* (1965, Cardiff, 1987); E. R. Wickham, *Church and People in an Industrial City* (1957, London, 1969); M. A. Smith, *Religion in Industrial Society: Oldham and Saddleworth, 1740–1865* (Oxford, 1994).

[115] The data on new saints' dedications by parish and period has been taken from F. Arnold-Forster, *Studies in Church Dedications, or England's Patron Saints*, 3 vols. (London, 1899). This magisterial source lists parish, dedication, county, diocese and period of dedication. I am grateful to my colleague Graham Jones for assistance in computerising these data.

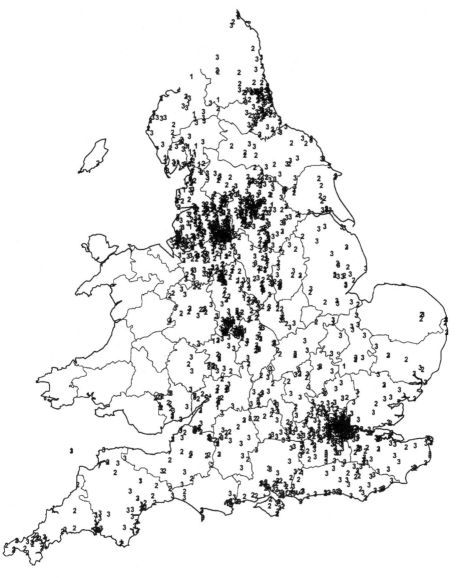

Figure 7.2   New saints' dedications, 1700–1899.
Key: 1 = 1700–99; 2 = 1800–49; 3 = 1850–99.

nineteenth-century new dedications; that is they have a key of either 2 or 3. This distribution is a very close match indeed to nineteenth-century urbanisation, or the density of population.[116] As such it underlines what an urban phenomenon new church building was. There were, for example, few new saints' dedications in largely rural counties like Bedfordshire, Rutland, Dorset, Herefordshire, Norfolk, Suffolk, or Lincolnshire outside its fenland areas. Indeed, the latter three counties, with their many large medieval churches, were suffering from a surfeit of saints already – many of their churches were later to be deemed 'redundant'. Rather, the areas that heavily predominate on the map are London and its immediate hinterland, Birmingham and the Black Country, Derbyshire, Staffordshire, Lancashire, the West Riding, the industrial north-east, the industrial west of Monmouthshire, the more industrial parts of Nottinghamshire, and the growing shipping and resort towns of the southern English coast. Along that south coast, one finds new church dedications in the Cornish mining areas, the enlarged naval dockyard town of Plymouth, the new resort town of Torquay, and other towns like Southampton, Bournemouth, Brighton or Eastbourne. Many rural areas like the Forest of Dean or the Fens feature noticeably, as one would expect from my earlier discussion of extra-parochial places. Yet the most striking characteristic of the map is its urban basis. The Church of England has often been criticised for failing to adjust to nineteenth-century urbanisation, but in fact this map suggests that it made a dramatic and expensive attempt to do so.

The Pennines mark another major division. With a line roughly between Ripon and Leicester, the map shows how concentrated the new church dedications were to the west rather than the east of these midland and northern counties. The western areas had more scattered or dispersed settlement, higher average rainfall, more temporary or permanent grass, an emphasis on pastoral and dairying farming, and much late eighteenth-century industrialisation. To the east one finds heavier nucleated village settlement, high arable acreages, larger farms, and one is into part of the triangular zone of first-phase (c. 1750–90) Parliamentary enclosure involving open-field arable

---

[116] For a map of population density in 1851, see Snell and Ell, *Rival Jerusalems*, p. 410.

(a triangle roughly between Dorchester, Whitby and Norwich). Comparatively few new saints' dedications occurred in that triangular zone of arable enclosure. The parishes to the east of the Ripon–Leicester line probably had firmer established boundaries as they contained higher proportions of arable-farming nucleated settlements, and so were less alterable for new parish creation. Their economies were less conducive to industrialisation, partly because valuable arable land did not entice them to industry. Many poorer pastoral parishes, to the west, found such industrialisation necessary or attractive, and were therefore more liable to parish changes, partly because their pastoral economies often involved extensive grazing lands, overlaid by parish boundaries that were relatively easily altered, and mainly because industrialisation brought urban growth, and thus the redundancy of earlier parish formations and the necessity for new churches, new parishes and parochial reforms to adjust religious and civil administration to major shifts in population settlement.[117]

The figure for new saints' dedications matches very closely indeed the geography of new parishes themselves. This is shown in figure 7.3. The source for this figure is the *Clergy List* of 1896, another very large source which was computerised to allow new parishes to be analysed and mapped from it.[118] It provided data on benefices, incumbents, types and values of livings, whether the income was supplemented by the Ecclesiastical Commissioners, clerical accommodation, patrons, the population of each benefice, and, among other information, the date of formation of each new parish. The data was supplied

---

[117] B. K. Roberts and S. Wrathmell, *An Atlas of Rural Settlement in England* (London, 2000), pp. 14, 15, 30; J. T. Coppock, *An Agricultural Atlas of England and Wales* (1964, London, 1976), pp. 39, 54–7, 73, 78, 81, 115, 118, 217; M. Turner, *English Parliamentary Enclosure: Its Historical Geography and Economic History* (Folkestone, 1980), p. 59; J. Caird, *English Agriculture in 1850–51* (London, 1852), map used as frontispiece; and see the pastoral–arable divides apparent in marriage seasonality, and used to measure agricultural specialisations, in E. A. Wrigley and R. S. Schofield, *The Population History of England, 1541–1871: A Reconstruction* (London, 1981), p. 302; A. Kussmaul, *A General View of the Rural Economy of England, 1538–1840* (1990, Cambridge, 1993), pp. 2, 12, 50, 127, 133.

[118] *The Clergy List: Alphabetical List of Benefices* (London, 1896). I am grateful to Paul Ell and Ian Gregory for their assistance in computerising this data, a project that was kindly funded by the British Academy. I analysed the data for figures 7.1–7.4 with SPSS and mapped it with GenMap.

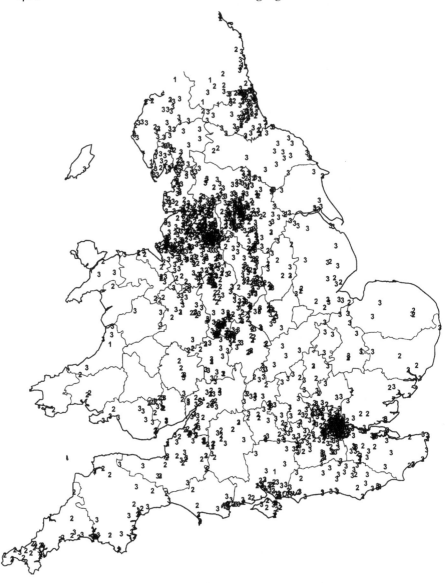

Figure 7.3   New ecclesiastical parishes formed, 1700–1896.
Key: 1 = 1700–99; 2 = 1800–49; 3 = 1850–99.

to the proprietors of the *Clergy List* directly by an official employed by the Ecclesiastical Commissioners, and the publication had a direct and unique link to the Commission. All the data was computerised, and the eighteenth- and nineteenth-century new parishes then extracted and mapped. Figure 7.3 is the result. It is constructed in the same manner as figure 7.2, and with the same key to show the broad period of new parish formation. In this case, the *Clergy List* also gave the information for Welsh parishes, and that was mapped too. The data cover 3,658 new parishes, and the extent of new parish formation is obvious from this map. The points made above with regard to new saints' dedications apply here as the main explanations for the distribution of new parishes. Once again, the urban geography is very apparent, and shows how town-based many of these new parishes were. The London and Middlesex area, Birmingham, the Black Country and other midland urban districts, Southampton and proximate districts, Lancashire and north Cheshire, the West Riding, and the urban north-east strongly predominate. The 1851 Religious Census commented upon how new churches and parishes had been formed 'as was to be expected and desired, in thickly-peopled districts', and this is borne out.[119] It would be too strong to say that 'the new parishes were almost exclusively urban',[120] as one can find very many rural areas that were affected – like parts of the Forest of Dean, the New Forest, Snowdonia, the Lake District, Exmoor, the Weald, Charnwood, Whittlewood, the Fens, and so on, some of them having been extra-parochial or detached – but, if one adopts a wide definition of 'town', a sizeable majority of these new parishes were urban.

In Wales there is the same concentration in west Monmouthshire as seen in figure 7.2, but the industrial regions in Glamorganshire, Carmarthenshire, Cardiganshire, Caernarvonshire or Anglesey, and rural Wales more generally, were not much affected by new parish creation. The Ecclesiastical Commission created very few parishes in Wales. This is perhaps surprising, but there was a near collapse of the parish in some areas of

---

[119] *Census of Great Britain, 1851. Religious Worship. England and Wales*, LXXXIX (1853), p. xxxix.
[120] Pounds, *History of the English Parish*, p. 508.

Welsh heavy industrialisation, where it could be virtually ignored by iron and coal masters.[121] The parish was probably not very central to people's lives in many Welsh regions of scattered settlement. The dominance of Welsh Nonconformity also raised doubts about what could be achieved by ecclesiastical parish reform. From the 1840s, new churches, church restorations, mission halls and the like were undertaken, but the scale of the Welsh changes was much smaller than in England, and never kept pace with the advance of Welsh Nonconformist chapels and institutions.[122]

THE CHRONOLOGY OF NEW PARISH FORMATION

The chronology of new parish formation may be seen in figure 7.4. This gives the numbers of new parishes formed each year, and is based on the precise dates given for each new parish in the *Clergy List* for 1896. That list also provided dates for eighteenth-century new parish formations, but they are so negligible in number (appearing throughout that century like the almost flat period 1800–15) that I have omitted the eighteenth century from this chart. One can readily document new church building and parish formation then, especially in areas like south Lancashire,[123] but that was slight nationally when compared to the nineteenth century. In the eighteenth century an Act of Parliament was needed to create a new parish which impinged upon an old one, and such legislation was fairly rare. Unlike in the nineteenth century, old parish boundaries were usually preserved in the eighteenth century when new churches were built, for example via use of the chapelry system. This helped to safeguard community identities, while allowing money for new churches to be collected from larger areas than was often

---

[121] I. G. Jones, *Communities: Essays in the Social History of Victorian Wales* (Llandysul, 1987), p. 181.

[122] I. G. Jones, 'Ecclesiastical economy: aspects of church building in Victorian Wales', in R. R. Davies (ed.), *Welsh Society and Nationhood: Historical Essays Presented to Glanmor Williams* (Cardiff, 1984); Brooks, 'Introduction', in Brooks and Saint (eds.), *Victorian Church*, p. 15.

[123] K. Clark, *The Gothic Revival: An Essay in the History of Taste* (1928, London, 1995), pp. 92–107; B. F. L. Clarke, *The Building of the Eighteenth-century Church* (London, 1963), pp. 50–89; Port, *Six Hundred New Churches*, p. 6; M. Smith, 'The reception of Richard Podmore: Anglicanism in Saddleworth, 1700–1830', in Walsh, Haydon and Taylor

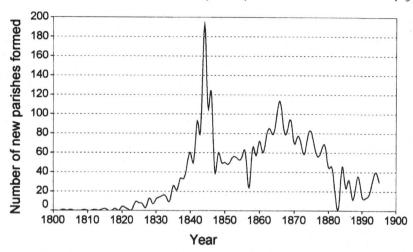

Figure 7.4   Number of new parishes formed, 1800–96.

the case with 'Peel districts' and other such 'parishes' in the nineteenth century. In some enclosure Acts, land was also set apart for church building, showing how enclosure could be intended as social reform or control as well as agricultural innovation.[124] However, new parish formation in the eighteenth and nineteenth centuries was overwhelmingly between 1820 and 1900. It took off very slowly after the formation of the Church Building Society (1817) and the 1818 Church Building Act, more rapidly in the 1830s, and then very steeply indeed in the 1840s, especially after Sir Robert Peel's 1843 'Act to Make Better Provision for the Spiritual Care of Populous Parishes'.[125] The year 1844 saw a massive peak, with 193 new parishes being

(eds.), *Church of England*, p. 115; and see the 1711 Church Building Act, 10 Anne, c. 20, planning fifty new London churches, although only ten churches were built under it.
[124] For example, the Act for the enclosure of Charnwood Forest and Rothley Plain, in which, out of 11,139 acres enclosed, 286 acres were designated for building churches, examples of which were at The Oaks, Copt Oak, and Woodhouse Eaves. W. E. Tate, *A Domesday of Enclosure Acts and Awards*, ed. M. E. Turner (Reading, 1978), p. 158. It is my impression that enclosure Acts making such provision were mainly ones in the second phase of such enclosure, after about 1790, those later phases of enclosure being more associated with less populous districts and hitherto 'waste' land, where churches were more likely to be lacking compared to the enclosures of open-field arable between *c.* 1750 and 1790. That second phase of enclosure was also more alive to social consequences and problems, as the adversities of the rural poor worsened in *c.* 1790–1840.
[125] 6 & 7 Vic., c. 37.

created. The figures then declined to about 50 per annum in the later 1840s, before rising gradually again to a new peak of 113 in 1866. The many Church Building Acts were clearly instrumental in encouraging this rise. The numbers of new parishes then slowly fell, but still with very substantial numbers of parishes being formed every year throughout the 1860s and 1870s. The numbers were much lower by the 1880s and thereafter: an average of 27 per annum in the 1880s and 1890s.

PROBLEMS OF THE NEW PARISHES

There were many problems arising from a new parish division, relating to the popular reception of such a move – which was often far from popular – the issue of who was to pay for church extension, and the rights of the original church. Advowsons, clerical freehold, glebe lands, tithes, moduses, surplice fees, pew rents, endowments, church rates, charities, and so on could all be affected, and reduced. Local people were usually conservative in their allegiance to their parish, and often resented its subdivision or alteration. There were even riots, protests or 'rough music' against new parishes. In one case, for example, when the bishop went to consecrate a new church his coach driver recalled that

we were met by two or three hundred men in holiday uniform, accompanied by the most discordant band which ever assailed mortal ears, and carrying a black banner with the inscription, 'More pigs, less parsons'. The hootings and shoutings were unimaginable and continued during the whole of the service. The tumult outside was incomprehensible – stones were thrown, the Bishop was hustled, and I never thought to get home alive.[126]

The clergyman in such a parish had an unenviable task ahead. The morale of many clergy in new parishes was very low, as was their income, and such parishes were often sited in the most working-class districts where anti-clericalism came with the pub spittoons. After all, during the extreme distress of the early 1840s, and with Chartism literally in its sights, a high-minded

---

[126] *Home Mission Field* (7 January 1887), p. 7, cited in Webster, *Joshua Watson*, p. 73. It is not clear where this incident occurred, other than that it was in a mill village in 1840.

State was moving beyond its unpopular 'Peelers' of 1828–30 to create large numbers of 'Peel districts', with expensive churches costing anything between £2,000 and £35,000, manned by pioneering 'missionary' clerics who spoke patronisingly of these districts as though they were inhabited by Hottentots or Eskimos. It also seems more than likely that some among the self-improving working classes were aware that a dictionary definition of 'to peel' was 'to pill, pillage, and plunder'; that 'peeled' could mean 'bald: tonsured'; that to 'peel off' meant to get one's hands on money; that a 'peeler' was 'a plunderer: a plant that impoverishes the soil'; and that a 'peel' was 'a palisaded enclosure ... a fortified house, usually entered by ladder to the first floor, with vaulted ground floor for cattle'.

However, it was not only the more anti-clerical among the working classes who had doubts about these developments. The provisions for new parish creation and endowment were intrinsically problematical. They were bound to create conflicts between vested clerical interests on the one hand, and the need for enhanced spiritual and administrative provision in neglected areas on the other. An advowson (the right of presentation to a church benefice) was heritable property, while a benefice and sources of clerical income were seen as akin to trust property and defended accordingly. Many of these assets were interdependent in complex legal and economic ways. For example, if clerical freehold and its benefits were in any way diminished, then the value of the advowson would fall. Countless examples can be found of clergymen objecting strongly to parish division on the grounds that it would diminish their income. One can imagine their feelings in those rare cases where their parish disappeared altogether, even if that was planned to occur after their retirement or death. Moreover, new parishes were usually unable for some time to benefit from Queen Anne's Bounty, which might otherwise have augmented the values of their livings. Church patronage was also directly affected. Rights to burial, and to vaults in an older church, were often an issue, especially if a new parish did not have a burial ground, and attempts were made to protect such rights, or to compensate for their loss. Parish charities also raised a perplexing array of legal difficulties. Primary documentation on new parishes and their churches often shows debate on levels of endowment, payment of costs, and the relation of the new church to the mother church.[127] The vested interests went much wider than those of incumbents. For example, one issue was the rights of Anglican pew-holders, whose pews resembled a species of private property, often being ancillary to property in the parish. Established interests in pews, which already caused much controversy and were subject to reforming endeavours, could be threatened by new churches with different geographical remits. Such churches also incorporated reformed and usually more egalitarian seating principles: avoiding box pews, with non-gallery seats facing east, and with provision of a specified proportion of free sittings for the poor.[128] In other words, earlier seating prerogatives or rights could be nullified or socially down-graded in a new church, even when private subscriptions to church building aimed to preserve them, and anticipation of this could arouse resistance.

Patrons of churches were especially suspicious of new church building. Church patronage was a form of investment and property, whether enjoyed by the Crown, bishop, dean and chapter, or a private person, and it could be sold or jealously defended. Private patrons controlled over half the total benefices, and that was only to decline significantly in the twentieth century.[129] The

---

[127] For example, Leics. CRO, DE 725/88 (Quorn: counsel's opinion on new districts under the Charnwood Enclosure Act; the relation of new churches to the mother church; doubts over the status of new churches; liability for repairs; controls by nearby rectors), DE 4224/17 (Donisthorpe: giving up of surplice fees; consents of patrons; provisions for fencing new churchyard), DE 4224/3 (Donisthorpe: land for a churchyard; adequacy of endowment and repair funds), DE 4224/21 (Donisthorpe: investments for repairs), DE 2216/9/8, 12, 21, 43, 45, 66 (Thorpe Acre: tenders for the parsonage; payment for bibles and prayer books; which land is in the new district; how the income is constituted; subscriptions for the endowment; payments for cast iron gates, posts, stone work, grates, pipes, etc.), DE 1760/87/12, 13, 19 (Whitwick: concerning terms of a grant from the Ecclesiastical Commission), DE 4502/16 (Bardon Hill: problems with the endowment).

[128] On denominational seating and appropriated pews, see Snell and Ell, *Rival Jerusalems*, pp. 321–63. For issues concerning pews in new churches, see Leics. CRO, DE 2216/9/15, 23 (Thorpe Acre: how many seats to be free; use of pew rents for church repairs), DE 4224/3, 17 (Donisthorpe: how many seats for the poor, compared to the minister, servants, proprietors, and owners of property; use to which seat rents will be put; varying sums chargeable as seat rents).

[129] Best, *Temporal Pillars*, pp. 46–7; M. J. D. Roberts, 'Private patronage and the Church of England, 1800–1900', *Journal of Ecclesiastical History*, 32 (1981), pp. 202–3. About 22 per cent of all patronage was episcopal by 1901. R. O'Day, 'The clerical renaissance in Victorian England and Wales', in G. Parsons (ed.), *Religion in Victorian Britain*, vol. 1: *Traditions* (Manchester, 1988), p. 197.

patron's permission had to be sought for a new parish, although different Acts gave patrons varying influence upon the outcome. Patronage of the parish church was usually allowed to extend to patronage of the new parish, although patronage could go to the current incumbent if a church was built by parish rate, or served a district rather than a parish, or was to be a chapel of ease.[130] Notice was served on patrons of intentions to build new churches,[131] and they could cause many difficulties, much more so than where the bishop was patron. The easiest parishes to divide were those that were wealthy, and controlled by the bishop. The hardest were poorly endowed parishes with low living values, with private patrons, where impropriators took much parish income. The extent of episcopal patronage varied regionally, for example being common in the Durham diocese, where about half the parishes were under the bishop's control.[132] Unification of parishes, if that was envisaged, was obviously made much easier if the churches were in the same patronage, preferably the bishop's, and this influenced some of the changes that occurred. Unification also had advantages in connection with parsonages, helping to cut housing and repair costs. There were many other patronal motives involved. Patrons were often worried about clergy being appointed (whether evangelical or ritualistic) who might be disruptive locally. Indeed, one motive among the evangelicals to build churches was to ensure that they could appoint like-minded clergy, and partly for this reason they established their own church extension fund, placing the right of presentation with a board of trustees.[133] Control over new parishes and their churches was, in this and other regards, fought over by different factions within the Church of England.

[130] 58 Geo. III, c. 45, ss. 16, 67–8, and see 59 Geo. III, c. 134, s. 16; Port, *Six Hundred New Churches*, pp. 107–8; Hodgson, *Steer's Parish Law*, pp. 18–20. Under the 1818 Act someone paying for a new chapel could appoint the curate for forty years, at which time the patronage would then revert to the old patron or incumbent.

[131] For an example, see Leics. CRO, DE 1224/77 (notice to patron of an intention to erect a chapel at Hinckley, 1835).

[132] W. B. Maynard, 'The response of the Church of England to economic and demographic change: the Archdeaconry of Durham, 1800–1851', *Journal of Ecclesiastical History*, 42 (1991), p. 440.

[133] Lewis, *Lighten their Darkness*, pp. 53, 87.

Church rates had historically been levied for the upkeep of parish churches, and they were defended as appropriate to a national church. With growing religious pluralism or secularisation their continuance was questioned, and their abolition would clearly have major repercussions for church mainten-ance. It was also feared within the church that ending church rates would lead to tithe abolition. They became even more of an issue with new parishes. New parish creation was never intended to discontinue church rates. The initial semi-parochial character of many new divisions frequently left inhabitants in new districts liable to repair the original church, even though they may not have identified with that parish church any more, feeling allegiance to a new one. They were also now under an obligation to repair that new church. Endowments for new churches often did not provide adequate funds for their upkeep in the years ahead, and in the case of beneficent private endow-ments this was a relatively invisible cost, for which little social credit could be gained. It was often therefore quietly ignored. Under the 1818 Act, repairs to the new church were to be paid for by a church rate levied upon inhabitants in the district (who might also be paying by subscription for the new church); and for twenty years from the new church's consecration the inhabitants of the new district still had to pay rates towards the old parish church. Inhabitants in many districts thus had to pay rates for two churches at the same time.[134] They had become a species of 'dual parishioner', belonging via their church rates to two churches and parishes. This may have been appropriate for a comparatively few property owners with holdings across parishes. The theme of 'multiple belonging' may be familiar to more people today, when work and home(s) have become so separated. However, it did not fit well with contemporary notions of local attachment, habitation and liability.

Such dual parochial responsibility, encapsulated in the church rate arguments, was condemned as a very unsound feature. It opened the way to considerable local difficulty. Many places, like Nottingham in 1828, Birmingham in 1832, or Braintree in

---

[134] 58 Geo. III, c. 45, s. 71; O. Chadwick, *The Victorian Church, Part I: 1829–1859* (1966, London, 1997), pp. 85–6; Traill, *New Parishes Acts*, p. 94; Port, *Six Hundred New Churches*, p. 26.

1836–53, refused to levy or pay church rates, either because of dissenting majorities, or because churchmen faced with double payment declined to attend such meetings and left them dominated by dissenters. Over 1,500 parishes refused such rates prior to their abolition in 1868, and they were not levied in many urban parishes after the 1840s.[135] In some cases, non-payers were imprisoned. Because of these issues associated with dual parishes, refusal to pay church rates was not only restricted to Nonconformists. Parties in the established church often sided with dissenters because they were sympathetic to their stance on church rates. Some dissenters had to pay two church rates to the Church of England, as well as their voluntary contributions to their own chapels. The campaign in England to abolish church rates probably started as a consequence of the 1818 Act, for it became apparent from the 1820s in some of the midland and northern cities, such as Nottingham, Sheffield, Leeds, Bradford and Dewsbury.[136] The first bill to abolish them had been in 1834, and many others followed. An additional problem was that where a new parish successfully relinquished its rate-paying to the old, the inhabitants of the latter were left with higher rates to pay, having to make up significant lost sums. There was also opposition to requests for church rates where they had not hitherto been levied.[137]

The church rate issue was to be highly contentious even among committed Anglicans. It set many new and old parishes at loggerheads with each other, sometimes with divisive consequences for parochial loyalty, notably when parishes were still in the same civil parish. Such issues muddled local allegiances, and were prominent in the arrangements for church repair

[135] Cornish, *English Church in the Nineteenth Century, Part I*, p. 170; Mole, 'Victorian town parish', p. 370.

[136] Abolition came with 31 & 32 Vic., c. 109. Thereafter voluntary rates were levied. Many towns had in fact already abandoned such rates before this. Chadwick, *Victorian Church, Part I*, p. 86 n. 1; Chadwick, *Victorian Church, Part II*, pp. 195–6; Port, *Six Hundred New Churches*, pp. 103–7; Best, *Temporal Pillars*, pp. 192–4; Cornish, *English Church in the Nineteenth Century, Part I*, pp. 158–72. I refer here to a formal English campaign against such rates; there had long been Nonconformist antagonism to church rates, especially among Quakers, and there was firmly established resistance to them in Ireland, and to a lesser extent in Wales.

[137] 'Church building and the New Parishes Acts Amendment Bill', *Times* (10 June 1864), p. 7, col. F.

caused by new church building. They were thought to detract from the development and efficiency of the parochial system, leading people to withdraw participation from 'the various administrations conducive to the public good', and reduce their contributions as public-spirited citizens.[138]

The endowment of new parishes was also a matter of much debate and a major concern for those sponsoring church building. There were, for example, the questions of how much endowment was needed, in what form, and how this related to the social standing of the benefice. How should glebe lands, tithes, rent-charges and other endowments be divided? How should the nature of the living be redefined if the tithes were redirected as payable to the incumbent as rector? Such matters were dealt with by the Commissioners in consultation with the bishop and local benefactors. The new churches and chapels could be augmented by a variety of sources. An Act in 1831 enabled ecclesiastical corporations to augment poor livings (those worth under £350 per annum) that they were connected with, which created some transfer of resources from bishops to parishes. In addition, there was the issue of new parsonages, which were always a problem to find sites and pay for.[139] Architectural plans for these also had to be drawn up and agreed.[140]

The Commission insisted that the churches to be built should be large: their rules variously stipulating seating for 1,200, 1,500 or even 1,800 people.[141] Requirements of this kind had adverse architectural effects. They resulted in some churches in which the clergyman could hardly be heard, with repercussions for attendances. Furthermore, such rules influenced the sizes of new parishes: where two new churches would have resulted in two new parishes, one church entailed one more populous parish. The character of a parish could be much changed by dividing it, for example, as fashionable urban areas became

---

[138] Traill, *New Parishes Acts*, pp. 36–7.
[139] For example, Leics. CRO, DE 2216/9/51 (new parsonage at Thorpe Acre, costing over £1,324 in 1848), DE 5057/62, 63, 65 (financial arrangements for building a parsonage at Glen Parva), DE 2790/37 (papers relating to a new parsonage at Thurmaston).
[140] An example relating to Leicester, the Martyrs, is Leics. CRO, DE 4922/18/1–10, 19.
[141] Port, *Six Hundred New Churches*, p. 102.

separated from a parish, and this could affect the composition of congregations and income from pew rents. This could lead to much argument over boundaries, which were usually contentious, and sometimes very oddly defined or inconvenient.[142] Such boundaries needed to be agreed, tightly specified, registered with the diocese, often described in the *London Gazette*, and drawn up on maps in very close detail to avoid future disputes.[143]

NEW PARISHES IN THE FOREST OF DEAN: A CASE STUDY

The Forest of Dean and its surrounding parishes in west Gloucestershire can be taken as an interesting regional example of new parish formation, illustrating how extensive such change could be, and showing some of the advantages, difficulties, and processes involved. No local example will ever prove 'typical' in this respect, because such a great diversity of areas, whether rural or urban, had their parishes recreated. Urban parish formation and church building in London, for example, differed greatly from the varying experiences of most of the manufacturing cities, or the resorts of the south coast, or more rural regions such as Charnwood Forest (Leics.), the Lincolnshire fenlands, or the Forest of Dean. On the other hand, there was also the very different parochial rationalisation and amalgamation that occurred in cities with extremely fragmented historic parish structures and a plethora of churches, such as Cambridge, Bristol or York. Nevertheless, the intense changes that could occur, often confusing the identities of local inhabitants, are well illustrated in the Forest of Dean.

The Forest was largely owned by the Crown, which because of gifts, assarting and encroachments gradually found its demesne reduced over the centuries. The extent of the Forest

---

[142] Welch, 'Bishop Blomfield', p. 208.

[143] Examples are Leics. CRO, DE 4502/16 (on the boundaries of Bardon Hill St. Peter, a district chapelry, with its boundaries closely marked up in green pencil, including along the middle of a railway line), DE 2451/47/5 (1852 map of the consolidated chapelry district of Oaks in Charnwood), DE 4811/40/3 (an account of the area of Christ Church, Mountsorrel), DE 2216/7 (Thorpe Acre, district described), DE 5057/58, 59 (extract from Orders in Council, concerning boundaries, with a map, of the consolidated chapelry of Glen Parva with South Wigston).

had changed considerably over time, enlarging or diminishing mainly in response to Crown initiatives or inaction, and neighbouring demographic pressures.[144] Back in *c.* 1300, the Forest had comprised most of the broad triangle lying between Monmouth, Ross-on-Wye, Newent, Gloucester and Chepstow. A map of the Forest and its surrounding region is shown in figure 7.5.[145] I will discuss its wider region, but pay most attention to its narrower limits in the nineteenth century, when it comprised about 23,000 acres, much the same as today.[146] The region was well known for its coal and iron-ore mining, for high-quality sandstone quarrying, and for metal industries such as tin-plate working in Lydney, Parkend and Lydbrook. In addition there were small but useful forest industries like charcoal burning, lime burning, tanning, wire, nail and pin-making, paper-making, and ochre and oxide mining.[147] The industrial features of the Forest, which expanded in the nineteenth century, its relative remoteness and inaccessibility – tucked between the lower reaches of the rivers Wye and Severn, with Wealden-like roads – and the cultures, rights and independent traditions of its 'free miners',[148] made it an area poorly served by the Church of England. Yet it proved attractive to the Baptists, Congregationalists, Wesleyan Methodists, Primitive Methodists and Bible Christians, and a compelling case was made here for 'missionary' work and parish reform.

[144] C. E. Hart, *The Extent and Boundaries of the Forest of Dean and Hundred of St. Briavels* (Woodgate, Glo., 1947); C. Hart, *The Verderers and Forest Laws of Dean (with Notes on the Speech House and the Deer)* (Newton Abbot, 1971), pp. 18, 42–3, 47, 68–9, 71–2, 80, 83–5, 99, 104, 108, 193, 199, 200, 207; Lord Eversley, *Commons, Forests and Footpaths* (1893, London, 1910), pp. 172, 176, 180.

[145] This map derives from J. C. Cox (revised by H. S. Davis), *Gloucestershire* (1914, London, 1949).

[146] H. P. R. Finberg, *The Gloucestershire Landscape* (London, 1975), p. 23; Hart, *Verderers*, p. 18.

[147] C. E. Hart, 'Charcoal-burning in the Royal Forest of Dean', *History of Metallurgy Bulletin*, 2 (1968), pp. 7–15; C. E. Hart, 'A résumé of the history of the Forest of Dean's ironworking industries', *History of Metallurgy Bulletin*, 2 (1968), pp. 33–9.

[148] On the 'free miners' see C. E. Hart, *The Free Miners of the Royal Forest of Dean and Hundred of St. Briavels* (Gloucester, 1953); C. Fisher, *Custom, Work and Market Capitalism: The Forest of Dean Colliers, 1788–1888* (London, 1981); Eversley, *Commons*, pp. 178–80; H. J. Hewson and I. Cohen, *The Homeland Guide to the Wye Valley and Forest of Dean* (London, 1951), p. 100. On the area's industrial history, see C. E. Hart, *The Industrial History of Dean* (Newton Abbot, 1971).

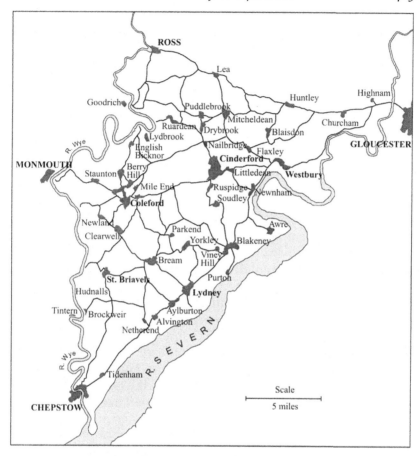

Figure 7.5   The Forest of Dean region.

That reform came especially in the shape of new churches, the creation of new parishes, augmented livings, and a bewildering array of much altered parochial divisions. The situation was complicated by a number of considerations. As royal demesne, the Forest had historically been extra-parochial, severely restricting habitations and making no formal provision for its poor. Many hamlets and other places remained extra-parochial. People living in them often had to be reluctantly relieved by surrounding parishes, like English Bicknor, Staunton, Westbury,

Flaxley, Ruardean, Littledean or Awre, and are recorded in their parish registers. The Forest had been very sparsely settled, and encroachments were invalidated, cottages cleared, and the boundaries supervised. As was usual in such places, the resistance against encroachments varied in different periods, the second half of the seventeenth and early eighteenth centuries seeing much ejection of squatters and settlers. Around 1658–9, for example, 400 houses and cabins were destroyed. Following the important Dean Forest (Reafforestation) Act of 1667, this was a period of considerable tree re-planting in the Forest, largely with Navy requirements in mind.[149] There were few Forest inhabitants in the early eighteenth century, largely as a result of efforts to sustain such growing timber.

However, assarting, small-scale encroachment, cabin building, garden and field extensions, movement of fences and hedges, expansion from detached parts of parishes, let alone the attractions of large-scale capital investment in the Forest's natural resources, subsequently proved irresistible. From the mid-eighteenth century in particular such actions eroded the older Forest boundaries, as became clear in the 1833 perambulation which delimited the statutory Forest. Areas like Harthill Common, Hewelsfield Common, Hudnalls, St Briavels Common, Joy's Green, or Pope's Hill, today bear unmistakable signs of such encroachments, with their small irregularly shaped closes, and complex networks of minor lanes and tracks. Surrounding parishes like Ruardean, Hewelsfield or Newland had many detached parts, often within the Forest, which owed their origins to practices of commoning, access to resources such as timber for mines, river frontages, sites for mills, and other considerations. This of course made the processes of intra-Forest enclosures and parochialisation difficult, as so many vested interests were at stake.

The major changes were initiated in 1842, with two Acts of Parliament, to provide for the relief of the poor in the Forest and other extra-parochial places in and near the Hundred of St Briavels, and to divide the Forest of Dean into ecclesiastical

---

[149] 19 & 20 Car. II, c. 8; Hart, *Verderers*, pp. 194, 206–13; Eversley, *Commons*, pp. 176–8; O. Rackham, *Trees and Woodland in the British Landscape* (1976, London, 1998), p. 173.

districts.[150] West Dean and East Dean were created as extensive townships, comprising respectively 10,035 acres and 20,393 acres. These were now to appoint overseers and maintain their poor. The townships were added to the Monmouth and Westbury-upon-Severn poor law unions, rates were to be levied and guardians appointed. Some extra-parochial areas were annexed to proximate parishes, such as St Briavels, Hewelsfield, Westbury and English Bicknor. Within West Dean there were the four new ecclesiastical parishes of St Pauls, All Saints, Holy Jesus, and Christ Church; and in East Dean were the three new ecclesiastical parishes of St John the Evangelist, Holy Trinity, and (from 1880) St Stephen's Woodside. In some cases, such as Holy Trinity, these parishes benefited from already constructed churches; in others, the churches were subsequently built and endowed. The Crown's rights in the Forest were not to be affected by these changes.

One of the strongest motivations behind these Acts was the 'Improvement of the religious and moral Habits of the Persons residing therein', and such comment and unease was frequent with regard to the Forest.[151] It was a moral concern often found elsewhere too, when extra-parochial places came to be 'parochialised', and it was hoped that new churches and clergy would remedy the apparent problem. R. M. Garnier later wrote about how this Forest's 'shady depths would have offered another sanctuary for outlawed Britons', and the *Imperial Gazetteer* commented that 'The inhabitants were long a lawless people, possessing peculiar rites.'[152] Richard Parsons, vicar of Driffield, thought that 'The inhabitants are, some of them, a sort of robustic wild people, that must be civilized by good discipline and government.'[153] The presence of deer inevitably encouraged poaching. There were riots in the Forest in 1831 by commoners against incursions by outside industrial interests, and against

---

[150] 5 & 6 Vic., c. 48; 5 & 6 Vic., c. 65. Revd H. G. Nicholls, *Nicholls's Forest of Dean: An Historical and Descriptive Account, and Iron Making in the Olden Times* (1858 and 1866, Dawlish, 1966), pp. 170–2.

[151] 5 & 6 Vic., c. 65.

[152] R. M. Garnier, *History of the English Landed Interest* (London, 1892), p. 24; Wilson (ed.), *Imperial Gazetteer*, under 'Dean Forest'.

[153] Cited in Nicholls, *Forest of Dean*, p. 56. Or, to similar effect, A. G. Bradley, *The Wye* (1910, London, 1926), p. 152.

enclosure. These prompted the Dean Forest Commission Act of that year,[154] and enquiries in 1832 by the Dean Forest Commissioners which resulted in greater regulation of mines, tenures, and advocacy of parochialisation.

Whether real or imaginary, a need for moral improvement was a recurrent motif among commentators on the Forest, although this was probably exaggerated by all religious denominations to enhance the missionary cause and achievements. The Revd P. M. Proctor of Newland described a low moral state in 1803: 'most deplorable – habitual profanation of the Sabbath-day, drunkenness, rioting, immodest dancing, revellings, fightings, an improper state of females on their marriages, and an absence and ignorance of the Holy Scriptures'.[155] However, after church building and 'parochialisation' it was often claimed that 'a great change has been wrought'; or 'the moral character of the inhabitants has been much improved by the building of churches'.[156] Other denominations partook of this self-commendation. The Independent minister John Horlick, speaking about the Blakeney area, commented: 'The moral scenery in this part of the Forest of Dean, about 34 years ago, presented a dark aspect, the generality of the people were veiled in thick darkness, the Sabbath was profaned by a variety of games and sports . . . until it pleased God in His mysterious providence' to bring in preachers who did something about it.[157] Viewing the lovely naturalistic scenery of the Wye, through woodlands to the shimmering Severn, left many commentators disturbed that words worthy of the scenery of Nature could not be matched by the 'moral scenery', even though some contemporaries trusted or hoped that beauty in Nature might induce moral perfectibility among inhabitants, or might be expedited to do so, even amid budding coal tips and tramways. Not to be outdone by

---

[154] 1 & 2 Wm IV, c. 12. On the 1831 rioting, see in particular R. Anstis, *Warren James and the Dean Forest Riots: Being the Story of the Leader of the Riots in the Forest of Dean in 1831, with an Account of the Riots and of their Causes* (Gloucester, 1986).

[155] Nicholls, *Forest of Dean*, pp. 155–6. To similar effect, see Fisher, *Custom, Work and Market Capitalism*, pp. 31–2: 'Ragged and dirty, the foresters were regarded as inferiors who had no rights of attendance at service with their respectable neighbours. The result was the development of what clergymen of all denominations saw as a wild, heathen race, as much in need of redemption as the Maori or Eskimo.'

[156] Two commentators cited in Nicholls, *Forest of Dean*, p. 149.

[157] T. Bright, *The Rise of Nonconformity in the Forest of Dean* (Coleford, 1953), pp. 28–9.

the Anglican Church or the Independents, the *Wesleyan Method-ist Magazine* quoted a petition from the Dean Forest Methodist Society of Colliers, from as early as 1823:

Our state was once that of lawless heathen, but now we have learned to fear God, honour the King and obey his laws. We no longer lay claim to his majesty's timber or deer, nor do we attack and murder his keepers. The rising plantations grow unmolested and our neighbours' flocks graze around us unassailed . . . We are no longer the terror of neighbouring towns, neither breaking their bones nor shedding their blood. Horrid blasphemies are changed into loud hosannas, and instead of the lewd drunkard's song we join in hymns of praise.[158]

Such statements and claims were made for many other regions experiencing new parishes, like the Fens, Charnwood, Manchester, or the East End of London, although some such places may not have shared the royally scenic qualities of Dean Forest.

Some improvements in 'moral scenery' probably did result from new churches and chapels, Sunday schools, other denominational schools, ministerial oversight, and inter-faith rivalry. It may be easy to smile at such contemporary avowals, especially given a few subsequent events in the area, but something like a 'reformation of manners' here was often commented upon, and one needs to respect the efforts and claims that were made. In Dean, as elsewhere, these claims probably had some justification. It has rightly been said, for example, that 'The educational system of the Forest of Dean has its roots principally in the missionary work of Anglican ministers in the early nineteenth century.'[159] Some of the churches were built by laudable personal efforts, as in Parkend, where the Revd Henry Poole was for almost forty years 'the first incumbent and [the church] was built chiefly by his labours'.[160]

However, there is another side to these parochial reforms, which I wish to stress here because of its relevance to the theme of belonging and local attachment. Just how practically difficult

---

[158] Cited in *Ibid.*, p. 35.
[159] A. R. J. Juřica, 'Education', in Herbert (ed.), *History of the County of Gloucester*, p. 405.
[160] Wording on his gravestone, Parkend. See also G. Waygood, 'St. Paul's Church, Parkend: the church in the woods and its association with the Crown Office of Woods and Forests', *The New Regard: The Journal of the Forest of Dean Local History Society*, 20 (2005); D. Verey and A. Brooks, *Gloucestershire 2: The Vale and the Forest of Dean* (1970, London, 2002), pp. 630–1.

and tortuous the parochial divisions of the Forest of Dean proved to be can be seen in Appendix 7.1.[161] This lists chronologically the administrative boundary changes that occurred, as seen only from the viewpoint of the civil authorities and the established church. (One can hardly begin to fathom the various shifting circuits and alternative organisational networks of the Nonconformists, draped over the Anglican and civil structures, and Nonconformity was arguably much more important than the established church in the Forest of Dean.) The appendix also shows some (by no means all) of the alterations that took place in the twentieth century. The list is not complete even for the nineteenth century. Even though most readers will be unfamiliar with the fine details of the Dean region, and where exactly some of these places are situated, it is worth perusing this lengthy list of parochial alterations, because such a reading conveys an important message. It shows how complex, pernickety and prone to re-evaluation nineteenth-century parochialisation and reformation often was. In this case, it is remarkable to think that all the many changes listed occurred in the triangular area of the old Forest, located within the rivers Wye and Severn, between Monmouth, Churcham (west of Gloucester) and Tidenham (north-east of Chepstow): an area that was only about eighty square miles.

This extraordinary process continued into the twentieth century – indeed, there were substantial changes in the 1930s and 1950s. The Forest was an area that for historical reasons was very open to administrative intervention and change. Clearly religious provision had been poor there. Yet faced with such evidence of so much change in parishes, nobody would wish to argue that the nineteenth century was lethargic in reforms. Nor can the Anglican Church be accused of inactive organisation or long-term neglect, because much of this civil and ecclesiastical change came at its instigation. Many urban areas, notably in the great cities, experienced change of a similar intensity and persistence. One

---

[161] This appendix has been put together from various sources, in particular Herbert (ed.), *History of the County of Gloucester*; *Kelly's Directory of Gloucestershire and Bristol* (London, 1885); the decadal censuses for Gloucestershire; Wilson (ed.), *Imperial Gazetteer*; and Youngs, *Guide to Local Administrative Units of England*, vol. 1. The appendix is incomplete in many slight ways, and many parish and benefice changes in the twentieth century have not been entered.

has to wonder what effects such levels of disruption had on local people's awareness of place and ideas of belonging, as proximate local communities found themselves twisted, re-shaped and subdivided into such an unforeseen sequence of variously overlapping and differently named ecclesiastical or civil districts, chapelries, townships, or 'parishes' over time.

This volatility of change was as marked with regard to places of religious worship. Figure 7.6 shows the chronology of Anglican Church and Nonconformist chapel building and major

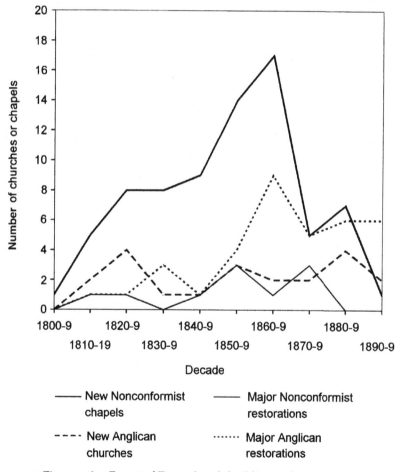

Figure 7.6   Forest of Dean church building and restoration.

restorations for the Forest of Dean area, which I have recon-
structed from many sources. There were twenty-one new Anglican churches built in this area during the nineteenth century,
and at least seventy-five new chapels built by Nonconformist
denominations. A few of these replaced earlier ones. The graph
shows the dating of thirty-six Anglican Church restorations, and
ten Nonconformist restorations. (The restorations shown here
were major structural renovations – smaller building items and
changes have not been included.[162]) As can be seen, there was
much vitality in church and chapel building and restoration.
Many of the Anglican churches were associated with parish
creations and reformulations. Indeed, as was widely the case
elsewhere, church building could precede and prompt the creation of a new parish, a district then being necessary for the
newly erected church, even when it was built by a private
patron with little regard to wider diocesan planning. In other
cases, the new ecclesiastical district or parish pre-dated the
church, and the latter was constructed soon after.

The Anglican Church and the Nonconformist denominations
were of course in ardent competition in this region. Earlier royal
enclosures and land sales under Charles I, and the unpopular
actions of Sir John Winter, had led many local people to support
the Parliamentary cause,[163] and dissenting attitudes continued.
The industrial growth of the area, with its consequent inflows of
labour, the creation of new settlements, expanded hamlets, and
urban growth in and around Coleford and Cinderford, offered
considerable scope for Nonconformists. The main denominations involved were the Primitive and Wesleyan Methodists,
numerically followed by the Independents and Baptists, and
then the Bible Christians. (The Moravians, Presbyterians and
Plymouth Brethren had a minor presence.) These denominations
built chapels mainly in 1800, 1813–14, 1818, the early 1820s, the
mid-1830s, throughout the 1840s, and heavily during the 1850s

---

[162] It does not therefore include new mission rooms, halls, Sunday schools, class rooms,
dual-purpose buildings or rooms also used for services, and building alterations such
as organ installations, minor repairs to spires, new porches, gallery building or
removal, window alterations, re-flooring, re-pewing, vestry construction, or the
addition of school rooms.

[163] Eversley, *Commons*, pp. 174–5.

and 1860s, when chapels were being built almost every year, some years seeing three or four chapels built in the Dean region. There was on-going Nonconformist chapel building between 1874 and 1886, after which new building was rare. These chapels commonly survived with active congregations until after the Second World War. The usual pattern was for closures thereafter, especially between 1955 and 1992, when in this region a chapel was (on average) closing every fifteen months, a decline that was tied in with the subsidence of the area's nineteenth-century mining and other industrial communities.

The Church of England in the Forest of Dean responded rather late to the challenge of Nonconformity. The Anglican Church built a handful of churches in 1812, 1816, and 1820–2. There was notable early missionary endeavour in the Forest led by some Anglican clergy from proximate parishes, like the Revd P. M. Proctor of Newland after 1803, or the Revd H. Berkin in 1812. Proctor had found the foresters 'destitute of churches or ministers whom they could properly call their own', and certainly many of them were over five miles from a church.[164] Important innovations affected ecclesiastical parishes in 1842–5. Even so, new Anglican church construction was spread fairly thinly throughout the century. Most of its church restorations occurred in and after the 1860s. The main activity of the Anglican Church, to judge from church building, restoration, and ecclesiastical parish changes, came between 1856 and 1896. Yet between 1800 and 1860 at least forty-eight Nonconformist chapels were built in the Forest region, and others had earlier origins. John Wesley had been preaching here long before the Anglican 'missionaries' from Gloucester, Mitcheldean or Newland, establishing a close rapport in 1756 and 1763 with the 'plain loving people' in Coleford, who apparently had almost no 'disorderly walker' among them.[165] Methodism expanded markedly in the Forest in the early nineteenth century. By 1850 the Nonconformists were firmly established, and the

---

[164] Nicholls, *Forest of Dean*, pp. 155–6, 159, 168.
[165] *Ibid.*, p. 155. Charles Wesley had rather less success than his brother, as he nearly drowned while crossing the river Severn at Newham, and was stoned at St Briavels. The Foresters were often said to be 'intensely suspicious of strangers'. Bright, *Rise of Nonconformity in the Forest of Dean*, p. 1.

inhabitants of this mining region had developed a very dissenting (notably Methodist) reputation. Such a woodland, mining, quarrying and metal-working area, and such workers, were always likely to lean strongly towards denominations like the Primitive Methodists. This was a repeated pattern in comparable mining-industrial and commoning areas elsewhere, and some Nonconformist preachers in the Forest came from such areas in south Wales, the midlands and Somerset.

In the face of such Forest proclivities perhaps the Anglican Church cannot be blamed. It did take many steps to counteract Nonconformity, and the new churches, restorations and copious reformulations of parish boundaries and identities bear witness to that. Evidence of success at some levels can be seen in the large graveyard of Holy Trinity, Drybrook, the so-called 'Forest Church' which opened in 1817, with an impressive late Georgian vicarage, and this is where the Forest's talented historian Revd H. G. Nicholls was vicar between 1847 and 1866. Yet the lateness of many of the Anglican churches, and their usually high church orientation, had a rather limited effect in dislodging an essentially Nonconformist culture. Building upon the traditions of the 'free miners', which became fully legalised in 1838, and the development of heavier industry subsequently, that culture came to express a working-class consciousness and a Forest of Dean identity that tended to eclipse loyalty to the parish or village, giving the Forest the special character and reputation for mutual support and assertive solidarity which it had up to the 1960s.

NEW PARISHES IN THE TWENTIETH CENTURY

The process of new parish formation continued strongly into the twentieth century, although often with new causes or problems to solve. The Union of Benefices Act (1919), the Union of Benefices Measures of 1923–36, the New Parishes Measures of 1939 and 1943, the Reorganization Areas Measure (1944) – dealing with war-destroyed churches, reorganisation and town renewal – the Pastoral Reorganization Measure (1949), the Pastoral Measures of 1968 and 1983, the innovations of team and group ministries, and provisions for very many redundant churches, notably in the 1960s and 1970s, all ensured that changing boundaries and new parish creation was on-going. To judge from Leicestershire, Rutland and Cambridgeshire, new ecclesiastical parishes were formed in a fitful manner, with small bursts of notable change in 1904, 1918–32, 1941, and from 1951 into the 1970s. Despite the nineteenth-century legislation, many places remained outside any ecclesiastical parish, which needed to be remedied. In some years during the inter-war period, 'new parishes were created at the rate of one a fortnight' by the Ecclesiastical Commission.[166] In only one year, 1936, the Commission spent £189,000 endowing new parishes.[167] The boundaries of ecclesiastical parishes became more of a quandary to local people. Divisions between civil and ecclesiastical parishes continued to open up as more of both types of parish were formed, especially as a result of the Divided Parishes Acts of 1876 and 1882.[168] The growing powers of the Church of England to legislate for itself, through the Church Assembly after 1910, facilitated further ecclesiastical parish formation, arguably taking less and less note of civil parish units and institutions.

There were many other problems faced by the church, which often resulted in changes to parish entities. Church finance became ever more problematical, and the relative incomes of its clergy compared with other professions like medicine or law continued to decline, as they had since at least the 1870s. Queen Victoria's Clergy Sustentation Fund aimed to raise their incomes, but not much was achieved.[169] The value of rural endowments fell in the late nineteenth century, largely as a result of the agricultural depression, and the rural slump in the inter-war period had a similar effect. These depressions further marginalised the clergy in country parish life. There were complaints within the church about shortages of clergy, their quality, and of a lack of money to train or pay

---

[166] Sir G. Middleton, 'Estates of the Church', *Times* (13 August 1936), p. 11, col. G. The same point was made in 'Lords and Coal Bill', *Times* (4 May 1938), p. 7, col. A. Other denominations using a parochial system also rapidly changed the local geography of their parishes. See for example 'Roman Catholic Church extension', *Times* (5 June 1939), p. 11, col. B.

[167] 'The Church in 1936', *Times* (29 December 1936), p. 17, col. C.

[168] 'Ecclesiastical news: Bishop of Carlisle on church finance', *Times* (24 September 1924), p. 15, col. D.

[169] K. S. Inglis, *The Churches and the Working Classes in Victorian England* (London, 1963), p. 39.

them.[170] Clerical incomes remained very unequal.[171] As during the Napoleonic Wars, the two World Wars much reduced the numbers of men who were ordained.[172] The planning of so many new parishes called into question how they were to be supplied with clergy, and how that could be done without reducing clergy numbers in the most densely populated districts. Returning clergy from overseas helped to fill benefices: apparently it did not matter 'whether his previous experience has been gained in Togoland or Tooting'.[173] But new parishes were hindered by the low stipends payable, which were often declining in real terms. This had been a long-term problem in Wales – being one factor in the low numbers of new parishes which we have seen formed there in the nineteenth century – and it was now a national issue.[174] 'A Vicar cannot live on £120 a year', wrote J. B. Everard indignantly to the Ecclesiastical Commissioners in 1918, and he also complained that £160 a year 'is not sufficient at the present time for a clergyman with wife and children to live in decent comfort'.[175] In fact, inter-war clerical income was often barely above that of a labourer.[176] Pension provision was also inadequate, especially for widows and orphans of clergy.[177] The merger of benefices

[170] 'Sponsors', *Times* (26 May 1928), p. 13, col. D; 'Training for the Ministry', *Times* (26 June 1939), p. 17, col. E.
[171] H. McLeod, *Class and Religion in the Late Victorian City* (London, 1974), pp. 105–6, 122–3.
[172] 'Aid for Ordinands', *Times* (22 June 1946), p. 5, col. C.
[173] 'Clergy from oversea', *Times* (5 July 1934), p. 15, col. D.
[174] 'Welsh church finances', *Times* (30 September 1925), p. 9, col. D; 'Finances of the Church. Successive serious losses of clergy's income', *Times* (12 February 1947), p. 5, col. F; A. T. P. Williams, *The Anglican Tradition in the Life of England* (London, 1947), p. 122; C. Garbett, *The Claims of the Church of England* (1947, London, 1948), p. 153; Snell and Ell, *Rival Jerusalems*, pp. 87–9, on the mid-nineteenth-century English and Welsh values.
[175] Leics. CRO, DE 4502/16 (Bardon Hill: correspondence of 24 December 1917, and 17 January 1918. Everard wanted £200 per annum, a figure he then raised to 'at least £240').
[176] Dr H. W. Bradfield, '£500 minimum stipend, Bishop's objective for Diocese', *Times* (10 October 1952), p. 3, col. A (the author was Bishop of Wells and Bath, and was discussing that diocese); T. Barnes, *My Dorset Days* (Sherborne, 1980), pp. 75–6. An agricultural labourer (among the lowest paid of all labourers) would earn an average of about £100 per annum in 1930. W. H. Pedley, *Labour on the Land: A Study of the Developments between the Two Great Wars* (London, 1942), p. 38.
[177] 'Urgent needs of the Church today', *Times* (4 October 1934), p. 14, col. E.

was therefore needed for reasons of efficiency, finance and clerical recruitment.[178]

A few people were willing to leave sums to help endow new parishes, like Horace Gummer of Bristol, who left £2,500 from his tobacco profits for this purpose in 1931.[179] Yet this was rarer than it had been in past centuries, and aid from the state was not now forthcoming for new churches. With so many inhabitants who were clerks, artisans and other such occupations, it was impossible for local people to build a church in a new parish around somewhere like London.[180] A unification of urban parishes also brought foreseeable problems with church schools, as rich and well-equipped parishes were sometimes united with poor or recent ones.[181] Above all, suburbanisation raised huge difficulties for the church, as indeed it did for the Nonconformists. The growth of suburbs around London was well under way from 1861, facilitated by transport improvements. It generated a need for new churches in areas which had hitherto lacked them, such as 'London-over-the-border' (Charles Dickens' term for south-west Essex), where ten new ecclesiastical parishes were formed between 1914 and 1925 (in places like Walthamstow, East Ham or Ilford).[182] Churches were lacking in many areas, such as to the south of London,[183] or in the new housing areas of Birmingham,[184] and such churches also needed sites, endowments, schools, and parsonages.[185] Moreover, as people moved to the suburbs, the working classes left behind in some cities formed something akin to one-class parishes, rendering futile the socially unifying qualities sometimes associated with parish life. As the centres of cities remained as slums or as commercial centres, it was also increasingly hard to attract people to city

---

[178] 'Church property and finance', *Times* (12 May 1924), p. 15, col. E; 'Dearth of young clergy', *Times* (24 August 1925), p. 7, col. B.

[179] 'Wills and bequests', *Times* (1 June 1931), p. 19, col. D.

[180] 'Judicial Committee of the Privy Council, All Hallows, Lombard Street: demolition scheme', *Times* (10 February 1937), p. 4, col. B.

[181] 'Oxford diocesan conference', *Times* (5 November 1925), p. 9, col. E.

[182] 'Ecclesiastical news', *Times* (27 May 1925), p. 19, col. D, 'Essex churches and schools', *Times* (2 February 1934), p. 15, col. D.

[183] 'Ecclesiastical news: Bishop of Southwark's appeal', *Times* (12 October 1925), p. 19, col. D; 'Bishop of London's Jubilee', *Times* (26 June 1935), p. 13, col. D.

[184] 'Church extension in Birmingham', *Times* (6 December 1933), p. 19, col. E.

[185] 'The Church in new areas', *Times* (21 April 1936), p. 9, col. A.

churches: 'the clergy have to rack their brains to do this'.[186] Organ recitals and midday services resulted. Sales of rectories and vicarages – even the sale of churches on valuable sites for commercial needs, for example in Exeter – resulted in some profits being reallocated to supplement the poor livings of new suburban parishes.[187] Many new parishes were formed in Middlesex, to cater for 'these great new towns which cluster on the circumference of London! . . . Gone are almost all the fields through which we used to bicycle before the War.'[188] Between 1901 and 1931 there were forty-seven new parishes created in London, mainly in the suburbs.[189] St Andrews church, Kingsbury, Middlesex, was built by moving a church, stone by stone, from the city,[190] but the central churches in cities like London or Liverpool could hardly be pulled down and moved like this in response to these major population shifts. Nor could their resources be easily transferred. Six Liverpool churches had to be demolished, and five of its churches were sold under the Liverpool and Wigan Churches Act (1904). Others in that city were demolished under the Union of Benefices Act (1923).[191]

Lingering hopes to move some of the more famous city churches – for example some of Wren's – to the suburbs were halted when they were bombed. Even if the church walls remained, bombing ruined many of their interiors.[192] The extent of Second World War damage to churches was horrific. Out of 2,258 churches and chapels located in the diocese of London, only 266 escaped war damage; 88 per cent of them were damaged, many wholly destroyed. Out of 701 Anglican churches, 624 were damaged, 91 of them completely devastated.[193] (By comparison, 86 churches were destroyed by the Great Fire of

---

[186] C. B. Marshall, 'Church and nation', *Times* (11 November 1925), p. 8, col. A.
[187] Revd A. P. Lancefield, 'Churches in cathedral cities', *Times* (19 September 1927), p. 8, col. D.
[188] G. Vernon Willesden, 'Changing Middlesex', *Times* (7 February 1934), p. 8, col. D.
[189] 'The new districts of London', *Times* (31 May 1932), p. 12, col. C.
[190] 'Church removed stone by stone', *Times* (15 October 1934), p. 19, col. D.
[191] 'City churches in Liverpool', *Times* (27 May 1929), p. 21, col. B; and see 'Church extension in Liverpool', *Times* (17 December 1935), p. 17, col. E.
[192] H. Baker, 'After the City fires', *Times* (15 January 1941), p. 5, col. E; J. M. Richards (ed.), *The Bombed Buildings of Britain: A Record of Architectural Casualties, 1940–41* (Cheam, 1942).
[193] Bishop of London, 'Churches for Londoners. Plans for new buildings and new parishes: war damage and population change', *Times* (22 May 1946), p. 5, col. F.

London in 1666.) Many of their parishes could not persist in their older shape, because, even with assistance from the War Damage Commission and appeals by the bishop and diocesan organisations, funds were lacking to rebuild or repair churches on this scale.[194] In London and elsewhere, war damage expedited further parochial changes, under the Reorganization Areas Measure, permanently re-arranging parishes and their clergy.[195] At least eighty-three London diocese parishes were merged into other parishes shortly after the war, creating many new parishes. The clergy and the parochial system proved their usefulness during the war, with clergy organising shelters, billeting, providing centres of rest and re-creation, supplementing local authorities' roles during air raids, using parish halls, arranging removals to the country, and so on. Yet the urban church emerged from war in real crisis, its churches often in ashes, its ordinations well under a third of what they had been in 1939, and many benefices vacant. Congregations continued to decrease, the meaning and visibility of the parish seemed persistently to diminish, and even more church social organisations and functions were about to be taken over by the state.

In the face of these urban problems in the first half of the twentieth century, there was less tolerance for small rural parishes, each traditionally manned by a clergyman.[196] The model of the rural parish continued to influence urban church planning, as it had done since Thomas Chalmers' days. Rural parishes still predominated numerically, despite the urban concentration of population. Yet there was less patience with the financial and administrative aspects of such rural-pastoral indulgence. The inter-war agricultural depression was severe in some regions – many fields reverted to waste, weeds, and wildlife – and rural depopulation occurred at an ever faster pace. 'Urban areas multiply; country areas become almost Deserted Villages.'[197] Adrian Bell wrote in 1932 of rural Suffolk and its abandoned farms that 'The country round us became lonely,

---

[194] 'London churches. Many parishes to be reorganized', *Times* (14 February 1946), p. 7, col. D; 'Restoring church life', *Times* (26 August 1946), p. 7, col. D.

[195] 'Church planning', *Times* (6 March 1943), p. 5, col. C; 'The post-war Church', *Times* (20 November 1943), p. 5, col. D.

[196] G. R. Y. Radcliffe, 'A financial policy for the church', *Times* (6 March 1930), p. 10, col. C.

[197] 'The parochial system', *Times* (20 October 1934), p. 13, col. C.

thinly populated. The old community I had known on coming here ten years ago or more was now almost all gone . . . It had died away – the old bluff, hospitable life of the countryside – like a summer's day. I saw it fade.'[198] As with the deserted villages of late medieval England, upkeep of small-congregation rural churches was an ever greater problem. The case for union of rural parishes became stronger. 'Small country parishes . . . are being amalgamated and wiped out of separate existence.'[199] At the same time, thousands of people were moving from city centres into suburbs. As W. J. Smith saw it in 1936:

During the Industrial Revolution England became mainly urban. To-day, there is rapidly proceeding the reverse process – de-urbanisation. People are moving their homes away from the places where they find work. The age-old parochial system is bearing a breaking strain. It is essentially a static system. It must become more fluid . . . Church authorities should be endowed with power to combine some of the older parishes and sell redundant churches and church sites, thereby releasing money and men for new parishes.[200]

This was an agenda for yet more new parishes, on top of and churning up what the nineteenth century had done, and that is essentially what happened.

Faced with such contrary tendencies – the rural exodus, and suburbanisation – it is no surprise that the rural parochial model was increasingly challenged by some authorities in the church, who came up with alternative models. Debate along these lines, raising many options, had occurred in the nineteenth century too. Horace Mann, for example, had intelligently discussed the problems of new parishes in large towns, especially the conundrum of reconciling urban pastoral supervision with running a church. He had advocated 'conventional' districts and additional clerical and lay 'agents' as auxiliaries to the regular incumbent, serving existing churches and parishes, rather than 'a much minuter subdivision of existing districts, with the erection of much smaller churches'.[201] Even by 1851, in other

[198] A. Bell, *The Cherry Tree* (1932, London, 1949), pp. 40–1.
[199] 'Clergy from oversea', *Times* (5 July 1934), p. 15, col. D.
[200] W. J. Smith, 'New building areas and the Church', *Times* (31 December 1936), p. 10, col. C.
[201] *Census of Great Britain, 1851. Religious Worship. England and Wales*, LXXXIX (1853), pp. clxii–clxiii.

words, there was implied criticism of what had become frequent practice over the past decade. These debates and policy options intensified subsequently. What were the alternatives to the parochial system? Could forms of congregationalism substitute for the urban parish? What should be the supervisory basis of mission activity? How might lay evangelists be organised? Was there a role for brotherhoods of clergy, as suggested by E. B. Pusey, an idea with intimations of revived monasticism? The Bishop of Worcester later argued for 'strong centres' serving comparatively wide districts. He felt that this was 'certainly preferable to the haphazard creation of new parishes'.[202] Others wanted the rural deanery to be such a centre. W. E. Tate predicted in 1946 that in the future the 'parson will have disappeared, as he is daily doing through the amalgamation of parishes, so that a future generation of villagers will have perhaps a quarter of a rector or 33⅓rd per cent of a vicar'.[203] That fraction for many parishes is in fact now well below what he predicted. Throughout the twentieth century, financial exigencies, apparent indecision and lack of consistent policy, short-term *ad hoc* remedies, rapid about-turns – all of them reasonably trying to adjust to the pace of change – have characterised an established church that once defined and prided itself in relation to a stable 'ancient' parish system which also embraced civil administration. One should not devalue the contribution that countless clergymen made in the twentieth century: the religious services, pastoral support, church music, Sunday schools, parish clubs and branches of national organisations, the parochial church council, fund-raising, church upkeep, and so much else. Yet stumbling through so many parochial changes, bewildered by adjustments to boundaries, having to deal with functionally varying and differently named districts, it is hardly surprising that many people discarded both a religious faith and a sense of belonging to 'their' parish, and looked elsewhere for their senses of identity.

---

[202] 'The parochial system', *Times* (20 October 1934), p. 13, col. C.
[203] W. E. Tate, *The Parish Chest: A Study of the Records of Parochial Administration in England* (1946, Cambridge, 1960), p. 3; to similar effect, and stressing loss of leadership and social life, see C. S. Orwin, *Problems of the Countryside* (Cambridge, 1945), p. 10.

CONCLUSION

The nineteenth century is sometimes seen as a period of declining conjoint secular/ecclesiastical functions of the parish, in which the parish was increasingly left with a largely religious role. In the twentieth century, the word 'parish' became highly coloured by religious connotations and usage, so it probably now has antiquarian associations to many people.[204] Yet, as we see in other chapters of this book, the parish continued through the nineteenth century as crucially important in many matters, as for example respecting the role of overseers, or as the venue where people received out-door poor relief, or as a key unit in people's identity, for example with regard to attitudes to local 'outsiders', or as informing ideas of belonging upon death. 'Civil' parishes were also altered in many ways by the Poor Law Board and other authorities – that is an important subject which, while overlapping with this discussion, has not been my main focus here, mainly because those alterations were not on such a large scale as those affecting ecclesiastical parishes. Civil parishes were probably weakened, but not greatly incapacitated, by the way in which ecclesiastical parishes were created, despite the problems that often resulted. In some ways parish administration expanded. For example, parochialisation or the assimilation of extra-parochial places or detached parts into adjoining parishes increased the administrative tasks and size of many parishes. In addition, the huge increase in ecclesiastical parishes and their churches can, in some regards, be judged as a token of the *vitality* of the parish in the nineteenth century. One does not create 4,000 or so new parishes, and adjust many more, if one does not value them highly. So many new parishes highlight the expectations that contemporaries had of the parish, underline the way in which they took it for granted as fundamental for communities, and show how they extolled the social, administrative and ecclesiastical life that it could encapsulate. The vitality of the parish is borne out too by the sweeping levels of church restoration, which occurred with or independently of

---

[204] Poole and Keith-Lucas, *Parish Government*, p. 207, citing the Minister of State (David Gibson-Watt), on the term parish having 'an ecclesiastical ring and is associated with workhouses and poverty. It may also be described as old-fashioned.'

these changes. One may bewail that restoration – many do – but it was done for a purpose beyond historical respect and antiquarian restorative precision. It was done in the nineteenth century out of continuing theological and parochial faith; while today when we (occasionally) restore churches we do so as architectural monuments. Which, asking objectively and as a historian, is preferable?

In these regards, one of the themes of this book – the on-going strength of the parish in the nineteenth century – is well displayed. In many cases, new churches and parishes were certainly needed. It is easy to point to features of parish division and geography in the late eighteenth century which were extremely odd, complex, or even corrupt. Many contemporaries did, some of them with radical agendas in mind. Plenty of these parishes needed to be 'tidied up', and reform aimed to do that. In some cases, the results were a major improvement, and came to mean much to local people, who identified with them. New churches were often funded heavily by local subscriptions, and their consecrations were often mass events, causes for local celebration, elaborate flower-bedecked occasions of local pride, and certainly these events did not always meet with cynical opposition, 'rough music', and a terrified bishop's coachman. In the case of London and other cities, some of the new churches were well attended.[205] They brought in their wake other assets, like new schools and a better framework for education, visiting societies, home missionary societies, mission churches or rooms, urban settlements (with their social services), charity organisations, dispensaries, and so on. The optimistic view of new parish creation may be summed up in the words of Robert Rodes, who wrote that 'by the last quarter of the nineteenth century the parish system was pretty well up to date, pretty well uniform, and capable of further updating as required'.[206] Many in the church saw it that way, and certainly one can see advantages in what had been achieved.

A less optimistic assessment would point to other characteristics and consequences. Robert Southey, poet laureate and 'defender of the poor', died in 1843, the year of the New Parishes

---

[205] Welch, 'Bishop Blomfield', p. 214.
[206] Rodes, *Law and Modernization*, p. 169.

Act. He had spoken of how 'The diseased growth of parishes frustrated the political as well as the religious purposes of our old parochial system, if we may be permitted to consider apart things which are, strictly speaking, inseparable.'[207] One can imagine, therefore, what he might have said about the subsequent expansion of new parishes. From his perspective, the danger was the growing separation of the civil from the ecclesiastical, and that was undeniably hastened by one-dimensional new parish creation, *either* for ecclesiastical *or* civil purposes. The mismatches between civil and ecclesiastical parishes, and the discontinuities and dissolving senses of local place that resulted, were perceived features on the ground and in communities of the growing separation of Church and State. They affected most people's lives in a way that conventional political discourse and arguments about 'Church and State' did not. These parochial disjunctures and reformulations increasingly left parish life weakened and shrivelled by comparison with previous centuries, while parish inhabitants tried to shrug off their frustrations and growing sense of powerlessness. The alternatives provided by the Nonconformist communities could also appear more attractive as the social benefits of the Anglican parish dwindled; while of course many people discarded religion altogether.

One can form these judgements despite the many initiatives that were taken by countless clergy to invigorate a more narrowly defined religious life in the parishes, which was often achieved in the half century or so after 1843. This separation of parochial functions coalesced with many other changes in the nineteenth century, and it was agreeable to the leanings of many churchmen. The growing functional divide between ecclesiastical and civil parishes was a corollary or parallel outcome of the Oxford Movement and its related interests affecting ecclesiology, liturgy, ritual, and the priestly role of the clergy. Furthermore, in making a case for people themselves, not the State, to build churches, as they imagined had been the medieval situation, the Oxford Movement and the high churchmen it

---

[207] R. Southey, in Coleman (ed.), *Idea of the City*, pp. 41–2.

influenced tacitly accepted the political strength of Nonconformity and contributed further to disengage church activity from civil affairs. In some new parishes this was welcomed, and may have been successful, perhaps even up to the mid-twentieth century. Yet it contributed to a *laissez-faire* exuberance of church building: 'sacred progress measured in ecclesiastical bricks and mortar', coupled with a 'free-enterprise system of parochial subdivision'.[208] Although this was, in a curious way, in harmony with much economic thinking, it left a demoralising legacy of redundant or nearly empty churches,[209] and a plethora of poorly planned or nearly unworkable urban parishes.

Other commentators believed that the industrial revolution had 'wrecked' the existing parochial system, partly through urbanisation shifting the balance of population, and partly through the patchy jumble of subdividing new parishes formed to deal with these problems.[210] Such subdivision, or coppicing, of parishes was said to be necessary to deal with high densities of population, but, as Gladstone pointed out, there was 'no adequate provision for a clergyman in many of these small parishes'.[211] Providing a living for a tithe-dependent clergyman had been a major determinant of parish sizes back in very early medieval times. Yet such a spatial criterion was utterly incompatible with practical clerical services to densely populated industrial cities, where the population of a street or two would exceed that of many Anglo-Saxon villages. Despite the efforts that were made, which were often heroic and self-sacrificing, historians might think that little could have been done to acclimatise traditionally conceived church and parish communities to the dramatic growth of some Victorian towns and cities. Lord Shaftesbury believed in 1857 that the population of large towns, particularly the metropolis, had outstripped the parochial

[208] The quotations are respectively from Green, *Religion in the Age of Decline*, p. 89; and A. Saint, 'Anglican Church building in London, 1790–1890: from state subsidy to the free market', in Brooks and Saint (eds.), *Victorian Church*, p. 47 (and see his whole chapter). Green, *Religion in the Age of Decline*, p. 129, also speaks of 'the largely unplanned, unintended and almost uncontrolled evolution of the urban ecclesiastical plan'.

[209] R. Gill, *The Myth of the Empty Church* (London, 1993), discusses the negative effects upon religious attendance of excessive church provision and empty seats.

[210] For example, Webster, *Joshua Watson*, p. 60.

[211] *Hansard*, CX (1 May 1850), 1081–3.

system, and many clergy probably felt that way.[212] 'However it busied itself in the city', wrote Chris Brooks, 'nineteenth-century Anglicanism had never lost the feeling that its true home was the rural parish.'[213] The suitability of the parochial system to urban life was widely disputed, given urban morphologies, population densities, slums, socio-economic structures, patterns of re-creation, internal migration, problems of public health, sanitation and burial grounds, the absence of paternalistic gentry, let alone the acute competition from rival denominations who ignored the parish system. Sir Edward Akroyd built All Souls Halifax in the 1850s partly to keep up 'the old notion of a village' within an industrial town: a hierarchical society of land-lord and labourers sharing a common faith.[214] In some indus-trial towns such urban paternalism seemed to perpetuate a rural model, but very often the rural parish ideal was conspicuously unsuccessful when transplanted in this way. Even in a town like Brighton, hardly notable for industrialisation, 'the parochial system may be said to be extinct'.[215] By 1890, many clergy themselves had lost faith in new parishes, some even thinking them 'a lost cause, an exploded method'.[216] The new parishes and their boundaries were often as unclear and unreal to local people as they were to dispirited census authorities, and many parish boundaries within the industrial cities must have had negligible practical or cultural significance to inhabitants. Such parochial units were rarely 'communities', and could do little to augment a sense of 'community', especially when they no longer meant much in terms of civil administration. For people already often suffering the trials of rural exodus and urban dislocation, the parochial discontinuities and vaguenesses offered very little in terms of reassurance or security. Some of the new churches were well attended, as indicated above – but many were not;

---

[212] G. B. A. M. Finlayson, *The Seventh Earl of Shaftesbury, 1801–1885* (London, 1981), pp. 387–91.
[213] C. Brooks, 'Building the rural church: money, power and the country parish', in Brooks and Saint (eds.), *Victorian Church*, p. 76.
[214] Green, *Religion in the Age of Decline*, pp. 102–3.
[215] The Revd Arthur Wagner, to the *Royal Commission on Ritual*, xx (1867), pp. 846ff, cited in E. P. Hennock, 'The Anglo-Catholics and church extension in Victorian Brighton', in M. J. Kitch (ed.), *Studies in Sussex Church History* (London, 1981), p. 178.
[216] H. J. Tebbut, in *Church Congress Report* (1889), p. 51, cited in Inglis, *Churches and the Working Classes*, p. 27.

in fact many in the diocese of London were said to have 'stood nearly empty', especially in the poorest districts.[217] Their large building debts (which often lasted decades), and the church repair costs, can hardly have helped to attract congregations either.

The church itself was becoming more separated from social services – whether these were schooling, the poor law, vestry matters, health care, charities, almshouses, the giving of legal advice, and so on – and the new parishes expedited this process. These were church units stripped threadbare of many earlier parochial functions. Government of the ancient parish, and parish welfare provision, in which the clergy in the seventeenth and eighteenth centuries had been prominent, came gradually under the aegis of a variety of different authorities, many of them distant from the parish itself, and having much stronger powers than the parish vestry. This administrative eclipsing of the parish was slower in the nineteenth century than most historians have recognised, but it was certainly underway. Rather than sympathetically adopt the older parish to new needs, as a fundamental local unit of belonging still largely commensurate with the lived ambit of everyday life, and one that was compatible with democracy, alternative administrative areas now escalated in an alarming manner. Their complexity is one reason why they have attracted so few historians. They included ecclesiastical *versus* civil parishes, distinct and separate parishes, district chapelries, particular districts, patronage districts, consolidated chapelries, surviving Gilbert unions, highway districts, census districts, poor law unions, relieving officer districts, medical officer districts, district parish wards, school board districts, burial board districts, police districts, sanitary districts, Parliamentary districts, county boroughs, municipal boroughs, metropolitan boroughs, rural and urban districts, registration or administrative *versus* historical counties, and so on, superadded to almost all the re-defined or re-used eighteenth-century entities, very few of which disappeared – in short, all the confusing geographical miscellanea of Victorian local government.

---

[217] P. T. Marsh, *The Victorian Church in Decline: Archbishop Tait and the Church of England, 1868–1882* (London, 1969), p. 7; Lewis, *Lighten their Darkness*, pp. 108–9.

These all had their own areas and boundaries, which some-times coincided, and usually did not. Multiplicities of boundar-ies and lines of division meant that boundaries became increasingly invisible. The ancient parish had usually been rela-tively clear-cut; it had been widely comprehended through local culture, custom and rating practices, its boundaries were well known, and for good or ill it was often strongly identified with. But what local unit of personal belonging, identity and attach-ment could survive as meaningful among all the farraginous bureaucratic districts of the nineteenth century? It was probably inevitable that people's ideas of belonging would gradually transfer from the ancient parish, to vaguer alternatives: subject-ive, residential, aesthetic, or broader areas which were person-ally rather than administratively defined; and senses of belonging were weakened because they now had less connec-tion with administrative districts, the latter having become so disparate, multi-layered and confusing to come to terms with.

There were further transitions which reduced the role of the parish and its traditional administrators in people's lives. Church rates were abolished in 1868. The Burial Laws Amend-ment Act of 1880 further diminished the responsibilities and powers of incumbents. Many churchyards were being closed and replaced by municipal cemeteries. The vestry itself became increasingly secular, especially in the 1880s and 1890s. The 1894 Local Government Act had a key effect. It reduced the role of the clergyman (who was now no longer necessarily the chairman, and who had to be elected to the parish council), took manage-ment of burial grounds from the vestry to the parish councils, transferred control over 'civil' charities to the council (causing many quarrels in the process), and in a number of other ways concluded the intimate connection between civil and religious matters that had been axiomatic since 1601 and earlier. As Rod Ambler has written, the 1894 Act was 'in effect a local disestab-lishment of the Church of England'.[218] The clergyman could still have a significant on-going place in parish governance, but this was being reduced, and it became less natural for him if his

---

[218] Ambler, *Churches, Chapels and the Parish Communities of Lincolnshire*, p. 2; Chadwick, *Victorian Church, Part II*, pp. 196–200; E. Norman, *Church and Society in England, 1770–1970: A Historical Study* (Oxford, 1976), p. 219.

benefice was no longer co-extensive with the civil parish. He had less authority on the vestry, the powers of which were being whittled down by 1900 mainly to ecclesiastical matters. The role of churchwardens also diminished markedly in nineteenth-century civil matters, for example in poor law administration, with them ceasing to act as 'overseers' from 1894. Owen Chadwick has rightly pointed out that 'the removal of the secular business left the vestry without a life . . . [which] forced the Church of England to remake its parish constitution'.[219]

These developments hastened the segregation of church and civil life, and at local level left both weaker. Society itself was shifting towards secular pluralism, and however invigorated the movement to subdivide and create new parishes was, in the context of wider ideological and scientific thought there was probably little that could be done to halt this trend. 'For the parish had meaning and vitality only in a society whose central core was the Christian Church',[220] and it was one of the tragedies of local history in the nineteenth and early twentieth centuries that, in moving away from such a Christian concept of local and parish identity, other less religious justifications for local governance, administration and local attachment were not retained or substituted. We have lived uneasily with the consequences for a long time.

[219] Chadwick, *Victorian Church, Part II*, p. 199.
[220] Brose, *Church and Parliament*, p. 206.

APPENDIX 7.1 FOREST OF DEAN CHANGES IN PARISH STRUCTURES

Place or parish	Parish creation or reforming	Composition and other details of district/parish and church building
Woolaston	1711	Chapelry of Lancaut attached to Woolaston.
Bream	1752, 1756	Ecclesiastical parish created, from Newland.
Coleford	1782	Ecclesiastical parish created, from Newland.
West Dean township	1844	Formed from extra-parochial Forest of Dean.
St Paul	1822, 1842	Parkend (church built in 1821–2), created from Whitecroft, Futterill.
All Saints	1842	Created from Yorkley and Viney Hill.
Holy Jesus	1842	Most of Lydbrook. Church built in 1850–1.
Christ Church	1817, 1842	Berry Hill, Joyford, Hillersland and Lane Ends. Church built 1812–13 and 1816.
East Dean township	1844	Formed from extra-parochial Forest of Dean.
Holy Trinity	1817, 1842, 1844	Including Drybrook, Ruardean Woodside, Ruardean Hill, Harrow Hill, part of Lydbrook. Church built in 1816–17 at Harrow Hill.
St John the Evangelist	1844/5	Comprising Bilson, Ruspidge, Soudley, part of Viney Hill. Church built in 1843–4 at Ruspidge. Given a district from the eastern part of the Forest of Dean, from Blaize Bailey to Cannop, including Ruspidge and Soudley.
English Bicknor	1842	Much of Mailscot added to English Bicknor.
Parkend	1842/4	Church of St Paul built in 1821–2. District (1844) in southern part of the Forest of Dean, between Blakeney Hill, Clearwell Meend, Cannop and the Speech House. (This district or parish was much altered later.)

Appendix (*cont.*)

Place or parish	Parish creation or reforming	Composition and other details of district/parish and church building
St Briavels	1842	Enlarged with the addition of detached parts of Forest of Dean extra-parochial area. Civil parish enlarged to include Mocking Hazel Wood, the Fence, Bearse Common, and most of Hudnalls.
Hewelsfield	1842	Tract of extra-parochial land (Hewelsfield Common and part of Hudnalls) added to Hewelsfield for civil purposes.
Berry Hill/Christ Church	1844	Assigned a district with Joyford, Hillersland and Lane Ends. Christ Church built in 1812–13 and 1816.
Cinderford	1845	Separate civil parish created.
Bishop's Wood	1845	Ecclesiastical parish created, from Ruardean and Walford.
Beachley	1850	Ecclesiastical parish created.
Highnam	1851	Churcham, and hamlets of Highnam, Over and Linton formed into the ecclesiastical parish of Highnam.
Lydbrook	1852	Consolidated chapelry created from parishes of English Bicknor, Newland, south-west Ruardean, parts of Holy Trinity, and townships of East and West Dean. Church of Holy Jesus built in 1850–1.
Blakeney	1853	Assigned a separate ecclesiastical district from the southern part of the parish of Awre.
Bream	1854	Ecclesiastical parish re-created from Newland and West Dean township, including from St Paul, Parkend.

Appendix (*cont.*)

Place or parish	Parish creation or reforming	Composition and other details of district/parish and church building
Hewelsfield	1855	Separate ecclesiastical parish and living created.
St Briavels	1855	Made a separate ecclesiastical parish.
Clearwell	1856	Consolidated chapelry formed. Included parts of Newland, and the ecclesiastical district of St Paul, Parkend.
Lea Bailey	1866	Separate civil parish created from earlier tithing.
Churcham/Highnam, Over and Linton	1866	Separate civil parish made from three hamlets.
Viney Hill/All Saints (later called Parkend)	1866	Made an ecclesiastical parish with Yorkley church (All Saints). Land taken from St Paul, including Blakeney Hill and Yorkley Slade. Church built in 1865–7.
Aylburton	1866	Made a separate civil parish, but having no separate ecclesiastical identity it stayed as a chapelry of Lydney.
Hinders Lane and Dockham	1858	Civil parish created from extra-parochial land (on Littledean Hill).
Coleford	1872	Ecclesiastical district re-created for Coleford chapel. New church opened in 1880.
Woodside	1873	Made into a district with its own curate.
Blakeney	1878	Formed from civil parish of Awre.
St Stephen's Woodside	1880	Ecclesiastical parish comprising Bilson Woodside (part of Cinderford), parts of Newland, St John, Hinders Lane, Dockham, Holy Trinity, and land taken from Flaxley. Church built in 1888–90.
Wick	1880	Ecclesiastical parish formed out of Abson. Church built in 1850 (St Bartholomew).

Place or parish	Parish creation or reforming	Composition and other details of district/parish and church building
Cinderford	1880	Parts of Holy Trinity transferred to Cinderford.
Westbury	1882/3	Part of Flaxley transferred to Westbury.
Mitcheldean	1882/3	Blackwell Meadows transferred to East Dean civil parish, under the Divided Parishes Act, 1882.
Blaisdon	1883	A portion of Flaxley absorbed by Blaisdon civil parish.
Littledean	1883, 1884	The civil parish took in parts of Flaxley, Newland and a small detached part of Westbury-on-Severn.
Flaxley	1883	A portion of Flaxley transferred to East Dean township or civil parish. Part of Blaisdon added to Flaxley.
Ruardean	1884	Two detached parts of Newland added to Ruardean. A detached part of Lydbrook added to Ruardean.
Yorkley Wood	1884	Church built in 1884.
Hinders Lane and Dockham	1884	Abolished and merged with East Dean civil parish.
Coleford	1890	Ecclesiastical parish enlarged to include Lane End district in the Forest of Dean, Broadwell, Clearwell, and the north-west of St Pauls, Parkend.
Coleford tithing	1894	Became a separate civil parish.

Newland detached parts:

Parts of Lea Bailey	1883, 1890	Transferred to Lea.
Parts of Lea Bailey	1883	Transferred to Weston under Penyard
Parts of Lea Bailey	1884	Transferred to Hope Mansell.
Parts of Lea Bailey	1884	Transferred to Walford.
Parts of Lea Bailey	1884	Transferred to East Dean.
Parts of Lea Bailey	1890	Transferred to Blaisdon.
Morse Grounds at Drybrook	1883	Transferred to East Dean.

Appendix (*cont.*)

Place or parish	Parish creation or reforming	Composition and other details of district/parish and church building
Area near Pope's Hill	1883	Transferred to Littledean.
Area at Ellwood	1883	Transferred to West Dean.
Whitemead Park	1883	Transferred to West Dean.
Oakwood Mill (north of Bream)	1883	Transferred to West Dean.
Hoarthorns farm (north-east of Berry Hill), and part of Joyford hamlet	1883	Transferred to West Dean.
Reddings (near Lydbrook)	1884	Transferred to Ruardean.

Twentieth century:

Place or parish	Parish creation or reforming	Composition and other details of district/parish and church building
St Paul	1909	Gained two detached parts of Newland at Yorkley.
Clearwell	1909	Ecclesiastical parish re-created.
Upper Soudley	1909–10	Church built at Upper Soudley.
Shapridge	1912	Parts of Edge Hill area and Plump Hill transferred to Holy Trinity for ecclesiastical purposes.
St Briavels	1932	Ecclesiastical parish extended to include former extra-parochial areas of the civil parish (St Briavels Castle, Bearse Common, Forest Fence and the Fence, Mocking Hazel Wood, part of Hudnalls with St Briavels Common).
Tidenham with Lancaut	1932	Ecclesiastical parish created, partly from Lancaut chapelry.
Hewelsfield	1932	Southern part of St Briavels Common and part of St Briavels added to Hewelsfield ecclesiastical parish.
Milkwall	1935	A small church built at Milkwall.
Mitcheldean	1935	Main area of Abenhall joined with Mitcheldean civil parish.
Newland	1935	Civil boundary changed.

Appendix (*cont.*)

Place or parish	Parish creation or reforming	Composition and other details of district/parish and church building
English Bicknor	1935	Part of Mailscot (in West Dean) transferred to English Bicknor.
Alvington	1935	Civil boundary altered.
Hewelsfield	1935	Civil boundary altered.
Awre	1935	Civil boundary altered.
Flaxley	1935	Flaxley civil parish was united with Blaisdon.
Lydbrook	1935	North-east part of English Bicknor transferred to Lydbrook civil parish, along with parts of Ruardean and West Dean. (A third of English Bicknor inhabitants were thus shifted to Lydbrook.)
Churcham	1935	Civil boundary altered.
Tidenham	1935	Civil boundary changed, adding Lancaut.
Lydney	1935	Church built near New Mills added to Lydney from West Dean.
Mitcheldean	1946	The benefice was united with Abenhall.
Littledean	1953	Parish enlarged, from East Dean.
Ruspidge	1953	Civil parish created from East Dean.
Awre	1953	Civil boundary altered, part added from East Dean.
Mitcheldean	1953	Civil parish gains part of East Dean.
Cinderford and Ruspidge	1953	Parish of East Dean was dismembered. New civil parishes of Cinderford and Ruspidge were created.
Drybrook	1953	New civil parish was created, from East Dean.
Drybrook	1957	Civil parish was altered.
Hewelsfield	1963	The living of Hewelsfield was joined to St Briavels.
Goodrich	1965	Part of English Bicknor transferred to Goodrich.
Mitcheldean	1965	Civil parish boundary altered.

CHAPTER 8

'Of this parish': gravestones, belonging and local attachment

I am a stranger and a sojourner with you: give me a possession of a burying place with you, that I may bury my dead out of my sight.[1]

Each in his narrow cell for ever laid, The rude Forefathers of the hamlet sleep.[2]

I

Anyone who looks at gravestones in church or chapel burial grounds will observe a very frequent feature. It was once extremely common to add to the name of the deceased further details about where they were 'of' or 'from'. Very frequently the phrase used was 'of this parish'. One typical inscription reads: 'Here lieth the Body of joan the wife of walter Williams of Baddon in the Parish of Brideftow', to take an example dated 1774 from Lydford in west Dartmoor. Other inscriptions may take the form of 'In Memory of [name], of this parish', or 'of the parish of . . .'. The wording can vary in a number of ways. Sometimes one finds the person, or his or her spouse or parents, being ascribed to a certain place rather than 'this parish', a place that may be a small settlement or even a house address, through to a large city. Assuming that the memorials have not suffered much erosion (which is often the case where limestone or sandstone monuments predominate), one will find such mention of place following many deceased people's names in most areas in the eighteenth and nineteenth centuries. In some regions, such as many parts of Norfolk and Suffolk, it is less striking, even though the imported Barnack stone, or the

---

[1] Genesis, 23: 4.
[2] Thomas Gray, 'Elegy written in a country church-yard' (1751), st. 4.

sandstone from north-east England that was often used along the north Norfolk coast, lent itself to fine carving of cherubs, symbols and lettering.[3] Statements of belonging may often have been superfluous in a region like this with high levels of parochial endogamy.[4] However, in many other regions – such as Leicestershire and its adjoining counties, Cumbria, Yorkshire, or north Devon – these statements are very prevalent indeed. There are even some parishes, such as Hartland on the north-west Devon coast, where this recording of place is on a majority of gravestones before the twentieth century. As one moves into that century such recording became less frequent in all regions of England. Indeed, from about the end of the First World War it ends as a widespread phenomenon.

This is a completely untouched historical subject, both as a commemorative practice and as something subject to remarkable change. Adding to the earlier chapters, it may reveal much about how ideas of 'belonging' were manifested in the past.[5] It relates closely to what the Suffolk writer Adrian Bell described as 'the lessening of the power of the spirit of place'.[6] As we saw

---

[3] Researchers on gravestones will know how variable types of stone are in their durability, and how prone to erosion Cotswold limestone, Bath and Portland stone, north-eastern sandstone and many other types are, especially when compared with the varieties of granite, slate and imported marble. Dioceses often controlled which stone was allowed, sometimes insisting on local stone. In Leicestershire and the surrounding counties, where much of my research has been conducted, slates from the Swithland and Groby quarries provided some of the most outstanding materials ever used for gravestone memorials, and the intensely fine rococo designs and calligraphy of the eighteenth-century carvers survive today in almost pristine clarity. However, it is not my impression that the prevailing stones used for memorials have much influenced the regional likelihood of place associations being mentioned on gravestones, although certainly they have affected the subsequent readability of such inscriptions.

[4] See pp. 188–92 of this book.

[5] I can find nothing in any of the extensive British or American historiography on death, memorials and gravestones that mentions this subject of place association on gravestones. This discussion will therefore be relatively and unusually free of historiographical references. On gravestone analysis, among a large literature, see F. Burgess, *English Churchyard Memorials* (1963, London, 1979); B. Bailey, *Churchyards of England and Wales* (1987, Leicester, 1994); M. Cox (ed.), *Grave Concerns: Death and Burial in England, 1700 to 1850* (York, 1998); S. Tarlow, *Bereavement and Commemoration: An Archaeology of Mortality* (Oxford, 1999); H. Lees, *English Churchyard Memorials* (Stroud, 2000); H. Mytum, *Recording and Analysing Graveyards* (York, 2000). On the legal framework, notably the many Victorian Burial Acts, see T. Baker, *The Laws Relating to Burials, with Notes, Forms, & Practical Instructions* (1855, London, 1873). For further reading, see the excellent bibliographies in the books by Tarlow and Cox.

[6] A. Bell, *By-Road* (London, 1937), p. 206.

in chapter 1, the idea of *attachment* today is very often discussed: attachment to place, to family, employment, institutions, community and neighbourhood. There is a strong presumption that it has declined over time. Rootlessness and a sense of 'non-identity', of having no established place in a community, are repeatedly linked to social disintegration, crime, and to an erosion of national, family and regional loyalties. Arguments for power to be devolved down to smaller units often have such concerns in mind. Multi-national capital, we are told, is mobile, cynical, inimical to locality and local attachment, destructive of local difference, habitat and wildlife, even when using local images and memories to sell products. 'Product strategies' are increasingly formulated with global markets in mind. Large corporations pay lip-service to local pride – and yet local people are used and discarded when a cheaper 'labour force' is found elsewhere. As 'globalisation' proceeds, perhaps we no longer see anything closely or well, in the style of Gilbert White, John Clare or Adrian Bell: while the past was often myopic in its local focus, it now seems as though whole societies are moving in the opposite direction, their presbyopic refraction often leaving them oblivious to what is immediately before their eyes. For the kinds of knowledge induced by modern travel are fleeting, transitory and superficial, shallow in memory and association, blurred in recall. De-localisation and advances in the technology of speed induce a sense of place that is poorly discerning and often indifferent, reducing local loyalties and mutual obligations, and influencing ideas of identity and selfhood. Localities lose their meanings and differences.[7] Given the rate of global change and mobility, the insecurity of work and (for many) the transience of residence and acquaintance, it is crucial for historians to stand back and take stock of what we are losing, and of how our ancestors' experiences compared with our own. In the quietude of parish churchyards and burial grounds, and as one of the concluding chapters of this book, it may be that gravestones have something to tell us in this regard – before even more of them are cleared by councils and business interests.

---

[7] Some of the literature on globalisation is referenced in chapter 1 n. 5.

The recording of personal details on gravestones entailed careful choice and deliberation among the gravestone-leaving classes. It could also add to the cost charged by monumental masons, who were (and still are) often paid by the incised letter.[8] On a long enduring monument of personal and family pride, one would not wish to enter details of little consequence, and there was limited space available. Names, ages, spouses, children and the like were commonly inscribed, alongside epitaphs and other fond phrases. Therefore when we see 'of this parish', or 'of the parish of . . .', or references to 'native parish', or to a particular place, added to details about the deceased, we must believe that such communication of belonging or place identity was important to people. What might it mean? Why was it done? What does it tell us about ideas of 'belonging' in the past, and about how those ideas and their expression may have changed?

'Of this parish': anyone familiar with parish registers will also immediately recognise this wording. As we saw in chapter 4, it was very common there, both before and after Hardwicke's Act in 1753. As was made clear in that Act, in registers it referred to *residence* in that place. While there could be some ambiguity about what was meant,[9] this interpretation has been the one adopted by historians. Some parish-register entries may occasionally also imply concepts such as legal settlement, or family lineage – 'of an ancient family here' – or ties established through ownership of property, or they may even say that a registered person was a 'stranger'. Such alternative meanings are rare.

---

[8] A gravestone might cost between £1 and £10 (usually about £5) in the eighteenth and early nineteenth centuries, and letters were charged at about 1d. each. Burgess, *English Churchyard Memorials*, pp. 273–5; C. Gittings, *Death, Burial and the Individual in Early Modern England* (London, 1984), pp. 143–6; R. Houlbrooke, *Death, Religion and the Family in England, 1480–1750* (Oxford, 1998), pp. 368–9 n. 91. They seem to have become more affordable in the early twentieth century, thus (like coffins over the previous three centuries) allowing a larger social range of people to use them. For example, headstones cost between 7s. 8d. and 25s. in 1915 in the Coleford area of Somerset. (Information kindly supplied by Julie Dexter.) Julie-Marie Strange cites a cost of 9d. per dozen letters in 1913 for pauper graves in Stretford. See her 'This mortal coil: death and bereavement in working-class culture, 1880–1914' (Ph.D., University of Liverpool, 2000), p. 134. There were additional but lesser costs of transportation and erection.

[9] See pp. 171–6.

In marriage registers, 'of this parish' can normally be taken to mean residence at the time of the wedding. It did not necessarily involve much longer-term residence, although that would frequently have been the case. Sometimes one suspects that the person was a fairly new arrival, or even temporarily resident for a few weeks prior to the marriage. That would have been sufficient to satisfy the terms of Hardwicke's Act, and to allow this term to be used. In many other cases the phrase describes people who had been long resident, even though we may often be unsure from this source what kind of local ties are represented.

However, when we read gravestones which say 'of this parish', we are surely receiving a stronger message: for this seems to indicate greater rootedness to locality than underlay some parish-register usage of the term. Nobody dying and being buried in a parish in which s/he was a temporary resident would have any obvious motive to have 'of this parish' inscribed on a monumental stone, nor would their relatives. A very certain, enduring and meaningful attachment to place was being chipped into stone and inscribed to posterity by such a memorial statement. The phrase usually had varying subjective rather than legal meanings; although it may have been buttressed in a family's thoughts by formal considerations such as legal settlement, or at least by the economic and social criteria (property ownership, renting for £10 per annum, serving local offices, etc.) underpinning legal settlement. The latter was something that could usually be taken for granted by the classes that concern us here, for it was legally contingent upon their propertied status. We saw in chapter 3 how property became more important as underpinning legal settlement in the nineteenth century.[10] Membership of a parish burial club or friendly society might also have influenced locally attached memorialisation. Yet most burial-club members were probably below the classes leaving gravestones, fearing a pauper burial and being concerned to provide for a respectable funeral.[11] Such clubs normally paid

[10] See pp. 120–3.

[11] P. H. J. H. Gosden, *The Friendly Societies in England, 1815–1875* (Manchester, 1961), pp. 58–9; M. D. Fuller, *West Country Friendly Societies* (Lingfield, Surr., 1964), pp. 83–7, 154; K. Y. Heselton, *The Oddfellows of Great Easton* (Great Easton, Leics., 1986), pp. 40–1; M. Scarth, *The Rules and Regulations of the Castle Eden Friendly Society* (London, 1798),

for the funeral, not for an enduring memorial. Motives to belong to such a parish club, and to belong to a parish in memorialisation, might have been closely connected – but not causally so. As for rights to burial, to be 'of this parish' was not a strict requirement for burial in the churchyard. All inhabitants had a right to be buried in the parochial churchyard. Furthermore, one could be buried there even though one came from elsewhere. There was also a necessity to bury the dead speedily in the interests of hygiene. Having obtained burial, there was little further need to have a stone inscribed to display one's entitlement to that grave.[12] Nor in English culture would there appear to have been a strong requirement of a superstitious nature to 'fix' the dead in their place – to ensure 'the grateful corpse', or the non-malevolent spirit that would not trouble the living – that

---

p. 61, and *Articles to be Observed by the Members of a Friendly Society held at the House of Mr. John Bamford, in Barton, Nottinghamshire* (Nottingham, 1807), p. 11, both reprinted in K. E. Carpenter (advisory ed.), *Friendly Societies: Seven Pamphlets, 1798–1839* (New York, 1972). The same thought applies to membership of local branches of the larger national societies, like the Royal Liver Friendly Society or the Liverpool Victoria Legal Society, and to funeral briefs, Local Collecting Burial Societies, or occupationally related levies upon death for the widow (e.g. among government dockyard workers). See J. F. Wilkinson, *Mutual Thrift* (London, 1891), pp. 75–7, 138–9, 197–9.

[12] One might qualify this in certain regards. Graves were allotted but, sentimental and related considerations aside, such allocation in churchyards did not normally confer a right of property over the grave for the allottee, beyond the right of temporary occupation. (I exclude here private burial grounds, and the terms of 15 & 16 Vic., c. 85, ss. 33–4, 'An Act to Amend the Laws concerning the Burial of the Dead in the Metropolis' (1852), where burial boards under this Act were permitted to sell the 'exclusive right to burial, either in perpetuity or for a limited period', in any part of their burial grounds.) In this regard, the dead may be thought of as akin to 'tenants'. This status affected many who in life had enjoyed freehold property, and this anomaly may illuminate some features of burial ground memorialisation. Subsequent disturbance of the grave remained a real possibility, for which there was huge historical precedent. One motive to erect a gravestone (or iron railings, raised ledger, pedestal, chest-, body-, table- or bale-tomb, etc.) may have been to avoid disturbance after the body had decomposed, or even to slow the process of decomposition, perhaps to similar ends. See A. J. Munby (ed.), *Faithful Servants: Being Epitaphs and Obituaries Recording their Names and Services* (London, 1891), 31; Baker, *Laws Relating to Burials*, p. 302, regarding covering stones, and *ibid.*, p. 32 note (b), on trespass in the removal of tombstones, even by the incumbent who had the freehold of the churchyard, as such stones remained the property of the persons who erected them. Any such monuments were inconsistent with the 'tenancy' of the corpse below, more so than a headstone, but were permitted out of courtesy or deference. These points are worth making because the claiming of indigenous parish attachment through an inscription might provide another disincentive to disturb the grave in the future – although such motivation has never been documented, and would probably not be assisted in the case of extra-parochial named attachments.

might have inclined people to use a terminology of local attachment as a spiritual means to this end: a stony *aide-mémoire* for
the dead.[13] In all periods there were always plenty of burials of
people with no such claim on their gravestones; and a majority
of burials in the eighteenth and nineteenth centuries were un-
marked by any long-lasting stone memorial, or even perhaps by
a significant wooden memorial.[14] Many other stones celebrated

---

[13] Compare C. Lévi-Strauss, *Tristes Tropiques* (1955, Harmondsworth, 1984), ch. 23, esp.
pp. 301–2; G. Kligman, *The Wedding of the Dead: Ritual, Poetics, and Popular Culture in
Transylvania* (Berkeley, 1988), pp. 157–8, 171, 193, 216, 245; G. H. Gerould, *The Grateful
Dead: The History of a Folk Story* (London, 1908); D. J. Davies, *A Brief History of Death*
(Oxford, 2005), pp. 146–7; J. Okely, *The Traveller-Gypsies* (1983, Cambridge, 1984),
ch. 12, esp. pp. 225–30. Among the gypsies, all possible means are taken to render
sedentary the *mulo* or spirit, and the accoutrements and trappings of the grave play a
crucial role in this. Such thinking seems not to have played any part in the gravestone
place attachments discussed here, despite cultural expressions like gothic horror
featuring the restless dead, or ideas from Roman law about a spirit's proximity to
its place of sepulture. On the latter, see J. M. Duncan, *Treatise on the Parochial Ecclesiastical Law of Scotland* (Edinburgh, 1864), p. 663. On staking into their graves suicides,
or fearful malefactors, who otherwise might not 'rest in their graves', or tying their
legs upon burial, or burning their goods (cf. the gypsies), see J. C. Atkinson, *Countryman on the Moors* (1891, Oxford, 1983), pp. 114–18.

[14] An analysis of Upper Broughton (Notts.) by Catherine Jones showed that 25–45 per
cent of burials (1790–1820) were commemorated with lasting stones. In Knighton
(Leics.), studied by Penny Smart, the memorials document under 4 per cent of the
entries in the parish register (1724–1850). This rose to 9 per cent in 1851–60, and to
34 per cent in 1911–18. In Kirby Muxloe (Leics.), Pam Fisher found that between
34 and 42 per cent of adult burials had their graves marked (1813–1920). In Bottesford
(Leics.), Max Bailey found 399 gravestone-recorded deaths, representing 8.7 per cent
of burials (1563–1837). In Roudham churchyard (Norf.), analysed by Peter Barry, 138
people were buried (1803–1922), but only 21 have surviving headstones (15 per cent).
In Deeping St James (Lincs.), analysed by John Lewis, about 50 per cent of those
buried (1920–50) were mentioned on a surviving memorial. Thereafter more than 60
per cent were so mentioned, while in recent years the percentage has risen to about 85.
Between 1674 and 1895 there were about 8,300 burials here, only a small fraction of
which have surviving gravestones. In Glasgwm (Radnorshire, now Powys), Adam
Fenn found that about 32 per cent of burials (1810–90) were thus memorialised, a
figure that gradually rose thereafter to 100 per cent in the 1970s. (These figures are
from unpublished work on burial grounds in the Centre for English Local History,
University of Leicester.) While there is some variation, and while the proportions of
burials with surviving memorials almost always rise into the twentieth century, it is
usually true that a large majority of those buried in the earlier two centuries have no
lasting memorial. On the early eighteenth century, see Houlbrooke, *Death, Religion and
the Family*, p. 365. There has of course been an unknown amount of burial ground
clearance or reorganisation in the past. Arthur Munby, for example, went back to
St James's, Jermyn Street (Mdx.), in 1867 to re-examine a stone to a servant buried in
1781, but 'looked for this in vain . . . the tombstones have all been levelled, misplaced,
or destroyed'. See his *Faithful Servants*, p. 154. Or see G. Orwell, *Coming Up for Air*
(1939, Harmondsworth, 1990), p. 200, on levelling of graves and clearance of old
wooden headpieces.

(if that is the right word) ties of the deceased to other places, which were sometimes far away. So while it could be argued that entries of local attachment in marriage registers had a formal and permissive aspect to them, legitimating the marriage, any such requirement seems to have been lacking in the case of burials and subsequent memorials to the dead.[15]

We need to look in more detail at these ties to place mentioned on gravestones, to explore issues of local attachment and its meaning to people. Let me give some illustrative examples. A churchyard replete with memorials stressing such links is that of Oaks-in-Charnwood in north-west Leicestershire, near Mount St Bernard's Abbey. The church is situated in Charnwood Forest, an upland region of thin and infertile soils, scattered farms and pastoral agriculture, which was poorly catered for historically by the religious establishment. Indeed, the small church here was built as late as 1815. It thus lacks examples of earlier monuments found elsewhere, but its graveyard memorials certainly make up for its short chronological span. Arrayed on a sloping ground, beneath pine trees, they present the pedestrian viewer with a quite bewildering array of addresses and geographical affiliations. Among them one inevitably finds people 'of this parish'. One also sees 'of Lubcloud Cottage'; 'of Waterworks Road, Bardon'; 'of one Barrow Lodge'; 'of the Oaks'; 'of Charnwood Heath'; the daughter of the late John Egremont Esq. of Reedness Hall, Yorkshire, who died at the Terrace Powyke near Worcester aged eighty-three, who 'was for many years resident in this parish'; 'of Lub Cloud'; Finney Hill; Charley; of Minehead, Somerset; of Green Hill; of Charnwood Forest; of Blackbrook; of Whittle Hill; of Upper Blackbrook – and so on. There are many more, all in a quite confined burial ground.

This example is of a non-nucleated parish of dispersed settlement, and it may be that such places had a greater proclivity to give isolated addresses rather than general mention of 'this parish'. 'The parish' in such an area may have meant less to

---

[15] One can also find similar wording in wills, and sometimes in book dedications. For example: 'To the abiding memory of my brother CHARLES TAYLOR KENDALL formerly of the parish of Shoreham in the County of Kent.' The dedication in S. G. Kendall, *Farming Memoirs of a West Country Yeoman* (London, 1944).

inhabitants than it did in regions where a central village provided the main focus for community life. A similar effect seems
apparent if one moves to Garsdale, a township and chapelry in
the parish of Sedbergh, on the Yorkshire–Lancashire border. This
is a more extreme example of upland settlement patterns. One
finds people buried there who are said to be of places such as Pike
Hill in Garsdale; Thrushgill; Grouse Hall; Badgerdub; Ruecrofts,
Sedbergh; Cannon House, Sedbergh; Aldershaw, Crisedale; Low
House; West Paradise; Low Smithy; Smorthwaite Hill, Garsdale;
West Rackenthwaite; Hawes Junction; Pryhill; Spital, Kendal;
Dandragarth; Castle Garsdale; Mudbecks; Moorland Cottage;
Paradise Farm; 10, Railway Cottages; Beckside Cautley; Wood
End, Garsdale; Longhouse; Wallasey; Whitbeck Cottage; Pinfold
Farm; Low Scale; Middle Paradise; East Cote Weggs, and other
such places. The churchyard also includes a few references to
where people died. A perambulation through this hilly township
soon identifies many of the houses and farms named in the
churchyard, and suggests in this case the key role of farms as
reference points in people's minds.

Many other such upland churchyards could be taken as fur-
ther examples of very detailed place referencing on gravestones.
Brathay, near Ambleside in the Lake District, is one such, a
churchyard which is also very notable for cases of footstones
being used with headstones. Here we find people being 'of
Heam Hurst in this parish'; Fishgarths; Ambleside; of the Leas
Hoylake; Brodsworth; Mill Brow; Burnt How Cottage; 'of Glen
Brathay, born at Lincoln'; of Broad Ings, Skelghyll, Ambleside;
Blackburn; Ashley Green, Loughrigg; Elterwater; Clappersgate;
Tarn Foot, Loughrigg; Brathay bank; Fleetwood; Cragg Head,
Loughrigg; Skelwith Fold; Gilbert Scar Foot, Ambleside; Mireside
Skelwith; Skelwith Bridge; Pull Wyke Cottage; Brathay hall;
The Nook, Fern Hill, Kendal; and then (perhaps a little incon-
gruously) someone of Bognor Regis, Sussex. Here too one can
find some references to where people died, wording that is
nevertheless usually rare.

I have quoted such examples extensively to give a flavour of
what is found in many churchyards. These cases are from
upland settlements, with scattered habitations, with perhaps
greater proclivity to give isolated addresses. Yet these are small
churchyards, and countless others supply a more extensive

range of places mentioned on memorials. For example, well over twenty places are mentioned in Clifton Campville churchyard, a very different type of parish in Staffordshire. Place referencing takes many forms, and can go well beyond 'of this parish'. It can be localised to a particular address, or it can relate to a township, chapelry, or part of a parish, to the whole parish, or to a large town or city – 'of London', 'of Manchester', 'of Birmingham', 'of Brighton', 'of Stafford', to take examples I have seen. It can even refer to a topographical region, or what were sometimes known as 'countries'. Thus one can find people being referenced to 'the Lakes', or 'the Downs', or 'the Forest of Dean'. In rare cases the monumental mason has even tried to give expression to such scenery on the stone, as in two cases of hill and lake depictions at Patterdale Church in the Lake District. More specific topographical references, for example at Long Sutton (Lincs.), can be to areas such as Holbeach Marsh, or Gedney Marsh. I have yet to find anyone addressed to 'the Fens', which seem not to inspire inscription. In Snelston (south Derb.), many people are 'of Snelston Common'. Precise addresses may be urban as well as rural: for example, 43 High Street, Bideford, as found in Hartland churchyard. In Long Sutton, as elsewhere, many stones commemorate people from named farms. This also tied them to kin in local understanding, if farm occupancy was long-standing. It helped to confirm their social status too, a consideration that may well have been as important, perhaps for similar reasons, as giving one's place of belonging or attachment. The grave may be one's 'last tenement', but in cases like these very clear indication was given of previous residence.

Sometimes one can view the residents of particular addresses over quite extensive periods from gravestones. This is so even though the memorials may not show the same surnames, and their disparate and scattered locations in the churchyard might suggest that the tenants or owners of the properties were unrelated, being buried alongside their kin, rather than near previous residents of the address chiselled on their gravestone. An example is that of 'Pull Wyke Cottage' (in 1888, 1905, and 1973) at Brathay churchyard in Cumbria. In such cases, the locational gravitation towards kin seems to have been stronger than a burial placement tied to a property affiliation, even though the latter was sufficiently important to warrant mention. Rather surprisingly, it is rare to find people said to be of a county (even where this can be an assertive statement, for example in post-1974 Rutland), although the name of a county is sometimes given after a place.[16] In some cases, most notably from the later nineteenth century, a dual location can occasionally be found. This often seems to indicate the widening phenomenon of second homes or of multiple property ownership among the gravestone-leaving classes, something that has not been studied by historians. As one might expect, it is particularly apparent in regions with romantic associations such as the Lake District. Thus at Hawkshead church one finds people 'of Fieldhead House and Manchester' (1874), or 'of Yewfield and Acton, Middlesex' (1901), or 'of Darcy Lever and Fair Oak Park, Hants' (1929). In some such instances, professional qualifications or occupational details suggest what had financed such disparate assets, as well as providing another form of identity. In addition, an ambiguity of locational belonging due to mobility in the Empire had long been visible on a few stones: such as that at Hawkshead of 'Anthony Gregg, M. L. of the Island of Barbadoes, who died at Hawkshead, the place of his Nativity, March 24th, 1807, aged 78 Years'. Many examples may be found of stones commemorating local people who died in distant places: 'of this parish, but died in Peking', is one such extreme example.[17] There was, throughout the last three centuries,

[16] David Hey rightly suggests that 'in addition to a firm identity with a parish . . . most people had a weaker sense of belonging to the surrounding neighbourhood that they called their "country". This is supported by demographic studies, surname distributions, the annual movements of farm servants, etc. and by the use of the term by Victorian novelists, especially George Eliot . . . this usage survived well into the twentieth century.' Surname distributions were usually restricted to much smaller districts than counties, i.e. to neighbourhoods or localised *pays* or 'countries', such as the Sheffield district, or that of the Potteries. The notion of 'our country' and 'distant countries' was one of the definitions of 'country' in the *OED*: 'A tract or district having more or less definite limits in relation to human occupation, e.g. owned by the same lord or proprietor, or inhabited by people of the same race, dialect, occupation, etc.' Hey suggests that attachments to *counties* were not strong until the close of the eighteenth century at the earliest, and probably not until the Victorian period, notably associated with county cricket (Correspondence: 12 August 2002; 4 September 2005); and see D. Hey, *Family Names and Family History* (London, 2000), pp. 126–30.

[17] Or there are stones in far-off places commemorating distantly belonging people buried locally, using the cultural phrasing discussed here. I found one in a small overgrown cemetery in the jungle five miles south of Sapele in Nigeria, where a late nineteenth-century memorial commemorates part of a Scotsman: 'native of Edinburgh, eaten by a crocodile'.

a widespread movement of corpses back to 'home' parishes, like that of Fanny Robin in *Far From the Madding Crowd*.[18] There was indeed much ambivalence as to where and who Thomas Hardy's own body belonged, which might be seen as a posthumous corollary of the persistent theme of belonging and outsiders in his writing.[19] However, for our purposes here we need to be aware that in cases of death elsewhere it is the site of commemoration which is significant, and this site may not be the same as the place of burial.

If the burial of people 'of this parish', or of a stated address within it, is made much of, so too is the burial of outsiders. Readers will have observed examples of this above. As perhaps when living, so also in death, outsider affiliations were frequently noted. For a while, I wondered whether this insider–outsider phenomenon was related to the issue of status and burial placement, and particularly to any north–south side distinctions within the churchyard. It is often said that the north side of the churchyard was reserved for the humble, the unbaptised, the social outcasts, the illegitimate (perhaps even for suicides and the excommunicated if they, the 'unholy dead',[20] were permitted burial in consecrated ground at all). In some areas there is evidence of labourers buried on 'the dreary north side', farmers on 'the sunny south side';[21] although the location of the church path was probably a more important determinant of status burial location. The neglected moss- and lichen-covered graves of 'outsiders' can certainly be found to the north in certain churchyards.[22] There may be a slight disposition for

---

[18] T. Hardy, *Far From the Madding Crowd* (1874, London, 1971), pp. 313–24. On the movement of corpses, which is important for questions in historical demography concerning the relation between residence and vital registration, see K. D. M. Snell, 'Parish registration and the study of labour mobility', *Local Population Studies*, 33 (1984); R. S. Schofield, 'Traffic in corpses: some evidence from Barming, Kent, 1788–1812', *Local Population Studies*, 33 (1984).

[19] There was debate over whether he should have been buried at Westminster Abbey, contrary to his wishes, or at Stinsford, where his heart was interred. Hardy was a keen devotee of gravestones, often carrying a small wooden scraper to help read them.

[20] The phrase is from J. Rugg, 'Defining the place of burial: what makes a cemetery a cemetery?', *Mortality*, 5 (2000), p. 266; Burgess, *English Churchyard Memorials*, p. 25.

[21] J. W. Robertson Scott, *The Land Problem (an Impartial Survey)* (London, n.d., c. 1913), p. 83.

[22] In Godmanchester, Nonconformists (another form of 'outsider') were buried in a reserved area on the north side. In some burial grounds, paupers were buried apart

this generally to occur, but inspection of large numbers of churchyards will show that 'outsiders' (as judged from statements on stones) were located in all parts of the churchyard, and in this regard there seems to have been no apparent discrimination against them.[23] In some cases of people said to be from elsewhere, a long-term local residence did not wholly eclipse an earlier distant affiliation. For example, 'Anthony Oughton, Gent, descended from an antient family of that name at Fillongley in Warwickshire, but for three-score and six years an inhabitant of this parish', was buried in St Margaret's, Canterbury, in 1750. Susannah Baker died on 9 March 1845 aged seventy-six, and was buried in St Brelade's, Jersey. She had lived on the island for fifty-three years – yet her stone tells us that she was a native of Edinburgh.[24] Many who were 'native of Ireland' are buried in English and Welsh churchyards, alongside others sometimes named 'hibernians'. Other strangers, 'from a foreign land, cut down by Death's relentless hand', are to be found in places such as Brinsley (Notts.), where 'Joseph Fallow, a native of Switzerland', died in 1855. In Ashby de la Zouch (Leics.) one discovers the burials of French prisoners of war from the Napoleonic Wars, who had stayed and married locally. Many

(for an example, J. C. Powys, *Wolf Solent* (1929, Harmondsworth, 1978), p. 29). In this discussion of churchyards, I am not considering the many cemeteries where some religious or ethnic groups (e.g. Jews, Poles, Latvians, or Italians) are buried in certain sections of the site.

[23] One can find occasional attempts to refuse burial to non-parishioners. See e.g. Leics. CRO, DE 5851/1 (Seagrave Parish Council minutes, 19 and 21 March 1896), where the Council is writing to the Home Secretary to ask if this can be done in the parish cemetery. Such non-parishioners could be charged more for their burial in the parish. For example, 'for every one who is buried in the Churchyard a fee of one shilling is due to the officiating Clergyman of the Parish . . . For every Person living in another Parish, a fee of six shillings & eight pence.' This was part of the 'custom of the parish of Cowfold'. P. S. Godman (ed.), *The Parish Register of Cowfold, Sussex, 1558–1812* (Lewes, 1916), pp. 57–8; or see J. Woodforde, *The Diary of a Country Parson, 1758–1802* (1924–31, Oxford, 1979), p. 594; J. Skinner, *Journal of a Somerset Rector, 1803–1834* (1930, Oxford, 1985), pp. 65–6; J. Litten, *The English Way of Death: The Common Funeral since 1450* (London, 1991), p. 225. Special fees have often been charged for burial of non-parishioners in the twentieth century. For example, see Leics. CRO, DE 5851/1 (Seagrave Parish Council minutes, 5 June 1901): 'no person non-parishioners shall be Buried in this Cemetery without the consent of the Council and that an extra charge be made'. Quite diverse prices operate in London cemeteries today, justified in part by residential differences.

[24] The phrase 'native of' is especially common in Canadian Presbyterian churches (e.g. in Nova Scotia or New Brunswick), often referring to people of Scottish descent.

stranger sailors are buried in coastal areas, such as Bideford, Appledore or St Just. 'Strangers' Hill' in Hartland refers to a part of the graveyard where dead sailors were given a Christian burial, their sodden bodies having been lugged up from the shore below. These men, of course, received no personal memorial other than the 'hill' named after them. Such an end was widespread for sailors whose names and homes were unknown, who were not indicatively tattooed, or initialled, or wearing tokens of their home parish such as name-and-parish pendants, or distinctive parochially patterned guernseys, knitted by pensive womenfolk.[25]

Total anonymity was the fate of most of the local poor also, even if they escaped pauper burial, and even if their families or burial clubs could afford an acceptably decent funeral, in an appropriate part of the graveyard. To George Crabbe 'the mingled relics of the parish poor' were jumbled, nameless, communal by default.[26] They became depersonalised in the collectivity of undifferentiated ancestors, in a way that is rare today. There were always a few commemorated exceptions to this among the poor, often the trusty servant whose long-lasting service to the gentry or aristocracy led him or her to be endowed with a gravestone (often on the north side of the church) by the employer.[27] One gained a memorialised personal identity via upward class service, and this helped to avoid subsequent grave disturbance. Jane Ryder, for example, who died in 1897 and was buried in Twyford churchyard (Leics.), deserved a particularly large memorial, having spent '41 years in the service

---

[25] In Staithes (North Yorks.), for example, guernseys were patterned in ways that displayed the wearer's parish, and garments and boots were also marked with initials, to identify men when they drowned. Dame L. Knight, *Oil Paint and Grease Paint: The Autobiography of Laura Knight*, vol. 1 (1936, Harmondsworth, 1941), p. 84.

[26] G. Crabbe, 'The pauper's funeral', in *The Penguin Book of English Verse* (1956, Harmondsworth, 1983), p. 249. On burial affecting the poor, see especially R. Richardson, *Death, Dissection and the Destitute* (1988, Harmondsworth, 1989).

[27] 692 epitaphs of servants were recorded in Munby, *Faithful Servants*. I am grateful to Barry Reay for this reference. While 'of this parish', or 'a native of . . .', are found in these servant entries, the stress on longevity of faithful service and the accompanying words (faithful, trusty, attached, fidelity, devoted, friend, affectionate, steady, true, etc.) frequently convey a sense of belonging to the employer's family as well as to place. Indeed, an initial mention of a servant's place of origin can often give way to tribute in these terms, hinting that praise is also due to someone who relinquished a local place attachment in preference for loyal service elsewhere to a person or family.

of the Dukes of Rutland. TRUST IN THE LORD AND DO GOOD.'[28] Such a morally edifying stone stood partly as a reminder, to others among the lower ranks, of the rewards of long and loyal service in one's allotted station, the length of employment often being mentioned. It probably also represented the employer's genuine gratitude. One may find mention of such a servant's origin, which was often at a considerable distance – hinting at loyalty to the employer rather than to place. While an identity of sorts was imparted retrospectively through such memorialisation, it was an identity by association and service – a point underscored by the way in which the deceased person's often diminutively inscribed name was dwarfed by the subsequent information that s/he 'was servant to THE DUKE OF RUTLAND', or some other regional luminary.

Such extreme cases of class transparency and juxtaposition bear upon questions of identity raised by this subject. They remind us of two important points. These are, first, that the dead do not bury themselves. Thomas Mann commented that ultimately a man's dying is more his survivors' affair than his own.[29] For our purposes, burials and inscriptions were conducted and made by the living. Sometimes they acted by following the dead person's instructions; but often the stones and their wording were clearly servicing (in many possible ways) the needs of the living. This has obvious relevance to issues of lineage, belonging and place attachment, where the claims of the living could so clearly be buttressed by statements about dead parents or relatives. Secondly, insofar as gravestones are indicative about ideas of belonging, they are so usually for those above the working class. In saying this, one should not rule out many examples of gravestones of working-class people. Even before the twentieth century, some of these displayed symbols or other explicit mention of occupations – this can be found, with some regional variation, throughout the era of gravestone commemoration studied here. Nevertheless, there is certainly a class bias to this

---

[28] Original capitalisation. Munby, *Faithful Servants*, p. 196, cites another example of morally instructive wording on servants' memorials: 'Watch ye therefore, for ye know not when the master of the house cometh.'
[29] Cited without reference in I. M. Lewis, *Social Anthropology in Perspective: The Relevance of Social Anthropology* (1976, Cambridge, 1985), p. 132.

source, one that is probably most apparent for church and chapel burial grounds before the mid-twentieth century. I have chosen not to analyse public or parish cemeteries, which may contain less of a class bias, although it almost certainly exists there as well. As we will see, these issues of social status frequently arise when we interpret gravestones.

II

I have referred to a lack of analysis of place association on gravestones, and to an apparent decline in this form of memorialisation over time. To explore the issue further I analysed about 16,000 gravestones in eighty-seven burial grounds, examining trends in the mention of places associated with the deceased. This was done for fifty-three Anglican churchyards, and for thirty-four Nonconformist and Catholic church and chapel burial grounds.[30] I separated Anglican and non-Anglican burial grounds, partly to see whether denominational affiliation has any bearing on the issue.[31] Anglican senses of place, it might be argued, were rather different from many Nonconformist attachments, because of the different organisational structures involved: for example, the Anglican parish as contrasted with the Baptist district or Methodist circuit. We still know little about how the parish was conceived of by the various dissenting groups, with regard to both its religious and secular roles.[32] Dissenters may have come more frequently from surrounding or more distant places, and this is quite evident

---

[30] For discussion of the burial grounds analysed here, see Appendix 8.1.

[31] It should be stressed that this division by no means reflects clear-cut segregation of burial, for many Nonconformists and Catholics were buried in Anglican churchyards (even including Nonconformist ministers), as was their right, frequently having to accept Anglican rites until the 1880 Burial Act. In some parishes rural incumbents tried to perpetuate this (or to exclude dissenters) as late as the 1890s. The matter was finally resolved by the Burial Grounds Act of 1900. Far fewer Anglicans, one suspects, were buried in dissenting burial grounds, although in some cases known to me kinship ties led to this.

[32] However, for the early modern period, much light has been shed on this issue by the essays in M. Spufford (ed.), *The World of Rural Dissenters, 1520–1725* (Cambridge, 1995). The Baptists appear to have had a clear sense of belonging to a 'family', of being a part of God's brethren and a common church membership – and this is a theme found in some of their epitaphs. Parish, and hierarchy, seem less significant in their case than for the Anglican Church.

in some cases, such as the Unitarians in Leicester.[33] We will need to keep questions about varied meanings of the parish in mind as we proceed. With regard to the location of these burial grounds, a small majority of the ones researched here were in Leicestershire, but they include a large number in other counties, some of them far removed from the English midlands. My main approach has been to record external memorials which linked the person to a place, whether 'of this parish', or another place such as the examples given above, to see how common such place associations were in different periods. For reasons of consistency, access, and to avoid greater class bias, I did not include memorials inside church or chapel buildings; these would in any case have been an insignificant fraction of the whole. I took the gravestone as my unit of analysis, rather than individual people. Thus if a stone commemorated a husband, for example, and then later a wife was added, this was treated as one. The point here is that if the husband was stated as being 'of this parish', there may have been little motive to inscribe the same about his wife. A sizeable minority of stones commemorate more than one person. Any mention of a named place, or 'this parish', 'this town[ship]', or 'this place', as associated with the person/family was tabulated. The date I recorded was the date of the death of the person commemorated, or, in cases of two or more people commemorated, the date of the person's death that had seemingly led to the stone being created. This is usually the first named person. One can, for example, have a wife dying first, only to be memorialised – 'together at last' – on a shared stone erected some years later when her husband died. Usually in such a case it would be the husband who is stated to be 'of this parish', or of another place, and his date and place has been used.

The results demonstrate some very remarkable trends. These are plotted by decade in figures 8.1–8.3. The first figure shows

---

[33] The burial ground of the Leicester Unitarian Great Meeting Chapel includes a significant number of people from towns like Derby, Loughborough, Coventry, Birmingham, Northampton, Bristol, Manchester, Glasgow, and London, and appears to illustrate an expansive network of Unitarian urban connections. Such a Unitarian burial site differs markedly from the significant co-extension between parish and inhabitants observed in many Anglican churchyards. The places mentioned are also more wide-ranging than is true of most other Nonconformist burial grounds.

the total numbers of gravestones mentioning people's associations with place, for Anglican and for Nonconformist (including Catholic) burial grounds. The data in this figure are from all the burial grounds listed in Appendix 8.1. The mentions of place are of the kind instanced above. The Anglican churchyards studied outnumber the Nonconformist – hence the greater numbers of Anglican memorials in figure 8.1, and no significance therefore attaches to the larger Anglican numbers in that figure. It is the rise and fall of this phenomenon that draws one's attention, a pattern shared by Anglican and non-Anglican burial grounds. The mention of place reaches a peak in the 1870s for the Anglican churchyards, and a decade earlier for the Nonconformists. There is thereafter a precipitous decline, as steep as the earlier rise. By the second half of the twentieth century it was very rare to find people being associated with any place on their gravestones. This situation had begun to arise from the 1880s, and the period of most rapid change away from such wording came between 1890 and 1930.

This decline is not due to the overall numbers of gravestones over time. Of course, there are comparatively few surviving external memorials for the early eighteenth century, and the upward trend in figure 8.1 until the later nineteenth century is to be expected, given greater accessibility, usage and numbers of stone memorials over that period. Such commemoration was increasingly common in the eighteenth century, and the memorials became large and more elaborate, being used where a century or less earlier only a wooden graveboard,[34] marker or small stone with initials and date would have been normal,[35] if a

---

[34] Almost none of these earlier wooden graveboards survive, apart from a few in Sussex, Surrey and Buckinghamshire. Burgess, *English Churchyard Memorials*, pp. 118, 148; Lees, *English Churchyard Memorials*, p. 55; M. Binney and P. Burman, *Change and Decay: The Future of our Churches* (London, 1977), p. 126, for a photograph of graveboards at Burstow (Surr.); *Gentleman's Magazine*, 82 (August 1812), pl. 1, pp. 102–3, for an engraving of Ditchling (Suss.) by Collyer after W. Hamper; G. Jekyll, *Old West Surrey: Some Notes and Memories* (1904, Chichester, 1999), pp. 235–6, for a further photograph. They were set above the length of the interred body, and sometimes painted black with white lettering. An 1832 example was referred to by Arthur Munby: 'The memorial is one of those old wood ones.' See his *Faithful Servants*, p. 82. Others like this were made of both wood and stone, and one can sometimes find stone memorials modelled on the wooden type. It is now impossible to analyse the content of such wood memorials, and to see how their wording compared with later stone ones.

[35] Small stones with only initials and no date may frequently have been footstones.

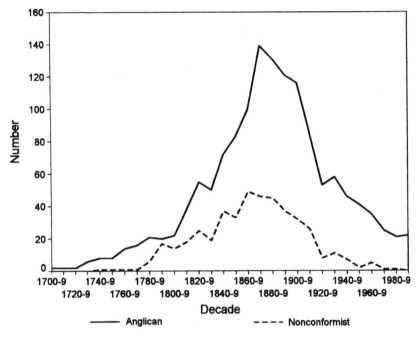

Figure 8.1 Gravestones mentioning people's association with place
(total number of gravestones).

memorial was present at all. Growing numbers among the middling and elite classes were adopting stone memorialisation in the course of the eighteenth century. This was probably true across all denominations.[36] The rise in numbers in figure 8.1 is

---

[36] There are in fact surprisingly few differences in memorial design, wording, symbols and other attributes across denominational burial grounds. Some examples of design differences are given in Mytum, *Recording and Analysing Graveyards*, pp. 10, 14, 24, 61. The Quakers in particular tended to retain small, modest and uniform memorials, regarding anything else as vain and overly eulogistic, and as attempting to create distinctions based upon rich and poor in the after-life. In my sample, over the entire period (1700–2000), about 19.9 per cent of memorials in Anglican burial grounds mentioned place associations, while in Nonconformist burial grounds the equivalent figure was a very similar 18.2 per cent. Such similarity occurs despite the strong sense of the parish among Anglicans, and the weaker ecclesiastical associations of the parish for many dissenters. The latter often adopted alternative, trans-parochial organisation, such as societies, circuits, districts, branches, alternative larger 'parishes', and so on, and for them the traditional parish may have had more to do with socio-economic administration rather than ecclesiastical community. Certainly one almost never finds

therefore predictable. However, the total numbers of *all* grave-stones in these burial grounds continued to grow thereafter, and in many burial grounds there are far more monuments in the twentieth century than in the nineteenth. This is true even though I excluded the increasingly used small plaques that commemorate those who have been cremated – a custom which has grown considerably in the twentieth century after the 1902 Cremation Act, and especially since 1945.[37] (I also excluded small initialled stones, or others of very small size, usually of the early or mid-eighteenth century, on which it would also have been hard to inscribe details of place.) In other words, the steep decline in place association on gravestones from the later nineteenth century, shown in figure 8.1, is certainly not because of falling numbers of memorials. Nor does it seem to owe anything to the inscription-carrying size of memorials. It is true that many Victorian gravestones are large and can transmit quite lengthy epitaphs and biblical texts, and the twentieth century saw greater economy and mass production in this regard.[38] However, many fulsome terms of family endearment

'of this parish' in Baptist or Congregational burial grounds, the preference there being for mention of a named place where the person was of or from. It is not yet clear whether this is also true for Methodist burial grounds. Even so, the frequent stresses in Spufford, *World of Rural Dissenters*, about the integration of Nonconformists into their local communities (even before the Toleration Act of 1689) appear relevant here.

[37] The campaign for cremation began in the 1870s, notably with the Cremation Society formed in 1874 by Sir Henry Thompson. The practice was earlier thought to be anti-Christian, and to defy ideas of resurrection. Cremations have been rising ever since 1902 as a proportion of all deaths, most sharply since the 1930s: from under 5 per cent in 1940, to about 40 per cent in 1960, and they now account for about three-quarters of cases. The scattering of ashes is now often said to be the most common post-cremation method, although firm evidence on this is lacking. On this subject and recent practice, see Richardson, *Death, Dissection and the Destitute*, pp. 259–60, fig. 5; D. Davies, *Reusing Old Graves: A Report on Popular Attitudes* (Crayford, Kent, 1995); P. C. Jupp, *From Dust to Ashes: The Development of Cremation in England, 1820–1997* (London, 2000).

[38] There have also been more attempts to control the size of monuments in the twentieth century by diocesan and particularly cemetery authorities. Conspicuous 'status graves' became less common from the 1920s. For example, a Hampstead Cemetery regulation in 1934 laid down that no monument should be over 5 foot 6 inches high. K. Hudson, *Churchyards and Cemeteries* (London, 1984), p. 25. Even so, such regulations still gave ample space for such inscriptions. Handbooks for the clergy and parochial church councils in the twentieth century usually refer to the need for 'sensible lettering', avoidance of 'doubtful taste' and 'ostentation', and sometimes recommend traditional rather than imported stone. For example, see C. R. Forder, *The Parish Priest at Work: An Introduction to Systematic Pastoralia* (1947, London, 1959), p. 130. Under 15 & 16 Vic., c. 85, s. 38 (relating to the metropolis), a dispute about the suitability of a

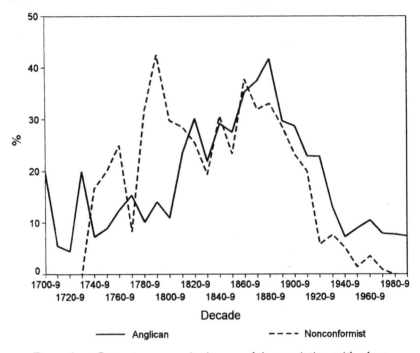

Figure 8.2   Gravestones mentioning people's association with place
(percentages).

and remembrance became more common in the twentieth century, as probably did lines from hymns, and such inscriptions took up more space than the usual two or three words needed to identify a deceased person with a place.

The trends through time are further confirmed by figure 8.2. This shows gravestones linking people to places expressed as a percentage of all gravestones. It therefore controls for the overall numbers of memorials. Once again, the trends are very similar for Anglican and non-Anglican burial ground memorialisation, and they confirm figure 8.1. The rise to the late nineteenth

monumental inscription, in a consecrated area of a burial ground, was to be determined by the bishop of the diocese. Yet this was hardly relevant to my discussion here: the churches and ecclesiastical authorities certainly had no moral or other objections to place associations being mentioned, and were indeed sympathetic to that, as many clerical gravestones show.

century is very clear, and the decline thereafter even more so. The numbers of stones in the eighteenth century are smaller, and this accounts for the fluctuations in percentages up to about 1820: readers therefore should not presume that those eighteenth-century fluctuations have much significance. Very generally, about 10 per cent of memorials associated people with place in the first half of the eighteenth century, rising to about 40 per cent by 1860–90, and this fell to well below 10 per cent by the late twentieth century. In fact, in many of the Anglican grave-yards analysed (e.g. Ashby Folville, Beeby, Belton, Clifton Campville, Harlaston, Knighton or Skegness) place association had effectively ceased by the 1940s, if not earlier. The same was often true for the Nonconformists. It has survived through to more recent decades mainly in the upland parishes or town-ships: places such as Brathay, Newlands, Patterdale, Garsdale or Hawkshead, and in these it often related people to farms and named property, rather than to a hamlet, parish or town. Finally, while we are looking at figure 8.2, we might note one further point. The trend for the Nonconformist burial grounds, par-ticularly the downward trend, seems slightly to predate the Anglican, and to be more resolute.

In figure 8.3 all Anglican and Nonconformist gravestones mentioning people's association with place have been com-bined, showing them as decadal percentages of all stones. This clarifies further the pattern of figure 8.2, and reveals very well the cross-denominational trends that require explanation. It will be seen that the phenomenon revealed is not a 'mechanical' artifact of the growth and decline of stone-commemorated corpse burial. Rather, the percentages show incised place asso-ciation to be a fashion or expectation that emerged gradually but strongly over time, only to fall almost completely out of favour during the early decades of the twentieth century. The pattern is so clear and so consistently found across all the burial grounds that I believe the overall trend must be broadly repre-sentative of most English regions, although this remains to be completely tested by other researchers.[39] The situation in Wales

---

[39] The *proportions* of stones across regions making place associations vary. For example, there seems to be greater frequency of such mention in upland, northern and westerly

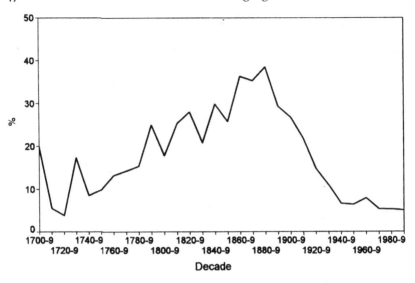

Figure 8.3 Percentage of all gravestones mentioning people's association
with place (Anglican and Nonconformist combined).

awaits research, and is likely to be intriguing given differences
in parochial structures, denominational emphases, Welsh regional contrasts and other cultural features, and may throw up
interesting comparisons with England.

areas than in the English midlands, and it is higher again in the midlands than in East
Anglia. It appears to be very common in south and west Wales, for both English and
Welsh language inscriptions. I suspect that it is most prevalent either in upland areas
of scattered settlement (often relating to townships, farms, etc.), or in highly nucleated
villages (e.g. many parishes in Leicestershire), but that it is less common in areas of
weak nucleation (as in many parts of Norfolk and Suffolk), where quite dispersed
settlement could lead to extra-parochial affiliations, notably for those living on parish
margins. This issue of regional variation also raises the question of how strong local
custom, or courtesy, was with regard to the rights of families to be buried in particular
places within the churchyard. In England such rights were weaker than those of
heritors in Scotland, for whom such places had a reserved status akin to English or
Scottish church seats customarily tied to parish-located property. The varying
customs bearing on rights to burial in specific plots might have influenced the use
of a tombstone language of belonging, because where such rights were firmly established, and determined burial location, such a language was more likely to have been
superfluous. On Scottish heritors' rights to burial, see A. Dunlop, *Parochial Law*
(Edinburgh, 1841), pp. 72–6. On rights affecting church seating, see K. D. M. Snell
and P. S. Ell, *Rival Jerusalems: The Geography of Victorian Religion* (Cambridge, 2000),
ch. 10. These speculations, and the types of place association, await further comparative research on gravestones and local custom.

III

Why did these changes occur? When we discuss manifestations of 'belonging' here or in other contexts, we are dealing with very subtle, subjective and personal themes. In the case of memorialisation, these themes were interwoven with fashions, social and familial expectations, ideas of decorum, precedence and pride in place. At such a distance in time, and with virtually no evidence available on personal motivations, or on dealings with monumental masons,[40] it is hard to explain trends like these. Burial board minute and account books, and other related documentation following the Victorian burial Acts, and parish council minute books from 1894, provide almost no illumination on this subject. Furthermore, there is still no historiographical consensus on the nature and chronology of centralisation affecting English society over this period, let alone subjective responses to it. This approach to gravestones is a new subject, with no interpretative documentation, and some of my explanation must therefore be tentative and subject to refinement by others. On some gravestones additional information was added,

---

[40] It would be interesting to know more about the influence of monumental masons and designers bearing upon these issues, and the extent to which they influenced regional differences and changes. Designs for monuments were certainly published, but these had limited impact upon inscriptions beyond sometimes circumscribing them. See e.g. Baker, *Laws Relating to Burials*, p. 302 note (a). The inscriptions appear to have been less formulaic than the designs and emblems that surrounded them, although there were clearly influential fashions, and socio-familial copying is also evident locally. No research in this connection has addressed the questions that concern me here, and indeed almost no work has been done on producer–client influences relating to extra-mural monuments of this type. This is partly because surviving records of the small craft businesses are usually so slight; and, where they exist, they do not cover this topic. (See e.g. Leics. CRO, DE 1670/1–4, records of William Allsop and Sons, monumental masons.) What little research exists may be found in Burgess, *English Churchyard Memorials* (esp. pp. 255–81, and see his index, pp. 320–3, on monumental masons), with very limited further information in R. Merriman, 'The use of Swithland slate gravestones and their engravers' (MA dissertation, Centre for English Local History, University of Leicester, 2000); M. W. Barley, 'Slate headstones in Nottinghamshire', *Transactions of the Thoroton Society of Nottinghamshire*, 52 (1948); J. C. Davies, 'The "tulip slates" of south Leicestershire and north-west Northamptonshire', *The Leicestershire Historian*, 4 (1993); S. Lewis, 'A family of stone carvers: the Coxes of Northamptonshire', *Northamptonshire Past and Present*, 1 (1953); D. Neave and V. Heron, 'Slate headstones and their engravers', *The Local Historian*, 8 (1969); R. C. Russell, *Headstones in Lincolnshire, as Works of Art and as Evidence of Craftsmanship* (Barton on Humber, 1981).

often involving moral approbation, allowing us more insight
into what was meant by statements of local attachment. The
person was 'for 45 years parish clerk here'; or he was 'minister
of this parish'; or was 'Alderman and once Mayor of this Ancient and Loyal Corporation'; or some other such wording may
be given. The Revd John Clark, for example, 'after long and
useful exertions as a Clergyman at Sleaford, Hull, and other
places died in this his native parish August 15, 1826 in the 73rd
year of his age', and was buried in St Margaret's, Leicester.
Internal church monuments sometimes provide more detail
on attachment to place. Such memorials often mention property, accounts of local office, services rendered to a parish or
town, philanthropy to the parish poor, and so on. However, we
usually know much less about the more numerous people memorialised in the graveyard. Genealogists may be able to help
interpret some gravestone inscriptions. Even so, we will still be
some way from knowing why one person, or his or her surviving family, chose to have chiselled into stone 'of this parish',
while many others with seemingly equal legal, demographic,
denominational, social or economic eligibility chose to omit it.

First of all, we can notice that there has been a tendency for
family-related statements and expressions of emotion to become
relatively more pronounced on gravestones than was true of
extra-mural memorials in the eighteenth and much of the nineteenth centuries. 'A loving husband, father and grandfather',
'our dear mother', 'much missed by her loving son', and words
to similar effect, appear to have become more common in the
twentieth century. 'A stone is a memorial to a relationship', as
Sarah Tarlow wrote.[41] Such sentiments were of course widely
felt in earlier periods, and may be found especially on larger
internal church monuments pertaining to higher classes. Many
monuments extolled virtues of femininity in almost all periods.
Familial sentiments expressed about men were fairly unusual
on external church gravestones before the mid-nineteenth century. Even so, there was an increasing tendency for men in
particular to be extolled, if extolled at all, by reference to the

---

[41] S. Tarlow, 'Romancing the stones: the graveyard boom of the later eighteenth
century', in Cox (ed.), *Grave Concerns*, p. 43.

contribution they made to the (surviving) family. To some extent, statements bearing on familial roles seem to take over from earlier affiliations with place. This was never a simple matter, and countless nineteenth-century gravestones state a place affiliation prior to giving further information about family, and that information may often be couched in a way that salutes familial virtues. Biblical quotation may be used to similar effect. Place affiliation can seem incidental in such inscriptions, and not attain the significance of the stated family ties. Except in very rare instances, it certainly has not done so in the twentieth century, when the family appears all important, and to have heavily eclipsed community and place references. Let us keep this point of general shifting emphasis in mind, prior to reminding ourselves of some key administrative and socio-economic changes which will help explain these findings.

The most obvious point to make is that the parish, once the key unit of local governance and the organising arena of most people's secular and religious lives, has become a relic of its former self. This is true in many fields of life and local government. There have been the poor law unions from 1834, the Poor Law and Local Government Boards, the highway districts from the Acts of 1835, 1862 and 1864, and later centralisation of transport planning, civil registration and its districts from 1836, the Union Chargeability Act in 1865, pauper irremovability and the growing irrelevance of settlement law and locality-derived entitlement to welfare in the twentieth century, the extremely limited powers and expenditures of parish councils, plus the manifold changes away from very local administration of hospital and medical services, sanitary inspection, unemployment assistance, policing, education, charities and the supply of many amenities. The expansion of the civil service and of professionalisation accompanied such changes. Then there was the growth in the eighteenth and nineteenth centuries of religious Nonconformity with its extra-parochial circuits and other structures,[42] the effects of secularisation upon the Church of

---

[42] Snell and Ell, *Rival Jerusalems*, esp. pp. 265–6, on the extent of Nonconformist growth between 1676 and 1851. For an illuminating study of circuits, see D. Garratt, 'Primitive Methodist circuits in the English–Welsh borderland', *Rural History*, 14 (2003).

England's identity and concept of the parish, along with the emergence of so many other extra-parochial organisations and administrative entities (insurance, trade unions, school boards, the shift from parish friendly societies to the larger affiliated orders, and so on). I have stressed in this book the continued vitality of the parish in the nineteenth century, for much longer than is often supposed. The trends in parish and place memorialisation bear that out as well, showing how late it was (after the 1880s) before decline eventually set in. Nevertheless, all these changes gradually transcended parishes and left them with a much reduced role. The creation of complex, variously defined types of 'new' parish (as discussed in chapter 7), and the functional separation of civil and ecclesiastical parishes, undercut the administrative importance and integrity of former parishes, enfeebling their perceived significance. The differentiation of areas between ecclesiastical and civil parishes was a particularly important development between 1818 and 1940. By the early twentieth century, only a minority of parishes were coterminous for ecclesiastical and civil purposes.[43] There were major boundary changes still to come, notably affecting civil parishes in the 1930s, which further disrupted historical continuities and accentuated these trends. Spatial transcendence of the parish – a sense of its ecclesiastical irrelevance – seems to have been experienced earliest in Nonconformist circles, as one would expect. (See figure 8.2.) The span of local consciousness was also being much expanded by technological advances in transport and communications. It is true that the Boer War, and then the First World War, were accompanied by use of parish ties to assist recruitment,[44] and commemoration of the dead was strongly tied to the parish, especially in rural and suburban areas. Nevertheless, these wars fostered national loyalties and a patriotism that went far beyond parochial or very local senses of pride and

---

[43] *Census of England and Wales, 1911. Area, Families or Separate Occupiers, and Population*, vol. III: *Parliamentary Areas*, p. v; *Census of England and Wales, 1911*, vol. II: *Registration Areas*, p. iv: 'there are now only about 6,000 instances in which the ecclesiastical and civil boundaries coincide' (out of 14,614 civil, and 14,387 ecclesiastical, parishes in England and Wales).

[44] N. Mansfield, *English Farmworkers and Local Patriotism, 1900–1930* (Aldershot, 2001); K. Grieves, '"Lowther's lambs": rural paternalism and voluntary recruitment in the First World War', *Rural History*, 4 (1993).

attachment. There was nothing new in such patriotism, as every eighteenth-century historian knows; but in the early twentieth century it was exceptionally intense and pervasive, and it was superimposed upon the de-localising changes of the previous eighty years.

There was nothing novel about high levels of migration either, but even so the cumulative forsaking of the land from the mid-nineteenth century was unprecedented in its scale and effects. We saw in chapter 4 the dramatic decline in rural parochial endogamy from the 1880s. Low wages, unemployment, anti-deferential attitudes, controls on religion and trade unions, and a general sense of better alternatives elsewhere produced a rural exodus in England, the relatively early chronology of which had almost no other European counterpart. This exodus particularly affected the poorer classes – and readers may suggest that these people rarely afforded a gravestone. Yet rural depopulation induced growing concern among employers, who felt that their own prestige, values and senses of rural community were being questioned. They complained about labour shortages, and rural trade unionism, and began to worry about the longer-term viability of the parish as a place to take pride in. Many rural Tories had opposed the new poor law, that seeming landmark in the decline of the parish, viewing its structure and centralised Poor Law Commission as a direct challenge to their own local influence. It may be no coincidence that 1834, and the next few years immediately following the new poor law, saw high proportions of gravestones proudly announcing 'of this parish', sometimes even in capital letters, which I have not found earlier. I have yet to see a gravestone proclaiming 'of this poor law union', and I do not expect that I ever will.

We have seen that notification of parish or place among the gravestone-leaving classes became more frequent over the first three-quarters of the nineteenth century. Affluent enough to afford a lasting monument, and often key players in parish governance, their prosperity gave them a proud stake in the immediate locality. This was much less apparent among many poorer 'parishioners', whose mobility, difficulty in gaining settlements, religious and political dissent, and associated values were a matter of growing and defensive concern among parish elites. The rural exodus from around the mid-century may have reduced poor rates, but it was also a challenge to the local pride and place loyalty of the propertied classes. Furthermore, the parish and its historic roles were being undercut by administrative reforms that started to diminish the power of local ratepayers and parish vestries. Local property owners commonly had, in the nineteenth century, an unprecedented legal security of property, especially after Parliamentary enclosure, and pride in their local position was probably enhanced by this. They faced some external subversion of their positions, through the centralising tendencies of administrative reforms. Nevertheless, to be 'of this parish', or of a place located within it, was still a message that enhanced the status of the family, and was felt to confer local benefit to it. Until the later nineteenth century, to be trenchantly 'parochial' even unto death was not usually a cause of disparagement and belittlement.

In our earlier decades, when attachment to place on gravestones was less frequent, it was something that hardly needed stating for those from the classes that concern us here. It was taken for granted, as normal and to be expected when so much life was parish-centred. Everyone in the mid-eighteenth century knew that John Brown, buried in the plot near his relatives, was of this parish. There was no need to chip the obvious into stone. Place association came to be thought increasingly necessary from the later eighteenth century, in an era of enlarging personal mobility among these classes. Thus 'of this parish' was inscribed more often when significant numbers of those in the burial ground were thought *not* to be 'of this parish', or perhaps (for example in the case of many Methodists) not fully of the Anglican persuasion.[45] A sense of *difference* and to some extent social precedence is revealed by this phrase, and a desire to emphasise such differences within the parish. The same applies to statements linking people to places elsewhere, and here

---

[45] It is just possible that 'of this parish' could also be an occasional code referring to those who were Anglicans in the parish – the phrase perhaps having a denominational connotation. This is certainly a possibility, one reinforced by the avoidance of the term by Baptists and Congregationalists as noted above (n. 36). If this is true, it would add another interesting slant to the meaning of 'belonging'. It would not rule out many Anglicans who chose to express themselves differently on their gravestones. Only very detailed nominal linkages from the relevant gravestones to other parish or Nonconformist sources could establish this.

aloofness, external place loyalty, genealogical statements laid down for posterity, and other such motives are implied.

The pace and chronology of centralisation (in all its economic, political, civil and cultural dimensions) is debated by nineteenth-century historians. One view is that the most significant changes occurred from the 1870s, and that 'the age of localism' lasted until around then.[46] The most common argument for peace-time conditions sees growing, if rather ineffective, centralisation from *c.* 1830, compounded more strongly by the late nineteenth- and early twentieth-century welfare, educational, transport, amenity provision and governmental reforms. This chronology invites one to view the rise in place-association inscriptions in the nineteenth century as being a response to early signs of centralisation in British society and local government. The stony responses of some people to the new poor law suggest this. Defensive loyalty to place coincided with initial signs of nineteenth-century centralisation. However, one also needs to stress the continued role of the parish in people's lives, notably in the countryside, for we have seen how important it remained long after 1834. As Alan Everitt expressed it, 'local attachments, far from declining with the growth of national consciousness, were in many ways becoming stronger: a fact which will cause no surprise to an observant reader of novelists like George Eliot and Mrs. Oliphant'.[47] There were significant reforms between 1830 and 1865, alluded to above, affecting in particular the poor law and parish administration; and, within multi-horizoned views of 'the local', it is certainly the *parish* that most concerns us in this explanation, given its centrality for burial and commemoration. The year 1834 was a watershed

---

[46] R. Price, *British Society, 1680–1880: Dynamism, Containment and Change* (Cambridge, 1999), p. 185.

[47] A. Everitt, 'Nonconformity in country parishes', in J. Thirsk (ed.), *Land, Church and People: Essays Presented to Professor H. P. R. Finberg* (Reading, 1970), supplement to the *Agricultural History Review*, 29 (1970), pp. 178–9. See also the important argument of J. Langton, 'The industrial revolution and the regional geography of England', *Transactions of the Institute of British Geographers*, 9 (1984); P. Hudson, 'The regional perspective', in her (ed.), *Regions and Industries: A Perspective on the Industrial Revolution in Britain* (1989, Cambridge, 1993), pp. 18–22; or, on the growth of local and regional fiction after *c.* 1800, K. D. M. Snell (ed.), *The Regional Novel in Britain and Ireland, 1800–1990* (Cambridge, 1998), ch. 1; and his *The Bibliography of Regional Fiction in Britain and Ireland, 1800–2000* (Aldershot, 2002), pp. 1–12.

for the parish with regard to poor law administration, even though the parish remained the funding unit and basis for local welfare, and overseers remained crucial. Yet the new poor law had limited import for sepulchral matters, and, despite the threat and fear of the workhouse, we have seen that 'out-door' poor relief in the parishes or townships remained the norm.[48] With hindsight it can be argued that the subsequent decades witnessed a fairly confined 'revolution in government': that local elites still had main control, and that central legislation often retained a permissive rather than mandatory form.[49] The parish or township also remained fundamental for matters such as church rates, some features of policing, or the management of by-roads. It was not until the post-1870 developments – affecting the international economy, education, local government, public health, trade unionism, the 'nationalising' of popular culture (e.g. football, rugby, the music hall), stronger trans-local class alignments,[50] and a widely held view of the Empire as central to national identity – that the most fundamental decline of localism set in. While it is impossible to prove personal motivations here, it seems likely that the rise up to the 1870s in gravestone place associations was an expression of the continuing strength of local attachments, and literally a defensive stand against early centralising trends. Thereafter the sharp reduction in monumental place association seems inevitably linked to ever greater mobility and asserted centralisation, which by then was affecting so many key features of English life.

Related to this was a cultural phenomenon, well summed up by Jan Marsh when she described 'a wish to claim an ancestral

---

[48] See chapter 5. In 1839–43, for example, 85 per cent of paupers were receiving out-relief rather than relief within the workhouse. Sir G. Nicholls, *A History of the English Poor Law, in Connection with the State of the Country and the Condition of the People*, vol. II (1854, New York, 1967), p. 351, and see *ibid.*, pp. 387, 390–1. 'Out-door' paupers were still 77–8 per cent of paupers in 1847–8, in effect being relieved in their parishes. Nicholls, as a Poor Law Commissioner and Secretary to the Poor Law Board, objected strongly to such deviation from 'the principles of 1834'; but with regional variations it remained a feature of the new poor law, highlighting the continuing role of the parish as the venue for relief, albeit now dispensed largely by guardians and relieving officers.

[49] Price, *British Society*, pp. 177–90.

[50] On the nineteenth-century survival of local xenophobia, in relation to arguments about class, see chapter 2.

connection with one particular region or county, in a way denying that very mobility which now enabled people to choose where to live'.[51] This was evident among the classes that concern us. In some cases – Marsh mentions Edward Thomas and Rupert Brooke – it was a transferable allegiance. Edward Thomas was attracted to a Wiltshire that was the literary creation of Richard Jefferies. Rupert Brooke punted into Grantchester, the subject of his poem acclaiming local patriotism, as quoted earlier[52] – after living there a few months he affirmed the place as 'my village'. Vicarious and fashionable though it was, such attachment and ideas of belonging were strongly extolled or prioritised by many regional authors, including Thomas Hardy, as indeed by many painters of Victorian country or fishing villages, such as Birket Foster, Samuel Palmer, H. C. Bryant, W. G. Foster or Thomas Barrett. Much of the appeal of 'regional' authors was linked to their own artistic sentiments about a particular locale, sentiments of local allegiance which clearly spoke (and often still speak) to a prevailing mood of nostalgic loss and displacement from community.[53] This was a mood quintessentially transferable to Victorian gravestone inscription, documenting a loss that was in every sense historical, communal and personal.

In the face of expanding personal mobility, it also became necessary in the nineteenth century for family survivors to identify their dead more accurately: to indicate that this person buried here was John Brown of *this* parish, not the one from the village in the adjoining valley, or across the river. Where kinship ties were especially dense, and where the range of surnames could be narrow – for example in some of the Lakeland communities, or in many Welsh rural neighbourhoods – the identification of people via their local habitations was always helpful to the living. Thus we find high and more enduring levels of gravestone place association in such areas. In England, these areas were also often liable to attract transferable outsider

---

[51] J. Marsh, *Back to the Land: The Pastoral Impulse in England, from 1880 to 1914* (London, 1982), p. 31.
[52] See pp. 43–4.
[53] The output of local and regional fiction was expanding greatly in the mid-late nineteenth century. Snell, *Regional Novel in Britain and Ireland*, p. 25; Snell, *Bibliography of Regional Fiction*, pp. 5–6.

allegiance for yearning-*cum*-aesthetic reasons, an allegiance often expressed in stone.

A number of further considerations help to explain the shift away from gravestone place association. Preoccupation after 1880 with national and imperial issues, in this most expansive phase of British history, came to make very local ties to place seem antiquated at all cultural levels. 'Parochial', like 'provincial', was one of the newly disparaging words of the later nineteenth century,[54] particularly among some of the more ambitious and meritocratically inclined in the property-owning or professional classes. The anti-parochial views of people like Edwin Chadwick, or Charles Dickens (to put two unlikely companions together),[55] became more prevalent through the nineteenth century. High levels of personal mobility among the middle classes, associated with education, career development, work, tourism, and new technologies of travel, reduced the numbers of those who felt a sufficiently strong place connection to justify mentioning it on a gravestone. Such 'far-sighted' people did not wish to replicate 'the return of the native', the man whom Thomas Hardy brought back to Egdon Heath from the Paris jewelry trade, and then blighted with diminishing eyesight. Outward-looking attitudes and migration increasingly counter-balanced the nostalgic tendencies induced by such mobility. This was the age of commercialised photographic travel albums, of the international tourist photography of Roger Fenton, Francis Firth and their many followers. Postcards were first used in 1863, although their general usage came a few decades later. Furthermore, the late nineteenth-century agricultural depression, extending for twenty or so years after 1876, must have reduced a desire to make place references among hitherto well-to-do rural classes, as rents declined, indebtedness increased, farms fell vacant, and tenants became bankrupt or moved elsewhere in search of lower rents. The later nineteenth century also saw more dual entries of place attachment on

---

[54] On the disparagement of the 'provincial', see Snell, *Regional Novel in Britain and Ireland*, pp. 48–52. The history of the word 'parochial' remains to be written.

[55] On Dickens, see for example the indictment of the parish beadle and a parish workhouse (of a kind founded before 1834) in *Oliver Twist, or, the Parish Boy's Progress* (London, 1837–9), chs. 1–7, or 17.

gravestones among elevated professional people (as noted above for the Lake District), and this bears witness to the mobility, affluence and varied regional property holding that more people were enjoying, which co-existed for a while with a desire to confirm ties to place. On some of the Hawkshead gravestones linking a person to two places there are professional qualifications added, which are further testimony to a link between mobility and an ambiguous or dual sense of belonging.

This disassociation from a single place during one's life persisted and intensified radically during the twentieth century. We have now reached a historical point at which comparatively few people could, or may even wish to, make any such claim. Nor would such a statement normally induce much solidarity or pride among survivors. 'Here lies K. D. M. Snell: of this parish': how bizarre, relatives and friends would think, as they travelled back to their distant and most recent home places. Many soon-to-die people might also worry that such a claim would reflect poorly on them if they left instructions to make it.[56] To be 'of this parish' no longer carries the moral approbation that it once did. This is largely because achievement has (for better or worse) become associated with migration away, with 'non-belonging', with qualifications, jobs and money obtained elsewhere. Many of us retain some ambivalence on the question of where (and whether) we 'belong'. Nevertheless, this society now appears to believe that to stay put is to be a failure, whatever one's local contribution. Indeed, we have developed many words and sayings that reveal this attitude: 'stick-in-the-mud', 'stay-at-home';[57] as contrasted with 'seeking

---

[56] I grant that in some circles, and among some advertisers, place attachment and its dialectal associations paradoxically convey an aura of solidity and integrity in the face of what may be thought of as ephemeral and morally dubious. Whether such an understanding and usage of 'the local' was equally prevalent in the late nineteenth and early twentieth centuries remains to be researched.

[57] Earlier negative appellations of clod-like fixity in the nineteenth century especially ridiculed the rural labourers, thought to be among the lowest of the low (and in many regions their smocks were seen to add feminine contours to such denigration). On chawbacons, clods, hobnails and swains, see A. Howkins, 'From Hodge to Lob: reconstructing the English farm labourer, 1870–1914', in M. Chase and I. Dyck (eds.), *Living and Learning: Essays in Honour of J. F. C. Harrison* (Aldershot, 1996), pp. 218–35; K. D. M. Snell, *Annals of the Labouring Poor: Social Change and Agrarian England, 1660–1900* (Cambridge, 1985), pp. 5–10; K. D. M. Snell, 'Deferential bitterness: the social outlook

the bright lights', 'getting on one's bike', 'on the move', 'going places', 'moving onwards and upwards', and so on. This increased disenchantment with local fixity became more apparent in the later nineteenth century, and it appears to be well mirrored by trends in gravestone memorials.

Coupled with increased mobility, and related to it, has been the growing estimation of people on their gravestones by their contribution to the nuclear family. This was noted earlier. No longer 'rooted' to place, nor identifying oneself with any such place, nor taking pride in any such association, one falls back upon the nuclear family that one helped to form, that shared some of one's personal mobility, and that has sometimes been strong enough to maintain its affective ties in the face of migration. One is remembered by that family, much more so now than by the people of a parish or community with whom one might have lived and worked over many decades. Many ex-community rituals (for example, Christmas) have also been taken over by the family.[58] This isolation of individuals and families, and crumbling of place-defined community, is seen by many theorists to be a feature of 'modernisation'. The change is shown well, and with chronological precision, in churchyard memorialisation. Unknown to so many in any 'local community', as is now so often the case, there seems little point in staking associations with it on a gravestone.[59] One is extolled instead as a loving husband or wife, father or mother, grandfather or grandmother, having apparently been that across *many* places. This emphasis owed something to the Victorian veneration of the family. Perhaps linked to that, long-term ties to a parish's inhabitants, or to a certain working community, have become so tenuous that there was often little credible alternative memorial. Where place association continued longest, in the

---

of the rural proletariat in eighteenth- and nineteenth-century England and Wales', in M. L. Bush (ed.), *Social Orders and Social Classes in Europe since 1500: Studies in Social Stratification* (Harlow, 1992), pp. 162–5.

[58] See also the perceptive comments by R. Hutton, *The Stations of the Sun: A History of the Ritual Year in Britain* (1996, Oxford, 1997), pp. 426–7, on the replacement of the community by the family as the principal unit of celebration in festive rituals.

[59] R. Price even argued that from around the 1880s 'The political subject was now regarded as a free-standing individual, not as a member of a community': *British Society*, p. 332; and certainly arguments for growing 'individuation' have been made in many ways by sociologists and theorists.

upland parishes, the places people associated with on memorials were very commonly the named farmsteads or residences. This was partly because of the nature of scattered settlement; but these places also served as proxies for 'family' in a way that 'of this parish' did not.

As place association on gravestones declined, therefore, we probably witness a very interesting series of linked phenomena. Death has become more of a private family matter, rather than a community one.[60] Changes in funeral and mourning customs throughout the British Isles suggest this. Private grief has very much eclipsed public or community grief, and familial affection for most classes has perhaps become more public, or even 'feminized', at least in memorial declarations.[61] Death itself has become privatised, even 'forbidden' or 'unnamable' as a subject: a social embarrassment and fear that is contrary to utilitarian general happiness.[62] The understanding of the churchyard as a 'visible centre of a community of the living and the dead', as Wordsworth put it, has been much eroded.[63] The use of more

---

[60] The same is sometimes said of marriages, with public participation waning in preference for privacy. It was arguably also true for welfare provision in the nineteenth century, where the stress went from local community provision, as under the old poor law, to some greater insistence upon family support as some of 'the principles of 1834' came to be enforced rather more strongly in the 1870s and 1880s.

[61] Among the aristocracy and gentry, from the sixteenth century onwards, expressions of affection and appreciation were often recorded on internal church monuments – but, even allowing for the cost and length of inscriptions, in the eighteenth and early nineteenth centuries such wording was less common on extra-mural monuments for people of somewhat lower status. Purely factual statements predominated at that level, and it was only later that one finds more frequent comments of familial endearment. I would not, of course, deduce anything about 'real' affection or 'romantic love' from this.

[62] P. Aries, *Western Attitudes towards Death: From the Middle Ages to the Present* (1974, London, 1976), pp. 85–107; Orwell, *Coming Up for Air*, p. 190: 'Every new town puts its cemetery on the outskirts. Shove it away – keep it out of sight! Can't bear to be reminded of death'; Davies, *Brief History of Death*, ch. 7. On deaths taking place more commonly in institutions over the late nineteenth and early twentieth centuries, see M. A. Crowther, *The Workhouse System, 1834–1929: The History of an English Social Institution* (London, 1983), pp. 57–8.

[63] W. Wordsworth, 'Essay upon epitaphs', in W. J. B. Owen and J. W. Smyser (eds.), *The Prose Works of William Wordsworth*, 3 vols. (Oxford, 1974), vol. II, p. 56; or see R. Morris, *Churches in the Landscape* (London, 1989), pp. 4–5. In some extreme departures from Wordsworth's description – Grasmere is an ironic example, where Wordsworth is buried near the stream – the churchyard is now a 'visible centre' for world tourists, a Japanese touchstone amid flowing internationalism. Presumably tourists find solace there for their nostalgic literary localism.

distant cemeteries, the growth of funerary transport, and the crowding out of parish churchyards have contributed to this development. Frequent resort to large urban cemeteries has obviated the idea of *parish* burial, going much wider geographically than that, and frequently having no possible relation to an experienced and personally known 'community' of local people. Such cemeteries often came to be situated outside towns (as in Roman times), partly for public health reasons. Edwin Chadwick argued for this in the 1840s, and here (as elsewhere) he had almost no respect for the parish or its authorities. The development of elaborate funeral transport in the nineteenth century, as the distances to burial increased, epitomised this rupture between a parish community and its dead. In the twentieth century, there was 'an increasing tendency to push [cemeteries] well away from the inhabited areas'.[64] In more distant funerals, close families were much more likely to attend than neighbours and others in a community. Indeed, the church often recommended that only a few family members (rather than a wider network of people) should attend at the cemetery graveside.[65] The use of such cemeteries was also encouraged by the perception that parish churchyards were steadily reaching saturation point. The adoption of enduring gravestones over recent centuries made such a conclusion almost inevitable, by helping to secure graves against future re-use. One might 'belong' most strongly in stone, and so provide durable evidence for historians, but one did so as an impediment to others 'belonging' that way subsequently. This form of belonging, unlike others we have discussed, was not transferable, or a niche vacated and refillable in due course, as arguably had been so for the dead in earlier centuries before stone memorialisation became frequent. Nor was it easily discarded, or anonymised, like church bequests, which were another expression of belonging, sustaining one's memory locally. Given this situation, the memorialised long-dead of the eighteenth and nineteenth centuries – some might call them 'the selfish dead' – hindered or pre-empted

---

[64] P. Dow (ed.), assisted by R. A. C. Drobig, *Hobson's Local Government* (London, 1951), p. 64.
[65] Forder, *Parish Priest at Work*, p. 295.

the hitherto close emotional ties between the living and the recently dead in their parish churchyard. They thwarted a strong link among the living to the parish, and obliged residents to look to more distant cemeteries or crematory options. Complaints about the impossibility of burying one's relatives or friends in one's own parish churchyard have been commonplace in the twentieth and twenty-first centuries, often becoming newspaper issues.[66] And even parish cemeteries had, under mid-nineteenth-century legislation, to be 100 yards or more away from the nearest house in a village, again to some extent displacing the dead from any central place in their community.[67] Chadwick's influence, as in poor law affairs so detrimental to parish belonging, reveals itself yet again; that is why in so many hundreds of villages today, one sees the parish cemetery well outside the village, beyond intervening fields. In sum, we see in the demise of place associations on gravestones some decline of local community association, the deriving of identities and status among survivors by other means than by asserting links between relatives and localities, and a growing tendency in the context of commemoration to believe that only one's family mattered.

It was not always so. At a level above the migratory labouring poor, many people once *were* their place: to have an 'occupation' originally meant to 'occupy' a place, and was used in that sense by poets such as Wordsworth, or by Thomas Hardy in his stress upon village craftsmen with customary leases as the backbone of village life. We sense this in some Welsh naming characteristics that were still current in the nineteenth and early twentieth centuries: Wil y Wern, or John Tŷ Uchaf (referring to an unmarried son by his Christian name and the name of his father's farm),[68] Wil Cwmcyrnach, Llew'r Garth, the speaking

---

[66] For example, 'Woman is refused burial place', *Leicester Mercury* (24 April 1996), pp. 1, 3; 'Still life in death', *Guardian* (8 January 1997).

[67] This was due to the operation of 18 & 19 Vic., c. 128, s. 9. Any parish cemetery within 100 yards of the nearest house had to be with the written consent of all affected owners, lessees and occupiers, which was often not worth trying to obtain. For a very similar clause in a Scottish Act of the same year (1855), see 18 & 19 Vic., c. 68.

[68] A. D. Rees, *Life in a Welsh Countryside: A Social Study of Llanfihangel yng Ngwynfa* (1950, Cardiff, 1996), p. 64. In Wales, a married occupier of a holding could be referred to as

of a person as the son of a farm,[69] Dai the smithy, Rachel the Pandy,[70] Jones the Chapel, Rhys the Swamp,[71] or in the somewhat stereotyped characters of Richard Llewellyn's *How Green Was My Valley* (1939). In England, one thinks of farms taking their names from former tenants – White's Farm, Dunn's Farm, Clark's Farm, and so on – or the naming of people in association with places in Mrs Gaskell's *The Life of Charlotte Brontë* – 'in many instances the person is designated by his residence', for example, Jonathan o' th' Gate[72] – the character referencing of a Kentish–Sussex novelist like Sheila Kaye-Smith,[73] or much earlier toponymic and locative naming patterns.[74] People were once described, given an identity, and their behaviour even accounted for, by their place and by their occupation in it, however parochial that might be.[75] In death, they were esteemed by mention of their local connections to their parish. 'A Welsh death, like marriage, was a celebration of history and community,' wrote the late David Jones,[76] and the same was true for many English areas. Yet for very many people, all this is now largely gone. Work and home are usually in different places: we no longer occupy our occupation. Our incomes now are not usually dependent upon our occupation of property, in the way for example of Hardy's woodlanders. Rather, we occupy property by virtue of our incomes. Furthermore, the parish is, at last, an economic and social irrelevance for most of us, both

the husband of such and such a farm, and descendants were often also referred to by the name of the farm where the ancestor lived.

[69] For example: 'My grandfather was the son of Y Fraich Esmwyth, a little farm on the side of Mynydd Pencarreg facing Lampeter and Cardiganshire. The place was a family freehold where they had been living for generations.' D. J. Williams, *The Old Farmhouse* (1961, Carmarthen, 1987), p. 203. See also T. J. Morgan and P. Morgan, *Welsh Surnames* (Cardiff, 1985).

[70] Williams, *Old Farmhouse*, pp. 126, 236.

[71] A. Lovins and P. Evans, *Eryri, the Mountains of Longing* (London, 1971), pp. 32–3.

[72] E. Gaskell, *The Life of Charlotte Brontë* (1857, Harmondsworth, 1983), pp. 567–8.

[73] S. Kaye-Smith, *Joanna Godden* (London, 1921), pp. 9–10.

[74] D. Hey and G. Redmonds, *Yorkshire Surnames and the Hearth Tax Returns of 1672–73* (York, 2002), pp. 16–28.

[75] In some other European regions today, like the Italian Dolomites, farmers often continue to be known by the name of their farm, and will frequently introduce themselves as such rather than by using their personal name. I am grateful to Margery Tranter for this information.

[76] D. J. V. Jones, *Rebecca's Children: A Study of Rural Society, Crime, and Protest* (Oxford, 1989), p. 77.

in religious terms and as a working community – and I say this with historical regret and with genuine respect for those who would hope or think otherwise.

We also witness these changes in other features of the disposal of the dead. The twentieth-century move towards cremation, and the frequent scattering of ashes to the winds or waters, epitomise the historical change that I am discussing here. Survivors often have no monument to help them remember the dead. 'Cremation excludes a pilgrimage.'[77] Even when some ashes are buried under a small plaque, the dead are hardly 'placed' by this process. I recently watched as the ashes of a friend were cast down into a swollen river Wye, near Symonds Yat. I stood among a small number of other people, some of whom I did not know and did not speak to. No memorial marks his passing, or could commemorate any local identity that he had. Like Wesley (that originator in so much) the world had been his parish. Unlike his ancestors, he had very diverse attainments and attachments, which had been gained in, and had taken him to, countless places. His attachment to place, or at least to this place, was aesthetic, wistful, post-nostalgic: a substitute for old familiarities, which he never had. Moving so far away from an Anglican or working historical conception of home place, it could never be said of such a person that he was 'of this parish'. He represents a growing multitude in the modern world, belonging nowhere in particular in life, nor in death: and he has no fixed memorial. His ashes simply dispersed out of sight in the swirling water. Alternative forms of memorial have taken over, and those alternatives (such as photography, publications, the recorded voice) are themselves more mobile. Today, we turn chapels into garages; and we tarmac over church and other burial grounds to create car parks: turning permanent resting places into transient lay-bys servicing mobility. How soon will it be before we discuss not the decline of gravestones mentioning place, but the decline of gravestones altogether? And what would that mean to us?

---

[77] Aries, *Western Attitudes towards Death*, p. 91.

The fifty-three Anglican churchyards analysed were:
Arthingworth (Northants.), Ashby Folville, *Ashby Magna, Austrey* (Warws.), Beeby, Belton (Rut.), Brathay (Cumb.), *Bruntingthorpe,* Clifton Campville (Staffs.), *Clipston* (Northants.), *Croxton Kerrial, Elford* (Staffs.), Foston, *Gaddesby,* Garsdale (West Riding, Yorks.), Gaulby, Goxhill (Lincs.), Great Stretton, *Hallaton,* Harby, Harlaston (Staffs.), *Harrington* (Northants.), *Hartland* (Devon.), *Hawkshead* (Cumb.), Hexham Abbey (Northumb.), *Horninghold,* King's Norton, *Kirby Muxloe,* Knighton, *Knipton, Knossington,* Lamport (Northants.), *Little Stretton,* Lockington, *Loddington* (Northants.), *Necton* (Norf.), Newlands (Cumb.), *Newton Regis* (Warws.), *Orton on the Hill, Owston, Patterdale* (Cumb.), Peatling Magna, *Peatling Parva, Ravensthorpe,* Ryal (Northumb.), *St Clements Skegness* (Lincs.), *Slawston, South Croxton,* Stoughton, Thorpe on the Hill (Lincs.), Tur Langton, *Twyford,* and *Welham.*

The following thirty-four Nonconformist and Catholic burial grounds were analysed; the denomination is given in brackets: Arnesby (Baptist), Bardon Park (United Reformed), Barton in the Beans (Baptist), Belton (Baptist), Billesdon (Baptist), Castle Donington (General Baptist), Clipston (Baptist, Northants.), Countesthorpe (Baptist), Crick (United Reformed, Northants.), Diseworth (General Baptist), Earl Shilton (Baptist), Earl Shilton (Independent, now United Reformed), East Leake (General Baptist, Notts.), Gretton (Baptist, Northants.), *Haunton* (Catholic, Staffs.), Husbands Bosworth (Catholic), Irthlingborough (Baptist, Northants.), Kegworth (General Baptist), Keyworth (United Reformed, Notts.), Kibworth Harcourt (Congregational), Leicester (Unitarian), Long Whatton (Baptist), Measham (Baptist), Quorndon (Baptist), Ringstead (Baptist; now Baptist and Methodist, Northants.), Shepshed (Baptist), Sutton in the Elms (Baptist), Theddingworth (Congregational), Walgrave (Baptist, Northants.), Woodford (Baptist, Northants.), Woodhouse Eaves (Baptist), Woodhouse Eaves (Methodist), Wymeswold (Wesleyan Methodist), and Yelvertoft (Congregational, Northants.).

All these places are in Leicestershire unless otherwise indicated. A full burial-ground survey was conducted for all the above named church or chapel burial grounds printed in roman, while a more straightforward tabulation only of stones giving place references was completed for the italicised places. Hence, in figure 8.1 in the text, the tabulations based on trends in total numbers alone refer to all the above places, while the decadal percentage calculations (figures 8.2–8.3) refer to the places printed above in roman type.

Most of the non-Anglican burial grounds pertain to old dissenting denominations. In part this is because the Baptists and Congregationalists tended to be strong in the midland areas I have researched most closely, and of course their chapels were frequently longer established than those of the Methodists, with a correspondingly greater likelihood of having their own burial grounds. Even so, it is not mentioned in the religious or graveyard historiography that only a very small minority of Methodist chapels, at least in the English midlands, have their own burial grounds, and Methodists would appear to be more prone to partial conformity to the Church of England than the old dissenters in matters relating to burial. Of 6,919 Methodist chapels in Great Britain in 1990, 577 have burial grounds (8 per cent), of which 189 are closed. I am grateful to Christopher Stell for this information, which he obtained from the 'Statistical Returns' for 1990 published by the Methodist Property Division, Oldham Street, Manchester. Equivalent statistics on this matter do not appear to be easily available for other denominations, although some guidance may be obtained from lists of non-parochial registers. Mr Stell comments that 'Many of the older chapels – Baptist, Congregational, Presbyterian (Unitarian) – had some facility for burial, often making use of whatever curtilage was available, however small', and 'Most Quaker meeting-houses will have had a burial-ground either attached or at a distance, sometimes shared, as a matter of principle' (personal correspondence, 21 May 2001). Christopher Stell's own impressive regional guides to Nonconformist chapels and meeting houses, published by the Royal Commission on the Historical Monuments of England, provide much assistance on the location of Nonconformist burial grounds. For example, covering the midlands, see *An Inventory of Nonconformist Chapels and Meeting-houses in Central England* (HMSO, 1986), or the published county fascicules from it.

CHAPTER 9

Conclusion – belonging, parish and community

This book has taken readers through a range of subjects relating to belonging and the parish in the past. It has covered the cultures of local xenophobia, the changing nature of the settlement laws, the decline of high parochial endogamy, the role of the parish and its overseers under the new poor law, the 'new parishes' and their problems, and how people showed their ideas of local belonging on their burial ground memorials. As I pointed out in the introduction and subsequently, ideas of 'belonging' are complex, subjective, culturally ingrained, based on different and often rival criteria, and intermeshed with administrative systems. They can be explored in a great variety of ways, and via many other themes than those chosen here. I am conscious of an enormity of possible themes. Some traverse the parish and take us into kinship and occupational regions beyond the parish, with their respective obligations and forms of mutuality. Many are addressed through important cultural variations involving ethnicity, language, dialect, religion, folklore and local calendars, collective actions, ritual and precedences, political dispositions, vernacular building and folk art. Others relate to senses of industrial community of the kinds established in countless textile, mining, shipbuilding, and other settlements associated with the Industrial Revolution.

It is obvious from these chapters that I do not believe that the word *community* should normally be put into inverted commas by historians speaking about the past, in the way of modern commentators who frequently search in vain for it now. Community in its main historical forms was comprised within a bounded or limited area in which almost everybody knew each other, to which people felt that they belonged, and in which someone who was not known was enquired about. It meant a district of inter-personal knowledge. This was often (but not always) a district that had formal administrative functions.[1] Such an understanding of the term covers a myriad of different but real communities in our past, notably parishes and townships. By comparison, 'community' today in most regions is a figment and flickering shadow of what it once was, something warranting the inverted commas that designate its questionable reality. There are many reasons for this. The decline of the parish or township as a proud self-administering neighbourhood of interconnected interests, the rural exodus, the First World War, the inter-war depression and its social effects, the crumbling of local forms of religious organisation, suburbanisation and the revolution in transport, work- and home-place separation, the collapse through de-industrialisation of solidaristic industrial communities, let alone the centralising penchants of left- and right-wing governments – these have all undercut forms of community and belonging, as many commentators from Richard Hoggart to Robert Colls have graphically shown.[2] Even if we take the broader notion of occupational communities, we have relatively few of those grounded in local place. The biotechnology networks around Cambridge, a few remaining car-manufacturing areas, or financial services in the City of London, are perhaps weak examples. They seem scarce and diffused compared with the agricultural, fishing, mining, quarrying, furniture-making, metal-working, pottery, cotton, woollen, lace, hosiery and other such occupational communities of early modern and industrial Britain. Cultural celebrations of local

---

[1] As communities not administering themselves, I think for example of some extra-parochial places, of some townships that relinquished their administration to a wider parish, or perhaps of sets of streets or districts within towns. There is a massive literature on defining 'community', a term fundamental to sociology as a discipline. See for example C. Bell and H. Newby, *Community Studies: An Introduction to the Sociology of the Local Community* (London, 1971), pp. 15–16, 21–2, 27–32, 49. Back in 1955 one article analysed ninety-four definitions of the term, and there are hundreds of rival ones now. G. A. Hillery, 'Definitions of community: areas of agreement', *Rural Sociology*, 20 (1955). The best one can do is simply to clarify one's own usage.

[2] R. Hoggart, *The Uses of Literacy: Aspects of Working-class Life with Special Reference to Publications and Entertainments* (London, 1957); R. Colls, *Identity of England* (Oxford, 2002); R. Colls, 'When we lived in communities: working-class culture and its critics', in R. Colls and R. Rodger (eds.), *Cities of Ideas: Civil Society and Urban Governance in Britain, 1800–2000* (Aldershot, 2004).

belonging have much diminished – such as Rogation perambulations, parochial calendrical rituals, doleing customs, parish feast days and festivals, Sunday school and friendly society marches, and the like. Furthermore, legal and administrative frameworks and criteria for local belonging have almost totally disappeared. They are now rarely based on personal service, repute or merit regardless of age or class – as they once often were, ranging from young farm servants or apprentices earning their settlements, to justices of the peace, affecting behaviour accordingly – and even where such criteria exist and are subjectively seen as such they are hardly publicly credited in that way. We have gladly left behind us much of the local xenophobia that once existed. Yet in the modern world we are individualised, isolated and disconnected compared to most of our counterparts in the rural and market-town societies of the past. As a historian I believe that we are much impoverished and beset by problems as a result. The rarity now of large families and their kin mutualities, and the increase of single-person households, has further isolated people from close networks of conversant support. The modern scenario is not historically impressive, and, as I suggested at the opening of this book, little in the experiences of centralisation, globalisation and modern communications look set adequately to replace the face-to-face parish community of the seventeenth to nineteenth centuries. One can now communicate almost instantaneously with people in other countries, but neighbours are often ignored, and it can take a week or more to contact a 'local' doctor or 'district' nurse. The predicament of isolated elderly people is ever more apparent, testimony to the lack of modern 'community'. In every street in the country there exist such persons bereft of local family, relatives, useful neighbours, and people with shared community memories. By comparison, the parish almshouses of earlier centuries lacked the facilities of modern medicine, and were materialistically basic, but they housed people usually bound together in the humorous or sad riches of collective local memory and folklore, in shared attachments to place, and in a righteous solidarity of entitled belonging.

I have shown in this book that the eventual decline of the parish, the erosion of strong senses of local belonging, and by implication what many term 'the collapse of community', were not concomitants of industrialisation or the early stages of 'modernisation'. I do not believe that industrialisation between *c.* 1750 and 1870 destroyed local attachment and community, however visible some urban examples of such collapse were. There was often more community in the epicentres of industrialisation than there ever was in those districts before. Across the country, the Industrial Revolution coincided with strong and often heightened senses of place and belonging, as well as with an intensification of regional cultures and local pride. The most striking manifestations of the latter are usually Victorian. By contrast, it has been the period of de-industrialisation that has most damaged community and pride in place. We are also embarrassed by much post-1945 architecture, and many resent the damage to our built and natural environment done for the sake of the motor car. Like local pride, however, community spirit remained a pervasive feature of English and Welsh local societies well into the early twentieth century, even though by then it often co-existed with, and was filtered through or augmented by, abrasive senses of class. It seems to me that community as a concept has failed to convince some historical commentators partly because they have not equated or bonded it to the parish: to the legal criteria for belonging, to insider–outsider divisions, precedences and suspicions, to parish office-holding and the enormous saliency of the parish in this country's historic welfare systems.

One should therefore stress how flourishing and long-enduring the parish was. We can all think of alternative past *foci* of community other than the parish – some larger, and some smaller than the parish, as for example a street or district in a town setting,[3] or even perhaps a small town itself. Yet in general terms I can think of no such community focus that had anything approaching the administrative, legal, social and cultural importance of the parish, or its frequent northern equivalent – the township. *Community* for most people *was the parish* in the

---

[3] For example, see J. White, *The Worst Street in North London: Campbell Bunk, Islington, Between the Wars* (London, 1986). The street had its own codes of honour, its own 'collective identity of belonging', and (as yet another manifestation of local xenophobia) 'strangers' or people from other streets were often derided or beaten up. *Ibid.*, pp. 79–82.

eighteenth and nineteenth centuries. It was usually an early medieval entity of great longevity, strength and meaning: 'one feature of a whole world constructed between *c.* 900 and *c.* 1200 that only reached the verge of extinction in the last century'.[4] As late as 1886, T. F. Bulmer in his *History, Topography, and Directory of Northumberland* rightly stated that the parish 'was at a very early date adopted by the state for civil purposes; and parishes are now, except, perhaps, in the centres of population, objects of primary interest to the inhabitants, especially in religious and ecclesiastical matters, and the concerns, spiritual and civil, of one's own parish, attract the attention before it diverges to the country at large'.[5] The parish's administration, customs and folklore were enduring and revivified in many ways, even with its divisions, its fluxes, its hierarchies and concentric circles of belonging, its outward looking dissenters, and its restless migrants moving elsewhere even though still regarding it as their 'home'. The parish as community came under pressure in some areas with industrialisation, producing responses which often damaged it further. Yet it was not simply an 'imagined' community. It had tangible boundaries, with its mere stones, boundary streams and pathways. Its boundary trees were deeply scored with carved and ever enlarging parish initials, from which the ivy was regularly stripped. Everyone knew these boundaries, and knew them from a young age, their information coming from the elderly. In addition, the parish church and churchyard were much restored by the Victorian masons, and were central symbols, albeit symbols that were often received differently by local inhabitants. The parish was a *legal* entity, a unit of responsibility and oversight, in which one built up respect and obligations – what would later be discovered and called 'social capital' – and this legal entity of the parish had ramifications for almost all features of everyday life. The senses of belonging to the parish were conspicuous and they flood at us from the historical evidence, even from evidence covering people of quite different social status. This is clearly

---

[4] This quotation is from Charles Phythian-Adams (personal communication, 1 December 2005).
[5] T. F. Bulmer, *History, Topography, and Directory of Northumberland (Hexham Division)* (Manchester, 1886), p. 238.

true of the early modern period, and I believe that it is very true of the nineteenth century as well.

To abandon the term community as a tool of social-historical analysis may be understandable, given what little we have now, but it is to shut one's eyes to the historical reality and pervasive importance of the parish, as well as to other forms of community. One might suppose that this parish role was least applicable to religious Nonconformists, because the topography of dissent was often extra-parochial. However, Nonconformists were usually well integrated into the civic, economic and social life of the parish, just as Margaret Spufford and others have shown for earlier periods.[6] In Wales they dominated that civic life. Even the Methodist denominations, most remarkable for their extra-parochial circuits, still customarily buried their dead in the parish churchyard – relatively few of their own chapels have separate burial grounds. The new poor law was based upon the bedrock of the parish system, and upon ideas of parochial belonging. Those ideas were fundamental to its decision-making at all levels, and to its accountancy. That poor law was funded and coordinated by the parishes right through to its end in the late 1920s. The overseers of the poor – those famous Elizabethan officers – were still the crucial enabling agents of the rating and welfare system in the reigns of Edward VII and George V. The guardians of the poor were parish-appointed – their elections were depicted as highly innovative in 1834, extended the franchise to women ratepayers, and even when they were contentious such elections often enhanced or framed a sense of the parish. Most paupers were relieved in their own 'home' parishes, not in union workhouses elsewhere. The laws of parish settlement lasted throughout the nineteenth century; indeed the settlement laws were only abolished in the mid-twentieth century, when in effect a 'national settlement' was created under the Attlee government. Few would dispute the emergence of class consciousness by the late nineteenth century, but it was delayed by parish pride, local allegiances and a suspicion of outsiders. Astonishingly high levels of parochial endogamy (marriage to people of the same parish)

---

[6] M. Spufford (ed.), *The World of Rural Dissenters, 1520–1725* (Cambridge, 1995).

persisted in rural areas through most of the nineteenth century, until horizons widened with the coming of the affordable safety bicycle in the 1880s, and the accumulating impact of the railways and the rural exodus. The dedication of middling-class people to local place might even seem to have intensified through the nineteenth century if we judge this from the incidence of statements attesting to place loyalty on gravestones. Even when the parish came to be reformed, most notably after about 1840, the response of civil and ecclesiastical authorities was massively to augment the numbers of parishes. The cultural and administrative importance of the parish was rarely questioned then, and was usually strongly extolled, not least by those who resisted new parish formation. In due course, the plethora of new and subdivided parishes, with their functional separations regarding the civil and the ecclesiastical, came to be major problems for the parish, and were among the factors that undermined its continuity, organic credibility and its utility as a coherent unit to which people could feel that they belonged.

These chapters have elaborated such views in much detail, and have stressed how real and fundamental the parish community was. Divisions within the parish about how it should be run, or about its transfers of wealth or countless other issues, do not undermine a stress upon its centrality as a unit – I am not arguing here for a romanticised view of its tensions or often conflictual affairs. After all, John Clare, one of the strongest exponents of parochial affection, also left us some of the bitterest statements about parochial animosities.[7] The sixteenth, seventeenth and eighteenth centuries are normally held to be the heyday of the parish, and its life and micro-politics in that period have been wonderfully explored by historians such as Keith Wrightson, Margaret Spufford and Steve Hindle.[8] Yet that long period – the second half of the parochial era – must be

---

[7] See for example his *The Parish: A Satire* (written 1820–7, Harmondsworth, 1986), also in J. W. and A. Tibble (eds.), *John Clare, Selected Poems* (London, 1965).

[8] K. Wrightson, *English Society, 1580–1680* (London, 1982), and his *Earthly Necessities: Economic Lives in Early Modern Britain* (New Haven, 2000); K. Wrightson and D. Levine, *Poverty and Piety in an English Village: Terling, 1525–1700* (Oxford, 1995); M. Spufford, *Contrasting Communities: English Villagers in the Sixteenth and Seventeenth Centuries* (Cambridge, 1974); Spufford, *World of Rural Dissenters*; S. Hindle, *On the Parish? The Micro-politics of Poor Relief in Rural England, c. 1550–1750* (Oxford, 2004).

extended to cover most of the Victorian age as well. It is impossible to judge the relative importance of the parish *versus* the nation in the nineteenth century – the two were in any case closely and mutually reinforcing. However, it would certainly be wrong to suggest that nationalism swept all before it, rendering parish belonging and localism a backwater preserve, confined to areas like the heathlands or vales of Dorset – of which Thomas Hardy wrote that it was 'among such communities as these that happiness will find her last refuge on earth, since it is among them that a perfect insight into the conditions of existence will be longest postponed'.[9] Even among those who emigrated, seemingly the least parochially attached of all, an intense interest in the parish world and its dealings persisted in their letters back 'home', letters which were often read from the pulpit or in public houses to fascinated listeners.[10]

Community could mean many things, sometimes in parallel or multiple forms, and it did so in the eighteenth and nineteenth centuries.[11] Yet above all during that period it meant the parish. This was an entity which shaped people's identities, which they spoke of as 'home', and one in which they desperately strove to end their days. The parish as a unit of community and belonging was a world of vitality, allegiance and administrative centrality, which seems to have satisfied a real human need. Historians therefore need to study the parish more closely, especially in the period 1834–1930, when it has so often been ignored. And those struggling with modern social problems, far too numerous to list, might also gain from a fuller appreciation of the benefits of local pride, personal local repute, and the integrated wholeness and quality of social life that the parish once contributed to. After all, given my arguments, the decline

[9] T. Hardy, 'The Dorsetshire labourer' (1883), reprinted in J. Moynahan (ed.), *The Portable Thomas Hardy* (1977, Harmondsworth, 1979), p. 716.

[10] For collections of such letters, see K. D. M. Snell, *Annals of the Labouring Poor: Social Change and Agrarian England, 1660–1900* (Cambridge, 1985), p. 10 n. 20.

[11] For thoughtful recent discussion on this, see D. Mills, 'Defining community: a critical review of "community" in *Family and Community History'*, *Family and Community History*, 7 (2004); and B. Deacon and M. Donald, 'In search of community history', *Family and Community History*, 7 (2004). I do not, of course, wish to deny alternative *foci* for community, or the utility of discussing them – yet I do not believe that any alternative focus approaches the historical dominance and importance of the parish.

of the parish and of the primacy of local belonging is a fairly recent phenomenon in historical time, one largely of the twentieth century. It may even be most associated with the period of widespread car ownership – let us not forget that people had often taken their communities with them by tram or train, char-à-banc or bus. Indeed, one could mention the village halls, war memorials, and other features of the inter-war period as signs of parochial allegiance then, and many from the Anglican Church could rightly point to areas of on-going vigour of the parish. Some modern writers – most notably Ronald Blythe – continue to celebrate it as a living entity.[12] The modernity of this decline suggests its selective recoverability and its capacity to influence reform today, and there is no doubt about the much stronger enduring localism and local government traditions of many other advanced countries. Whether, in the face of modern centralisation and globalisation, it is too late for the English and Welsh past to be instructive on these issues is for others to decide.

---

[12] Foremost among Ronald Blythe's fine local writing on this theme are his *Word from Wormingford: A Parish Year* (1997, Harmondsworth, 1998), *Out of the Valley: Another Year at Wormingford* (London, 2000), and *Borderland* (Norwich, 2005).

Select bibliography

A complete bibliography of all items referenced in this book would be very extensive indeed. The following bibliography is therefore a select one, which indicates some among the referenced items that are interesting or helpful for the particular themes of this book. No judgement is therefore implied on referenced or other items omitted here, and there are many of them, given the expansive historiography. For referenced items not included in this select bibliography, readers should concentrate on footnotes, which are 'self-contained' within each chapter. In other words, for any short-titled reference, referral back within that chapter will obtain the full reference. Acts of Parliament, Hansard, Parliamentary papers, official publications, poor law circulars, record office documents, newspaper articles and the like have not been included in this bibliography, as they are too numerously referenced. They are almost always of considerable value, notably the Select Committee Reports on settlement, the poor law, and boundaries, or the Official Circulars of the Poor Law Commission and Board.

Aitchison, J. and Carter, H., 'Rural Wales and the Welsh language', *Rural History*, 2 (1991).

Ambler, R. W., 'Preachers and the plan: patterns of activity in early Primitive Methodism', *Proceedings of the Wesley Historical Society*, 46 (1987–8).

Churches, Chapels and the Parish Communities of Lincolnshire, 1660–1900 (Lincoln, 2000).

Anstruther, I., *The Scandal of the Andover Workhouse* (1973, Gloucester, 1984).

Archbold, J. F., *The Act for the Amendment of the Poor Laws, with a Practical Introduction* (London, 1839).

The Poor Law, Comprising the Whole of the Law of Relief, Settlement, and Removal of the Poor, Together with the Law relating to the Poor Rate (1853, London, 1872).

Archer, J. E., *'By a Flash and a Scare': Arson, Animal Maiming, and Poaching in East Anglia, 1815–1870* (Oxford, 1990).

Aries, P., *Western Attitudes towards Death: From the Middle Ages to the Present* (1974, London, 1976).

Armstrong, H. B. J. (ed.), *A Norfolk Diary: Passages from the Diary of the Rev. Benjamin John Armstrong, Vicar of East Dereham, 1850–88* (London, 1949).

Armstrong's Norfolk Diary: Further Passages from the Diary of the Reverend Benjamin John Armstrong, Vicar of East Dereham, 1850–1888 (London, 1963).

Ashforth, D., 'Settlement and removal in urban areas: Bradford, 1834–71', in Rose, M. E. (ed.), *The Poor and the City: The English Poor Law in its Urban Context, 1834–1914* (Leicester, 1985).

Augé, M., *Non-places: Introduction to an Anthropology of Supermodernity* (1995, London, 2000).

Bailey, B., *Churchyards of England and Wales* (1987, Leicester, 1994).

Baker, T., *The Laws Relating to Burials, with Notes, Forms, & Practical Instructions* (1855, London, 1873).

Barrell, J., *The Idea of Landscape and the Sense of Place, 1730–1840: An Approach to the Poetry of John Clare* (Cambridge, 1972).

English Literature in History, 1730–80: An Equal, Wide Survey (London, 1983).

Bates, H. E., *The Vanished World: An Autobiography of Childhood and Youth* (1969, London, 1987).

Bauman, Z., *Globalization: The Human Consequences* (Cambridge, 1998).

Bell, A., *Men and the Fields* (London, 1939).

Bell, C. and Newby, H., *Community Studies: An Introduction to the Sociology of the Local Community* (London, 1971).

Bellamy, C., *Administering Central–Local Relations, 1871–1919: The Local Government Board in its Fiscal and Cultural Context* (Manchester, 1988).

Best, G. F. A., *Temporal Pillars: Queen Anne's Bounty, the Ecclesiastical Commissioners, and the Church of England* (Cambridge, 1964).

Blythe, R., *Word from Wormingford: A Parish Year* (1997, Harmondsworth, 1998).

Out of the Valley: Another Year at Wormingford (London, 2000).

Borderland (Norwich, 2005).

Borrow, G., *Wild Wales* (1862, London, 1970).

Bosanquet, H., *The Poor Law Report of 1909* (1909, London, 1911).

Boyson, R., 'The new poor law in north-east Lancashire, 1834–71', *Transactions of the Lancashire and Cheshire Antiquarian Society*, 70 (1960).

Brereton, Revd C. D., *A Practical Enquiry into the Number, Means of Employment and Wages of Agricultural Labourers* (Norwich, 1824).

Briggs, K. M., *A Dictionary of British Folk-tales in the English Language, Part A, Folk Narratives* (Bloomington, 1970).

Brooks, C. and Saint, A. (eds.), *The Victorian Church: Architecture and Society* (Manchester, 1995).

Brose, O. J., *Church and Parliament: The Reshaping of the Church of England, 1828–1860* (Stanford, 1959).

Burgess, F., *English Churchyard Memorials* (1963, London, 1979).

Burn, R., *The History of the Poor Laws, with Observations* (London, 1764).

Bushaway, B., *By Rite: Custom, Ceremony and Community in England, 1700–1880* (London, 1982).

Castles, S. and Davidson, A., *Citizenship and Migration: Globalization and the Politics of Belonging* (Basingstoke, 2000).

Chadwick, O., *The Victorian Church, Part I: 1829–1859* (1966, London, 1997).

The Victorian Church, Part II (1970, London, 1980).

Checkland, S. G. and Checkland, E. O. A. (eds.), *The Poor Law Report of 1834* (1834, Harmondsworth, 1974).

Clare, J., *The Parish: A Satire* (written 1820–7, Harmondsworth, 1986), also in Tibble, J. W. and Tibble, A. (ed.), *John Clare, Selected Poems* (1965).

Clifford, J., *Routes: Travel and Translation in the Late Twentieth Century* (London, 1997).

Cobbett, W., *Rural Rides* (1830, Harmondsworth, 1975).

Cohen, A. P. (ed.), *Belonging: Identity and Social Organisation in British Rural Cultures* (Manchester, 1982).

Symbolising Boundaries: Identity and Diversity in British Cultures (Manchester, 1986).

Colley, L., *Britons: Forging the Nation, 1707–1837* (London, 1992).

Colls, R., *Identity of England* (Oxford, 2002).

'When we lived in communities: working-class culture and its critics', in Colls, R. and Rodger, R. (eds.), *Cities of Ideas: Civil Society and Urban Governance in Britain, 1800–2000* (Aldershot, 2004).

Constant, A., 'The geographical background of inter-village population movements in Northamptonshire and Huntingdonshire, 1754–1943', *Geography*, 33 (1948).

Cox, K. R. (ed.), *Spaces of Globalization: Reasserting the Power of the Local* (New York, 1997).

Cox, M. (ed.), *Grave Concerns: Death and Burial in England, 1700 to 1850* (York, 1998).

Crewe, Sir G., *A Word for the Poor, and Against the Present Poor Law* (London, 1843).

Crowther, M. A., *The Workhouse System, 1834–1929: The History of an English Social Institution* (London, 1983).

'Paupers or patients? Obstacles to professionalization in the Poor Law Medical Service before 1914', *Journal of the History of Medicine and Allied Sciences*, 39 (1984).

Cuttle, G., *The Legacy of the Rural Guardians* (Cambridge, 1934).

Daunton, M. (ed.), *Charity, Self-interest and Welfare in the English Past* (New York, 1996).

Davey, H., *Poor Law Settlement (Local Chargeability) and Removal* (1908, London, 1925).

Davies, D. J., *A Brief History of Death* (Oxford, 2005).

Davies, E. T., *Religion and the Industrial Revolution in South Wales* (1965, Cardiff, 1987).

Davis, H. J. and Owston, H. A., *Overseers' Manual, Showing their Duties, Liabilities, and Responsibilities* (London, 1864).

Deacon, B. and Donald, M., 'In search of community history', *Family and Community History*, 7 (2004).

Digby, A., 'The labour market and the continuity of social policy after 1834: the case of the eastern counties', *Economic History Review*, 28 (1975).

'Recent developments in the study of the English poor law', *The Local Historian*, 12 (1977).

Pauper Palaces (London, 1978).

Making a Medical Living: Doctors and Patients in the English Market for Medicine, 1720–1911 (Cambridge, 1994).

Dow, P. (ed.), assisted by Drobig, R. A. C., *Hobson's Local Government* (London, 1951).

Drage, G., *Public Assistance* (London, 1930).

Driver, F., *Power and Pauperism: The Workhouse System, 1834–1884* (Cambridge, 1993).

Dunbabin, J. P. D., *Rural Discontent in Nineteenth-century Britain* (London, 1974).

Duncan, J. M., *Treatise on the Parochial Ecclesiastical Law of Scotland* (Edinburgh, 1864).

Dunlop, A., *Parochial Law* (Edinburgh, 1841).

Dyck, I., 'From "Rabble" to "Chopsticks": the radicalism of William Cobbett', *Albion*, 21 (1989).

William Cobbett and Rural Popular Culture (Cambridge, 1992).

'Local attachments, national identities and world citizenship in the thought of Thomas Paine', *History Workshop Journal*, 35 (1993).

Dymond, D., 'God's disputed acre', *Journal of Ecclesiastical History*, 50 (1999).

Eastwood, D., *Government and Community in the English Provinces, 1700–1870* (London, 1997).

Eden, Sir F. M., *The State of the Poor*, 3 vols. (1797, Bristol, 2001).

Edgerley, J. T. (ed.), *Ecclesiastical Law, Being a Reprint of the Title Ecclesiastical Law from Halsbury's Laws of England* (London, 1957, Church Assembly edn).

Edwards, G., *From Crow-Scaring to Westminster* (London, 1922).

Eliot, G., *Silas Marner* (1861, Harmondsworth, 1969).

Felix Holt (1866, Harmondsworth, 1975).

Englander, D., *Poverty and Poor Law Reform in Britain: From Chadwick to Booth, 1834–1914* (London, 1998).

Evans, G. E., *Ask the Fellows Who Cut the Hay* (1956, London, 1962).
The Strength of the Hills: An Autobiography (1983, London, 1985).

Evans, E. J. (ed.), *Social Policy, 1830–1914: Individualism, Collectivism and the Origins of the Welfare State* (London, 1978).

Everitt, A., 'Nonconformity in country parishes', in Thirsk, J. (ed.), *Land, Church and People: Essays Presented to Professor H. P. R. Finberg* (Reading, 1970).

The Pattern of Rural Dissent: The Nineteenth Century (Leicester, 1972).

Fawcett, H., *Pauperism, its Causes and Remedies* (1871, Bristol, 1996).

Findler, G., *Folk Lore of the Lake Counties* (Clapham, Yorks., 1968).

Fisher, C., *Custom, Work and Market Capitalism: The Forest of Dean Colliers, 1788–1888* (London, 1981).

Forder, C. R., *The Parish Priest at Work: An Introduction to Systematic Pastoralia* (1947, London, 1959).

Foster, G. M., 'Peasant society and the image of the limited good', *American Anthropologist*, 67 (1965).
'The anatomy of envy: a study in symbolic behavior', *Current Anthropology*, 13 (1972).

Frankenberg, R., *Village on the Border: A Social Study of Religion, Politics and Football in a North Wales Community* (London, 1957).

Freeman, M., *Social Investigation and Rural England, 1870–1914* (Woodbridge, 2003).

Galt, J., *Annals of the Parish; or the Chronicle of Dalmailing during the Ministry of the Rev. Micah Balwhidder* (1821, Oxford, 1986).

Garbett, C., *The Claims of the Church of England* (1947, London, 1948).

Garratt, D., 'Primitive Methodist circuits in the English–Welsh borderland', *Rural History*, 14 (2003).

Gilbert, A. D., *Religion and Society in Industrial England: Church, Chapel and Social Change, 1740–1914* (1976, London, 1984).

Gittings, C., *Death, Burial and the Individual in Early Modern England* (London, 1984).

Gosden, P. H. J. H., *The Friendly Societies in England, 1815–1875* (Manchester, 1961).

Green, F. E., *The Tyranny of the Countryside* (London, 1913).

Green, S. J. D., *Religion in the Age of Decline: Organisation and Experience in Industrial Yorkshire, 1870–1920* (Cambridge, 1996).

Grose, F., *A Provincial Glossary, with a Collection of Local Proverbs and Popular Superstitions* (1787, Menston, Yorks., 1968).

Halévy, E., *A History of the English People in the Nineteenth Century: England in 1815* (1913, London, 1970).

Hall, E. H., *A Description of Caernarvonshire (1809–1811)* (Caernarvon, 1952).

Hampson, E. M., 'Settlement and removal in Cambridgeshire, 1662–1834', *Cambridge Historical Journal*, 2 (1926–8).

Hardy, T., *Far From the Madding Crowd* (1874, London, 1971).

The Return of the Native (1878, London, 1971).

The Woodlanders (1887, London, 1971).

Harling, P., 'The power of persuasion: central authority, local bureaucracy and the New Poor Law', *English Historical Review*, 107 (1992).

Hart, C. E., *The Free Miners of the Royal Forest of Dean and Hundred of St. Briavels* (Gloucester, 1953).

Havinden, M., *Estate Villages Revisited: A Second, Up-dated Edition of a Study of the Oxfordshire (formerly Berkshire) Villages of Ardington and Lockinge* (1966, Reading, 1999).

Head, Sir E., 'The law of settlement', *Edinburgh Review*, 87 (April 1848).

Herbert, N. M. (ed.), *A History of the County of Gloucester, vol. v: Bledisloe Hundred, St. Briavels Hundred, The Forest of Dean* (Victoria County History, Oxford, 1996).

Hey, D., *Family Names and Family History* (London, 2000).

Hindle, S., 'Exclusion crises: poverty, migration and parochial responsibility in English rural communities, c. 1560–1660', *Rural History*, 7 (1996).

'Power, poor relief, and social relations in Holland Fen, c. 1600–1800', *Historical Journal*, 41 (1998).

'A sense of place? Becoming and belonging in the rural parish, 1550–1650', in Shepard, A. and Withington, P. J. (eds.), *Communities in Early Modern England* (Manchester, 2000).

On the Parish? The Micro-politics of Poor Relief in Rural England, c. 1550–1750 (Oxford, 2004).

Hines, C., *Localization: A Global Manifesto* (London, 2000).

Hitchcock, T., King, P. and Sharpe, P. (eds.), *Chronicling Poverty: The Voices and Strategies of the English Poor, 1640–1840* (Basingstoke, 1997).

Hodgson, H. J., *Steer's Parish Law, Being a Digest of the Law relating to the Civil and Ecclesiastical Government of Parishes, Friendly Societies, etc., and the Relief, Settlement, and Removal of the Poor* (1830, London, 1857).

Holderness, B. A., '"Open" and "close" parishes in England in the eighteenth and nineteenth centuries', *Agricultural History Review*, 20 (1972).

Holdsworth, W. A., *The Handy Book of Parish Law* (n.d., c. 1859, London, c. 1872).

Houlbrooke, R., *Death, Religion and the Family in England, 1480–1750* (Oxford, 1998).

Howell, P., 'Church and chapel in Wales', in Brooks, C. and Saint, A. (eds.), *The Victorian Church: Architecture and Society* (Manchester, 1995).

Howkins, A., 'From Hodge to Lob: reconstructing the English farm labourer, 1870–1914', in Chase, M. and Dyck, I. (eds.), *Living and Learning: Essays in Honour of J. F. C. Harrison* (Aldershot, 1996).

Hudson, P., 'The regional perspective', in her (ed.), *Regions and Industries: A Perspective on the Industrial Revolution in Britain* (1989, Cambridge, 1993).

Hurren, E., 'Labourers are revolting: penalising the poor and a political reaction in the Brixworth Union, Northamptonshire, 1875–1885', *Rural History*, 11 (2000).

'Agricultural trade unionism and a crusade against out-door relief: poor law politics in the Brixworth Union, Northamptonshire, 1870–1875', *Agricultural History Review*, 48 (2000).

'Welfare-to-work schemes and a crusade against outdoor relief in the Brixworth Union, Northamptonshire, in the 1880s', *Family and Community History*, 4 (2001).

Hutton, R., *The Rise and Fall of Merry England: The Ritual Year, 1400–1700* (1994, Oxford, 1996).

The Stations of the Sun: A History of the Ritual Year in Britain (1996, Oxford, 1997).

Inglis, K. S., *Churches and the Working Classes in Victorian England* (London, 1963).

Jones, D. J. V., *Rebecca's Children: A Study of Rural Society, Crime, and Protest* (Oxford, 1989).

Jones, I. G., 'Ecclesiastical economy: aspects of church building in Victorian Wales', in Davies, R. R. (ed.), *Welsh Society and Nationhood: Historical Essays Presented to Glanmor Williams* (Cardiff, 1984).

Communities: Essays in the Social History of Victorian Wales (Llandysul, 1987).

Jupp, P. C., *From Dust to Ashes: The Development of Cremation in England, 1820–1997* (London, 2000).

Kendall, Revd H. B., *The Origin and History of the Primitive Methodist Church* (London, n.d., c. 1905).

Kendall, S. G., *Farming Memoirs of a West Country Yeoman* (London, 1944).

Kidd, A., *State, Society and the Poor in Nineteenth-century England* (Basingstoke, 1999).

Kidd, A. J., '"Outcast Manchester": voluntary charity, poor relief and the casual poor, 1860–1905', in Kidd, A. J. and Roberts, K. W. (eds.), *City, Class and Culture: Studies of Social Policy and Cultural Production in Victorian Manchester* (Manchester, 1985).

King, S., *Poverty and Welfare in England, 1700–1850: A Regional Perspective* (Manchester, 2000).

'"It is impossible for our Vestry to judge his case into perfection from here": managing the distance dimensions of poor relief, 1800–1840', *Rural History*, 16 (2005).

King, S. and Tomkins, A. (eds.), *The Poor in England, 1700–1850: An Economy of Makeshifts* (Manchester, 2003).

King, S., Tomkins, A. and Nutt, T. (eds.), *Narratives of the Poor in the Long Eighteenth Century* (London, 2006).

Kussmaul, A., *Servants in Husbandry in Early Modern England* (Cambridge, 1981).

Langton, J., 'The industrial revolution and the regional geography of England', *Transactions of the Institute of British Geographers*, 9 (1984).

Lawson, J., *Progress in Pudsey* (1887, Firle, 1978).

Lees, L. H., *The Solidarities of Strangers: The English Poor Laws and the People, 1700–1948* (Cambridge, 1998).

Lewis, D. M., *Lighten their Darkness: The Evangelical Mission to Working-class London, 1828–1860* (Westport, Conn., 1986).

Lidbetter, E. J., *Settlement and Removal* (London, n.d., c. 1932).

Mabey, R., *Gilbert White* (1986, London, 1999).

Macfarlane, A., *Marriage and Love in England: Modes of Reproduction, 1300–1840* (Oxford, 1986).

Mackay, T., *A History of the English Poor Law, vol. III: from 1834 to the Present Time; Being a Supplementary Volume to 'A History of the English Poor Law' by Sir George Nicholls* (1854, London, 1900).

MacKinnon, M., 'English poor law policy and the crusade against outrelief', *Journal of Economc History*, 47 (1987).

McLeod, H., *Class and Religion in the Late Victorian City* (London, 1974).

Malcolmson, R. W., *Popular Recreations in English Society, 1700–1850* (Cambridge, 1973).

Mansfield, N., *English Farmworkers and Local Patriotism, 1900–1930* (Aldershot, 2001).

Marsh, J., *Back to the Land: The Pastoral Impulse in England, from 1880 to 1914* (London, 1982).

Massey, D. and Jess, P. (eds.), *A Place in the World? Places, Cultures and Globalization* (Oxford, 1995).

Maynard, W. B., 'The response of the Church of England to economic and demographic change: the Archdeaconry of Durham, 1800–1851', *Journal of Ecclesiastical History*, 42 (1991).

Midwinter, E. C., *Social Administration in Lancashire, 1830–60: Poor Law, Public Health and Police* (Manchester, 1969).

Millard, J., 'A new approach to the study of marriage horizons', *Local Population Studies*, 28 (1982), also in Drake, M. (ed.), *Population Studies from Parish Registers* (Matlock, 1982).

Mills, D., *Lord and Peasant in Nineteenth-century Britain* (London, 1980).

Mitson, A., 'The significance of kinship networks in the seventeenth century: south-west Nottinghamshire', in Phythian-Adams, C. (ed.), *Societies, Cultures and Kinship, 1580–1850: Cultural Provinces and English Local History* (Leicester, 1993).

Morgan, P., 'From long knives to blue books', in Davies, R. R., Griffiths, R. A., Jones, I. G. and Morgan, K. O. (eds.), *Welsh Society and Nationhood: Historical Essays Presented to Glanmor Williams* (Cardiff, 1984).

Mytum, H., *Recording and Analysing Graveyards* (York, 2000).

Neeson, J. M., *Commoners: Common Right, Enclosure and Social Change in England, 1700–1820* (Cambridge, 1993).

Newby, H., *The Deferential Worker* (1977, Harmondsworth, 1979).

Nicholls, Sir G., *A History of the English Poor Law, in Connection with the State of the Country and the Condition of the People* (1854, London, 1898, 1904, New York, 1967).

Nicholls, H. G., *Nicholls's Forest of Dean: An Historical and Descriptive Account, and Iron Making in the Olden Times* (1858 and 1866, Dawlish, 1966).

Nolan, M., *A Treatise of the Laws for the Relief and Settlement of the Poor*, 2 vols. (1805, London, 1808).

Northall, G. F., *English Folk Rhymes: A Collection of Traditional Verses Relating to Places, Persons, Customs, and Superstitions* (London, 1892).

O'Dowd, A., *Spalpeens and Tattie Hokers: History and Folklore of the Irish Migratory Agricultural Worker in Ireland and Britain* (Dublin, 1991).

Okely, J., *The Traveller-Gypsies* (1983, Cambridge, 1984).

Owen, T. M., *The Customs and Traditions of Wales* (Cardiff, 1991).

Parry-Jones, D., *My Own Folk* (Llandysul, 1972).

Pashley, R., *Pauperism and Poor Laws* (London, 1852).

Peel, R. F., 'Local intermarriage and the stability of rural population in the English Midlands', *Geography*, 27 (1942).

Pelling, M. and Smith, R. M. (ed.), *Life, Death, and the Elderly: Historical Perspectives* (London, 1991).

Perry, P. J., 'Working-class isolation and mobility in rural Dorset, 1837–1936: a study of marriage distances', *Transactions of the Institute of British Geographers*, 46 (1969).

Phythian-Adams, C., *Re-thinking English Local History* (Leicester, 1987).

Phythian-Adams, C. (ed.), *Societies, Cultures and Kinship, 1580–1850: Cultural Provinces in English Local History* (Leicester, 1993).

Poole, K. P. and Keith-Lucas, B., *Parish Government, 1894–1994* (London, 1994).

Port, M. H., *Six Hundred New Churches: The Church Building Commission, 1818–1856* (London, 1961).

Potter, D., *The Changing Forest: Life in the Forest of Dean Today* (London, 1962).

Pounds, N. J. G., *A History of the English Parish: The Culture of Religion from Augustine to Victoria* (Cambridge, 2000).

Poynter, J. R., *Society and Pauperism: English Ideas on Poor Relief, 1795–1834* (London, 1969).

Price, R., *British Society, 1680–1880: Dynamism, Containment and Change* (Cambridge, 1999).

Pryce, W. T. R., 'Welsh and English in Wales, 1750–1971: a spatial analysis based on the linguistic affiliations of parochial communities', *Bulletin of the Board of Celtic Studies*, 28 (1978).

Purdy, F. W., 'The statistics of the English poor rate before and since the passing of the Poor Law Amendment Act', *Journal of the Statistical Society*, 23 (1860).

Rack, H. D., *Reasonable Enthusiast: John Wesley and the Rise of Methodism* (1989, London, 1992).

Reay, B., *Microhistories: Demography, Society and Culture in Rural England, 1800–1930* (Cambridge, 1996).

Redford, A., *Labour Migration in England, 1800–1850* (1964, Manchester, 1976).

Rees, A. D., *Life in a Welsh Countryside: A Social Study of Llanfihangel yng Ngwynfa* (1950, Cardiff, 1996).

Ribton-Turner, C. J., *A History of Vagrants and Vagrancy, and Beggars and Begging* (London, 1887).

Richardson, R., *Death, Dissection and the Destitute* (1988, Harmondsworth, 1989).

Rider Haggard, H., *Rural England*, 2 vols. (London, 1906).

Roberts, M. J. D., 'Private patronage and the Church of England, 1800–1900', *Journal of Ecclesiastical History*, 32 (1981).

Robertson Scott, J. W., *The Land Problem (an Impartial Survey)* (London, n.d., c. 1913).

Robinson, E. (ed.), *John Clare's Autobiographical Writings* (1983, Oxford, 1986).

Rogers, A., 'Parish boundaries and urban history: two case studies', *Journal of the British Archaeological Association*, 35 (1972).

Rose, M. E., 'The allowance system under the New Poor Law', *Economic History Review*, 19 (1966).
   'The new poor law in an industrial area', in Hartwell, R. M. (ed.), *The Industrial Revolution* (Oxford, 1970).
   'Settlement, removal and the new poor law', in Fraser, D. (ed.), *The New Poor Law in the Nineteenth Century* (London, 1976).

Shaw, J., *The Parochial Lawyer; or, Churchwarden and Overseer's Guide and Assistant* (1829, London, 1833).

Sibley, D., *Geographies of Exclusion: Society and Difference in the West* (London, 1995).

Sklair, L., *Globalization: Capitalism and its Alternatives* (Oxford, 2002).

Smith, M. A., *Religion in Industrial Society: Oldham and Saddleworth, 1740–1865* (Oxford, 1994).

Smith, R. (ed.), *Land, Kinship and Life-Cycle* (Cambridge, 1984).

Snell, K. D. M., 'Parish registration and the study of labour mobility', *Local Population Studies*, 33 (1984).
   Annals of the Labouring Poor: Social Change and Agrarian England, 1660–1900 (Cambridge, 1985).
   'Settlement, poor law and the rural historian: new approaches and opportunities', *Rural History*, 3 (1992).

'The apprenticeship system in British history: the fragmentation of a cultural institution', *History of Education*, 25 (1996).

(ed.), *The Regional Novel in Britain and Ireland, 1800–1990* (Cambridge, 1998).

Snell, K. D. M. and Ell, P. S., *Rival Jerusalems: The Geography of Victorian Religion* (Cambridge, 2000).

Sokoll, T., 'Negotiating a living: Essex pauper letters from London, 1800–1834', *International Review of Social History*, 45 (2000).

Sokoll, T. (ed.), *Essex Pauper Letters, 1731–1837* (Oxford, 2001).

Solar, P., 'Poor relief and English economic development before the industrial revolution', *Economic History Review*, 48 (1995).

Song, B. K., 'Agrarian policies on pauper settlement and migration, Oxfordshire 1750–1834', *Continuity and Change*, 13 (1998).

'Landed interest, local government, and the labour market in England, 1750–1850', *Economic History Review*, 51 (1998).

Spufford, M. (ed.), *The World of Rural Dissenters, 1520–1725* (Cambridge, 1995).

Stapleton, B., 'Inherited poverty and life-cycle poverty: Odiham, Hampshire, 1650–1850', *Social History*, 18 (1993).

Stevenson, J., *Popular Disturbances in England, 1700–1870* (London, 1979).

Stewart, J. and King, S., 'Death in Llantrisant: Henry Williams and the New Poor Law in Wales', *Rural History*, 15 (2004).

Strathern, M., *Kinship at the Core: An Anthropology of Elmdon, a Village in North-west Essex in the Nineteen-sixties* (Cambridge, 1981).

Styles, P., 'The evolution of the law of settlement', *University of Birmingham Historical Journal*, 9 (1963–4).

Symonds, J. F., Scholefield, J. and Hill, G. R., *The Law of Settlement and Removal, with a Collection of Statutes* (1882, London, 1903).

Synnott, Revd E. F., *Five Years' Hell in a Country Parish* (London, 1920).

Tarlow, S., *Bereavement and Commemoration: An Archaeology of Mortality* (Oxford, 1999).

Tate, W. E., *The Parish Chest: A Study of the Records of Parochial Administration in England* (1946, Cambridge, 1960).

Taylor, J. S., 'The impact of pauper settlement, 1691–1834', *Past and Present*, 73 (1976).

Poverty, Migration, and Settlement in the Industrial Revolution: Sojourners' Narratives (Palo Alto, Calif., 1989).

'"Set down in a large manufacturing town": sojourning poor in early nineteenth-century Manchester', *Manchester Region History Review*, 3 (1989).

'A different kind of Speenhamland: nonresident relief in the Industrial Revolution', *Journal of British Studies*, 30 (1991).

Thane, P., 'Old people and their families in the English past', in Daunton, M. (ed.), *Charity, Self-interest and Welfare in the English Past* (New York, 1996).

Old Age in English History: Past Experiences, Present Issues (2000, Oxford, 2002).

Thomas, F. G., *The Changing Village: An Essay on Rural Reconstruction* (1939, London, 1945).

Thomas, T., *Poor Relief in Merthyr Tydfil Union in Victorian Times* (Cardiff, 1992).

Thompson, E. P., *The Making of the English Working Class* (1963, Harmondsworth, 1975).

Customs in Common (1991, Harmondsworth, 1993).

Thompson, K. A., *Bureaucracy and Church Reform: The Organizational Response of the Church of England to Social Change, 1800–1965* (Oxford, 1970).

Thompson, R., 'A breed apart? Class and community in a Somerset coal-mining parish, *c.* 1750–1850', *Rural History*, 16 (2005).

Thomson, D., 'The decline of social welfare: falling state support for the elderly since early Victorian times', *Ageing and Society*, 4 (1984).

'"I am not my father's keeper": families and the elderly in nineteenth-century England', *Law and History Review*, 2 (1984).

'The welfare of the elderly in the past: a family or community responsibility?', in Pelling, M. and Smith, R. M. (eds.), *Life, Death, and the Elderly: Historical Perspectives* (London, 1991).

A World without Welfare: New Zealand's Colonial Experiment (Auckland, 1998).

Toulmin Smith, J., *Local Self-Government and Centralization: The Characteristics of Each* (London, 1851).

The Parish: Its Obligations and Powers, its Officers and their Duties (1854, London, 1957).

Traill, J. C., *The New Parishes Acts, 1843, 1844, & 1856, with Notes and Observations, Explanatory of their Provisions* (London, 1857).

Trower, C. F., *The Law of the Building of Churches, Parsonages, and Schools; and of the Divisions of Parishes and Places* (London, 1867).

Tyson, B., 'The Mansion House, Eamont Bridge, Cumbria: a tercentenary history of its owners, occupiers and associations', *Transactions of the Ancient Monuments Society*, 31 (1987).

Underdown, D., *Revel, Riot and Rebellion: Popular Politics and Culture in England, 1603–1660* (Oxford, 1985).

Vialls, C., 'The laws of settlement: their impact on the poor inhabitants of the Daventry area of Northamptonshire, 1750–1834' (Ph.D., University of Leicester, 1998).

Virgin, P., *The Church in an Age of Negligence: Ecclesiastical Structure and Problems of Church Reform, 1700–1840* (Cambridge, 1989).

Vulliamy, A. F., *The Law of Settlement and Removal of Paupers* (1895, London, 1906).

Walmsley, L., *Phantom Lobster* (1933, Harmondsworth, 1948).

Waters, M., *Globalization* (1995, London, 2001).

Webb, S. and Webb, B., *English Local Government: The Parish and the County* (1907, London, 1963).

English Poor Law Policy (1910, London, 1963).

English Local Government: English Poor Law History, Part 1: The Old Poor Law (London, 1927).

Welch, P. J., 'Bishop Blomfield and church extension in London', *Journal of Ecclesiastical History*, 4 (1953).

Wells, R. (ed.), *Victorian Village: The Diaries of the Reverend John Coker Egerton of Burwash, 1857–1888* (Stroud, 1992).

Wesley, J., *The Journal of John Wesley, 1735–1790*, ed. Ratcliff, N., (London, 1940).

White, G., *The Natural History of Selborne* (1788–9, Harmondsworth, 1987).

White, J. M., *Parochial Settlements: An Obstruction to Poor Law Reform* (London, 1835).

Wickham, E. R., *Church and People in an Industrial City* (1957, London, 1969).

Williams, K., *From Pauperism to Poverty* (London, 1981).

Williams, M. W., *The Sociology of an English Village: Gosforth* (London, 1956).

Williams, S., 'Caring for the sick poor: poor law nurses in Bedfordshire, *c.* 1770–1834', in Lane, P., Raven, N. and Snell, K. D. M. (eds.), *Women, Work and Wages in England, 1600–1850* (Woodbridge, 2004).

Williamson, T., *Polite Landscapes: Parts and Gardens in Georgian England* (Stroud, 1995).

Williamson, T. and Bellamy, L., *Property and Landscape: A Social History of Land Ownership and the English Countryside* (London, 1987).

Wilson, J. M. (ed.), *The Imperial Gazetteer*, 6 vols. (Edinburgh, n.d., *c.* 1872).

Winchester, A., *Discovering Parish Boundaries* (Princes Risborough, 1990).

Wood, P., *Poverty and the Workhouse in Victorian Britain* (Stroud, 1991).

Wright, P., *The Village that Died for England: The Strange Story of Tyneham* (1995, London, 1996).

Wrigley, E. A., 'Men on the land and men in the countryside: employment in agriculture in early-nineteenth-century England', in Bonfield, L., Smith, R. M. and Wrightson, K. (eds.), *The World We Have Gained: Histories of Population and Social Structure* (Oxford, 1986).

People, Cities and Wealth: The Transformation of Traditional Society (Oxford, 1987).

Continuity, Chance and Change: The Character of the Industrial Revolution in England (1988, Cambridge, 1990).

Wrigley E. A. and Schofield, R. S., *The Population History of England, 1541–1871: A Reconstruction* (London, 1981).

Wrigley, E. A., Davies, R. S., Oeppen, J. E., and Schofield, R. S., *English Population History from Family Reconstitution, 1580–1837* (Cambridge, 1997).

Youngs, F. A., *Guide to the Local Administrative Units of England, vol. I: Southern England* (London, 1979).

Guide to the Local Administrative Units of England, vol. II: Northern England (London, 1991).

Subject and persons index

Places index

Places are entered in their own right, and not also under their counties. The spelling of place names here and in the text is as generally found in my sources: hence, for example, the 'Carnarvon union' and other often English spellings of places in Wales.

Places index

Lightning Source UK Ltd.
Milton Keynes UK
UKOW01f0623270218
318544UK00001B/43/P